THINK
AMERICAN GOVERNMENT

2012 Edition

THINK
AMERICAN GOVERNMENT

2012 Edition

NEAL TANNAHILL
Houston Community College

PEARSON

Boston   Columbus   Indianapolis   New York   San Francisco   Upper Saddle River
Amsterdam   Cape Town   Dubai   London   Madrid   Milan   Munich   Paris   Montreal   Toronto
Delhi   Mexico City   São Paulo   Sydney   Hong Kong   Seoul   Singapore   Taipei   Tokyo

Executive Editor: Reid Hester
Executive Digital Producer: Stefanie Snajder
Digital Project Manager: Janell Lantana
Senior Digital Editor: Paul DeLuca
Editorial Assistant: Emily Sauerhoff
Executive Marketing Manager: Wendy Gordon
Production Manager: Eric Jorgensen
Project Coordination, Development, Text Design, Photo Research, and Electronic Page Makeup: PreMediaGlobal
Cover Designer: John Callahan
Cover Image: nico_blue /iStockphoto
Manufacturing Manager: Mary Fischer
Printer and Binder: RR Donnelley
Cover Printer: Lehigh-Phoenix Color/Hagerstown

For permission to use copyrighted material, grateful acknowledgment is made to the copyright holders on pp. 405–406, which are hereby made part of this copyright page.

Library of Congress Cataloging-in-Publication Data

Tannahill, Neal R.
Think : American government / Neal Tannahill. — 2012 ed. [4th ed.]
    p. cm.
  Includes index.
  ISBN 978-0-205-85600-8
  1. United States—Politics and government. I. Title.
JK275.T36 2012a
320.473—dc23

2 3 4 5 6 7 8 9 10—V003—14 13 12

PEARSON

ISBN-13: 978-0-205-85600-8
ISBN-10:   0-205-85600-4

BRIEF CONTENTS

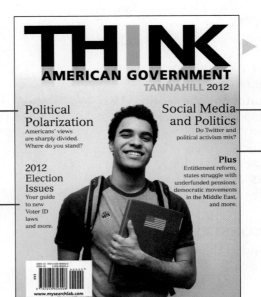

The Great Recession
Response of the Federal Government and the Fed p.309–310, 317–319
The Debt Crisis in Greece p.319
Executive Compensation at TARP Companies p.285

Midterm Elections
States Adopt Voter ID Laws Just in Time for 2012 Election p.134
The Tea Party Movement p.129–130
Impact of the Results p.184–186, 191–192

THINK
AMERICAN GOVERNMENT
TANNAHILL 2012

Political Polarization
Americans' views are sharply divided. Where do you stand?

Social Media and Politics
Do Twitter and political activism mix?

Plus
Entitlement reform, states struggle with underfunded pensions, democratic movements in the Middle East, and more.

2012 Election Issues
Your guide to new Voter ID laws and more.

www.mysearchlab.com

▶ **on the cover:**

Healthcare Reform
Passing Healthcare Reform p.221–222
The Patient Protection and Affordable Care Act p.321

Arizona's Immigration Law p.11–12
Challenges to California's Proposition 8 p.40, 85–86
New FDA regulations on Cigarette Packages in Texas p.269–270

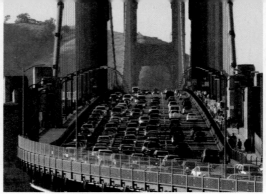

DETAILED CONTENTS

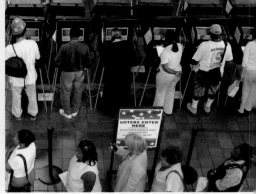

PREFACE

To the Instructor

I have written *Think American Government* with the goal of creating an academically solid textbook that students actually want to read. Although I recognize that most of our students will not major in political science, I believe it is important to expose them to political science research and to expect them to be able to relate political science concepts to current political developments and controversies. Students who master the material in *Think American Government* will have a solid introduction to American government and politics. They will also know how to participate in American government.

My principle objection to magazine-style textbooks is that they sometimes sacrifice content for style. My editors and I have created a text that will catch the attention of students with engaging photos, colorful images, interesting graphics, and interesting features but not at the expense of academic depth. The photos, images, and graphics have been chosen to enhance the text rather than distract from it. The features, meanwhile, are designed to help students understand course concepts. The Breaking News feature, for example, uses a current event, such as the lawsuit filed by several states against healthcare reform, as a vehicle for explaining course concepts in depth.

The new 2012 edition focuses on a number of important new issues and political developments, and contains several new features geared toward student learning:

- **Stronger pedagogy:** Each chapter is framed with *What We Will Learn* key concepts for the chapter and *What We Learned* summaries to help students navigate the chapters and understand the main concepts.

- **Richer content:** The revision provides students with a fuller explanation of concepts and more background information (a history of American foreign policy, a history of the Supreme Court, etc.) to help them better understand course content. Reorganization within chapters promotes better student comprehension, and reorganization among chap-

ters moves the discussion of civil liberties and civil rights to the front part of the book to group together the chapters that deal with Constitutional issues.

- **New features:** As mentioned, Breaking News! uses an important political issue in the news to explain course concepts in more depth. Office Hours boxes respond to the kinds of questions students typically ask as they attempt to apply the chapter concepts to the real world. Tips for Success offers practical advice from the author designed to help students not only pass the course but also eventually graduate from college.

- Revised, **streamlined design**: Every aspect of the design (photos, features, graphics, etc.) has been chosen with the goal of helping students better understand the text.

- **New issues and developments:** The new edition focuses on a number of important new issues and political developments, including the unsuccessful Republican efforts to repeal healthcare reform, the impact of state budget cuts on higher education, the Supreme Court ruling in the Westboro Baptist Church free speech case, state voter ID laws, partisan media and political polarization, the impact of Americans for Tax Reform and the Taxpayer Protection Pledge on the policymaking process, congressional redistricting, medicare reform proposals, presidential powers and the use of force in Libya, FDA regulations requiring more prominent health warnings on cigarette packages, public employee pension funding, the U.S. Supreme Court's refusal to allow the Walmart gender discrimination case to proceed as a class action lawsuit, and Congress's vote to raise the debt ceiling after a protracted struggle.

I hope that you will enjoy using *Think American Government* and that it effectively supports your teaching. I am interested in your feedback and will be happy to answer any questions you have. My e-mail address is neal.tannahill@hccs.edu.

Neal Tannahill

To the Student

I designed this textbook with students in mind. I have been a member of the political science faculty at Houston Community College for more than 30 years, teaching hundreds of introductory American government classes, probably much like the one you are taking now. I have learned from experience that students want a textbook that is easily read. Consequently, my primary goal as a textbook author is to write clearly. I want students to be able to understand every sentence, every paragraph, and every chapter without having to read them over and over again.

I also know that students want a textbook that is interesting. In order to catch and hold student interest, I have organized the textbook around the major policy controversies of today, including Arizona's immigration law, healthcare reform, and the war in Afghanistan. The text also includes colorful features and photographs selected not just to entertain but to enhance your understanding of course concepts.

Students want a textbook that will guide their study. Each chapter is framed with *What We Will Learn* key concepts and *What We Learned* summaries to help students navigate the

chapters and understand the main concepts. Other features include key terms, a glossary, a self-test after each chapter, a Breaking News! feature designed to use a current event to elaborate on a course concept, an Office Hours feature that answers the questions students typically ask, a Take Action feature that allows students to learn by doing, and a Tips for Success feature that guides students toward success in their course and in college. Another feature that I think you will find most helpful is a set of short podcasts that I have recorded discussing course concepts, called Talking About American Government. These podcasts can be accessed through the book's companion website, www.TheThinkSpot.com. My own students tell me that the podcasts are invaluable for helping them understand course material and I think you will find them beneficial as well. The website also contains quizzes, flashcards, and other study aids.

I am proud to have the opportunity to be part of your education. If you have questions about the text or about American government, you can write to me at neal.tannahill@hccs.edu or ntannahill@aol.com. I hope to hear from you!

ACKNOWLEDGMENTS

Many people contributed to the writing and production of this book. Donna Garnier, Eric Jorgensen, and the whole team at PreMediaGlobal gave me sympathetic and professional help from the beginning of my work on the edition to its completion.

I am grateful to my friends and colleagues among the government faculty at Houston Community College for their friendship and support. I have learned most of what I know about teaching from them. I wish to dedicate this book to the people who are close to me personally, especially Anup Bodhe, Anderson Brandao, Jason Orr, and Kim Galle.

Finally, this edition has profited from the informed and professional suggestions of colleagues around the country, and I would like to thank the following individuals for their reviews of the book:

Ward Albro, University of Texas at San Antonio
Catherine Bottrell-Tomerlin, Tarrant County College Southeast Campus
Paul Davis, Truckee Meadows Community College
Fred Lokken, Truckee Meadows Community College
Melinda Mueller, Eastern Illinois University
Leah Murray, Weber State University
Gary Sokolow, College of the Redwoods
Robert Wood, University of North Dakota

NEAL TANNAHILL

intro **GOVERNMENT,**

THE IMPORTANCE OF GOVERNMENT

Learning Objective **1** How does government affect the lives of individuals and society as a whole?

GOVERNMENT AND POLITICS

Learning Objective **2** What is the difference between government and politics?

THE POLICYMAKING PROCESS

Learning Objective **3** What are the stages of the policymaking process?

The **Americans with Disabilities Act (ADA)** is a federal law designed to end discrimination against people with disabilities and eliminate barriers to their full participation in American society. The ADA protects people with disabilities from discrimination in all employment practices, including hiring, firing, promotions, and compensation. The ADA does not force employers to hire unqualified individuals who happen to be disabled, but it does require companies to make "reasonable accommodation" for otherwise qualified job applicants or current employees who happen to be disabled unless the business can show that the accommodation would put an "undue hardship" on its operation. The ADA also requires that private businesses that are open to the public—such as restaurants, hotels, theaters, retail stores, funeral homes, healthcare offices, pharmacies, private schools, and daycare centers—be accessible to persons with disabilities. Business owners may have to modify their premises or change their way of doing business so long as the necessary modifications or accommodations do not unduly burden the business or force business owners fundamentally to alter the nature of the goods or services they provide.[1]

Americans with Disabilities Act (ADA) a federal law designed to end discrimination against people with disabilities and eliminate barriers to their full participation in American society.

POLITICS, AND THE POLICYMAKING PROCESS

THE IMPORTANCE OF GOVERNMENT

The ADA illustrates the importance of government. For millions of Americans with disabilities, the act offers the promise of opportunity to compete in the workplace without discrimination and it guarantees access to restaurants, hotels, shops, and clinics. The ADA forces employers to review their employment practices to ensure compliance with the law and to take reasonable steps to accommodate the needs of workers and customers with disabilities. For society as a whole, the ADA gives millions of people with disabilities the opportunity to become full participants in the nation's economy, both as workers and consumers.

Government affects individual Americans through regulations, taxes, and services. Government regulates many aspects of daily life, either directly or indirectly. The government sets speed limits and other driving regulations, establishes a minimum age to purchase and consume alcoholic beverages, and determines the educational and technical qualifications required for practicing many occupations and professions. Government regulations affect the quality of air and water, gasoline mileage performance of automobiles, and working conditions in factories. In addition, regulation attempts to protect consumers from unsafe products, untested drugs, misleading package labels, and deceptive advertising.

Government services provide benefits to all Americans. Public hospitals, schools, and transportation networks serve millions of people. Many college students receive financial aid and attend institutions that benefit from public funding. Government welfare programs assist millions of low-income families.

think *Do you favor a small government that provides relatively modest services but holds down taxes, or an active government that provides more services but costs more?*

Older people and many individuals with disabilities receive Social Security and Medicare benefits.

Government regulations and services cost money. In 2009, federal, state, and local governments combined raised nearly $3.5 trillion in taxes and fees, a figure representing 25 percent of the nation's gross domestic product (GDP), which is the value of goods and services produced by a nation's economy in a year, excluding transactions with foreign countries.[2] Workers pay income and payroll taxes on the wages they earn. Consumers pay sales taxes on retail purchases and excise taxes on tobacco, alcohol, tires, gasoline, and other products. Homeowners and business owners pay property taxes on their homes and businesses.

Government not only touches the lives of individual Americans, but it also affects the nation's quality of life. Most people would not want to live, work, or run a business in a country without a fully functioning government. Government regulations and services help ensure safe neighborhoods, a healthy environment, an efficient transportation system, and an educated workforce. The tax system provides a mechanism for government to spread the cost of its operation over a broad range of individuals and groups in society. In times of emergency, such as a terrorist attack or a natural -

Speed limit laws and other government regulations affect the daily lives of all Americans.

disaster, people turn to government to respond to the crisis, assist the victims, and rebuild damaged communities.

Studying American government is important because of its great impact on individuals and society. People who understand how government works will be better equipped to take advantage of the benefits and services government provides and more able to prepare themselves to live effectively under government regulation and taxation. Studying American government helps citizens understand how they can influence government policies through voting, participating in political organizations, and contacting public officials.

GOVERNMENT AND POLITICS

2 *What is the difference between government and politics?*

Government and *politics* are distinct but closely related terms. **Government** is the institution with authority to set policy for society. Congress, the presidency, courts, and government agencies, such as the Social Security Administration (SSA) and the Food and Drug Administration (FDA), are all structures of American national government. Each state has a governor, legislature, court system, and administrative departments in addition to a series of local governments, such as municipalities, townships, counties, and school districts.

Whereas government is an *institution*, politics is a *process*. One political scientist says that **politics** is the way in which decisions for a society are made and considered binding most of the time by most of the people.[3] Another scholar declares that the study of politics is "the attempt to explain the various ways in which power is exercised in the everyday world and how that power is used to allocate resources and benefits to some people and groups, and costs and burdens to other people and groups."[4] We

could add a third definition: politics is the process that determines who shall occupy the roles of leadership in government and how the power of government shall be exercised.

Each of these definitions of politics emphasizes different aspects of the concept. Taken together, they enable us to identify certain key elements of politics as well as the relationship between politics and government:

- Government and politics are entwined. The selection of government personnel and the adoption of government policies are political. The enactment of the ADA, for example, took place through the political process.
- Politics is broader than government. In addition to the institutions of government and government officials, politics also involves individuals, groups, and organizations that are not officially part of the government, such as individual political activists, voters, the media, interest groups, political parties, and policy experts.
- Politics involves making decisions about the distribution of government benefits and the allocation of their costs.
- Politics is competitive. In American politics, individuals and groups compete with one another over the selection of the people who will occupy government office and over the policies government will enact and enforce.

Politics
also involves
**individuals,
groups, and
organizations**
that are **not officially**
part of the
government.

government the institution with authority to set policy for society.

politics the process that determines who shall occupy the roles of leadership in government and how the power of government shall be exercised.

Public policy is what government officials choose to do or not to do about public problems. Government policies can take the form of laws, executive orders, administrative regulations, court decisions, or, in some cases, no action at all. The ADA is a law aimed at addressing the problem of access to buildings open to the general public and to employment opportunities for people with disabilities. Some public policies may take the form of government programs. A government program is a system of projects or services intended to meet a public need. For example, the Supplemental Nutrition Assistance Program (SNAP) was created to address the problem of hunger in America. In late 2009, more than 37 million people received SNAP benefits.[5]

The **policymaking process** is a logical sequence of activities affecting the development of public policies. It takes place within the context of American society and includes seven stages: agenda setting, policy formulation, policy adoption, policy legitimation, policy implementation, policy evaluation, and policy change.

The Context of Policymaking

The policymaking process takes place within a context of the factors that determine problems that government addresses, the set of policy alternatives that decision-makers are willing to consider, and the resources available to the government for addressing the problems. Political scientists Michael E. Craft and Scott R. Furlong identify several aspects of the context for policymaking in the United States:

- The social context includes the diversity of the nation's people, population growth, population movement within the United States, and immigration from abroad. The proportion of the population with disabilities or with friends or family members with disabilities influences the policymaking process for disability rights because it determines the number of people who must be accommodated, as well as the potential strength of forces advocating disability rights.
- The economic context includes the strength of the nation's economy and the government's budgetary situation. The likelihood of the adoption of disability rights legislation is greater when the economy is strong than when it is weak because business and governments are able to afford the architectural adjustments necessary for making facilities accessible during good economic times.
- The political context refers to the strength of the two major parties and public opinion. The emergence of organized groups advocating disability rights was a key factor in the passage of the ADA. Furthermore, public opinion generally supported the goals of the disability rights movement.
- The governing context includes the constitutional system and the structures of government. Adoption of the ADA involved approval by both chambers of Congress and the president.
- The cultural context involves the political values of the nation and its people.[6]

Agenda Setting

Agenda setting is the process through which problems become matters of public concern and government action. The politics of agenda setting involves government officials and groups outside of the government competing to determine which problems government will address. Whereas some interests want to promote the consideration of certain issues, forces opposing change work to block discussion by denying that a problem exists or by arguing that the government either cannot or should not address it. Consider the controversy surrounding global warming, which is the gradual warming of the Earth's atmosphere reportedly caused by the burning of fossil fuels and industrial pollutants. Many scientists believe that global warming is a threat to the planet which, if left unchecked, will lead to serious consequences for life in the United States and around the world. Environmentalists want the government to take action to reduce the greenhouse gas emissions that cause global warming. In contrast, people who oppose government efforts to address global warming are skeptical that it exists, doubt that it is caused by human action, and/or question the effectiveness of government actions to address the problem. They want government to take no action or minimal action.

> The likelihood of the **adoption of legislation** such as that for disability rights is **greater** when the **economy is strong** than when it is **weak**.

public policy what government officials choose to do or not to do about public problems.

policymaking process a logical sequence of activities affecting the development of public policies; it takes place within the context of American society and includes seven stages: agenda setting, policy formulation, policy adoption, policy legitimation, policy implementation, policy evaluation, and policy change.

agenda setting the process through which problems become matters of public concern and government action.

Agenda setting not only identifies problems for government attention but also defines the nature of those problems, and therefore the eventual direction for a policy solution. Consider the issue of disability rights. During the debate in Congress on the ADA, spokespersons for advocacy groups for the disabled, such as the Disability Rights Education and Defense Fund (DREDF) and the Americans Disabled for Attendant Programs Today (ADAPT), noted that the employment rate for persons with severe disabilities was only 23 percent compared to an employment rate for adults without disabilities of nearly 80 percent.[7] The supporters of disability rights argued that discrimination or a lack of access to public facilities prevented many persons with disabilities from working. They proposed passage of federal legislation prohibiting discrimination against people with disabilities and ensuring access to business facilities as a solution to the problem. In contrast, business groups opposed government regulation. They denied that employment discrimination against people with disabilities was a major problem, suggesting instead that the employment rate for people with disabilities was low because many people with disabilities either cannot work or do not want to work. Furthermore, they said, individuals with disabilities who have few skills can make more money from government disability payments than they can earn in low-wage jobs.

Policy Formulation

Policy formulation is the development of strategies for dealing with the problems on the official policy agenda. Government officials as well as individuals and organizations outside of government, such as interest groups, political parties, policy experts, and the media, participate in policy formulation. The formulation of ADA legislation, for example, involved negotiations among members of Congress, executive branch officials, business interests, and advocacy groups for

people with disabilities. Although most business groups supported the goals of the ADA, they were concerned that the law would require businesses to hire unqualified applicants or make extensive (and expensive) physical modifications in their facilities. Business owners also worried that the new law would subject them to lawsuits and the possibility of expensive jury settlements.

The wording of the ADA reflects a compromise between the supporters of people with disabilities and business interests. The advocacy groups succeeded in writing a broad definition of disability into the law. The ADA declares that an individual with a disability is "a person who has a physical or mental impairment that substantially limits one or more major life activities, a record of such an impairment, or is regarded as having such an impairment."[8] Major life activities include the ability of individuals to care for themselves, perform manual tasks, walk, see, hear, speak, breathe, learn, work, sit, stand, lift, and reach. Under the law, persons with learning disabilities, epilepsy, mental illness, muscular dystrophy, HIV infection, cancer, diabetes, mental retardation, alcoholism, and cosmetic disfigurement are all considered disabled.

Business groups succeeded in limiting the scope of the law. Although the ADA prohibits discrimination, it does not establish

Disability rights activists crawl across the plaza of the U.S. Supreme Court building to protest court rulings limiting the scope of the ADA.

a quota system for hiring people with disabilities. It requires only that employers hire and promote qualified candidates without regard to disability. Furthermore, the ADA declares that a business need only make "reasonable accommodation" for employees and customers with disabilities that do not place an "undue hardship" on its operations.

Policy Adoption

Policy adoption is the official decision of a government body to accept a particular policy and put it into effect. The ADA, for example, was enacted through the legislative process. Congress passed the measure and the president signed it into law.

Not all policies are drafted into formal legislation and adopted through the legislative process. Courts adopt policies when they decide cases. Government agencies, such as the Environmental Protection Agency (EPA), adopt policies by issuing regulations. The president can adopt policy by issuing executive orders. Government officials also make policy when they decide either to take no action or continue policies already in place.

policy formulation the development of strategies for dealing with the problems on the official policy agenda.

policy adoption official decision of a government body to accept a particular policy and put it into effect.

Agenda setting **identifies problems** for government attention and **defines the direction for a policy solution**.

Policy Legitimation

Policy legitimation refers to the actions taken by government officials and others to ensure that most citizens regard a policy as a legal and appropriate government response to a problem. The president, congressional leaders from both political parties, and disability rights spokespersons helped to legitimize the ADA by hailing its passage as a step toward fairness and equal opportunity for millions of Americans with disabilities. Although not everyone agreed with all the details of the ADA, the measure itself enjoyed broad support. In other words, the ADA was widely regarded as a legitimate use of government power. Not all policies enjoy such a high level of legitimacy. For example, nearly 40 years after *Roe v. Wade*, the Supreme Court decision that legalized abortion throughout the United States, the country's abortion policy remains illegitimate in the eyes of millions of Americans.

Policy Implementation

Policy implementation is the stage of the policy process in which policies are carried out. Implementation involves not just government officials but also individuals and groups outside of the government. Private businesses, individual with disabilities, the Equal Employment Opportunity Commission (EEOC), and the courts all participate in the implementation of the ADA. The law requires private businesses to take reasonable steps to accommodate employees and customers with disabilities. If individuals with disabilities believe they have suffered discrimination, the law allows them to file a lawsuit against the offending business and/or file a complaint with the EEOC. Penalties for violators can be as high as $110,000 for repeat offenders.[9] During 2009, the EEOC, which also hears charges of racial, ethnic, gender, and age discrimination, handled 21,451 complaints based on the ADA, more than a fifth of the total complaints filed with the agency.[10]

The implementation process often involves supplying details and interpretations of policy that are omitted, either intentionally or unintentionally, during policy formulation. The ADA, for example, requires businesses to make "reasonable accommodations" for employees and customers with disabilities that do not place an "undue hardship" on their operations. How these terms apply to hundreds of specific circumstances depends on their interpretation by the EEOC and the courts. The EEOC, for example, has ruled that employers may not refuse to hire people with disabilities because of concerns about their impact on health insurance costs.[11] More often than not, the courts have sided with employers, narrowing the scope of the ADA and making it difficult for individuals to prevail in disability discrimination lawsuits filed against businesses. Employers win more than 90 percent of the workplace discrimination cases filed under the ADA.[12]

Policy Evaluation

Policy evaluation is the assessment of policy. Is a policy working well? Is it achieving its goals? Are there unintended consequences? Is it cost effective? Evaluation studies show that the ADA has had a mixed impact:

- A survey of corporate executives found that the median cost of making the workplace more accessible was only $223 per individual

policy legitimation the actions taken to ensure that most citizens regard a policy as a legal and appropriate government response to a problem.

policy implementation the stage of the policy process in which policies are carried out.

policy evaluation the assessment of policy.

TAKE ✓ ACTION
Government and You

Government policies affect each of us everyday in some ways that are obvious and in other ways that may not always be readily apparent. If a police officer stops you for speeding on your way to class, the government has touched you in a fashion that is direct and clear. In contrast, when you pick up a relative at the airport for a holiday visit, it may not occur to you that tax dollars paid to build the airport.

An important goal of this course is for students to recognize the relevance of government to their own lives and to the life of their community. Your assignment is to keep a journal documenting the impact of government on your daily life, directly or indirectly, throughout the semester. Your instructor will grade your journal on the following criteria:

- Number and frequency of entries. Your journal must include at least four dated entries for each week of the course.
- Evidence of growth in your understanding of American government. As the course progresses, your journal entries should reveal a higher level of sophistication than do entries made in the first few weeks of the term.
- Quality of journal entries. Some of your entries should identify a connection to concepts discussed in your textbook or in the classroom. At least one entry a week should include a personal evaluation of the role of government, displaying evidence that you have thought critically about the role of government in your life and in society as a whole.

with disabilities. Two-thirds of the executives surveyed reported that the ADA had not spawned an increase in lawsuits.[13]

- A majority of ADA complaints filed with the EEOC have involved issues that members of Congress did not discuss in drafting the law, such as back problems and psychological stress. Only 10 percent of the complaints have come from people with spinal cord injuries or other neurological problems—the conditions most frequently mentioned when the ADA was written.[14]
- Despite the ADA, the employment rate for people with disabilities actually declined between 1992 and 2000.[15]

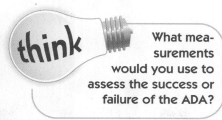

think What measurements would you use to assess the success or failure of the ADA?

Policy Change

Policy change refers to the modification of policy goals and means in light of new information or shifting political environments. Policy change is frequently the result of policy evaluation. Programs that are successful may no longer be needed; unsuccessful programs may be eliminated because of their failure. Partially successful programs or programs with unintended negative consequences may be modified in hopes of improving their operation. Policies may also be changed because the political landscape changes. Programs adopted by Democratic Congresses and presidents may be revised when Congress and the presidency are in the hands of the Republicans and vice versa.

policy change the modification of policy goals and means in light of new information or shifting political environments.

what we LEARNED

THE IMPORTANCE OF GOVERNMENT

1 *How does government affect the lives of individuals and society as a whole?*

Government affects individual Americans both directly and indirectly. Government adopts regulations such as speed limits and consumer protection laws, and provides services such as public hospitals and schools. These services are paid for through taxes and fees on workers and consumers. Government also influences the nation's quality of life.

GOVERNMENT AND POLITICS

2 *What is the difference between government and politics?*

Government is the institution with authority to set policy for society. Politics is the process that determines who shall occupy the roles of leadership in government and how the power of government shall be exercised. Although politics and government are intertwined, politics is broader than government. It involves the distribution of government benefits and the allocation of their costs. Politics is also competitive.

THE POLICYMAKING PROCESS

3 *What are the stages of the policymaking process?*

The policymaking process is a logical sequence of activities affecting the development of public policies. The policymaking process takes place within a context of factors, including the social, economic, political, governing, and cultural contexts. It includes seven stages:

agenda setting, policy formulation, policy adoption, policy legitimation, policy implementation, policy evaluation, and policy change.

MySearchLab®

1 A CHANGING

THE AMERICAN PEOPLE

Learning Objective **1.1** How is the population of the United States described in terms of age distribution, diversity, income distribution, and poverty?

THE UNITED STATES AND THE WORLD

Learning Objective **1.2** How does the United States compare with other nations of the world, and how does the global economy affect the economy of the United States?

AMERICAN POLITICAL CULTURE

Learning Objective **1.3** What are the most important elements of American political culture?

Throughout American history, the population center of the United States has been shifting steadily to the South and the West.[1] Although the population has increased in all regions of the country, it has grown more rapidly in the South and West, the region known as the **Sunbelt,** than it has in the Northwest and Midwest, the **Frostbelt.** According to the 2010 Census, 60 percent of the nation's population lives in the Sunbelt compared with 40 percent located in the Frostbelt. A century earlier in 1910, the figures were reversed—60 percent of the nation's people were in the Frostbelt compared with 40 percent in the Sunbelt.[2] As recently as 1950, three of the nation's four most populous states (New York, Pennsylvania, California, and Illinois) were Frostbelt states compared with only one of the four largest states in 2010 (California, Texas, New York, and Florida).[3]

The population of the Sunbelt has grown more rapidly than the population of the Frostbelt because of climate and economy. Florida, Arizona, and other Sunbelt states have

Sunbelt the southern and western regions of the United States.

Frostbelt the northeastern and mid-western regions of the United States.

AMERICA

become the retirement home for millions of retirees fleeing the cold winters of the Northeast and Midwest. Relative economic strength is the other factor driving population movement. The economies of Sunbelt states have grown rapidly, attracting immigrants in search of jobs from both other regions of the United States and other countries.

In contrast, Frostbelt economies have grown slowly because the automotive, steel, and other major industries of the region have been in decline.

The story of U.S. population movement introduces Chapter 1, which examines some of the important elements of the policymaking context. The chapter begins with a profile of the nation's population, considering immigration, illegal immigration, and population diversity. It examines the United States's place in the world as well as the global economy. The chapter next looks at the distribution of wealth, poverty, and healthcare. Finally, it discusses the political culture of the United States, focusing on democracy and capitalism.

THE AMERICAN PEOPLE

1.1 *How is the population of the United States described in terms of age distribution, diversity, income distribution, and poverty?*

According to the Census Bureau, the United States has more than 310 million people. The figure to the right traces the population growth rate of the United States since 1900. The nation's population increased rapidly in the early decades of the century before the Depression years of the 1930s, when the growth rate fell sharply. The population growth rate accelerated in the late 1940s and 1950s with the birth of the **baby-boom generation**, which is the exceptionally large number of Americans born after the end of World War II. Many American families delayed having children during the Great Depression in the 1930s and World War II in the early 1940s. After the war, the birthrate soared because families reunited and people grew optimistic about the future. With the end of the baby boom in the early 1960s, the rate of population growth slowed in each subsequent decade until the 1990s, when the nation's population increased more rapidly than it had in any decade since the 1950s. Even though birthrates continued falling in the 1990s, the population growth rate climbed because of increased immigration.

baby-boom generation the exceptionally large number of Americans born during the late 1940s, 1950s, and early 1960s.

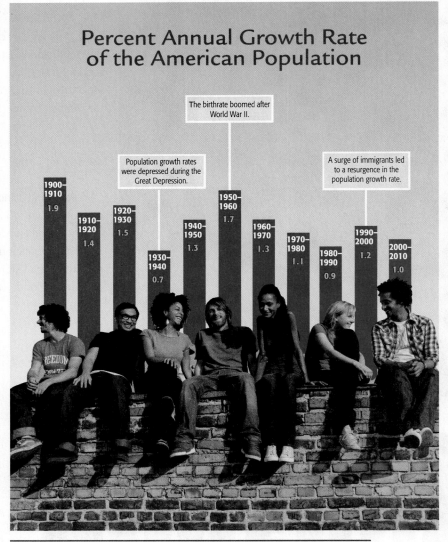

Percent Annual Growth Rate of the American Population

The birthrate boomed after World War II.

Population growth rates were depressed during the Great Depression.

A surge of immigrants led to a resurgence in the population growth rate.

1900–1910 1.9
1910–1920 1.4
1920–1930 1.5
1930–1940 0.7
1940–1950 1.3
1950–1960 1.7
1960–1970 1.3
1970–1980 1.1
1980–1990 0.9
1990–2000 1.2
2000–2010 1.0

The 2010 Census found that the population of the United States increased by 1 percent during the first decade of the twenty-first century.

State Governments Get Tough on Illegal Immigration

Some states, frustrated with Congress's failure to pass comprehensive immigration reform legislation, have adopted their own immigration laws. In 2010, Arizona enacted a measure making failure to carry immigration papers a crime for noncitizens. The law authorized the police to stop an individual if an officer has a "reasonable suspicion" that the person may be undocumented. Several other states have subsequently adopted more stringent measures. Georgia, for example, forces employers to check on the immigration status of potential employees. Some states have even taken the Arizona approach a step further. Alabama bars illegal immigrants from enrolling in any public college or university after high school. The Alabama measure also makes it a crime to rent to illegal immigrants.

DISCUSSION

Have all states adopted anti-illegal immigrant measures? No. In general, the states that have acted have been states with Republican legislatures and Republican governors. Opposition to illegal immigration is a big issue for Republican activists, and less so for Democratic voters who tend to favor a more comprehensive approach.

Are Latino rights organizations concerned that Arizona-style measures will lead to racial profiling? Yes. Racial profiling is the practice of police officers targeting individuals as suspected criminals on the basis of their race or ethnicity. Even though states that adopt Arizona-style measures typically prohibit racial profiling, Latino groups contend that authorities will target people with brown skin. They also worry that landlords and business owners will avoid the risk of breaking the law by employing or renting to an illegal alien by turning away all Latinos.

Are many business interests opposed to the anti-immigrant measures? Yes. In Georgia, for example, agriculture and landscaping interests warn that they may not be able to find enough documented workers to stay in business. Business groups in general complain about the expense involved in verifying worker status. Landlords in Alabama argue that having to verify the immigration status of tenants will add significantly to their cost of doing business. Tourist industry spokespersons fear the possibility of boycotts organized by groups opposed to the immigration measures.

Does the Constitution allow states to have their own immigration laws? That's the question currently before the courts. Civil liberties and immigrant rights groups filed suit against each of the state laws as soon as they were enacted. Federal judges responded by putting enforcement of the measures on hold, pending court review. Business groups support many of the lawsuits as well, arguing that allowing states to create their own immigration laws would create a crazy-quilt pattern of laws across the nation that would burden employers and be unfair to employees. It is likely that the issue will eventually reach the U.S. Supreme Court.

An Aging Population

The population of the United States is aging. In 2010, 40.2 million Americans were age 65 and older. The U.S. Census Bureau estimates that the number of older Americans will increase steadily for at least the next two decades. The number of people age 65 or older will be 54.8 million in 2020 and 72 million in 2030. As a percentage of the total population, the group of people age 65 and older will steadily increase from 13 percent in 2010 to 19.3 percent in 2030. While the older population is increasing rapidly, the number of people between 20 and 64 years of age, the prime working years, is growing slowly and actually falling as a percentage of the total population. According to the U.S. Census Bureau, the number of people age 20 to 64 will fall from 60 percent of the total population in 2010 to only 54.5 percent in 2030.[4]

The aging of the population threatens the financial solvency of the government's major healthcare and pension programs—Medicare, Medicaid, and Social Security. **Medicare** is a federally health insurance program for the elderly. As the population ages, the number of people eligible for Medicare will climb and the cost of the program will grow. **Medicaid** is a federal health insurance program for low-income persons, people with disabilities, and elderly people who are impoverished. Although older people are a minority of Medicaid recipients, the cost of their healthcare is greater than it is for other groups of beneficiaries. **Social Security** is a federal pension and disability insurance program funded through a payroll tax on workers and their employers. Its costs will rise as more people reach retirement age and begin collecting benefits. Because the traditional working age population is growing slowly, payroll tax revenues will be unable to keep up with program expenditures, forcing the government to cut benefits or find other revenue sources to fund the program.

Population Diversity

The United States is a multiracial/multiethnic society. The Census Bureau estimates that the nation's population is 65 percent white, 16 percent Latino, 13 percent African American, 5 percent Asian American, and 1 percent American Indian or Alaska Native. Latinos are the fastest growing American ethnic group.[5] Because of continued immigration and relatively high birthrates for Latino women, demographers expect that the Latino population will continue to grow rapidly, increasing from 16 percent of the population in 2010 to 24.4 percent in 2050.[6]

Immigrants constitute an eighth of the nation's population.[7] Whereas earlier waves of immigration to the United States were primarily from Europe, most recent immigrants come from Latin America or Asia. The primary countries of origin for recent legal immigrants to the United States are, in order of importance, Mexico, Philippines, India, and China. The states in which immigrants most frequently settle are California, New York, Texas, Florida, New Jersey, and Illinois.[8]

In 2009, 11.1 million people lived in the United States illegally, down from 12 million in 2007.[9] The undocumented population is evenly divided between people who entered the country legally on temporary visas, such as student visas and tourist visas, and people who crossed the border illegally. Mexico accounted for 60 percent of unauthorized immigrants in 2009. A fifth of illegal immigrants are from other Latin American countries, particularly Honduras, El Salvador, Guatemala, Nicaragua, and Brazil. The rest comes from Canada, Europe, Asia, and Africa. Although undocumented immigrants are found in every region of

Medicare a federally funded health insurance program for the elderly.

Medicaid a federal program designed to provide health insurance coverage to low-income persons, people with disabilities, and elderly people who are impoverished.

Social Security a federal pension and disability insurance program funded through a payroll tax on workers and their employers.

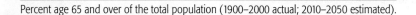
Percent age 65 and over of the total population (1900–2000 actual; 2010–2050 estimated).

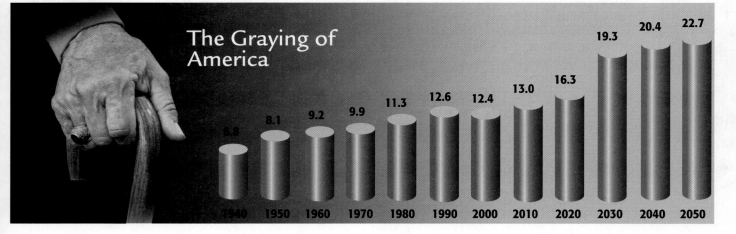

The Graying of America

| 6.8 | 8.1 | 9.2 | 9.9 | 11.3 | 12.6 | 12.4 | 13.0 | 16.3 | 19.3 | 20.4 | 22.7 |
| 1940 | 1950 | 1960 | 1970 | 1980 | 1990 | 2000 | 2010 | 2020 | 2030 | 2040 | 2050 |

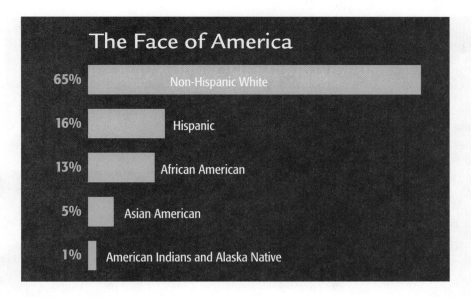

The Face of America

65%	Non-Hispanic White
16%	Hispanic
13%	African American
5%	Asian American
1%	American Indians and Alaska Native

Illegal immigration is controversial. Critics charge that undocumented workers drive down wage rates for American citizens while overcrowding schools and hospital emergency rooms. They argue that unauthorized immigrants undermine the nation's cultural integrity because they create cultural enclaves that resemble their home countries instead of learning English and adopting the customs of the United States. The opponents of illegal immigration favor tighter border controls, strict enforcement of immigration laws, and punishment for American citizens who provide unauthorized immigrants with jobs, housing, healthcare, and other services.

In contrast, immigration advocates contend that the United States benefits from immigration, even illegal immigration. They argue that undocumented workers take jobs that citizens do not want and that they pay more in taxes than they receive in government services. An influx of hard-working, well-motivated manual workers enhances the competitiveness of American industry and provides additional jobs for citizens as managers. The defenders of immigration believe that today's immigrants enrich the nation's culture just as did earlier waves of immigrants from Great Britain,

the country, a majority lives in the states of California, Texas, Florida, New York, Arizona, Illinois, and New Jersey.

People migrate to the United States primarily for economic reasons. The number of illegal immigrants declined in 2008–2009 because the weak job market. Unauthorized workers account for 5.1 percent of the civilian workforce. They are concentrated in low-wage occupations such as farming, cleaning, construction, and food preparation. Although unauthorized workers in the United States earn only about half as much as do American citizens and permanent residents, they make substantially more money than they earned in their home countries.

Most undocumented immigrants in the United States live in families rather than alone as single adults. The ratio of men to women is 58 percent to 42 percent. Undocumented families include four million children who are U.S. citizens because they were born in the United States. Most unauthorized families live at or near the poverty level and lack health insurance.[10]

Illegal immigrants are concentrated in low-wage occupations such as farming, cleaning, construction, and food preparation.

After World War II, in which France suffered 600,000 casualties, the government of France encouraged immigration to provide labor for postwar reconstruction. Over the next 30 years, millions of foreign workers migrated to France, often joined by their families. Immigrants came to France from southern Europe, especially Italy and Portugal, and from North Africa, particularly Algeria, which had been a French colony prior to its independence in 1962.[11]

The presence in France of a large number of North African immigrants has been controversial. Some French see North Africans as a threat to social cohesion and even national security. North Africans, most of whom are Arab Muslims, are ethnically and culturally different from the French European majority, most of which is non-observant Catholic. Some French also consider North Africans a threat to national security because of the association of some European Islamic immigrants with 9/11 and other terrorist acts.[12]

France has adopted a series of laws and regulations aimed at addressing the issue of non-European immigration. It has halted the immigration of non-European workers but continues to allow family reunification. In order to reduce the size of the immigrant population, France has offered financial incentives to immigrants to return home, but the program has had little success. It has also attempted to pressure North African immigrants to assimilate into French culture. A 2004 law, for example, bans headscarves from public schools, preventing Muslim girls from covering their heads.[13] In 2010, Belgium,

France, and several other European countries considered legislation that would ban Muslim women from wearing niqabs or burqas, which cover the full body and face, calling them a symbol of denigration and subjugation of women.

QUESTIONS

1 How important is it for immigrants to adopt the culture of the majority of people in their new country?

2 Are Mexican immigrants in the United States as culturally different as North African immigrants are in France?

3 Is opposition to non-European immigration in France (and in the United States) racist?

Muslim schoolgirls gather in Strasbourg to protest a ruling banning headscarves in French public schools.

Germany, Ireland, Italy, and Poland. Furthermore, the proponents of immigration contend that most recent immigrants are quick to learn English and eager to become citizens so they can participate in the nation's political life. Immigration advocates believe that the United States should grant legal status to undocumented workers who have helped build the nation's economy while enacting a realistic immigration system to enable foreign workers to enter the country legally to find jobs.

Geography

As we discussed in the introduction to this chapter, the population of the United States has been shifting to the South and the West,

the region known as the Sunbelt, and away from the Northeast and Midwest, the Frostbelt. In 1970, a bare majority of the nation's population, 52 percent, lived in the Frostbelt. Today, the figure is 60 percent.

Population changes have affected the political balance in the U.S. House of Representatives. Because the Northeast and Midwest have lost population, they have lost seats in the House. After the 2010 Census, New York and Ohio each lost two U.S. House seats. Illinois, Iowa, Louisiana, Massachusetts, Michigan, Missouri, New Jersey, and Pennsylvania each lost one seat in the House. In contrast, Sunbelt states have gained representation in the House. Texas was the big

winner after the 2010 Census, gaining four seats in the House. Florida added two seats. Arizona, Georgia, Nevada, South Carolina, Utah, and Washington gained one seat each. As Sunbelt states have gained influence in Congress, issues important to the region, such as immigration and energy, have become more prominent on the nation's official policy agenda.

Sunbelt politicians have also dominated the race for the White House. Every elected president between John Kennedy from Massachusetts, who won office in 1960, and Barack Obama from Illinois, who won in 2008, has been from the Sunbelt. Lyndon Johnson (1964) was from Texas, Richard Nixon (1968 and 1972) was from California, Jimmy Carter (1976) was from Georgia, Ronald Reagan (1980 and 1984) was from California, and George H.W. Bush (1988) was from Texas.

The United States is an urban country. Census data show that 80 percent of the nation's people reside in metropolitan areas, with a majority of Americans living in urban centers of more than a million residents. Furthermore, metropolitan areas are growing more rapidly than non-metropolitan areas.

Income Distribution

The table below shows the share of national income earned by each of five income groups, from the poorest fifth of American families through the wealthiest fifth. Over a 29-year period from 1980 through 2009, the proportion of national income received by the wealthiest fifth of the population increased from 41.4 percent to 50.3 percent. The rich got richer. In the meantime, the share of national income earned by the four other groups of families declined. In particular, the share of income earned by the poorest families fell by more than

"The wealthiest 4,000 Americans earned more money in 2000 than more than half a million retail clerks earned combined."

Donald L. Barlett and James B. Steele, "Has Your Life Become a Game of Chance?" *Time*, February 2, 2004, p. 42.

35 percent, from 5.3 percent of the total in 1980 to 3.4 percent in 2009. The poor got poorer.

Economist Robert H. Frank attributes the growth of income inequality to changes in the economy and tax policy. Professor Frank says that the United States has a winner-take-all economy in which small differences in performance often translate into huge differences in economic reward. Corporate executives, sports stars, and well-known entertainers earn huge paychecks, many times greater than the earnings of ordinary workers, average athletes, and entertainers without the star power. In the meantime, income tax cuts adopted during the Ronald Reagan and George W. Bush administrations significantly reduced income tax rates for upper-income earners, effectively shifting wealth toward the top of the income ladder.[14]

Household income in the United States varies, depending on race, ethnicity, residence, region, and gender. Whites and Asian Americans/Pacific Islanders are better off than Latinos and African Americans. In 2009, the median household income in the United States was $49,777. Asian American/Pacific Islander households had the highest average income: $65,469. The average income for white households was $54,461. In contrast, the average household income for African Americans and Latino households was significantly lower: $32,584 and $38,039 respectively. The average household income for families living in metropolitan areas was higher than it was for families located outside big cities, and suburban households had higher incomes than families living in the inner city. Household income was lowest in the South, and highest in the Northeast. Income also varies by gender. In 2009, the average income of male full-time, year-round workers was $47,127 compared with $36,278 for women.[15]

Income differences among racial and ethnic groups and between men and women reflect disparities in education and training, social factors, and discrimination. As a group, Asian Americans and whites are better educated than African Americans and Latinos. Women often fall behind their male counterparts on the career ladder because many women leave the workforce for years to raise children. Jobs that are traditionally held by women, such as nursing and education, typically pay less than jobs that are traditionally male. Finally, many observers believe that the incomes of women and minorities lag behind those of white males because of employment discrimination.

Share of National Income Received by Each Fifth of Families, 1980–2009

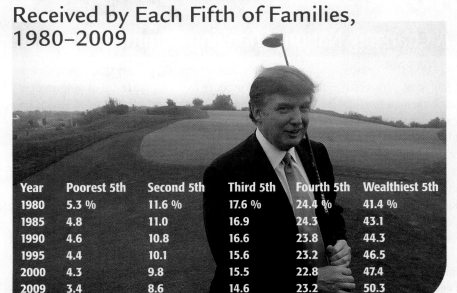

Year	Poorest 5th	Second 5th	Third 5th	Fourth 5th	Wealthiest 5th
1980	5.3 %	11.6 %	17.6 %	24.4 %	41.4 %
1985	4.8	11.0	16.9	24.3	43.1
1990	4.6	10.8	16.6	23.8	44.3
1995	4.4	10.1	15.6	23.2	46.5
2000	4.3	9.8	15.5	22.8	47.4
2009	3.4	8.6	14.6	23.2	50.3

Source: U.S. Census Bureau, *2009 Statistical Abstract*, available at www.census.gov; U.S. Census Bureau, "Income and Earnings Summary Measures by Selected Characteristics: 2007 and 2008," *Income, Poverty, and Health Insurance Coverage in the United States: 2008*, available at www.census.gov.

Poverty

The government measures poverty on a subsistence basis. The **poverty threshold** is the amount of money an individual or family needs to purchase basic necessities, such as food, clothing, healthcare, shelter, and transportation. The actual dollar amount varies with family size, and rises with inflation. In 2009, the official government poverty threshold was $22,050 for a family of four.[16] More than 43 million Americans lived in poverty in 2009, 14.3 percent of the population.[17]

Although the poverty rate for racial and ethnic minority groups and for families headed by women has declined over the last 50 years, it is still higher than it is for other groups. In 2009, the poverty rate for Latinos, African Americans, and Asian Americans stood at 25.3 percent, 25.8 percent, and 12.5 percent, respectively, compared

think

Should the government do more to reduce poverty?

with 9.4 percent for whites. Poverty also affects children and families headed by women in disproportionate numbers. Nearly 21 percent of the nation's children under 18 lived in families that were poor in 2009. The poverty rate for families headed by women was 29.9 percent.[18]

poverty threshold the amount of money an individual or family needs to purchase basic necessities, such as food, clothing, healthcare, shelter, and transportation.

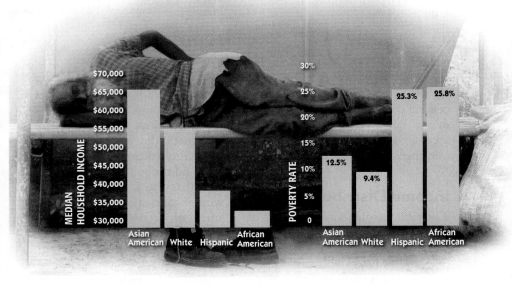

U.S. Income and Poverty Rate, by Ethnicity, 2009

TAKE ✓ ACTION

A Changing Nation, Changing Communities

Data from the 2010 U.S. Census show that the United States is changing. Is your local community changing as well? Your assignment is to research the ways in which your community has changed by interviewing one or more people who have lived in the community for at least 15 or 20 years. They can be relatives, friends, coworkers, or fellow students. Your questions should cover the following topics:

- **Population change**. Has the population of the area grown? Have people immigrated to the community from other states or other nations? How has the racial/ethnic makeup of the population changed? Has the population as a whole grown younger or older?

- **Economic change**. Has the mix of businesses and industries changed? Have any major employers gone out of business? Are there new industries?

- **Cultural change**. Does the community have places of worship for religious faiths that are new to the area? Are there

new types of restaurants? Do grocery stores carry different varieties of produce to match the tastes of new residents? Does the community celebrate different or additional holidays and festivals?

Take careful notes on what you are told because your instructor plans to organize a class discussion around the research that you and other students have completed. The instructor will ask students to relate the information they learned from their interviews and then analyze the impact of socioeconomic change on the policymaking process. Prepare for the discussion by considering the following questions: Would you expect different political issues to emerge today as compared with 20 years ago based on the changes that have taken place in your community? Do you think the capacity of government to respond to policy demands has changed? Would you expect that the community's standard for evaluating government performance has changed?

THE UNITED STATES AND THE WORLD

How does the United States compare with other nations of the world, and how does the global economy affect the economy of the United States?

The United States is the one of the largest countries in the world, both in terms of population and physical size. It is the third most populous country, after China and India, each of which has well over a billion people. In terms of land area, the United States ranks third, after Russia and China.[19]

The United States is the foremost nation in the world, militarily, economically, and culturally. Since the collapse of the Soviet Union in 1991, the United States has emerged as the world's only **superpower**, which is a country powerful enough to influence events throughout the world. The U.S. defense budget

A newsstand in Beijing displays the Chinese version of *Rolling Stone* magazine, demonstrating the pervasiveness of American culture around the world.

accounts for more than 40 percent of world military spending, more than seven times as much as China, the second place country, spends on its military.[20]

American culture permeates the world. American fashion, music, and entertainment are pervasive. People around the world eat at McDonald's restaurants, wear Levi jeans, drink Pepsi or Coke, watch Hollywood movies, and have Facebook pages.

The U.S. Economy

The United States is also the foremost economic power with the world's largest and most productive economy. The **gross domestic product (GDP)** is the value of goods and services produced by a nation's economy in a year, excluding transactions with foreign countries. The U.S. GDP stood at $14.9 trillion in late 2010, substantially greater than that of China ($5.9 trillion) and Japan ($5.5 trillion). Even though the United States contains only 4.6 percent of the world's population, it generates 23.6 percent of world economic output.[21]

The figure to the right shows gross national income (GNI) per capita (per person) adjusted for purchasing power differences for China, Mexico, Germany, Japan, the United Kingdom, and the United States. Because the cost of goods and services varies from country to country, the same amount of money does not purchase the same quantity of goods and services from one nation to another. Adjusting GNI per capita to reflect

differences in purchasing power is a good measure of a nation's **standard of living**, which is a term that refers to the goods and services affordable by and available to the residents of a nation. As the figure indicates, the average American enjoys greater purchasing power than people living in the other countries listed in the table. Americans are somewhat better off than people living in other industrialized countries, such as, Germany, Japan, and the United Kingdom. Meanwhile, the standard of living in the United States is substantially higher than it is in Mexico and other **developing countries**, which are nations with relatively low levels of per capita income. Even though the rapidly growing Chinese economy is the second largest in the world after the United States, per capita purchasing power is relatively low in China because the nation has a huge population.

Average Annual Per Capita Purchasing Power

United States	$46,790
UK	$36,240
Japan	$35,190
Germany	$35,950
Mexico	$14,340
China	$6,010

superpower a country powerful enough to influence events throughout the world.

gross domestic product (GDP) the total value of goods and services produced by a nation's economy in a year, excluding transactions with foreign countries.

per capita per person.

standard of living the goods and services affordable to and available to the residents of a nation.

developing countries nations with relatively low levels of per capita income.

General Motors is neck and neck with Volkswagen as the leading automobile seller in China. GM now sells more cars in China than in the United States.

The Global Economy

The United States emerged from World War II as the world's foremost economic power. With European and Asian competitors devastated by war, American companies dominated the domestic market and shipped manufactured goods around the globe. Millions of Americans with only a high school education found good-paying jobs working in steel plants or on automobile assembly lines.

Today, the United States is part of a **global economy**, which is the integration of national economies into a world economic system in which companies compete worldwide for suppliers and markets. International treaties and agreements have reduced the barriers to trade among the world's countries. The move toward free trade has allowed American companies to compete for business abroad, but it has forced them to compete at home as well against overseas competitors.

Some American companies and workers have prospered in the global economy. American agriculture, major retailers such as Wal-Mart, and the nation's biggest makers of automobiles and automobile

parts have benefited from international trade. For example, although General Motors (GM) has been steadily losing market share in the United States to foreign competitors, it is doing very well abroad, especially in China where it has become that nation's leading automobile seller. In fact, GM now sells more cars in China than in the United States.[22] Companies that have lowered their cost of doing business through outsourcing or the use of modern technology have also done well. Their investors have profited from higher stock prices, and their managers and executives have reaped the reward in higher salaries and bonuses. Skilled workers who understand and can operate the latest technology in their fields are in high demand, especially workers who have the ability to adapt quickly as technology changes.

In contrast, international trade has been a disaster for workers in fields that have been unable to compete against low-wage competition from abroad. Less expensive transportation and communication systems make it possible to produce goods in areas of the world where production costs are low and then

transport those goods to markets worldwide. How can an American manufacturer afford to pay $15 an hour to low-skill assembly workers in the United States if low-skill workers in Indonesia, China, or the Caribbean will do the same work for less than $2 an hour? The American firm must either move its production process to a country with lower wage costs or lose market share because it cannot compete.

American companies have also begun to cut costs by outsourcing information technology work and some business process functions to India, China, and Russia—countries that have a large number of college-educated workers who will work for much lower wages than will their counterparts in the United States. While General Motors is reducing its workforce in the United States, it is hiring in China. Analysts estimate that wages and benefits per factory

global economy the integration of national economies into a world economic system in which companies compete worldwide for suppliers and markets.

Outsourcing may be more prevalent in your daily life than you realize. Some McDonald's restaurants utilize "remote order-taking," in which call centers field and place drive-through orders over the Internet.

worker in China are about a tenth of what they are in the United States. GM plans to open a new factory in China within the next few years and may begin exporting vehicles from there to the United States.[23]

Low-skill, poorly educated American workers have also been damaged by technological change. Modern technology has enabled companies to replace low-skill workers with machines, generating the same output or more with fewer workers. Between 1979 and 2000, U.S. factory output nearly doubled, even though the number of manufacturing jobs fell by more than 2 million. A quarter century ago, General Motors employed 454,000 workers to manufacture 5 million vehicles. Today, the GM payroll has shrunk to 75,000 employees and its sales are less than 3 million vehicles a year.[24] Even though the American workers who lose their jobs because of international trade and technological change usually find new positions, their new jobs typically pay $2 or more an hour less than their old jobs and often come without benefits.[25] In 1979, General Motors, Ford, and General Electric were the nation's largest employers; today the companies employing the most workers are Wal-Mart, McDonald's, and UPS.[26]

AMERICAN POLITICAL CULTURE

1.3 *What are the most important elements of American political culture?*

Political culture refers to the widely held, deeply rooted political values of a society. These values are important for the policymaking process because they define the terms of political debate and establish the range of acceptable policy options available to policymakers.

Democracy

Attitudes toward democracy and capitalism constitute the core of America's political culture. A **democracy** is a system of government in which ultimate political authority is vested in the people. Political scientist Robert A. Dahl identifies eight criteria of a democratic society:

1. *The right to vote.* All or nearly all citizens enjoy the right to vote and have their votes counted equally. In the United States, every adult citizen has the right to vote except people who have lost their voting rights because they have been convicted of a serious crime. Significant restrictions on the right to vote are undemocratic. For example, Saudi Arabia held elections for the first time in 2006 to select members of municipal councils but only allowed men to cast ballots. Although holding an election is a step toward democracy, excluding women is undemocratic.
2. *The right to be elected.* Citizens have the right to compete for elective office, including people who oppose the policies of the current government. In 2007, Vietnam held elections for the National Assembly with 876 candidates competing for 500 positions. The election fell short of democracy, however, because all but two independent candidates were either members of the Communist Party or nominated by organizations affiliated with the party.[27]
3. *The right of political leaders to compete for support and votes.* Candidates have an opportunity to conduct campaigns in order to win support. If candidates cannot campaign, voters are unable to make informed choices.
4. *Free and fair elections.* All candidates compete under the same set of rules, without legal advantage or disadvantage. Democratic governments respect the outcomes of elections, peacefully stepping down from office and allowing opposition political parties and leaders to take power.
5. *Freedom of association.* Citizens have the right to form political parties and organize groups. They can attend meetings, participate in political rallies, and take part in peaceful demonstrations. In 2009, the government of Iran proved itself undemocratic: when demonstrators took to the streets to protest the outcome of an election that they considered stolen, the government responded with violence, brutally suppressing the demonstrations and arresting protest leaders.
6. *Freedom of expression.* People living in a democracy have the right to express their political views without censorship or fear of government retaliation. Governments that jail their critics are not democracies. For example, an Egyptian court sentenced an opposition political leader to five years in prison at hard labor for allegedly forging the signatures on the petition he used to create his own political party, including those of his wife and father.[28]
7. *Alternative sources of information.* The citizens in a democracy have access to information sources that are not controlled by the government. Elections cannot be free and fair if the only information voters have about government policies and candidates is information supplied and controlled by the government. In Russia, for example,

political culture the widely held, deeply rooted political values of a society.

democracy a system of government in which ultimate political authority is vested in the people.

Many Americans were infuriated by the government bailout of the banking and auto industries because they blamed poor executive decisions for the decline of the auto industry and overly aggressive home mortgage lending by banks for the Great Recession of 2008–2009. The government acted because policymakers believed that the failure of either of these industries would make the economy worse.

the government has taken over private television networks, and journalists who dare to report information that contradicts the official government line face the danger of lawsuits, imprisonment, and even death.[29]

8. *Institutions for making public policies depend on votes and other expressions of citizen preference.* In a democracy, citizens elect policymakers. Free and fair elections are meaningless if military leaders or religious figures that do not answer to the voters are the real policymakers.[30] For example, Saudi Arabia, despite its recent elections for municipal councils, is still ruled by King Abdullah.

Capitalism

Capitalism, the other principal element of America's political culture, is an economic system characterized by individual and corporate ownership of the means of production, and a market economy based on the supply and demand of goods and services. Under capitalism, businesses and industries are privately owned rather than controlled by the government. The marketplace, in which buyers and sellers freely exchange goods and services, determines what goods and services are produced, how they are produced, and for whom they are produced. The proponents of capitalism argue that it is good for consumers because businesses compete to provide quality goods and services at prices that consumers are willing to pay. They believe that capitalism promotes economic growth because only the most efficient business enterprises survive the competition of the marketplace.

The primary alternative to capitalism is **socialism,** which is an economic system characterized by governmental ownership of the means of production and control of the distribution of goods and services. In a socialist economy, the government owns and operates business and industry. It makes decisions about the production and distribution of goods and services in the public interest without regard for the profit motive. The proponents of socialism believe that it is a better system than capitalism because, they say, it prevents the unfair concentration of wealth and power in a small segment of society. In contrast, capitalists contend that socialism retards economic growth because economic decisions reflect the political biases of government bureaucrats rather than the law of supply and demand.

The economy of the United States and that of other capitalist nations is best described as a **mixed economy,** which is an economic system that combines private ownership with extensive governmental intervention. Although most business and industry are in private hands, the government owns and operates some sectors of the economy and closely regulates other. The industries most frequently owned by the governments around the world are telecommunications, power, petroleum, railways, airports, airlines, public transport, healthcare, postal service, and sometimes banks. In the United States, the **public sector,** which is the government-owned segment of the economy, is relatively small. Nonetheless, the **private sector,** which is the privately owned segment of the economy, is closely regulated by the government.

capitalism an economic system characterized by individual and corporate ownership of the means of production and a market economy based on the supply and demand of goods and services.

socialism an economic system characterized by governmental ownership of the means of production and control of the distribution of goods and services.

mixed economy an economic system that combines private ownership with extensive intervention.

public sector the government-owned segment of the economy.

private sector the privately owned segment of the economy.

TAKING SIDES

Illegal Immigrants and American Politics

How important a role do illegal immigrants currently residing in the United States play?

Should the Constitution be altered so that children born of illegal immigrants are not U.S. citizens?

OVERVIEW

While most Americans and government officials would like to stop illegal immigration, there is no widespread consensus as to what to do with the people who are already living here. Illegal immigrants may have crossed the borders with no or fraudulent documents, or have overstayed or violated the rules on their visas. According to a Pew Hispanic Center study, nearly 12 million unauthorized immigrants live in the United States.[31] The cost of illegal immigrants to the government is somewhere between $11 billion and $22 billion a year, as a result of their paying less in taxes but consuming social services.[32] Arizona recently passed a highly controversial law that empowers local law enforcement to check the papers of anyone suspected of being in the country illegally.

Hispanic Americans have recently taken to the streets in mass marches to protest the unjust treatment of illegal aliens, who are vital to many U.S. industries. Hispanic Americans are beginning to gain political power in the United States, as their legal population and number of representatives in Congress are increasing. As Hispanics are gaining a foothold in American politics, neither party can afford to alienate these voters.

Some propose to provide amnesty to all illegal aliens currently residing in the United States. After paying back-taxes, the alien's illegal entry would be overlooked and he or she would be placed on the five-year citizenship path that legal immigrants travel.

 ## SUPPORTING amnesty for illegal immigrants

 ## AGAINST amnesty for illegal immigrants

Illegal immigrants benefit the U.S. economy. People who have come here looking for a better life generally work in jobs that are unattractive to most Americans. They provide a necessary labor pool, which keeps the country running smoothly and bolsters the economy.

Children of illegal immigrants born while in the United States are citizens. Being born to an American citizen or being born on American soil grants citizenship in this country. Many illegal immigrants have children while here, and these children are Americans. Granting the parents amnesty allows them to better provide for their children.

The states are overly burdened with what is a federal issue. Border states are bearing the full brunt of the difficulties arising from the federal government's inaction. Putting illegal aliens on the path to citizenship would free up resources the states are using to police what is essentially a national issue.

Offering amnesty would encourage more illegal behavior. People who are in this country without a visa or are in violation of their visas are criminals. We should not condone the violation of law, and offering amnesty would encourage more people to come illegally.

The United States is stretched thin economically taking care of its people. Illegal immigrants and their children become burdens on the social structure because they are more likely to need government-provided health care, and will overburden schools that were not prepared for those numbers of children. If we are to take care of people here well, we need to regulate who is here and contain the numbers.

We have no idea who has crossed our borders and is living within them. Illegal aliens have crossed our borders without proper documents, so we don't know enough about these individuals to grant blanket amnesty. As terrorism is becoming more of a threat, particularly from people inside our borders, it is in our interest to know who is here.

what we LEARNED

THE AMERICAN PEOPLE

1.1 *How is the population of the United States described in terms of age distribution, diversity, income distribution, and poverty?*

The population of the United States stood at 310 million in 2010. The population grew rapidly in the post–World War II years with the birth of the baby-boom generation. Population growth rates subsequently fell before increasing in the 1990s, primarily because of immigration. In the first decade of the twenty-first century, population growth was 1 percent. Immigration, both legal and illegal, has added substantially to the nation's growth rate and to its diversity. In 2010, the population of the United States was 65 percent white, with Latinos representing the largest and fastest growing minority group. A majority of Americans live in the Sunbelt. As a result, Sunbelt states now hold a majority of seats in the U.S. House of Representatives.

Although the United States is a wealthy country, many Americans live in poverty. Whites and Asian Americans/Pacific Islanders are better off than are Latinos and African Americans. They earn higher incomes and are less likely to be poor. People living in metropolitan areas earn more than do people outside metro areas. Suburban residents are more affluent than are people living in the inner city. The South is the poorest region; the Northeast is

the wealthiest. Families headed by women are worse off than are other families.

THE UNITED STATES AND THE WORLD

1.2 *How does the United States compare with other nations of the world, and how does the global economy affect the economy of the United States?*

The United States is third among nations in land area and population, but it is the world's foremost military and economic power. With the collapse of the Soviet Union, the United States has emerged as the world's lone military superpower. It has the world's largest economy by far and, among large nations, the world's highest standard of living. Meanwhile, American cultural influences are pervasive.

The global economy is the integration of national economies into a world economic system in which companies compete worldwide for suppliers and markets. It increases competition for companies and workers. Companies that are able to compete effectively do very well because their potential market has increased, whereas inefficient companies risk losing out to international competitors. Meanwhile, creative managers and highly skilled workers do well because their services are in demand, whereas low-skill American workers suffer a loss in wages in competition with low-skill workers

around the globe who will work for less money.

AMERICAN POLITICAL CULTURE

1.3 *What are the most important elements of the political culture of the United States?*

Attitudes toward democracy and capitalism constitute the core of America's political culture. A democracy is a system of government in which ultimate political authority is vested in the people. Professor Robert Dahl identifies eight criteria of democracy that focus on voting rights, fair election procedures, and freedom of expression and association. Capitalism is an economic system characterized by individual and corporate ownership of the means of production, and a market economy based on the supply and demand of goods and services. The primary alternative to capitalism is socialism, which is an economic system characterized by governmental ownership of the means of production and control of the distribution of goods and services.

The economy of the United States and that of other capitalist nations is best described as a mixed economy, which is an economic system that combines private ownership with extensive governmental intervention. Although most business and industry are in private hands, the government owns and operates some sectors of the economy and closely regulates other.

Send   Save   Delete

From: Professor Tannahill
Add Cc | Add Bcc

Subject: Tips for Success

📎 Attach a file

BUYING TEXTBOOKS:
Don't sign up for a course unless you can afford the textbook as well as the course tuition and fees. Students without textbooks don't pass.

MySearchLab®

1.1 *How is the population of the United States described in terms of age distribution, diversity, income distribution, and poverty?*

1. Which of the following statements is true about the baby-boom generation?
   a. The baby-boom generation is smaller than preceding or succeeding generations.
   b. The baby-boom generation retired just before 2000.
   c. The baby-boom generation was born after World War II.
   d. None of the above

2. Demographers expect which of the following racial/ethnic group will grow most rapidly in the years ahead?
   a. Latinos
   b. Whites
   c. African Americans
   d. Asian Americans

3. After the 2010 Census, Texas gained seats in the U.S. House of Representatives. Knowing that fact, which of the following statements must therefore be true?
   a. Texas is the most populous state in the nation.
   b. The population of Texas increased at a faster rate in the 2000s than did the population of the United States as a whole.
   c. Texas is in the Sunbelt.
   d. All of the above

4. Which of the following statements is true about income distribution in the United States?
   a. Since 1980, the proportion of national income received by the wealthiest fifth of the population has increased.
   b. Since 1980, the proportion of income received by the poorest fifth of the population has fallen.
   c. The income gap between the wealthiest and poorest families has been increasing.
   d. All of the above

5. Median household income in the United States is highest for which of the following groups?
   a. Asian Americans
   b. Whites
   c. African Americans
   d. Latinos

6. Which of the following statements is true?
   a. Household income is higher in the South than it is in any other region.
   b. On average, women earn more than men.

   c. The average income for people living in metropolitan areas is lower than it is for people living outside metropolitan areas.
   d. None of the above

7. How is the official poverty threshold determined?
   a. The poverty threshold is set at 30 percent of average household income. Anyone earning less than 30 percent of the average is considered poor.
   b. The official poverty rate was set in 1950 at $8,000 and changes each year based on the inflation rate.
   c. The poverty threshold is based on the amount of money an individual or family needs to purchase basic necessities.
   d. People declare whether they are poor based on their perception of their a bility to buy the things they need.

1.2 *How does the United States compare with other nations of the world, and how does the global economy affect the economy of the United States?*

8. The term superpower accurately describes which of the following nations today?
   a. Russia
   b. China
   c. United States
   d. All of the above

9. Which of the following nations spends the most money on its military?
   a. United States
   b. China
   c. Russia
   d. India

10. Which of the following nations has the largest economy?
   a. China
   b. Russia
   c. India
   d. United States

11. How have low-skilled workers been affected by the global economy?
   a. They have been harmed because global competition has led to price increases for many of the products that they purchase.
   b. They have been harmed because American companies cannot afford to pay high wages to low-skill workers and still compete effectively against foreign competitors with lower wage costs.

   c. They have been helped because the number of good jobs available to low-skill workers has increased.
   d. All of the above

1.3 *What are the most important elements of the political culture of the United States?*

12. Which of the following terms is defined as "the widely held, deeply rooted political values of a society?"
   a. Socialism
   b. Political culture
   c. Democracy
   d. Capitalism

13. According to Robert A. Dahl, which of the following is a criterion of democracy?
   a. Citizens have the right to form political parties and organize groups.
   b. All businesses and industry are privately owned.
   c. All citizens enjoy a minimum standard of living, including access to healthcare.
   d. All of the above

14. In Country A, the government owns and operates business and industry. It makes decisions about the production and distribution of goods and services in the public interest without regard for the profit motive. Which of the following terms best describes Country A?
   a. Democracy
   b. Mixed economy
   c. Socialism
   d. Capitalism

15. In Country B, most business and industry are privately owned, but they are subject to extensive regulation. Which of the following terms best describes Country B?
   a. Mixed economy
   b. Socialism
   c. Constitutional monarchy
   d. Democracy

KNOW the score

14–15 correct:	Congratulations—you know your Arican government!
12–13 correct:	Your understanding of this chapter is weak—be sure to review the key terms and visit TheThinkSpot.
<12 correct:	Reread the chapter more thoroughly.

Answers: 1) c, 2) a, 3) b, 4) d, 5) a, 6) d, 7) c, 8) c, 9) a, 10) d, 11) b, 12) b, 13) a, 14) c, 15) a

2 AMERICAN

The first priority of the newly elected U.S. House of Representatives in 2011 was to vote to repeal the healthcare reform legislation passed by Congress in 2010 and signed into law by President Barack Obama. Republicans in Congress unanimously opposed healthcare reform in 2010, and the party made repeal a leading issue in that year's election. When Republicans won a majority of seats in the House, they were in position to fulfill a campaign promise, but their victory was merely symbolic. The repeal measure had no chance of passing in the Senate where Democrats still held a majority. Moreover, even if the Senate were to vote to repeal healthcare reform, President Obama would certainly veto the

CONSTITUTION

measure, and Republicans would not have the votes to override the veto.

The battle over the repeal of healthcare reform illustrates the interplay between the U.S. Constitution and contemporary politics. The Constitution establishes the roles officials play in the policy process, determines the powers they can exercise, and outlines the procedures for policy adoption. A measure cannot become law unless it passes both houses of Congress and the president signs it into law or allows it to become law without signature. If the president vetoes a bill, the Constitution provides that it can become law only if both houses of Congress vote to override the veto by a two-thirds margin.

Healthcare repeal failed in 2011 because one mid-term election was not enough to change the political balance in Washington. Republican hopes to repeal healthcare reform would depend on the future willingness of voters to change not just the party in control of the House but of the Senate and the White House as well.

THE BACKGROUND OF THE
CONSTITUTION

2.1 *What historical events and philosophical principles influenced the development of the new government?*

A **constitution** is the fundamental law by which a state or nation is organized and governed, and to which ordinary legislation must conform. It establishes the framework of government, assigns the powers and duties of government bodies, and defines the relationship between the people and their government. The U.S. Constitution, which is more than 220 years of age, is the oldest written national constitution still in effect in the world today.

English colonists advertised opposition to the hated stamp act on everyday items, such as this teapot.

Historical Setting

The Americans who wrote the Constitution of 1787 had lived through two difficult periods: the late colonial period under British rule and the period under the government created by the Articles of Confederation. To a considerable degree, the Constitution was a reaction to these two experiences.

The Colonial Period. The American colonists were initially satisfied with the political relationship with Great Britain. Preoccupied with matters at home, the British authorities allowed the Americans a substantial measure of self-government. Each colony had a governor, appointed by the king, and a legislative assembly whose members were locally elected. The colonial assemblies could levy taxes, appropriate money, approve or reject the governor's appointments, and pass laws for their colony. Although the governor had the power to veto legislation, the assemblies exercised considerable leverage over the governor by virtue of their control of the budget.

This **power of the purse**, which is the authority to raise and spend money, made the locally elected legislative assemblies the dominant bodies of colonial government.

After 1763, the British chose to reorganize their colonial system. The French and Indian War (1756–1763), in which the British and the Americans fought against the French and their Indian allies for control of North America, left the British with a sizable war debt. The British also faced the problem of governing Canada and enforcing treaties with the Indians, which limited westward expansion by the colonists.

British officials decided that the American colonists should pay part of the cost of defending and administering the empire in North America. The British imposed new taxes, and to enforce their policies, they increased the number of officials in North America and permanently stationed troops in the colonies.

constitution the fundamental law by which a state or nation is organized and governed, and to which ordinary legislation must conform.

power of the purse the authority to raise and spend money.

To the surprise of the British, the Americans were outraged. Over the years, the colonists had grown accustomed to self-government and they were unwilling to surrender the privilege. They regarded the new policies as a violation of local traditions and an abridgment of their rights as British citizens. Before 1763, the only taxes the Americans paid to London were duties on trade, and the colonists interpreted the duties as measures to regulate commerce rather than taxes. Now, however, London attempted to impose levies that were clearly taxes. The Americans argued that as English citizens they could be taxed only by their own elected representatives and not by the British Parliament. No taxation without representation, they declared. This argument made no sense to the British. In their view, every member of Parliament represented every British citizen; it was irrelevant that no Americans sat in Parliament. The dispute over taxation and other issues worsened, leading eventually to revolution and American independence.

During the Revolutionary War, the American colonies became the United States, loosely allied under the leadership of the Continental Congress, which was a **unicameral** (one-house) **legislature** in which each state had a single vote. Although the Continental Congress had no official governing authority, it declared America's independence, raised an army, appointed George Washington commander in chief, coined money, and negotiated with foreign nations. The Continental Congress also drafted a plan for national union. This plan, known as the Articles of Confederation, went into effect in 1781, upon approval by the 13 states.

The Articles of Confederation. The Articles of Confederation created a league of friendship, a "perpetual union" of states, with a unicameral congress. Although state legislatures could send as many as seven delegates to the Confederation Congress, each state possessed a single vote, and 9 states (of 13) had to approve decisions. Amending the Articles required unanimous approval of the states. The Articles provided for no independent national executive or national judiciary.

The states were the primary units of government in the new nation rather than the Confederation government. Each of the 13 states had its own state constitution that established a framework for state government. These state constitutions typically provided for a **bicameral** (two-house) **legislature**, a governor, and a court system. Because Americans feared executive power as a source of tyranny, they adopted state constitutions that limited the powers of state governors, making legislatures the dominant branch of state government.[1]

The Americans who wrote the Articles of Confederation were determined to create a government whose powers would be strictly limited. Having just freed themselves from British rule, they did not want to create a strong national government that might become as oppressive as the British colonial government. The Americans who wrote the Articles apparently went too far, however, because the Confederation proved too weak to deal effectively with the new nation's problems. It lacked the power to collect taxes from individuals, having to rely instead on contributions from the states. When state

Alexander Hamilton was a strong critic of the weak central government of the Articles of Confederation. He was one of the leaders of the movement to strengthen the national government and became the new nation's first secretary of the Treasury.

unicameral legislature
a one-house legislature.

bicameral legislature a two-house legislature.

The right to protest, essential for a democracy and rooted in the history of the country's founding, is protected in the First Amendment. Here, Tea Party activists voice their opposition to government spending.

governments failed to pay—as many did—the Confederation government was left without financial support. The Confederation also lacked authority to regulate commerce, prohibit states from printing worthless currency, enforce the provisions of the peace treaty with Great Britain, or even defend itself against rebellion. When small farmers in western Massachusetts engaged in an armed uprising against the government over debt and taxes in 1786–1787, the Confederation government failed to respond. After a private army finally crushed the insurrection, which was known as Shay's Rebellion after its leader, Daniel Shay, public opinion began to coalesce in favor of a stronger national government than

The ABC hit series, *Lost*, featured numerous characters that share the names of famous philosophers, including John Locke. In what ways does the fictional character of John Locke adhere to or reject the motivations and principles of the philosopher? (You can view old episodes online at abc.com.)

People create government to **protect their rights,** not to abridge them.

the one provided by the Articles of Confederation.

American Political Thought

The Americans who wrote the Constitution were educated people who studied the important political writings of their day. The work of Englishman John Locke (1632–1704) was particularly influential. In his Second Treatise on Government (1689), Locke declared that people in their natural state were born free and equal, and possessed certain natural rights, which were life, liberty, and property. Unfortunately, Locke said, evil people disrupt the good life of the state of nature by conspiring to deprive others of their life, liberty, or property. In order to protect their rights, people voluntarily join together to form governments. The power of government, then, stems from the consent of the governed, who entrust the government with responsibility for protecting their lives, liberty, and possessions. Should government fail in this task, Locke declared, the people have the right to revolt and institute a new government. The colonists used Locke's theories to justify their revolution and inform the creation of their new government based on three important principles they drew from Locke's thought:

1. *Justification of revolution* In the Declaration of Independence, which is reprinted in the Appendix of this text, the founders used Locke's theory of revolution to justify independence from Great Britain. The Americans were justified in revolting against the King because the King deprived them of their rights to "Life, Liberty, and the pursuit of Happiness."

2. *Government as a positive force in society* According to Locke, the people create government in order to accomplish certain goals, that is, to protect life, liberty, and property from the dangers inherent in a state of nature. In theory, then, government is not just a necessary evil but can play an active, positive role in society.

3. *Protection of individual rights* Locke's doctrine of **natural rights** is the belief that individual rights transcend the power of government. Thus, government authority over the individual should be limited; people create government to protect their rights, not to abridge them. Locke's theory of natural rights provided a basis for a bill of rights, which is a constitutional document guaranteeing individual rights and liberties.

Although the nation's founders frequently cited the writings of European philosophers such as Locke, they did more than just apply the theories developed in Europe to the United States. They created a nation and wrote a Constitution that was also based on American events, experiences, and ideas.[2]

The most important element of American political thought was the changing conception of the nature of politics and government. At the time of the Revolution, American political theorists believed that politics was a never-ending struggle between the people and the government. In their view, the people were virtuous and united in support of the public good. In contrast, the government, personified by the king, was corrupt and oppressive. After declaring their independence, the Americans knew that they needed a national government, but they did not want a strong one. The government established by the Articles of Confederation fit the bill nicely.

natural rights the belief that individual rights transcend the power of government.

After a few years of independence, many Americans recognized that they were wrong about the nature of the people and the role of government. Instead of society being united behind a common perception of the public good, they saw that it was composed of a variety of interests or factions, which opposed each other on a number of policy issues. Furthermore, practical political experience in the states demonstrated that the people were not so virtuous after all. When one faction gained control of the government of a particular state or locality, it would often use its power to enforce its will over opposing interests.

By 1787, many Americans had decided that a strong national government could play a positive role in society. First, the national government could reconcile the divergent concerns of various groups in society to produce policies designed to achieve the public good. A large nation, such as the United States,
includes a wide range of interests competing for power. Although a particular group or faction might be strong enough to control the government in one state or a local area, no single group would be able to dominate nationwide. A strong national government would provide a forum in which groups would be able to reconcile their differences. The result would be policies that would be acceptable to a broad range of interests.

Second, a strong national government could protect individual liberty and property from the power of oppressive majorities. At the state or local level, a dominant faction could adopt policies designed to advance its own religious or economic interests at the expense of the minority. At the national level, however, no one group or faction would be powerful enough to enforce its will on the entire nation. Because every group held minority status in one state or another, it would be in each group's interest to

A **large nation,** such as the United States, includes a **wide range of interests** competing for power.

protect minorities against the power of oppressive local majorities.[3] For example, the framers of the Constitution included a provision prohibiting a state-supported church because of the multiplicity of religious sects in America. Although many of the early American religious groups would have liked nothing better than to establish their faith as the official state religion, they lacked the power to achieve that goal. Consequently, they preferred an official government policy of religious freedom to risking the possibility that another religious group would gain official recognition.[4]

CONSTITUTIONAL PRINCIPLES

 What kind of government does the Constitution create, and how does it divide political power?

To understand the American Constitution, we must study the principles behind it. Let's look in detail at some of the constitution's most important themes.

Representative Democracy

A **democracy** is a system of government in which the people hold ultimate political power. Although the framers of the Constitution favored a government that would answer to the people, they did not want to give too much power to majority opinion. The framers were particularly wary of **direct democracy**, which is a political system in which the citizens vote directly on matters of public concern. The framers of the Constitution worried that ordinary
citizens lacked the information to make intelligent policy decisions. They feared that direct democracy would produce policies reflecting hasty, emotional decisions rather than well-considered judgments.

The framers also worried that direct democracy would enable a majority of the people to enact policies that would silence, disadvantage, or harm the minority point of view, thus producing a **tyranny of the majority**, which is the abuse of the minority by the majority. The danger of majority rule is that the majority may vote to adopt policies that unfairly disadvantage the minority. The challenge for the framers of the Constitution was to create a form of government that would provide for majority rule while protecting the rights and liberties of minorities.

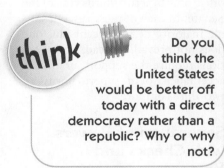

Do you think the **United States** would be better off today with a direct democracy rather than a republic? Why or why not?

democracy a system of government in which ultimate political authority is vested in the people.

direct democracy a political system in which the citizens vote directly on matters of public concern.

tyranny of the majority the abuse of the minority by the majority.

Instead of a direct democracy, the framers created a **representative democracy** or a **republic**, which is a political system in which citizens elect representatives to make policy decisions on their behalf. The framers believed that elected representatives would act as a buffer between the people and government policies. Representatives would be more knowledgeable than ordinary citizens about policy issues. They would also be more likely than the general public to recognize the legitimate interests of different groups in society and to seek policy compromises designed to accommodate those interests.

To further guard against the tyranny of the majority, the framers provided that some policy actions could be taken only with the consent of a **supermajority**, a voting margin which is greater than a simple majority. Constitutional amendments must be proposed by two-thirds of the members of both the House and the Senate and ratified by three-fourths of the states. Treaties must be approved by two-thirds of the Senate. Presidential vetoes can be overridden only by a two-thirds vote of each chamber of Congress. Executive and judicial officials can be removed from office only by a two-thirds vote of the Senate. In each of these cases, a simple majority of 50 percent plus one does not prevail. Instead, policy actions require the support, or at least acceptance, of a supermajority of two-thirds or more.

Separation of Powers with Checks and Balances

The Constitution creates a representative democracy that divides political power among the branches of government, between the chambers of Congress, and between the national government and the state governments. The framers of the U.S. Constitution adopted separation of powers with checks and balances as a means for controlling the power of government. Although the roots

of these concepts went back a century, their modern development was the work of Baron de Montesquieu, an eighteenth-century French political philosopher. Montesquieu identified three kinds of political power: the power to make laws (**legislative power**), enforce laws (**executive power**), and interpret laws (**judicial power**). Montesquieu warned against allowing one person or a single group of people from exercising all three powers because that person or group would become so powerful as to pose a threat to individual liberty. To protect freedom, Montesquieu advocated **separation of powers**, that is, the division of political power among executive, legislative, and judicial branches of government. He called for a system of checks and balances to prevent any one of the three branches from becoming too strong. **Checks and balances** refer to the overlapping of the powers of the branches of government designed to ensure that public officials limit the authority of one another.

James Madison was the principal architect of America's system of separation of powers with checks and balances. In fact, scholars sometimes refer to the nation's constitutional apparatus as the Madisonian system. Madison and two other proponents of the new constitution, Alexander Hamilton and John Jay,

James Madison is the principal architect of the U.S. Constitution, so much so that America's system of government is sometimes called the Madisonian system.

wrote a series of essays known as the *Federalist Papers* to advocate the ratification of the Constitution of 1787. In *The Federalist* No. 51, Madison identified two threats to liberty: 1) **factions,** which are special interests who seek their own good at the expense of the common good, and 2) the excessive concentration of political power in the hands of government officials. Madison's remedy for these dangers was the creation of a strong national government with separation of powers and checks and balances.

Madison believed that the nation needed a strong national government to control the power of factions. In this regard, Madison noted the advantage of a large nation with many diverse interests.

representative democracy/republic a political system in which citizens elect representatives to make policy decisions on their behalf.

supermajority a voting margin that is greater than a simple majority.

legislative power the power to make laws.

executive power the power to enforce laws.

judicial power the power to interpret laws.

separation of powers the division of political power among executive, legislative, and judicial branches.

checks and balances the overlapping of the powers of the branches of government designed to ensure that public officials limit the authority of each other.

Federalist Papers a series of essays written by James Madison, Alexander Hamilton, and John Jay advocating the ratification of the Constitution.

factions special interests who seek their own good at the expense of the common good.

At the local or state level, he said, a single faction might be powerful enough to dominate. It could unfairly force its will on the minority, creating a tyranny of the majority. Over the breadth of the entire nation, however, the narrow perspectives of that faction would be checked by the interests of other factions entrenched in other areas. A strong national government would provide an arena in which factions would counterbalance one another. National policies, therefore, would reflect compromise among a range of interests.

Madison also favored separation of powers with checks and balances as a means to control the power of government officials. Madison said that the goal of the system was "to divide and arrange the several offices [of government] in such a manner as that each may be a check on the other."[5] In this fashion, the selfish, private interests of officeholders would counterbalance each other to the public good. "Ambition," Madison wrote, "must be made to counteract ambition."[6]

The Constitution contains an elaborate network of checks and balances. The executive branch, for example, checks the judicial branch through the power of the president to appoint members of the Supreme Court and other federal courts. Congress, in turn, checks the president and the courts in that the Senate must confirm judicial appointments. Similarly, the Constitution declares that Congress has the authority to declare war, but it names the president commander in chief of the armed forces. The president negotiates treaties, but the Senate must ratify them.

Separation of powers with checks and balances creates tension among the branches of government because the framers of the Constitution refused to draw clear lines of demarcation among Congress, the president, and the judiciary. In fact, the phrase *separation of powers* is misleading. What really exists is a system in which separate institutions *share* power.[7] Friction is inevitable.

Bicameralism

The framers of the Constitution expected the legislative branch to be the dominant institution of American national government because it was the most important branch of state governments. To prevent the national legislature from becoming too powerful, the framers divided Congress into two houses with different sizes, terms of office, responsibilities, and constituencies. The precise organization of America's bicameral Congress was the product of an agreement between large-state and small-state forces known as the Connecticut Compromise. Members of the House of Representatives would be chosen by direct popular election to serve two-year terms with the number of representatives from each state based on population. This pleased large states. Each state would have two senators chosen by their state legislatures to serve six-year terms. This pleased small states. (The adoption of the Seventeenth Amendment in 1913 provided for direct popular election of senators.)

The framers expected that the popularly elected house would be constrained by a more conservative senate. With a two-year term, members of the house would be closer to the people and more likely to act hastily in accordance with short-term popular sentiment. In contrast, senators, chosen by state legislatures and serving longer terms, would be insulated from popular pressures, thus enabling them to act more cautiously and put the national interest ahead of short-term political gain.[8]

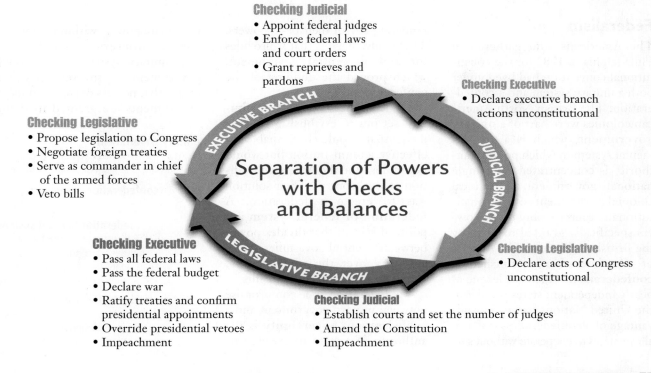

Checking Judicial
- Appoint federal judges
- Enforce federal laws and court orders
- Grant reprieves and pardons

Checking Executive
- Declare executive branch actions unconstitutional

Checking Legislative
- Propose legislation to Congress
- Negotiate foreign treaties
- Serve as commander in chief of the armed forces
- Veto bills

Separation of Powers with Checks and Balances

EXECUTIVE BRANCH

JUDICIAL BRANCH

LEGISLATIVE BRANCH

Checking Executive
- Pass all federal laws
- Pass the federal budget
- Declare war
- Ratify treaties and confirm presidential appointments
- Override presidential vetoes
- Impeachment

Checking Judicial
- Establish courts and set the number of judges
- Amend the Constitution
- Impeachment

Checking Legislative
- Declare acts of Congress unconstitutional

Most of the world's democracies are patterned after the British parliamentary system rather than the checks and balances system of the United States. A parliamentary system is a system of government in which political power is concentrated in a legislative body and a cabinet headed by a prime minister. The British legislature, which is called the Parliament, has two chambers, a House of Commons and a House of Lords. Real power is in the hands of the House of Commons, which is composed of 660 members elected from districts. The House of Lords, which includes the bishops of the Church of England and other members appointed for life by the king or queen, is now little more than a debating society with the power only to delay legislation, not to defeat it.

British voters understand that when they vote for members of Parliament that they are also choosing a government. A vote for a particular parliamentary candidate is also a vote for the policies offered by that candidate's political party and a vote for the election of that party's leader as prime minister.

The primary check on the government in Great Britain is the electorate. The government must hold a new parliamentary election within five years, giving voters the opportunity to keep the current government in power or to turn the government over to the opposition. In 2010, British voters ended 13 years of Labour Party rule, but failed to give the opposition Conservative Party enough seats for an outright majority. Subsequently, the Conservatives formed a coalition government with the smaller Liberal Party and Conservative leader David Cameron became prime minister.

Prime Minister David Cameron, right, works closely with Nick Clegg, the head of the Liberal Party and Deputy Prime Minister.

QUESTIONS

1 Which political system is more responsive to citizen demands—the American or the British system?

2 Which political system is more likely to produce dramatic policy change?

3 Which political system is better equipped to protect the rights of minorities?

Federalism

The Americans who gathered in Philadelphia in 1787 for the constitutional convention had lived under both a unitary system and a confederation. The British North American colonies were part of a **unitary government**, which is a governmental system in which political authority is concentrated in a single national government. The local colonial governments could constitutionally exercise only those powers specifically granted to them by the British parliament. The Articles of Confederation established a **confederation,** which is a league of nearly independent states, similar to the United Nations today. The advantage of a confederation is that it allows states to cooperate without surrendering any of their basic powers. The disadvantage is that it provides for a weak central government, which proved the undoing of the confederation.

The framers of the Constitution set out to establish a government that would be capable of effective administration but would not undermine the American tradition of local control. Their solution was to create a federation. A **federation or federal system** is a political system that divides power between a central government, with authority over the whole nation, and a series of state governments.

A federation is a compromise between unitary government and a confederation. **Sovereignty** is the authority of a state to exercise its legitimate powers within its boundaries, free from external interference. In a unitary system, the national government is sovereign, which means that powers of state and local governments are granted to them

unitary government a governmental system in which political authority is concentrated in a single national government.

confederation a league of nearly independent states.

federation/federal system a political system that divides power between a central government, with authority over the whole nation, and a series of state governments.

sovereignty the authority of a state to exercise its legitimate powers within its boundaries, free from external interference.

by the national government. In a confederation, the states are sovereign, and the national government's authority flows from the states. In a federal system, the national (or federal) government and the state governments are both sovereign. They derive their authority not from one another but from the Constitution. Both levels of government act directly on the people through their officials and laws, both are supreme within their proper sphere of authority, and both must consent to constitutional change.

A federation offers Americans several advantages. A federal system provides a means of political representation that can accommodate the diversity of American society. Individual Americans are citizens of their states and the nation as well, and participate in the selection of representatives to both levels of government. In a federal system, local interests shape local policy. The national government, meanwhile, is an arena in which local interests from different regions

think Which do you think is the best form of government for the United States—a unitary government, a confederation, or a federal government?

can check and balance one another, permitting the national interest to prevail.

Federalism can help protect against the tyranny of the majority. The federal system creates a series of overlapping state and district election systems that select both members of Congress and the president. The federal election system gives minorities of all kinds—racial, ethnic, religious, regional, local, occupational, social, and sexual—the opportunity to be part of a majority because together they may make up the swing vote in a closely divided state or district. Consequently, they must be consulted; their interests must be considered.[9]

Nonetheless, a federal system imposes certain disadvantages. Local variations confuse citizens and hinder business. Traveling Americans face different traffic laws in each state. People who move from one state to another must adapt to different laws regarding such matters as marriage, divorce, wills, and occupational licensing. A couple approved as foster parents in one state may have to go through the approval process again if they move to another state. Businesses must adjust to variations in tax laws and regulations. Federalism also sets the stage for conflict. American history is filled with examples of disputes between states and the national government; the Civil War was the most serious. Issues such as the 55 mile-per-hour speed limit requirement and the 21-year-old minimum legal drinking age are contemporary examples of conflicts between states and the national government.

TAKE ✓ ACTION
Service Learning

Service learning is based on the concept that students can learn more about a subject through participation and experience, combined with traditional coursework, than they can through classroom instruction alone.

Use the following checklist to guide you through your service-learning project:

1. Identify a government office or agency that welcomes student volunteers. You may wish to begin with the mayor's office, school district, hospital district, or state legislator. They can give you referrals to agencies that deal with issues related to your career goals.
2. Call the agency or department that interests you and ask to speak to the volunteer coordinator. Explain that you are completing a service-learning project for your college and want to know about volunteer opportunities.
3. Your instructor will set the number of hours you should volunteer. Normally, students should expect to work from 20 to 40 hours over a semester to receive full benefit from the activity.

4. As you complete your assignment at the agency, ask the volunteer coordinator to provide you with documentation of the hours of your work to present to your instructor.

You will be required to keep a reflective journal documenting your service. Journal entries should discuss your work on the project and your reaction to the experience, covering the following topics:

1. What you did for the organization.
2. What you thought of the organization, including the clients served, the work done, and the other employees or volunteers.
3. How your experience relates to course materials.
4. How your experience relates to topics in the news.

Write at least one journal entry for every two hours you spend at your placement. You will be evaluated on the amount of time you spent at your placement, the number and length of your journal entries, and the quality of your entries.

LIMITATIONS ON THE POWER OF GOVERNMENT

2.3 *How does the Constitution limit the power of government?*

imited government is the constitutional principle that government does not have unrestricted authority over individuals. The framers of the Constitution created a government whose powers over the individual would be limited. The **rule of law** is the constitutional principle that holds that the discretion of public officials in dealing with individuals is limited by the law.

The very existence of a written Constitution implies the rule of law, but certain constitutional provisions deserve special notice. In Article I, Section 9, the Constitution guarantees the privilege of the writ of *habeas corpus* except in cases of invasion, rebellion, or threat to public safety. A **writ of** *habeas corpus* is a court order requiring that government authorities either release a person held in custody or demonstrate that the person is detained in accordance with law. *Habeas corpus* is designed to prevent arbitrary arrest and imprisonment. The Constitution protects Americans from being held in custody by the government unless they are charged and convicted in accordance with the law.

The Constitution prohibits the passage of bills of attainder and *ex post facto* laws. A **bill of attainder** is a law declaring a person or a group of persons guilty of a crime and providing for punishment without benefit of a judicial proceeding. An *ex post facto law* is a retroactive criminal statute that operates to the disadvantage of accused persons. It makes a crime out of an act that was not illegal when it was committed.

Due process of law is the constitutional principle holding that government must follow fair and regular procedures in actions that could lead to an individual's suffering loss of life, liberty, or property. In both the Fifth and Fourteenth Amendments, the Constitution provides that neither Congress (the Fifth Amendment) nor the states (the Fourteenth Amendment) may deprive any person of "life, liberty, or property, without due process of law." Due process of law generally protects individuals from the arbitrary actions of public officials. Before individuals may be imprisoned, fined, or executed, they must be given their day in court in accordance with law. Among other rights, the Constitution guarantees accused persons the right to a speedy, public trial by an impartial jury, the right to confront witnesses, and the right to legal counsel.

The Bill of Rights

Perhaps the most important constitutional restriction on the authority of government is the **Bill of Rights**, the first ten amendments to the Constitution. The Bill of Rights was not part of the original Constitution because a majority of the framers of the Constitution believed that such a provision was unnecessary, redundant, useless, and possibly even dangerous. The framers thought that a bill of rights would be unnecessary because each state constitution had a bill of rights and the national government lacked sufficient power to threaten individual liberty. They considered a bill of rights redundant because the Constitution already contained a number of provisions designed to protect individual liberty, such as the prohibition against *ex post facto* laws and bills of attainder, and the guarantee of due process of law. They thought that a bill of rights would be useless because they believed that a paper guarantee of individual liberty would mean little in the face of public pressure. Finally, the framers resisted the inclusion of a bill of rights in the Constitution because they worried that some rights might be inadvertently left out and that any right omitted from the document would be lost.[10]

---

limited government the constitutional principle that government does not have unrestricted authority over individuals.

rule of law the constitutional principle that holds that the discretion of public officials in dealing with individuals is limited by the law.

writ of *habeas corpus* a court order requiring government authorities either to release a person held in custody or demonstrate that the person is detained in accordance with law.

bill of attainder a law declaring a person or a group of persons guilty of a crime and providing for punishment without benefit of a judicial proceeding.

ex post facto law a retroactive criminal statute that operates to the disadvantage of accused persons.

due process of law the constitutional principle holding that government must follow fair and regular procedures in actions that could lead to an individual's suffering loss of life, liberty, or property.

Bill of Rights the first ten amendments to the U.S. Constitution.

---

think Should the government be allowed to arrest American citizens and hold them without charges and without trial if it believes that they are involved in planning terrorist attacks against the United States?

The failure of the proposed Constitution to include a bill of rights became a political issue during the debate over ratification. After the Constitution was written in 1787, it still had to be approved (or ratified) by 9 of the 13 states. The **Antifederalists** were Americans opposed to the ratification of the Constitution of 1787 because they thought it gave too much power to the national government. They raised the issue of a bill of rights in hopes of defeating the Constitution and forcing the convening of a new constitutional convention. The **Federalists** were Americans who supported the ratification of the Constitution of 1787. Although most Federalists initially opposed inclusion of a bill of rights in the constitution, they switched sides on the issue in order to secure ratification and prevent a new convention. They promised to add a bill of rights once the Constitution was ratified and the new government took office.[11]

The Federalists kept their promise. In 1789, the First Congress of the United States proposed 12 amendments, 10 of which were ratified by a sufficient number of states to become part of the Constitution by 1791. One of the rejected amendments, a provision requiring that a congressional pay raise could not go into effect before an intervening election take place, was finally ratified in 1992 to become the Twenty-seventh Amendment.

The authors of the Bill of Rights intended that it would apply only to the national government and not the states because the states already had bills of rights. The U.S. Constitution and the national Bill of Rights would protect individual rights against abuse by the national government. State constitutions and state bills of rights would secure individual rights from infringement by state governments.

The Fourteenth Amendment, which was added to the Constitution immediately after the Civil War, provided the constitutional basis for applying the national Bill of Rights to the states. Congress proposed the Fourteenth Amendment in 1866 to protect the rights of the former slaves from infringement by state governments. The amendment defined U.S. citizenship, making it clear that all Americans are citizens of both the United States and the state in which they live. The amendment declared that

Antifederalists Americans opposed to the ratification of the new Constitution because they thought it gave too much power to the national government.

Federalists Americans who supported the ratification of the Constitution.

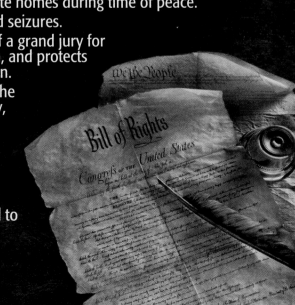

PROTECTIONS GUARANTEED BY THE
Bill of RIGHTS

FIRST AMENDMENT Protects freedom of speech, press, assembly, and petition, and prohibits Congress from creating an establishment of religion or restricting the free exercise of religion.

SECOND AMENDMENT Guarantees the right to keep and bear arms.

THIRD AMENDMENT Prohibits forced quartering of troops in private homes during time of peace.

FOURTH AMENDMENT Protects against unreasonable searches and seizures.

FIFTH AMENDMENT Guarantees due process of law and the use of a grand jury for serious crimes, prohibits double jeopardy and self-incrimination, and protects against the seizure of private property without just compensation.

SIXTH AMENDMENT Protects the rights of the accused, including the right to counsel, to a speedy and public trial, to an impartial jury, to be informed of charges, to face accusers, and to obtain witnesses.

SEVENTH AMENDMENT Guarantees the right to a civil trial by jury.

EIGHTH AMENDMENT Prohibits excessive bail, excessive fines, and cruel and unusual punishments.

NINTH AMENDMENT Declares that individual rights are not limited to those rights specifically enumerated in the Constitution.

TENTH AMENDMENT Stipulates that the powers not delegated to the national government or denied to the states are reserved to the states or to the people.

Creation and Incorporation of the Bill of Rights

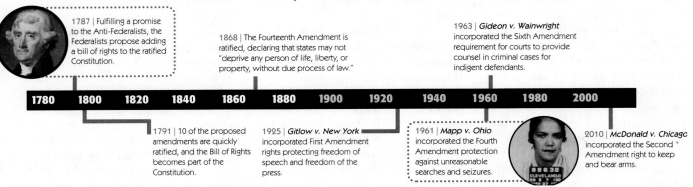

1787 | Fulfilling a promise to the Anti-Federalists, the Federalists propose adding a bill of rights to the ratified Constitution.

1868 | The Fourteenth Amendment is ratified, declaring that states may not "deprive any person of life, liberty, or property, without due process of law."

1963 | *Gideon v. Wainwright* incorporated the Sixth Amendment requirement for courts to provide counsel in criminal cases for indigent defendants.

1780	1800	1820	1840	1860	1880	1900	1920	1940	1960	1980	2000

1791 | 10 of the proposed amendments are quickly ratified, and the Bill of Rights becomes part of the Constitution.

1925 | *Gitlow v. New York* incorporated First Amendment rights protecting freedom of speech and freedom of the press.

1961 | *Mapp v. Ohio* incorporated the Fourth Amendment protection against unreasonable searches and seizures.

2010 | *McDonald v. Chicago* incorporated the Second Amendment right to keep and bear arms.

state governments could not take life, liberty, or property without "due process of law," or deny to any person within their jurisdiction "equal protection of the laws." The Fourteenth Amendment also prohibited states from making laws abridging the "privileges or immunities" of citizens.

The Fourteenth Amendment did not play a major role in the protection of individual rights until the twentieth century. Initially, the Fourteenth Amendment had little impact on individual rights because the Supreme Court of the United

States refused to interpret its provisions to protect individual rights. Not until the twentieth century did the Court begin the process known as the **selective incorporation** of the Bill of Rights against the states. This is the process through which the U.S. Supreme Court interpreted the Due Process Clause of the Fourteenth Amendment of the U.S. Constitution to apply most of the provisions of the national Bill of Rights to the states. Although the Supreme Court has never ruled that the Bill of Rights as a whole applies to the states, it has selectively held

that virtually all of its key provisions apply against the states through the Due Process Clause of the Fourteenth Amendment. As a result, the national Bill of Rights now protects individual rights against infringement by both the national government and the state governments as well.

selective incorporation the process through which the U.S. Supreme Court interpreted the Due Process Clause of the Fourteenth Amendment of the U.S. Constitution to apply most of the provisions of the national Bill of Rights to the states.

CONSTITUTIONAL CHANGE

2.4 *How does the Constitution change?*

The Constitution has not merely survived for more than 220 years. It has grown and matured with the nation, serving as the fundamental framework for policymaking to this day. When the original document was written in 1787, the United States was a nation of only about four million people, most of which lived on farms and in small towns. Many Americans—slaves, women, and individuals without property—were denied full rights of participation in the policymaking process. Today the country is dramatically changed, but the Constitution, with only 27 official amendments, endures as the centerpiece of policymaking.

The genius of the Constitution lies in its ability to adapt to changing times while maintaining adherence to basic principles. The Constitution is a brief, generalized document that is full of phrases lacking clear definition. The Eighth Amendment, for example, prohibits "cruel and unusual punishments." Article I, Section 8 gives Congress the power to regulate "commerce." Article II, Section 4 declares that the president may be impeached and removed from office for "treason, bribery, or other high crimes and misdemeanors." The Fourth Amendment prohibits "unreasonable searches and seizures." What do these terms mean? What punishments

are "cruel and unusual?" What is "commerce?" What are "high crimes and misdemeanors"? Which searches and seizures are "reasonable" and which are "unreasonable"?

The Constitution is often vague, and this is what the framers intended. They set down certain basic, fundamental principles, but omitted details in order to allow succeeding generations to supply specifics in light of their own experiences. The basic idea behind the concept of "cruel and unusual punishments," for example, is that government must not go too far in punishing criminals. The prohibition against "unreasonable searches and seizures" places limits on the police. Had the framers of the Constitution decided to spell out everything in detail, they would have produced a document far longer and less satisfactory than the one we have. Eventually, the nation would have outgrown it and either cast it aside or been forced to amend it repeatedly.

Is the Constitution too general? What are the advantages and disadvantages of a less specific Constitution?

Change Through Amendment

A **constitutional amendment** is a formal, written change or addition to the nation's governing document. A major flaw of the Articles of Confederation was that the articles could be amended only by unanimous vote. In practice, this made change impossible because of the obstinacy of only one or a few states. In 1787, then, the Constitution's framers were careful to include a reasonable method of

amendment that permitted change but was difficult enough to preclude hasty, ill-conceived changes.

The Constitution provides two methods for proposing amendments and two methods for their ratification. An amendment may be proposed by either a two-thirds vote of each house of Congress or by a constitutional convention called by Congress upon petition by two-thirds of the states. The former method has been used many times; Congress proposed all 27 amendments that have been added to the Constitution. The convention procedure has never been used.

After an amendment is proposed, by either Congress or a convention, three-fourths of the states must ratify it. Ratification can be accomplished either by vote of the state legislatures or by specially called state conventions. The former method has been used successfully 26 times, the latter only once, to ratify the Twenty-first Amendment repealing Prohibition. The road to constitutional amendment is difficult, and Congress has considered but failed to pass numerous proposed amendments in recent years dealing with such issues as prayer in schools, flag burning, term

limitation, abortion, Electoral College reform, a balanced budget, and gay marriage.

Is amending the Constitution too difficult, too easy, or just right?

Change Through Practice and Experience

The Constitution has adapted to changing times through practice and experience. Consider the role of the presidency. The historical development of the office has given definition to the powers of the presidency beyond the scope of the office that was foreseen by the framers. Other elements of American government have developed despite slight mention in the Constitution. Even though the federal bureaucracy is barely discussed in the Constitution, its importance in American government has grown to the point that some observers refer to it as the fourth branch of government. Furthermore, some important contemporary features of American government are not mentioned at all in the Constitution, including the committee system in Congress, the president's cabinet, and the political party system. To an important extent, the meaning of the Constitution is found in its historical development over time as succeeding generations of Americans have addressed policy issues within its framework.

Change Through Judicial Interpretation

A final means of constitutional change is judicial interpretation. In fact, it may be no exaggeration to say that what counts most in constitutional law is the interpretation of the Constitution by the courts, particularly the U.S. Supreme Court, rather

Constitutional Change

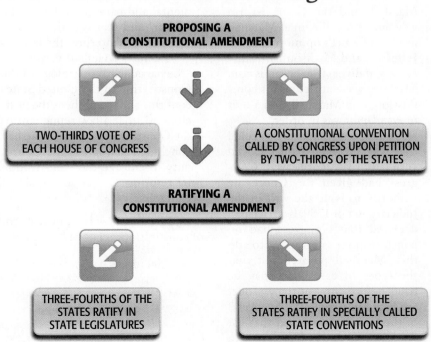

PROPOSING A CONSTITUTIONAL AMENDMENT

TWO-THIRDS VOTE OF EACH HOUSE OF CONGRESS

A CONSTITUTIONAL CONVENTION CALLED BY CONGRESS UPON PETITION BY TWO-THIRDS OF THE STATES

RATIFYING A CONSTITUTIONAL AMENDMENT

THREE-FOURTHS OF THE STATES RATIFY IN STATE LEGISLATURES

THREE-FOURTHS OF THE STATES RATIFY IN SPECIALLY CALLED STATE CONVENTIONS

constitutional amendment
a formal, written change or addition to the nation's governing document.

than the words of the document itself. Many phrases important to constitutional law are not even in the Constitution, including "war power," "clear and present danger," "separation of church and state," "right of privacy," "separate but equal," and "police power." These famous words appear not in the Constitution but in judicial opinions.

Judicial interpretation of the Constitution is inevitable because of the document's generalized nature. Many of the phrases of the Constitution are purposely ambiguous, requiring continuous reinterpretation and adaptation. Indeed, one constitutional scholar says that we have an unwritten constitution, whose history is the history of judicial interpretation.[12]

The power of courts to declare unconstitutional the actions of the other branches and units of government is known as **judicial review**. Although the Constitution is silent about the power of judicial review, many historians believe that the founders expected the courts to exercise the authority. Ironically, the Supreme Court assumed the power of judicial review through constitutional interpretation, first holding an act of Congress unconstitutional in 1803 in the case of *Marbury v. Madison*.[13]

- **The Case** President John Adams and his Federalist Party lost the election of 1800. In the remaining months of his presidency, Adams appointed a number of loyal Federalists to various judicial positions. One of these appointments went to William Marbury, who was named justice of the peace for the District of Columbia.

    President Adams signed and sealed Marbury's commission the day before he left office, but the secretary of state neglected to deliver it. The new president, Thomas Jefferson, ordered his secretary of state, James Madison, not to deliver the commission. Marbury sued, asking the Supreme Court to issue a writ of *mandamus* to force Madison to

deliver the commission. A **writ of mandamus** is a court order directing a public official to perform a specific act or duty.

- **The Decision** The Supreme Court had a problem. Chief Justice John Marshall and the other members of the Court were Federalists. They would have liked to force Madison to deliver the commission. However, Jefferson might well have defied the order, damaging the Court's prestige.

    Judicial review provided Marshall and the Court with a way out of the dilemma. Marshall used the Court's opinion to scold Jefferson and Madison for refusing to deliver the commission. Marbury was entitled to his commission, said Marshall, and a writ of *mandamus* was in order.

    However, Marshall also ruled that the Supreme Court lacked authority to issue the writ. Congress had given the Court the authority to issue the writ in the Judiciary Act of 1789, but Marshall declared that Congress had no constitutional authority to do this. Marshall pointed out that the types of cases that may be tried before the Supreme Court are listed in Article III, Section 2 of the Constitution, and that list does not include the power to

issue writs of *mandamus* to federal officials. Therefore, the section of the Judiciary Act that gave the Court the power to issue writs of *mandamus* was unconstitutional. By this means, Marshall was able to attack Jefferson but keep the president from defying the Court.

- **The Significance** *Marbury v. Madison* is the first case in which the Supreme Court ruled an act of Congress unconstitutional. In his ruling, Marshall stated that the Constitution is the "fundamental and paramount law of the nation" and that it is the duty of the courts to interpret the law.

    "Thus," Marshall continued, "the particular phraseology of the Constitution of the United States confirms and strengthens the principle . . . that a law repugnant to the Constitution is void." Marshall concluded that it was the Court's duty to enforce the Constitution by refusing to uphold the act of Congress.

    Judicial review is an instrument of constitutional change because the

judicial review the power of courts to declare unconstitutional the actions of the other branches and units of government.

writ of mandamus a court order directing a public official to perform a specific act or duty.

process involves constitutional interpretation. Professor Richard H. Fallon, Jr., says that today's justices interpret the Constitution in light of history, precedent (that is, earlier interpretations), and considerations of moral desirability and practical workability.[14]

Consider the history of judicial interpretation of the **Equal Protection Clause**, which is the provision found in the Fourteenth Amendment of the U.S. Constitution that declares that "No State shall . . . deny to any person within its jurisdiction the equal protection of the laws." The U.S. Supreme Court's initial interpretation of the Equal Protection Clause came in 1896 in *Plessy v. Ferguson*. The case centered on the constitutionality of a Louisiana law that required racial segregation (separation) in passenger railcars. Could a state government prohibit African American travelers from sharing a railcar with white passengers without violating the Equal Protection Clause? The Supreme Court answered that it could as long as the accommodations were equal. "Separate but equal" facilities, said the Court, were sufficient to satisfy the requirements of the Fourteenth Amendment.[15] Almost 60 years later, the Supreme Court addressed a similar issue in the case of *Brown v. Board of Education of Topeka* (1954). The *Brown* case involved a

"A law repugnant to the Constitution is void."
— Chief Justice John Marshall

constitutional challenge to a Kansas law requiring racial segregation in public schools. Could a state government prohibit African American youngsters from sharing a school with white children without violating the Equal Protection Clause? In this case, the Supreme Court overruled *Plessy*, holding that the Equal Protection Clause of the Fourteenth Amendment prohibits state laws requiring racial segregation in public schools. The Court declared that "separate but equal" was a con-

tradiction because the legal requirement of separation placed the stamp of inferiority on the black race.[16] And so the Constitution was changed, not through the adoption of a constitutional amendment (the wording of the Equal Protection Clause remained the same), but because of changing judicial interpretation.

Equal Protection Clause a provision of the Fourteenth Amendment of the U.S. Constitution that declares that "No State shall ... deny to any person within its jurisdiction the equal protection of the laws."

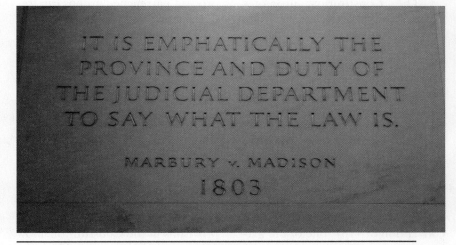

A excerpt from John Marshall's decision establishing judicial review is engraved in the wall of the Supreme Court Building in Washington, D.C.

THE CONSTITUTION, POLITICS, AND PUBLIC POLICY

 How does the Constitution affect the policymaking process?

The U.S. Constitution affects the policymaking process by fragmenting political power. Separation of powers divides power at the national level among legislative, executive, and judicial branches. Bicameralism splits power between the House and Senate. Federalism distributes power between the national government and the states.

The fragmentation of political power in the United States produces slow, incremental change.

Presidents need the cooperation of Congress to have their programs enacted. In turn, Congress has difficulty acting without presidential initiative. Both the president and Congress need the support of the bureaucracy if their policies are to be faithfully executed. Frequently, they require the cooperation of state and local officials as well. The courts, meanwhile, can reverse or delay policies adopted at other levels or by other branches of government. When policy changes occur, they are generally incremental and gradual, reflecting compromise among the various political actors involved in the process.

The framers of the U.S. Constitution were cautious people, wary of rapid change and none too confident about the judgment of popular majorities. Consequently, they created a constitutional apparatus that would work slowly. The founders feared that rapid, major change would too often produce more harm than good.

The Constitution promotes policy stability.[17] The election of a new president or a change in control of Congress is unlikely to produce dramatic policy change. A new president with bold new ideas must convince both Congress and the federal courts that the policy ideas are not only wise but constitutional.

The framers of the Constitution wanted to ensure that the diversity of political interests in American society would be represented in the policy process. During the debates at the constitutional convention of 1787, one of the major issues was how best to protect the small states from large-state domination. In response to the controversy, the authors of the Constitution established a system that would provide opportunity for the varied groups and interests of American society to participate in policymaking. Today, many Americans still consider this as a virtue.

Nonetheless, America's constitutional arrangements have their critics. The oldest complaint, first voiced by the Antifederalists, is that the Constitution favored the rich and wellborn over the common people. In the early twentieth century, historian Charles Beard echoed the position of the Antifederalists by arguing that the framers of the Constitution had been members of a small group of wealthy Americans who set out to preserve and enhance the economic and political opportunities of their class.[18] Although modern historians have refuted most of Beard's research, a number of contemporary observers nonetheless believe that the Constitution benefits special interests. The constitutional fragmentation of power that presents a range of forums in which different groups may be heard also provides a series of power centers that interest groups can control. Because of the complexity of the constitutional process, entrenched groups can frequently muster the influence to halt policy changes they consider unfavorable, sometimes overriding the wishes of a majority in Congress

The **fragmentation** of political power in the United States produces **slow, incremental** change.

and the nation. The supermajority provisons in the Constitution allow a determined minority to block the will of the majority.

The most basic criticism of the Constitution is that it is a blueprint for political deadlock among the branches and units of government. By dividing government against itself, the founders ensured that all proposals for policy change must pass through a maze of power centers. The complexity of the arrangement not only slows the policymaking process but also gives most of the trump cards to the forces opposing whatever measure is under consideration. It is easier to defeat policy proposals than to pass them.

Professor James Sundquist believes that American history is filled with the failures of the system to respond effectively to policy crises. Consider the dilemma of the Vietnam War. Congress and the president were unable to agree either to withdraw American forces or do what was necessary to win the war. As a result, the nation was condemned to a half-in, half-out compromise policy that satisfied no one. Sundquist says the same constitutional paralysis hindered the nation's ability to deal with secession in the 1860s, the Great Depression in the 1930s, and federal budget deficits of the 1980s.[19]

Nonetheless, constitutional stalemate is not inevitable. Sundquist's list tells only half the story. The nation did eventually rise to the challenge of secession and preserved the Union. The constitutional deadlock over the Great Depression ended. The budget deficit of the 1980s was finally eliminated. Furthermore, we can point to national crises such as World War II and the Cuban Missile Crisis that the American government was able to address in a forthright, spirited manner without constitutional gridlock.

Policy deadlocks are as much political as they are constitutional. The Constitution structures the policy process by setting the ground rules. It does not dictate the outcome of the policy process. The failure of American government to resolve the Vietnam War reflected a lack of political consensus rather than a constitutional breakdown.[20] We could say the same about the failure of Congress to dictate the withdrawal of American combat forces from Iraq. Whereas public opinion polls showed that a majority of Americans believed that the war was a mistake, they found the public conflicted on the best course to end American involvement.[21]

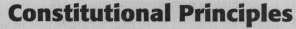

TAKING SIDES

Constitutional Principles

What is the best way of understanding the Constitution? Does it embody universal values, or should it be understood in terms of contemporary society?

Is there a difference between the founding conceptions of equality and those of today?

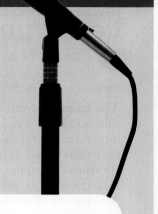

OVERVIEW

When the Constitution was ratified in June 1788, the United States had a population of roughly 3.9 million, and the right to vote was limited to those property owners. Today, the United States has a population of over 300 million, a very different makeup in terms of race, ethnicity, and religion, and much more inclusive voting rights. How is it that the Constitution can incorporate the differing social and political views of a multicultural and diverse nation?

Some scholars argue that the Constitution has been a successful document because it is based upon the principles of natural law and natural rights—principles holding that all human beings are created equal and endowed with certain inalienable rights, that these principles do not change over time, and that political institutions can be created to reflect natural equality and human dignity. Others argue that the Constitution is a flexible instrument created to adapt

to social, historical, and political change. This view holds that constitutions and laws should reflect prevailing social convention and thought, and it is in this way that the Constitution has been able to be interpreted to allow for equality and social justice.

Just what does the Constitution mean, and how will this question determine the near future of American history?

SUPPORTING
a natural rights interpretation of the Constitution

AGAINST
a natural rights interpretation of the Constitution

Natural rights theory assumes a higher moral law. It is through liberty and justice that individuals can realize their potential and approach happiness, and the Constitution was created to embody these values, which do not change over time.

A natural rights interpretation assumes the use of reason. Alexander Hamilton argues in the *Federalist Papers* that the Constitution represents "good government" created by "reflection and choice." This new form of government is based on the natural rights principle that all political power is derived from the people exercising their right to create government and to live under laws of their own choosing.

Natural rights theory embodies the principle of political equality. The Constitution should be interpreted as incorporating the principle found in the Declaration of Independence that "all men are created equal" and should have equal political rights. This allows the rich and the poor, the highly educated and the ignorant, and the secular and the religious to have a say and a share in government.

The founders simply used the prevailing philosophies of their times. There is no way to determine if natural rights theory is true, and the founders had no way of knowing what the future held in the way of new philosophies and science of government. For example, they did not consider that government could be used for social purposes, such as ensuring social welfare through government policy.

The Constitution must be interpreted in light of advances in technology and social organization. The United States of the twenty-first century is a different nation than the America of the eighteenth century. It is highly unlikely that the founders could envision the complex evolution of human society and technology—how could they consider freedom-of-speech issues and the Internet? To apply constitutional law to Internet speech issues necessarily means interpreting the Constitution in a way undreamed of by the founders.

Natural rights theory as understood by the founders leads to inequality. For example, the Declaration of Independence declares all men are equal, yet it allowed for slavery and unregulated free markets. The Constitution must be interpreted with a view to new understandings of social and political equality.

BACKGROUND OF THE CONSTITUTION

2.1 *What historical events and philosophical principles influenced the development of the new government?*

The framers of the U.S. Constitution of 1787 lived through two important historical periods that influenced their approach to constitutional development—the colonial era and the period under the Articles of Confederation. The experience under British rule made Americans wary of strong central authority, so the first American constitution, the Articles of Confederation, created a confederation. However, the government established under the Articles proved too weak, and the stage was set for the constitutional convention of 1787.

The political theories of John Locke were important for the Americans who wrote the declaration of independence. Locke said that the power of government flows from the consent of the governed and that people form governments to protect their life, liberty, and property. The framers embraced Locke's theory to justify their revolution. After a few years of independence, many Americans recognized that society was composed of a variety of interests or factions, which opposed one another on a number of policy issues. A strong national government could reconcile the divergent concerns of various groups in society to produce policies designed to achieve the public good. A strong national government could protect individual liberty and property from the power of oppressive majorities.

CONSTITUTIONAL PRINCIPLES

2.2 *What kind of government does the Constitution create, and how does it divide political power?*

The Constitution creates a representative democracy in which citizens elect representatives to make policy on their behalf. It established separation of powers—the division of the powers of government into legislative, executive, and judicial branches. The concept of checks and balances—the overlapping of the powers of the branches of government—is designed to ensure that public officials limit the authority of one another. Federalism is the division of power between a national government and a series of state governments. Bicameralism is the division of the legislative branch into two chambers, a House and a Senate. It too is designed to limit the power of government by dividing political authority.

LIMITATIONS ON THE POWER OF GOVERNMENT

2.3 *How does the Constitution limit the power of government?*

In addition to the separating of powers and checks and balances, power is further limited through the concept of rule of law, which means that the discretion of public officials in dealing with individuals is limited by law. The Bill of Rights protects individual rights from the government, including freedom of speech, freedom of religion and the like. It was not included in the original constitution, but added immediately after. It initially applied only to the federal government, but the Supreme Court subsequently incorporated most of its provisions to apply to the states.

CONSITUTIONAL CHANGE

2.4 *How does the Constitution change?*

The Constitution changes through amendment, experience, and judicial review. The Constitution has been amended a mere 27 times. Amendments must be proposed and ratified. Some elements of the Constitution have developed through practice and experience, such as the role of the president as commander in chief. Judicial review, which is the power of courts to declare unconstitutional the actions of the other branches and units of government, is another way the Constitution has changed.

THE CONSTITUTION, POLITICS, AND PUBLIC POLICY

2.5 *How does the Constitution affect the policymaking process?*

The U.S. Constitution fragments political power. Separation of powers divides national government among branches, bicameralism divides Congress into chambers, and federalism divides political power between a national government and a series of state governments. Political fragmentation produces slow, incremental change. It promotes stability and facilitates the representation of diverse interests. Although fragmentation can lead to political deadlock, the gridlock often reflects a lack of political consensus rather than constitutional failure.

Send	Save	Delete

From: Professor Tannahill
Add Cc | Add Bcc

Subject: Tips for Success
📎 Attach a file

KEY TERMS ARE KEY:
If you are looking for a study shortcut, focus on the key terms. Learn the meaning of each key term in the context of the chapter (rather than memorizing a definition) and you will have come a long ways toward mastering the course material.

TEST yourself

2.1 *What historical events and philosophical principles influenced the development of the new government?*

1 The fundamental law by which a state or nation is organized and governed, and to which ordinary legislation must conform is the definition of which of the following?
a. Bicameralism
b. Separation of powers
c. Constitution
d. Federalism

2 Which of the following was *not* a criticism of the Articles of Confederation?
a. The Articles were too difficult to amend.
b. The Articles gave too much power to the president.
c. The Articles failed to give the national government adequate authority to raise revenue.
d. The Articles failed to give the national government adequate authority to regulate commerce.

3 The political thought of John Locke had the most influence over which of the following documents?
a. Articles of Confederation
b. Declaration of Independence
c. Constitution of 1787
d. Fourteenth Amendment

2.2 *What kind of government does the Constitution create, and how does it divide political power?*

4 The voters in Country A elect legislators who make policy decisions on their behalf. Which of the following terms best describes Country A?
a. Federalism
b. Direct democracy
c. Unitary government
d. Representative democracy

5 According to James Madison, what constitutional principle was designed to prevent the concentration of power in the hands of one government official or set of officials?
a. Separation of powers with checks and balances
b. *Federalist Papers*
c. *Tyranny of the majority*
d. Bill of Rights

6 The president nominates Person A to the U.S. Supreme Court, but the Senate rejects the nomination. This scenario is an example of which of the following?
a. Federalism
b. Bicameralism

c. Checks and balances
d. Tyranny of the majority

7 A political system that divides power between a central government, with authority over the whole nation, and a series of state governments is known as which of the following?
a. Unitary government
b. Confederation
c. Federal system
d. Authoritarian government

8 Why did the framers of the Constitution divide Congress into two chambers?
a. They wanted to ensure that the executive branch would be the dominant branch of government.
b. They wanted to prevent the legislative branch from becoming too powerful.
c. They wanted to prevent the judicial branch from becoming too powerful.
d. They wanted to strengthen the legislative branch.

2.3 *How does the Constitution limit the power of government?*

9 The Constitution guarantees accused persons the right to a speedy, public trial by an impartial jury, the right to confront witnesses, and the right to legal counsel. These provisions embody which of the following constitutional principles?
a. Separation of powers
b. Tyranny of the majority
c. Checks and balances
d. Due process of law

10 The constitutional principle that government does not have unrestricted authority over individuals is the definition for which of the following terms?
a. Limited government
b. Due process of law
c. Separation of powers
d. Bicameralism

11 Do the provisions of the Bill of Rights apply to state governments?
a. No. The Bill of Rights applies only to the actions of the federal government.
b. Yes. The Supreme Court has ruled that the entire Bill of Rights applies to state governments as well as the national government.
c. Yes. The Supreme Court has ruled that the Bill of Rights applies to the states but not to the national government.
d. Yes, for the most part. The Supreme Court has ruled that most of the provisions of the Bill of Rights apply to the states.

2.4 *How does the Constitution change?*

12 Which of the following is a means through which the Constitution changes?
a. Practice and experience
b. Constitutional amendment
c. Judicial interpretation
d. All of the above

13 Which of the following branches of government has the role of interpreting the meaning of the Constitution?
a. Legislative branch
b. Judicial branch
c. Executive branch
d. All three branches play an equal role.

14 What was the significance of *Marbury v. Madison*?
a. It was the first case in which the U.S. Supreme Court declared an act of Congress unconstitutional.
b. The U.S. Supreme Court ruled that racial segregation was constitutional.
c. The U.S. Supreme Court ruled that state laws requiring racially segregated schools were unconstitutional.
d. The U.S. Supreme Court ruled that federal law takes precedence over state law.

2.5 *How does the Constitution affect the policymaking process?*

15 In which of the following ways does the Constitution affect policymaking?
a. Policies change rapidly, sometimes without sufficient deliberation.
b. A narrow majority, 50 percent plus one, can almost always force through major changes over the objections of the minority.
c. Government is sometimes unable to adopt solutions to problems when no consensus exists in the nation as to the direction that should be taken.
d. All of the above

KNOW the score

14–15 correct:	Congratulations—you know your American government!
12–13 correct:	Your understanding of this chapter is weak—be sure to review the key terms and visit TheThinkSpot.
<12 correct:	Reread the chapter more thoroughly.

Answers: 1) c, 2) b, 3) b, 4) d, 5) a, 6) c, 7) c, 8) b, 9) d, 10) a, 11) d, 12) d, 13) b, 14) a, 15) c

test yourself 45

3 THE FEDERAL

SYSTEM

THE CONSTITUTIONAL STRUCTURE OF FEDERALISM

Learning Objective **3.1** What are the powers of the national government and the states in America's system of federalism?

NATIONAL SUPREMACY AND THE SUPREME COURT

Learning Objective **3.2** How has the Supreme Court addressed the debate between states' rights and national government supremacy?

FEDERAL GRANT PROGRAMS

Learning Objective **3.3** How does the federal government distribute money to the states?

Medicaid is a federal program designed to provide health insurance coverage to low-income persons, people with disabilities, and elderly people who are impoverished. It covers such services as inpatient and outpatient hospital care, health screening, dental care, hearing evaluations, physician services, family planning services, laboratory fees, x-ray work, and prescription drugs. Although children from low-income families compose the largest single group of Medicaid recipients, most Medicaid expenditures go to provide services for the blind, persons with disabilities, and impoverished elderly people because their medical needs are greater and therefore more expensive to meet.

Medicaid is the nation's largest healthcare program, even bigger than **Medicare**, which is a federally funded healthcare program for the elderly. The states and the federal government share the cost of Medicaid, with the size of the state share depending on the state's average personal income. Medicaid is a large and rapidly growing part of every state's budget. The cost of Medicaid for both the national government and the states will soon increase significantly because the new healthcare reform law is expanding the program to cover more low-income people.

State officials are ambivalent about Medicaid. On one hand, Medicaid enables states to provide healthcare coverage to vulnerable populations, including elderly nursing home residents, people with disabilities, and children in low-income families. On the other hand, state budgets are strained by rapidly increasing Medicaid costs, driven not just by higher medical costs but also by congressionally mandated increases in program eligibility and coverage.

The Medicaid program introduces this chapter on the federal system. It begins with a discussion of the constitutional structure of the federal system. It then examines the ongoing controversy over the relative power of the national government and the states. It ends with a discussion of federal programs.

THE CONSTITUTIONAL
STRUCTURE of FEDERALISM

 3.1 *What are the powers of the national government and the states in America's system of federalism?*

The United States has a **federal system** of government, which is a political system that divides power between a central government with authority over the whole nation and a series of state governments. The Constitution delegates certain powers to the national government while leaving other powers to the states.

Powers of the National Government

The powers explicitly granted to the national government by the Constitution are known as the **delegated** or **enumerated powers**. The Constitution gives the legislative branch the most extensive list of powers and the judicial branch the least extensive.

Powers of the Legislative Branch. The Constitution vests the *legislative power*, the power to make laws, in Congress. In Article I, Section 8, the Constitution gives Congress broad legislative authority. Congress has the *power of the purse*, the authority to raise money (typically through taxes or borrowing) and to spend it. The Constitution charges Congress with providing for the "common defense and general welfare."

The Constitution grants Congress the power to promote economic development. Congress can regulate commerce among the states and trade with other nations. It can coin money, enact laws governing bankruptcy, set standards for weights and measures, provide for the punishment of counterfeiters, create post offices and post roads, and establish rules for copyright and patent protection. The Constitution also gives Congress an important role in foreign affairs and the nation's defense. Congress can suppress insurrection and repel invasion. It can declare war, raise and support armies, and maintain a navy.

Article I, Section 8 concludes with the **Necessary and Proper Clause** or **Elastic Clause**. "[Congress shall have the power] to make all laws which shall be necessary and proper for carrying into execution the foregoing powers, and all other powers vested by this Constitution in the government of the United States, or in any department or office there-of." The Necessary and Proper Clause is the basis for much of the legislation passed by Congress because it gives Congress the means to exercise its delegated authority.

The Necessary and Proper Clause is the constitutional basis for the doctrine of **implied powers,** which are those powers of Congress not explicitly mentioned in the Constitution but derived by implication from the delegated powers. Because the Constitution explicitly

federal system a political system that divides power between a central government, with authority over the whole nation, and a series of state governments.

delegated or enumerated powers the powers explicitly granted to the national government by the Constitution.

Necessary and Proper Clause/Elastic Clause the Constitutional provision found in Article I, Section 8 that declares that "[Congress shall have the power] to make all laws which shall be necessary and proper for carrying into execution the foregoing powers, and all other powers vested by this Constitution in the government of the United States, or in any department or office thereof."

implied powers those powers of Congress not explicitly mentioned in the Constitution, but derived by implication from the delegated powers.

The Necessary and Proper Clause **gives Congress the means** to exercise its delegated authority.

The authority of Congress to regulate offshore drilling is based on the Commerce Clause. In 2010, Congress conducted an investigation of the explosion of the Deepwater Horizon rig and resulting oil spill in the Gulf in order to assess regulation and oversight of offshore drilling. Here, former British Petroleum CEO Tony Hayward testifies before Congress.

grants Congress the authority to raise armies, the power to draft men and women into the armed forces would be an example of an implied power. The authority to draft is not explicitly granted as a delegated power, but it can be inferred as an action "necessary and proper" for carrying out one of the delegated powers—raising armies.

Several constitutional amendments expand the authority of Congress beyond those powers listed in Article I. The Fourteenth Amendment contains the Due Process Clause, which declares that no state shall "deprive any person of life, liberty, or property, without due process of law," and the Equal Protection Clause, which declares that "No State shall . . . deny to any person within its jurisdiction the equal protection of the laws." The Fifteenth Amendment declares that the rights of citizens to vote shall not be abridged on account of race, color, or previous condition of servitude, and the Sixteenth Amendment grants Congress the authority to levy an income tax. Congress has the power to enforce all of these provisions through "appropriate legislation."

Powers of the Executive Branch. The Constitution grants *executive power*, the power to enforce laws, to the president, declaring that the president should "take Care that Laws be faithfully executed." In Article II, the Constitution says that the president shall be commander in chief of the nation's armed forces. It states that the president may require reports from the heads of the executive departments, grant pardons and reprieves, make treaties with "the Advice and Consent" of the Senate, and appoint ambassadors, judges, and other officials. The president may make policy recommendations to Congress, receive ambassadors, and convene special sessions of Congress.

Powers of the Judicial Branch. The Constitution vests *judicial power*, the power to interpret laws, in a Supreme Court and whatever other federal courts Congress sees fit to create. In Article III, the Constitution declares that the judicial power extends to all cases arising under the Constitution, federal law, and treaties. The Constitution gives the Supreme Court of the United States the authority to try a limited range of cases, such as cases affecting ambassadors and cases in which a state is a party.

National Supremacy. The Constitution addresses the question of the relative power of the national and state governments in Article VI in a passage known as the **National Supremacy Clause**. This is the constitutional provision that declares that the Constitution and laws of the United States take precedence over the constitutions and laws of the states. The U.S. Constitution is superior to national law, state constitutions, and state laws. National law is superior to state constitutions and state laws.

The federal laws and regulations that have the greatest impact on state and local policymaking take the form of federal preemption and federal mandates. **Federal preemption of state authority** *prevents* states from

National Supremacy Clause the constitutional provision that declares that the Constitution and laws of the United States take precedence over the constitutions and laws of the states.

federal preemption of state authority an act of Congress adopting regulatory policies that overrule state policies in a particular regulatory area.

Encouraged by the allied powers, Germany created a federal system after World War II. Having fought two world wars against Germany, the allies wanted the Germans to create a political system that would disperse power among the national government and a series of states, rather than concentrate it in a central government.

The German federal system divides power between a national government and 16 states called *länder*.[1] Unlike the American states, the *länder* are more accurately described as administrative units rather than historically or culturally distinct regions. Public opinion favors centralized education policy-making with a uniform national policy because German society is culturally homogeneous, and the public wants the schools to promote national unity. The German public also believes that a consistent national educational policy promotes academic excellence, whereas educational diversity produces mediocrity.

The *länder* use the Standing Conference of Ministers of Culture (KMK) to circumvent the constitutionally required decentralization of educational policy. The KMK has negotiated an agreement to standardize the curriculum, establish uniform educational assessment criteria, and coordinate the timing and duration of the school year among the *länder*. Consequently, Germany has a uniform national education policy despite the constitutional requirement of decentralization.[2]

QUESTIONS

1 Would the German public favor or oppose an educational initiative such as No Child Left Behind? Why or why not?

2 Why do Americans, unlike the Germans, resist a national set of educational policies?

3 Do you believe states should be able to set their own education policies or should education policy be determined at the national level?

Students in German schools follow a national curriculum.

adopting their own policies in selected policy areas. Congress has passed more than a hundred laws preempting state regulation, including policies dealing with cellular phone rates, nuclear power safety, pension plans, automobile safety standards, and trucking rates.[3] A **federal mandate** is a legal requirement placed on a state or local government by the national government *requiring* certain policy actions. For example, the Americans with Disabilities Act (ADA), discussed in the Introduction chapter, mandates requirements intended to end discrimination against persons with disabilities and eliminate barriers preventing their full participation in American society. Because of

the ADA, colleges and universities typically provide special assistance to students with disabilities, such as sign-language interpreters for students who have hearing impairments and additional time to take exams for students with learning disabilities.[4]

The Role of States in the Federal System

The Constitution discusses the relationship of states with one another and with the national government. The **Full Faith and Credit Clause** is the constitutional provision requiring that states recognize the official acts of other states, such as marriages, divorces, adoptions, court orders, and other legal decisions. The

constitutional meaning of the Full Faith and Credit Clause may soon be tested by the controversy over gay marriage. Gay couples who marry in states where it is legal may move to other states and then ask their new home states to recognize their marriage under the Full Faith and Credit

federal mandate a legal requirement placed on a state or local government by the national government requiring certain policy actions.

Full Faith and Credit Clause the constitutional provision requiring that states recognize the official acts of other states, such as marriages, divorces, adoptions, court orders, and other legal decisions.

Clause. Consequently, the U.S. Supreme Court may eventually be asked to rule on the meaning of the Full Faith and Credit Clause.

Article IV also address the concepts of privileges and immunities, and extradition. The **Privileges and Immunities Clause** is a constitutional provision prohibiting state governments from discriminating against the citizens of other states. This provision ensures that visitors to a state are accorded the same legal protection, travel rights, and property rights as a state's own citizens. **Extradition** is the return from one state to another of a person accused of a crime. A person charged with a crime in California who flees to Nevada, for example, could be extradited back to California.

The Constitution prohibits states from taking certain actions. States may not negotiate international treaties, form alliances with foreign countries, or engage in war unless they are invaded. States may not create their own currency or levy taxes on commerce with other states or foreign nations.

The Constitution includes a number of guarantees to the states. It declares that states may not be divided or consolidated without their permission. The Constitution also promises states defense against invasion, protection from domestic violence when requested, equal representation in the U.S. Senate, and a republican form of government. The Eleventh Amendment prohibits foreign residents or the citizens of other states from suing a state in federal court.

The best-known constitutional guarantee given to the states is the Tenth Amendment: "The powers not delegated to the United States by the Constitution, nor prohibited by it to the states, are reserved to the states respectively, or to the people." The powers of the national government are enumerated in the Constitution— the delegated powers. According to the Tenth Amendment, the powers not delegated to the national government are reserved to the states or to the people. **Reserved**, or **residual powers**, then, are the powers of government left to the states. In other words, the national government may exercise only those powers granted to it by the Constitution, whereas state governments possess all the powers not given to the national government, except those that are prohibited to the states by the Constitution.

This description of the federal system implies that the division of powers between the national government and the states resembles a layer cake, with each level of government exercising authority in its own sphere without overlap. In practice, however, the authority of the national government and the powers of the states overlap considerably. For example, both the states and the national government participate in education policymaking. The powers of government that are jointly exercised by the national government and state governments are known as **concurrent powers**. Both levels of government have authority to tax, spend, and regulate. Instead of a layer cake, the federal system today more closely resembles a marble cake with its overlapping textures.

Privileges and Immunities Clause the constitutional provision prohibiting state governments from discriminating against the citizens of other states.

extradition the return from one state to another of a person accused of a crime.

reserved/residual powers the powers of government left to the states.

concurrent powers powers of government that are jointly exercised by the national government and state governments.

NATIONAL POWERS
(ENUMERATED)

- COIN MONEY
- CONDUCT FOREIGN RELATIONS
- REGULATE COMMERCE WITH FOREIGN NATIONS AND AMONG THE STATES
- RAISE AND SUPPORT ARMIES
- PROVIDE AND MAINTAIN A NAVY
- DECLARE AND CONDUCT WAR
- ESTABLISH A NATIONAL COURT SYSTEM
- MAKE LAWS NECESSARY AND PROPER TO CARRY OUT THE DELEGATED POWERS

CONCURRENT POWERS
(SHARED)

- TAX
- BORROW MONEY
- MAKE AND ENFORCE LAWS
- CHARTER BANKS AND CORPORATIONS
- SPEND MONEY FOR THE GENERAL WELFARE
- TAKE PRIVATE PROPERTY FOR PUBLIC PURPOSES, WITH JUST COMPENSATION

STATE POWERS
(RESERVED)

- ESTABLISH LOCAL GOVERNMENTS
- REGULATE COMMERCE IN THE STATE
- CONDUCT ELECTIONS
- RATIFY AMENDMENTS TO THE FEDERAL CONSTITUTION
- ADOPT MEASURES FOR PUBLIC HEALTH, SAFETY, AND MORALS
- EXERCISE POWERS THE CONSTITUTION DOES NOT DELEGATE TO THE NATIONAL GOVERNMENT OR PROHIBIT THE STATES FROM USING

States Cut Their Budgets and Higher Education Takes a Hit

The recession of 2008–2009, the steepest economic decline since the Great Depression, was a disaster for state governments. Revenues shrank because of a decrease in the income, sales, and property tax collections on which state governments depend, while the demand for services increased, especially for welfare benefits and unemployment compensation programs that are jointly funded by the federal government and the states. Although money from the federal government helped make up for some of the shortfall, states were forced to cut expenditures and increase taxes and fees to balance their budgets. State governments furloughed employees, periodically closed state offices, and reduced public services. Higher education was hit particularly hard. Colleges and universities around the nation were forced to reduce scholarship money, cut faculty pay, lay off employees, increase tuition and fees, and cap enrollment to meet the budget challenge. For example, the state of California reduced higher education funding by 20 percent in 2009, forcing universities and community colleges to turn away hundreds of thousands of students.[5] In Nevada, meanwhile, colleges and universities suffered a 20 percent cut in funding in 2010 and then another 15 percent cut in 2011.[6]

DISCUSSION

Now that we are moving toward economic recovery, has funding been restored? Recovery has been slow. Unemployment remains high in most states and consumers are reluctant to spend, so tax revenues have not recovered and may not come back anytime soon. Moreover, the federal stimulus money that cushioned the blow of declining tax revenues in 2009 is now gone.

Why don't states do what the federal government does and borrow the money to fund services? Almost every state is constitutionally required to balance its budget. Although state officials have some budget gimmicks they can use to make it through a rough patch, the gimmicks aren't effective when the budget shortfall continues for a number of years.

Why are states cutting higher education? Isn't that the last thing anyone would want to do during a recession? Cutting higher education in a recession is shortsighted, but the alternatives are equally unattractive. Most state budgets don't have a lot of fat. The biggest expenditure categories for state governments are public education, healthcare, transportation, higher education, and prisons. None of those budget areas is easily trimmed.

Why not just raise taxes? Many state governments have raised taxes, but the increases have generally been insufficient to close the budget gap completely. Moreover, raising taxes is politically unpopular, so much so that many governors and state legislators refuse to consider the option, preferring instead to cut the budget. Government should learn to live within its means, they say, just as ordinary families have had to reduce their spending to match their incomes.

NATIONAL SUPREMACY
AND THE SUPREME COURT

How has the Supreme Court addressed the debate between states' rights and national government supremacy?

Constitutional controversies about the relative powers of the states and the national government are a recurrent theme of American history. The supporters of states' rights and the proponents of national government supremacy have long debated the role of the states and the national government in the federal system.

The States' Rights Debate

The doctrine of **states' rights** is an interpretation of the Constitution that favors limiting the authority of

think Which side more closely reflects your point of view: the supporters of a strong national government or the advocates of states' rights? Why?

the federal government while expanding the powers of the states. The advocates of states' rights believe that the Constitution is a compact among the states that restricts the national government to those powers explicitly granted to it by the Constitution, that is, to the delegated powers. They would question, for example, whether the federal government should be involved in public education at all. The advocates of states' rights argue that the scope of the implied powers should be strictly limited.

In contrast, the supporters of national government supremacy contend that the Constitution is a contract among the people rather than the states. They note that the document begins with the following phrase: "We the people ..." The supporters of a strong national government believe that the implied powers should be construed broadly in order to further the interests of the people. The federal government has a role to play in public education, they say, because it has a duty to "promote the general Welfare."

The controversy over the respective roles of the national government and the states has also been argued on the basis of practical politics. States' rights advocates believe that local control makes for more efficient government because state and local governments are closer to the people and know and can act upon their policy preferences. The supporters of a strong national government believe that national control makes for better public policy. Some problems such as healthcare, education reform, and climate change are too big and complex to be resolved at the state level because state governments may lack the financial resources or the political will to address the issues.

The Role of the Supreme Court

The Supreme Court first addressed the controversy over the relationship between the states and the national government in the famous case of *McCulloch v. Maryland* (1819). The Court ruled that states do not have the right to interfere in the constitutional operations of the national government.

- **Background** In 1791, Congress chartered a national bank, the First Bank of the United States, amid great controversy. Secretary of State Thomas Jefferson opposed the bank because the authority to create it was not among the powers specifically enumerated by the Constitution. In contrast, Secretary of the Treasury Alexander Hamilton supported the bank and the power of Congress to establish it. He believed that the action of Congress was justified as an exercise of authority reasonably implied by the delegated powers. Despite the controversy, no legal challenge to the bank arose, and it operated until its charter expired in 1811.

- **The Case** Congress chartered the Second Bank of the United States in 1816. It, too, became the object of controversy, particularly in the West and South. Critics accused the bank of corruption and inefficiency. The most serious charge was that the bank was responsible for an economic downturn that ruined thousands of investors. Several states responded to the public outcry against the bank by adopting restrictions on it or levying heavy taxes against it. Maryland, for example, required payment of an annual tax of $15,000 on the bank's Baltimore branch, which, in those days, was a sum large enough to drive the bank out of business in the state. When James W. McCulloch, the bank's cashier, refused to pay the tax, Maryland

states' rights an interpretation of the Constitution that favors limiting the authority of the federal government while expanding the powers of the states.

sued. The case presented two important constitutional issues: 1) Does the national government have authority to charter a bank?; and 2) Does a state have the power to tax an arm of the national government?

- **The Decision** Chief Justice John Marshall wrote the unanimous opinion of the U.S. Supreme Court, answering both questions. First, the Court upheld the authority of Congress to charter a bank on the basis of the doctrine of implied powers. Marshall noted that although the Constitution does not specifically grant Congress the power to incorporate a bank, the Constitution does say that Congress may lay and collect taxes, borrow money, and raise and support armies. What if, Marshall asked, tax money collected in the North is needed in the South to support an army? The creation of a national bank to transport that money would be a "necessary and proper" step to that end. The power to charter the bank, Marshall held, was implied by the Necessary and Proper Clause.[8] Second, the Court ruled that Maryland's tax was unconstitutional. The power to tax, said

Marshall, is the power to destroy because a high tax can drive the object of the taxation out of existence. If Maryland or any state has the authority to tax an arm of the national government, it could effectively shut it down and that would be contrary to the nature of the federal union as stated in the National Supremacy Clause.

- **The Implications** The Supreme Court's decision in *McCulloch v. Maryland* supported the position of those who favored national government supremacy. By giving broad scope to the doctrine of implied powers, the Court provided the national government with a vast source of power. By stressing the importance of the National Supremacy Clause, the Court denied states the right to interfere in the constitutional operations of the national government.

The Supreme Court has not always been as receptive to the

exercise of federal power as it was in *McCulloch v. Maryland*. In 1857, a few years before the outbreak of the Civil War, the infamous *Dred Scott* decision held that the national government lacked authority to regulate slavery in the territories.[9] Similarly, in the early 1930s, the Supreme Court limited the power of the national government to respond to the Great Depression by striking down much of the **New Deal** as unconstitutional. The New Deal was a legislative package of reform measures proposed by President Franklin Roosevelt for dealing with the Great Depression. It involved the federal government more deeply in the nation's economy than ever before.

Both the Supreme Court's decisions in *Dred Scott* and its anti–New Deal rulings were all eventually reversed. Congress and the states overturned the *Dred Scott* decision

By stressing the importance of the National Supremacy Clause, **the Court denied states the right** to interfere in the constitutional operations of the national government.

New Deal a legislative package of reform measures proposed by President Franklin Roosevelt for dealing with the Great Depression.

Supreme Court Decisions: National Supremacy vs. States' Rights

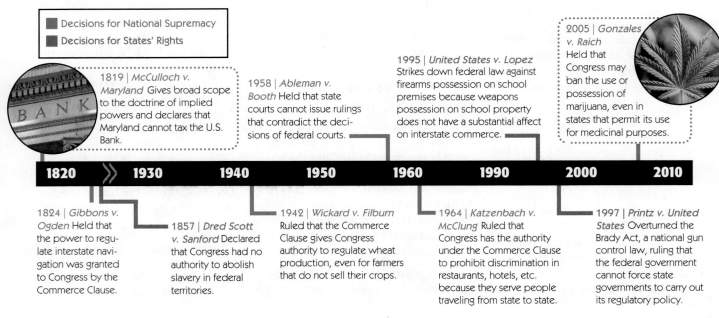

- ■ Decisions for National Supremacy
- ■ Decisions for States' Rights

1819 | McCulloch v. Maryland Gives broad scope to the doctrine of implied powers and declares that Maryland cannot tax the U.S. Bank.

1958 | Ableman v. Booth Held that state courts cannot issue rulings that contradict the decisions of federal courts.

1995 | United States v. Lopez Strikes down federal law against firearms possession on school premises because weapons possession on school property does not have a substantial affect on interstate commerce.

2005 | Gonzales v. Raich Held that Congress may ban the use or possession of marijuana, even in states that permit its use for medicinal purposes.

1820 » 1930 1940 1950 1960 1990 2000 2010

1824 | Gibbons v. Ogden Held that the power to regulate interstate navigation was granted to Congress by the Commerce Clause.

1857 | Dred Scott v. Sanford Declared that Congress had no authority to abolish slavery in federal territories.

1942 | Wickard v. Filburn Ruled that the Commerce Clause gives Congress authority to regulate wheat production, even for farmers that do not sell their crops.

1964 | Katzenbach v. McClung Ruled that Congress has the authority under the Commerce Clause to prohibit discrimination in restaurants, hotels, etc. because they serve people traveling from state to state.

1997 | Printz v. United States Overturned the Brady Act, a national gun control law, ruling that the federal government cannot force state governments to carry out its regulatory policy.

by ratifying the Thirteenth, Fourteenth, and Fifteenth Amendments. The Supreme Court reversed itself in the late 1930s, eventually holding New Deal legislation constitutional. For half a century thereafter, the Supreme Court found few constitutional limitations on the exercise of federal power.

Congress took advantage of the Supreme Court's broad interpretation of the doctrine of implied powers to exercise authority in a wide range of policy areas using the Commerce Clause to justify legislation. The **Commerce Clause** is the constitutional provision giving Congress authority to "regulate commerce . . . among the several states." Congress used the Commerce Clause as a basis for legislation dealing with such diverse subjects as child labor, agricultural price supports, and racial discrimination in public places. In each instance, Congress argued that the particular activity it sought to regulate was part of interstate commerce, which Congress is empowered to regulate, and in each instance, the Supreme Court eventually accepted the argument.

In recent years, however, the Supreme Court has issued a series of states' rights rulings. In 1995, the Supreme Court ruled that Congress had overstepped its authority when it enacted the Gun-Free School Zones Act of 1990, banning firearms within 1,000 feet of a school. The Court found the act unconstitutional, ruling that Congress can regulate only the economic activity that "substantially affects" interstate commerce, and that the possession of a firearm in the vicinity of a school does not meet that criterion.[10] In 1997, the Supreme Court overturned a provision in the Brady Act, a federal gun control law that requires a background check on an unlicensed purchaser of a firearm. The Court ruled unconstitutional a provision in the bill that required local law enforcement agencies to conduct background checks on potential gun purchasers. The Court said that the national government did not have the authority to force state governments to carry out its regulatory policies.[11] In 2000, the Supreme Court threw out a provision in the federal Violence Against Women

Act that gave the victims of sexual assault the right to sue their attackers for damages. Congress based the measure on its constitutional power to regulate interstate commerce, but the Court ruled that violent crime is insufficiently connected to interstate commerce to justify Congress taking action.[12]

The constitutional relationship between the federal government and the states is an area of constitutional law that is clearly evolving. Twenty years ago the national government was the dominant partner in the federal system, as the Supreme Court's interpretation of the implied powers was broad enough to enable the federal government to justify almost any action. Today, however, the pendulum has begun to swing back toward the states' rights position. In several recent cases, the Supreme Court has made it clear that it will not uphold the constitutionality of federal actions unless they are closely tied to one of the delegated powers.

Commerce Clause the constitutional provision giving Congress authority to "regulate commerce . . . among the several states."

FEDERAL GRANT PROGRAMS

 How does the federal government distribute money to the states?

A **federal grant program** is a program through which the national government gives money to state and local governments to spend in accordance with set standards and conditions. Medicaid is a federal program that deals with healthcare. Other federal programs address such policy areas as transportation, public education, childhood nutrition, public housing, vocational education, airport construction, hazardous waste disposal, job training, law enforcement, scientific research, neighborhood

preservation, mental health, and substance abuse prevention and treatment. In 2010, the federal government gave $654 billion in grants to state and local governments, which made up 17.6 percent of federal outlays.[13]

The figure on the following page graphs the allocation of federal grant money to state and local governments in billions of dollars from 2000 through 2010. Federal funding levels increased steadily in the early years of the decade, leveled off in the middle years, and then rose dramatically in

2009 and 2010. The significant increase in federal grant funding to state and local governments in 2009 and 2010 came with the adoption of the Economic Recovery and Reinvestment Act of 2009, which allocated billions of dollars to state and local governments. The recession of 2008–2009 was a disaster for state finance. The most important revenue

federal grant program a program through which the national government gives money to state and local governments to spend in accordance with set standards and conditions.

Despite an influx of federal grant money in 2009 and 2010 from the stimulus package, states still struggled to balance their budgets. Declining state revenue during the recession combined with rigid budgeting policies forced state officials in California to drastically slash state spending and increase fees. University of California students protested a 32 percent increase in tuition.

Federal Grant Money to State and Local Governments*

*in billions of dollars

sources for state and local governments are sales, income, and property taxes. During a recession, sales tax revenues fall because people have less money to make purchases. Income tax receipts shrink because personal income falls, and property tax collections fall because property values decline. Meanwhile, state and local government expenditures rise during a recession because more people qualify for unemployment compensation and welfare benefits. Congress and the president provided state and local governments with billions of stimulus dollars in order to help them maintain services and avoid layoffs of state and local employees without increasing their taxes.

Program Adoption

Congress and the president adopt federal programs through the legislative process. Both houses of Congress must agree to establish a program and the president must either sign the legislation or allow it to become law without signature. If the president vetoes the measure, it can become law only if Congress votes to override the veto by a two-thirds margin in each house.

Federal programs must be authorized and funds appropriated for their operation. The **authorization process** is the procedure through which Congress legislatively establishes a program, defines its general purpose, devises procedures for its operation, specifies an agency to implement the program, and indicates an approximate level of funding for the program but does not actually provide money. Although Congress authorizes some federal programs on a permanent basis, it

stipulates that other programs must be re-authorized periodically.

The **appropriations process** is the procedure through which Congress legislatively allocates money for a particular purpose. The appropriations process takes place annually. Federal programs do not function unless Congress authorizes them *and* appropriates money for their operation. Without money, programs go out of business or, if they are new programs, never begin functioning. Even if opponents of a federal program cannot prevent its authorization, they can accomplish

authorization process the procedure through which Congress legislatively establishes and defines a program, but does not actually provide funding for it.

appropriations process the procedure through which Congress legislatively allocates money for a particular purpose.

the same goal by cutting or eliminating the program's funding.

Types of Federal Programs

Federal programs come in a variety of forms.

Categorical and Block Grants. A **categorical grant program** is a federal grant program that provides funds to state and local governments for a narrowly defined purpose, such as removing asbestos from school buildings or acquiring land for outdoor recreation. In this type of program, Congress allows state and local officials little discretion as to how the money is spent. Categorical grants comprise more than 90 percent of all federal grants and provide nearly 90 percent of federal grant money to state and local governments.[14] Most federal education programs are categorical grant programs. A **block grant program** is a federal grant program that provides money for a program in a broad, general policy area, such as childcare or job training. State and local governments have more discretion in spending block grant funds than they have in spending categorical grant money.

Officials at different levels of government hold contrasting views about categorical and block grants. Most state officeholders favor block grants because they allow states more discretion in implementation. In contrast, members of Congress usually prefer categorical grants because they enable Congress to exercise more control over implementation. Members of the U.S. House, in particular, like categorical grants because they entail special projects that can be targeted to individual congressional districts.[15]

Project and Formula Grants. Federal grants differ in the criteria by which funding is awarded. A **project grant program** requires state and local governments to compete for available federal money. The Department of Education, for example, administers project grants dealing with a range of educational initiatives, such as teacher training, math and science education, bilingual education, and preparing students for the demands of today's workforce. Public schools, colleges, and universities submit applications to the agency which then decides which grant proposals merit funding.

A **formula grant program** awards funding on the basis of a formula established by Congress. In contrast to project grants, formula grants provide money for every state and/or locality that qual-

ifies under the formula. The Community Development Program, for example, is a federal grant program that awards annual grants to urban communities for neighborhood revitalization, economic development, and improved community facilities and services. The program awards funds based on a formula that includes population, poverty, and overcrowded housing. Most formulas are based on state population with modifications designed to focus on areas of greater need and to ensure that every state receive at least a minimal amount of money. Formula grants outnumber project grants by a four-to-one ratio, and most federal money is awarded through formula grants.

> **think** If you were a member of Congress, would you prefer block grants or categorical grants?

categorical grant program a federal grant program that provides funds to state and local governments for a fairly narrow, specific purpose.

block grant program a federal grant program that provides money for a program in a broad, general policy area.

project grant program a grant program that requires state and local governments to compete for available federal money.

formula grant program a grant program that awards funding on the basis of a formula established by Congress.

TAKE ✓ ACTION

Federal Programs and You

Federal grants and loans are important for students and the institutions they attend. Many students depend on federal financial aid to complete their degrees. Students need not repay grant money, but loans must be repaid. Pell Grants provide federal financial assistance to students based on their financial need. The amount of money that students can receive depends on the cost of their education and their available financial resources. Federal Family Education Loans (FFEL) and the Stafford Loan Program enable students to borrow money to attend college. Depending on their financial need, students may be eligible for subsidized federal loans, which do not begin assessing interest until recipients begin repayment.

Your assignment is to complete the paperwork to apply for federal financial aid. Visit your college's financial aid office or go to its website to obtain the appropriate documents. You may wish to attend a financial aid seminar to learn what aid is available and whether you are eligible. Complete the paperwork and submit the original or a copy to your instructor to document that you have completed the assignment.

Grant Conditions

Federal grants usually come with conditions. A **matching funds requirement** is the legislative provision that the national government will provide grant money for a particular activity only on condition that the state or local government supplies a certain percentage of the total money required for the project or program. For example, the federal government covers only 75 percent of the cost of highway construction projects, requiring states to provide a 25 percent match. About half of all federal grant programs require funding participation by the recipient. Even federal programs that do not mandate financial participation by state and local governments usually require the state to manage the program.

Matching funds requirements sometimes force states and localities to devote ever-growing sums of money to particular programs. Consider the impact on state budgets of Medicaid, a federal program designed to provide health insurance coverage to low-income persons. The federal government and the states split the cost of Medicaid, with the federal government picking up 50 to 80 percent of the cost, depending on a state's wealth. Healthcare costs, especially the cost of prescription drugs, are rapidly rising. Medicaid is the fastest growing item in most state budgets, accounting for 21 percent of state general fund expenditures.[16]

Congress also imposes mandates on recipients of federal funds. One kind of federal mandate, an **unfunded mandate**, is a requirement imposed by Congress on state or local governments without providing federal funding to cover its cost. As discussed earlier, federal mandates are often provisions in the area of equal rights or equal access for the disabled. Individual programs often have particular strings attached as well. In order to receive federal law enforcement grants, for example, states must collect data on sex offenders, include DNA samples, and prepare a statewide sex offender registry database.[17] In 1995, Congress passed and the president signed the Unfunded Mandates Reform Act to curb the growth in unfunded mandates, but it has been ineffective.

Grant conditions and federal mandates impose substantial costs on state and local governments. The National Conference on State Legislatures estimates the annual cost of federal mandates to states at $30 billion.[18] The most expensive federal programs for states and localities are federally mandated special education programs and prescription drug costs for people eligible for both Medicare and Medicaid.[19]

matching funds requirement the legislative provision that the national government will provide grant money for a particular activity only on the condition that the state or local government involved supplies a certain percentage of the total money required for the project or program.

unfunded mandate requirement imposed by Congress on state or local governments without providing federal funding to cover its cost.

federal GRANTS

	Purpose	Discretion given to state and local governments	Example
Categorical Grant	Narrowly defined purpose	Very little flexibility	Food Stamp Program
Block Grant	For a broad, general policy area	Some flexibility	Community Development Program
	How is money allocated?		**Example**
Project Grant	• State and local governments compete for available federal money • Doesn't provide money for every state/locality that qualifies		National Sciences Foundation grants for biological sciences
Formula Grant	• Funding awarded based on formula established by Congress to focus on areas of greater need • Provides money for every state/locality that qualifies		School Lunch Program, Unemployment Insurance, Temporary Assistance for Needy Families (TANF)

TAKING SIDES

Medicinal Marijuana and Federalism

Does the federal government have the power to overturn a state's right to legalize medicinal marijuana?

Do citizens and their doctors have the right to employ any relief possible when in pain?

OVERVIEW

In 1999, the Institute of Medicine released a report finding that marijuana's active components were "potentially effective in treating pain, nausea and vomiting, AIDS-related loss of appetite" and therefore should be tested for their benefits. The chemical in marijuana, THC, has been found by some doctors to be effective in slowing Alzheimer's disease, treating nausea in patients undergoing chemotherapy, and relieving pain in patients with multiple sclerosis or glaucoma.[20] The identified health risks of marijuana use are related to the delivery of the drug—smoking—and not necessarily to the drug components that produce the benefits for the sick.

As of 2010, 14 states have enacted laws that legalized medical marijuana for residents of the state, and patients can grow their own marijuana in all but one. Nine of these states passed the laws by ballot proposal, which means the laws were directly approved by a majority of the voters. However, in 2005, the Supreme Court ruled in *Raich v Gonzales* that the federal government can prosecute medical marijuana patients, even in states with compassion use laws. This ruling did not overturn state law, but the federal government, if it wishes, can shut down medical marijuana dispensaries in states where medicinal marijuana is legal.

 SUPPORTING
medicinal marijuana use

 AGAINST
medicinal marijuana use

Physicians know best what is good for their patients and should be allowed to prescribe medicinal marijuana. The federal government should not come between a doctor and his ability to best treat his patients. If states have laws that allow doctors to prescribe medicinal marijuana use, then the Drug Enforcement Agency should not get involved.

The Food and Drug Administration (FDA) has not moved quickly enough on the recent medical evidence. The Institute of Medicine released findings in 1999 that marijuana was potentially effective in helping patients, and recent studies have corroborated those findings. The FDA should adjust its controlled substance list based on medical findings, not politics.

States should be the locus of legislation about the health of its citizens. Most of these states legalized the use of marijuana through ballot proposals, which require support from a majority of voters to pass. The federal government should not intervene in what the people in the various states want regarding their drug policy.

The FDA lists marijuana on the strictest controlled substance list. As of 2006, the FDA indicates that marijuana has a high potential for abuse, and no medically accepted benefits. Therefore, given the potential harm of smoking marijuana, the federal government should block its use, regardless of state law.

Illegal trafficking of drugs is a dangerous problem for the United States. Marijuana is one of many drugs that are illegally trafficked. If we allow some people to smoke and overlook the occasional recreational use of marijuana, we are sending a mixed message that might destabilize the efforts to keep kids off of all drugs.

According to the Office of National Drug Control Policy, marijuana is bad for people's health. It impairs short-term memory, and has been the cause of automobile crashes and workplace accidents. The federal government has the responsibility to intervene to prevent this kind of negative impact on its citizens.

what we LEARNED

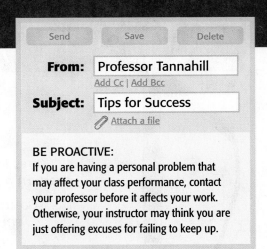
THE CONSTITUTIONAL STRUCTURE OF FEDERALISM

3.1 *What are the powers of the national government and the states in America's system of federalism?*

The Constitution specifically grants certain powers to the national government—the delegated powers. The list granted the legislative branch is the most extensive. The Necessary and Proper Clause is the basis for the implied powers, which enable Congress to put its delegated powers into operation. The National Supreme Clause declares that the national government is the dominant partner in the federal system. The federal laws and regulations that have the greatest impact on state and local policymaking take the form of federal preemption and federal mandates.

The Full Faith and Credit Clause requires that states honor the official acts of other states, such as divorces and deeds. The Privileges and Immunities Clause prevents states from discriminating the residents of other states. Extradition provides for the return of criminal suspects from one state to another. The Tenth Amendment says that the powers not granted to the national government are reserved to the states. In practice, both the national government and the states are involved in a broad range of policy areas.

NATIONAL SUPREMACY AND THE SUPREME COURT

3.2 *How has the Supreme Court addressed the debate between states' rights and national government supremacy?*

States' rights advocates want to limit the role of the federal government strictly to the delegated powers. They believe that local officials better understand local problems and know the policy preferences of local residents. In contrast, the advocates of national government supremacy believe that state governments may lack the financial resources and the will to tackle major national issues, such as healthcare and education reform.

In *McCulloch v. Maryland*, the U.S. Supreme Court endorsed an expansive interpretation of the implied powers and stressed the importance of the National Supremacy Clause. In subsequent years, the Court has not always been a consistent proponent of national government authority. Today, the Court generally requires that the exercise of federal power be tied relatively closely to one of the delegated powers.

FEDERAL GRANT PROGRAMS

3.3 *How does the federal government distribute money to the states?*

A federal grant program is a program through which the national government gives money to state and local governments to spend in accordance with set standards and conditions. Categorical grants provide money for fairly narrow purposes, whereas block grants give state and local officials more discretion by providing money for a broad policy area. State and local governments submit proposals to compete for project grants; formula grants award funds based on a formula. Federal grants typically come with strings attached, including matching funds requirements and mandates.

MySearchLab®

TEST yourself

3.1 *What are the powers of the national government and the states in America's system of federalism?*

1 Article I, Section 8 of the U.S. Constitution declares that Congress has the authority to coin money. Coining money is an example of which of the following?
   a. Delegated powers
   b. Implied powers
   c. Checks and balances
   d. Concurrent powers

2 In Article I, Section 8, the Constitution grants Congress authority to "regulate commerce among the several states." Congress passes legislation establishing regulations for inter-state trucking, including safety standards for trucks and drivers. Which of the following constitutional provisions or principles gives Congress the authority to set standards for trucks and truck drivers?
   a. National Supremacy Clause
   b. Implied powers
   c. Concurrent powers
   d. Equal Protection Clause

3 The Elastic Clause is another name for which of the following constitutional provisions?
   a. National Supremacy Clause
   b. Equal Protection Clause
   c. Necessary and Proper Clause
   d. Commerce Clause

4 Suppose Congress passes a law which conflicts with the state constitution of Georgia. Which takes precedence—the U.S. law or the Georgia Constitution?
   a. The Georgia Constitution, because of the Tenth Amendment
   b. The Georgia Constitution, because all constitutions take precedence over all laws
   c. The U.S. law, because of the delegated powers
   d. The U.S. law, because of the National Supremacy Clause

5 Because of the Americans with Disabilities Act (ADA), colleges and universities are required to provide special assistance to students with disabilities. This requirement is an example of which of the following?
   a. Federal mandate
   b. Matching funds requirement
   c. Federal preemption of state authority
   d. Project grant

6 Mr. and Mrs. Brown are residents of Louisiana. They fly to Nevada and get divorced. Are they legally divorced in the eyes of the state of Louisiana? Why or why not?
   a. They are not divorced. Because they were married in Louisiana, they must get divorced in Louisiana.
   b. They are not divorced unless the two states have an extradition treaty recognizing marriages and divorces.
   c. They are divorced because the Privileges and Immunities Clause requires states to honor the official actions of other states.
   d. They are divorced because the Full Faith and Credit Clause forces states to honor the official actions of other states.

7 The Tenth Amendment is the constitutional basis for which of the following?
   a. Reserved powers
   b. Delegated powers
   c. Implied powers
   d. Concurrent powers

8 Both state governments and the national government have the constitutional authority to tax and spend. Therefore, the power to tax and spend is an example of which of the following?
   a. Reserved powers
   b. Delegated powers
   c. Implied powers
   d. Concurrent powers

3.2 *How has the Supreme Court addressed the debate between states' rights and national government supremacy?*

9 Which of the following statements would most likely be made by an advocate of a strong national government as opposed to a supporter of states' rights?
   a. The Constitution is a compact among the states, and the powers of the national government should be narrowly interpreted.
   b. The powers of the national government should be closely limited to the delegated powers.
   c. National control makes for better public policies.
   d. All of the above

10 Which of the following was part of the Supreme Court's ruling in *McCulloch v. Maryland*?
   a. The Supreme Court ruled that Congress lacked the constitutional authority to charter a bank.
   b. The Supreme Court ruled that the powers of Congress were limited to the delegated powers.
   c. The Supreme Court upheld the Maryland tax on the bank.
   d. None of the above

11 Which of the following constitutional provisions has played the most prominent role in the modern expansion of federal government authority?
   a. Equal Protection Clause
   b. Full Faith and Credit Clause
   c. Privileges and Immunities Clause
   d. Commerce Clause

3.3 *How does the federal government distribute money to the states?*

12 A federal grant program that provides funds to state and local governments for a fairly narrow, specific purpose is known as which of the following?
   a. Block grant
   b. Formula grant
   c. Categorical grant
   d. Project grant

13 A federal grant program that provides money for a program in a broad, general policy area, such as childcare or job training, is known as which of the following?
   a. Block grant
   b. Formula grant
   c. Categorical grant
   d. Project grant

14 A grant program that requires state and local governments to compete for available federal money is known as which of the following?
   a. Block grant
   b. Formula grant
   c. Categorical grant
   d. Project grant

15 In order to qualify for a federal grant, a unit of local government is required to spend a certain amount of its own money on the activity supported by the grant. This is an example of which of the following?
   a. Matching funds requirement
   b. Federal preemption of state authority
   c. Appropriations process
   d. Formula grant program

KNOW the score

14–15 correct:	Congratulations—you know your American government!
12–13 correct:	Your understanding of this chapter is weak—be sure to review the key terms and visit TheThinkSpot.
<12 correct:	Reread the chapter more thoroughly.

Answers: 1) a, 2) b, 3) c, 4) d, 5) a, 6) d, 7) a, 8) d, 9) c, 10) d, 11) d, 12) c, 13) a, 14) d, 15) a

test yourself 61

4 CIVIL

The Reverend Fred Phelps, the pastor of Westboro Baptist Church in Topeka, Kansas, preaches that God hates homosexuals (Phelps uses a different word) and that the Biblical punishment for homosexuality is death and damnation to hell.[1] Phelps believes that God is angry with the United States because it tolerates homosexuality and that God uses natural disasters, such as Hurricane Katrina and the wars in Afghanistan and Iraq, as punishment.

Phelps and his small congregation, mostly family members, are best known for picketing the funerals of American servicemen killed in action, displaying signs such as "Thank God for Dead Soldiers," "God Hates You," and "You Are Going to Hell." One of the funerals that Phelps chose to picket was that of Marine Lance Corporal Matthew Snyder, who was killed in Iraq.[2] On the day of

LIBERTIES

the service, Westboro Church members picketed on public land adjacent to public streets roughly 1,000 feet from the church where the funeral was held. None of the demonstrators entered the church or set foot on church property. Phelps and his group displayed their signs, sang hymns, and recited Bible verses. No violence was associated with the demonstration.[3] Albert Snyder, the father of the deceased Marine, was largely unaware of the demonstration until he saw an account of it on the evening news. He subsequently filed suit against Phelps and his church, accusing them of intentional infliction of emotional distress, invasion of privacy, and conspiracy. A jury ruled in Snyder's favor and awarded him more than $2 million in damages. Phelps appealed on the grounds that he and his fellow church members had a constitutional right to express themselves. An appeals court overturned the verdict and ordered Snyder to pay Phelps's court costs. Snyder then appealed to the U.S. Supreme Court.[4]

The legal controversy over the Westboro Baptist Church introduces this chapter on **civil liberties**, which is the protection of the individual from the unrestricted power of government. The chapter begins by examining the constitutional basis of civil liberties in the United States, and then discusses a number of important civil liberties issues.

civil liberties the protection of the individual from the unrestricted power of government.

THE CONSTITUTION
AND CIVIL LIBERTIES

4.1 *What is the constitutional basis for civil liberties in America?*

Both the U.S. Constitution and state constitutions affect civil liberties policymaking.

The U.S. Constitution

The Bill of Rights and the Fourteenth Amendment are the most important constitutional provisions affecting civil liberties policymaking. The **Bill of Rights**, which is contained in the first ten amendments to the Constitution, is a constitutional document guaranteeing individual rights and liberties. Initially, the Bill of Rights restricted the national government but not the states. It prohibited Congress from passing laws abridging the freedom of speech, for example, but it did not affect the actions of state and local governments.

As discussed in Chapter 2, Section 1 of the Fourteenth Amendment reads, "No State shall . . . deprive any person of life, liberty, or property, without due process of law." The Due Process Clause provided the mechanism by which the U.S. Supreme Court eventually applied most of the provisions of the Bill of Rights to the states through the process of selective incorporation. As a result, most of the rights protected by the Bill of Rights now apply not just to the national government but to state and local governments as well.

The Supreme Court has held that the guarantees of the Bill of Rights are not absolute. Note the wording of the Due Process Clause: "No State shall . . . deprive any person of life, liberty, or property, *without due process of law*" (emphasis added). The government can restrict individual rights and liberties when it can demonstrate sufficient reason. Furthermore, the Bill of Rights applies only to the actions of government, not to those of individuals or private employers. Consider the controversy surrounding actor Charlie Sheen. CBS fired Sheen after he called the cocreator of his show, *Two and a Half Men*, a "contaminated little maggot." The First Amendment's guarantee of freedom of expression protects individuals from the power of government, but it does not protect them from losing their jobs because of their statements. CBS may have violated Sheen's employment contract, but it did not violate his First Amendment rights.

The Supreme Court has determined that some rights are more important than other rights. A **fundamental right** is a constitutional right that is so important that government cannot restrict it unless it can demonstrate a compelling or overriding public interest for so doing. To restrict rights that are not fundamental, government need show only that it is acting in pursuit of a legitimate public purpose. Suppose a city government prohibited both holding political rallies and drinking alcoholic beverages in a public park. Because the U.S. Supreme Court has recognized freedom of expression as a fundamental right, the city would have to show a compelling or overriding public interest in prohibiting political rallies for that policy to survive legal challenge. In contrast, because the Supreme Court has not held that drinking alcoholic beverages is a

Bill of Rights the first ten amendments to the U.S. Constitution.

fundamental right a constitutional right that is so important that government cannot restrict it unless it can demonstrate a compelling or overriding public interest for so doing.

fundamental right, the city government would need to demonstrate only a legitimate public purpose to justify its policy on alcohol consumption.

State Constitutions

State constitutions affect civil liberties policymaking as well. In America's federal system of government, states must grant their residents all the rights guaranteed by the U.S. Constitution (as interpreted by the Supreme Court). If state governments so choose, they may offer their residents *more* rights than are afforded by the U.S. Constitution.[5] All state constitutions include bills of rights, many of which are longer and use more expansive language than the national document. Since 1970, state supreme courts around the nation have issued hundreds of rulings in which they have granted broader rights protection under state constitutions than the U.S. Supreme Court has allowed under the U.S. Constitution.

Actor Charlie Sheen lost his job with CBS after calling the cocreator of his show, *Two and a Half Men*, a "contaminated little maggot."

FIRST AMENDMENT FREEDOMS

4.2 *What freedoms does the First Amendment guarantee?*

The First Amendment reads: "Congress shall make no law respecting an establishment of religion, or prohibiting the free exercise thereof; or abridging the freedom of speech, or of the press; or the right of the people peaceably to assemble, and to petition the Government for a redress of grievances." The most controversial of these freedoms are those regarding religion, expression, and the press.

Government and Religion

The First Amendment clause addressing the relationship between church and state has two elements. On one hand, the First Amendment prohibits the "establishment of religion." It concerns the degree to which the government may constitutionally support religion or promote religious belief. On the other hand, the First Amendment prohibits the government from interfering with the "free exercise" of religion. It addresses the extent to which government actions may constitutionally interfere with individual religious practice.

Establishment of Religion. The First Amendment prohibits government from making laws "respecting an establishment of religion." Historians agree that the authors of this provision intended to prohibit the naming of an official state church, but they disagree as to what other forms of church/state involvement constitute "establishment." Some experts believe that the Framers intended to build a wall of separation between church and state so that the affairs of government and the affairs of religion should never intermix. In contrast, other scholars argue that the founders never envisioned so extreme an interpretation of the Establishment Clause. They believe that the authors of the Constitution favored a society in which government would accommodate the interests of religion, especially Christian religion.[6]

The Supreme Court has adopted a middle ground on the issue of establishment of religion, attempting to balance the concerns of groups favoring a strict separation of church and state and the values of groups calling for accommodation between government and religion.[7] Consider the controversy over state aid to parochial schools. In 1941, the New Jersey legislature authorized school districts to subsidize the transportation of students to and from school and, if districts chose, to extend the aid to parochial school students as well. When Ewing Township did just that, a taxpayer named Everson sued, challenging the constitutionality of the action. The Supreme Court decision in *Everson v. Board of Ewing Township* set an important precedent on the meaning of the Establishment Clause. The Court ruled that New Jersey's transportation plan was constitutional because it had a "secular legislative purpose"—safe transportation for school children—and "neither advance[d] nor inhibit[ed] religion." Thus, the Court created a standard for determining the constitutionality of state aid to parochial schools: Aid that serves a public purpose is constitutional; aid that serves a religious purpose is not.[8]

think

Do you believe in the strict separation of government and religion, or should the government accommodate the interests of religion?

The controversy over parental choice and school vouchers is a recent manifestation of the battle over public funding for church-related schools. **Parental choice** is an educational reform aimed at improving the quality of schools by allowing parents to select the school their children will attend. The theory behind the concept is that public schools will have to improve in order to hang onto students and funding. Under a parental choice program, the state gives parents a voucher that provides a type of scholarship to be paid to the school that the parents choose for their child to attend. Some parental choice programs allow parents to select not only among public schools but also among private schools, including parochial schools. For example, the state of Ohio created a parental choice program for low-income families residing in the Cleveland City school district. Students who qualified could attend the private school of their parents' choice or a public school in an adjacent district and receive tuition assistance grants from the state. Although the overwhelming majority of private schools chosen by parents for student transfer were religiously affiliated, the U.S. Supreme Court ruled the program constitutional. The Court upheld the program because it had a valid secular purpose (providing educational assistance to poor children in a weak school system), it was neutral toward religion (parents could choose any private school or even another public school), and it provided assistance to families rather than to the schools.[9]

School prayer is perhaps the most controversial Establishment Clause issue. In *Engel v. Vitale* (1962), the Supreme Court ruled that the daily classroom recitation of a prayer written by New York's State Board of Regents violated the First Amendment. "[I]t is no part of the business of government to compose official prayers for any group of the American people to recite as part of a religious program carried on by the government," declared the Court. Furthermore, it was irrelevant that the prayer was voluntary and students were not forced to recite it. "When the power, prestige, and financial support of government [are] placed behind a particular religious belief," the Court said, "the indirect coercive pressure upon religious minorities to conform to the prevailing officially approved religion is plain."[10]

The Supreme Court has consistently ruled against government efforts to introduce religious

A CLOSER LOOK
The Ten Commandments and the Establishment Clause

The Supreme Court is divided over the constitutionality of public displays of religious symbols. In 2005, the Court ruled 5–4 that a six-foot-tall monument of the Ten Commandments on the grounds of the Texas Capital was constitutional because it was erected to achieve a valid secular purpose—reducing juvenile delinquency.[11] In the same year, the Court also ruled 5–4 that a display of framed copies of the Ten Commandments on the walls of two courthouses in Kentucky was *unconstitutional*, because the county governments in Kentucky posted them to advance a religious agenda, which was a violation of the Establishment Clause.[12]

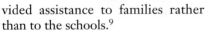

parental choice an educational reform aimed at improving the quality of schools by allowing parents to select the school their children will attend.

observances into the public schools. Consider the school prayer controversy in Santa Fe, Texas. The school district allowed students at Santa Fe High School to vote on whether to have an invocation before home football games and then held a second election to select a student to deliver the prayer. Two families—one Mormon and the other Catholic—sued the school district, and the case reached the Supreme Court in 2000. The Court ruled that the invocation was an unconstitutional infringement on the Establishment Clause, rejecting the school district's argument that the student delivering the invocation was exercising her free speech rights. "The delivery of a message such as the invocation here—on school property, at school-sponsored events, over the school's public address system, by a speaker representing the student body, under the supervision of school faculty, and pursuant to a school policy that explicitly and implicitly encourages public prayer—is not properly characterized as 'private' speech."[13]

think Do you agree with the Supreme Court's decision regarding school prayer in *Engel v. Vitale*? Why or why not?

Free Exercise of Religion. The First Amendment prohibits the adoption of laws interfering with the free exercise of religion. In practice, disputes concerning free exercise fall under two general categories. The first category involves the deliberate effort of government to restrict the activities of small, controversial religious groups. Many localities have also enacted local laws aimed at preventing Jehovah's Witnesses and other religious groups from distributing religious literature door-to-door. The Supreme Court has upheld these sorts of restrictions on religious practice only when the government has been able to justify

its action on the basis of a compelling or overriding government interest that could not be achieved in a less restrictive fashion. Because the compelling interest test is a high standard, the Supreme Court more often than not has struck down laws and regulations aimed against particular religions or religious practices.[14] The Court has ruled, for example, that Jehovah's Witnesses may distribute religious literature door to door and in public places without the permission of local authorities and without paying license taxes.[15]

The second category of disputes concerns the impact on religious practice of general laws and government procedures that are otherwise neutral with respect to religion. Prison inmates who are Muslim or Jewish, for example, demand that they be provided meals that do not violate the dietary restrictions imposed by their religious faiths. Amish parents protest school attendance laws. For years, the Supreme Court subjected these sorts of incidental restrictions on religious practice to the compelling government interest test. Since *Employment Division v. Smith* (1990), however, the Supreme Court has held that states can enact laws that have an incidental impact on

religious freedom so long as they serve a valid state purpose and are not aimed at inhibiting any particular religion. The *Smith* case involved a decision by the state of Oregon to deny unemployment benefits to state employees who were fired because a drug test showed that they had used peyote, which is an illegal hallucinogenic drug that is used in Native American religious practices. The Court upheld the firing and denial of unemployment benefits because the law under which they were dismissed served a valid state purpose, was not aimed at any particular religion, and had only an incidental impact on religious belief.[16]

Freedom of Expression

The First Amendment guarantees freedom of expression. "Congress shall make no law . . . abridging the freedom of speech, or of the press; or the right of the people peaceably to assemble to petition the government for a redress of grievances." People have a constitutional right to criticize the government and its officials, even if the criticism is outrageous, intemperate, and unfair.[17] They also have a constitutional right to express their political views even if

Demonstrators protest the planned construction of an Islamic center with a prayer room in lower Manhattan, a few blocks from Ground Zero. Is the planned center an affront to the memory of the people who died on 9/11 or is it the legitimate application of the Free Exercise Clause of the First Amendment?

those views are hateful, hurtful, or controversial.

In *Snyder v. Phelps* (2011), the U.S. Supreme Court ruled that Phelps and his congregation could not be held liable for inflicting emotional distress on the Snyder family because their picket signs dealt with issues of public concern rather than private matters. The Court held that the First Amendment protected the Westboro picket signs because they dealt with important national issues, including the political and moral conduct of the United States and its citizens, the fate of the nation, and homosexuality in the military. The Court further held that Phelps and his congregation were expressing their well-known views, which are apparently sincerely held. Phelps and his congregation chose the site of the marine's funeral to draw attention to their position, not to target the Snyder family. Snyder may have been offended, but that does not diminish the protection afforded to the Westboro picket signs.[18]

Antigovernment Speech. People have a constitutional right to criticize the government and its officials, even if the criticism is outrageous, intemperate, and unfair. The courts have ruled that the government can restrict political expression only if it has a compelling interest that cannot be achieved by less restrictive means. Consider the case of Clarence Brandenburg, a Ku Klux Klan leader from Ohio, who was convicted under an Ohio law for making a speech at a Klan cross-burning rally in which he threatened the president, Congress, and the Supreme Court for suppressing the white race. In 1969, the Supreme Court overturned Brandenburg's conviction, saying that the mere advocacy of lawless action was not sufficient to sustain a conviction because the state does not have a compelling interest in outlawing "mere abstract teaching." Instead, the state must prove that the "advocacy is directed to inciting or producing imminent

lawless action and is likely to incite or produce such action."[19]

Expression That Threatens the Public Order. Can the government punish expression that may lead to a disruption of public order? Consider the controversy generated by Paul Cohen and his jacket. In 1968, during the Vietnam War, Cohen wore a jacket into the Los Angeles County Courthouse upon which the words "F____ the Draft" were clearly visible. Cohen was arrested and subsequently convicted by a local court for disturbing the peace. The judge reasoned that the jacket might provoke others to commit acts of violence and sentenced Cohen to 30 days in jail. Cohen appealed, and the case eventually reached the Supreme Court, which overturned the conviction. The Court held that government cannot forbid shocking language that is not legally obscene and that is not directed at an individual listener (or reader) in such a way as to provoke violence.[20] Otherwise, government risks the unconstitutional suppression of ideas.[21]

The Supreme Court distinguishes between expression and action. Protestors do not have a constitutional right to disrupt traffic, block sidewalks, or impede access to public places. The Supreme Court has upheld lower court orders preventing anti-abortion

Protecting the civil liberties of even those we disagree with is an essential component of a democratic government. As Supreme Court Justice Felix Frankfurter (1939–1962) noted, "It is a fair summary of history to say that the safeguards of liberty have been forged in controversies involving not very nice people."

protesters from blocking access to abortion clinics because the government has an interest in "ensuring public safety, . . . promoting the free flow of traffic, . . . protecting property rights, and protecting a woman's freedom to seek pregnancy related services."[22]

Hate-Crimes Legislation. A **hate-crimes law** is a legislative measure that increases penalties for persons convicted of criminal offenses motivated by prejudice based on race, religion, national origin, gender, or sexual orientation. Suppose a group of young white men beat up an African American man who has just moved his family into a predominantly white neighborhood. During the assault, the white men use racial slurs and warn the man to move out of the area. The white men could be charged with the crime of assault. Because they acted out of racial animosity, they could also be charged with a hate crime. In recent years, many states have adopted hate-crimes legislation, enhancing penalties for persons convicted of crimes motivated by bias.

Yet hate-crimes legislation is controversial. Critics charge that hate-crimes laws infringe on freedom of expression. They also believe that hate-crimes provisions

The Supreme Court has upheld hate-crimes legislation, drawing a **distinction between speech and action**.

inhibit expression because they rely on speech as evidence of biased motive. In contrast, the proponents of hate-crimes laws claim they are justified because crimes motivated by hate inflict not only physical harm but also psychological damage on their victims. Furthermore, they argue that violent crimes aimed at groups of persons are more threatening to society than crimes against particular individuals

because they increase racial and social divisions.[23]

The Supreme Court has upheld hate-crimes legislation, drawing a distinction between speech and action. Although biased speech is constitutionally protected, violent behavior motivated by bias is not. "A physical assault is not by any stretch of the imagination . . . protected by the First Amendment," said the Court. Because hate crimes are perceived as inflicting "greater individual and societal harm" than ordinary crimes, states are justified in providing greater penalties for their commission.[24]

Symbolic Expression

Symbolic expression, such as flying the flag or burning a cross, enjoys the same constitutional protection as speech or written communication. Congress and the states can restrict symbolic expression only when they can demonstrate a compelling government interest that cannot be achieved in a less restrictive fashion. Consider the issue of flag burning. In 1989, the Supreme Court overturned a Texas flag desecration law under which Gregory Lee Johnson was convicted for burning an American flag at the 1984 Republican convention in Dallas, ruling that Johnson's action was a form of symbolic speech. "If there is any bedrock principle underlying the First Amendment," wrote Justice William Brennan in the majority opinion, "it is that the government may not prohibit the expression of an idea simply

because society finds the idea itself offensive or disagreeable."[25] Congress responded to the uproar over the Court's decision by passing a federal statute that outlawed flag burning. A year later, the Court declared it unconstitutional as well.[26]

Freedom of the Press

Freedom of the press is a fundamental right, which means that government cannot restrict it unless it can demonstrate a compelling or overriding public interest for so doing. The U.S. Supreme Court has ruled that the government has a compelling interest in prohibiting obscenity and protecting individuals from defamation of character.

"The government may not prohibit the expression of an idea simply because society finds the idea itself offensive or disagreeable.**"**

—Justice William Brennan

Obscenity. The U.S. Supreme Court narrowly defines obscenity. In order for material to be legally obscene, it must meet all three elements of the following criteria:

1. It must depict or describe sexual conduct. Although depictions of graphic violence may offend many people, the legal definition of obscenity does not encompass violent images.
2. The material must be such that the "average person, applying contemporary . . . standards,

hate-crimes law a legislative measure that increases penalties for persons convicted of criminal offenses motivated by prejudice based on race, religion, national origin, gender, or sexual orientation.

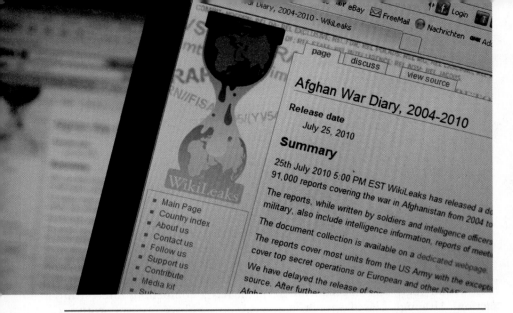

Wikileaks is a website that publishes sensitive material from governments and other high-profile organizations. In 2010, Wikileaks published classified documents on the Afghan war that were apparently leaked to the organization by an American soldier. Even though the U.S. government believed that the leak compromised national security, it could do nothing against Wikileaks because it is based in Sweden with servers located around the world.

would find that the work taken as a whole appeals to prurient interest." (The word *prurient* is defined as an excessive interest in sex.)

3. The work taken as a whole must lack serious literary, artistic, political, or scientific value.[27]

The definition of obscenity is so narrowly drawn as to exclude most material that ordinary citizens consider pornographic. With the exception of cases involving child pornography, obscenity prosecutions are rare and seldom successful.

Defamation. Defamation involves false written (**libel**) or spoken (**slander**) statements that lower a person's reputation or expose a person to hatred, contempt, or ridicule. The U.S. Supreme Court long held that the First Amendment does not protect defamatory expression, but in recent decades, it has adopted a relatively strict standard for the defamation of public figures. Because they have access to channels of effective communication to combat allegations, public figures must show not only that a statement is false and lowers their reputation, but that it was made with malice or reckless disregard for the truth.[28] Consequently, elected officials and high-profile government appointees seldom file

defamation suits against the media and are almost never successful.

Prior Restraint. Expression involving defamation or obscenity can be held punishable *after* its utterance or publication; the issue of **prior restraint** considers whether government can block the expression of objectionable material

before the fact. The Supreme Court has held that prior restraint—government action to prevent the publication or broadcast of objectionable material—is such an extreme limitation on freedom of the press that it can be used only in exceptional circumstances, such as times of war.[29]

The Supreme Court has had difficulty deciding prior restraint cases involving national security. In the *Pentagon Papers Case* (1971), the Court refused to block newspaper publication of government documents detailing the history of American involvement in Vietnam. Although the Nixon administration claimed that the documents included military secrets, the newspaper charged that the government's only real concerns were political because no national security issues were at stake. The Court was deeply divided, however, and its opinion gave little guidance as to how similar disputes might be resolved in the future.[30]

libel false written statements

slander false spoken statements

prior restraint government action to prevent the publication or broadcast of objectionable material

A CLOSER LOOK
The Right to Bear Arms

Amendment II

A well regulated Militia being necessary to the security of a free State, the right of the people to keep and bear Arms, shall not be infringed.

Historically, the courts have interpreted the Second Amendment to guarantee the right of states to maintain an armed militia, rather than protecting an individual right to own a firearm. In a 5–4 decision in 2008, however, the U.S. Supreme Court declared that the Second Amendment protects an individual right to possess a firearm in the home for purposes of self-defense.[31] In another 5–4 decision in 2010, the Court ruled that that right applies to state and local governments as well as to the federal government.[32] The Court made clear that the right to bear arms is not absolute, and that the rulings should not cast doubt on the constitutionality of "longstanding prohibitions on possession of firearms by felons and the mentally ill, or laws forbidding the carrying of firearms in sensitive places such as schools and government buildings, or laws imposing conditions and qualifications on the commercial sale of arms."[33]

PRIVACY RIGHTS

Do Americans enjoy a constitutional right of privacy? Although the Constitution does not specifically mention privacy, the Supreme Court has interpreted the Due Process Clause of the Fourteenth Amendment to include a right of privacy. In 1965, the Court struck down a seldom-enforced Connecticut law that prohibited the use of contraceptives and the dispensing of birth control information, even to married couples, on the grounds that its enforcement would involve government's invading "the privacy of the bedroom." The Court declared that various constitutional guarantees found in the Bill of Rights create "zones of privacy." The Third Amendment's prohibition against quartering soldiers in private homes and the Fourth Amendment's protection against unreasonable searches and seizures imply a right of privacy.[34] In contrast, conservative legal scholars believe that the Supreme Court simply invented a right of privacy that does not exist in the Constitution because a majority of the justices disagreed with the Connecticut law and wanted to find an excuse to strike it down. Although few conservatives want to defend Connecticut's statute against contraception, which some label "an uncommonly silly law," they have been outraged that the Court has used the right of privacy as the basis for major decisions involving abortion and gay rights.

The Supreme Court based *Roe v. Wade*, its landmark abortion decision, on a right of privacy. The case dealt with a challenge by an anonymous Dallas woman, "Jane Roe," to a Texas law prohibiting abortion except to save the life of a woman. The Court found the Texas statute unconstitutional, declaring that a woman's right to personal privacy under the U.S. Constitution included her decision to terminate a pregnancy. The Court said, however, that a woman's right to privacy was not absolute and must be balanced against the state's interest in protecting health, medical standards, and prenatal life.

The Supreme Court balanced these competing interests by dividing a pregnancy into trimesters. During the first trimester, state governments could not interfere with a physician's decision, reached in consultation with a pregnant patient, to terminate a pregnancy. In the second trimester, the state could regulate abortion, but only to protect the health of a woman. In the third trimester, after the fetus had achieved viability (the ability to survive outside the womb), the Court ruled that state governments could prohibit abortion except when it was necessary to preserve the life or health of a woman.[35]

In the years since *Roe* was decided, the Supreme Court has upheld its original decision while allowing states leeway to regulate abortion. In 1989, the Court upheld a Missouri law limiting access to abortion. The statute prohibited the use of public employees or facilities to perform or assist an abortion except to save a woman's life, and outlawed the use of public funds, employees, or facilities to encourage or counsel a woman to have an abortion not necessary to save her life. Citing recent medical advances, the Court abandoned the trimester system adopted in *Roe* by allowing Missouri to require physicians to perform medical tests to determine fetal viability beginning at 20 weeks.[36] The Court subsequently ruled that a state could regulate

Abortion Should Be:
Legal under any circumstances—24%
Legal under certain circumstances—54%
Illegal in all circumstances—19%

An abortion opponent kneels amid mock cemetery crosses to dramatize the loss of life through abortion.
Source: Gallup Poll, 2010

Fred Phelps would not be welcome in France. At about the time the U.S. Supreme Court ruled that the First Amendment protected Phelps, French police were arresting John Galliano, the well-known Christian Dior fashion designer, for making anti-Semitic remarks to a couple during an incident in a Paris café. Alcohol was apparently involved. French hate-speech laws protect individuals and groups from being insulted because of their ethnicity, nationality, race, religion, sex, or sexual orientation, or because of a disability. Persons convicted of hate-speech violations may be fined or sentenced to prison. French law also allows the government to outlaw groups that advocate racism.

The U.S. approach to hateful speech is the exception rather than the rule. Many of the nations of Western Europe passed hate-speech laws after World War II in the aftermath of the Holocaust. Hate-speech laws typically make it a crime to incite hatred against any identifiable group. In Canada, Germany, and France, it is illegal to deny that the Holocaust occurred. Many countries make it a crime to display Nazi symbols. Criticizing Islam is against the law in France.

The policy toward free speech in the United States makes it a haven for international hate groups. Anti-Semitic, racist, antigay, anti-Muslim, and other hate-based organizations set up their websites in the United States, where they are protected by the First Amendment. Were they to maintain similar websites in Europe, they could be prosecuted for violating the hate-speech laws.

QUESTIONS

1 If you lived in a country with hate-speech laws, would you call authorities if someone insulted you because of your race, gender, or sexual orientation, or would you just let it go?

2 Is it better to outlaw racist groups and possibly drive them underground or to attempt to discredit them by exposing them to public scrutiny?

3 Would you rather live in a country with hate-speech laws or with near absolute freedom of speech?

---

access to abortion as long as the regulations did not place an "undue burden" on a woman's right to choose. The Court's majority defined an undue burden as one that presented an "absolute obstacle or severe limitation" on the right to decide to have an abortion. State regulations that simply "inhibited" that right were permissible.

The Court has upheld a number of restrictions on abortion, including the following:

• Women seeking abortions must be given information about fetal development and alternatives to ending their pregnancies.
• Women must wait at least 24 hours after receiving that information before having an abortion.

• Doctors must keep detailed records on each abortion performed.
• Abortion records must be subject to public disclosure.
• Unmarried girls under the age of 18 must get the permission of one of their parents or the certification of a state judge that they are mature enough to make the decision on their own.

The only provision in the law that the Court considered an undue burden was a requirement that married women notify their husbands of their plans to have an abortion.[38]

The Supreme Court's most recent application of the right of privacy involved a legal challenge to the Texas sodomy law, which

criminalized private, consensual sexual conduct between two adults of the same gender. When police in Houston, Texas, arrived at the home of John Lawrence because of an unrelated call, they found Lawrence and another man engaged in sexual intercourse. They arrested the men and charged them with violating the Texas homosexual conduct law for "engaging in deviant sexual intercourse with another person of the same sex." In *Lawrence v. Texas*, the Court ruled that the Texas law violated the Due Process Clause of the Fourteenth Amendment because it intruded into the personal and private lives of individuals without furthering a legitimate state interest.[39]

DUE PROCESS OF LAW AND THE
RIGHTS OF THE ACCUSED

What are the constitutional rights of people accused of crimes?

Several provisions of the Bill of Rights, including the better part of the Fourth, Fifth, and Eighth Amendments, protect the rights of persons under investigation or accused of crimes. The key constitutional phrase is found in the Fifth Amendment and repeated in the Fourteenth Amendment: No person shall be deprived of "life, liberty, or property, without due process of law." **Due process of law** is the constitutional provision that declares that government must follow fair and regular procedures in actions that could lead to an individual's suffering loss of life, liberty, or property. Neither the national government nor the states may resort to stacked juries, coerced confessions, self-incrimination, denial of counsel, cruel and unusual punishments, or unreasonable searches and seizures.

Searches and Seizures

The Fourth Amendment guarantees the "right of the people to be secure in their persons, houses, papers, and effects, against unreasonable searches and seizures . . . and no warrants shall issue, but upon probable cause . . . and particularly describing the place to be searched, and the persons or things to be seized." In general, this provision means that the police need a **warrant** (that is, an official authorization issued by a judicial officer) for most searches of persons or property. Judges or other magistrates issue warrants after the law-enforcement authorities have shown probable cause that certain items will be found. **Probable cause** is the reasonable suspicion based on evidence that a particular search will uncover contraband.

Through the years, the Supreme Court has permitted a number of exceptions to the basic warrant requirement. The police do not need a warrant, for example, to search suspects who consent to be searched or to search suspects after valid arrests. If police officers have a reasonable suspicion of criminal activity, they may stop and search suspicious individuals. The Court has ruled, for example, that the police are justified in searching an individual in a high-crime area who flees when the police appear.[40] The authorities can also search luggage in airports and may fingerprint suspects after arrests.

The Supreme Court has been more willing to authorize searches of automobiles without warrants than it has offices and homes. Consider the 1982 case, *United States v. Ross*. An informant tipped off the District of Columbia police about a narcotics dealer known as Bandit, who sold drugs from the trunk of his purplish-maroon Chevrolet Malibu. When the police spotted a car fitting the description, they pulled it over and searched the trunk, even though they did not have a warrant. Sure enough, they found heroin and cash in the trunk. The car's driver, Albert Ross, Jr., was subsequently tried and convicted of possession of narcotics with intent to distribute. He appealed his case to the Supreme Court. Did the police search of Ross's car trunk without a warrant violate his constitutional rights? The Court said that it did not because the police had legitimately stopped the car and had probable cause to believe it contained contraband. As a result, the police could

due process of law the constitutional principle holding that government must follow fair and regular procedures in actions that could lead to an individual's suffering loss of life, liberty, or property.

warrant an official authorization issued by a judicial officer.

probable cause the reasonable suspicion based on evidence that a particular search will uncover contraband.

In June 2009, the Supreme Court ruled in *Safford Unified School District v. Redding* that a strip search of middle-schooler Savana Redding, suspected of distributing prescription drugs, violated her Fourth Amendment right to be secure against "unreasonable searches and seizures."

search the vehicle as thoroughly as if they had a warrant. The Court added, however, that a search "must be limited by its object," that is, the police cannot conduct a general search to see what might turn up.[41] If authorities have probable cause to believe that illegal aliens are being transported in a van, for example, they may search the van, but they have no justification for searching the glove compartment or luggage where no illegal aliens could possibly be hiding.[42]

The Exclusionary Rule

The **exclusionary rule** is the judicial doctrine stating that when the police violate an individual's constitutional rights, the evidence obtained as a result of police misconduct or error cannot be used against the defendant in a criminal prosecution. In 1914, the Supreme Court established the exclusionary rule in federal prosecutions in the

Weeks v. United States case. The police arrested Fremont Weeks at his place of business and then searched his home. Both of these actions were taken without a warrant. Papers and articles seized in the search were used in federal court against Weeks, and he was convicted. He appealed his conviction, arguing that the judge should not have admitted into evidence illegally seized materials. The Supreme Court agreed. In 1961, the Supreme Court extended the exclusionary rule to the states in the case of *Mapp v. Ohio*.[43]

The exclusionary rule is controversial. Its defenders say that is a necessary safeguard to ensure that police authorities do not intentionally violate individual rights. In contrast, critics point out that the United States is the only country to take the position that police misconduct must automatically result in the suppression of evidence. In other countries, the trial judge determines whether the misconduct

is serious enough to warrant the exclusion of the evidence.[44]

In recent decades, the Supreme Court has weakened the exclusionary rule without repealing it by carving out major exceptions to its application. In 1984, the Court adopted a "good faith" exception to the exclusionary rule requirement, allowing the use of illegally seized evidence in criminal prosecutions as long as the police acted in good faith.[45] Subsequently, the Court added a "harmless error" exception, allowing a criminal conviction to stand despite the use of illegally obtained evidence when other evidence in the case was strong enough to convict the defendant anyway.[46] In 2009, the Court ruled that evidence obtained from an unlawful arrest based on careless record keeping rather than intentional police misconduct could be used in a prosecution.[47]

exclusionary rule the judicial doctrine stating that when the police violate an individual's constitutional rights, the evidence obtained as a result of police misconduct or error cannot be used against the defendant.

TAKE ✓ ACTION

Talking About *Miranda*

Is the *Miranda* warning a meaningful constitutional safeguard or a technical formality that has no impact on justice? The class project is to research the implementation of the *Miranda* warning by interviewing police officers or members of the campus police at your college. Before conducting the interviews, prepare a set of questions designed to focus on the following topics:

- **Police training.** How do police academies cover the topic of *Miranda*? Is it presented as a necessary evil or as an important element of civil liberties in a free society?
- **Police supervision.** How seriously does management take the *Miranda* warning? Do police supervisors frequently review implementation procedures or is that left to the discretion of individual officers?
- ***Miranda* implementation.** When, if ever, do officers recite the *Miranda* warning to suspects? Do they read the warning from a card, or do they have it memorized? What steps, if

any, do officers take to ensure that suspects understand the meaning of the warning?

- ***Miranda* impact.** Do law enforcement officers believe that the *Miranda* warning has an impact on their work? Do they think the warning discourages guilty persons from confessing? Do they believe that *Miranda* plays a positive role in law enforcement by reminding innocent people of their constitutional rights? Or do they believe that the *Miranda* warning is meaningless, a waste of time to satisfy the courts that has no impact in the real world of law enforcement?

After the interviews are complete, students should organize their notes and prepare to participate in class discussion. In particular, the instructor will invite students to discuss their assessment of the *Miranda* warning. Is it harmful or beneficial, or is it just a meaningless technicality that neither police officers nor criminal suspects take seriously?

The *Miranda* Warning

Ernesto Miranda was an Arizona man arrested for kidnapping and raping a young woman. Under questioning, Miranda confessed. On appeal, Miranda challenged the use of his confession as a violation of the Fifth Amendment's guarantee against self-incrimination because the police had not informed him of his constitutional rights to remain silent and consult an attorney.

The Supreme Court reversed Miranda's conviction. The Court's majority held that the prosecution could not use a statement against an accused person in a court of law unless the authorities observe adequate procedural safeguards to ensure that the statement was obtained "voluntarily, knowingly, and intelligently." The *Miranda* **warning** is the requirement that police inform suspects of their rights before questioning them. Before questioning, accused persons must be warned that 1) they have a right to remain silent; 2) that any statements they give may be used against them; and 3) that they are entitled to the presence of an attorney, either retained or appointed.[48]

The Court's *Miranda* ruling has sparked an ongoing debate. Critics say that it makes law enforcement more difficult by preventing police from interrogating suspects quickly before they have a chance to concoct an alibi or reflect on the consequences of telling the truth.[49] In contrast, *Miranda*'s defenders call it the "poor person's Fifth Amendment." Educated, middle-class defendants do not need the *Miranda* warning—they know their rights. *Miranda* protects poor, uneducated, and first-time offenders from police coercion.

The Supreme Court has undermined the *Miranda* ruling without reversing it. The Court has held that in cross-examining defendants, prosecutors can use statements that do not meet the *Miranda* standard.[50] The Court has also ruled that police need not give the *Miranda* warning before questioning a suspect when the public safety is immediately and directly threatened.[51] The Court even upheld a conviction when the police refused to allow an attorney hired by a suspect's relatives to see him because the suspect had not asked to see a lawyer.[52] In 2010, the Court ruled that defendants must assert their right to remain silent after receiving and understanding the *Miranda* warning (see Breaking News!).

Double Jeopardy

The Fifth Amendment prohibits **double jeopardy**, which involves the government trying a criminal defendant a second time for the same offense after an acquittal in an earlier prosecution. No person shall be "twice put in jeopardy of life and limb" for the same criminal offense, the amendment declares. The goal of this provision is to protect individuals from the harassment of repeated prosecutions on the same charge after an acquittal. Because of the Double Jeopardy Clause, no one who has been acquitted of an offense can be retried for the same crime even if incontrovertible evidence of the person's guilt is discovered.

The Supreme Court has held that the Double Jeopardy Clause does not protect persons convicted of child molestation from involuntary commitment to mental hospitals after they have served their prison sentences. Consider the case of *Kansas v. Hendricks*. Leroy Hendricks was a pedophile, an adult who sexually abuses children. He had five convictions for child molestation in the state of Kansas and admitted that he could not stop trying to have sex with children. In 1994, after Hendricks finished serving his most recent sentence for child molestation, the state of Kansas transferred him to a mental health facility, where he was confined indefinitely under

> **"Who is it tomorrow that we're going to label as abnormal and potentially dangerous?"**
>
> —*Steven Shapiro*, ACLU

provisions of the state's Sexually Violent Predator Act. A state judge ruled that Hendricks was "mentally abnormal" and likely to commit additional crimes. Hendricks and his attorneys filed suit against the state, charging that his continued confinement was a sort of double jeopardy in that he was tried and punished twice for the same crime. The case eventually reached the U.S. Supreme Court, which declared that Hendricks could be confined against his will because he was being held in a mental institution rather than a prison. Technically, he was no longer being punished.[53] Although no one was sympathetic with Hendricks, a number of observers worried about the precedent set by the case. "Today we're dealing with sexual predators," said Steven Shapiro of the ACLU. "Who is it tomorrow that we're going to label as abnormal and potentially dangerous?"[54]

Fair Trial

A number of provisions in the Sixth Amendment are aimed at guaranteeing that defendants receive a fair trial. The amendment promises a speedy and public trial. Although the Supreme Court has been reluctant to set timetables for trials, the federal government and many states have adopted "speedy trial laws" to ensure that justice will not be long delayed. As for the public trial requirement, the Supreme Court has held that the public (and the press) may not

Miranda warning Before questioning, accused persons must be warned that 1) they have a right to remain silent; 2) that any statements they give may be used against them; and 3) that they are entitled to the presence of an attorney, either retained or appointed.

double jeopardy the government trying a criminal defendant a second time for the same offense after an acquittal in an earlier prosecution.

Supreme Court Weakens *Miranda* Warning

The U.S. Supreme Court has ruled that defendants must assert their right to remain silent after receiving and understanding the *Miranda* warning. Otherwise, the police may question them and use any statements they make against them. Van Chester Thompkins was arrested in connection with a fatal shooting in Southfield, Michigan. The police gave Thompkins a written form containing the *Miranda* warning, but he refused to acknowledge either that he received and understood his rights, or that he was waiving them. Officers began to question Thompkins about the crime, but Thompkins remained mostly silent. After nearly three hours, a detective asked Thompkins if he had ever asked God to forgive him "for shooting that boy down." Thompkins said yes and his statement was used to help convict him of murder. The lawyers for Thompkins argued that the statement should not have been allowed in evidence because Thompkins had not waived his right to remain silent. In a 5–4 decision, the Supreme Court rejected the argument because Thompkins never expressed a wish to end the interrogation. Furthermore, he effectively waived his right to remain silent by speaking up in answer to the detective's question.[55]

DISCUSSION

Does this decision overturn **Miranda?** No. Police are still required to read suspects held in custody their *Miranda* rights before questioning them and suspects still have the right to remain silent. The police are not required, however, to get suspects to explicitly waive their right to remain silent before beginning an interrogation.

So what is the point of this decision? Suspects must declare that they do not want to talk and ask that the interrogation end. It's not enough just to say nothing, as Thompkins did for nearly three hours.

So defendants must speak up to remain silent? No. Thompkins and other criminal suspects have a constitutional right to say nothing, but they must speak up to end the interrogation.

Why do some commentators believe that this ruling undermines the **Miranda** *decision?* The original rationale for *Miranda* was to create a procedural safeguard to protect the Fifth Amendment rights of defendants held in police custody. Being held in police custody is psychologically intimidating; in fact, it's so intimidating that defendants, especially inexperienced, poorly educated defendants, may have difficulty demanding their constitutional rights. They may even confess to crimes that they did not commit. The purpose of the *Miranda* decision was to establish a set of procedures to ensure that unassertive defendants know their rights and can easily invoke them. The *Thompkins Case* undermines *Miranda* by forcing defendants to assert their right to remain silent in order to end an interrogation. Unassertive suspects, the people that *Miranda* was designed to protect, are unlikely to speak up.

be excluded from the courtroom except in rare circumstances.[56] Furthermore, the Court has said that states may permit the unobtrusive use of television in a courtroom if they wish.[57]

The Sixth Amendment guarantees trial by an impartial jury. Although juries are traditionally 12 people, the Supreme Court has said that juries with as few as 6 people are acceptable.[58] The Court has also held that jury selection processes must ensure that the jury pool represents a cross-section of the community, holding, for example, that prosecutors may not systematically exclude racial minorities from jury service.[59]

The Sixth Amendment grants defendants the right to legal counsel. In *Gideon v. Wainwright*, the Supreme Court ruled that states must provide attorneys for indigent defendants charged with serious crimes.[60] The Court has also held that assigned counsel must meet a standard of reasonable competence.[61]

Cruel and Unusual Punishments

Should mentally retarded offenders be held fully accountable for their crimes? Daryl Renard Atkins is a murderer, convicted and sentenced to death by the state of Virginia for the robbery and slaying of a U.S. airman in 1996. Atkins is also severely retarded, at least according to his defense attorneys. Would executing Atkins violate the prohibition against cruel and unusual punishments contained in the Eighth Amendment to the U.S. Constitution? In general, the Supreme Court has interpreted this provision to mean that the punishment must fit the crime. The Court, for example, has held that a life sentence without the possibility of parole for a series of nonviolent petty offenses is cruel and unusual.[62] The Court has also ruled that it is unconstitutional to impose the death penalty on a defendant who rapes a child but does not kill the victim.[63] Furthermore, in 2010, the Supreme Court ruled in *Graham v. Florida* that sentencing juveniles to life in prison without the possibility of parole for crimes other than murder violates the constitutional prohibition against cruel and unusual punishments. The ruling gave inmates sentenced as juveniles the possibility of release but not a guarantee.

No issue has generated more controversy under the Eighth Amendment than the death penalty (**capital punishment**). In 1972, the opponents of capital punishment won a temporary victory in the case of *Furman v. Georgia*. By a 5–4 vote, the Supreme Court declared that the death penalty, *as then applied*, was unconstitutional because it allowed too much discretion, thereby opening the door to discriminatory practices. Which crimes and individuals received the death penalty was so arbitrary, the Court said, that it was similar to being struck by lightning.[65]

Many state legislatures responded to *Furman* by adopting new capital punishment laws designed to satisfy the Court's objections. As the states implemented their new death penalty statutes, cases began to make their way through the court system. In 1976, the U.S. Supreme Court ruled in the case of *Gregg v. Georgia*, which involved a constitutional challenge to Georgia's new death penalty statute, that capital punishment was constitutional.[66] Thirty-eight states

capital punishment the death penalty.

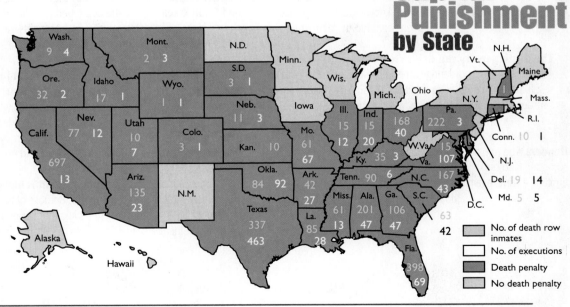

Capital Punishment by State

Green states employ the death penalty. Yellow numerals show the current number of death row inmates, and white numerals show the number of executions carried out since 1976

Source: www.deathpenaltyinfo.org. Data as of Jan 1, 2010.

TAKING SIDES

The Death Penalty

*Is the death penalty an effective
punishment or deterrent for crimes?*

*Does the death penalty violate the Eighth Amendment
clause against cruel and unusual punishments?*

OVERVIEW

Capital punishment is one of the most controversial political issues in American politics. Use of the death penalty varies across the states. Although 35 states have death penalty laws on the books, many states seldom if ever employ it. In 2009, only 11 states carried out executions, with Texas leading the way with 24 executions. Since 1976, Texas alone has executed 457 convicted murderers.

Critics charge that the death penalty is unfair and inefficient. Since 1976, 15 white defendants have been executed for murdering black victims compared with 243 black defendants who were executed for murdering white victims. Furthermore, since 1973, over 130 people have been released from death row because they were eventually found innocent.[67]

Support for the death penalty has held steady since 2003 at around 65 percent. However, when respondents are given the choice of life without parole as an alternative to execution, slightly more people choose life than death—47 percent favored the death penalty compared with 48 percent who preferred life without parole.[68]

 SUPPORTING
use of the death penalty

 AGAINST
use of the death penalty

Victims and their families deserve justice. The United States uses the death penalty only if a life has been taken. People who have lost a loved one gain closure from knowing that justice has been served to the perpetrator.

The death penalty can deter violent crime. If a person is considering murdering someone, knowing that the act will result in death could deter the person from committing the murder. Harsh punishments reduce the incidence of crime.

Only the death penalty guarantees against repeat offenders. The role of punishment in the legal system is to catch someone who broke the law and prevent that person from ever committing a crime again. The only way to guarantee that criminals do not offend again is to execute them.

This punishment has been abandoned in all but three industrialized democracies. Only the United States, Japan, and South Korea still use the death penalty. The United States should be a leader on an issue of human rights, not one of the last countries to make the change.

The death penalty is too final a punishment for a faulty legal system. The United States legal system is built on an adversarial model, which means it is not necessarily the finding of fact that leads to a conviction, but the quality of lawyers. Wealthy defendants who can afford the best attorneys avoid the harshest punishments whereas poor people end up on death row.

The financial cost of capital punishment is higher than the cost of keeping a prisoner for life. Because of the high cost of death penalty trials and appeals, it is less expensive to keep prisoners in jail for the rest of their lives than to seek the death penalty.

and the federal government adopted capital punishment statutes; 32 states conducted executions, with Texas taking the lead, carrying out more than a third of the nation's executions.[69] The federal government executed one convicted murderer, Timothy McVeigh, the convicted Oklahoma City bomber.

The increased rate of executions was accompanied by increased controversy. The opponents of the death penalty charged that the process of trials and appeals was so flawed that innocent people might face execution. A study published by Columbia University law professor James S. Liebman found that two-thirds of the death sentences given by American courts between 1973 and 1995 were overturned on appeal. When death penalty cases were retried, 7 percent of defendants were found not guilty.[70] Furthermore, the critics of the death penalty argued that it was inefficient because only 5 percent of death sentences were actually carried out and then only after years of evaluation.[71] In contrast, the proponents of capital punishment defended the process, saying that it was scrupulously fair. They pointed out that people given the death penalty were entitled to an appeals process that lasts for years. According to the Bureau of Justice Statistics, the average time on death row for the convicted murderers before their executions

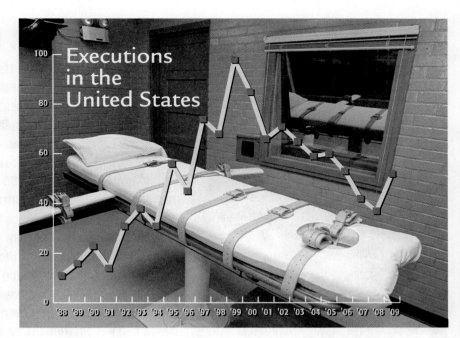

is more than 12 years, long enough for their cases to be thoroughly examined for error.[72]

The renewed debate over capital punishment has been accompanied by a decline in the implementation of the death penalty. As the figure above shows, the number of people executed in the United States peaked in 1999 at 99 and then fell steadily until 2009, when the number of executions increased to 52 nationwide. In some states, executive officials have slowed or halted capital punishment because of concerns about efficacy. New Jersey and New Mexico have repealed the death penalty statute entirely, and 18 states have adopted laws to prohibit the execution of mentally retarded criminals.[73]

In this context, the U.S. Supreme Court declared that the execution of mentally retarded defendants violated the Cruel and Unusual Punishment Clause of the Eighth Amendment. The Court argued that a national consensus had developed against executing the mentally retarded and reversed the position it had taken in 1989 when only two states excluded mentally retarded individuals from the death penalty.[74] The Court returned the Atkins case to a trial court in Virginia to determine whether the defendant was indeed mentally retarded. Ironically, a jury found Atkins mentally competent, and a judge sentenced him to death. His case is once again on appeal.

CIVIL LIBERTIES AND THE
WAR ON TERROR

 What civil liberties issues are raised by the conduct of the war on terror?

Executive authority grows during wartime, sometimes at the expense of civil liberties. In the midst of war, presidents exercise extraordinary powers and declare that their actions are necessary to defend the nation and win the war. Although civil libertarians often challenge the president's actions as infringements on personal liberty, other political actors and the general public either support the president's initiatives or mute their criticism for fear of being accused of failing to stand up to the enemy. Over time, public passions over the war recede and either a new administration or the other branches of government reverse

if you talk too much

THIS MAN MAY DIE

Civil Liberties in Times of War

1861 (Civil War) President Lincoln suspends the writ of *habeas corpus* to protect troop movements along the railroad lines.

1918 (WWI) Congress passes the Sedition Act, which makes it a crime to say or publish anything "disloyal, profane, scurrilous, or abusive" about the government or the military.

1942 (WWII) President Roosevelt issues Executive Order 9066, which forces nearly 120,000 people of Japanese ancestry— 70,000 of them American citizens—from their homes and businesses into internment camps until the war's conclusion in 1945.

1950 (Cold War) Congress passed the Subversive Activities Control Act (also known as the McCarran Act), which authorizes the president to detain without the benefit of *habeas corpus* anyone considered likely to engage in espionage or sabotage.

2001 (War on Terror) Congress passes the USA PATRIOT Act, which loosens restrictions on domestic surveillance, investigations without probable cause, and detention without judicial review when there is deemed to be a threat to national security.

the policies that compromised civil liberties.[75]

Consider the Japanese internment during World War II. In early 1942, shortly after the Japanese attack on Pearl Harbor, President Franklin Roosevelt issued an executive order to forcibly relocate nearly 120,000 people of Japanese ancestry living on the West Coast into internment camps until the end of the war. Most were American citizens. The president justified the order as necessary to prevent sabotage and espionage. When Fred Korematsu, an American citizen of Japanese descent, challenged his detention, the U.S. Supreme Court upheld the constitutionality of the executive order.[76] The U.S. government eventually began to regard the Japanese internment with regret. In 1988, Congress passed and President Ronald Reagan signed legislation officially apologizing for the internment and providing reparation payments of $20,000 each to the survivors or their heirs.

After 9/11, President George W. Bush took actions that critics charged threatened civil liberties. He approved wiretapping of overseas telephone calls without benefit of court order. He ordered terror suspects captured in the war on terror to be held at Guantánamo Bay, Cuba, without benefit of prisoner-of-war status or the rights of suspected criminals under the U.S. Constitution. The president authorized the use of aggressive interrogation techniques against terror suspects, and had some detainees transported to third countries, where they were allegedly tortured. American citizens suspected of terrorism were held indefinitely without trial. Bush also declared his intent to try some enemy combatants

The events of 9/11 as well as recent terror threats highlight the need for strict security measures at airports, including passenger screenings. The American Civil Liberties Union (ACLU) and other rights groups contend that airport security authorities should not target travelers based on their ethnicity or religion, and that security procedures should intrude on individual's privacy only as necessary based on the level of risk.

in military tribunals without many of the civil liberties guarantees afforded by civilian courts.[77]

The U.S. Supreme Court overturned or modified many of the Bush administration's actions. In a case involving Yaser Esam Hamdi, an American citizen who was taken into custody in Afghanistan, the Court held that the president could not deprive detainees of their right to due process.[78] The Court ruled against Bush's plan to put detainees on trial before military tribunals because Congress had not authorized the action.[79] In *Boumediene v. Bush*, the Supreme Court also declared that terror suspects held at Guantánamo have a constitutional right to seek their release in federal court.[80]

Similarly, President Obama reversed many Bush administration policies concerning the war on terror. In addition to banning the use of aggressive interrogation techniques, Obama ordered the closure of the Guantánamo prison within a year and made plans to try terror suspects in civilian courts within the United States. In particular, Obama wanted to try Khalid Sheik Mohammed, the alleged al-Qaeda mastermind of the 9/11 attacks, in New York City. Obama soon discovered the difficulty of implementing his plans. The prison at Guantánamo

CIVIL LIBERTIES AND TERRORISM

In order to curb terrorism in this country, do you think it will be necessary for the average person to give up some civil liberties?

Yes ▭ No ▭ Unsure ▭

Source: Pew Research Center for the People & the Press.

Bay remained open more than a year after he called for its closure because the U.S. government was unable to find countries willing to take all the inmates and American communities opposed efforts to transfer them to federal prisons in the United States.

President Obama ran into a similar problem with his plan to try Khalid Sheik Mohammed in New York City when Mayor Michael Bloomberg rejected the proposal because of concerns over security and the trial's effect on traffic congestion.

what we LEARNED

THE CONSTITUTION AND CIVIL LIBERTIES

4.1 *What is the constitutional basis for civil liberties in America?*

The Bill of Rights and the Fourteenth Amendment are the most important constitutional provisions affecting civil liberties policymaking. The Due Process Clause of the Fourteenth Amendment is the basis for the selective incorporation of the Bill of Rights to the states. The rights guaranteed by the Bill of

Rights are not absolute; the government can restrict individual rights and liberties when it has sufficient reason. A fundamental right, such as freedom of expression or freedom of religion, is a constitutional right that is so important that government cannot restrict it unless it can demonstrate a compelling or overriding public interest for so doing. To restrict rights that are not fundamental, government need only show that it is acting in pursuit of a legitimate public purpose.

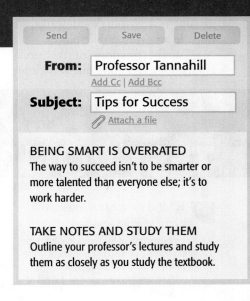

| Send | Save | Delete |

From: Professor Tannahill
Add Cc | Add Bcc
Subject: Tips for Success
📎 Attach a file

BEING SMART IS OVERRATED
The way to succeed isn't to be smarter or more talented than everyone else; it's to work harder.

TAKE NOTES AND STUDY THEM
Outline your professor's lectures and study them as closely as you study the textbook.

FIRST AMENDMENT
FREEDOMS

4.2 *What freedoms does the First Amendment guarantee?*

The First Amendment declares that government should not make laws "respecting an establishment of religion" or prohibiting the "free exercise" of religion. The Supreme Court has always ruled government-sponsored school prayer unconstitutional, but has adopted a middle ground on establishment issues such as school vouchers, balancing a separation of church and state with accommodation between government and religion. It is unconstitutional for the government to deliberately restrict the activities of religious groups without a compelling government interest, but states can enact laws that have an incidental impact on religious freedom as long as they serve a valid state purpose and are not aimed at inhibiting any particular religion.

The First Amendment also protects freedom of expression. The Supreme Court has held that the government can restrict political expression only if it has a compelling interest that cannot be achieved by less restrictive means. The Court has ruled that symbolic expression, such as flying a flag or burning it, should be treated the same as other types of expression. The Supreme Court distinguishes between expression and action. Protestors do not have a constitutional right to disrupt traffic, block sidewalks, or impede access to public places.

Finally, freedom of the press is considered a fundamental right, which means that government cannot restrict it unless it can demonstrate a compelling or overriding public interest for so doing. The U.S. Supreme Court has ruled that the government has a compelling interest in prohibiting obscenity and protecting individuals from defamation of character. The Supreme Court has held that prior restraint is such an extreme limitation on freedom of the press that it can be used only in exceptional circumstances, such as times of war.

PRIVACY RIGHTS

4.3 *What is the basis for a constitutional right to privacy and to what sorts of controversies has the right to privacy been applied?*

Although the Constitution does not specifically mention privacy, the Supreme Court has interpreted the Due Process Clause of the Fourteenth Amendment to include a right of privacy. After striking down a Connecticut law that prohibited the use of contraceptives, the Supreme Court based *Roe v. Wade*, the famous abortion decision, on a right to privacy. The Supreme Court also based its decision to overturn the Texas sodomy law on a constitutional right of privacy.

DUE PROCESS OF LAW AND THE RIGHTS OF THE ACCUSED

4.4 *What are the constitutional rights of people accused of crimes?*

Due process of the law is the key constitutional provision protecting the rights of persons investigated for or accused of crimes. The Fourth Amendment protects against unreasonable searches and seizures. The Courts have upheld the exclusionary rule and the *Miranda* warning, but in recent decades have weakened both. The Constitution prohibits double jeopardy and guarantees a fair trial. The death penalty is the most controversial issue arising under the prohibition against cruel and unusual punishments, and there is growing debate over the fairness of capital punishment.

CIVIL LIBERTIES AND THE WAR ON TERROR

4.5 *What civil liberties issues are raised by the conduct of the War on Terror?*

Executive authority grows during wartime, sometimes at the expense of civil liberties. In the midst of war, presidents exercise extraordinary powers and declare that their actions are necessary to defend the nation and win the war. Once the war has ended, civil libertarians are typically able to reverse actions taken during wartime. After 9/11, President George W. Bush took actions that some critics charged threatened civil liberties protections. Subsequently, the U.S. Supreme Court and the Obama administration overturned or modified many of the Bush administration's actions.

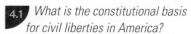

TEST yourself

4.1 *What is the constitutional basis for civil liberties in America?*

1 The protection of the individual from the unrestricted power of government is the definition for which of the following?
- a. Selective incorporation of the Bill of Rights
- b. Fundamental rights
- c. Civil rights
- d. Civil liberties

2 The selective incorporation of the Bill of Rights against the states is based on which of the following?
- a. Due Process Clause of the Fourteenth Amendment
- b. First Amendment
- c. Equal Protection Clause of the Fourteenth Amendment
- d. Thirteenth Amendment

3 Attorneys for Terrance Graham asked the U.S. Supreme Court to overturn their client's sentence as a violation of the constitutional prohibition against cruel and unusual punishments. On what basis would the Supreme Court hear the appeal?

a. None. The U.S. Supreme Court has no authority to review state court decisions.
b. The attorneys had a right to ask the U.S. Supreme Court to intervene because Graham was convicted in a federal court.
c. The Supreme Court heard the case because it was an interesting case and the justices enjoy deciding interesting cases.
d. The attorneys had a right to ask a federal court to intervene because the Eighth Amendment's prohibition against cruel and unusual punishments applies not just to the actions of the national government but to state governments as well (because of selective incorporation).

4 Which of the following statements is true about the fundamental rights protected by the Bill of Rights?

a. They are absolute and may never be abridged by the government.
b. They can be abridged but only when the government can demonstrate a plausible justification.
c. They are guidelines, but government officials can abridge them when they determine it is in the public interest.
d. They cannot be abridged unless the government can demonstrate a compelling or overriding public interest for so doing.

4.2 *What freedoms does the First Amendment guarantee?*

5 Disputes over school prayer are based on which of the following provisions of the U.S. Constitution?

a. The freedom of religion clause in the First Amendment
b. The establishment of religion clause in the First Amendment
c. The freedom of expression clause in the First Amendment
d. The freedom of assembly clause in the First Amendment

6 A dispute over a local law aimed at preventing a religious group from passing out literature door-to-door would involve which of the following constitutional provisions?

a. The freedom of religion clause in the First Amendment
b. The establishment of religion clause in the First Amendment
c. The freedom of expression clause in the First Amendment
d. The freedom of assembly clause in the First Amendment

7 Which of the following is an example of a content-neutral regulation of expression?

a. A school district prohibits students from wearing t-shirts with political messages but allows other messages
b. A school district prohibits students from wearing "controversial" t-shirts

but allows shirts with non-controversial messages
c. A school district prohibits students from wearing t-shirts with message or symbols of any kind
d. All of the above

8 Which of the following is an example of a hate crime?

a. A group of young Latino and African American men break into the home of an Asian family. While robbing the family, they use racial/ethnic slurs, threatening the Asian family with violence if they don't move out of the neighborhood.
b. A woman publishes a newsletter in which she attacks homosexuals as "godless pagans who spread disease."
c. A white man who is fleeing from the scene of a crime shoots and wounds a police officer who is African American.
d. All of the above

9 A supermarket tabloid newspaper prints a story in which stating that a prominent U.S. senator is having an affair with a married woman. It names both parties. As it turns out, the accusation is false. Both the senator and the woman sue the newspaper for defamation. Which of them is more likely to win?

a. Neither can win a lawsuit because the First Amendment protects the newspaper's right to publish.
b. The senator and the woman are equally likely to win because the courts treat all parties the same.
c. The senator is more likely to win because he has more to lose than the woman, who is just an ordinary citizen.
d. The woman is more likely to win because it is easier for an ordinary citizen to prove defamation than it is for a public figure.

4.3 *What is the basis for a constitutional right to privacy and to what sorts of controversies has the right to privacy been applied?*

10 Which of the following statements is true regarding a right to privacy?

a. The First Amendment guarantees people the right to personal privacy.
b. The Supreme Court has interpreted various provisions of the Bill of Rights to create "zones of privacy."
c. A right to privacy is the basis for *Brown v. Board of Education*.
d. All of the above

11 *Roe v. Wade* was based on which of the following constitutional provisions?

a. A constitutional right to privacy
b. The Equal Protection Clause of the Fourteenth Amendment
c. The Establishment Clause of the First Amendment

d. The Free Exercise Clause of the First Amendment

4.4 *What are the constitutional rights of people accused of crimes?*

12 The constitutional principle that government cannot deprive someone of life, liberty, or property without following fair and regular procedures is known as which of the following?

a. Selective incorporation
b. Parental choice
c. Exclusionary rule
d. Due process of law

13 What is the rationale for the exclusionary rule?

a. If the evidence proves a defendant's guilt, then the evidence should be used against the defendant regardless of how the evidence was obtained.
b. If the government is allowed to use evidence that was obtained illegally, then the government has no incentive to follow the law in collecting evidence.
c. Defendants should be informed of their rights so they can knowingly choose to exercise them or not to exercise them.
d. All of the above

4.5 *What civil liberties issues are raised by the conduct of the war on terror?*

14 *Boumediene v. Bush* dealt with which of the following issues?

a. Exclusionary rule
b. Freedom of religion
c. The rights of terror suspects held at Guantánamo Bay, Cuba
d. Abortion rights

15 Why was President Obama initially unable to keep his promise to close the prison at Guantánamo Bay, Cuba?

a. The Supreme Court ruled that Guantánamo had to remain open.
b. Congress refused to approve funds for the transfer of prisoners.
c. Neither foreign countries nor American communities were willing to accept the transfer of prisoners.
d. All of the above

KNOW the score

14–15 correct:	Congratulations—you know your American government!
12–13 correct:	Your understanding of this chapter is weak—be sure to review the key terms and visit TheThinkSpot.
<12 correct:	Reread the chapter more thoroughly.

Answers: 1) d, 2) a, 3) d, 4) d, 5) b, 6) a, 7) c, 8) d, 9) d, 10) b, 11) a, 12) d, 13) b, 14) c, 15) c

5 CIVIL

The battle over gay marriage has been fought state by state. Massachusetts became the first state to legalize same-sex marriage in 2004 when the Massachusetts Supreme Judicial Court (SJC) ruled that the state could not discriminate against same-sex couples when it issued marriage licenses. The SJC, which is the state's highest court, based its decision on the Massachusetts state constitution rather than the U.S. Constitution. Four additional states subsequently legalized gay marriage, including Vermont, Connecticut, New Hampshire, and Iowa.[1] Two states, California and Maine, approved gay marriage and then repealed it by referendum, which is an election in which state voters can approve or reject a state law or constitutional amendment. After the California Supreme Court had ruled in favor of gay marriage, opponents gathered signatures to put the issue to a vote. California voters approved aballot measure known as Proposition 8, 52 percent to 48 percent, which repealed same-sex marriage.

RIGHTS

In 2010, gay rights forces launched a legal battle aimed at establishing a national constitutional right to marry for gay couples. The lawsuit, which was filed on behalf of two same-sex couples in California, challenged the constitutionality of Proposition 8 under the U.S. Constitution. Court cases take years to work their way through the court system, but if the U.S. Supreme Court eventually agrees that state bans on same-sex marriage violate the U.S. Constitution, gay men and lesbians in every state will have the right to marry. Furthermore, the U.S. government will be required to recognize the validity of those marriages for Social Security survivor benefits, income tax filing status, and other legal matters.[2]

The legal and constitutional battle over same-sex marriage introduces this chapter on **civil rights**, which is the protection of the individual from arbitrary or discriminatory acts by government or by other individuals based on an individual's group status, such as race or gender. Whereas civil liberties issues involve individual rights, civil rights issues concern group rights. The chapter examines the constitutional basis of civil rights and then considers a number of important civil rights issues, including equal rights, voting rights, freedom from discrimination, and affirmative action.

civil rights the protection of the individual from arbitrary or discriminatory acts by government or by individuals based on that person's group status, such as race and gender.

THE CONSTITUTION AND
CIVIL RIGHTS

5.1 *What is the constitutional basis for civil rights in America?*

Both the U.S. Constitution and state constitutions affect civil rights policymaking. The most important provisions dealing with civil rights in the U.S. Constitution are the Fourteenth and Fifteenth Amendments. The Fourteenth Amendment includes the **Equal Protection Clause:** "No State shall . . . deny to any person within its jurisdiction the equal protection of the laws." The Fifteenth Amendment declares that the right to vote "shall not be denied or abridged by the United States or by any State on account of race, color, or previous condition of servitude." Both the Fourteenth and Fifteenth Amendments contain sections granting Congress authority to pass legislation to enforce their provisions.

Most state constitutions include provisions prohibiting discrimination and/or guaranteeing equal protection of the laws. In recent years, a number of state supreme courts have interpreted their state constitutions to require equitable funding for public schools, guarantee equal rights for women, and, as discussed in the opener, grant marriage rights to same-sex couples. In each of these cases, state courts adopted policy positions embracing a more expansive interpretation of civil rights than were taken at the time of writing either the U.S. Constitution or federal law.

Do you support same-sex marriage? Why or why not?

Equal Protection Clause a provision of the Fourteenth Amendment of the U.S. Constitution that declares that "No State shall . . . deny to any person within its jurisdiction the equal protection of the laws."

EQUAL RIGHTS

5.2 *How does the Equal Protection Clause affect civil rights for African Americans and other groups?*

Although the Fourteenth Amendment guarantees individuals equal protection under the law, the U.S. Supreme Court has never required that laws deal with everyone and everything in precisely the same fashion. By their nature, laws distinguish among groups of people, types of property, and kinds of actions. The Court has recognized that most distinctions are necessary and desirable, and hence permissible under the Constitution. Only certain types of classifications that the Court considers arbitrary and discriminatory violate the Equal Protection Clause.

Most distinctions are **necessary and desirable,** and hence permissible under the Constitution.

The Supreme Court has ruled that policy distinctions among persons based on their race, ethnicity, and citizenship status are **suspect classifications**, which are distinctions among persons that must be justified on the basis of a compelling government interest. The Supreme Court has declared that it will apply "strict judicial scrutiny" to any law that distinguishes among persons based on their race and ethnicity or citizenship. **Strict judicial scrutiny** is the judicial decision rule holding that the Supreme Court will find a government policy unconstitutional unless the government can demonstrate a compelling interest justifying the action. Furthermore, the government must prove that a policy that distinguishes among persons based on their race, ethnicity, or citizenship status is the least restrictive means for achieving the compelling policy objective.

The Supreme Court has chosen not to look so closely at laws that discriminate against persons on grounds other than race and ethnicity or citizenship status. It has held that government need only demonstrate some "reasonable basis" in order to justify public policies that distinguish among persons on the basis of such factors as relative wealth, physical ability, marital status, residency, or sexual orientation. As for gender, the Court has ruled that the government must offer an "exceedingly persuasive justification" that gender-based distinctions are necessary to achieve some "important governmental objective." Commentators see this standard as somewhere between "compelling government interest" and "reasonable basis."[3]

Racial Equality

Although the Equal Protection Clause of the Fourteenth Amendment was intended to protect the civil rights of freed slaves, it initially did little to shelter African Americans from discrimination. In the late nineteenth and early twentieth centuries, southern state legislatures enacted **Jim Crow laws,** which were legal provisions requiring the social segregation of African Americans in separate and generally unequal facilities. Jim Crow laws prohibited blacks from sharing schools, hospitals, hotels, restaurants, passenger railcars, and a wide range of other services and public facilities with whites.

Did Jim Crow laws violate the Equal Protection Clause? The U.S. Supreme Court addressed the question in 1896 in the famous case of *Plessy v. Ferguson.* Homer Plessy, an African American, purchased a first-class ticket on the East Louisiana Railway to travel from New Orleans to Covington, Louisiana, and took a seat in the rail car reserved for whites. He was arrested and charged with violating a state law that prohibited members of either race from occupying accommodations set aside for the other. Plessy contended that the Louisiana law violated his rights under the U.S. Constitution to equal protection. By an 8–1 vote, the U.S. Supreme Court ruled that the law was a reasonable exercise of the state's power, holding that states can require separate facilities for whites and African Americans as long as the facilities are equal. Thus, the Court adopted the policy known as **separate but equal**, the judicial doctrine holding that separate facilities for whites and African Americans satisfy the equal protection requirement of the Fourteenth Amendment . . . as long as the facilities are the same.[4]

The Supreme Court allowed state and local governments to determine whether racially segregated facilities were actually equal. In 1899, for example, the Court held that a Georgia school district's decision to close the only African American high school in the county did not violate the Equal Protection Clause even though two white high schools remained open.[5]

"Separate but equal" schools were never equal for African American students. They were underfunded and neglected by white-run school boards.

The Supreme Court began to reassess the constitutional status of racial segregation in the late 1930s. The Court started chipping away at the *Plessy* precedent in 1938 in

suspect classifications distinctions among persons that must be justified on the basis of a compelling government interest that cannot be achieved in a less restrictive fashion.

strict judicial scrutiny the judicial decision rule holding that the Supreme Court will find a government policy unconstitutional unless the government can demonstrate a compelling interest justifying the action.

Jim Crow laws legal provisions requiring the social segregation of African Americans in separate and generally unequal facilities.

separate but equal the judicial doctrine holding that separate facilities for whites and African Americans satisfy the equal protection requirement of the Fourteenth Amendment.

Missouri ex rel Gaines v. Canada, the beginning of a long line of test cases brought by the National Association for the Advancement of Colored People (NAACP). A **test case** is a lawsuit initiated to assess the constitutionality of a legislative or executive act. Gaines, who was an African American citizen of Missouri, applied to attend the University of Missouri law school. The state denied him admission, but offered to pay his tuition at a law school in a neighboring state where he could be accepted. Gaines sued, charging that the arrangement violated the Equal Protection Clause, and the Court agreed. Separate but equal had to be in the same state.[6]

The Supreme Court further undermined *Plessy* in two cases decided in 1950. In *Sweatt v. Painter*, it ruled that Texas's hasty creation of an African American law school did not satisfy the constitutional criterion of equal protection.[7] In *McLaurin v. Oklahoma State Regents*, the Court ruled against segregation within an institution. The University of Oklahoma admitted G. W. McLaurin, an African American man, to graduate school but forced him to sit in a particular seat, study in a particular carrel in the library, and eat at a particular table in the cafeteria—all labeled, "Reserved for Colored." The Supreme Court ordered that McLaurin be treated like other students.[8]

In 1954, the Court took the final step, unanimously overturning *Plessy* with the landmark decision known as *Brown v. Board of Education of Topeka*. The case involved a lawsuit brought by the parents of Linda Brown, an African American youngster who was denied admission to a "whites only" school near her home. The Court ruled that racial segregation mandated by law denied African American students equal educational opportunity. "Segregation of white and colored children in public schools has a detrimental effect upon the colored children," wrote Chief Justice Earl Warren in the Court's majority opinion. The Court declared that "separate but equal" was a contradiction in terms. Once the law requires racial separation, it stamps the badge of inferiority on the minority race.[9]

The *Brown* decision may have been the most important judicial ruling of the twentieth century, but it left two important questions unanswered. One concerned the distinction between *de jure* and *de facto* segregation. **De jure** segregation means racial separation required by law, whereas **de facto** segregation is racial separation resulting from factors other than law, such as housing patterns. In *Brown*, the Court ruled that *de jure* segregation was unconstitutional, but it left the issue of *de facto* segregation undecided. The second problem left unsettled by *Brown* was implementation. How was desegregation to be achieved and at what pace? The Court delayed its implementation decision until 1955, when it ordered the lower federal courts to oversee the transition to a nondiscriminatory system "with all deliberate speed."[10]

Implementation proved more deliberate than speedy. For years, *Brown* was a hollow victory for civil rights forces. Congress did nothing. Although states in the Upper South made some progress toward desegregation, public officials in the Deep South responded to the *Brown* decision with delay, evasion, defiance, and massive resistance. President Dwight Eisenhower finally took action in 1957, ordering federal troops into Little Rock, Arkansas, to enforce a school desegregation order against a stubborn Governor Orval Faubus and an angry mob. Nonetheless, a decade after the *Brown* decision, only 1 percent of African American students living in the South attended public schools

(From left to right) George E. C. Hayes, Thurgood Marshall, and James M. Nabrit were the NAACP Legal Defense Fund attorneys who represented the Brown family in *Brown v. Board of Education* (1954). The Court declared that "separate but equal" was a contradiction in terms.

test case a lawsuit initiated to assess the constitutionality of a legislative or executive act.

de jure segregation racial separation required by law.

de facto segregation racial separation resulting from factors other than law, such as housing patterns.

that were not racially segregated.[11] Alabama Governor George Wallace spoke for many white Southerners in 1963: "I say segregation now, segregation tomorrow, segregation forever."[12]

The civil rights movement of the 1960s succeeded in rallying support for the cause of African American civil rights. African American protest demonstrations, vividly displayed on the television evening news, moved public opinion to support the cause. Presidents John Kennedy and Lyndon Johnson called for action, and Congress responded with the Civil Rights Act of 1964, which authorized the government to cut off federal money to school districts practicing segregation. The department set guidelines and some progress took place. Furthermore, the Supreme Court lost patience with the slow pace of school desegregation, declaring an end to "all deliberate speed" and ordering immediate desegregation.[13] By the 1972–1973 school year, 91 percent of African American students living in the South attended integrated schools.[14]

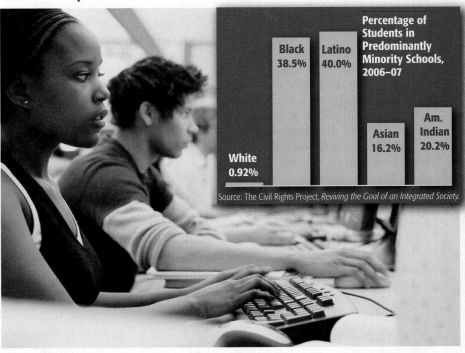

think How important is it for children to attend schools that are racially diverse?

The Court's decision to order an end to racial segregation forced the justices to deal with the issues left unresolved by the original *Brown* case. How could integration be achieved? In *Swann v. Charlotte-Mecklenburg Board of Education* (1971), the Court unanimously held that busing, racial quotas, school pairing or grouping, and gerrymandered attendance zones could all be used to eliminate the vestiges of state-supported segregation.[15] Two years later, the Court expanded the definition of *de jure* segregation to include segregation fostered by administrative policies even in the absence of segregation laws. Consequently, the Court ordered the integration of Denver schools, not because they were segregated by force of law, but because the local school board had manipulated attendance zones to create one-race schools.[16]

Today, racial segregation no longer has a legal basis. Few issues of constitutional law are more firmly established than the principle that any law or procedural requirement compelling the physical separation of people by race or ethnicity is unconstitutional. The old Jim Crow laws are now all gone, either repealed or rendered unenforceable by court rulings.

Nonetheless, the end of legal segregation has not necessarily brought about meaningful racial integration in the public schools. Today, African American and Latino students have less contact with white students than their counterparts had in 1970. In the 2006–2007 school year, nearly

The end of **legal segregation** has not necessarily brought about meaningful **racial integragation**.

40 percent of African American and Latino youngsters attended schools where minority students composed 90 percent to 100 percent of the student body.[17] Racial segregation in the schools is growing because of a major increase in enrollment by minority students, continued migration of white families from urban neighborhoods, and housing patterns that isolate racial and ethnic groups.[18]

Furthermore, the Supreme Court is no longer willing to order state and local officials to act aggressively to achieve racial integration. In *Millikin v. Bradley* (1974), the Court ruled that a district judge in Michigan lacked authority to order student busing between Detroit's predominantly African American inner-city school district and 53 predominantly white suburban school districts. Suburban school districts could not be forced to help desegregate a city's schools unless the

Diversity in Public Schools

White 0.92%	
Black 38.5%	
Latino 40.0%	
Asian 16.2%	
Am. Indian 20.2%	

Percentage of Students in Predominantly Minority Schools, 2006–07

Source: The Civil Rights Project, *Reviving the Goal of an Integrated Society.*

More than 50 years after *Brown v. Board of Education*, many public schools, especially in urban areas, remain racially segregated.

suburbs had been involved in illegally segregating them in the first place.[19] Although most Americans favor school desegregation in principle, busing for the purposes of achieving racial balance in schools is unpopular, even with many minority parents.

In *Missouri v. Jenkins* (1995), the Supreme Court overturned a district court order requiring the state of Missouri to pay for a plan to upgrade predominantly African American schools in Kansas City, Missouri. The goal of the district court order had been to improve the inner-city schools in hopes of enticing white parents who live in the suburbs voluntarily to send their children to the inner city. The Supreme Court held that local desegregation plans could not go beyond the purpose of eliminating racial discrimination.[20]

Finally, in *Parents Involved in Community Schools v. Seattle School District No. 1* (2007), a closely divided Supreme Court struck down a Seattle school assignment procedure that used race as a "tiebreaker" in making student assignments to high schools, even though the goal of the plan was to achieve racial integration rather than segregation.[21] Instead of using the *Brown* precedent to further efforts to achieve racial integration of public schools, the Court declared that *Brown* required school districts to follow color-blind school assignment policies.

Other Equal Rights Issues

Not all equal-protection claims involve African Americans or school desegregation. Other groups have also struggled for equal protection under the law on issues including citizenship, gender, and sexual orientation.

Citizenship Status. The Supreme Court has declared that citizenship

Demonstrators protest the adoption of SB1070, the Arizona law designed to crack down on illegal immigration. Critics charge that Senate Bill 1070 will lead to racial profiling.

status is a suspect classification similar to race, justifiable only by a compelling government interest. For example, the Court has struck down state laws that prohibited non-citizen permanent residents from becoming lawyers, engineers, or notary publics, and ruled that states may not deny legal residents who are not citizens the opportunity to apply for financial aid for higher education.[22] In each case, the Court ruled that the government had failed to establish that it had a compelling interest in making the distinction. In contrast, the Court has held that states do indeed have a compelling interest in excluding noncitizens from playing a role in government, either by voting, running for office, or working as police officers.

After the terrorist attacks of September 11, 2001, Congress passed and President George W. Bush signed the Aviation and Transportation Security Act, which included a provision restricting employment as airport screeners to U.S. citizens. Thousands of non-citizen legal residents who had been employed as airport screeners lost their jobs

because of the measure and several of them filed suit, attacking the constitutionality of the new law. A federal district judge ruled that the provision was unconstitutional. The judge concluded that although the government had a compelling interest in protecting aviation security, excluding non-citizens from screening jobs was not the "least restrictive means" for achieving that goal.[23]

Gender. Over the years, the Supreme Court has considered a number of equal protection issues raised on the basis of gender. For nearly a century after the adoption of the Fourteenth Amendment, the Court refused to apply the Equal Protection Clause to gender discrimination. Instead, the Court accepted discrimination against women as a necessary protection for the weaker sex. In 1873, for example, the Supreme Court upheld an Illinois law denying women the opportunity to practice law with the following explanation: "The natural and proper timidity and delicacy which belong to the female sex evidently unfit it for many of the occupations of civil life."[24]

think Is the male-only draft registration requirement gender discrimination?

Within the last 30 years, the Supreme Court has begun to look closely at claims of gender discrimination. Although the Court has not added gender to its list of suspect classifications, it has required that state governments prove that sex-based distinctions are necessary to achieve some "important governmental objective." The Court has also declared that the government must offer an "exceedingly persuasive justification" for gender-based distinctions if they are to be held constitutional.[25] The Court ruled, for example, that the Virginia Military Institute (VMI), a state-supported military university, could not constitutionally exclude women, and that the state's offer to create a separate military college for women was unacceptable. The Court held that the state of Virginia had failed to show an exceedingly persuasive justification for maintaining a male-only university.[26] Nonetheless, the Court still upholds some gender-based laws, such as Congress's decision to exclude women from having to register for military service, on the basis of traditional attitudes about the respective roles of men and women in society.[27]

Sexual Orientation. In 1996, the Supreme Court issued its first equal-protection ruling favoring gay and lesbian rights in the case of *Romer v. Evans*. The legal dispute concerned a challenge to an amendment to the constitution of Colorado approved by state voters in 1992. Amendment Two, as it was known, not only repealed all local ordinances and

These female GIs are stationed at Wagram Air Base near Kabul, Afghanistan. Women, who make up 15 percent of military personnel, now serve in most areas of the U.S. military, but they are prohibited from serving in ground combat units, including armor, artillery, infantry, and special forces units.

AROUND THE WORLD

Women's Rights in Saudi Arabia

Under Saudi law, which is based on a conservative interpretation of Islam, women are socially and legally dependent on their male guardians—their fathers at birth and their spouses upon marriage. Women cannot even have their own legal identity cards. Their names are added to their father's identify card when they are born and transferred to their husband's identity card when they marry. As a result, a woman cannot travel, purchase property, or enroll in college without the written permission of a male relative.[28]

Women must cover themselves fully in public and wear a veil. They cannot attend classes with men or work with men. Women's education is aimed at making women better wives and mothers; they cannot study law, vote, or drive a vehicle. Women who fail to conform to societal norms may be arrested, imprisoned, and even caned.

Nonetheless, Saudi Arabia has a women's rights movement. Many Saudi women are now more aware of the status of women in other countries because of the Internet, satellite TV, and traveling abroad. Young Saudi women in particular, who are better educated than most of the older women, are challenging their society's conservative interpretation of Islam. They are demanding access to education and employment opportunities.

The Saudi government has made some concessions to women's rights. Even though some leading universities continue to admit only men, women now constitute a majority of university students.[29] The Saudi government is also reportedly considering lifting the ban against women driving.[30]

QUESTIONS

1 Is the treatment of women in Saudi Arabia a concern for people around the world, or should it be an internal matter for the Saudis alone to address?

2 Should the United States pressure Saudi Arabia to improve the status of women?

3 Do you think most women in Saudi Arabia are comfortable with their legal and social status?

Although Saudi women cannot drive, they can own cars. These two saleswomen work in a women-only car dealership in Saudi Arabia.

statewide policies protecting gay men and lesbians from discrimination, but also prohibited the future enactment of similar measures. The Supreme Court declared that the state of Colorado would have to demonstrate that the amendment bore a rational relationship to some legitimate end in order to meet the requirements of the Equal Protection Clause. The amendment was so broadly drawn, however, that the only logical explanation for its enactment was animosity toward gay men and lesbians. The real purpose of the measure was evidently "to make homosexuals unequal to everyone else," which, the Court said, is not a legitimate goal of state government. Consequently, Amendment Two violated the Equal Protection Clause of the Fourteenth Amendment.[31]

As discussed in the opener, the current lawsuit challenging the constitutionality of California's Proposition 8 is based on the Equal Protection Clause. The groups bringing the lawsuit hope that the Supreme Court will conclude that the government lacks a reasonable basis for limiting marriage to opposite sex couples.

VOTING RIGHTS

5.3 *What is the history of voting rights in America?*

Although the right to vote is a fundamental civil right, universal adult **suffrage** (the right to vote) is a relatively recent development in the United States. The original Constitution (Article I, Section 2) allowed the states to establish voter qualifications, and initially most states limited the right to vote to adult white males who owned property. Popular pressure forced states to drop the property qualification in the early decades of the nineteenth century. Women won the right to vote with the ratification of the Nineteenth Amendment in 1920.

The struggle for voting rights for African Americans was particularly difficult despite the Fifteenth Amendment, which declared that the right to vote could not be abridged on account of race or color. In the late nineteenth and early twentieth centuries, Southern white authorities adopted an array of devices designed to **disenfranchise** African Americans, or prevent them from exercising meaningful voting rights.

The **white primary** was an electoral system used in the South to prevent the participation of African Americans in the Democratic primary. (A primary election is an intra-party election held to select party candidates for the general-election ballot.) Because Democrats dominated Southern politics from the 1870s through the

In the early 20th century, women held demonstrations to call for suffrage. Women received the right to vote with the ratification of the Nineteenth Amendment in 1920.

1950s, the Democratic Party primary was, by far, the most important election in most Southern states. By excluding African Americans from the Democratic primary, Southern officials effectively prevented them from participating meaningfully in state politics. The Supreme Court invalidated the white primary in 1944.[32]

Tests of understanding, literacy tests, and poll taxes were often used in combination with a grandfather clause. A **test of understanding** was a legal requirement that citizens must accurately explain a passage in the United States or state constitution before they could register to vote. A literacy test was a legal requirement that citizens demonstrate an ability to read and write

suffrage the right to vote.

disfranchisement the denial of voting rights.

white primary an electoral system used in the South to prevent the participation of African Americans in the Democratic primary.

test of understanding a legal requirement that citizens must accurately explain a passage in the U.S. Constitution or state constitution before they could register to vote.

before they could register to vote. A poll tax was a tax levied on the right to vote. A **grandfather clause** was a provision that exempted those persons whose grandfathers had been eligible to vote at some earlier date from these difficult-to-achieve voter qualification requirements. The effect of the grandfather clause was to allow prospective white voters to escape voter requirements used to discourage or disqualify prospective African American voters.

Although the Supreme Court invalidated the grandfather clause in 1915,[33] tests of understanding, literacy tests, and poll taxes survived constitutional challenge for decades. The Court finally knocked down the use of tests of understanding in 1965, holding that they were often used to deny African Americans the right to vote.[34] In the same year, Congress passed, and the president signed, legislation that suspended the use of literacy tests throughout the South. Five years later, Congress extended the ban on literacy tests to the entire nation. The poll tax lasted until the mid-1960s. The Twenty-fourth Amendment, ratified in 1964, eliminated the use of poll taxes for elections to federal office. In 1966, the Supreme Court held that the poll tax was an unconstitutional requirement for voting in state and local elections as well.[35] The **Voting Rights Act (VRA)**, signed by President Johnson in 1965, makes it illegal for state and local governments to enact and enforce election rules and procedures that diminish racial and ethnic minority voting power. As we will discuss in Chapter 11, the VRA also affects redistricting plans by preventing discrimination in the drawing of electoral districts.

grandfather clause a provision that exempted those persons whose grandfathers had been eligible to vote at some earlier date from tests of understanding, literacy tests, and other difficult-to-achieve voter qualification requirements.

Voting Rights Act (VRA) a federal law designed to protect the voting rights of racial and ethnic minorities.

A History of Voting Rights

1776 | Suffrage limited to white men with property

1870 | Fifteenth Amendment guarantees suffrage to freed male slaves and other African American men

1915 | *Guinn v. United States* declares the grandfather clause unconstitutional

1920 | Nineteenth Amendment gives women the right to vote

1944 | *Smith v. Allwright* rules the white primary system unconstitutional

1964 | Twenty-fourth Amendment outlaws poll taxes in federal elections

Civil Rights Act of 1964 makes it illegal to discriminate on the basis of race, religion, color, gender, or national origin, in voting, public accommodations, the workplace, and schools

1965 | Voting Rights Act protects the voting rights of racial and ethnic minorities

1971 | Twenty-sixth Amendment lowers the voting age to 18

| 1776 | 1870 | 1915 | 1920 | 1944 | 1964 | 1965 | 1971 |

FREEDOM FROM DISCRIMINATION

Civil rights concerns the protection of the individual, not just against government action, but also against discrimination by *private* parties, such as hotels, restaurants, theaters, and business firms. Most individual rights claims against private discrimination are based on **statutory law,** law written by a legislature, rather than constitutional law.

After the Civil War, Congress enacted two important laws designed to protect the civil rights of former slaves. The Civil Rights Act of 1866 declared that citizens "of every race and color" were entitled "to make and enforce contracts, to sue . . . , give evidence, to inherit, purchase, lease, sell, hold, and convey real and personal property."[36] The Civil Rights Act of 1875 declared that "all persons within the jurisdiction of the United States shall be entitled to the full and equal enjoyment of the accommodations . . . of inns, public conveyances on land or water, theaters, and other places of public amusement."[37]

In the *Civil Rights Cases* (1883), however, the U.S. Supreme Court found the Civil Rights Act of 1875 unconstitutional. These cases involved disputes over theaters that would not seat African Americans, hotels and restaurants that would not serve African Americans, and a train that refused to seat an African American woman in the "ladies" car. The Court held that the Fourteenth Amendment protected individuals from discrimination by government but not by private parties.[38] The Court's decision in the *Civil Rights Cases* opened the door for private individuals, businesses, and organizations to discriminate in public accommodations, housing, and employment, and it took civil

Three young African Americans challenge segregation laws forbidding them to eat at a white lunch counter in North Carolina in 1960.

rights forces more than 80 years to overcome the precedent set in the *Civil Rights Cases*.

Public Accommodations

Civil rights forces used litigation and legislation to attack forms of private discrimination. In the late 1950s and early 1960s, African American activists staged sit-ins at segregated dime store lunch counters and refused to leave until served. Local police would arrest the protesters, charging them with disturbing the peace or breaking a local Jim Crow ordinance. With NAACP legal assistance, the demonstrators would appeal their convictions to the federal courts, where they would be reversed and the local segregation ordinance overturned. This case-by-case approach desegregated many public facilities, but it was slow and expensive.

> Civil rights forces used **litigation and legislation** to attack private discrimination.

The Civil Rights Act of 1964 was a more efficient tool for fighting discrimination. Title II of the act outlawed discrimination based on race, religion, color, sex, or national origin in hotels, restaurants, gas stations, and other public accommodations. Congress based Title II on the Interstate Commerce Clause in order to overcome the precedent set in the *Civil Rights Cases* that the Fourteenth Amendment prohibits discrimination by the government but not discrimination by private individuals and firms. Because hotels, restaurants, gas stations, and the like serve individuals traveling from state to state, and because they purchase products that have been shipped in interstate commerce, Congress reasoned that they are part of interstate commerce and, consequently, subject to regulation by Congress. In *Heart of Atlanta Motel*

statutory law law that is written by the legislature.

v. United States and *Katzenbach v. McClung* (1964), the Supreme Court upheld the constitutionality of Congress's action.[39]

Housing

Although the Supreme Court ruled in 1917 that cities could not establish exclusive residential zones for whites and blacks,[40] housing developers often achieved the same result through **racially restrictive covenants,** which were private deed restrictions that prohibited property owners from selling or leasing property to African Americans or other minorities. The NAACP finally succeeded in undercutting restrictive covenants in *Shelley v. Kraemer*, a test case that reached the Supreme Court in 1948. The Court held that private contracts calling for discrimination could be written, but state courts could not constitutionally enforce them because enforcement would make the state a party to discrimination.[41]

The executive and legislative branches of government participated in the battle against housing discrimination as well. In 1962,

President Kennedy issued an executive order banning discrimination in property owned, sold, or leased by the federal government. Subsequently, Title IV of the Civil Rights Act of 1964 extended nondiscrimination provisions to all public housing and urban renewal developments receiving federal assistance. The most important legislative move against housing discrimination was the Fair Housing Act of 1968, which prohibited discrimination in all transactions involving realtors.

Employment

The Civil Rights Act of 1991 dealt with hiring practices that are not overtly discriminatory but which nonetheless limit employment opportunities for women and minorities. Suppose a city government requires prospective police officers to stand at least 5'5" tall. That requirement would disproportionately reduce the number of women eligible to apply for jobs because women are typically shorter than men. The Civil Rights Act of 1991 declared that hiring practices that have a disproportionate impact on women and minorities must be

"job-related for the position in question and consistent with business necessity." The city's height requirement for police officers would be illegal unless the city could show that a height of at least 5'5" was necessary to do the job. Furthermore, the Civil Rights Act of 1991 allowed women, minorities, and the disabled to sue for monetary damages in cases of intentional job discrimination and harassment.

The concept of sexual harassment is based on federal laws prohibiting gender discrimination in employment.[42] Employers who sexually harass their employees or permit sexual harassment in the workplace are guilty of illegal employment discrimination.[43] The federal courts have identified two categories of sexual harassment: *quid pro quo* harassment and harassment based on a hostile environment. *Quid pro quo* harassment involves a supervisor threatening an employee with retaliation unless

racially restrictive covenants private deed restrictions that prohibited property owners from selling or leasing property to African Americans or other minorities.

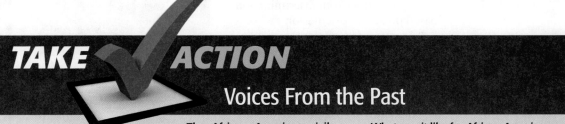

TAKE ✓ ACTION

Voices From the Past

The African American civil rights movement was one of the most important U.S. political developments of the twentieth century. Laws that once prevented African Americans from voting were repealed, and today more African Americans hold elective office than ever before. Nonetheless, racism and its vestiges have not been eliminated. African Americans are disproportionately affected by unemployment and poverty. They are underrepresented in corporate boardrooms but overrepresented in prison.

Your class project is to interview older African American adults in your community—friends, relatives, acquaintances, or coworkers—to ascertain their perspective on the impact of the civil rights movement on their lives and on the United States. Plan and conduct interviews that cover the following topics:

- What was it like for African Americans where you lived when you were growing up? What was good, and what was bad? What events do you remember?
- What are the most important changes that have taken place? Have all the changes been positive?
- What do you see as the biggest remaining barrier to full equality for African Americans?
- How do you feel about the election of Barack Obama?
- Are you optimistic or pessimistic about the future? Why?

Students will want to compare and contrast the recollections of different interview subjects who may have different perspectives. The instructor will also ask students to relate the content of their interviews to information contained in the textbook. To what extent do their experiences of and concerns about African American civil rights mirror the discussions in the text?

the employee submits to sexual advances. Defining sexual harassment based on a hostile environment is more difficult. Even though no sexual demands are made, an employer may be guilty of sexual harassment if an employee is subjected to sexual conduct and comments that are pervasive and severe enough to affect the employee's job performance.

Expanding and Limiting Protections

Congress and the president have enacted legislation extending civil rights protection to groups based on criteria other than race, gender,

OFFICE HOURS
with PROFESSOR TANNAHILL

QUESTION: I understand that federal and state laws protect individuals against private discriminatory behavior. Given that, how can a restaurant or a bar have a BIG SIGN saying, "We reserve the right to refuse service to anyone"? I don't get it!

ANSWER: Restaurants can post signs because restaurant owners and managers have freedom of speech, but that doesn't mean that they can act on the sign in all respects. The 1964 Civil Rights Act outlaws discrimination based on race, religion, color, sex, or national origin in hotels, restaurants, gas stations, and other public accommodations. If the restaurant owner refuses to serve someone because that person is Italian, female, Jewish, etc., then the restaurant is breaking the law, and the aggrieved party can file suit against the restaurant. In contrast, the restaurant can legally refuse to serve someone with bare feet, flip-flops, or a tank top because the law does not protect those people from discrimination.

or national origin. The Americans with Disabilities Act (ADA) is a federal law intended to end discrimination against disabled persons and to eliminate barriers to their full participation in American society. Other federal legislation prohibits age discrimination and protects families with children from housing discrimination. Title IX of the Education Amendments of 1972 is a federal law that prohibits gender discrimination in programs at educational institutions that receive federal funds. Because of Title IX, high schools, colleges, and universities have expanded athletic opportunities for women.

State and local governments have also adopted policies protecting various groups from discrimination which often go beyond federal law. As discussed in the opener, a number of states have legalized gay marriage, and numerous others have enacted legislation to allow gay men and lesbians to form **civil unions**, legal partnerships between two men or two women that give the couple all the benefits, protections, and responsibilities under law that are granted to spouses in a traditional marriage. In addition, some states offer protection from discrimination based on sexual orientation and sexual identity (to protect transgendered persons from discrimination).

The U.S. Supreme Court has held, however, that state and local civil rights laws must be balanced against individual rights. Consider the case of *Boy Scouts of America v. Dale* (2000). James Dale had been a scout since he was eight, earning the rank of Eagle Scout at the age of eighteen. Dale became an adult member of the scouts and served as an assistant scoutmaster while he was a student at Rutgers University. After a story appeared in a local newspaper identifying Dale as the co-president of the Rutgers University Lesbian/ Gay Alliance, the Boy Scouts sent him a letter revoking his membership, stating that the organization specifically forbids membership by homosexuals. Dale sued the Boy Scouts, charging that their action

Should gay men and lesbians enjoy the same legal protection from discrimination that women and the members of racial and ethnic minority groups have?

violated a New Jersey law prohibiting discrimination in public accommodations on the basis of sexual orientation. The U.S. Supreme Court ruled that applying the New Jersey law to the Boy Scouts would violate the organization's First Amendment right of "expressive association." The Boy Scouts claimed that opposition to homosexuality was an integral part of its organizational message. The Court decided that forcing the Scouts to include an openly gay member would unconstitutionally violate the organization's freedom of expression because it would make it difficult for the Scouts to convey their value system to members and the general public.[44]

Title IX is a federal law that prohibits gender discrimination in programs at educational institutions that receive federal funds. Since Title IX became law in the early 1970s, the number of women on athletic scholarships at Division I colleges and universities has increased from fewer than a hundred to more than 65,000.

civil union a legal partnership between two men or two women that gives the couple all the benefits, protections, and responsibilities under law as are granted to spouses in a traditional marriage.

Polls Show Majority Support for Same-Sex Marriage

For the first time, a majority of Americans support gay marriage. A poll conducted by the Gallup organization in May 2011 found that Americans favored same-sex marriage by 53 to 45 percent.[45] The Gallup survey mirrored the results of a *Washington Post*–ABC News poll conducted two months earlier that showed support for gay marriage stood at 53 percent compared with 44 percent opposed.[46] Public support for gay marriage has grown significantly. When national survey research firms first began asking about same-sex marriage in the middle 1990s, two-thirds were opposed. As recently as 2009, only 40 percent supported gay marriage. The latest shift in attitudes in favor of same-sex marriage has been driven by women under 35 and men under 50, both of which are now much more supportive of gay marriage than they were just a few years ago.

DISCUSSION

Why are attitudes changing? Massachusetts began marrying same-sex couples in 2004, and several other states have been conducting gay marriages for at least a few years. When same-sex marriage began, the opponents predicted dire consequences for marriage, family, and civilization as we know it, but the predictions have not come true. Same-sex couples are also increasingly visible in society, making the concept of same-sex marriage less threatening.

Is it true that attitudes toward gay rights issues reflect generational differences? Yes. Young people are considerably more supportive of same-sex marriage than older people. Approval for gay marriage stands at 70 percent for people under 35 compared with only 39 percent for people 55 and older.

Will polls showing increased support for same-sex marriage have any effect on court rulings concerning the constitutionality of state laws limiting marriage to opposite sex couples? Poll data that show increasing acceptance of gay marriage should encourage the proponents of same-sex marriage. The U.S. Supreme Court is usually careful not to get too far out in front of public opinion on major social issues. No one can predict how the Supreme Court will deal with the challenge to California's Proposition 8, of course, but these sorts of poll numbers are encouraging to the advocates of marriage equality.

Does the issue still divide people along party lines? It does, and that division should discourage the proponents of same-sex marriage. Whereas Democrats and independents strongly favor gay marriage, Republicans are just as strongly opposed. In 2011, the U.S. Supreme Court included four justices appointed by Democratic presidents and five appointed by Republican chief executives. If the justices were to vote on the Proposition 8 case along party lines, gay marriage would lose 5–4.

AFFIRMATIVE ACTION

5.5 *How can universities and employers use affirmative action to increase enrollment and employment of women and minorities?*

Few issues in American government are more controversial than **affirmative action**, which refers to steps taken to ensure equal opportunities in employment and college admissions for racial minorities and women. The proponents of affirmative action believe that race- and gender-based preferences are necessary to remedy the effects of past discrimination. Colleges and universities assert that they benefit from a diverse student body. Employers value a diverse workforce. In contrast, the opponents of racial and gender preferences argue that the only fair way to determine college admissions and employment decisions is merit. It is wrong, they say, to hire or promote someone simply because of race or gender.

> Colleges and universities assert that they benefit from a **diverse student body**.

Affirmative action takes a number of forms. A corporation may target colleges and universities with substantial minority enrollments in hopes of increasing the number of African Americans, Latinos, and Asians in its applicant pool. A local government taking bids for the construction of a new sports stadium may stipulate that contractors make a good faith effort to ensure that at least 25 percent of subcontracts go to firms owned by women or minorities. A federal grant program designed to provide scholarships to college students studying to become teachers may be limited to students who are members of racial and ethnic minority groups. A law school may reserve 20 percent of the places in its first-year class for African Americans and Latinos.

Employment

Federal government efforts to remedy the effects of discrimination in employment began in the early 1960s. Presidents Kennedy and Johnson ordered affirmative action in federal employment and hiring by government contractors, and in the late 1960s the Department of Labor began requiring government contractors to employ certain percentages of women and minorities. However, affirmative action underwent a major setback during the administrations of Ronald Reagan and George H. W. Bush. In Reagan's view, civil rights laws should offer relief not to whole groups of people, but only to specific individuals who could prove that they were victims of discrimination. Hiring goals, timetables, and racial quotas, the administration argued, were reverse discrimination against whites. The Equal Employment Opportunity Commission (EEOC), under the leadership of Clarence Thomas, dismantled affirmative action programs and anything that resembled a quota system for women and minorities.

Reagan and Bush appointees to the Supreme Court created a majority that shared this conservative philosophy on affirmative action issues.

In *City of Richmond v. J. A. Croson Co.* (1989) and *Adarand Constructors v. Pena* (1995) the Supreme Court put many affirmative policies in constitutional jeopardy. The *Croson* case dealt with a minority business set-aside program for municipal construction contracts established by the city of Richmond, Virginia. A **minority business set-aside** is a legal requirement that firms receiving government grants or contracts allocate a certain percentage of their purchases of supplies and services to businesses owned or controlled by members

affirmative action steps taken by colleges, universities, and private employers to remedy the effects of past discrimination.

minority business set-aside a legal requirement that firms receiving government grants or contracts allocate a certain percentage of their purchases of supplies and services to businesses owned or controlled by members of minority groups.

The Gender Gap in Wages

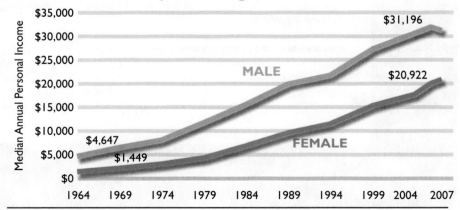

Despite significant gains for women in the workplace over the last half century, the median annual income for women is still over $10,000 less than that of men.

Source: U.S. Census Bureau, *The 2010 Statistical Abstract*, available at www.census.gov.

of minority groups. Even though African Americans constituted half of Richmond's population, less than 1 percent of city government construction dollars had typically gone to minority-owned firms. In light of this history, the city council passed an ordinance requiring that prime contractors awarded city construction contracts over the following five years must subcontract at least 30 percent of the dollar amount of their contracts to one or more minority-business enterprises.

When an exam used to qualify firefighters for promotions in New Haven, Connecticut, resulted in no eligible black candidates, the city threw out the results based on the test's disparate impact on a protected racial minority. The firefighters who passed the exam sued the city, and in its June 2009 decision in *Ricci v. DeStefano*, the Supreme Court held 5–4 that New Haven's decision to ignore the test results violated Title VII of the Civil Rights Act of 1964.

Richmond's minority business set-aside program soon became the target of litigation. J. A. Croson Co., a contracting company whose bid for a city project was rejected for failing to meet the minority set-aside, filed suit against the ordinance, charging that it was unconstitutional. The U.S. Supreme Court ruled that Richmond's set-aside ordinance unconstitutionally violated the Equal Protection Clause of the Fourteenth Amendment because it denied certain persons an opportunity to compete for a fixed percentage of city contracts based solely on their race.

The most significant aspect of the *Croson* decision was that the Court applied strict judicial scrutiny to race-conscious efforts to remedy the effects of past discrimination. The Court's majority opinion declared that although minority set-aside programs can be justified as a remedy for discrimination in some instances, the Richmond city council failed to demonstrate a specific history of discrimination in the city's construction industry sufficient to justify a race-based program of relief. The mere fact that few city construction contracts had gone to minority firms was not sufficient evidence to prove discrimination

either by the city government or in the city's construction industry. Instead of comparing the number of city contracts going to minority businesses with the proportion of minority citizens in Richmond, the Court ruled that the city council should have compared contracts with the proportion of minority-owned enterprises in the city's construction industry.

The Court also held that Richmond's set-aside program was constitutionally unacceptable because it was not narrowly tailored to achieve any goal except "outright racial balancing." The plan gave absolute preference to minority entrepreneurs from anywhere in the country, not just the Richmond area. Furthermore, the Court said, the program made no effort to determine whether particular minority businesspersons seeking a racial preference had themselves suffered the effects of discrimination.[47]

The Court affirmed this conservative interpretation of affirmative action in *Adarand Constructors v. Pena* (1995), which involved a discrimination lawsuit by Adarand Constructors, a Colorado construction company, against the federal Department of Transportation (DOT).

Adarand's low bid on a contract to build highway guardrails was rejected in favor of a higher bid by Gonzales Construction Company, which was certified by the DOT as a small business controlled by "socially and economically disadvantaged individuals." Based on the same reasoning as in *Cronin*, the Supreme Court ordered the *Adarand* case returned to the trial court for reconsideration in light of the standard of strict judicial scrutiny. All racial classifications must serve a compelling government interest and must be narrowly tailored to further that interest.[48]

College Admissions

The Supreme Court first dealt with affirmative action in college admissions in *Regents of the University of California v. Bakke* (1978). Allan Bakke, a white male, sued the university after he was denied admission to medical school. The university had a minority admissions program in which it set aside 16 of 100 places each year for minority applicants. Because he was not allowed to compete for any of the slots reserved for minority applicants, Bakke charged that he was the victim of illegal racial discrimination, and the Court agreed. The Court ordered Bakke admitted, saying that a numerical quota for minority admissions violated the Equal Protection Clause of the Fourteenth Amendment. The Court added, however, that race and ethnicity could be considered as one of several factors in admissions decisions as a "plus factor" in an individualized admissions process.[49]

The Supreme Court reaffirmed the *Bakke* precedent in *Grutter v. Bollinger* (2003) and *Gratz v. Bollinger* (2003). Barbara Grutter, a white woman, had a college grade point average of 3.8 and a high score on the Law School Admissions Test (LSAT), but she was rejected from University of Michigan Law School. The law school looks for academically capable students, but also strives to ensure that its student body is racially and ethnically diverse by enrolling a critical mass of students from groups that have historically suffered discrimination—African Americans, Latinos, and Native Americans. When the law school rejected her application, Grutter accused it of favoring minority applicants who were less qualified academically. She filed suit, charging

Public Opinion on Affirmative Action

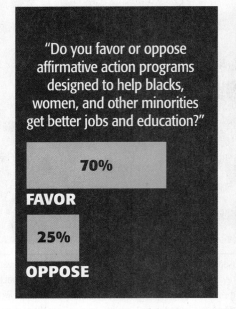

"Do you favor or oppose affirmative action programs designed to help blacks, women, and other minorities get better jobs and education?"

70%
FAVOR

25%
OPPOSE

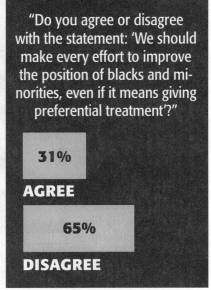

"Do you agree or disagree with the statement: 'We should make every effort to improve the position of blacks and minorities, even if it means giving preferential treatment'?"

31%
AGREE

65%
DISAGREE

Today, the American public is generally supportive of efforts to improve the position of minorities in this country, but is decidedly opposed to the idea of providing preferential treatment.

Source: Pew Research Center, *Public Backs Affirmative Action, But Not Minority Preference.*

that the school discriminated against her on the basis of race in violation of the Fourteenth Amendment and the Civil Rights Act of 1964.[50] Similarly, Stephanie Gratz, also a white woman with strong academic credentials, was denied admission to the University of Michigan. However, unlike the law school, the undergraduate affirmative action program used a point system for admission that automatically awarded points to underrepresented ethnic groups.

The Court ruled that the university, which is a government agency, could consider race in its admissions program because the government has a compelling interest in promoting racial and ethnic diversity in higher education. The law school's admissions process was constitutional, the Court held, because it considered race and ethnicity as only one of numerous factors in the admissions process. However the undergraduate program was unconstitutional, because it awarded points to every minority applicant rather than considering race as part of an individualized review of applications.[51]

Barbara Grutter (left) and Stephanie Gratz (right) both filed affirmative action lawsuits against University of Michigan admissions procedures. Grutter lost her lawsuit against the University of Michigan Law School, but Gratz won her fight for undergraduate admission.

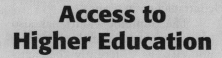

TAKING SIDES

Access to Higher Education

Can discrimination against minority groups be overcome by using affirmative action?

Should colleges be required to admit certain numbers of students of diverse demographic backgrounds?

OVERVIEW

Attending college is important for many reasons, not least among them the financial return on the investment. According to the Census Bureau, high school graduates earn an average of $1.2 million over their working lives, while bachelor's degree holders earn about $2.1 million. A report published by the Higher Education Policy Institute found that college graduates enjoy increased personal and professional mobility, improved quality of life, and better health for themselves and their children.

According to the American Council on Education, there are significant gaps among groups in higher education achievement. In 2006, 61 percent of college-age Asian Americans were in college, compared to 44 percent of whites, 32 percent of blacks, and 25 percent of Latinos.[52] The number of minority students in college has increased from 15 percent of students in 1976 to 32 percent of students in 2007, but those numbers are less than minority representation in society.[53] Should colleges and universities take affirmative action to increase minority enrollment?

 SUPPORTING affirmative action

 AGAINST affirmative action

SUPPORTING affirmative action

Associating with diverse groups of people benefits all students. The world is smaller than ever before, so being exposed to people with different backgrounds puts students on the path toward successfully navigating a global marketplace. It is in an institution's best interest to admit many people with diverse backgrounds because all students benefit.

History has stacked the odds against certain population groups. Many disadvantaged groups, including women, African Americans, and Latinos, have not historically had equal access to education, and there are fewer people in these groups on admissions boards. In order to guarantee equal access, decision-making bodies need to be encouraged to look more closely at applicants from minority groups.

Equality is an American value worth striving for. Generally, Americans consider themselves committed to equality of opportunity. If it is the case that most students attending college are white and/or economically privileged, it is important to achieve equality by guaranteeing spots for individuals from groups who would not otherwise have the support necessary to take advantage of this opportunity.

AGAINST affirmative action

Admitting students who have earned it is fair. Americans are committed to fairness in procedures. Admissions quotas mean that some less-qualified applicants will be admitted rather than better qualified applicants. Americans would prefer that higher education institutions try harder to find qualified minority applicants,[54] which is a more fair way to guarantee diversity in the college classroom.

Affirmative action programs breed resentment. Instead of righting old racist wrongs, admitting lower achieving students into a program because of their race or gender, while denying admission to other students, who have also worked hard, will just make the problems worse.

Affirmative action is the wrong policy to gain equality. People who argue for affirmative action make a case that every citizen should be treated equally under the Fourteenth Amendment. Thus, any policy that favors one group over another simply because of the identity of that group is a violation of equality under the law.

what we LEARNED

THE CONSTITUTION AND CIVIL RIGHTS

5.1 *What is the constitutional basis for civil rights in America?*

The most important provisions in the U.S. Constitution dealing with civil rights are the Fourteenth Amendment, which includes the Equal Protection Clause, and the Fifteenth Amendment, which protects the right to vote from abridgement on account of "race, color, or previous condition of servitude." Many state constitutions include civil rights protections as well.

EQUAL RIGHTS

5.2 *How does the Equal Protection Clause affect civil rights for African Americans and other groups?*

The Supreme Court has ruled that policy distinctions among persons based on their race, ethnicity, and citizenship status are suspect classifications, which are distinctions among persons that must be justified on the basis of a compelling government interest. Government need only demonstrate some "reasonable basis" in order to justify public policies that distinguish among persons on the basis of such factors as relative wealth, physical ability, marital status, residency, or sexual orientation. As for gender, the Court has ruled that the government must offer an "exceedingly persuasive justification" that gender-based distinctions are necessary to achieve some "important governmental objective."

The Equal Protection Clause initially had little effect on African American civil rights. States adopted Jim Crow laws and the Supreme Court endorsed them in *Plessy v. Ferguson* and other cases. Eventually, the Court overturned the *Plessy* decision in *Brown v. Board of Education*, ruling that separate-but-equal, the standard adopted in *Plessy* to satisfy the Equal Protection Clause, was a contradiction in terms.

The Supreme Court has also struck down most state laws treating non-citizens differently than citizens, and has invalidated most distinctions based on gender. The Supreme Court applied the protections of the Equal Protection Clause to gay men and lesbians for the first time in the case of *Romer v. Evans*. Gay rights groups hope that the Supreme Court will eventually rule that limiting marriage rights to opposite sex couples violates the Equal Protection Clause.

VOTING RIGHTS

5.3 *What is the history of voting rights in America?*

States initially limited suffrage to white male property owners. Property qualifications were dropped in the nineteenth century and women won the right to vote in the early twentieth century. The struggle for African American voting rights was more difficult despite the adoption of the Fifteenth Amendment after the Civil War. Tests of understanding, literacy tests, the white primary, grandfather clauses, and poll taxes were all used to disfranchise African Americans. All of these and other restrictions on minority voting rights eventually fell because of court rulings, a constitutional amendment to outlaw the poll tax, and the passage of the Voting Rights Act.

FREEDOM FROM DISCRIMINATION

5.4 *What steps has government taken to protect women and minorities from discrimination?*

In *Shelley v. Kraemer* the Supreme Court ruled that racially restrictive covenants are unenforceable. The Civil Rights Act of 1964 outlawed discrimination based on race,

religion, color, sex, or national origin in hotels, restaurants, gas stations, and other public accommodations. The ADA protects disabled persons against discrimination and eliminates barriers to their full participation in American society. The Civil Rights Act of 1991 dealt with hiring practices that limit employment opportunities for women and minorities. In recent years, however, the Supreme Court has held that state and local civil rights laws must be balanced against individual rights.

AFFIRMATIVE ACTION

5.5 *How can universities and employers use affirmative action to increase enrollment and employment of women and minorities?*

An affirmative action program is a program designed to ensure equal opportunities in employment and college admissions for racial minorities and women. The Supreme Court applies strict judicial scrutiny to affirmative action programs, which means that those programs must be justified by a compelling government interest and be narrowly tailored to further that interest. As for college and university admissions, the Court ruled quotas unconstitutional, but said that race and ethnicity could be considered as one of several factors in admissions decisions as a "plus factor" in an individualized admissions process.

5.1 *What is the constitutional basis for civil rights in America*

1   Which of the following constitutional provisions has the greatest impact on civil rights policymaking?
    a.   Equal Protection Clause of the Fourteenth Amendment
    b.   First Amendment
    c.   Second Amendment
    d.   Due Process Clause of the Fourteenth Amendment

2   Does the U.S. Constitution require that government treat all persons identically, regardless of their race, ethnicity, gender etc.?
    a.   Yes. The Equal Protection Clause requires that everyone be treated identically by government.
    b.   Yes. The Bill of Rights requires that the government not make distinctions among persons on the basis of race, gender, or religion.
    c.   No. The Supreme Court has long recognized that the government can make distinctions among person if it can justify the distinctions.
    d.   No. The Constitution does not address the issue of equal treatment.

3   Which of the following distinctions among persons is not a suspect classification?
    a.   Ethnicity
    b.   Race
    c.   Citizenship status
    d.   Sexual orientation

4   Under what circumstances would it be constitutionally permissible for the government to deal differently with individuals based on whether they smoke? (For example, the government might prohibit smokers from becoming foster parents.)
    a.   No circumstances. The government must treat everyone alike.
    b.   The government must demonstrate a compelling government interest to treat people differently.
    c.   Because smoking status is not a suspect classification, the government need only demonstrate a reasonable basis for making the distinction.
    d.   The government must offer an exceedingly persuasive justification for making the distinction.

5.2 *How does the Equal Protection Clause affect civil rights for African Americans and other groups?*

5   Which of the following statements about *Brown v. Board of Education* is/are true?
    a.   It was a test case promoted by the NAACP.
    b.   It overturned *Plessy v. Ferguson*.

c.   It outlawed *de jure* segregation but not *de facto* segregation.
    d.   All of the above

6   Why is it that many public schools in the United States have student bodies that are all or almost all members of the same racial/ethnic group?
    a.   The Supreme Court overturned *Brown v. Board of Education* in *Parents Involved in Community Schools v. Seattle School District No. 1*.
    b.   The federal courts no longer enforce the *Brown Decision*.
    c.   Housing patterns in many cities isolate racial and ethnic groups.
    d.   Public opinion is heavily opposed to racial integration in public schools.

7   Suppose the government reinstates the military draft, but only drafts men. Would it be possible for the government to adopt the policy constitutionally?
    a.   Yes, but it would have to demonstrate a rational basis for making the distinction.
    b.   Yes, but it would have to offer an "exceedingly persuasive justification" to make the distinction.
    c.   Yes, but it would have to demonstrate a compelling government interest in making the distinction.
    d.   No. Because of the Equal Protection Clause, any draft would have to include both men and women.

5.3 *What is the history of voting rights in America?*

8   How did the White Primary discriminate against African American voters?
    a.   African Americans were allowed to vote in primary elections but not general elections, thus minimizing their electoral influence.
    b.   African Americans were prevented from voting in the Democratic primary, which was the only election that mattered in the South.
    c.   African Americans were prevented from voting in the Republican primary, which was the only election that mattered in the South.
    d.   African Americans had to pay a tax in order to vote and that discouraged their electoral participation.

9   What was the purpose of a grandfather clause?
    a.   To exempt white people from voting restrictions placed on African Americans.
    b.   To limit voting to older people.
    c.   To prevent older people from voting.
    d.   To establish different voting requirements based on age.

10   Which of the following is a federal law designed to protect the voting rights of racial and ethnic minorities?
    a.   Americans with Disabilities Act (ADA)
    b.   Poll tax
    c.   Grandfather clause
    d.   Voting Rights Act (VRA)

5.4 *What steps has government taken to protect women and minorities from discrimination?*

11   Which of the following outlawed discrimination based on race, religion, color, sex, or national origin in hotels, restaurants, gas stations, and other public accommodations?
    a.   *Brown v. Board of Education*
    b.   Civil Rights Act of 1964
    c.   Voting Rights Act
    d.   Equal Protection Clause

12   Does the federal government have the authority to outlaw discrimination against racial and ethnic minorities in private businesses such as restaurants and hotels?
    a.   Yes. The Supreme Court has ruled that Congress can legislate on the basis of its constitutional authority to regulate interstate commerce.
    b.   Yes. The Supreme Court has ruled that Congress can legislate as part of its authority to enforce the Equal Protection Clause of the Fourteenth Amendment.
    c.   Yes. The First Amendment gives the federal government the authority to prohibit discrimination.
    d.   No. These are state issues, not federal issues.

5.5 *How can universities and employers use affirmative action to increase enrollment and employment of women and minorities?*

13   Which of the following cases dealt with affirmative action?
    a.   *Shelly v. Kraemer*
    b.   *Brown v. Board of Education*
    c.   *City of Richmond v. J. A. Croson Company*
    d.   All of the above

14   Why did the U.S. Supreme Court uphold the admissions program at the University of Michigan Law School?
    a.   The Court ruled that the government has a compelling interest in promoting racial and ethnic diversity in higher education.
    b.   The admissions program did not establish a quota system for admissions.
    c.   The admissions program did not award a set number of points to applicants based on their race or ethnicity.
    d.   All of the above

Answers: 1) a, 2) c, 3) d, 4) c, 5) d, 6) c, 7) b, 8) b, 9) a, 10) d, 11) b, 12) a, 13) c, 14) d

6 PUBLIC

A mericans are growing increasingly polarized on a broad range of issues. Consider public attitudes toward **global warming**, the gradual warming of the Earth's atmosphere reportedly caused by the burning of fossil fuels and industrial pollutants. As recently as 2007, more than 70 percent of Americans surveyed agreed that the climate was warming and that it was caused at least in part by human activity. A large majority of survey respondents indicated that they considered global warming an urgent threat and favored government action to address the issue, including higher automobile fuel efficiency standards, increased use of renewable energy, and improved energy efficiency standards for new homes.[1]

Today, public opinion on global warming is sharply divided between conservatives and liberals. Many people no longer

OPINION

accept that global warming is real and that it is man-made. Only 36 percent of the respondents to a 2011 opinion survey said that they believed that there was evidence of global warming and that it was primarily caused by human activity. Moreover, the differences of opinion between conservatives and liberals were dramatic. According to the survey, 75 percent of "staunch conservatives" said there was no evidence of global warming compared with only 10 percent of "solid liberals" who took that position. Only 5 percent of the conservatives attributed global warming to human activity compared with 70 percent of the liberals.[2]

The topic of attitudes toward global warming provides a good introduction to the study of **public opinion,** the combined personal opinions of adults toward issues of relevance to government. This chapter begins by explaining how scholars measure public opinion on issues such as abortion rights, and whether opinion surveys are accurate. It examines what factors account for the development of individual attitudes and beliefs to explain why different groups of Americans hold different views. Finally, it assesses the extent to which public opinion influences public policy.

> **public opinion** combined personal opinions of adults toward issues of relevance to government.

POLITICAL SOCIALIZATION

6.1 *What factors influence the political socialization process?*

The process through which individuals acquire political knowledge, attitudes, and beliefs is called **political socialization**. Socialization is a learning process, but it does not always take place in a classroom. Filling out an income tax return, serving on a jury, and standing for the National Anthem at a sporting event are all opportunities for political socialization.

> **think**
>
> Would you vote for a presidential candidate that does not share your position on abortion if you agree with the candidate on most other issues? Why or why not?

Process of Socialization

Grade-school students recognize terms such as *Congress, political party,* and *democracy,* but they do not understand their meanings. Many youngsters can name the political party their family supports, but they are unable to distinguish between the two major parties on issues. Almost all young children have a positive attitude toward government and its symbols. They see police officers as friends and helpers, and tell researchers that the president is someone who is smarter and more honest than other people are. Most can distinguish the American flag from other flags, for example, and say they like it best.

In adolescence, young people begin to separate individuals from institutions. They understand, for example, that one can criticize the president while supporting the presidency. Adolescents are aware of processes such as voting and lawmaking, and their general understanding of these processes is more sophisticated.

Attitudes begin to diverge in the adolescent years. For example, many African American children grow less trustful of authority figures, especially police officers.[3] Political events can also drive adolescent socialization. For example, young people gain knowledge and develop party attachments during a presidential campaign. The more intense the political event, the more enduring the political views it creates. The Civil War and the Great Depression had a lifelong impact on generations of Americans.[4]

Political socialization continues in adulthood. Attitudes and basic political knowledge crystallize during early adulthood and tend to persist throughout life.[5] Nonetheless, as adults go to work, start families, and retire, they may change their views on specific political issues.

Agents of Socialization

The factors that contribute to political socialization by shaping formal and informal learning are known as **agents of socialization**. In American society, the agents of socialization include the family, school, peer groups, religious institutions, and the media.

Family. Children acquire attitudes toward politics from their families. Individuals whose parents were politically active are more likely to be involved in politics themselves as compared with their peers whose parents were uninvolved in the political system. Voters, for example, are usually the children of voters.[6] Children of politically knowledgeable parents are themselves more likely to be well informed about government and politics than are other youths.[7]

Families influence at least the initial development of political party affiliation. As parents talk with one another and with their children, they are unconsciously constructing a family identity that may include party identification.[8] The effective-

> **political socialization** the process whereby individuals acquire political knowledge, attitudes, and beliefs.
>
> **agents of socialization** those factors that contribute to political socialization by shaping formal and informal learning.

ness of the political party identification transmission from parent to child is strongest when parental attitudes are consistent across time and between parents, and when parental convictions are strongly held. Parents who are strong Democrats or strong Republicans tend to raise children who with similar attachments.[9]

Political similarities between parents and children diminish over time. Young adults frequently change their political views and party affiliation in response to new socializing experiences. By the age of 25, young adults often adjust their political party identification to place it in line with the party they prefer on the issues about which they care.[10]

School. Civics classes enhance student knowledge of American government and politics. Coursework may lead students to watch news programs or read about current events online. Students may ask their parents more questions about political affairs.[11] Furthermore, young people who volunteer to work in community organizations,

Children acquire attitudes toward politics from their parents.

think

Should schools celebrate the cultural differences of students or focus primarily on teaching the cultural history of the United States?

perhaps as part of a high-school course requirement, often develop a lifetime habit of civic engagement that includes participation in community organizations and voting.[12]

Schools teach patriotism. In the classroom, students pledge allegiance to the flag, sing patriotic songs, commemorate national holidays, and study the lives of national heroes. Schools may provide extracurricular activities, including student government organizations. Young people who learn participatory skills in school typically become participatory adults.[13]

Schools teach young people how to work within a power structure. A school is a self-contained political system, with peers, authorities, rules, awards, rewards, and punishments. Youngsters inevitably develop attitudes about authority and their roles as participants in a system. Schools are not democracies, of course; principals and teachers are often more interested in discipline than participation. Some scholars believe that a primary focus of schools on compliance with rules hinders the development of political participation skills. This phenomenon is particularly true of schools in low-income areas.[14]

College students differ politically from high-school graduates. College life does appear to influence political attitudes as students are exposed to a variety of new ideas and people. As a result, they are less likely than non-college graduates to share their family's political views. However, college-bound youngsters already tended to vary from non-college peers even before they entered college. High-school graduates who go to college are more knowledgeable and interested in politics

Importance of Religion

Is religion an important part of your daily life?

- United States: 65%
- Germany: 40%
- France: 30%
- United Kingdom: 27%
- Japan: 24%

*Percentage who answered "yes"

Americans are more religious than are people in most industrial nations. Nearly two-thirds of Americans tell survey researchers that religion is an important part of their daily life.

Steve Crabtree, "Religiosity Highest in World's Poorest Nations," August 31, 2010, available at www.gallup.com.

Although the proportion of Americans who declare that they are religious has decreased since the 1950s, Americans are more religious than are the people in most other industrialized nations. According to the Gallup Poll, 41 percent of Americans report that they attend religious services once a week compared with 26 percent of Canadians and 17 percent of people living in the United Kingdom.[15]

People who are active in religious organizations are more likely to be politically engaged as well.[16] This association between religious and political activism is particularly important for African Americans.[17] Historically, the black church has been an important training ground for political leadership.

People tend to join religious organizations that promote their own political beliefs, but these can also influence political views.[18] This is particularly true for religious groups demanding an intense commitment of faith and a belief

and feel more capable of influencing the policy process than do young people who are not college-bound.

Religious Institutions. Churches, synagogues, mosques, and other religious institutions are important agents of political socialization for many Americans. Sixty-five percent of Americans tell survey researchers that religion is very important in their lives. Nearly two-thirds belong to a church, synagogue, or another religious body.

think Should churches and other religious institutions take positions on political issues and candidates?

TAKE ✓ ACTION

Family Politics

Political scientists believe that families play an important role in the socialization process. Politically active families typically raise children who become politically active adults. Families also pass along their party identification to their offspring, at least initially. How did your family impact your political socialization, particularly your level of political involvement and your party identification? Prepare to join a class discussion on this topic by taking the following steps:

1. Jot down some information about your own level of political involvement and party affiliation. Are you registered to vote? Are you a regular voter? Have you ever joined a political group or participated in a political campaign? How closely do you follow current events? Do you consider yourself a member of a political party? Have you always had the same party affiliation?

2. Speak with your parents or other members of your family and record your family's political involvement and party loyalties. Were your parents or the adults who raised you politically active? What was their political party allegiance?

3. Finally, consider the role your family played in your personal political socialization and be prepared to discuss the topic in class.

> Discussions **among friends** are more important than the media in **influencing voter decisions.**

in religion as a source of truth. Members who accept the religious organization as the authoritative interpreter of the word of God often respect the political pronouncements of religious leaders as well.[19]

Peer Groups. Friends and coworkers also shape political attitudes and beliefs. Individuals who personally know someone who is gay or lesbian are more supportive of gay rights than are other people.[20] Studies show that discussions among friends are more important than the media in influencing voter decisions.[21] When adults change jobs or neighborhoods, new peer groups may change their political views as well.[22]

The impact of a peer group on an individual's political views depends on the significance of the group to the individual. People are more likely to share the values of a group that is important to them than they are those of a group that is less significant. Nonetheless, not all members of a group think alike. Many persons remain in a group even though they disagree with its values because they overlook the conflict. A study of conservative Christian churches found that nearly 40 percent of women members held feminist views that were contrary to the values of their church. The feminist women remained in the church despite the conflict because they perceived little or no connection between their religious beliefs and their political views.[23]

Media. Mass media outlets are important agents of socialization. Political participation is closely associated with media usage, especially newspaper and newsmagazine readership. Nearly everyone who votes reads a newspaper. Young people who use media frequently understand American government and are more supportive of American values, such as free speech.[24]

The media, especially television, have been shown to determine the importance that Americans attach to issues. In other words, the media help set the policy agenda. Television news stories influence the priorities that Americans assign to various national problems.[25] Media reports also shape public opinion of a president. The more the media focus on a policy issue, the more the public incorporates its knowledge of that issue into its overall judgment of a president.[26]

Can Political Attitudes Be Genetically Transmitted?

Political scientists have begun to explore whether differences in political attitudes and beliefs have a genetic basis. Researchers compared the political attitudes of monozygotic (identical) and dizygotic (non-identical) twins in the United States and Australia. They found a genetic basis for the way individuals respond to environmental conditions. Political similarities between parents and children, then, may have as much to do with genetics as with socialization. The researchers suggest that the ideological division in American politics may have a genetic basis. They identify two distinct ideological orientations. People with an "absolutist" orientation are suspicious of immigrants, yearn for strong leadership and national unity, and seek an unbending moral code. They favor punishment for those who violate society's moral code, tolerate economic inequality, and hold a pessimistic view of human nature. In contrast, people with a "contextualist" orientation are tolerant of immigrants and seek a context-dependent approach to proper social behavior. They dislike predetermined punishments, distrust strong leaders, disapprove of economic inequality, and hold an optimistic view of human nature.[27]

MEASURING PUBLIC OPINION

6.2 *How is public opinion measured, and what factors affect the accuracy of public opinion polls?*

Survey research, the measurement of public opinion, is a familiar part of the American scene. Businesses use market surveys to assess public tastes for their products and services. Political campaigns employ polls to plan strategy. Public officials use surveys to assess public understanding of problems and issues.[28] The media use opinion surveys to gauge public reaction to political events and assess the popularity of officeholders and candidates. Scholars rely on survey research as a tool for studying public opinion and political behavior.

Sampling

In survey research, a **universe** is the population researchers wish to study. It may consist of all adult Americans, or Californians, or likely voters. Survey research enables scholars to examine the characteristics of the universe by studying a subset of that group, a sample. A properly chosen sample will reflect the universe within a given **margin of error (or sample error)**, which is a statistical term

survey research the measurement of public opinion.

universe the population survey researchers wish to study.

sample a subset of a universe.

margin of error (or sample error) a statistical term that refers to the accuracy of a survey.

Margins of Error*

Margin of error	Sample size
+/– 4%	600
+/– 3%	1,065
+/– 2%	2,390
+/– 1%	9,425

* for a universe greater than 500,000, 95% of the time

that refers to the accuracy of a survey. The margin of error's size depends on the size of the sample. The table above lists the margins of error for various sample sizes for a large universe. The margin of error decreases as the sample size increases and vice versa. The margin of error for samples of under 100 is so large as to make the survey meaningless. Researchers can reduce the margin of error by increasing the sample size. However, they can never eliminate error unless they survey every member of the universe. In practice, most professional survey research firms aim for a margin of error of plus or minus 3 to 4 percentage points.

The margin of error for a sample of 1,065 persons out of a universe of 500,000 or more is plus or minus 3 percentage points, 95 percent of the time. For example, suppose that we know that 10 percent of all adults are left-handed. Sampling theory tells us that, 95 percent of the time, a randomly selected sample of 1,065 people will include 7 to 13 percent left-handers, that is, plus or minus 3 percentage points from 10, or the true proportion of left-handed people in this universe. Five percent of the randomly selected samples of 1,065 persons will produce an error that is greater than 3 percentage points. In other words, 5 samples out of 100 will contain a proportion of left-handed people less than 7 percent or more than 13 percent.

Survey research is not exact. Suppose one survey shows that Candidate X is leading Candidate Y by a 48 percent to 46 percent margin, while another survey indicates that Candidate Y is leading by 49 percent to 45 percent. The margin of error in each survey is a plus or minus 4 percentage points. Statistically, the surveys show the same result—support for the two candidates is within the margin of error. Neither candidate is actually ahead.

Statistical chance dictates that 5 percent of samples taken will have a margin greater than the margin of error. For example, even if two candidates are actually tied in voter support, an occasional sample will show one or the other with a lead greater than the margin of error. Over the course of an election campaign, surveys may show a good deal of small voter movement between candidates, with an occasional major shift in public support even if no actual change in voter support for the two candidates takes place.

An accurate sample must be representative of its universe. If researchers are interested in the views of all Americans, a sample of a thousand people from Atlanta, a thousand women, or a thousand callers to a radio talk show would not likely be representative. An unrepresentative sample is a **biased sample,** that is, a sample that tends to produce results that do not reflect the true characteristics of the universe because it is unrepresentative of the universe. For example, radio talk programs present a distorted picture of public opinion because callers and listeners are disproportionately conservative Republican men with strong opinions on political issues.[29]

Internet polls are notoriously (and sometimes hilariously) unreliable because the sample consists of people who choose to participate, sometimes more than once. For example, *People* magazine once conducted an online poll to select the Most Beautiful Person of the Year. The editors at *People* expected that the winner would be a glamorous celebrity. When Howard Stern, a nationally syndicated radio talk show host, heard about the poll, he encouraged his listeners to vote for Hank, the Angry, Drunken Dwarf. Wrestling fans got into the act as well, flooding the *People* website with votes for Ric "Nature Boy" Flair, a professional wrestler. Hank, the Angry, Drunken Dwarf won the vote as *People*'s Most Beautiful Person and Flair finished second.[30]

Most Beautiful People?

A biased sample led to one of the most famous polling mistakes in history. During the 1920s and 1930s, a magazine called *Literary Digest* conducted presidential polls every four years. In 1936, the magazine mailed 10 million ballots to names taken from telephone directories and automobile registration lists. About two million people responded. On that basis, *Literary Digest* predicted that Alf Landon, the Republican challenger, would defeat Democrat Franklin Roosevelt by a resounding 57 percent to 43 percent margin. In fact, Roosevelt was re-elected by the largest landslide in American history!

> Surveys conducted before relatively low-turnout elections are frequently inaccurate because pollsters are unable to separate actual voters from nonvoters.

What went wrong? *Literary Digest*'s sample was unrepresentative of the universe of likely voters. In the midst of the Great Depression, most of the people who owned telephones and automobiles were middle- and upper-income, who tended to vote Republican. In contrast, many poor and working-class people could not afford cars and telephones, and were not sampled by the poll. Most of them voted for Roosevelt.

Although nothing can guarantee a representative sample 100 percent of the time, the ideal approach is to employ a **random sample**. A random sample is a sample in which each member of a universe has an equal likelihood of being included; it is unbiased. If the universe were composed of students of a particular college, researchers could select a random sample by picking every tenth or twentieth student from a master list. In contrast, taking a random sample of Roman Catholics or people who will vote in the next election is difficult because no master list exists. Identifying samples of likely voters is especially challenging for pollsters because people tend to overestimate the probability that they will cast a ballot. Surveys conducted before relatively low-turnout elections are frequently inaccurate because pollsters are unable to separate actual voters from nonvoters.

National survey research firms generate samples starting from a list of all telephone exchanges in the United States and an estimate of the number of households served by each exchange. A computer creates a master list of telephone numbers and then selects a random sample from its list. The computer creates a list of possible numbers rather than using actual telephone numbers so that unlisted telephone numbers will be as likely to be included as listed numbers. To correct for the possible bias of including only people who are usually home and answer their telephones, polling firms call back repeatedly at different times over several days. Once someone answers, the researchers do not necessarily interview that person. They ask for all the adults in the household and then randomly select a name.

Many people refuse to participate in opinion polls. The response rate for major national surveys is less than 30 to 40 percent. It is even less for snapshot polls taken overnight. Cell phones are another problem for survey researchers, as cell phone users are less likely to participate than people using landlines.[31] Scholars are concerned that low response rates may make surveys inaccurate because the people who respond to surveys differ demographically from the people who refuse to participate. Researchers attempt to compensate for differing response rates by adding men, young adults, and other demographic groups, which would otherwise be underrepresented in the sample.[32]

As an increasing number of young people opt out of landlines, survey researchers must find ways to ensure this demographic group is not under-represented.

biased sample a sample that tends to produce results that do not reflect the true characteristics of the universe because it is unrepresentative of the universe.

random sample a sample in which each member of the universe has an equal likelihood of being included.

Question Wording

The best sample is worthless if survey questions are invalid. Questions that are confusing, oversimplified, or biased are unlikely to produce valid results. Question wording can affect survey responses because it provides a frame of reference for a question.[33] Consider the issue of granting legal status to same-sex couples. Although a majority of Americans say that they oppose gay marriage, the nation is evenly divided on whether homosexual couples should be allowed "to legally form civil unions, giving them some of the legal rights of married couples." If the wording mentions "healthcare benefits and Social Security survivor benefits," approval rises to more than 60 percent.[34] Many Americans react negatively to the use of the word *marriage* because it has a religious frame of reference and they are reluctant to sanction homosexuality in that context. In contrast, questions that mention healthcare and Social Security benefits frame the issue in a legal rather than a religious context.

Question Sequencing

The order in which questions are asked can affect a survey's results because question sequence can determine the context within which respondents consider a question. For example, asking about presidential job performance following questions about a particular government policy may affect a president's popularity depending on whether the policy is perceived as successful or unsuccessful. Professional researchers attempt to control for the impact of question sequencing by rotating the order in which questions are asked among survey respondents.[35]

Phantom Opinions

A survey sponsored by the *Washington Post* newspaper asked a national sample of Americans the following question: "Some people say the 1975 Public Affairs Act

FRAMING THE QUESTION

 survey questions

1 Do you believe that waterboarding is torture and that the U.S. has a moral responsibility to not engage in or condone any form of torture?
a) Yes
b) No
c) Unsure

... and the problems with these survey questions:

This question is *confusing*. The stem of the question raises at least two issues: whether waterboarding is torture and whether the U.S. should not engage in or condone torture. How do people answer if they disagree with the first part and agree with the second of the question, or vice versa?

2 Do you believe that abortion should be legal?
a) Yes
b) No
c) No Opinion

This question is *oversimplified*. Many people believe that abortion should be legal under certain circumstances but illegal under others. The question, with its oversimplified answer alternatives, forces these people to misstate their views.

3 Should the Obama administration step back from the rush to create "cap-and-trade" energy legislation that will cost jobs, harm future economic growth, and impose an estimated $1,761 new energy tax on America's families?
a) Yes
b) No
c) Not Sure

This question is *biased*, which means it will produce results that are tilted to one side or another. The question is clearly not a fair assessment of whether people favor or oppose cap-and-trade legislation. After all, who would be in favor of a program that costs jobs, hurts future economic growth, and imposes a high tax?

should be repealed. Do you agree or disagree that it should be repealed?" The survey found that 24 percent of the sample agreed that the act should be repealed, while 19 percent said that it should not be repealed. The other 57 percent had no opinion. Ironically, the people with no opinion were the best informed because the Public Affairs Act was a totally fictitious law. The survey researchers made it up in order to test how many respondents would express an opinion on an issue about which they obviously had no knowledge.[36]

Phantom opinions are made-up responses from respondents who do not want to appear uninformed. Professional pollsters guard against distorting their poll

results with uncommitted opinions by offering respondents a relatively painless opportunity to confess that they have not heard of an issue or do not have an opinion. Some survey researchers also ask respondents to indicate the intensity with which they hold their views and then take that intensity into account in interpreting the results of a survey.

Interviewer–Respondent Interaction

The race or gender of an interviewer can affect survey results when sensitive issues are involved because respondents sometimes attempt to say the right thing based on the race or gender of the interviewer. For example, a survey measuring racial attitudes found black respondents were much more likely to say that white people could be trusted when the interviewer was white than when asked the same question by an African American.[37] Similarly, women are more likely to give pro-choice responses to questions about abortion to female interviewers than they are to male interviewers.[38]

Timing

Even the most carefully conducted survey is only a snapshot of public opinion on the day of the poll. In March 1991, for example, following the American victory in the first Gulf War, the Gallup Poll showed that the approval rating of the President H. W. Bush was 89 percent. Many political observers predicted the president would win reelection easily. By August 1992, however, Bush's popularity rating had fallen below 35 percent, and three months later he was defeated for reelection.[39]

Using poll results to predict the future can be risky: ask Thomas E. Dewey. In 1948, Democratic President Harry Truman was running for election against Dewey, the Republican Party nominee. Throughout the summer and early fall, the polls showed Dewey well ahead and it was generally assumed that Dewey would win handily. In fact, the major polling firms stopped surveying voters more than a week before the election, so they missed a late voter shift in favor of

President Truman. Consequently, Truman's election victory was a surprise to many people, including the editors of the *Chicago Tribune* rushed to press on election night with the famous headline: "Dewey Defeats Truman."

AROUND THE WORLD

Survey Research in Afghanistan

If survey research is challenging under the best of conditions, consider how difficult it must be in a developing country at war. In the last few years, Gallup and some other survey research firms have begun working in Afghanistan. International aid organizations, the U.S. government, and firms interested in marketing their products in Afghanistan are all willing to purchase survey research data on public opinion in Afghanistan.

Afghanistan has a diverse population composed of four major ethnic groups speaking different languages and an illiteracy rate of nearly 50 percent. To build trust, interviewers should share the ethnic background of the person being interviewed and, of course, should speak the same language. For cultural reasons, in an Islamic country such as Afghanistan, women should interview women, and men should interview men. A survey research firm consequently must hire a multi-ethnic, multi-lingual staff that includes both men and women.

Afghanistan is geographically large with few paved roads; because of the war, travel is dangerous. Survey research supervisors must closely review the survey data produced by field teams to ensure that contract workers don't simply make up the results rather than actually conduct the interviews.[40]

Despite the obstacles, survey research firms are already publishing the results of their work. In September 2009, Gallup released the results of a survey asking Afghans whether they believed that additional American troops would help stabilize the security situation. The survey showed that 49 percent of Afghans said that more troops would help compared with 32 percent who said they would not help.[41]

QUESTIONS

1 Would you enjoy working for a survey research firm doing surveys in other countries? Why or why not?

2 Would it be appropriate in the United States for a survey research firm to match the racial/ethnic background of interviewers and interviewees?

3 How confident are you in the accuracy of surveys conducted in Afghanistan?

Afghan men guide their donkeys carrying election supplies in the rugged mountains of the Panjshir valley.

POLITICAL KNOWLEDGE AND ATTITUDES

What do Americans know and believe about politics and government?

Political scientists use survey research to measure what Americans know and believe about politics and government.

Knowledge and Interest

Public knowledge about and interest in politics and government has grown. Not long ago, survey research found that most Americans were poorly informed about politics and government. Although some Americans were quite knowledgeable about public affairs, a majority of the nation's adults could not accurately name their own representative in Congress or even one of the U.S. senators from their state. Most Americans were unable to identify the Bill of Rights. Less than a fifth could name the current chief justice of the United States.[42]

In contrast, recent students show that both political interest and knowledge are on the rise. The percentage of Americans who tell survey researchers that they follow the news about national politics very closely increased from 26 percent in 2000 to 43 percent in 2008. It jumped from 19 percent in 2001 to 36 percent in 2009. (Political interest is typically higher in presidential election years such as 2000 and 2008 than it is in non-election years such as 2001 and 2009.) In addition to the 36 percent who indicated that they followed the national news very closely in 2009, another 42 percent declared that they followed the news somewhat closely. Only 6 percent said that they followed the news not at all.[43]

Interested people are also knowledgeable people. According to a study conducted by the Pew Research Center in 2007, most Americans knew which political party controlled Congress (the Democrats), could name of the Speaker of the House (Nancy Pelosi), and could identify the two branches of Islam struggling for control of Iraq (Shia and Sunni). The study found that 26 percent of respondents could answer all 10 of its political questions correctly, whereas only 14 percent could correctly answer three or fewer questions.[44]

Some groups of Americans are more interested and better informed than are other groups. As a group, men are more interested and knowledgeable than are women. Republicans have more interested and know more than do Democrats. Older Americans are better informed and more interested in politics than younger people. Men over 50 are the most knowledgeable and attentive segment of the population; younger women are the least.[45]

*Americans are **more likely** to endorse democratic principles in the **abstract** than in specific application.*

Political interest and information affect political behavior and beliefs. Knowledgeable Americans are more likely to vote and more likely to cast an informed ballot than are the uninformed. Furthermore, knowledgeable respondents usually vote for candidates whose views on issues of importance to them coincide with their own. In contrast, there is almost no relationship between the political issues that low-knowledge voters say matter most to them and the issue positions of the candidates for whom they voted.[46]

Support for Democratic Principles

Do Americans support the democratic principles of majority rule and minority rights? Political scientists have studied this question for decades. During the 1950s, Professor Samuel Stouffer conducted a study to evaluate public opinion toward individual rights. He found a high level of intolerance toward persons with unpopular views. For example, only 27 percent of the persons interviewed would permit "an admitted communist" to make a speech.[47]

In 1960, political scientists James W. Prothro and C. W. Grigg published what has become a classic study of political tolerance. They conducted a survey in which respondents overwhelmingly endorsed the sentiment that public officials should be chosen by majority vote, and stated that people whose opinions were in the minority should have the right to convince others of their views. When Prothro and Griff asked about specific, concrete situations, however, they found dramatically less support for the practice of majority rule and minority rights. Many respondents said that a communist should not be allowed to take office, even if legally elected. Many persons also stated that atheists should not be allowed to speak publicly against religion.[48] In the years since the Prothro and Grigg study first appeared, other research has confirmed that Americans are more likely to endorse democratic principles in the abstract than in specific application. One study found that a majority of Americans opposed many of the specific guarantees of individual rights found in the Bill of Rights.[49]

A number of studies conducted in the 1970s concluded that Americans were becoming more tolerant of political diversity. Using questions almost identical to Stouffer's of two decades before, researchers found significantly more Americans willing to tolerate atheists, socialists, and communists. Some concluded that this trend reflected the views of a younger, more urban, and better-educated population.[50]

Subsequent research contradicted this conclusion that Americans have grown more accepting of political diversity. Although attitudes toward socialists, communists, and atheists have generally become more tolerant, many Americans express intolerant attitudes toward racists and persons advocating military rule in the United States. Americans are apparently no more tolerant of persons with unpopular views today than they were in the 1950s. The difference is that the targets of intolerance have changed.[51]

A number of political scientists believe that the general public has little understanding or concern for civil liberties. "[T]he only time many people consider . . . [civil liberties]," one scholar says, "is when they are being queried about it in public opinion surveys."[52] Consequently, people respond to questions about civil liberties based on their perception of a particular group's threat to society. In the 1950s, many Americans favored limiting free speech for communists because they feared communism. Americans today feel less threatened by communists than by racist groups such as the Ku Klux Klan. When answering survey questions, then, they express more tolerance for communists than for members of the Klan.[53] In sum, Americans favor civil liberties for groups they like; they oppose them for groups they dislike.

The apparent indifference of many Americans to civil liberties, at least as they apply to controversial groups, disturbs a number of observers. Tolerance for people of other races, ethnicities, religions, and political beliefs is an important underpinning of democracy.[54] Many political theorists believe that a free society requires a high degree of popular support for civil liberties. How, then, can we explain the stability of our democracy when research has often found a lack of support for the fundamental principles of democracy?

Political scientists identify three factors accounting for the preservation of political freedom in the United States, despite the ambivalence and occasional hostility of many Americans to civil liberties. First, the Constitution protects individual rights.[55] Although paper guarantees are not sufficient to ensure civil liberties, they provide an important foundation for individual rights. Second, Americans do not agree on the target groups to be suppressed. Some people believe that members of the Klan should be kept from expressing their views, whereas others favor silencing people how oppose abortion rights. Since Americans

what didn't AMERICA KNOW?

	Knew it	Blew it
1. Who delivered the Gettysburg Address?	67%	33%
2. Who was the first president of the U.S.?	92%	8%
3. What is the name of the National Anthem?	58%	42%
4. Two of the three branches of the U.S. government are called the executive and the legislative branches. What is the third branch called?	59%	41%
5. How many U.S. senators are there from each state?	34%	66%
6. In what document are these words found? "We hold these truths to be self-evident, that all men are created equal."	34%	64%
7. Who wrote the "Letter from Birmingham Jail"?	33%	67%
8. What are the first 10 amendments of the U.S. Constitution called?	47%	53%
9. Who is the current vice president of the U.S.?	69%	31%
10. Who is the current chief justice of the U.S. Supreme Court?	17%	83%

ANSWERS: 1. Abraham Lincoln 2. George Washington 3. The Star-Spangled Banner 4. Judicial 5. Two 6. Declaration of Independence 7. Martin Luther King, Jr. 8. The Bill of Rights 9. Joe Biden 10. John C. Roberts

While political knowledge is on the rise in America, there are still some people poorly informed about politics. How's your political knowledge? Try to answer these questions, and then see how you compare to the country as a whole.

Source: George H. Gallup, Jr., "How Many Americans Know U.S. History? Part I," October 21, 2003, available at www.gallup.com.

cannot agree on target groups, they are unable to unite behind undemocratic public policies. Finally, a number of political scientists believe that the attitudes of the general public about civil liberties issues are not nearly as important as the views of **political elites**, who are persons that exercise a major influence on the policymaking process. Support for democratic principles is stronger among people who are politically active and well informed than it is among individuals who are politically uninvolved. Democracy endures because those who are most directly involved in policymaking—political elites—understand and support the principles of majority rule and minority rights.[56]

Political Trust and Political Legitimacy

Many scholars believe that political trust is essential to political legitimacy in a democracy. **Political legitimacy** is the popular acceptance of a government and its officials as rightful authorities in the exercise of power. For the most part, democracy depends on the voluntary cooperation of its citizens rather than coercion. People pay taxes and obey laws because they accept the authority of the government. They seek political change through the electoral process and peacefully accept the outcomes of election contests because they recognize the decisions of the electoral process as binding. If a significant proportion of the population loses trust in the political system, the quality of democracy declines. Tax evasion and disrespect for the rule of law increase. The potential for a revolutionary change in the political order may develop. Political battles may be fought with bullets, not ballots.

Political scientists attempt to measure the level of political trust in society through a set of questions developed by the Center for Political Studies (CPS), which is a social science research unit housed at the

think Should racist groups be allowed to hold political rallies?

University of Michigan. The questions probe the degree to which citizens believe that government leaders are honest (or crooked) and competent (or incompetent). One question asks, "How much of the time do you think you can trust the government in Washington to do what is right—just about always, most of the time, or only some of the time?" Another question reads, "Do you think that quite a few of the people running the government are a little crooked, not very many are, or do you think hardly any of them are crooked at all?"[57]

Political scientists average the answers to the questions to create a Trust Index. The index fell during the 1960s and 1970s, rose in the 1980s, fell again in the 1990s, increased dramatically after the terrorist attacks on September 11, 2001, and then dropped yet again. In 2010, only 22 percent of Americans told survey researchers that they trusted the government to do what is right just about always or most of the time, a record low.[58] The survey found that 56 percent of Americans were frustrated with the federal government; another 21 percent were angry. Only 19 percent answered that they were basically content with the government. Other surveys taken in 2010 indicated low levels of approval/high levels of disapproval for Congress and both major political parties.[59]

Recent studies show that both political interest and knowledge are on the rise.

political elites the people who exercise a major influence on the policymaking process.

political legitimacy the popular acceptance of a government and its officials as rightful authorities in the exercise of power.

In 2010, only 22 percent of Americans told survey researchers that they trusted the government to do what is right just about always or most of the time, a record low.

Source: ANES, Trends from Pew Research Center, American National Election Studies, Gallup, ABC/*Washington Post*, CBS/New York Times, and CNN Polls.

Political Efficacy

Political efficacy is the extent to which individuals believe they can influence the policymaking process. Political efficacy is related to participation. People who believe that they can affect government policies are more inclined to participate

> **❝**Sometimes politics and government seem so complicated that a person like me can't really understand what's going on.**❞**

politically than people who have no confidence in their ability to influence what government does.

Political scientists identify two components of this concept. **Internal political efficacy** is the assessment by an individual of his or her personal ability to influence the policymaking process. The concept addresses knowledge of the political system and ability to communicate with political decision-makers. Scholars measure internal political efficacy by asking this agree/disagree question: "Sometimes politics and government seem so complicated that a person like me can't really understand what's going on." Agreement with the statement indicates a low level of internal political efficacy. In 2000, 60 percent agreed with the

statement compared with 32 percent who disagreed.[60] Internal political efficacy rose during the 1980s and 1990s, when voting turnout was in decline. So it appears that the concept is not related to voter participation. Low levels of internal political efficacy may explain why many Americans do not participate politically in other ways, but they apparently do not account for changes in voter participation rates.

political efficacy the extent to which individuals believe that they can influence the policymaking process.

Internal political efficacy the assessment by an individual of his or her personal ability to influence the policymaking process.

External **political efficacy** refers to the assessment of an individual of the responsiveness of government to his or her concerns. This concept deals with an individual's evaluation of the willingness of government officials to respond to the views of ordinary citizens. Political scientists have created a Government Responsiveness Index based on responses to questions such as the following: "Over the years, how much attention do you feel the government pays to what the people think when it decides what to do?" The index generally declined from the mid-1960s through the early 1980s, but it has subsequently increased.[61] Scholars believe that external political efficacy is associated with voter participation.[62]

external political efficacy the assessment of an individual of the responsiveness of government to his or her concerns.

POLITICAL PHILOSOPHY

6.4 *Are Americans liberal or conservative?*

In American politics, the terms *liberalism* and *conservatism* are used to describe political philosophy. **Liberalism** is a political philosophy that favors the use of government power to foster development of the individual and promote the welfare of society. Liberals believe that the government can (and should) advance social progress by promoting political equality, social justice, and economic prosperity.

Liberals usually favor government regulation and government spending for social programs. Liberals value social and cultural diversity, and defend the right of individual adult choice on issues such as access to abortion. In contrast, **conservatism** is the political philosophy that government power undermines the development of the individual and diminishes society as a whole. Conservatives argue that government regulations and social programs generally do harm rather than good. Charities, private businesses, and individuals can solve problems if the

liberalism the political philosophy that favors the use of government power to foster the development of the individual and promote the welfare of society.

conservatism the political philosophy that government power undermines the development of the individual and diminishes society as a whole.

"If a free society cannot help the many who are poor, it cannot save the few who are rich.**"**
–John F. Kennedy

President John Kennedy, an unapologetic liberal, believed in the power of government to address social problems.

government leaves them alone. Conservatives also believe that the government should actively defend the traditional values of society.

The terms *right* and *left* are also used to describe political ideology. In American politics, the **political right** or **right wing** refers to conservatism, the **political left** or **left wing** to liberalism. The use of these terms comes from the traditional practice in European legislatures of seating members of liberal parties on the left side of the meeting hall, whereas members of conservative parties sit on the right side.

Liberals and conservatives disagree about the capacity of government to solve problems. Although liberals and conservatives both acknowledge that the nation faces certain social problems, they disagree as to whether those problems can be best addressed by the government or private initiative. Liberals advocate government action to assist disadvantaged groups in society, such as the elderly, poor, minorities, and people with disabilities. They generally support such programs as Social Security, Medicare, welfare assistance for the poor, national health insurance, federal aid for education, and affirmative action programs for women and minorities.

In contrast, conservatives argue that government, especially the national government, is too inefficient to solve the nation's social problems. They believe that government should reduce spending on social programs and cut taxes in order to promote economic growth, which, the conservatives argue, benefits everyone.

Liberals and conservatives disagree about the efficacy of government regulation. Liberals believe in the use of government power to regulate business in the public interest. They support environmental-protection laws, consumer-protection regulations, and occupational safety and health standards. Liberals are more likely than conservatives are to endorse trade restrictions to protect American companies and workers from foreign competition. In contrast, conservatives warn that government

think

Do you consider yourself a liberal, conservative, or moderate?

political left or left wing liberal.

political right or right wing conservative.

> **"**Government is not the solution to our problem; government is the problem.**"**
> –Ronald Reagan

Ronald Reagan championed the conservative principles of limited government, with lower taxes, reduced regulation, and fewer services.

QUESTION: Isn't political science just a matter of opinion?

ANSWER: The purpose of a political science course isn't primarily to debate the issues of the day but to understand them in the context of American politics and government. The textbook deals with the issue of abortion, for example, not to discuss whether it is right or wrong, but to consider the role of public opinion, the media, interest groups, political parties, elections, Congress, the president, and the courts in setting abortion policy in the United States.

regulations usually involve undue interference with the market economy. They believe that government regulations drive up the cost of doing business, increasing prices for consumers and lowering wage rates for workers.

Consider the issue of the environment. Liberals value a clean environment even if it means sacrificing some economic growth. They advocate government regulation to ensure clean air and water. They favor government responses to the threat of global warming, which is the gradual warming of the Earth's atmosphere caused by burning fossil fuels and industrial pollutants. In contrast, conservatives want to proceed slowly in addressing environmental issues such as global warming so as not to negatively impact economic growth. They prefer market-oriented solutions to the pollution problem rather than government mandates.

On social issues, conservatives and liberals trade positions on the role of government. Conservatives favor more active government intervention, whereas liberals prefer less government involvement. Conservatives define social issues in terms of traditional family values. They generally support the adoption of a constitutional amendment against abortion and the enactment of an amendment permitting school prayer, and they oppose assisted suicide, most stem cell research, and laws protecting gay men and lesbians from discrimination. They also reject efforts to legalize same-sex marriage.

In contrast, liberals generally prefer that government stay out of these questions except to protect the rights of the individual. Liberals hold that women should be allowed to pursue the career goals of their choice and should be treated equally with men under the law. They believe that women should not be forced to bear unwanted children; gay men and lesbians should not suffer discrimination; and the government should not dictate prayers for children to recite in the public schools. They favor government support for stem cell research aimed at finding cures for disease.

Ironically, both liberals and conservatives criticize government. Liberals believe that the government should act more aggressively to promote the democratic value of equality by helping disadvantaged individuals and groups gain economic and political power. In contrast, conservatives criticize government for undercutting capitalism by interfering with the efficient working of the free enterprise system, thus lowering economic productivity. Conservatives believe that government economic intervention hurts everyone, including the poor.

Although the terms *liberalism* and *conservatism* help define the contours of the policy debate in America, their usefulness is limited. The real-life differences between liberals and conservatives are often matters of degree and emphasis rather than dramatic contrast. Also, a number of policy issues cannot easily be defined along liberal/conservative lines. Finally, few Americans are consistently liberal or conservative with most people holding conservative views on some issues, liberal opinions on others.

Are Americans Liberal or Conservative?

More Americans self-identify as conservatives than as liberals. In 2010, the ratio of conservatives to liberals was 42 percent to 20 percent with another 35 percent declaring that their political views were moderate.[63] Nonetheless, political scientists caution about putting too much stock into self-appraisals of political philosophy because many Americans are unable accurately to define the terms liberal and conservative. For example, when asked to choose between "more government services and more spending" or "fewer services to reduce spending," survey respondents favored more services and spending (the liberal position) 43 percent to 20 percent, with the rest either in the middle or declaring they don't know.[64] Furthermore, relatively few Americans are consistently liberal or conservative on the full range of political issues.

It is unclear whether Americans are growing more liberal or more conservative. Although the success of the Democratic Party in the 2006 and 2008 elections implies that Americans are turning to the left (Democrats typically take more liberal positions on most issues

Whether Americans are liberal or conservative **depends on the issue.**

than do the Republicans), Americans by a 39 percent to 18 percent margin tell survey researchers that their views have been growing more conservative in recent years as opposed to more liberal, with another 42 percent indicating that their thinking has not changed. In looking at specific issues, however, polls show that while Americans have grown more conservative on some issues, such as protecting the environment and gun control, they have become less conservative on other issues, such as immigration and tax rates.[65]

Opinion Differences Among Groups

Surveys show that political attitudes vary among individuals according to such factors as social class, race, and gender. For example, support for abortion rights is greater among women, college graduates, young people, African Americans, higher income earners, Democrats and people who lack a religious affiliation. In contrast, opposition to abortion rights is greatest among men, older adults, Republicans, people with relatively little formal education, lower-income groups, and regular church goers.[66]

Social Class. On social welfare issues and many economic issues, lower-income people tend to be more liberal than middle- and upper-income Americans. Lower income people tend to be more supportive of programs such as Medicare and Social Security, and are considerably more supportive of raising taxes on upper-income wage earners. In contrast, lower-income individuals are often more conservative than other income groups on such non-economic issues as abortion, teaching creation in public schools, and stem cell research.

In foreign policy matters, lower-income individuals are more isolationist than middle-income people, but also more supportive of the use of military force in dealing with other nations. Isolationism is the view that the United States should stay away from the affairs of other nations. Working-class people often oppose free trade, fearing the loss of jobs to international competition. In contrast, middle- and upper-income people have a more international perspective; they tend to favor free trade, foreign aid, and negotiated settlements of disputes.[67]

Race and Ethnicity. African Americans and Latinos favor activist government. Members of both minority groups typically favor welfare programs and support affirmative action, a program designed to ensure equal opportunities in employment and college admissions for racial minorities and women. African Americans, in particular, perceive widespread racial discrimination in society and believe that it is the major reason that many African Americans have trouble finding good jobs and adequate housing. They want government to play an active role in the quest for racial equality.

Many whites believe that African Americans have already

VERY LIBERAL OR LIBERAL	MODERATE	VERY CONSERVATIVE OR CONSERVATIVE
20	35	42

ARE AMERICANS LIBERAL OR CONSERVATIVE?

DON'T KNOW — 3

More Americans self-identify as conservatives than identify as liberals, but over a third of Americans consider themselves moderate.

Source: Gallup Poll, 2009

achieved equality.[68] When asked whether they believe that blacks have as good a chance as whites to get any kind for job for which they are qualified, 82 percent of whites and Hispanics agree with the statement compared with only 49 percent of blacks who agree.[69] In fact, African Americans continue to lag behind whites in employment, income, education, and access to healthcare.

African Americans and Latinos are more conservative than whites on some social issues. Although African Americans and Latinos are less likely to support the death penalty than whites, they are more likely to hold conservative views than the general population on the issues of homosexual relations, gay marriage, and stem cell research. African American and Latino conservatism on these issues reflects relatively high rates of church attendance for both minority groups.[70]

Religion. Religious beliefs motivate many Americans to participate in politics. The **religious left** refers to individuals who hold liberal views because of their religious beliefs, whereas the phrase **religious right** refers to those who hold conservative views because of their religious beliefs. Both groups feel motivated by their religious beliefs to participate in politics. Most members of the religious left are associated with mainline Protestant Christian churches, such as the Presbyterians, Episcopalians, and Church of Christ (Disciples), or with the Jewish faith. It also includes Buddhists and many people who declare that they are "spiritual" but not associated with organized religion.[71] Christian conservatives tend to be associated with white evangelical Protestant churches, such as Assemblies of God and the Southern Baptist Convention.[72]

Not all religious groups are firmly in the camp of the left or right. For example, although Roman Catholics oppose gay marriage, a position associated with the religious right, they also oppose the death penalty, support civil rights and immigrant rights, and favor government efforts to end poverty. The latter positions are typically associated with the religious left. Ironically, Roman Catholics are actually somewhat more supportive of abortion rights than are Protestants, despite the official opposition of the Catholic Church to abortion.[73]

In contemporary American politics, the religious right is more influential than the religious left. This development reflects the relative strength of the religious organizations associated with each cause. Whereas most mainline Protestant churches have been losing members for years, conservative evangelical churches have been growing. Furthermore, church attendance is higher among conservative evangelicals.[74]

Because of the growth of conservative Christian churches, active church participation is now associated with political conservatism. At least among whites, the more actively involved people are with religious organizations, the more likely they are to hold conservative politi-

religious left those who hold liberal views because of their religious beliefs.

religious right those who hold conservative views because of their religious beliefs.

African Americans are relatively conservative on the issues of abortion and gay and lesbian rights, reflecting their high rates of church attendance.

cal views. For African Americans, the church is a basis for liberal activism on economic issues. Nonetheless, African Americans who are active church members hold more conservative views on social issues, such as abortion and gay marriage, than do African Americans who do not participate actively in a church.[75]

Generation. Younger Americans are considerably more likely than middle-aged and older Americans to label themselves liberal.[76] They are more tolerant of ethnic, racial, and social diversity than older adults. They are also more sympathetic to affirmative action programs that aid minorities than are older people, and are more likely to favor gay and lesbian rights.[77] Despite conventional wisdom, studies find no evidence that people grow more conservative with age. Instead, age-related differences in political views reflect the impact of socializing events common to a generation. Younger Americans today, for example, came of age after the appearance of individual rights movements for African Americans, women, and homosexuals. In contrast, older people grew up at a time when African Americans were segregated, most women worked at home, and gay men and lesbians were in the closet. Younger Americans may also be more tolerant because they are better educated than previous generations.[78]

> Younger Americans are more tolerant of ethnic, racial, and social diversity than older adults.

Region. In general, people from the East and West coasts are more liberal than people from the South, Midwest, or Rocky Mountain regions. Most regional differences can be explained by class, race, and religion, but some genuine regional variations based on unique cultural and historical factors may also play a role. The South's lingering identification with the Old Confederacy is perhaps the most notable example of how history can affect the political thinking of a region.

Gender. Men and women are differently politically. The phrase **gender gap** refers to differences in party identification and political attitudes between men and women. Women are more likely to vote for Democratic candidates and to favor government programs to provide healthcare and education, and to protect the environment. They are also more likely to support abortion rights and gay marriage. Women are less tolerant of employment discrimination than are men,[79] and less likely to favor increased defense spending and to believe that the wars in Afghanistan and Iraq are worth it.[80]

gender gap differences in party identification and political attitudes between men and women.

PUBLIC OPINION AND PUBLIC POLICY

 6.5 *To what extent does public opinion influence public policy?*

Years ago, political scientist V.O. Key, Jr., introduced the concept of latent opinion to explain the relationship between public opinion and policy. **Latent opinion** is not what voters think about an issue today, but what public opinion would be by election time if a political opponent made a public official's position on the issue the target of an attack.[81] Elected officials make thousands of policy decisions. Except for a relatively few high-profile actions, such as President Barack Obama signing healthcare reform, most of these decisions are invisible to the overwhelming majority of Americans. Nonetheless, public officials consider public opinion during policy formulation and adoption because they recognize that a future political opponent could raise the issue during an election campaign.

Contemporary political scientist James A. Stimson introduced the concept of a **zone of acquiescence,** which is the range of policy options acceptable to the public on a particular issue. Stimson says that some policy options are either too conservative or too liberal to be acceptable to a majority of the public. The zone of acquiescence encompasses policy options that lie between the two extremes. The size of the zone varies from issue to issue and may change if public opinion grows more conservative or more liberal. Policymakers tend to choose policy options within the zone of acquiescence; otherwise they risk electoral defeat.[82]

latent opinion what public opinion would be at election time if a political opponent made a public official's position on the issue the target of a campaign attack.

zone of acquiescence the range of policy options acceptable to the public on a particular issue.

think

Should public officials use opinion surveys to determine what policies are most popular and then adopt those policies?

The concept of a zone of acquiescence draws attention to a number of important points about the relationship between public opinion and public policy. First, public opinion affects policy by limiting options. On most issues, the zone of acquiescence is broad enough to include a number of options from which public officials may choose. Public opinion sets this range of acceptable alternatives, but it does not determine which options are selected. Other factors, including the influence of interest groups and political parties, come into play.

Second, the concept of a zone of acquiescence does not imply that policies are not controversial. The zone of acquiescence is based on majority preferences, but may alarm minorities. For example, although abortion is legal in the United States, it remains controversial for many Americans.

Third, the zone of acquiescence is affected by the policymakers constituency. A **constituency** is the district from which an officeholder is elected. A member of Congress elected from a district with a majority of African American constituents, for example, faces a more liberal zone of acquiescence on economic issues than does one whose constituents are mostly upper-income whites. The president, meanwhile, must deal with a nationwide constituency.

Finally, the zone of acquiescence for a particular issue changes as public opinion changes. During the 1980s, as public opinion grew more conservative on law and order issues such as the death penalty, so too did the range of acceptable policy options available to officials. States adopted laws giving harsher sentences to violent criminals and more states began implementing the death penalty. On other issues, such as gay and lesbian rights, public policy became more liberal as public opinion grew more liberal, especially in large urban areas where residents are more likely to hold liberal views on the issue than people living in small towns and rural areas.[83] Policy positions that were not acceptable in the 1950s have now become acceptable.

constituency the district from which an officeholder is elected.

At the Quinnipiac University Polling Institute, students man the computers and phone lines to help conduct public opinion polls.

TAKING SIDES

Governing and Public Opinion

Should elected officials consider public opinion when making decisions?

Should President Obama consider public opinion when deciding war policy in Iraq and Afghanistan?

OVERVIEW

Public opinion is important to democracy because our government derives its authority from the "consent of the governed." We believe that our elected officials should behave in a manner that reflects the will of the majority of the people. But to what extent should public opinion govern policy? Should our elected officials act in direct compliance with the will of the majority, or should they make decisions based on what they think is best for the people?

Making policy decisions based on public opinion can be problematic. Americans are often misinformed or lack knowledge about events on which they express their opinions. For example, in a March 2002 ABC News/*Washington Post* poll, 62 percent of Americans expressed support for the war in Iraq.[84] Yet polls conducted during that period by the Program on International Policy showed that nearly half of Americans believed that links between Iraq and al-Qaeda had been found, 22 percent believed that weapons of mass destruction were discovered in Iraq, and 25 percent thought that the world favored going war with Iraq. Sixty percent of Americans held at least one of these incorrect beliefs, which surely influenced their expressed opinion on the war.[85]

 SUPPORTING
close adherence to public opinion

Technology allows for greater inclusion of citizens in the policymaking process. Citizens today can read the latest news at the touch of a button, and can respond to their representative in real time on social networking sites. Citizens have greater opportunities to share informed, valuable opinions on policy issues, and elected officials should hear them.

Elected officials can rarely claim a mandate to govern. Representatives or even presidents often win with less than a majority of the votes, which means that over half the people are likely to disagree with their policies. Between elections, public opinion is how Americans can check their elected officials and thus have some control over the direction of the country.

Polling is scientifically valid. Public opinion polling today is a multi-million dollar industry managed by people firmly committed to delivering accurate numbers. If elected officials know that the majority of the people feel something, then it is the obligation of the elected official to deliver on that attitude.

 AGAINST
close adherence to public opinion

Citizens are too ignorant or ill informed to make good decisions. In a representative democracy, citizens elect officials to make decisions for them. If they are unhappy with the decisions, they will choose someone else next time. Representatives should make decisions that they feel are in the best interest of their constituents.

Our country believes in minority rights. While our nation operates generally on the principle of majority rule, we have a firm commitment to minority rights. Governing based solely on the opinions of the majority would undermine the protections of minority opinions provided for in the structure of our government.

Public opinion changes over time on controversial issues. Public opinion tends to fluctuate, particularly when issues are new and relatively little is known about them. Governing should be based on long-term goals, and public opinion today does not always reflect where the people will eventually land on an issue.

POLITICAL SOCIALIZATION

 6.1 *What factors influence the political socialization process?*

Political socialization is the process whereby individuals acquire political knowledge, attitudes, and beliefs. It begins in childhood and continues throughout the lifespan. The family, school, peer groups, religious institutions, and the media are all agents of socialization. For example, the family influences the initial development of political party affiliation. School civics classes enhance student knowledge of American government and politics. Schools also teach patriotism through patriotic rituals and symbols. Finally, political scientists have begun to explore whether differences in political attitudes and beliefs have a genetic basis.

MEASURING PUBLIC OPINION

6.2 *How is public opinion measured, and what factors affect the accuracy of public opinion polls?*

Survey research is based on the concept that a carefully drawn sample will allow a researcher to assess the characteristics of a universe within a given margin of error. To be an accurate reflection of a universe, a sample must be representative of the universe. Even a perfectly drawn sample is worthless if survey questions are confusing or biased. Question sequencing can influence survey results. People will sometimes profess to hold an opinion even when they do not just to keep from appearing uninformed. Sometimes the race or gender of the interview affects survey responses. Finally, even at its best, a survey is a snapshot of opinion on the day it is taken.

POLITICAL KNOWLEDGE AND ATTITUDES

6.3 *What do Americans know and believe about politics and government?*

Political knowledge and interest in politics have both increased over the last decade. Knowledgeable Americans are more likely to vote and more likely to cast an informed ballot than are the uninformed.

Research indicates that Americans overwhelmingly endorse democratic principles in the abstract, but show considerably less support when presented with concrete situations. Democracy in America persists in part because political elites show greater support for democratic principles in concrete situations than do Americans as a whole.

Political scientists believe that trust is essential to political legitimacy in a democracy. Many scholars believe that data measuring political trust reflect support for the current set of officeholders rather than support for the political system. Surveys taken in 2010 show that levels of political trust are at a record low point.

Internal political efficacy is the assessment by an individual of his or her personal ability to influence the policymaking process. External political efficacy refers to the assessment of an individual of the responsiveness of government to his or her concerns. Scholars believe that external political efficacy is associated with political participation.

POLITICAL PHILOSOPHY

 6.4 *Are Americans liberal or conservative?*

Liberalism is the political philosophy that favors the use of government power to foster the development of the individual and promote the welfare of society. In contrast, conservatism is the political philosophy that government power undermines the development of the individual and diminishes society as a whole. Political scientists caution about putting too much stock into self-appraisals of political philosophy because many Americans are unable accurately to define the terms liberal and conservative, and relatively few Americans are consistently liberal or conservative on the full range of political issues. Surveys show that political attitudes vary among individuals according to such factors as social class, race, and gender.

PUBLIC OPINION AND PUBLIC POLICY

 6.5 *To what extent does public opinion influence public policy?*

Political scientist James A. Stimson discusses the impact of public opinion on the decision-making calculus of public officials by introducing the concept of a zone of acquiescence, which is the range of policy options acceptable to the public on a particular issue. Rational policymakers choose policy options within the zone of acquiescence; otherwise they risk electoral defeat.

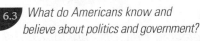

Send	Save	Delete

From: Professor Tannahill
Add Cc | Add Bcc

Subject: Tips for Success

Attach a file

DON'T BE HELD BACK:
The president is African American, the Speaker of the House is a woman, President Obama's first Supreme Court appointee is Hispanic, the mayor of Houston is lesbian, and the attorney general of Texas is in a wheelchair. Don't let anything keep you from succeeding.

MySearchLab®

6.1 *What factors influence the political socialization process?*

1 Which of the following statements about the socialization process is NOT true?
a. Political socialization ends when individuals reach their early 20s.
b. Young children typically identify with the same political party as their parents.
c. Schools teach the children of immigrants to be patriotic Americans.
d. Personal involvement in religious organizations is associated with political participation.

2 Which of the following agents of socialization plays the most important role in shaping the party identification of youngsters?
a. Family   c. Peers
b. School   d. Media

6.2 *How is public opinion measured, and what factors affect the accuracy of public opinion polls?*

3 What would be the universe for a study measuring the attitudes of college students toward politics and government?
a. The group of individuals who are actually interviewed for the study
b. All college-age adults
c. All college students
d. All Americans

4 A professionally administered survey has a margin of error of plus or minus 3 percentage points. How often will a sample differ from the universe by more than 3 percentage points, merely on the basis of chance?
a. Never. If the sample is truly random, it will never differ by more than the margin of error.
b. One time in 20. Even a perfectly drawn sample will by chance be outside the margin of error 5 percent of the time.
c. Three percent of the time. The margin of error indicates the error factor built into a survey.
d. One time in five. A well-conducted survey will be wrong 20 percent of the time.

5 A public opinion poll taken a month before the election has a margin of error of 3 percentage points. The poll shows Candidate A ahead of Candidate B by 46 percent to 44 percent. What is the best analysis of the result of the poll?
a. Candidate A is ahead by at least 2 percentage points but may actually be ahead by 5 percentage points.

b. Candidate A is ahead but it is impossible to know by how much.
c. Candidate B is actually ahead because Candidate A did not reach the 50 percent support level.
d. The candidates are in a statistical tie because the difference in their support is within the margin of error.

6.3 *What do Americans know and believe about politics and government?*

6 Which of the following statements about interest in and knowledge about government and politics is/are true?
a. People who are interested and informed are more likely to vote than people who are not.
b. Republicans as a group are better informed than Democrats.
c. Over the last decade, interest in politics and government has increased.
d. All of the above

7 On which of the following questions would you expect a survey to find the highest level of public support?
a. The public library should include all books, including books advocating racism and atheism.
b. People should enjoy freedom of speech, regardless of their political views.
c. A professor who condones the terror attacks of Sept. 11, 2001, should be allowed to teach at a public university.
d. The Ku Klux Klan should be allowed to hold a rally in the city park.

8 Which of the following would likely be a result of a low level of political legitimacy in a society?
a. Election turnout would be high.
b. Most people would voluntarily obey laws and regulations.
c. People wanting to bring about political change would turn to the electoral system rather than violence.
d. None of the above

9 Which of the following statements reflects a high level of internal political efficacy?
a. "I don't believe that government officials care what I think."
b. "I have a good understanding of how government works."
c. "I think that most of the people running the government are crooks."
d. "Sometimes politics seems so complicated that a person like me can't really understand what's going on."

6.4 *Are Americans liberal or conservative?*

10 Which of the following positions would most likely be taken by a conservative?

a. "Government has a responsibility to ensure that all Americans have access to affordable healthcare."
b. "Government should act aggressively to adopt regulations to slow global warming."
c. "Government has a responsibility to protect the unborn by limiting access to abortion."
d. "Government should address the problem of homelessness by providing more public housing."

11 Which of the following statements reflects a liberal ideology?
a. "The government that governs least governs best."
b. "Government regulations often do more harm than good."
c. "The government has no business telling women that they must carry a fetus to term."
d. "Churches and private charities do a better job than the government at solving social problems."

12 Which of the following statements about political ideology is true?
a. Southerners as a group are more conservative than people in other regions of the country.
b. Lower-income people are more liberal on social welfare issues than are middle- and upper-income people.
c. African Americans and Latinos are more liberal than are whites on economic issues.
d. All of the above

6.5 *To what extent does public opinion influence public policy?*

13 The range of policy options acceptable to the public on a particular issue is the definition for which of the following concepts?
a. Zones of acquiescence
b. Latent opinion
c. Political efficacy
d. Political legitimacy

14 How would Professor James Stimson explain the relationship between public opinion and the policymaking process?
a. Elected officials can adopt whatever policies they want because most Americans are too uninformed about politics to know or care.
b. Policymakers must follow public opinion or risk being voted out of office.
c. Public opinion sets limits on policymakers, but within those limits policymakers are free to adopt policies of their choosing.
d. The public does not care what policies officials adopt, but if they turn out badly, the public punishes the officials by voting them out of office.

Answers: 1) a, 2) a, 3) c, 4) b, 5) d, 6) d, 7) b, 8) d, 9) b, 10) c, 11) c, 12) d, 13) a, 14) c

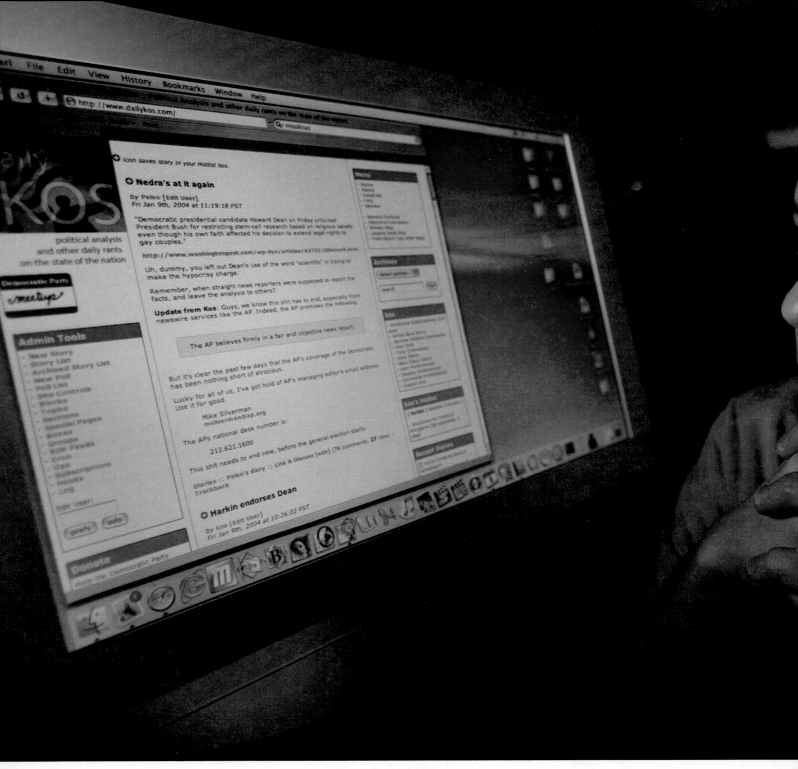

7 POLITICAL

FORMS OF PARTICIPATION

Learning Objective **7.1** How do individuals participate in the policy process?

PATTERNS OF PARTICIPATION

Learning Objective **7.2** What factors influence participation, and who tends to participate?

TRENDS IN VOTER TURNOUT

Learning Objective **7.3** How has voter turnout in the United States changed in recent elections, and how does it compare with turnout in other democracies?

DOES LOW TURNOUT MATTER?

Learning Objective **7.4** How do the patterns of participation in the United States affect public policies, and what can be done to increase participation?

The social media have enabled individual political activists to become increasingly influential participants in the policymaking process. Activists can use Twitter and Facebook updates to alert other activists about campaign developments or an impending vote in Congress. They can write weblogs to gather support for their points of view and advocate policy positions. They can e-mail lawmakers about pending legislative decisions and use Meetup to organize rallies to dramatize their position.

Social media activism has helped make Congress more polarized politically and thus less willing to make the compromises necessary to tackle major policy problems, such as the budget deficit. Because Republican activists are more conservative than the general Republican voter, they push their party's officials toward the right. Similarly, Democratic activists drive Democratic lawmakers in a liberal direction. These outside pressures make compromise less likely. Republican members of Congress who vote for a tax increase, for example, or Democrats who support cutting Social Security or Medicare can expect to be immediately

PARTICIPATION

attacked in their party's blogosphere and may be targeted for election defeat.[1]

Social media activism introduces this chapter on political participation. The chapter discusses voting and other forms of political participation in the United States. It examines why people participate and looks at patterns of participation. The chapter identifies recent trends in voter participation and compares turnout in the United States with participation rates in other democracies. It evaluates proposals for increasing participation and compares the policy perspectives of voters and non-voters.

FORMS OF PARTICIPATION

7.1 *How do individuals participate in the policy process?*

Political participation is an activity that has the intent or effect of influencing government action. Voting is the most common form of political participation. More than three-fourths of the respondents to the American National Election Studies (ANES) report casting ballots for president in 2008. (Reported turnout typically exceeds actual turnout because people do not want to admit to an interviewer that they neglected to vote.)[2]

Election turnout is closely related to the level of interest in a particular contest. Presidential races typically attract more voters on a percentage basis than other types of elections because of their high-profile nature. In contrast, voter turnout for congressional elections held in non-presidential (midterm) election years seldom exceeds 40 percent of the voting eligible population. The voter participation rate in the 2010 midterm election was 42 percent. Even though that was the highest midterm election turnout since 1970, the figure was substantially less than the turnout in the presidential election years of 2004 and 2008, which exceeded 60 percent of eligible adults.[3]

People participate in election contests in ways other than voting. Individuals who want to do more for a candidate or political party than just casting a ballot contribute money, prepare campaign mailers, telephone potential voters, put up yard signs, and work the polls on Election Day. Political participation is not only about elections. At any time, people may attempt to influence the policy process by writing, phoning, or e-mailing public officials. Surveys show that about a third of Americans have contacted public officials, usually at the state or local level.[4] (See figure below for rates of participation in other political activities.)

Americans also try to influence the policy process by joining or supporting interest groups. People interested in the reform of laws dealing with drunk driving join Mothers Against Drunk Driving (MADD), and opponents of gun control laws join the National Rifle Association (NRA).

Some Americans participate through unconventional political acts, such as protest demonstrations, sit-ins, or violence. Political movements, such as the Tea Party movement, often engage in protest demonstrations because they lack the organization to employ the political tactics typically associated with interest groups or political parties. A **political movement**

Is political violence every justified?

political participation an activity that has the intent or effect of influencing government action.

political movement a group of people that wants to convince other citizens and/or government officials to take action on issues that are important to the group.

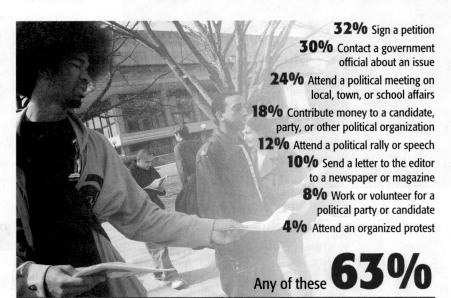

32% Sign a petition

30% Contact a government official about an issue

24% Attend a political meeting on local, town, or school affairs

18% Contribute money to a candidate, party, or other political organization

12% Attend a political rally or speech

10% Send a letter to the editor to a newspaper or magazine

8% Work or volunteer for a political party or candidate

4% Attend an organized protest

Any of these **63%**

Although voting is the most common form of political participation, it is not the only way that citizens participate in the policymaking process.

Source: Pew Internet & American Life Project, August 2008 Survey, available at http://www.pewinternet.org. Margin of error is +/−2%.

is a group of people that wants to convince other citizens and/or government officials to take action on issues that are important to the group. Some individuals and groups resort to violence to further their political cause, including bombing federal buildings and shooting physicians who perform abortions.

Sixteen percent of Americans reported attending a political rally or protest in the last year. Here, people participate in a pro-healthcare reform demonstration organized by the Service Employees International Union (SEIU).

PATTERNS OF PARTICIPATION

7.2 *What factors influence participation, and who tends to participate?*

ot all citizens participate politically, and participation rates vary among Americans in a number of ways.

Factors That Influence Participation

The most important factors influencing individual participation are personal resources, psychological engagement, voter mobilization, and community involvement.[5]

Personal Resources. The personal resources most closely associated with political participation are time, money, and civic skills, such as communication skills and organizational ability. Each form of political activity requires a different configuration of resources. People who want to contribute money to candidates and political parties must have financial resources. Individuals who work in campaigns or participate in political groups and activities must have both time and civic skills.[6] Participation rates are higher for activities that require relatively little time, few skills, and little or no expense. Voting is the most common form of political participation because it requires a relatively small amount of time and no expense. In contrast, relatively few people work in political campaigns or give money to

candidates because those activities require significant amounts of time, civic skills, and money.

Psychological Engagement. People take part in the policymaking process when they are knowledgeable, interested, and have a strong sense of political efficacy, or confidence that their participation can make a difference. People participate in political campaigns for candidates and parties in whom they are interested, contact public officials over issues about which they are knowledgeable, and join political groups whose causes they support. Individuals who believe that a particular government policy affects their personal welfare are more likely to participate.[7] For example, lower-income Social Security recipients are more likely to participate on that issue than are upper-income recipients, probably because they are more dependent financially on their Social Security checks.[8] In contrast, people who are uninformed or disinterested in politics are also usually uninvolved. Participation also depends on a sense of **political efficacy**, which is the extent to which individuals believe that they can influence the policymaking process.[9] People are more likely to participate when they

Voting is the **most common** form of political participation—it requires a **small amount of time** and **no expense.**

have confidence in their ability to affect the policy process and believe that policymakers are willing to accept their input.[10]

Voter Mobilization. Political participation depends on **voter mobilization**, the process of motivating citizens to vote. The likelihood that individuals will vote, participate in an election campaign, join a political group, or engage in some other form of political participation increases if those individuals are asked to participate.[11] Political parties encourage people to vote and volunteer for campaigns. Interest groups educate citizens about political issues and urge their involvement in the policy process. Door-to-door and live telephone

political efficacy the extent to which individuals believe they can influence the policymaking process.

voter mobilization the process of motivating citizens to vote.

contacts (as opposed to recorded messages) increase the likelihood that individuals will go to the polls, especially if the contacts take place near Election Day.[12]

Community Involvement. Finally, people participate politically because of their involvement in their communities. Individuals who have close community ties, such as homeownership and membership in community organizations, are more likely to participate. They regard voting and other forms of political participation as their civic duty because they can see the connection between participation and the quality of life in their community.[13]

think

Under what circumstances, if any, would you consider joining a protest demonstration?

Who Participates

Participation rates vary among individuals based on such factors as income, age, race/ethnicity, and gender.

Income. Affluence and activity go together for every form of political participation. The higher the family income, the more likely a person is to vote. According to the U.S. Census Bureau, the reported rate of voter turnout in 2008 for people in families earning more than $100,000 a year was 79.8 percent, compared with a turnout rate of 54 percent for people with family incomes less than $30,000.[14] The gap between high- and low-income groups is even greater for other types of participation. People who are well-off financially are more likely than low-income people to give money to candidates and parties, join organizations, contact public officials, and engage in political protests.[15] (See figure below.)

Participation rates and income are associated because resources and psychological attachment rise with income. Obviously, people in higher-income groups have more money to contribute to political causes. Because income and education are closely related, more affluent citizens are better informed about government and politics than are less wealthy individuals. They have better communication and organizational skills as well. Wealthy citizens are also more likely to have a relatively high level of political efficacy.

Age. Voter turnout is typically lowest for younger adults because they tend to have fewer resources

Reported Voting Turnout by Age Group 2008

18–24	49%
25–44	60%
45–64	69%
65–74	72%
75+	68%

Hip-hop personality Russell Simmons urges high school students to register to vote at a rally in New Jersey.

and are less interested in the policy process than older adults. As adults mature, their incomes increase and their skills develop. Older adults establish roots in their communities that increase their interest and awareness of the political process. Consequently, participation increases with each successive age group, with the peak voting years coming between 65 and 74 years of age. After age 75, voter participation begins to decline because illness and infirmity force the elderly to reduce their involvement in the policy process. The figure above shows reported voter participation rates by age group in the 2008 presidential election.

Race/Ethnicity. Participation varies among racial and ethnic groups. Voter turnout is higher for whites and African Americans; lower for Latinos and Asian Americans. The voter turnout in 2008 was 66 percent of eligible voters for whites, 65 percent for African Americans, 50 percent for Latinos, and 48 percent for Asian Americas.[16] (See figure on the following page.) Although the overall voter turnout in 2008 was up only slightly from 2004, minority voter turnout increased substantially, especially African American turnout. Whereas the number of whites who voted in 2008 was roughly the same as it was in 2004, two million more African Americans, two million more

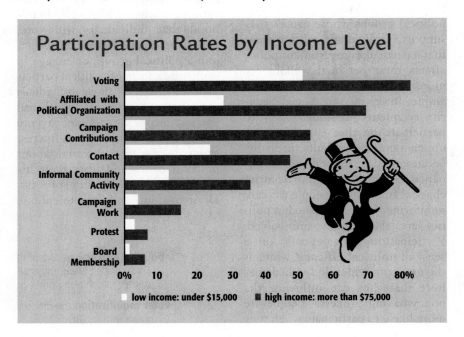

Participation Rates by Income Level

- Voting
- Affiliated with Political Organization
- Campaign Contributions
- Contact
- Informal Community Activity
- Campaign Work
- Protest
- Board Membership

0% 10 20 30 40 50 60 70 80%

□ low income: under $15,000   ■ high income: more than $75,000

Latinos, and 600,000 more Asian Americans participated in the 2008 election than took part in 2004. The historic candidacy of Barack Obama not only drew record numbers of African Americans to the polls but increased minority voter turnout in general.[17]

Nonetheless, voting rates of minority groups lag behind that of whites. Many members of racial/ethnic minority groups are ineligible to vote either because they are not citizens or are disqualified by criminal convictions. Only 8 percent of whites 18 years of age or older were unable to register and vote in 2008 because they were not citizens. The percentage of non-citizens among African Americans was 6 percent. It was 33 percent for Asian Americans and 37 percent for Latinos.[18] Meanwhile, 5.3 million Americans are disqualified from voting because they are incarcerated or have prior criminal convictions. Eleven states permanently disenfranchise individuals convicted of serious crimes. The policy of denying voting rights to criminal offenders disproportionately affects minority Americans, particularly African American males, 14 percent of whom are disenfranchised because of criminal convictions.[19]

Racial/ethnic patterns of participation also reflect the importance of recruitment to political participation. We would expect that participation rates for African American and Latino citizens would be lower than participation rates for whites because of income and age differences. As a

Reported Voting Turnout by Race 2008

white 66%
african american 65%
hispanic 50%
asian 48%

Minority voter turnout surged in 2008 in part because of the historic candidacy of Barack Obama. First-time voters (many of them young people and minorities) overwhelmingly supported Obama, 68 percent to 31 percent for McCain.

group, minority citizens are less affluent and younger than whites Nonetheless, participation rates for African Americans exceed expectations because of the effectiveness of organizations in the African American community, such as churches and political groups, at stimulating participation. Latino voter turnout, meanwhile, increases when Latino candidates are on the ballot.[20]

Gender. Women are more likely to vote than are men, but men are more likely to engage in many other forms of political participation. In 2008, 66 percent of women reported that they cast ballots compared with 62 percent of men.[21] Substantially more men than women are disquali-

fied from voting because of criminal convictions. Women are just as likely as men to participate in election campaigns, but they are less likely to contribute money to political campaigns, contact public officials, or join political organizations.[22]

These data reflect differences in resources and psychological engagement between men and women. Women on average have lower average incomes than do men. As you have read, income is closely associated with forms of participation other than voting. Furthermore, surveys indicate that men are more informed about and interested in politics and government than are women, even when they have the same level of education.[23]

TRENDS IN VOTER TURNOUT

7.3 *How has voter turnout in the United States changed in recent elections, and how does it compare with turnout in other democracies?*

Political scientists who study election participation measure voter turnout relative to the size of the **voting eligible population (VEP),** which is the number of residents who are legally qualified to vote. The VEP differs from the **voting age population (VAP),** which is the number of residents who are 18 years of age or older, because it excludes individuals who are ineligible to cast a ballot. In contrast to the VAP, the VEP does not include non-citizens, convicted criminals (depending on state law), and people who are mentally incapacitated.

voting eligible population (VEP) the number of U.S. residents who are legally qualified to vote.

voting age population (VAP) the number of U.S. residents who are 18 years of age or older.

States Adopt Voter ID Laws Just in Time for 2012 Election

Several states enacted voter ID laws during 2011, requiring prospective voters to prove their identity with a photo ID before casting a ballot. In Texas, for example, voters must present one of five acceptable forms of ID—a driver's license, military ID, passport, concealed handgun permit, or a special state-issued voter ID card provided free of charge by the state. College and university IDs are not permitted.[24] The supporters of voter ID legislation, almost all Republicans, believe that it is necessary to prevent fraud and enhance public confidence in the integrity of elections. In contrast, voter ID opponents, almost all Democrats, argue that it is designed to suppress the turnout of low-income and elderly voters who tend to vote Democratic.[25]

DISCUSSION

Why is voter ID such a big deal for Republicans? Many Republican activists as well as elected officials are firmly convinced that voter fraud is a serious problem in the United States, especially in minority communities. They believe that Democrats steal elections by busing unqualified voters to the polls. They argue that showing a photo ID to cast a ballot is not a major inconvenience. After all, people are routinely asked for a photo ID when they pay bills with a check, complete a bank transaction, or board an airplane. Why not require similar identification for something as important as voting?

Why are Democrats so adamantly opposed to voter ID laws? The Democrats believe that the Republicans push voter ID laws in order to suppress Democratic voter turnout. Many elderly low-income people, especially minority citizens who typically vote Democratic, do not have a driver's license or other forms of picture identification and may lack the means to travel to a state office to apply for a state-issued photo ID card. Furthermore, Democrats contend that there is no credible evidence that voter impersonation is a problem in American elections.

Are voter ID laws constitutional? In 2008, the U.S. Supreme Court upheld a legal challenge to Indiana's voter ID law. The Court held that states have a legitimate interest in ensuring the integrity of the election process and that a voter ID requirement placed a minimal burden on the right to vote.[26] Many of the more recent voter ID laws are more restrictive than the Indiana measure and will likely face legal challenges.

What effect have voter ID laws had in Indiana and other states that have had them for a while? Political scientists have researched the effect of voter ID laws. Although one study finds that voter ID reduces turnout by 3 to 4 percent, most studies find that the laws have no impact on voter participation. They also indicate that voter ID laws have no effect at reducing fraud or enhancing confidence in election procedures. Ironically, voter ID laws apparently have little impact on the electoral process despite the emotion surrounding their adoption.[27]

Voter Turnout in the United States

The figure below charts changes in presidential election turnout relative to the size of the VEP from 1964 through the 2008 election. More than 62 percent of the VEP cast ballots in the 1964 presidential election, capping a steady 36-year rise in voter turnout in the United States. For the next 30 years, voter participation rates generally fell, reaching a 70-year low in 1996 at 51.7 percent of the VEP. Election turnout subsequently rebounded, increasing to 54.2 percent in 2000, 60.3 percent in 2004, and 61.6 percent of in 2008.

Recent presidential elections suggest that the United States is experiencing a voting revival. The increase in voter turnout rates is the result of massive voter mobilization efforts coupled with high public interest in the recent elections. The two major political parties, supported by their interest group allies, organized sophisticated get-out-the-vote (GOTV) campaigns in 2004 and 2008. Campaign volunteers and paid organizers telephoned, mailed, e-mailed, or visited millions of potential voters, encouraging them to go to the polls. Exposure to intense campaign activity increases political engagement,

especially among low-income voters, a group with typically low voter turnout rates.[28] In the meantime, hot-button issues such as the war in Iraq and Afghanistan, gay marriage, healthcare reform, taxes, and the economy energized citizens to go to the polls. The percentage of Americans who told survey researchers that they closely follow national political news increased from 26 percent in 2000 to 43 percent in 2008.[29] People who are psychologically engaged are more likely to vote than people who are not.

> Recent presidential elections suggest that the **United States** is experiencing a **voting revival**.

Participation Rates in Comparative Perspective

Voting turnout in the United States is relatively low compared to other democracies. According to data collected by the International Institute for Democracy and Electoral Assistance, the United States lags behind most other countries in the world in electoral participation in national legislative elections. (See figure on the following page.)[30]

Political scientists identify three factors as primarily responsible for the United States having a lower voter turnout rate than do most other established democracies. First, American election procedures are more cumbersome than they are in most other democracies. Before Americans can cast a ballot in most states, they must register to vote, usually no later than 30 days before an election. In most other democracies, the government takes the initiative to register eligible voters. According to the U.S. Census Bureau, 29 percent of American citizens are not registered to vote. American elections traditionally take place on Tuesday, whereas other countries declare a national holiday so citizens can vote without missing work. The United States also holds more frequent elections and elects larger numbers of public officials. Many Americans stay home, confused by the length and complexity of the ballot.[31]

Second, voter participation rates in the United States are relatively low because the nation's political parties are weaker than those of other democracies. Strong political parties enhance voter turnout by educating citizens about candidates and issues, stimulating interest in election outcomes, and mobilizing citizens to go to the polls. Political scientist

Voter Turnout in Presidential Elections

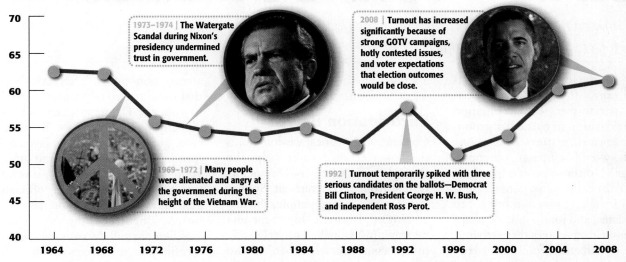

1973–1974 | The Watergate Scandal during Nixon's presidency undermined trust in government.

2008 | Turnout has increased significantly because of strong GOTV campaigns, hotly contested issues, and voter expectations that election outcomes would be close.

1969–1972 | Many people were alienated and angry at the government during the height of the Vietnam War.

1992 | Turnout temporarily spiked with three serious candidates on the ballots—Democrat Bill Clinton, President George H. W. Bush, and independent Ross Perot.

The 1964 presidential election capped a steady 36-year rise in voter turnout. For the next 30 years, voter participation rates declined, reaching a 70-year low in 1996. Election turnout has since rebounded, with 2008 having the highest turnout since 1968.

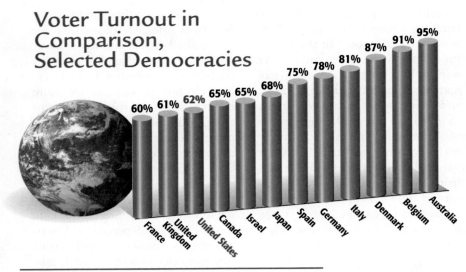

Voter Turnout in Comparison, Selected Democracies

France 60%
United Kingdom 61%
United States 62%
Canada 65%
Israel 65%
Japan 68%
Spain 75%
Germany 78%
Italy 81%
Denmark 87%
Belgium 91%
Australia 95%

Source: Institute for Democracy and Electoral Assistance, available at www.idea.int.

"I was just too busy."

The #1 reason Americans give for not voting is that they couldn't find the time.

G. Bingham Powell Jr. estimates that if American political parties were more centralized and had stronger ties to other social organizations, such as labor unions, religious bodies, and ethnic groups, then voter participation would rise by as much as 10 percent.[32] Labor unions in particular have an effect on voter turnout of low- and middle-income people.[33]

Finally, many citizens in the United States stay home from the polls because they do not perceive that elections have much impact on policy. Winning candidates may not be able to keep promises because of the separation of powers among the executive, legislative, and judicial branches of government. For example, during the 2006 election campaign, Democratic congressional candidates called for the withdrawal of American combat forces from Iraq. Even though the Democratic Party captured majorities in both the House and Senate, it could not keep its promise, either because proposals to bring home the troops failed to pass both chambers of Congress or because President George W. Bush vetoed them.

Ironically, Americans are at least as active as are the citizens of other countries when it comes to forms of political activity other than voting. People in the United States are more likely to engage in campaign activity, contact public officials, attend political meetings, and participate in non-political organizations than are people in other countries.[34] Political scientists have done relatively little research on the question of why participation rates for forms of political participation other than voting are greater in the United States than they are in other countries. Perhaps the best explanation is that Americans have more resources, including time, money, and civic skills, than people in other countries. As a group, Americans are better educated, more affluent, and more experienced at working in non-political groups such as clubs and religious institutions than the citizens of other democracies.[35]

DOES LOW TURNOUT MATTER?

7.4 *How do the patterns of participation in the United States affect public policies, and what can be done to increase participation?*

Does the low turnout of Americans, in particular the disparate rates of participation of participation of particular groups of Americans, matter? If everyone voted, would election outcomes change? Do those people who participate in campaigns, contact public officials, give money to candidates, and join political groups have issue preferences that are similar to all citizens? If political participation biases public policy toward candidates and policy preferences that are not shared by Americans as a whole, what, if anything, should we do about it?

Participation Bias

Conventional political wisdom holds that low election turnout helps the Republicans, whereas Democrats benefit from a large turnout. Studies indicate that young people, the unemployed, laborers, lower-income persons, individuals with relatively little formal education, people who are not married, Latinos, and people who seldom attend religious services are disproportionately represented among non-voters.[36] Surveys show that these groups of people also tend to vote for Democratic candidates more frequently than for Republicans. So, Democrats often favor reforming registration laws and other voting procedures to enhance voter turnout, and Republican officials generally oppose election law reform. Nonetheless, the 2004 election demonstrated that higher voter turnout does not necessarily benefit the Democratic Party. Even though the Kerry campaign increased the Democratic vote by 16 percent over

Compulsory voting is the legal requirement that citizens participate in national elections. It is a low-cost, efficient remedy to the problem of low turnout. Voter participation rates are almost 20 percent higher in nations with compulsory voting than they are in other democracies.[37] Almost everyone votes in Australia, a nation that has had compulsory voting since 1924. For example, voter turnout was 95 percent in the 2007 national election.[38]

The Australian Election Commission (AEC) enforces the nation's compulsory voting law. Election no-shows can either pay a fine or offer an explanation. The courts settle disputes between the AEC and individual non-voters over the validity of excuses. The proportion of Australians fined for failing to vote never exceeds 1 percent of the electorate.[39]

Political scientists believe that compulsory voting strengthens political parties. Because parties do not have to devote resources to turning out the vote, they can focus on persuasion and conversion. You have read that lower-income people are normally less likely to vote than middle-income citizens. So, compulsory voting also benefits political parties representing the working-class interests because lower-income people then vote at the same rate as middle-income citizens.

Australians who fail to turn out to vote may be fined for violating the nation's compulsory voting law.

QUESTIONS

1 Is non-voting such an important problem that it needs a legal remedy?

2 Would you resent or appreciate a compulsory voting law that forced you to cast a ballot or face a fine?

3 Do you think that the United States will ever adopt compulsory voting? Why or why not?

think
Does it really matter that many Americans do not vote?

Al Gore's showing in 2000, it was not enough, because the Republican presidential vote grew by 23 percent.[40]

Political scientists are skeptical that increased voter turnout would have much impact on the fortunes of either political party.[41] Many non-voters are disinterested and uninformed. Two-thirds of non-voters (compared with half of voters) see no difference between parties and candidates on the issues.[42] Furthermore, scholarly studies rarely uncover evidence that non-voters would have chosen a different president from the person actually elected.[43] Increased voter turnout will change the outcome of an election only when the election is closely fought, the increased turnout is relatively large in comparison with the normal electorate, and most of the new voters support the same candidate or party.[44] These three conditions are seldom met in American presidential politics and only occasionally met at the state and local level.

Research does, however, show a bias in political attitudes. Political activists are more conservative than is the population as a whole on economic issues. Compared with the general population, people who participate in the policy process are less likely to support government spending for public services, government help for minority groups, and programs to assist the poor. Individual campaign contributors tend to be more conservative and more Republican than is the electorate as a whole.[45] In sum, political activity underrepresents those people who favor government programs for disadvantaged groups and over-represents those who oppose them.[46] To the extent that elected officials respond to the demands of voters, public policies will be consistent with the interests of middle- and upper-income groups rather than the working class.

> **Political activists** *are more* **conservative** *than the population as a whole.*

Interest group and political party activities contribute to the participation bias as well. In the nineteenth and early twentieth centuries, the nation's most important interest groups were large membership organizations that drew people from all strata of society, rich and poor alike. These groups advocated government policies that benefited people across class lines, such as Social Security, Medicare, public schools, and programs for war veterans. Since the middle of the twentieth century, large membership organizations, such as labor unions, have declined, whereas professionally managed advocacy groups composed mainly of middle- and upper-middle class professionals have proliferated.

compulsory voting the legal requirement that citizens participate in national elections.

Voters use electronic touch screens in Miami, Florida. While electronic voting machines will prevent the problems Florida experienced in 2000 with its punch-card paper ballots, some worry about the potential for electoral fraud.

These groups push middle-class agendas.[47] Political parties contribute to the imbalance in participation rates as well by targeting their campaigns at people with voting histories. With rare exceptions, political campaigns focus on turning out their core supporters rather than trying to expand the electorate.[48]

Increasing Voter Turnout

Those observers who worry about low voter turnout favor the enactment of election law reforms to enhance participation rates. The Government Accountability Office (GAO), an investigative arm of Congress, recommends the adoption of the following three election procedures: 1) Registration deadlines that fall on or close to election day; 2) toll-free telephone numbers to allow voters to request absentee ballots; and 3) the increased use of mail balloting.[49] The state of Oregon has been using mail elections since the mid-1990s. Research indi-

cates that mail elections have increased election participation by 10 percent.[50] Some states have also begun experimenting with Internet voting. Seven states allow same-day registration, which means that citizens can register to vote on Election Day.

In 1993, Congress passed and President Clinton signed the **National Voter Registration Act (NVRA)**, which is also known as the Motor Voter Act. It is a federal law designed to make it easier for citizens to register to vote by requiring states to allow mail registration and provide an opportunity for people to register when renewing driver's licenses or visiting federal, state, or local agencies, such as welfare offices. The law also prohibited states from removing names from the voter registration rolls merely for failure to vote.

Although the NVRA dramatically increased the number of people registered to vote, it did not increase voter turnout. The NVRA helped add 11.5 million people to the voter rolls between January 1995, when states were required to implement the law, and November 1996. Nonetheless, the voter turnout rate hit a 70-year low in 1996. "You may be able to spoon-feed someone and make it almost automatic to get them registered," said one election official, "but if it takes that much effort just to get them registered, how do you expect them to take the initiative to actually come out and vote?"[51]

The NVRA failed to increase voter turnout in 1996 because it

think Should the United States reform its voting procedures to make it easier and more convenient for citizens to cast their ballots?

affected only the ease with which people can register. It did not make anyone more interested in politics or better informed about candidates and issues. The NRVA did not increase political efficacy or strengthen the efforts of political parties and groups to draw citizens to the polls. Voter registration reform alone is not sufficient to increase citizen participation in the electoral process.[52]

Nonetheless, the NRVA may have set the stage for the substantial increase in voter turnout that began with the 2000 presidential election by making the job of voter mobilization easier for the political parties and their interest group allies. The NRVA increased the voter registration rates of groups that traditionally turn out to vote in relatively low numbers, especially young people who tend to move frequently and often neglect to update their voter registration.[53] Consequently, the get-out-the-vote campaigns could focus on getting already registered people to the polls rather than having to spend valuable resources on extensive registration efforts.

National Voter Registration Act (NVRA)
a federal law designed to make it easier for citizens to register to vote; also known as the Motor Voter Act.

TAKE ✓ ACTION

Registering to Vote

Voting is a two-step process. Before Americans can vote, they must register. Registration is important because most people who register do subsequently vote. Your assignment is to learn how the voter registration process works in your state. You can obtain voter registration information from an office of county government, driver's license bureau, wel-

fare office, and some public libraries. Complete the voter registration card and submit it to your instructor to document that you have done the assignment. This may be your opportunity to register to vote. If you are not eligible to vote (you might not yet be 18 or are not an American citizen) or are already a registered voter, write VOID or DO NOT PROCESS on the card.

TAKING SIDES

Compulsory Voting

Should the U.S. government follow Australia's lead and mandate voting by law?

Should civic responsibility be a legal obligation?

OVERVIEW

Voter turnout in the United States is considerably lower than in most other industrialized democratic nations. According to the Institute for Democracy and Electoral Assistance, the United States averaged below 50 percent in voter turnout from 1945–2001,[54] while every country in the European Union averaged between 70 and 90 percent voter turnout.[55]

Voting affects policy. Nations with high voter turnout rates tend to adopt more labor-friendly policies. Who votes is also important because elected officials target their campaigns and policies to groups that vote. In the United States, people aged 18 to 24 make up 13 percent of the population, but only 9 percent of the voters, whereas people aged 65 to 74 represent 9 percent of the population, yet 11 percent of the voters. In recent elections, 49 percent of 18-to 24-year-olds cast ballots while 72 percent of 65- to 74-year-olds voted.[56] It's no wonder that the priorities of elected officials are much more focused on prescription drugs for the elderly than on the costs of college.

Some countries, such as Australia, have compulsory voting, which means that every citizen must cast a ballot or pay a fine. Australia has been mandating voting since 1924, and averages 95 percent turnout.[57] Some argue that the United States should consider mandatory voting as well.

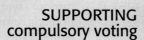

SUPPORTING compulsory voting

A functioning democratic republic requires participation from the people. If the United States is committed to being a democratic republic, then it should require citizens to engage in the political process just as it requires people to pay taxes. If the common good demands it, then the government coercing citizens to act is appropriate.

Representation is not representative with low voter turnout. Some groups are under-represented in the political process because of relatively low voter turnout. Forcing people to participate would in turn force elected officials to represent the interests of all groups in society.

Access to voting is a problem in the United States. Some states have registration and voting laws that make it difficult for people to vote, such as registration deadlines or inconvenient poll hours. The easing or elimination of these difficulties would ensure equal access to the polls for all citizens.

AGAINST compulsory voting

The United States is committed to individualism. To require someone to fulfill his or her civic duty would be an intrusion of the government on an individual's right to choose. Just because we have freedom of speech, for example, does not mean we have to speak.

State governments would be overburdened. State governments run and finance all the elections in the United States. Would states also be tasked with implementing compulsory voting, engaging law enforcement, and tracking and collecting fines?.

Not voting does not necessarily equal apathy. Choosing not to vote could signify satisfaction with the system and the status quo. In times of crisis, or when there's a particularly controversial issue on the ballot, turnout increases.

FORMS OF PARTICIPATION

7.1 *How do individuals participate in the policy process?*

Voting is the most common form of participation. People also participate in election campaigns, contact public officials, join interest groups, take part in protest demonstrations, or engage in unconventional acts, sometimes including violence.

PATTERNS OF PARTICIPATION

7.2 *What factors influence participation, and who tends to participate?*

The most important factors influencing individual participation are personal resources, psychological engagement, voter mobilization, and community involvement. Personal resources include time, money, and civic skills, such as communication skills and organizational ability. People take part in the policymaking process when they are knowledgeable, interested, and have a strong sense of political efficacy. Participation also depends on voter mobilization. Finally, people participate politically because of their involvement in the community.

Participation rates vary among individuals based on such factors as income, age, race/ethnicity, and gender. The higher the family income, the more likely a person will vote and participate in other ways. Voting participation increases with age until the latter years of life when participation declines because of ill health and infirmity. Voter participation rates are highest for whites and African Americans, but lower for Asian Americans and Latinos. Women are more likely to vote than men, but men are more likely to engage in other forms of participation.

TRENDS IN VOTER TURNOUT

7.3 *How has voter turnout in the United States changed in recent elections, and how does it compare with turnout in other democracies?*

Political scientists who study election participation measure voter turnout relative to the size of the voting eligible population (VEP), which is the number of U.S. residents who are legally qualified to vote. Rates of voter participation fell from 1968 through the 1996 election, but they have subsequently rebounded because of sophisticated voter mobilization campaigns coupled with increased public interest.

Voter participation rates in the United States are relatively low compared with turnout rates in many other democracies because American election procedures are relatively cumbersome, political parties and interest groups are relatively weak, and many citizens do not perceive that elections have much effect on public policy.

DOES LOW TURNOUT MATTER?

7.4 *How do the patterns of participation in the United States affect public policies, and what can be done to increase participation?*

People who participate in the policy process are more conservative than is the population as a whole on economic issues. Compared with the general population, political activists are less likely to support government spending for public services, government help for minority groups, and programs to assist the poor. Those observers who worry about low voter turnout favor the enactment of election law reforms to enhance participation rates, including streamlined registration procedures, easy access to absentee ballots, and mail voting.

MySearchLab®

7.1 *How do individuals participate in the policy process?*

1 Which of the following is the most common form of political participation?
   a. Contributing money to candidates
   b. Joining an interest group
   c. Contacting an elected official
   d. Voting

2 For which election will turnout be higher as a proportion of eligible voters—a presidential election or a local election for mayor?
   a. The presidential election, because interest will probably be greater in that contest.
   b. The presidential election, because more people are eligible to vote for president than are eligible to vote for mayor.
   c. The local election for mayor, because local officials have a more direct impact on the lives of ordinary people.
   d. Turnout will be the same for each type of election.

7.2 *What factors influence participation, and who tends to participate?*

3 Which of the following is a reasonable explanation why more people vote than volunteer to work in a political campaign?
   a. Voting requires less time and effort than volunteer work.
   b. Voting has a greater impact on the outcome of an election than volunteer work.
   c. Most political campaigns don't want volunteer help because they prefer to rely on professional campaign consultants.
   d. None of the above

4 Is political efficacy related to political participation?
   a. No. People vote out of civic duty regardless of other factors.
   b. Yes. People who think they can impact government policies are more likely to participate than are other people.
   c. Yes. People who express a high level of trust in public officials are more likely to vote than are people who do not trust the government to do what is right.
   d. No. One vote seldom impacts the outcome of an election.

5 Would you expect the average voter turnout rate to be higher for people earning $80,000 or $30,000 a year?
   a. Turnout would be the same for both groups.
   b. Turnout would be greater for the higher-income group.
   c. Turnout would be greater for the lower-income group.
   d. Turnout would be greater for the higher-income group in all elections but presidential elections, where the turnout rate would be the same.

6 What is the relationship between age and political participation?
   a. Participation rates fall as people age.
   b. Participation rates increase as people age.
   c. Participation increases through middle age and then gradually declines throughout the last half of the individual lifespan.
   d. Participation rates increase until individuals reach old age and then turn downward.

7 Which of the following groups is the least represented in all areas of political participation compared with the other groups?
   a. Latinos
   b. Whites
   c. African Americans
   d. The groups participate at roughly the same rate.

8 Voter turnout increased for which of the following racial/ethnic groups in 2008 compared with 2004?
   a. Turnout increased for all groups in roughly the same proportion.
   b. Turnout increased for whites and African Americans, but declined for other groups.
   c. Turnout increased for African Americans while holding steady for all other groups.
   d. Turnout increased for African Americans, Asian Americans, and Latinos, but not for whites.

9 Which of the following groups is most seriously impacted by state laws that disqualify individuals with serious criminal offenses from voting?
   a. White women
   b. Latino males
   c. African American males
   d. White males

7.3 *How has voter turnout in the United States changed in recent elections, and how does it compare with turnout in other democracies?*

10 Why is the voting age population (VAP) an imperfect database to measure voter participation?
   a. The census has a fairly accurate count of the population, but measures of the population by age group are imprecise.
   b. Voter turnout numbers are often inaccurate.
   c. The VAP includes large numbers of people who are not eligible to vote, including non-citizens and people who are incarcerated.
   d. All of the above

11 Which of the following statements best describes recent trends in voter turnout?
   a. Voter turnout in presidential elections has been falling consistently since the early 1960s.
   b. Voter turnout in presidential elections has been rising consistently since the early 1960s.
   c. Voter turnout in presidential elections has fallen in each of the last three presidential elections.
   d. Voter turnout in presidential elections has increased in each of the last three presidential elections.

12 Which of the following factors accounts for the United States having a lower voter turnout rate than in many other democracies?
   a. American political parties are relatively weak.
   b. The United States has a relatively cumbersome voter registration system.
   c. American labor unions are relatively weak.
   d. All of the above

13 Which of the following statements about compulsory voting in Australia is true?
   a. People who do not vote in Australia can go to jail for as much as a year.
   b. Voter turnout in Australia is much higher than it is in the United States.
   c. Political scientists believe that compulsory voting in Australia harms working class parties because it weakens the advantage labor unions enjoy in turning out their vote.
   d. All of the above

7.4 *How do the patterns of participation in the United States affect public policies, and what can be done to increase participation?*

14 Political activists are more likely than is the population as a whole to favor which of the following policies?
   a. Programs that benefit minority groups
   b. Programs that assist the poor
   c. Increased spending for public services
   d. None of the above

15 What impact did the National Voter Registration Act have on participation?
   a. It failed to increase registration rates or voter turnout.
   b. It succeeded in increasing both voter registration rates and voter turnout.
   c. It succeeded in increasing voter registration rates, but had no immediate effect on voter turnout.
   d. It failed to increase voter registration rates, but it increased voter turnout by spreading awareness of election issues.

Answers: 1) d, 2) a, 3) a, 4) b, 5) b, 6) d, 7) a, 8) d, 9) c, 10) c, 11) d, 12) d, 13) b, 14) d, 15) c

8 THE NEWS

THE MEDIA LANDSCAPE

Learning Objective **8.1** How is the media landscape in the United States changing?

GOVERNMENT REGULATION OF THE NEWS MEDIA

Learning Objective **8.2** What is the relationship between the government and the media?

MANAGING THE MEDIA

Learning Objective **8.3** How do politicians attempt to influence the tone and content of media coverage?

MEDIA BIAS

Learning Objective **8.4** Are the media biased?

THE MEDIA AND PUBLIC POLICYMAKING

Learning Objective **8.5** What is the role of the media in the policymaking process?

Where do you get most of your news about the 2012 presidential election? If you answered CNN or MSNBC, the chances are that you are a Democrat. If you said Fox or talk radio, you are probably a Republican.[1]

Before the Internet and cable TV, the three television networks dominated the news audience, capturing 90 percent of viewers.[2] Now, there are more options. People who do not care about politics can avoid the news altogether in favor of sports and entertainment. Political junkies, meanwhile, can stay with network news or tune to a cable station devoted to news and information. More and more, Americans are choosing media outlets that reflect their points of view. Although members of both political parties have been shifting to friendly news sources, the Republican switch is more striking. Journalism professor Barry Hollander puts it this way:

MEDIA

"Republicans have dramatically dropped news sources that they perceive as being biased against their position."[3]

The polarization of the media contributes to the polarization of American politics. The partisan media present extreme views because they attract higher ratings than moderate voices. People who get their news from the partisan media are given facts and interpretations of facts that confirm their own biases.[4]

They learn not only that they are right and the other side wrong, but that the other side is badly motivated, perhaps even willing to crash the economy in hopes it will enable them to capture the White House. Compromise between the political parties becomes difficult because many party activists see compromise as an agreement with the devil.[5]

Media polarization introduces our discussion on the place of the media in

the policymaking environment. The chapter begins by describing the news media in the United States and discussing how the media are changing. It examines the relationship between the government and the media. It explores the attempts of candidates and officeholders to shape news coverage and examines the question of media bias. Finally, the chapter assesses the role of the media in public policymaking.

THE MEDIA LANGUAGE LANDSCAPE

 8.1 *How is the media landscape in the United States changing?*

The news media are changing because of consolidation and the emergence of new media.

Media Ownership and Consolidation

In contrast to much of the world, direct government ownership of media outlets in the United States is relatively limited. The federal government operates the Armed Forces Radio and Television Service, which provides news and entertainment to members of the U.S. armed forces worldwide. Many local governments, including cities, schools, and colleges, operate cable television stations. City governments may use their cable television channels to air city council meetings and other public service programming. Universities and colleges sometimes operate radio stations.

The Corporation for Public Broadcasting is a government agency chartered and funded by the U.S. government with the goal of promoting public broadcasting. It provides some funding for both the Public Broadcasting Service (PBS) and National Public Radio (NPR), private non-profit media services. Public radio and television stations also benefit from corporate donations and financial contributions from the general public. PBS and NPR regularly interrupt their programming to ask their viewers and listeners to pledge their financial support.

Private businesses, often large corporations, own and operate most media outlets in the United States. Most **print media** (newspapers and magazines) and **broadcast media** (television and radio) outlets are part of large chains. Consolidation is an important trend in media ownership. The 10 largest newspaper groups control a majority of newspaper circulation in the nation. Most television stations belong to national networks, such as CBS, NBC, ABC, Fox, Univision, WB, or UPN. Clear Channel Communication and Cumulus Media own hundreds of radio stations, including many in the same city.[6]

Cross-media ownership is common as well, in which one corporation owns several types of media. For example, the Tribune Company, the parent company of the *Chicago Tribune* and *Los Angeles Times*, owns and operates 10 daily newspapers, 23 major-market television stations, several radio stations, and more than 50 websites.[7]

The major goal of news media outlets is to attract as large an audience as possible. Advertising rates in newspapers and magazines, on television and on the radio, and even

print media newspapers and magazines.

broadcast media television and radio.

Rupert Murdoch is the chairman, CEO, and founder of News Corporation, the world's second largest media conglomerate. He appeared before a committee of the British Parliament along with his son, James Murdoch, to apologize for the actions of News Corporation reporters who were accused of hacking the phones of accident and crime victims.

AROUND THE WORLD — Government Control of the Media in Cuba

The Cuban government owns the electronic media and tightly controls its content. Foreign news agencies are forced to hire local journalists through government offices if they wish to cover news stories in Cuba. Independent journalists are subject to harassment, detention, and physical attacks. Journalists found guilty of publishing anti-government propaganda or of insulting government officials can be sentenced to long prison terms. According to Reporters Without Borders, an international non-profit organization that advocates freedom of the press, 25 journalists were held in Cuban prisons in poor conditions in 2009.[8]

The Cuban government attempts to control Internet access by banning private Internet connections. As a result, less than 2 percent of the Cuban population has Internet access. People who want to surf the web or check their e-mail must go to Internet cafés, universities, or other public sites where their activities can be closely monitored with software installed to alert police whenever it spots "subversive" words. Cuban residents who write articles critical of the Cuban government for foreign websites are subject to 20-year prison terms.[9]

The U.S. government attempts to break the Cuban government's monopoly on information with Radio Martí, which broadcasts in Spanish from transmitters in Miami, Florida. However, the Cuban government typically jams the Radio Martí broadcasts throughout the island, so its effectiveness is questionable.

QUESTIONS

1 Can a country be a democracy without a free press? Why or why not?

2 Is it ever appropriate for a government to manage the news media?

3 Should the United States continue to fund Radio Martí?

Young Cubans cheer for a singer protesting against Cuban police methods at a rally.

---

online depend on the size and strength of the audience. Therefore television networks and big city newspapers aim to attract as large an audience as possible. They cover mainstream news from a middle-of-the-road perspective, with an eye to entertainment value by highlighting dramatic events and celebrities. Stories about Tiger Woods get more coverage than do in-depth analyses of budget policy. Reports on crime, traffic accidents, and severe weather dominate local news to the near exclusion of serious coverage of local policy issues. Other media outlets try to build a niche audience by targeting audiences based on political philosophy, issue focus, or religious values. These groups cater largely to only one viewpoint or set of ideas, and therefore encourage selective rather than comprehensive exposure to issues. Consumers can find a set

of websites, blogs, radio talk shows, magazines, and television shows that all reinforce their point of view.

Media consolidation impacts news coverage. Because of chain ownership, newspaper stories written for the *New York Times* or *Washington Post* may appear in local newspapers around the nation in identical form. In any given week, both *Time* and *Newsweek* may feature the same cover story. Meanwhile, local radio and television stations rely on network news feeds for national news. As a result, news outlets around the country tend to focus on the same handful of national stories each day, often told

think — What effect might media consolidation have on the content of the news you consume?

from the same perspective and sometimes in the same words. Because of staff reductions, local media outlets focus on national election coverage than rather than state and local contests.[10]

The Rise of New Media

The media landscape is changing. Many mainstream media outlets, especially newspapers, newsmagazines, and the network evening news, have been in decline for years, at least in terms of circulation and ratings. Between 2001 and 2008, daily newspaper circulation fell by 13.5 percent; Sunday newspaper circulation dropped by 17.3 percent. Newspaper circulation fell by an additional 10 percent in 2009 alone.[11] Circulation for the "big three" newsmagazines (*Time*, *Newsweek*, and *U.S. News*) is falling, with readership down by a third since 1994. In fact, one of the big three, *U.S. News*, ceased publishing as a weekly, converting to a monthly. Ratings for the network evening news and morning news shows are in a long decline as well. Over the past 25 years, the combined audience for the network evening news has fallen on average by a million viewers a year.[12]

While traditional media sources are losing readers, listeners, and watchers, the **new media**, which is a term used to refer to alternative media sources, such as the Internet, cable television, and satellite radio, are growing in importance. Young people in particular are turning away from traditional media sources in favor of the new media.[13] Fox News, CNN, and MSNBC offer news coverage around the clock. Radio talk shows offer news and opinion much of the day. In the meantime, anyone with a computer can create a website, write a blog, post a YouTube video, sign up for a Twitter account, or create a Facebook page.

The figure below shows the relative importance of news media sources in 2000 and 2008. As the figure shows, traditional media sources (newspapers, radio, and network TV) declined in importance between the two years, whereas new media sources (cable TV and the Internet) grew in importance. In 2000, the most important news sources were local TV news, followed by newspapers and radio news. In 2008, local TV news continued to lead, but cable TV news and the Internet emerged as the second and third most important sources for news.

Although online news sources vary considerably in quality and credibility, some of them have become important sources of information. The Matt Drudge website, the Drudge Report, was the first media source to break the news about the relationship between White House intern Monica Lewinsky and President Bill Clinton. Blogs in particular are important opinion outlets. In fact, liberal bloggers have become such an important source of opinion leadership in the Democratic Party that presidential candidates hired bloggers to write for their campaign websites during the 2008 election campaign.

Candidates and elected officials have adapted to the new media environment by using the Internet for communication and fundraising. Most candidates for office and most elected officials have a basic webpage with pictures, a biography, issue positions, and, for candidates, a

> **Young people** in particular are turning away from **traditional media** sources in favor of the **new media.**

new media alternative media sources, such as the Internet, cable television, and satellite radio.

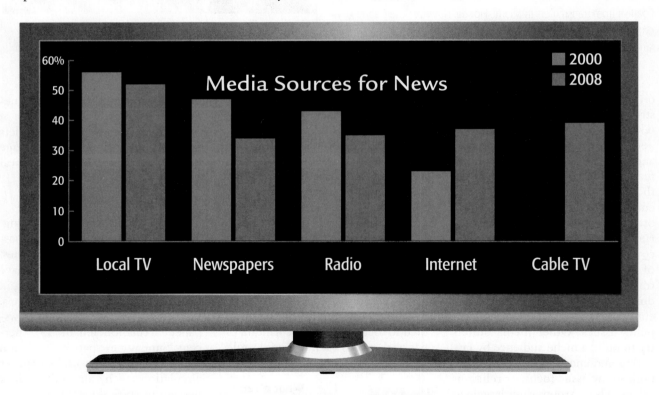

Media Sources for News

| | 2000 | 2008 |

Local TV   Newspapers   Radio   Internet   Cable TV

Today, more Americans get their national and international news from the Internet than from traditional newspapers. For young people, the Internet now rivals television as their predominant source of news, with 59 percent of Americans under 30 saying they get most of their news online.

Source: Pew Research Center for the People & the Press, available at http://people-press.org

fundraising link that accepts major credit cards. Technologically sophisticated candidates and officeholders go beyond a basic Internet site by utilizing the full array of social media.

No politician uses technology more effectively than Barack Obama. In 2008, the Obama campaign created an e-mail list of more than 13 million addresses. The most popular Obama Facebook page had 6.4 million supporters. Obama used his online network to deliver campaign messages, organize volunteers, and raise money. The Obama campaign broke all fundraising records by collecting more than half a billion dollars from three million online donors.[14] After becoming president, Obama used his online network to organize support for his legislative initiatives and appointments. In 2009, for example, the White House used its e-mail list to mobilize support for Sonia Sotomayor, the president's nominee to serve on the U.S. Supreme Court. Vice President Joe Biden e-mailed Obama supporters,

asking them to sign an online petition in support of Sotomayor. Visitors to Obama's webpage could e-mail their senators about the nomination without leaving the site.[15]

Technology enables candidates and officeholders to communicate directly with their supporters without having to go through a news media filter. Social media in particular have the ability to engage campaign supporters because they are immediate, targeted, and interactive. Political consultant Matt Glazer says that the value of the social media is to turn casual supporters into informed supporters, and informed supporters into donors and volunteers.[16]

The emergence of the new media has also helped produce the 24-hour news cycle, or round-the-clock news reporting. Cable television and the Internet allow for immediate reporting and continuous updating of a news story. Major stories that used to take days or weeks to develop now unfold in a matter of hours.

During his campaign, Barack Obama's savvy use of technology and new media helped him build and mobilize a network of supporters. As president, he is rarely seen without his BlackBerry.

Politics and the Internet

1991 High Performance Computing and Communication Act of 1991 (sponsored by then Senator Al Gore) leads to the Information Superhighway.

1998 MoveOn.org is founded as a news source and fundraiser for liberal causes.

2003 Howard Dean's campaign depends on online giving and makes extensive use of Meetup to organize volunteers.

2005 Bloggers expose fraudulent documents in a CBS News report on George W. Bush, leading to Dan Rather's resignation.

2010 Senator Scott Brown (R-MA) wins in Massachusetts with the help of a smartphone app called Walking Edge, which uses Google maps to show where undecided voters and supporters live.

| 1990 | 1992 | 1994 | 1996 | 1998 | 2000 | 2002 | 2004 | 2006 | 2008 | 2010 |

1998 The online Drudge Report breaks the news of President Bill Clinton's affair with intern Monica Lewinsky.

2004 Rock the Vote launched, registering an estimated 1.2 million new voters.

2008 Obama's website collects $500 million in political contributions during the 2008 campaign.

2006 Senator George Allen's (R-VA) racial gaff goes viral on the new video-sharing website, YouTube, leading to his electoral defeat.

The importance of the Internet has grown over the last two decades, not just for politicians but also for citizens and journalists

GOVERNMENT REGULATION
OF THE NEWS MEDIA

As discussed in Chapter 4, the U.S. Constitution guarantees freedom of the press. "Congress shall make no law," declares the First Amendment, "abridging the freedom of speech, or of the press." As a result, the news media enjoy broad freedom to report the news, even news that is critical of the government.

The FCC and Broadcast Media

Congress created the **Federal Communications Commission (FCC)** in 1939 to regulate the broadcast media using the public airwaves. The Supreme Court has allowed government regulation of these media, despite the First Amendment, because the public airwaves spectrum is limited.[17] FCC regulation of broadcast frequency and transmission power ensures that stations do not

The FCC fined CBS $550 million for Janet Jackson's "wardrobe malfunction" during the 2004 Super Bowl halftime show.

interfere with one another. The FCC has no authority to regulate cable TV, satellite radio, or the Internet.

In recent years, the FCC has adopted a more aggressive approach to regulating indecency. For example, the FCC fined CBS for Janet Jackson's "wardrobe malfunction" during the 2004 Super Bowl halftime show. Congress subsequently passed legislation to allow the FCC to impose fines as high as $325,000 for each violation of its decency standard.[18] Howard Stern, a radio talk show host famous for off-color remarks and sexual humor, moved his syndicated broadcast radio show to Sirius Satellite Radio to escape FCC scrutiny.

Some media observers favor greater government regulation of the broadcast media, particularly in regard to political neutrality. They want Congress or the FCC to reenact the **Fairness Doctrine**, which was an FCC regulation requiring broadcasters to present controversial issues of public importance in an honest, equal, and balanced manner. The FCC repealed the Fairness Doctrine in 1987, arguing that it inhibited rather than enhanced public debate and that it appeared to violate the First Amendment. The proponents of the Fairness Doctrine believe that it is needed to provide for the public discussion of controversial issues and to ensure that all voices are heard. In contrast, critics of the Fairness Doctrine argue that it inhibits free speech because broadcasters sometimes will not discuss controversial political issues because they want to avoid having to provide free airtime for opposing views. Fur-

thermore, they say, the Fairness Doctrine is unnecessary because the proliferation of media outlets, including Internet websites and blogs, ensures broad exposure to all sorts of competing points of view.

Reporters and Confidential Sources

Journalists frequently base their stories on information received from confidential sources, typically government officials who request that their identities be kept secret. Reporters honor the request because they know that their information sources will dry up if they cannot maintain their anonymity. The issue of confidential sources becomes especially troublesome if the reporter has information that may be relevant in a criminal prosecution or may impact national security. In 2005, for example, a federal judge ordered Judith Miller, a *New York Times* reporter, jailed for contempt of court for refusing to reveal her information source in the investigation of who illegally leaked the information that Valerie Plame was a covert Central Intelligence Agency (CIA) agent.

A **shield law** is a statute that protects journalists from being forced to disclose confidential information in a legal proceeding. A majority of states have enacted shield laws, but the federal government has

Federal Communications Commission (FCC) government agency that regulates the broadcast media using the public airwaves.

Fairness Doctrine an FCC regulation repealed in 1987 that required broadcasters to present controversial issues of public importance in "an honest, equal, and balanced manner."

shield law a statute that protects journalists from being forced to disclose confidential information in a legal proceeding.

not.[19] The proponents of shield laws believe that they protect the public's right to know. Without shield laws, confidential sources would hesitate to reveal government inefficiency and corruption to reporters for fear that they will lose their jobs when their identities are revealed. In

Do you favor or oppose the adoption of shield laws?

contrast, the opponents of shield laws argue that journalists should not be above the law. They should be required to appear in court and present evidence just like other citizens.

A **majority of states** have enacted shield laws, but the **federal government has not**.

MANAGING THE MEDIA

8.3 *How do politicians attempt to influence the tone and content of media coverage?*

Campaign organizations attempt to manage news coverage to present their candidates in the most positive light. Indeed, the presidential campaigns of Reagan in 1980 and 1984 and George H.W. Bush in 1988 were the prototype of campaign control of news media coverage. The Reagan–Bush strategy, which most campaigns now attempt to copy, was based on several principles. First, campaign managers choose a single theme to emphasize each campaign day, such as crime, the environment, or defense. If the candidate and the members of the candidate's team address the same issue and only that issue, the news media will be more likely to focus on that issue in their daily campaign reports.

Second, the campaign selects an eye-catching visual backdrop for its candidate that reemphasizes the theme of the day, such as the Statue of Liberty, a retirement home, or a military base. In 1988, George H.W. Bush even staged a campaign event in a factory that made American flags. Campaign organizers try to ensure that everyone in the audience is friendly so that television images convey the impression of popular support. When President George W. Bush ran for reelection in 2004, he typically appeared at invitation-only rallies to ensure that news reports would be filled with pictures of smiling faces and cheering crowds.

Finally, campaign managers carefully brief the candidate to stick with the campaign script. Each speech includes one or two carefully worded phrases that can be used as sound bites on the evening news. A **sound bite** is a short phrase taken from a candidate's speech by the news media for use on newscasts. "Read my lips," said Bush in 1988, "no new taxes." Candidates who lack discipline or who are prone to gaffes distract from their own message.

Once in office, elected officials establish sophisticated communications operations to manage the news. The George W. Bush administration's communications strategy attempted to tie policy, politics, and communications together. Professor Bruce Miroff says that the Bush administration depicted the war in Iraq as if it were a professional wrestling match in which the audience (the American people) watched the good guy (President Bush) overpower the bad guy (Saddam Hussein). President Bush declared victory on May 1, 2003, after landing in a jet on the deck of the aircraft carrier *Abraham Lincoln*. Bush, dressed in a green flight suit, used the aircraft carrier as a stage to announce that combat operations in Iraq were over. A large banner over the president's head read "Mission Accomplished."[20]

President Obama used the media in an effort to shape the public debate over healthcare reform legislation by giving five back-to-back interviews on a single day to network correspondents. The interviews, which aired on CNN, NBC, ABC, CBS, and Univision on the same Sunday in September 2009, were remarkably similar, with Obama making the same points, often in the same words, to each reporter.

President Bush used an aircraft carrier as a backdrop to declare "mission accomplished" and victory in the War in Iraq.

sound bite a short phrase taken from a candidate's speech by the news media for use on newscasts.

Obama's goal was to counter criticism of healthcare reform and build support for its adoption.[21]

Candidates and officeholders do not always succeed in managing the media. The proliferation of media outlets along with the emergence of new communications technologies such as YouTube and blogging increases the likelihood that candidate bloopers will be caught on tape and broadcast widely. Events sometimes overwhelm an officeholder's communications strategy. Hurricane Katrina, for example, was a communications catastrophe for the George W. Bush administration. Rather than interrupt his vacation to address the crisis, President Bush left Secretary of Homeland Security Michael Chertoff in charge. While television viewers saw images of thousands of people stranded on roofs and huddled in the New Orleans Superdome, Chertoff declared his pleasure with the response of the federal government to the disaster. When President Bush finally arrived in the region, several days after the hurricane struck, his rhetoric seemed out of touch with the reality in New Orleans. "Brownie," he said to Federal Emergency Management Administration (FEMA) Director Michael Brown, "you're doing a heck of a job."[22]

On July 16, 2010, BP executives Carl-Henric Svanberg, Tony Hayward, Robert Dudley, and Lamar McKay made a brief statement to the media outside of the White House at President Obama's request. Their "perp walk" was in response to the oil spill in the Gulf of Mexico.

MEDIA BIAS

8.4   *Are the media biased?*

Objective journalism is a style of news reporting that focuses on facts rather than opinion, and presents all sides of controversial issues. Major newspapers, broadcast television news, and the major cable news networks pride themselves on their commitment to objective journalism. The trademark slogan for Fox News is "fair and balanced." Even though newspapers endorse candidates on their editorial page, the ideal of objective journalism is that candidate endorsements have no impact on the content or tone of their news coverage.

Nonetheless, most Americans believe that the media are biased. According to a 2009 survey conducted by the Pew Center for the People & the Press, 60 percent of Americans think that the press is politically biased. Sixty-three percent believe that stories in the media are often inaccurate, 74 percent think that media stories tend to favor one side, and 74 percent say that the media are influenced by powerful people and organizations. People who identify with the Republican Party are more critical and less trusting of the media than are Democrats and independents.[23]

Research suggests that media sources may indeed play favorites. The network evening news treats Democratic candidates more favorably than it does Republicans. The Democratic candidate for president enjoyed more favorable coverage on the network evening news than did the Republican candidate in three of the five presidential elections from 1998 through 2004. Coverage was balanced in the other two elections. In 2004,

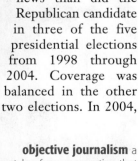

"We know that polls are just a collection of statistics that reflect what people are thinking in 'reality.' And reality has a well-known liberal bias.**"**

Stephen Colbert, popular host of the mock-news show, *The Colbert Report*. Colbert coined the term "truthiness," which he uses to describe things that a person claims to know intuitively or "from the gut" without regard to evidence, logic, intellectual examination, or facts.

objective journalism a style of news reporting that focuses on facts rather than opinion, and presents all sides of controversial issues.

for example, 57 percent of the network news reports on Democratic presidential candidate John Kerry were positive compared with 37 percent of the news reports on President George W. Bush.[24] Similarly, a study of 2008 election coverage conducted by the Pew Research Center's Project on Excellence in Journalism found that press coverage of John McCain's presidential campaign was more negative than was coverage of the Obama campaign. The study, which examined campaign stories from 48 news outlets, categorized the tone of 57 percent of the stories on McCain as negative compared with 14 percent that were positive in tone and 29 percent that were neutral. In contrast, the tone of Obama coverage was more closely balanced between positive (36 percent), neutral (35 percent), and negative (29 percent) stories.[25]

Nonetheless, scholars have no evidence that news coverage affects election outcomes. Kerry lost the 2004 election, for example, despite receiving more favorable network news coverage than Bush. As we have noted, survey research indicates that many voters distrust the accuracy of media reports and suspect a media bias. If voters do

not trust what the media have to say, they are unlikely to be swayed by bias. Furthermore, citizens have more news sources available to them than just the network news, including newspapers, radio, Internet websites, and cable television. Fox News coverage of the 2004 presidential election was decidedly Bush-friendly. Fifty-three

Bad news is now the **dominant theme** of political news coverage.

percent of Fox News stories on the president were positive compared with only 21 percent of the Kerry stories.[26] In practice, news consumers often choose media sources that match their political predispositions. Whereas Democrats regularly watch TV network news and CNN, Republicans prefer Fox.[27] (See figure below.)

You Are What You Watch—Selective Viewing

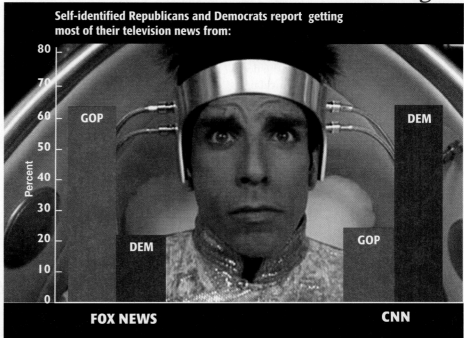

Self-identified Republicans and Democrats report getting most of their television news from:

People tend to seek out media sources that reinforce their own points of view. Republicans prefer news from the more conservative Fox News, and Democrats prefer watching the more liberal CNN.

Source: Pew Research Center for the People & the Press. http://pewresearch.org

TAKE ✓ ACTION
News and Information Exposure

How varied are the online sources you visit for information and opinion? Your assignment is to create an annotated inventory of online sites in each of the below categories. For each entry, indicate the name of the site, give its URL, and describe it. Compare your list with your classmates to expand the breadth of sites you go to for news and political information:

• National news source that practices objective journalism;
• State and local news source that practices objective journalism;
• Political commentary, combining news and opinion; and
• Issue-oriented website that focuses on a particular issue, either objectively or subjectively.

Political science research has also identified media biases that are not based on party affiliation or political ideology. Research on Senate races has found that newspapers tend to slant the information on their news pages to favor the candidate endorsed by the paper on its editorial page, regardless of that candidate's party affiliation.[28] Furthermore, studies show that the press is biased against presidential incumbents (current officeholders), without regard for party and ideology. All recent presidents, Democrats and Republicans alike, received more negative press coverage than did their opponents when they ran for reelection.[29]

In addition, the press has grown increasingly negative overall. Since the 1960s, bad news has increased by a factor of three and is now the dominant theme of national political news coverage. Thirty years ago, press coverage of public affairs emphasized the words of newsmakers and stressed the positive. The press grew more critical during the 1970s as journalists began to counter the statements of government officials rather than just report them. By the late 1970s, the focus of the Washington, D.C press corps was **attack journalism**, which is an approach to news reporting in which journalists take an adversarial attitude toward candidates and elected officials. Reporters decided to critically examine the actions of newsmakers, countering the statements of public officials with the responses of their critics and adversaries.[30] As a result, campaign coverage has grown negative. In 1960, 75 percent of press references to both major party presidential candidates (Richard Nixon and John Kennedy) were positive. In contrast, only 40 percent of references to the major party presidential candidates in 1992 (George H.W. Bush and Bill Clinton) were positive.[31]

attack journalism an approach to news reporting in which journalists take an adversarial attitude toward candidates and elected officials.

THE MEDIA AND
PUBLIC POLICYMAKING

8.5 *What is the role of the media in the policymaking process?*

Political scientists say that the press plays a **signaling role**, which is a term that refers to the accepted responsibility of the media to alert the public to important developments as they happen. The media may be unable to tell people what to think, but they generally succeed in telling people what to think about. In early 2007, the *Washington Post* published a series of stories about the poor quality of care injured service personnel had been receiving at Walter Reed Army Medical Center in Washington, D.C. Other media outlets quickly picked up on the coverage and the issue of medical care for Iraq war veterans soon rose to the forefront of the policy agenda. Several congressional committees held hearings on the issue, the Bush administration called for an investigation, and the Secretary of Defense removed the military commanders in charge of veterans' care at Walter Reed.

The media also influence policymaking through **framing**, which is the process by which a communication source, such as a news organization, defines and constructs a political issue or public controversy. The way the media present an issue helps define the approaches that policymakers will take to its resolution. The vivid images of flooded homes and people seeking shelter in the New Orleans Superdome along with accounts of bureaucratic bungling ensured that policymakers would regard Hurricane Katrina as not just a natural disaster but also the failure of the government to respond effectively to a crisis.

signaling role a term that refers to the accepted responsibility of the media to alert the public to important developments as they happen.

framing the process by which a communication source, such as a news organization, defines and constructs a political issue or public controversy.

TAKING SIDES

Political Punditry

Should talk show hosts be held accountable for their punditry?

To what extent should people get their information from talk shows that are essentially entertainment?

OVERVIEW

According to a 2008 Pew Research Report, 70 percent of Americans got most of their national and international news from television,[32] and among those viewers, 39 percent regularly watched cable news.[33] During the week leading up to Super Tuesday, 75 percent of available airtime on the major cable news networks was political punditry offering comments on the campaign, far more than the coverage given to any other stories, including reporting on the campaign events themselves.[34] Today, talk show hosts like Keith Olbermann, Glenn Beck, Rachel Maddow, and others vie for viewership and present political punditry almost around the clock. While some argue that these pundits provide viewpoints for consideration from both sides, others argue that they're allowed to provide inaccurate assessments or offcolor remarks, largely unchallenged.

The first show to pit a liberal and conservative against each other to argue about politics was CNN's *Crossfire*, which aired from 1982 to 2005. One of the factors in the show's cancellation was an appearance by comedian Jon Stewart in 2004, who berated the show for hurting America by engaging in "partisan hackery" that encouraged divisiveness. While the hosts argued that they were hosting a serious debate program, Stewart countered, "You're doing theatre, when you should be doing debate."

 ## SUPPORTING
holding pundits accountable

 ## AGAINST
holding pundits accountable

Political pundits polarize the American people. Talk show hosts are primarily focused on increasing ratings, so they advocate extreme positions. Instead of encouraging open-minded debate about issues, they present only one skewed angle, which people identify with as the only way to see an issue.

Pundits discourage compromise and hinder policymakers from doing their job. Pundits create an audience that doesn't want its legislators to deliberate and make the compromises necessary for making policy. In addition, public officials are forced to respond to the often inaccurate slurs or unworkable ideas of pundits rather than focus on their jobs.

Talk show hosts spread false information with no accountability. Unlike newspapers or broadcast journalists, pundits have no obligation to fact-check their information or speak objective truth. Generally their lies are caught by media watchdogs, but it's often too little too late, and tends to have no impact on their credibility with their audiences.

One of the most important rights in the U.S. Constitution is the right to free speech. Political speech needs to be protected for a free exchange of ideas. We should not infringe on the right of free speech, even if we disagree with what a pundit is saying.

Political pundits are not news reporters. Pundits are paid to give informed opinion, not report objectively. People have numerous places to get their news and information; some will choose not to listen to particular pundits, but others value hearing their opinion.

Democratic debate is good for democracy. Political pundits offer competing ideas that range across the political spectrum. No one idea is being aired to the detriment of some other idea, and these pundits encourage people to form opinions about and get involved with the workings of our government.

THE MEDIA LANDSCAPE

8.1 *How is the media landscape in the United States changing?*

Private businesses, often large corporations, own and operate most media sources in the United States. Many mainstream media outlets, especially newspapers, news-magazines, and the network evening news, have been in decline for years, at least in terms of circulation and ratings. In contrast, the new media, which is a term used to refer to alternative media sources, such as the Internet, cable television, and satellite radio, are growing in importance. A major goal of news media outlets is to attract as large an audience as possible. The mainstream media seek to draw an audience by focusing on stories with entertainment value, such as crime stories and celebrity news. Other media outlets try to build a niche audience by targeting audiences based on political philosophy, issue focus, or religious values.

GOVERNMENT REGULATION OF THE NEWS MEDIA

8.2 *What is the relationship between the government and the media?*

The Constitution guarantees freedom of the press. As a result, the news media enjoy considerable leeway to report the news, even news that is critical of the government. The FCC regulates the broadcast media, but not cable TV, satellite radio, or the Internet. A number of controversies arise over the relationship between government and the media, including the issue of whether reporters should be required to reveal the names of confidential sources to the government. Many states have adopted shield laws, which are statutes that protect journalists from being forced to disclose confidential information in a legal proceeding.

MANAGING THE MEDIA

8.3 *How do politicians attempt to influence the tone and content of media coverage?*

Campaign organizations attempt to manage news coverage to present the candidates they favor in the most favorable light with sound bites and visual images all designed to support a theme of the day. Once in office, elected officials try to manipulate media coverage to build support for their policy initiatives and eventual reelection campaigns.

MEDIA BIAS

8.4 *Are the media biased?*

Although major newspapers, broadcast television news, and the major cable news networks pride themselves on their commitment to objective journalism, most Americans believe that the media are biased. Research suggests that media sources may indeed play favorites, but scholars have no evidence that news coverage affects election outcomes.

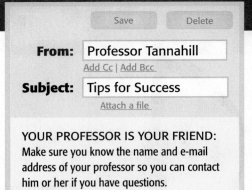

YOUR PROFESSOR IS YOUR FRIEND: Make sure you know the name and e-mail address of your professor so you can contact him or her if you have questions.

THE MEDIA AND PUBLIC POLICYMAKING

8.5 *What is the role of the media in the policymaking process?*

Political scientists say that the press plays a signaling role in that it alerts the public to important developments as they happen. The media also influence the policymaking process through framing, which is the process by which a communication source, such as a news organization, defines and constructs a political issue or public controversy.

8.1 *How is the media landscape in the United States changing?*

1 Which of the following media outlets is owned by the U.S. government?
   a. *New York Times*
   b. CBS Evening News
   c. National Public Radio
   d. None of the above

2 Cross-media ownership refers to which of the following?
   a. A corporation owning several different types of media outlets
   b. A corporation owning a chain of television stations in more than one city
   c. A corporation owning multiple radio stations in the same city
   d. A newspaper jointly owned by several corporations

3 Which of the following media outlets have been suffering from a loss of viewers or readers?
   a. Daily newspapers
   b. Network evening news shows
   c. Newsmagazines
   d. All of the above

4 Which of the following would be characterized as new media?
   a. *Time* magazine
   b. CBS television
   c. Chicago Tribune
   d. None of the above

8.2 *What is the relationship between the government and the media*

5 Which of the following media outlets is regulated by the FCC?
   a. Network television
   b. Cable television
   c. Satellite radio
   d. All of the above

6 A major newspaper carries a series of articles discussing the backgrounds and issue orientations of all the major candidates running for the presidency. The paper's decision to cover all of the candidates and not just its favorite candidate can be explained by which of the following?
   a. The Fairness Doctrine requires that all candidates be covered.
   b. The newspaper is following guidelines established by the FCC.
   c. The newspaper is voluntarily practicing objective journalism.
   d. None of the above

7 What is the purpose of a shield law?
   a. To protect journalists from being sued for negative reporting
   b. To protect journalists from being forced to disclose confidential information in a legal proceeding
   c. To protect journalists from being charged with violating FCC indecency standards
   d. None of the above

8.3 *How do politicians attempt to influence the tone and content of media coverage?*

8 "Read my lips: No new taxes." This is an example of which of the following?
   a. Objective journalism
   b. Attack journalism
   c. Equal-time rule
   d. Sound bite

9 Which of the below is NOT one of the strategies politicians employ to try to manage their news coverage?
   a. Emphasize several themes in hopes that the media will pick up at least one of them
   b. Select an eye-catching visual backdrop to reinforce the message
   c. Ensure the candidate sticks with the campaign script
   d. All of above are strategies of campaign organizations

8.4 *Are the media biased?*

10 Which of the following groups is most likely to distrust the media and believe that the media are biased?
   a. People who identify with the Democratic Party
   b. People who say they are independent
   c. People who identify with the Republican Party
   d. The three groups above are equally likely to distrust the media and believe they are biased

11 Which of the following statements most accurately describes media coverage of the 2008 presidential election?
   a. Most media coverage of the McCain campaign was negative, whereas coverage of the Obama campaign was balanced.
   b. Most media coverage of the Obama campaign was negative, whereas coverage of the McCain campaign was balanced.
   c. Coverage of both the Obama and the McCain campaign was negative.
   d. Coverage of both the Obama and the McCain campaign was balanced.

12 In 2008, a Republican was more likely than a Democrat to regularly watch which of the follow news sources?
   a. MSNBC
   b. CNN
   c. Fox
   d. Democrats and Republicans have similar viewing habits

13 "The media have a responsibility to present all sides of controversial issues." This statement best reflects which of the following concepts?
   a. Attack journalism
   b. Objective journalism
   c. Framing
   d. Signaling role

8.5 *What is the role of the media in the policymaking process?*

14 Which of the following is best defined as a term that refers to the accepted responsibility of the media to alert the public to important developments?
   a. Attack journalism
   b. Objective journalism
   c. Framing
   d. Signaling role

15 Which of the following terms is best defined as the process by which a communication source, such as a news organization, defines and constructs a political issue or public controversy?
   a. Attack journalism
   b. Objective journalism
   c. Framing
   d. Signaling role

KNOW the score

14–15 correct: Congratulations—you know your American government!

12–13 correct: Your understanding of this chapter is weak—be sure to review the key terms and visit TheThinkSpot.

<12 correct: Reread the chapter more thoroughly.

Answers: 1) d, 2) a, 3) d, 4) d, 5) a, 6) c, 7) b, 8) d, 9) d, 10) c, 11) a, 12) c, 13) b, 14) d, 15) c

9 INTEREST

MERICANS FOR TAX REFORM

President of the United States

Taxpayer Protection Pledge

Rick Santorum _____, pledge t

...payers of the United States of Ameri

that I will oppose and veto

...any and all efforts to increase taxes.

WHY PEOPLE JOIN GROUPS

Learning Objective **9.1** Why do people join interest groups?

TYPES OF INTEREST GROUPS

Learning Objective **9.2** What types of interest groups are active in American politics, and what are their goals?

INTEREST GROUP STRATEGIES AND TACTICS

Learning Objective **9.3** What strategies and tactics do interest groups use to achieve their goals?

THE STRENGTH OF INTEREST GROUPS

Learning Objective **9.4** What factors determine the relative strength of interest groups?

A mericans for Tax Reform (ATR) is the most powerful force in American politics on the issue of taxes. The group's position can be summarized briefly: No tax increases for any reason, ever. The ATR asks candidates for national, state, and local office to sign a Taxpayer Protection Pledge that they will never vote to increase tax rates and will only agree to reduce tax credits and deductions if the money saved goes dollar for dollar to lowering tax rates. The ATR endorses candidates who take the pledge and opposes candidates who refuse. If an elected official breaks the pledge and votes for higher taxes, the ATR targets him or her for defeat in the next election.

The ATR is closely allied with the Republican Party. Although it invites candidates of both parties to sign the pledge, almost all of the signers are Republicans. In the 112th Congress, which met in 2011–2013, all but 13 of the 288 Republican members of the House and Senate had signed the pledge. More than a dozen governors and hundreds of state legislators have signed the pledge as well.[1]

GROUPS

The ATR pledge increases the chances that Congress and the president will deadlock over the federal budget deficit. Because of the pledge, most Republicans insist that the budget deficit be reduced entirely with spending cuts. In contrast, most Democrats are unwilling to agree to deep spending reductions unless Republicans agree to close some tax loopholes and increase taxes on business and upper-income earners.

The ATR's role in American politics introduces this chapter on interest groups. The chapter begins by considering why people join groups. It then identifies the various types of interest groups in American politics, discusses their political goals, and assesses their relative strengths. Finally, the chapter examines the tactics interest groups employ to achieve their goals and discusses the factors that affect the relative strength of groups.

WHY PEOPLE JOIN GROUPS

9.1 *Why do people join interest groups?*

George and Inez Martinez are an older couple living in El Paso, Texas. They recently received a letter from AARP inviting them to join that organization. AARP, formerly known as the American Association of Retired Persons, is an interest group representing the concerns of older Americans. Mr. and Mrs. Martinez have heard of AARP and approve of its work on behalf of older people. Annual AARP dues are relatively low. Nonetheless, why should Mr. and Mrs. Martinez join? Surely, the few dollars that they would contribute in dues will be too little to have any appreciable effect on the fortunes of the organization. Furthermore, as senior citizens, Mr. and Mrs. Martinez stand to benefit from whatever legislative gains AARP achieves whether or not they join the organization.

The situation facing Mr. and Mrs. Martinez illustrates what Professor Mancur Olson calls the **free-rider barrier** to group membership, which is the concept that individuals will have little incentive to join a group and contribute resources to it if the group's benefits go to members and non-members alike. Olson says that groups attempt to compensate for the free-rider barrier by offering selective benefits that go only to group members.[2] AARP, for example, provides members with a number of selective benefits, including the opportunity to purchase discounted dental, health, and long-term care insurance.

Political scientists identify three types of incentives that individuals have for joining and participating in a group: material, solidary, and purposive incentives, which are sometimes also called expressive incentives. Material incentives to group membership are tangible benefits that can be measured monetarily. For example, the NRA offers its members firearms training classes, life insurance for the families of police officers killed in the line of duty, gun-loss insurance, and discounts on car rentals, hotel reservations, and airline tickets. Solidary incentives to group membership are social benefits arising from association with other group members. The NRA has more than 10,000 state associations and local clubs. Members participate in training programs, clinics, and shooting tournaments. Purposive incentives to group membership are the rewards that individuals find in working for a cause in which they believe. Many members of the NRA believe passionately in a constitutional right to keep and bear arms.[3] Some groups offer members one type of incentive to join, whereas other groups offer two types or all three kinds of incentives.

 think What kinds of incentives do the student groups or organizations at your school provide to help overcome the free-rider barrier?

free-rider barrier the concept that individuals will have little incentive to join and contribute to a group if benefits go to members and nonmembers alike.

TYPES OF INTEREST GROUPS

9.2 *What types of interest groups are active in American politics, and what are their goals?*

An **interest group** is an organization of people who join together voluntarily on the basis of some shared interest for the purpose of influencing policy. Sometimes the shared interest is economic. Dairy farmers, for example, work through the National Milk Producers

interest group an organization of people who join together voluntarily on the basis of some interest they share for the purpose of influencing policy.

Federation. Small business owners join the National Federation of Independent Business (NFIB). At other times, the interests that unite people involve morals, culture, and social values. Individuals concerned about safeguarding the environment may become involved in an environmental organization, such as the Sierra Club or Greenpeace.

Business Groups

Business groups are the most numerous, and probably the most potent, of America's interest groups. Although their voices are heard on virtually every major policy issue, business interests are especially concerned with tax laws, interest rates, environmental regulations, trade policy, labor laws, government contracts, and other matters that affect the way they conduct business. For example, energy companies, such as Exxon Mobil, Chevron, and ConocoPhillips, favor offshore drilling but worry about the cost of environmental regulations imposed after the BP oil spill. Citigroup, Bank of America, and JP Morgan Chase are concerned with the implementation of financial

*Business groups are the most **numerous** of America's interest groups.*

regulatory reform legislation. The health insurance industry focuses on the implementation of healthcare reform.

Business interests join together across industry lines to promote pro-business public policies. The Chamber of Commerce is a business federation representing the interests of more than three million businesses of all sizes, sectors, and regions.[4] It has a national organization with headquarters in Washington, D.C., organizations in every state, and chapters in thousands of cities throughout the nation. The National Federation of Independent Business (NFIB) is a federation representing the interests of small and independent businesses. The Business Roundtable is an association of chief executive officers of major U.S. corporations.

Business groups also work through **trade associations**, which are organizations representing the interests of firms and professionals in the same general field. Large financial institutions, such as Bank of America and JPMorgan Chase, belong to the American Bankers Association. Other trade associations include the National Association of

Manufacturers (NAM), the National Restaurant Association, and the National Association of Wholesaler-Distributors.

Business groups are well positioned to influence policy. They are numerous, dispersed throughout the country, organized, and well funded. Small business owners and corporate executives are prominent figures in communities around the nation. They often know their member of Congress personally and understand how to articulate their views effectively to policymakers. Furthermore, business groups have funds to contribute to political causes. In 2010, business interests contributed more than $1.2 billion to candidates and political parties, substantially more than the $77 million given by organized labor.

Labor Unions

Organized labor is an important political force in America, although it is not as powerful as it once was. More than a fourth of the civilian labor force belonged to a union in 1970 compared with only 12 percent in 2008.[5] The manufacturing industries, such as automobile assembly and steel manufacturing, in which unions have historically had their best organizing successes, now

FedEx Corp., the world's largest express delivery service, has developed a close relationship with members of Congress and the White House. FedEx is not only a major campaign donor to Democrats and Republicans, but it keeps its fleet of private planes on stand-by for lawmakers who need to jet off at a moment's notice. In 2001, the company's political efforts paid off when the U.S. Postal Service contracted with FedEx to delivery all of its overnight packages and express deliveries.

trade associations organizations representing the interests of firms and professionals in the same general field.

right-to-work laws statutes that prohibit union membership as a condition of employment.

Grover Norquist, pictured above, is the founder and president of Americans for Tax Reform (ATR). He developed the Taxpayer Protection Pledge in order "to shrink government to the size where we can drown it in a bathtub."

employ significantly fewer workers than they did 40 years ago. More than 20 states have adopted **right-to-work laws**, which are statutes that prohibit union membership as a condition of employment.[6] Furthermore, many employers aggressively resist unionization. For example, Wal-Mart, the nation's largest employer, has successfully fought off efforts to unionize its workforce. The unions that have had the most organizing success in recent years have been unions targeting public sector (government) employees and low-wage workers, such as janitors, agricultural workers, and people employed by nursing homes.

The largest union group in the nation is the American Federation of Labor-Congress of Industrial Organizations (AFL-CIO). It is composed of 57 separate unions with a combined membership of 11.5 million. Some of the better known unions affiliated with the AFL-CIO are the American Federation of Teachers (AFT), American Postal Workers Union, International Brotherhood of Teamsters, United Mine Workers of America (UMWA), and the American Federation of State, County, and Municipal Employees (AFSCME).[7]

Organized labor is strongest in the industrialized states of the Northeast and Midwest (the

Frostbelt), and weakest in the South and West (the Sunbelt). In Michigan, for example, the United Auto Workers (UAW) may be the state's single most potent political force. In contrast, in many Sunbelt states, organized labor is hurt by anti-union laws and by a diverse and divided work force, many of whose members are hostile to organized labor. Unionization in the South and Southwest has taken hold in only a few places.

Organized labor favors government policies aimed at making it easier for unions to organize. In particular, unions want Congress to pass the Employee Free Choice Act, which would allow the use of the card check method in union authorization elections. Under current law, workers form a union in a particular workplace by majority vote, usually by secret ballot. **Card check** is a method of union authorization that allows union organizers to collect employee signatures on authorization forms instead of holding a secret ballot election. Once a majority of worker signatures have been collected, the National Labor Relations Board (NLRB) certifies the union and the employer is forced to recognize it as the official representative of the workers. Organized labor favors card check because it makes it easier for workers to join a union. In contrast, business groups argue that card check denies workers their right to a secret ballot.

Organized labor supports programs and policies designed to improve the quality of life for working people and their families. Unions favor increasing the federal **minimum wage**, which is the lowest hourly wage

*At times, big business and big labor find themselves **on the same side** in policy disputes.*

that an employer can legally pay covered workers. They want the government to aggressively enforce workplace health and safety regulations, and to require the use of union labor and union wage scales on construction projects built with federal funds.

Conventional wisdom holds that organized labor and big business counterbalance each other, invariably taking opposing views on public policy issues. At times, that is the case. Management and labor generally disagree on labor relations laws, occupational safety and health regulations, and minimum wage laws. At other times, however, big business and big labor find themselves on the same side in policy disputes. Labor leaders and business executives both favor higher defense spending, for example, because it means more defense contracts and more jobs. The United Steelworkers and steel manufacturers join forces to push for import restrictions on foreign competition. Both business and labor oppose environmental regulations that could threaten the closing of offending plants and the loss of jobs.

Professional Associations

Doctors, lawyers, real estate agents, and other professionals form associ-

minimum wage the lowest hourly wage that an employer can legally pay covered workers.

card check a method of union authorization that allows union organizers to collect employee signatures on authorization forms instead of holding a secret ballot election.

In Orange County, California, teachers of the Capistrano Unified School District go on strike against pay cuts imposed to reduce a budget deficit.

The American Academy of Pediatrics advocates for children's health issues. In 2010, it partnered with the White House, Major League Baseball, and others in an initiative called Let's Move, which works to reduce childhood obesity.

ations to advance their interests. Professional associations are influential because of the relatively high socioeconomic status of their membership. Professionals have the resources to make their voices heard, and they enjoy an added advantage because many elected officials come from the ranks of the professions, especially the legal profession.

Professional associations are concerned with public policies that affect their members. The American Medical Association (AMA), an interest group representing the concerns of physicians, would like government to limit the amount of money that judges and juries can award in medical malpractice lawsuits. The American Bar Association (ABA), a lawyers' group, opposes the AMA on the issue. Professional associations sometimes take stands on policy issues outside the immediate concerns of their membership, such as tax policy, defense spending, and women's rights.

Agricultural Groups

Agricultural groups are influential on farm issues at the national level and in state legislatures in farming states. The most important farm groups include the American Farm Bureau and the National Farmers Union. Associations representing farm interests related to a particular crop or commodity, such as the National Milk Producers Federation, are important as well.

In general, agricultural groups want government loan guarantees, crop subsidies, and the promotion of farm exports. Of course,

Much of agriculture has become **agribusiness,** with all the advantages that business interests enjoy.

each farm group has its own particular cause. Western cattle interests want to ensure continued low-cost access to public lands to graze their herds. Fruit and vegetable growers favor immigration policies designed to ensure a steady supply of farm workers.

Racial and Ethnic Minority Rights Groups

African Americans, Latinos, Asian Americans, Native Americans, and other racial and ethnic minority groups have created interest groups to promote their political causes. The National Association for the Advancement of Colored People (NAACP) is an interest group organized to represent the concerns of African Americans. The League of United Latin American Citizens (LULAC) is a Latino interest group. The American Indian Movement (AIM) is a group representing the views of Native Americans.

Racial and ethnic minority groups share the goals of equality before the law, representation in elective and appointive office, freedom from discrimination, and economic advancement. Minority groups are interested in the enforcement of laws against discrimination; the election and appointment of minorities to federal, state, and local offices; and the extension of government programs to fight poverty. Racial and ethnic minority groups generally support the enforcement of the Voting Rights Act and the implementation

of affirmative action programs. In addition, LULAC and other Latino-rights organizations favor immigration reforms that would allow longstanding undocumented workers to work in the United States legally and eventually to become citizens.

Organizations that represent the interests of racial and ethnic minorities are an important political force in most big cities and in states where minority populations are large enough to translate into political power. In addition, minorities, especially African Americans and Latinos, play an important role in national politics.

The League of United Latin American Citizens (LULAC) holds educational and advocacy events to promote Latino civil rights. Here Telemundo VJ "Crash" (left) and Vice President Alfredo Richard (right) address the youth awards dinner at LULAC's 79th Annual National Convention and Exposition in Washington, D.C.

Religious Groups

Throughout American history, religious organizations have been actively involved in the policy process. Both the abolition (of slavery) and the prohibition (of alcoholic beverages) movements had strong religious overtones, as did the civil rights and anti-Vietnam War movements of the 1960s and early 1970s.

Today, the most active religiously oriented political groups are associated with the religious right—people who hold conservative views because of their religious beliefs. Focus on the Family, Family Research Council,

"Healthcare reform is fundamentally an issue of social and economic justice—one of the most critical moral issues of our time.**"**

—Jim Wallis, founder of Sojourners

Religious interest groups on both sides were involved in the healthcare debates. Faith for Health, a progressive coalition of more than thirty Protestant, Catholic, Jewish, and other religious organizations, campaigned in favor of healthcare reform.

and other conservative religious organizations are concerned with such causes as abortion, same-sex marriage, and prayer in school. Since the 2004 presidential election, religious liberals have begun organizing to counter the influence of the religious right. This religious left—people who hold liberal views because of their religious beliefs—has established a number of organizations, including the Center for Progressive Christianity. The religious left opposes the wars in Iraq and Afghanistan, while supporting immigration reform and the adoption of government programs to fight poverty and protect the environment.[8]

Conservative Christian organizations have been more successful at the ballot box than they have been in building influence in Washington, D.C., because many Christian conservatives are uncomfortable with the policy compromises necessary to move legislation through Congress.[9]

"Any healthcare policy that destroys our freedom and does not protect human life is unacceptable.**"**

—Mathew D. Staver, founder of Liberty Counsel

On the other side, the Freedom Federation, a consortium of about thirty-five conservative Christian organizations, campaigned against the healthcare bill.

AROUND THE WORLD

Church and State in Mexico

Mexico is an overwhelmingly Catholic country. In 2000, 85 percent of the population told surveyors that they were Roman Catholic. Furthermore, most Mexicans are practicing Catholics. More than 40 percent of Mexican Catholics attend church on a weekly basis; another 20 percent attend at least once a month.[10]

Nonetheless, the political system in Mexico has a strong history of **anti-clericalism**, or opposition to the involvement of the church in political life. Even though individual citizens enjoyed the right to worship as they pleased, the government restricted the power of the Catholic Church for years. The Mexican Constitution of 1917 limited the role of the church in education and deprived clergy of the right to vote. Public education incorporated anti-church rhetoric in student lessons.[11] The Mexican government suppressed the Roman Catholic Church in order to keep it from becoming a threat to state authority. Government officials regarded it as a potential threat to their control because the overwhelming majority of Mexicans are practicing Catholics.

As Mexico has become more democratic, the government has eased restrictions on the church, and the church's political involvement has grown. Clergy now enjoy the right to vote and speak out on political issues. As a result, the church has become an important interest group in Mexican politics.[12] It has addressed a number of political issues including the distribution of wealth, illicit drugs, and democratization.

QUESTIONS

1 Should churches take positions on political issues?

2 Do religious organizations play the role of interest groups in American politics?

3 Are interest groups essential to democratic development?

Many Mexicans are deeply religious. Here, men and boys carry crosses on Good Friday in a working-class neighborhood of Mexico City.

anti-clericalism a movement that opposes the institutional power of religion, and the involvement of the church in all aspects of public and political life.

Conservative Christian groups benefit from a core of highly committed supporters who can be mobilized to go to the polls and to contact members of Congress over issues, that are important to them, such as abortion and gay marriage. In 2008, for example, the Roman Catholic Church and the Church of Jesus Christ of Latter-Day Saints (LDS) led the successful effort to overturn gay marriage in California. Nonetheless, many conservative Christian activists are frustrated by the inability of Congress and the president to outlaw abortion and prohibit gay marriage through constitutional amendment.

Citizen, Advocacy, and Cause Groups

Citizen groups are organizations that support government policies that they believe will benefit the public at large. For example, Common Cause, which calls itself "the citizen lobby," is a group that works for campaign finance reform and other good government causes. Other citizen groups include the Sierra Club, an environmental organization, and the American Civil Liberties Union (ACLU), a group defending the rights of individuals as outlined in the U.S. Constitution.

Advocacy groups are organizations that seek benefits for people who are in some way incapacitated or otherwise unable to represent their own interests. The Children's Defense Fund, for example, promotes the welfare of children. The Coalition for the Homeless is an organization that works on behalf of homeless persons. Other examples of advocacy groups include the Alzheimer's Association and the American Cancer Society.

Cause groups are organizations whose members care intensely about a single issue or a small group of related issues. The National Right to Life Committee is an organization opposed to abortion, whereas NARAL Pro-Choice America favors abortion rights. The ATR is a cause group organized to oppose any and all tax increases.

MADD officials counter that alcohol-related fatal car accidents have fallen 60 percent since the drinking age was raised to 21 in 1984, and that lowering the drinking age would reverse this trend.

More than 100 college presidents who believe students drink in excess because of age restrictions have called on lawmakers to lower the minimum legal drinking age from 21 to 18.

Other cause groups include the NRA, AARP, the National Organization for Women (NOW), a cause group organized to promote women's rights, and the Human Rights Campaign (HRC), an cause group formed to promote the cause of gay and lesbian rights.

Citizen, advocacy, and cause groups have achieved some victories in American politics. Many of these groups are expert at attracting media attention to their issues by releasing research reports or conducting high-profile public demonstrations. Earth Day, for example, is an annual event designed to call attention to environmental concerns. The National Right to Life Committee holds a demonstration in Washington, D.C., every year on the anniversary of *Roe v. Wade*, the Supreme Court decision that recognized that a woman's constitutional right to privacy includes the right to an abortion during the first two trimesters of a pregnancy.

Many public policies reflect the policy values of citizen, advocacy, and cause groups. The Endangered Species Act, the Clean Air Act, and other pieces of environmental legislation testify to the effectiveness of the Sierra Club and other environmental organizations. Mothers Against Drunk Driving (MADD), which is a cause group that supports the reform of laws dealing with drunk driving, is the motivating force behind a successful effort to stiffen the nation's DWI laws. AARP is influential on policy issues affecting older Americans, such as Social Security and Medicare.

citizen groups organizations created to support government policies that they believe will benefit the public at large.

advocacy groups organizations created to seek benefits on behalf of groups of persons who are in some way incapacitated or otherwise unable to represent their own interests.

cause groups organizations whose members care intensely about a single issue or small group of related issues.

INTEREST GROUP
STRATEGIES AND TACTICS

Interest groups employ a variety of tactics in an effort to achieve their goals, including electioneering, lobbying, creating public pressure, protest demonstrations, litigation, and political violence.

Electioneering

Many interest groups seek policy influence by **electioneering**, or participating in the electoral process through endorsements or financial support of candidates. A number of groups try to affect election outcomes by targeting enemies and endorsing friends. Each congressional election year, Friends of the Earth, an environmental group, targets a "Dirty Dozen," 12 members of Congress who voted consistently against the group's positions on environmental legislation. The group publicizes its list in hopes that environmentally conscious citizens will vote against the representatives on the list. Other groups endorse candidates friendly to their causes. During

the 2008 presidential campaign, the AFL-CIO and NARAL Pro-Choice America endorsed Democrat Barack Obama, while the NRA and the National Right to Life Committee threw their support behind Republican John McCain.

Some interest groups focus on educating their members and supporters about the candidates. The AFL-CIO uses newsletters, phone banks, and rallies to encourage union members to support endorsed candidates. Many interest groups keep scorecards, showing how members of Congress voted on issues important to the group and assigning scores to senators and representatives indicating whether they are friend or foe. Groups hope that people sympathetic to group goals will consult the scorecards before deciding how to vote and for whom to contribute campaign contributions.

Groups with financial resources participate in the electoral process financially. Federal law requires that

think How does political action committee spending affect democracy? Does it make elections more democratic, or less so?

interest groups contributing money directly to candidates must make their contributions through a **political action committee** (PAC), which is an organization created to raise and distributes money in election campaigns. Although organized labor created the first PACs in the 1940s, the modern PAC era did not begin until the 1970s, when Congress passed the Federal Election Campaign Act (FECA) to reform campaign finance. Since the 1970s, the number of PACs active in American politics at the national level of government has grown from fewer than a thousand to more than 5,200.[13] The biggest spenders among PACs during the 2007–2008 election cycle were PACs associated with ActBlue ($54 million), Service Employees International Union ($46 million), MoveOn.org ($38 million), and EMILY's List ($25 million). The NRA Victory Fund spent $16 million.[14] ActBlue and MoveOn.org are liberal advocacy groups. EMILY's List (EMILY is the acronym for Early Money Is Like Yeast) is a PAC whose goal is the election of pro-choice Democratic women to office.

Interest groups follow different campaign-funding strategies. Labor

---

PARTY LEADERS' SCORES

SENATE

DEMOCRATS	SCORE	REPUBLICANS	SCORE
Reid (NV), Majority Leader	100	McConnell (KY), Minority Leader	0
Durbin (IL), Majority Whip	100	Kyl (AZ), Minority Whip	14
Schumer (NY), Conference Vice Chair	100	Alexander (TN), Conference Secretary	0
Leadership Average	100	Leadership Average	5

HOUSE

DEMOCRATS	SCORE	REPUBLICANS	SCORE
Pelosi* (CA), Speaker of the House	NA	Boehner (OH), Minority Leader	0
Hoyer (MD), Majority Leader	100	Cantor (VA), Minority Whip	0
Clyburn (SC), Whip	100	Mc Cathy	0
Larson (CT), Caucus Chair	100	Pence (IN), Conference Chair	0
Leadership Average	100	Leadership Average	0

* Nancy Pelosi was still Speaker in 2010, and by tradition the speaker seldom votes.

2009 National Environmental Scorecard · LCV | www.lcv.org   7

Some interest groups publish scorecards showing how frequently members of Congress side with the position of the group. The League of Conservation Voters is an environmental organization that wants the government to take action to protect the environment. Most Democrats in Congress earn high scores from the group; most Republicans earn low scores.

electioneering participating in the electoral process through endorsements or financial support of candidates.

political action committee (PAC) an organization created to raise and distribute money in election campaigns.

unions work to increase the number of members of Congress (usually Democrats) sympathetic to their point of view. In the 2007–2008 election period, PACs associated with organized labor made 92 percent of their contributions to Democratic candidates for Congress. Although most labor money goes to incumbent members of Congress, unions are willing to fund challengers and candidates for open seats if they stand a reasonable chance of winning. During the 2007–2008 election cycle, 33 percent of labor PAC donations went to challengers and candidates for open seats.[15]

Many cause groups pursue strategies similar to that of organized labor in that they are primarily interested in increasing the number of elected officials who share their views. Although some cause groups work to elect friends and defeat enemies regardless of party affiliation, most groups are closely associated with one political party. The bulk of NRA support goes to Republican Party candidates, for example, whereas most of the candidates backed by NOW are Democrats. Some cause groups aggressively fund challengers to incumbents who vote against their interests.

Business groups have broad policy interests, so they are more pragmatic than organized labor or most cause and advocacy groups. Business interests recognize that a public official who opposes them today on one issue may support them tomorrow on another. Business PACs contribute money to candidates with the goal of obtaining **access,** which is the opportunity to communicate directly with legislators and other government officials in hopes of influencing the details of policy. Many business-oriented PACs follow the **Friendly Incumbent Rule**, which is a policy whereby an interest group will back any incumbent who is generally supportive of the group's policy preferences, without regard for the party or policy views of the challenger. In 2007–2008, 90 percent of corporate PAC money went to in-

cumbents, with most of the rest going to candidates for open seats. Because business-oriented groups favor incumbents, they tend to divide their contributions between the two political parties, despite the traditional alliance between business interests and the Republican Party. In 2007–2008, corporate PACs gave 52 percent of their contributions to Republican candidates and 48 percent to Democrats.[16]

Interest groups in general, not just business-oriented groups, tend to support incumbents. Most interest groups would rather give to a strong candidate who is only somewhat supportive of their cause than throw their money away on an almost certain loser who completely supports the group's goals. Most PAC money goes to incumbents, especially in races for the House, because they win more often than challengers.

> Most pac money
> goes to **incumbents,**
> especially in races for the
> House, because **they**
> **win more often**
> than challengers.

The figure on the right shows the distribution of PAC contributions for seats in the House during the 2007–2008 election period. PACs gave nearly $332 million to incumbents compared with $49 million to challengers and $32 million to candidates for open seats.

Some interest groups funnel money to candidates they support through **bundling**, a procedure in which an interest group gathers checks from individual supporters made out to the campaigns of targeted candidates. The group then passes the checks along to the candidates. The advantage of bundling is that it allows the interest group to route more money to a candidate than it could legally contribute under its own name because the group is simply acting as a clearinghouse for checks written by hundreds of individuals.

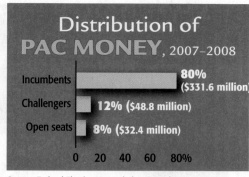

Distribution of **PAC MONEY**, 2007–2008

Incumbents	80% ($331.6 million)
Challengers	12% ($48.8 million)
Open seats	8% ($32.4 million)

Source: Federal Election Commission, www.fec.gov.

Some interest groups participate in elections through **527 committees**, which are organizations created by individuals and groups to influence the outcomes of elections by raising and spending money that candidates and political parties cannot raise and spend legally. Federal law limits the amount of money that individuals and groups can legally give to candidates and parties, but those limits do not apply to 527 committees. Groups can contribute as much money as they like to a 527 committee, which can then use the money for voter mobilization and "issue advocacy." Although the law prevents 527 committees from running advertisements either for or against particular candidates, it allows issue advertisements that are typically designed to influence voter opinion on

access the opportunity to communicate directly with legislators and other government officials in hopes of influencing the details of policy.

Friendly Incumbent Rule a policy whereby an interest group will back any incumbent who is generally supportive of the group's policy preferences, without regard for the party or policy views of the challenger

bundling a process in which an interest group gathers checks from individual supporters and sends them to candidates in a bundle, allowing an interest group to route more money than the group alone could contribute.

527 committees organizations created by individuals and groups to influence the outcomes of elections by raising and spending money that candidates and political parties cannot legally raise.

U.S. Supreme Court Overturns Campaign Finance Limits

The U.S. Supreme Court has ruled that corporations and labor unions have a constitutional right to fund political advertisements for or against candidates as long as they do not coordinate their actions with the campaigns they are promoting or with other groups. The ruling in *Citizens United v. Federal Election Commission*, which came on a five-to-four vote, struck down provisions of the Bipartisan Campaign Reform Act (BCRA) that prohibited corporations and unions from using funds from their general treasuries to advocate for or against candidates. The Court based its decision on the First Amendment guarantee of freedom of speech.

DISCUSSION

What does this decision mean? It means that if a corporation wanted to see Joe Smith elected, it could spend an unlimited amount of money running political ads supporting Smith or trashing Smith's opponent as long as the ads are independent expenditures, that is, not coordinated with the Smith campaign.

The First Amendment protects corporations? Yes. The U.S. Supreme Court has held for decades that corporations are legal persons.

Why did the Court equate campaign expenditures with freedom of speech? The Court's majority contends that campaign contributions provide the means for individuals and groups to express their views. Any restriction on the amount of money they can spend on political communication limits expression by reducing the scope of the discussion or the size of the audience addressed.

Aren't corporate voices already louder than other groups? Yes. Corporate PACs already contribute more money to candidates than other types of PACs, and now corporations and unions will be able to make unlimited independent expenditures for or against candidates.

Is that why the advocates of campaign finance reform are upset with the ruling? Yes. They believe that the decision will give moneyed interests even more influence in the political process. Suppose Exxon Mobil, which reported $45 billion in profits last year,[19] wanted Congress to cut taxes on oil companies or reduce environmental regulations. It could easily spend millions of dollars to support the candidates for Congress who agreed with it and defeat those candidates that disagreed. How many members of Congress would dare to vote against the position of a corporation with such deep pockets?

It sounds like the decision opens the floodgates to millions of dollars of campaign corporate expenditures. That could happen, but not necessarily. Many corporate executives welcomed campaign finance restrictions because they want to reduce political expenditures. Furthermore, corporations that get involved in election campaigns risk alienating large numbers of consumers and shareholders.

the candidates without explicitly telling people how to cast their votes.

Lobbying

Interest groups attempt to influence policymaking by **lobbying**, the communication of information by a representative of an interest group to a government official for the purpose of influencing a policy decision. Groups lobby both the legislative and executive branches of government, attempting to influence every stage of the policy process. The number of Washington, D.C., lobbyists, including their support staffs, is estimated at more than 250,000.[17] Some interest groups have full-time lobbyists on their professional staffs, whereas other groups hire Washington law firms or consulting agencies to lobby on their behalf. More than 150 former members of Congress are lobbyists.[18] Former senator and presidential candidate Bob Dole, for example, became a lobbyist with the firm of Alston & Bird after his unsuccessful run for the White House in 1996, earning far more money as a lobbyist than he would have made had he been elected president. Other lobbyists are former congressional staff members, former employees of the executive branch, and even relatives of current members of Congress.

While many people associate lobbyists with the likes of Jack Abramoff, a former lobbyist who was sentenced to federal prison for fraud, conspiracy, and tax evasion, most lobbyists are honest and important sources of information for government officials.

Lobbying is expensive whether interest groups employ full-time lobbyists or contract with established Washington lobbyists. In 2010, interest groups reported spending more than $3.5 billion for lobbying expenses. The U.S. Chamber of Commerce, for example, spent $756 million on its lobby activities. The AMA spent $248 million.[20]

Information is the key to lobbying. Successful lobbyists provide members of Congress with accurate facts and figures. Although lobbyists offer their own interpretation of data and voice arguments to support their group's particular policy preferences, they are honest because they know that their effectiveness depends on their credibility. In fact, lobbyists are an important information source for government officials.[21]

The most successful lobbying efforts of Congress are those supported by campaign contributions and buttressed by pressure from people living in a representative's district or a senator's home state.[22] Interest groups lay the groundwork for effective lobbying by giving money to political campaigns. Lobbyists sometimes serve as campaign treasurers for members seeking reelection. Major trade associations have purchased Capitol Hill townhouses for fundraisers so that members of Congress can attend events and go quickly back to the Capitol to cast votes.[23] Although campaign contributions do not necessarily buy votes, they do generally guarantee access to decision-makers by lobbyists. Once Congress is in session, well-organized groups support their lobbyists in Washington by encouraging group members in the home districts of key legislators to contact their representatives.

Interest groups use different approaches to influencing policy. Most labor unions and business groups employ what might be called an insider's approach to achieving influence. These groups have a long-range interest in several policy areas. They give PAC contributions to gain access for their

Corporations that get involved in election campaigns risk alienating large numbers of consumers and shareholders. For example, in 2010, gay and lesbian rights groups organized a boycott against Target after the Minnesota-based retailer gave $150,000 to an organization so it could run political advertisements in support of a pro-business Republican candidate for governor who opposed gay marriage.

lobbyists who then work to get to know the public officials on a personal basis. Whatever pressure these groups bring to bear on public officials is subtle and unspoken. They believe threats are counterproductive and harmful to the construction of a long-term relationship between the interest group and the

total lobbying spending

2009 $3.5*
2007 $2.8
2005 $2.41
2003 $2.04
2001 $1.63
1999 $1.44

* in billions of dollars

lobbying the communication of information by a representative of an interest group to a government official for the purpose of influencing a policy decision.

Top Spenders on Lobbying Activities, 2010

Lobbying Client	Total Spent
U.S. Chamber of Commerce	$132,067,500
Pharmaceutical Rsrch & Mfrs of America	$21,740,000
General Electric	$39,290,000
American Hospital Association	$19,488,358
Blue Cross/Blue Shield	$20,343,141
AARP	$22,050,000
American Medical Assn	$22,555,000
Northrup Grumman	$15,740,000
National Assn of Realtors	$17,580,000

Source: Center for Responsive Politics, www.opensecrets.org.

officeholder. In fact, interest groups give highest priority to lobbying their allies on the committees that formulate legislation. Lobbyists give friendly legislators facts, figures, and talking points in order to counter arguments raised by legislative opponents. Groups taking an insider's approach are usually able to take the outcome of elections in stride because they cultivate relationships with members of both political parties.

Lobbyists using the insider approach do not expect to affect the way in which members of Congress vote on final passage of high-visibility legislation. Instead, their goal is to influence the details of legislation to include loopholes that benefit the interest group they represent. For example, a recent tax bill contained a provision limited to a single company, identified as a "corporation incorporated on June 13, 1917, which has its principal place of business in Bartlesville, Oklahoma. The only company fitting that description is Phillips Petroleum.

In contrast, other groups, whose policy goals are more narrowly focused, follow an outsider's approach to influencing policy. The NRA, the National Right to Life Committee, and some other cause groups focus on a relatively small set of high-profile issues. Members of Congress either support them or oppose them on their pet issues. Groups using an outsider's strategy are more heavy-handed in dealing with public officials than are interest groups with a broader range of policy concerns. Groups taking an outside approach are less willing to compromise on policy issues than are insider groups, and more likely to threaten (and attempt to carry out) political reprisals against officeholders who oppose them.

Creating Public Pressure

Some interest groups attempt to achieve their goals by generating public support for their policy positions and focusing it on government officials. Groups launch public relations campaigns to convince the general public that their particular point of view embodies the public interest. The NRA, for example, purchased a series of magazine advertisements designed to improve the public image of the group. The advertisements featured hunters, police officers, and business people with the caption, "I am the NRA." Some tobacco companies have conducted high-profile media campaigns against underage smoking to counter criticism that tobacco advertisers have targeted youngsters.

Sometimes interest groups with negative public images will support other, less controversial groups that share their issue concerns. For ex-

ample, Americans for Prosperity is a cause group that favors lower taxes and less government regulation. It opposes healthcare reform, tobacco regulations, and tries to cast doubt on global warming. Although Americans for Prosperity declares that it is a grassroots organization, the group was founded and heavily funded by the Koch Family Foundation, which is headed by two brothers who control Koch Industries, an oil-and-gas company.[24]

The most sophisticated public relations campaigns are aimed at orchestrating citizen pressure on members of Congress and other public officials. The AFL-CIO ran radio and television advertisements in selected congressional districts attacking Republican members of the House for preventing legislation to raise the minimum wage from coming to a vote. More than 20 Republican House members broke with their party leadership and voted to increase the minimum wage. Their votes proved the difference. The legislation passed the House and eventually became law.[25]

Interest groups also use their membership lists to influence the legislative process. Lobbyists first identify which senators and representatives are the swing votes in Congress on issues important to the group. The professional staff of the interest group then sends direct mail or e-mail messages to members who live in the states and districts of the targeted lawmakers, asking them to contact their senator or representative in support of the group's goals.[26]

Protest Demonstrations

Groups use protest demonstrations to show policymakers that a number of people have strong feelings regarded a particular policy or program, usually negative feelings. Protests organized by the Tea Party movement, which is a loose network of conservative activists organized to protest high taxes, excessive government spending, and big government in general, were designed to draw attention to opposition to healthcare reform, government bailouts, and

Members of PETA (People for the Ethical Treatment of Animals) offer free gas and sandwiches to people who pledge to try vegetarianism.

high taxes. Other contemporary protest movements focus on gay marriage, immigration reform, and the wars in Iraq and Afghanistan. In general, protest demonstrations are a tactic used by groups unable to achieve their goals through other means. Sometimes the protest catches the attention of the general public, which brings pressure to bear on behalf of the protesting group. Tea Party activists hope that their movement will change the direction of American politics. In many cases, however, protests have only a marginal impact on public policy.

Litigation

A number of interest groups specialize in the use of litigation (i.e., lawsuits) to achieve their goals. The American Civil Liberties Union (ACLU) provides legal assistance to individuals and groups in controversies involving individual rights and liberties, including disputes over freedom of religion, free speech, and the death penalty. The American Center for Law and Justice and the Liberty Counsel are organizations that litigate in support of conservative Christian goals, such as opposition to abortion rights and gay marriage. Other interest groups use litigation as one of several approaches to achieving their policy goals.

Both business organizations and environmental groups, for example, file suit against government agencies, charging that the executive branch is either going too far or not going far enough to implement the nation's environmental laws. Although courts generally defer to federal agencies in the implementation of policy, they will overrule an agency decision if it appears that the agency acted on the basis of politics rather than the law. Consider the legal battle over a six-month moratorium imposed by the Department of the Interior on deepwater drilling in the Gulf of Mexico after the BP oil well blowout in April 2010. Although the Obama adminis-

tration said that the moratorium was necessary because of uncertainty of the cause of the blowout and a lack of available cleanup equipment if another spill were to occur, a dozen oil companies filed suit to block enforcement of the moratorium. They argued that the government lacked justification for the moratorium and that its imposition would cripple the industry financially. A federal judge agreed with the oil companies and his decision was upheld on appeal.[27] The Department of the Interior responded to the court ruling by issuing a revised six-month moratorium, designed to overcome the objections of the courts. The oil industry promised to go back to court to ask a judge to block the new moratorium.[28]

Political Violence

Some groups employ unconventional methods to achieve their goals. The Animal Liberation Front, Stop Animal Exploitation Now, and some other animal rights groups take aggressive action to oppose animal research. Although most animal rights demonstrations are peaceful and legal, some opponents of animal research resort to violence. Protestors have broken into university laboratories, released lab animals, and destroyed property. Some researchers have been threatened with physical assault and death, and had their homes vandalized.[29]

TAKE ✓ ACTION
Politics at the Movies

Some filmmakers aim not just to entertain but also to convey political messages. View a film with political themes and answer the following questions:

1. What is the title of the film and when was it released?
2. What is the film about? Summarize the storyline of the movie in your own words.
3. What political issue or issues does the film address?
4. What point of view does the film express?
5. Do you agree or disagree with the political views presented in the film? Why or why not?

Select one of the following films with political themes:

Absence of Malice, All the King's Men, American History X, An Inconvenient Truth, Apocalypse Now, Avatar, Boys Don't Cry, Charlie Wilson's War, Capitalism: A Love Story, Citizen Kane, District 9, Do the Right Thing, Dr. Strangelove, Fahrenheit 451, Fahrenheit 9/11, Frost/Nixon, Goodnight and Good Luck, Inherit the Wind, JFK, Man of the Year, Milk, Mississippi Burning, Mr. Smith Goes to Washington, The Manchurian Candidate, Network, No End in Sight, Nothing but the Truth, Once Were Warriors, Philadelphia, Platoon, Primary Colors, Recount, Sicko, Syriana, Thank You for Smoking, W., or *Wag the Dog.*

THE STRENGTH OF INTEREST GROUPS

What factors determine the relative strength of interest groups?

The policymaking influence of interest groups depends on several factors, including alliances with political parties, alliances with members of Congress and executive branch officials, public opinion, alliances among groups, opposition from other groups, and resources.

Alliances with Political Parties

In American politics, some interest groups have loose, informal alliances with political parties. Labor unions, African American rights groups, women's organizations, environmentalists, gun-control groups, abortion-rights organizations, and gay and lesbian rights groups are generally aligned with the Democratic Party. Business groups, the NRA, the National Right to Life Committee, anti-tax organizations, and conservative Christian organizations are tied to the Republican Party. Interest groups have more policymaking influence when the party with which they are allied is successful than when it is out of office. For example, after the Democrats took control of Congress in the 2006 election, labor unions, consumer groups, environmental organizations, and minority rights groups saw their influence rise, whereas business groups and trade associations lost influence.

Alliances with Congress and Executive Officials

The policymaking influence of interest groups depends on their ability to cultivate relationships with key officials in the legislative and executive branches of government, regardless of which party controls Congress or the White House. Business groups compensate for Democratic control of Congress by establishing ties with committee and subcommittee chairs through campaign contributions and effective lobbying. Frequently, business lobbyists succeed in softening

the impact of regulatory legislation on their particular industry.

Public Opinion

Public opinion affects the ability of interest groups to achieve their policy goals. Interest groups are most successful when their policy goals enjoy strong public support. The chief goal for the president and most members of Congress is reelection. They will not support policy proposals that the public strongly opposes or adopt programs that they believe will prove unpopular, regardless of PAC contributions, lobbying, or other interest group activities.

Allliances among Groups

Interest groups have more influence when organizations representing the same or similar interests or points of view share goals and speak with one voice. For example, at least 11 major environmental organizations participate in national politics, but they emphasize different aspects of the cause and disagree on tactics and strategy, sometimes quite vocally.[30] On those issues on which environmental groups agree, members of Congress who are already predisposed to be friendly to the environmental cause have clear direction for their efforts. When environmental groups disagree about policy, however, members of Congress who usually support their cause are less likely to proceed with enthusiasm.

Opposition from Other Groups

A group's policy influence depends on the extent of opposition from other groups. Interest groups are most successful on issues in which there is little conflict between groups.[31] Conflict is most likely on major policy issues that are high profile. Doctors' groups and lawyers'

associations, for example, butt heads over the issue of medical malpractice insurance reform. On many issues, public officials can choose which interests to court, playing one group off against another.

> The **most effective** interest group tactics all require **financial resources**.

Resources

Finally, groups with resources, especially money, organization, and volunteers, are more influential than groups without resources. The most effective interest group tactics—electioneering, lobbying, and creating public pressure—all require financial resources. Groups with a substantial number of committed members can generate pressure on Congress on behalf of group goals. Well-organized groups can provide campaign assistance to favored candidates through communications to members and perhaps volunteer support.

Outside groups unconnected to political parties or interest groups spent millions of dollars trying to influence election outcomes in 2010. Karl Rove, former advisor to President Bush, helped found American Crossroads, a conservative group that raised and spent $21 million trying to defeat Democratic candidates. Rove also helped found Crossroads GPS as a nonprofit organization that is not legally required to disclose its donors, which raised and spent $16 million on political advertising in 2010.

TAKING SIGHTS

Politics and Religion

Should the Morman Church have been allowed to fund the effort to repeal gay marriage in California?

To what degree does the Constitution establish a separation of church and state?

OVERVIEW

The First Amendment of the U.S. Constitution establishes the separation of church and state. It forbids Congress from creating a national church, and establishes an individual's right to freely practice his or her religion. The amendment does not, however, separate politics from religion. Religion has long impacted politics. It was the core of both the abolition and civil rights movements.

The nation is divided as to whether religions should be actively engaged in politics in a public way.

According to a 2008 poll conducted by the Pew Research Center, 45 percent of Americans believe that churches should express views on political issues compared with 52 percent who believe that they should keep out of political matters.[32]

This issue became particularly important in 2008 when the Mormon Church became involved in Proposition 8, a ballot initiative in California to ban gay marriage. The leadership of the Mormon Church sent a letter to be read at all churches saying that the "Church's teachings and position on this moral issue are unequivocal." The letter went on to ask "that you do all you can to support the proposed constitutional amendment by donating of your means and time." Some reports estimated the Mormon Church donated $190,000 to the cause to ban gay marriage. Many people believe that the Mormon Church's intervention in the California ballot made the difference in the 52 percent vote for the ban.

SUPPORTING
religious group involvement in political issues

Churches do public good. Where churches are engaged in changing the world for the better, they must engage in political action. Not allowing them to do so hinders the church's ability to do good.

The First Amendment protects the free speech of everyone. The freedom to speak politically is one of the most vitally important parts of being a free nation, and to block the free speech of religious leaders or institutions would be an infringement of their rights.

The black churches in the South were a central part of the civil rights movement. When Martin Luther King, Jr. called for congregation members to boycott the buses, he was asking them to behave politically. The church provided a space for political action that mobilized a very important movement in history.

AGAINST
religious group involvement in political issues

Churches have tax-exempt status. Because the primary purpose of a church is to do public good, the church can earn money without paying taxes on it. When a church uses its money to support or oppose political causes, that money should be taxed. In addition, the IRS prohibits the use of funds for political campaigns if the church has taxexempt status.

Churches should be spiritual, not political. Political issues are often nuanced, and don't benefit from unequivocal stands. Churches should not be making political decisions, which dilute their important function of educating people about their faith.

Church leaders do not speak for every member of the congregation. Individual members have differences of opinions from each other and from their leaders on political issues. For example, 46 percent of Presbyterians are Republican, while 50 percent of Presbyterian pastors are Democratic.[33] Leaders cannot speak for their laity as a monolithic church.

what we LEARNED

WHY PEOPLE JOIN GROUPS

9.1 *Why do people join interest groups?*

The free-rider barrier to group membership is the concept that individuals will have little incentive to join a group and contribute resources to it if the group's benefits go to members and non-members alike. Professor Mancur Olson says that groups attempt to compensate for the free-rider barrier by offering selective benefits that go only to group members, including material, purposive, and solidary incentives.

TYPES OF INTEREST GROUPS

9.2 *What types of interest groups are active in American politics and what are their goals?*

An interest group is an organization of people who join together voluntarily on the basis of some interest they share for the purpose of influencing policy. Business groups are concerned with government actions that affect their profits, costs, and operations, such as tax laws, environmental regulations, labor laws, and government contracts. Organized labor favors government policies aimed at making it easier for unions to organize and backs programs and policies designed to improve the quality of life for working people and their families. Professional associations are concerned with public policies that affect their members. Agricultural groups want government loan guarantees, crop subsidies, and the promotion of farm exports. Racial and ethnic minority groups share the goals of equality before the law, representation in elective and appointive office, freedom from discrimination, and economic advance-

ment. Interest groups that are part of the religious right are concerned with such causes as abortion, same-sex marriage, and prayer in school, whereas groups associated with the religious left focus on the wars in Iraq and Afghanistan, immigration reform, environmental protection, and poverty relief. Citizen groups support government policies that they believe will benefit the public at large. Advocacy groups seek benefits on behalf of groups of persons who are in some way incapacitated or otherwise unable to represent their own interests. Members of cause groups care intensely about a single issue or small group of related issues.

INTEREST GROUP STRATEGIES AND TACTICS

9.3 *What strategies and tactics do interest groups use to achieve their goals?*

Interest groups employ a variety of tactics in an effort to achieve their goals, including electioneering, lobbying, creating public pressure, protest demonstrations, litigation, and political violence. Interest groups endorse candidates for office and form political action committees (PACs) to support them financially. They employ professional lobbyists to commu-

nicate the viewpoint of the group to government officials. They may organize public relations campaigns to promote policies they favor or organize protests to broaden and deepen their support. Some groups file lawsuits to achieve their goals, whereas others organize protest demonstrations or engage in political violence.

THE STRENGTH OF INTEREST GROUPS

9.4 *What factors determine the relative strength of interest groups?*

A number of factors affect the relative strength of interest groups, including alliances with political parties, alliances with members of Congress and executive branch officials, public opinion, unity among groups representing the same cause, opposition from other groups, and resources.

MySearchLab®

TEST yourself

9.1 Why do people join interest groups?

1 "I don't see any point in joining the neighborhood civic association. My $25 annual dues aren't enough to make much difference. At any rate, I will benefit from the association's activities whether I am a member or not." The above statement reflects which of the following concepts?
a. Friendly Incumbent Rule
b. Free-rider barrier to group membership
c. Material incentives to group membership
d. Purposive incentives to group membership

2 Eric joined the American Legion because he enjoys hanging out at the Legion Hall with his buddies. This action illustrates which of the following concepts?
a. Free-rider barrier to group membership
b. Material incentive for joining a group
c. Purposive incentive for joining a group
d. Solidary incentive for joining a group

3 Which of the following is an example of a purposive incentive for joining an interest group?
a. Lee joins Greenpeace because he feels strongly about protecting the environment.
b. Diego joins the NRA because he wants to enroll his sons in NRA gun safety classes.
c. Luisa joins the American Federation of Teachers because many of her fellow teachers belong and she enjoys spending time with her friends.
d. None of the above

9.2 What types of interest groups are active in American and what are their goals?

4 Which of the following organizations would be most likely to favor legislation to allow offshore drilling off California and the East Coast?
a. Chamber of Commerce
b. AFL-CIO
c. Exxon Mobil
d. AARP

5 Which of the following statements is true about organized labor?
a. The percentage of the workforce that belongs to labor unions has been in decline for years.
b. Wal-Mart, the nation's largest employer, has successfully resisted unionization efforts.
c. Organized labor is stronger in the Frostbelt and weaker in the Sunbelt.
d. All of the above

6 Which of the following organizations would be most likely to favor affirmative action in college and university admissions?
a. NAACP
b. AFL-CIO
c. AARP
d. Sierra Club

7 Which of the following organizations would be most likely to celebrate Earth Day?
a. NARAL Pro-Choice America
b. The Sierra Club
c. The Human Rights Campaign
d. Common Cause

9.3 What strategies and tactics do interest groups use to achieve their goals?

8 What are political action committees (PACs)?
a. They are organizations representing the interests of firms and professionals in the same general field.
b. They are organizations whose members care intensely about a single issue or small group of related issues.
c. They are organizations created to raise and distribute money in election campaigns.
d. They are organizations created to seek benefits on behalf of groups of persons who are in some way incapacitated or otherwise unable to represent their own interests.

9 Which of the following candidates would you expect to benefit the most from PAC contributions?
a. A Republican challenger
b. A Democratic challenger
c. A candidate from either party running for an open seat
d. An incumbent from either party running for reelection

10 A PAC representing Interest Group A contributed to Congressman B's reelection campaign even though the congressman sides with the interest group's issue positions only about 60 percent of the time. The PAC is acting in accordance with which of the following principles?
a. Friendly Incumbent Rule
b. Free-rider barrier to group membership
c. Bundling
d. Material incentive to group membership

11 Which of the following statements about lobbying and lobbyists is true?
a. Groups lobby the legislative branch of government but not the executive branch.
b. Interest group lobbyists frequently focus on the details of legislation rather than the vote on final passage.
c. Former members of Congress are prohibited by law from becoming lobbyists.
d. None of the above

12 What is the best assessment of the relationship between campaign contributions and interest group lobbying?
a. Money buys votes. Members of Congress vote for the causes supported by the groups that give them the most money.
b. Money buys access. Members of Congress are willing to meet with lobbyists representing groups that provide them with campaign contributions.
c. Money and lobbying are unrelated. Members of Congress are open to consider all views regardless of political contributions.
d. Because of campaign finance regulations, interest groups are prohibited from contributing money to help members of Congress run for reelection.

9.4 What factors determine the relative strength of interest groups?

13 Which of the following types of interest groups is typically allied with the Republican Party?
a. Organized labor
b. Environmental organizations
c. African American rights groups
d. Anti-tax groups

14 Which of the following types of interest groups is typically allied with the Democratic Party?
a. Business groups
b. Abortion rights organizations
c. Conservative Christian organizations
d. None of the above

15 Which of the following factors contributes positively to the strength of an interest group?
a. Public opinion support for the group's goals
b. An alliance with the political party that controls Congress and the White House
c. No or only weak opposition from other interest groups
d. All of the above

KNOW the score

14–15 correct:	Congratulations—you know your American government!
12–13 correct:	Your understanding of this chapter is weak—be sure to review the key terms and visit TheThinkSpot.
<12 correct:	Reread the chapter more thoroughly.

Answers: 1) b, 2) d, 3) a, 4) c, 5) d, 6) a, 7) b, 8) c, 9) d, 10) a, 11) b, 12) b, 13) d, 14) b, 15) d

10 POLITICAL

What Will We Learn?

THE PARTY SYSTEM

Learning Objective **10.1** Why does the United States have a two-party system?

PARTY ORGANIZATION

Learning Objective **10.2** What role do the national organizations play in promoting the success of their political parties?

VOTING PATTERNS

Learning Objective **10.3** What groups of people typically vote Democratic or Republican?

PARTY STRENGTH AND THE PARTY BALANCE

Learning Objective **10.4** What factors **affect the position of a party** in the American political system?

The Tea Party movement has become a major force in American party politics. In 2009, conservative activists organized Tea Party groups around the nation to oppose government bailouts, high taxes, economic stimulus spending, budget deficits, environmental regulations, and health-care reform. The activists took their inspiration from the Boston Tea Party of 1773, when American colonists protested the British tax on tea by dumping three shiploads of it into Boston Harbor. TEA is also an acronym for "taxed enough already." Although most Tea Party activists identified with the Republican Party, they directed their anger not just at President Barack Obama and the Democrats but also at the establishment of the Republican Party because it had failed to rein in government spending during the George W. Bush administration.

The dilemma facing the Republican Party is how to harness the energy of the Tea Party without allowing it to push the Republican Party so far to the right that it alienates swing voters. In 2010, the Tea Party backed conservative challengers against establishment-supported candidates in several U.S. Senate primary elections. A number of Tea Party favorites won, including

PARTIES

Christine O'Donnell in Delaware and Sharron Angle in Nevada. In the November general election, the energy of the **Tea Party movement** increased the turnout of conservative voters, helping the Republican Party capture a majority of seats in the U.S. House, reduce the size of the Democratic majority in the U.S. Senate, and win hundreds of seats in state legislatures around the nation. Both O'Donnell and Angle lost, however, leading some critics to charge that the

Tea Party may have cost the Republicans their chance to capture a majority in the U.S. Senate. Will Republicans face a similar problem in 2012 in races for Congress and even the White House?[1]

The role of the Tea Party in American politics introduces this chapter on political parties. The chapter describes the party system and discusses how parties are organized. It examines the concepts of political cycles and party realignment. It compares and contrasts the

Democratic and Republican Parties in terms of party identifiers, support groups, and issue positions. Finally, the chapter explores the phenomenon of divided government.

Tea Party movement: A loose network of conservative activists organized to protest high taxes, excessive government spending, and big government in general.

THE PARTY SYSTEM

10.1 *Why does the United States have a two-party system?*

A **political party** is a group of individuals who join together to seek government office in order to make public policy. A party differs from an interest group in its effort to win control of the machinery of government. Both parties and interest groups participate in election campaigns, but only parties actually run candidates for office. Candidates for Congress run as Democrats or Republicans, not as representatives of labor unions or corporations.

The number of political parties varies from country to country. The United States has a **two-party system**, which is the division of voter loyalties between two major political parties, resulting in the near exclusion of minor parties from seriously competing for a share of political power. After the 2010 election, 98 of 100 U.S. senators were elected as either Democrats or Republicans. (Bernie Sanders of Vermont and Joe Liebermann of Connecticut won office as independents, but both caucus with the Democrats and are counted as Democrats for the purpose of committee assignments.) The two major parties held all 435 seats in the U.S. House and 49 of 50 offices of state governor. Independent Lincoln Chafee was governor of Rhode Island.

A **third party** is a minor party in a two-party system. Third-party

A **CLOSER** LOOK
Are Third-Party Candidates Spoilers?

Ralph Nader has been an independent candidate for president in several elections, but his most controversial run came in 2000. In the hotly contested state of Florida, George W. Bush beat Al Gore by 537 votes, securing Bush the presidency. Nader received 97,421 votes in Florida, and exit polls showed that most Nader supporters would have chosen Gore over Bush. Although other factors played a role in the 2000 election, many Democrats blamed Nader for Gore's loss. Are they justified?

candidates and independents may compete for office in a two-party system, but usually with a notable lack of success. The roster of third parties in the United States includes Green, Reform, Libertarian, Natural Law, Official Constitution, Workers World, Socialist, and Socialist Equality Parties. The Green and the Libertarian Parties are the most successful, winning a handful of local races.

Why does the United States have a two-party system rather than a system with three or more major political parties, as in many other

democracies? Political scientists offer two sets of explanations—the electoral system and the absence of deep-seated political divisions in American society. Maurice Duverger, a French political scientist,

political party a group of individuals who join together to seek government office in order to make public policy.

two-party system the division of voter loyalties between two major political parties.

third party a minor party in a two-party system.

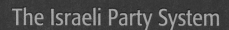
Israel has a **multiparty system**, which is the division of voter loyalties among three or more major political parties. The Knesset, the lower house of the Israeli national legislature, included 12 parties after the 2009 elections. Kadima, the largest party in the Knesset, held 28 of 120 seats. In order to achieve a majority in the Knesset, Kadima had to form a coalition with several smaller parties.

Israel has **proportional representation (PR)**, which is an election system that awards legislative seats to each party approximately equal to its popular voting strength. In 2009, for example, Kadima won 23 percent of the seats in the Knesset based on 22 percent of the popular vote. Proportional representation is related to multiparty systems because voters know that their votes will count. Unless a party has almost no popular support, each vote it receives will enable it to increase its representation in the Knesset.

Democracies with multiparty systems are countries with intense social and political divisions. People who disagree fundamentally about the nature of society and the role of government are less likely to form broad-based coalition parties such as those that exist in the United States. Instead, they create smaller, more narrowly based parties and electoral systems based on proportional representation in order to allow the democratic expression of those divisions at the ballot box.[2]

This menorah sculpture outside of the Knesset building is a symbol of Israel's statehood and sovereignty.

QUESTIONS

1 If the United States were to adopt proportional representation, do you think that a multiparty system would soon develop? Why or why not?

2 If Israel were to adopt a plurality election system, do you think a two-party system would eventually emerge in that country? Why or why not?

3 What are the advantages and disadvantages of each type of party system?

wrote in the 1950s that a **plurality election system**, which is a method for choosing public officials by awarding office to the candidate with the most votes, favors a two-party system.[3] Candidates for executive and legislative office in the United States run from geographic areas and the candidate with more votes wins the office. Candidates who finish second or third win nothing, no matter how

Would you vote for a third-party candidate that you liked even if you thought that he or she had no real chance of winning the election?

close the race. The **Electoral College**, which is the system established in the Constitution for indirect election of the president and vice president, is especially inhospitable to third-party candidates because it awards electoral votes, the only votes that really count, to candidates who win the most popular votes in a state. In 1992, for example, Reform Party candidate Ross Perot won no electoral votes, despite taking 19 percent of the popular vote, because he carried no states. The dilemma for minor parties in the United States is that if they do not quickly develop enough popular support to win elections, the voters will not take them seriously. If voters believe that a party and its candidates are unlikely to win, they often decide to choose between the major party candidates

because they do not want to throw away their votes.[4]

Scholars also believe that a nation's party system reflects the fundamental social and political divisions of society. The more intense the divisions, the more likely it is

multiparty system the division of voter loyalties among three or more major political parties.

proportional representation (PR) an election system that awards legislative seats to each party approximately equal to its popular voting strength.

plurality election system a method for choosing public officials that awards office to the candidate with the most votes; it favors a two-party system.

Electoral College the system established in the Constitution for indirect election of the president and vice president.

that the nation will have a multiparty system. The United States has a two-party system, they say, because Americans are relatively united. Americans may disagree about the role of government in society, but they generally share the basic values of capitalism and democracy. People with opposing views on some issues can unite under the same party banner because they agree on other issues.

PARTY ORGANIZATION

10.2 *What role do the national organizations play in promoting the success of their political parties?*

The organization of political parties in the United States reflects the federal system, with organizations at both the state and national levels of government. At the state level, the Democratic and Republican Party organizations are led by executive party committees, which are elected by party activists who participate in local party meetings, district conventions, and state party conventions. The executive committee usually elects the state party chair.

A national committee and a national chair lead the national party organizations. The national committee consists of a committeeman and committeewoman chosen by the party organizations of each state and the District of Columbia. The

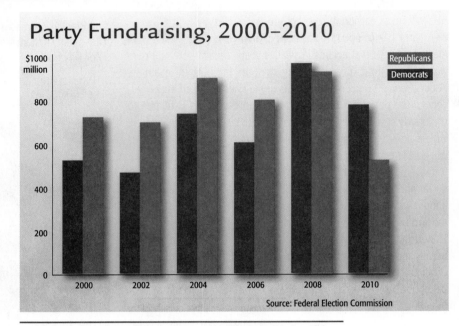

Party contributions are an important source of funding for political candidates.

national committee elects the national committee chair. When the party controls the White House, the president usually handpicks the national chairperson.

Parties Support their Candidates

The Democratic National Committee (DNC) and Republican National Committee (RNC) work to increase the number of party officeholders. Each party tries to recruit a strong list of candidates for the next election. Although the national party organizations do not control nominations, they can encourage potential candidates to run. They also provide candidates with technical assistance and campaign advice. The DNC and RNC support their candidates with polling data, issue research, media assistance, and advice on campaign strategy. Both national parties offer campaign seminars, teaching inexperienced candidates how to do everything from raising money to dealing with the media. The most important service the national party organizations provide for their candidates is money.

The Republicans have historically enjoyed a significant fundraising advantage over the Democrats because of the socioeconomic status of their support base. People who identify with the Republican Party have more money than those who consider themselves Democrats. Moreover, the Republicans have also benefited from a more efficient fundraising operation, especially direct mail. As the figure above

The Republican Party reacted to the election of Barack Obama by choosing former Maryland Lieutenant Governor Michael Steele as the first African American chair of the Republican National Committee.

shows, however, the Democrats closed the fundraising gap by 2008, primarily because they took better advantage of the Internet than did their Republican opponents. The Democratic Party and its candidates now raise substantially more money online than do the Republican Party and its candidates.[5] In 2010, Republicans benefitted more than Democrats from spending by outside groups.[6]

Political parties take a different approach to campaign finance than do interest groups. Most interest groups contribute primarily to incumbent officeholders because they want to develop positive relationships with influential members of Congress. Their goal is access, the opportunity to communicate directly with legislators and other government officials in hopes of influencing the details of policy. In contrast, the goal of political parties is to control the government itself. Consequently, they contribute most of their money to candidates in competitive races, whether incumbents or challengers.[7]

Parties Adopt Platforms

The DNC and RNC are also responsible for producing **party platforms**, statements of party principles and issue positions. These platforms help guide voters and candidates in knowing where the party stands on

Every four years, each of the two major political parties holds a national convention to formally select presidential and vice presidential candidates and to adopt a party platform.

important issues. The 2008 Democratic and Republican Party platforms show clear philosophical differences between the parties on many issues. The parties disagreed on tax policy, labor laws, abortion, gay and lesbian rights, and affirmative action. By no means, however, do the parties take opposite sides on all issues. Some differences are nuanced. Consider gun control. Both parties endorse a right of gun ownership, but they disagree on the efficacy of gun regulation. The Democrats endorse "reasonable regulation," while the Republicans declare that gun control penalizes the law-abiding without having an impact on crime. Finally, the two parties take similar positions on some issues. Both the Democratic and the Republican platforms declare support for Israel, even using the same phrase to pledge that the United States would ensure that Israel would always have better weapons ("a qualitative edge") than its adversaries. You can view the full Republican Party platform at www.gop.com, and the Democratic Party platform at www.democrats.org.

party platform a statement of party principles and issue positions.

TAKE ✓ ACTION

Party Politics at the Grassroots

State and local party organizations are responsible for building grassroots support for candidates and getting out the vote on Election Day. Your assignment is to learn about the organization and activities of a political party in your area by visiting its local office. Go online find the office location and hours, and when you arrive at the office, chat with the office staff, ask questions, collect any literature that might be available, and observe the layout. Do your best to learn the answers to the following research questions:

- What does the local party office do?
- Had you been a potential volunteer, ready to get involved in

party activities, would the local party have been able to take advantage of your energy?
- Was the office well supplied with literature and information about party officeholders, candidates, and issue positions?
- Would you describe the office as well organized or disorganized? Why?

Once you return from your visit, write a short essay describing your experience at the local party office. Discuss the answers to the questions above. Conclude the essay with your personal evaluation of the activity.

VOTING PATTERNS

Voting patterns reflect differences in income, race and ethnicity, education, gender, age, family and lifestyle status, religion, region, place of residence, and political ideology.

Income

Economic status is one of the most enduring bases for voting divisions in America. Since the 1930s, Republican candidates have typically done better among upper-income voters, whereas Democrats have scored their highest vote percentages among lower-income groups. In 2008, **exit polls**, which are surveys based on random samples of voters leaving the polling place, found that Obama outpolled McCain among voters with family incomes less than $50,000 a year by 60 percent to 38 percent. The two candidates evenly split the votes of people in families with annual incomes greater than $50,000.[8]

> **Economic status**
> is one of the most
> **enduring bases for
> voting divisions**
> in America.

Race and Ethnicity

Voting patterns reflect the nation's racial divisions. White voters lean Republican. In 2008, whites backed McCain 55 percent to 45 percent for Obama. In contrast, minority voters support the Democrats. African Americans supported Obama over McCain by a lopsided 95 percent to 4 percent. Asian Americans gave Obama 61 percent of their votes compared with 35 percent who supported McCain. Democratic candidates also enjoy strong support from most Latinos. In 2008, Obama won the Latino vote 66 percent to 32 percent for

McCain.[9] Latino voters were especially important for Obama because they apparently provided his margin of victory in Colorado, Florida, Nevada, and New Mexico, four hotly contested states that George W. Bush won in 2004.[10] Not all groups of Latinos share the same perspective on party affiliation. Whereas Mexican Americans and Puerto Ricans typically vote Democratic, most Cuban Americans support the GOP because of the Republican Party's strong anti-Castro position.[11]

Education

The Democratic Party is strongest with voters at either end of the education ladder. In 2008, Obama led McCain by 63 percent to 35 percent among voters who had not graduated from high school. Obama won the votes of high school graduates, as well, by a more modest 52 percent compared to 46 percent for his Republican opponent. The two parties evenly split the votes of college graduates. Among voters with postgraduate degrees, however, Obama led his Republican opponents by 58 percent to 40 percent.[12] For the most part, the relationship between education and party support reflects differences in income. As people move up the education ladder, they also move up the income ladder. Individuals in higher income brackets are more likely to vote Republican than are lower-income voters. The pattern holds true through college but not into graduate and professional school.

exit polls surveys based on random samples of voters leaving the polling place.

In 2008, young people and minority voters turned out in large numbers to support Barack Obama and Democratic candidates for Congress, but in 2010, not so much. Exit polls showed that Democrats carried the youth vote and the minority vote, but their turnout in 2010 lagged compared with 2008.

People who have postgraduate college degrees tend to vote Democratic because many of them hold liberal positions on social issues such as abortion rights, environmental protection, and gay and lesbian rights.

Gender

For more than 40 years, American voters have divided along gender lines, producing a gender gap, the differences in party identification and political attitudes between men and women. The **gender gap** has emerged in American politics because men have moved away from the Democratic Party. In 1952, a majority of both men and women identified with the Democratic Party. Since then, the percentage of women identifying with the Democrats has risen while the proportion of men has declined In 2008, Democrat Obama won the support of half of the male voters while taking 56 percent of the women's vote, a 6 percentage point gender gap.[13]

Age

Polling data reveal that younger voters have been moving toward the Democratic Party. In fact, Obama won the presidency in 2008 because of his support from younger voters. He outpolled McCain among voters under the age of 30 by 66 percent to 32 percent. Obama won the 30-to-44 age bracket as well, but by a closer margin of 52 percent to 46 percent. The two candidates split the votes of people age 45 to 64. McCain won a majority of voters over the age of 65, 53 percent to 45 percent for Obama.[14]

Family and Lifestyle Status

People who are members of traditional families tend to vote Republican, whereas unmarried adults and people who are gay, lesbian, or bisexual generally back the Democrats. In 2008, married voters supported McCain by 51 percent to 47 percent for Obama. In contrast, Obama led his Republican opponent among single people by 65 percent

Michelle Bachmann (R, MN), announcing her candidacy for the 2012 Republican presidential nomination, hoped to win the nomination with strong Tea Party support.

to 33 percent. Voters who identified as gay, lesbian, or bisexual supported Obama by 70 percent to 27 percent for McCain.[15]

Religion

Religion and party support are closely related. Before the 1980s, voting patterns reflected religious affiliation. Protestants generally supported the Republican Party, Catholics leaned to the Democratic Party, and Jews were strongly Democratic. Today, party divisions based on religion have grown more complex. Although most Jews still vote for Democrats, Catholics have become a swing group. Conservative white evangelical Protestants (including Southern Baptists, Pentecostals, and members of the Assemblies of God) are firmly Republican, as are members of the Church of Jesus Christ of Latter-day Saints (the Mormons). Latinos as a whole typically support the Democrats, but the GOP is stronger among Latino evangelicals than among Latino Catholics, who remain firmly Democratic.[16] White members of mainline Protestant denominations (including Methodists, Episcopalians, and Presbyterians) lean Republican as well, but less so than do evangelicals. Most African Americans are Democrats, regardless of their religious preferences.[17] In 2008, Jews supported Obama over McCain by 78 percent to 21 percent. Catholics backed Obama as well, but the margin was more narrow: 54 percent to 45 percent. Protestants voted for McCain by 54 percent, compared to 45 percent for Obama.[18]

> Voting patterns are also based on **frequency of attendance** at religious services.

In the current party system, voting patterns are also based on frequency of attendance at religious services. White Protestants and Catholics who attend worship services regularly are more likely to vote Republican than are people in the same group who attend services less frequently.[19] In 2008, McCain

gender gap differences in party identification and political attitudes between men and women

the suburbs was 50 percent for Obama to 48 percent for McCain.[22]

Political Ideology

The Democratic and Republican parties are ideologically polarized. In 2008, liberals supported Obama over McCain by a substantial 88 percent to 10 percent. In contrast, conservatives backed McCain by an impressive 78 percent to 20 percent. Moderates tend to be swing voters. Obama won the White House because he captured the votes of moderates, 60 percent, compared to 39 percent for McCain.[23]

The political parties were once more ideologically diverse than they are today. Many conservatives identified with the Democratic Party, especially in the South, whereas the Republican Party had a liberal wing based principally in the Northeast. Important legislation frequently passed Congress with the support of bipartisan coalitions. For example, the Civil Rights Act of 1964 passed Congress because moderate and liberal Republicans joined liberal Democrats to overcome the intense opposition of conservative Southern Democrats.

> Since 1960, the parties have **grown further apart** ideologically.

The political parties are more ideologically distinct today because their coalitions of supporters have changed. The move of Southern white conservatives from the Democratic Party to the GOP has made the Democrats more liberal and the Republicans more conservative. The Democratic Party has adopted liberal positions on a range of social issues in order to appeal to middle-class voters concerned with abortion rights, the environment, and gay and lesbian rights. The Republican Party, meanwhile, has taken conservative positions on social issues to bolster its support among conservative Christians.[24]

Joel Osteen—pastor, best-selling author, and televangelist—preaches at Lakewood Church in Houston. It is the largest "megachurch" in the country, drawing over 40,000 people to services each week. Religion and party support are closely related.

led among voters who said that they attended religious services more than once a week by 55 percent to 43 percent for Obama. In contrast, voters who declared that they seldom attended religious services voted for Obama by 59 percent to 40 percent. People who never attended services backed the Democrat by 67 percent to 30 percent.[20]

Region

Regional voting patterns have changed. The South was once the strongest region for the Democratic Party, whereas the Midwest was a stronghold for the GOP. Today, Democrats run best in the Northeast and on the West Coast. The GOP is strongest in the South, the Great Plains, and the Rocky Mountain West. The Midwest has become

a battleground region between the two parties. In 2008, Obama was strongest in the Northeast, winning 59 percent of the vote and carrying every state in the region. McCain ran best in the South, outpolling Obama 53 percent to 46 percent, and winning every southern state except Florida, North Carolina, and Virginia.[21]

Place of Residence

Voting patterns reflect place of residence. Generally, Democrats win urban areas, Republicans carry rural areas, and the suburbs are a battleground between the two parties. In 2008, Obama outpolled McCain in large urban areas by 63 percent to 35 percent, whereas the Republican candidate won rural areas by 53 percent to 45 percent. The vote in

PARTY STRENGTH AND THE PARTY BALANCE

10.4 *What factors affect the position of a political party in the American political system?*

The strength of a political party depends on its level of support among the electorate and the offices it holds.

Party Identification

Political scientists measure party identification by asking survey respondents if they consider themselves Democrats, Republicans, or Independents. In early 2010, Democrats outnumbered Republicans by a margin of 32 percent to 28 percent, with another 39 percent declaring that they were Independents. However, when asked whether they leaned more to the Democratic Party or the Republican Party, most of the Independents expressed a preference for one party or the other. Adding together party identifiers and leaning independents, the Democratic advantage shrunk to just one percentage—46 percent to 45 percent. Since the 2008 election, the party identification margin between the two parties has narrowed. In November 2008, Democrats and independents leaning to the Democratic Party outnumbered Republicans and independents leaning to the GOP by 51 percent to 40 percent, a difference of 11 percentage points.[27]

think *Is it better to identify with a political party or to be an independent? Why might a voter choose not to identify with a particular party?*

Political Cycles

The political party or party coalition holding the reins of government in a democracy is the **governing party**. The governing party formulates, adopts, and implements government policies. Although the nature of America's political system typically prevents the governing party from enacting all (or sometimes even most) of its policy agenda, it is able to take the policy lead on most issues. The political party out of power in a democracy is the **opposition party**. The opposition party criticizes the policies of the governing party and offers alternatives. Opposition parties help make democracy work by providing information to citizens and offering voters alternative policies and alternative sets of leaders to those put forward by the governing party. If the voters approve of government policies and believe the country is on the right track, they can return the governing party to power at election time. In contrast, if voters are unhappy with the state of the nation and blame the party in power, they can vote the governing party out of office and turn over the reins of government to the opposition party.

Alternation in power among political parties is an inevitable and essential element of democracy because it is the mechanism for holding the government accountable to the voters. The president and members of Congress have an incentive to do their best to provide an effective government because they know that they will eventually be held accountable at the ballot box.

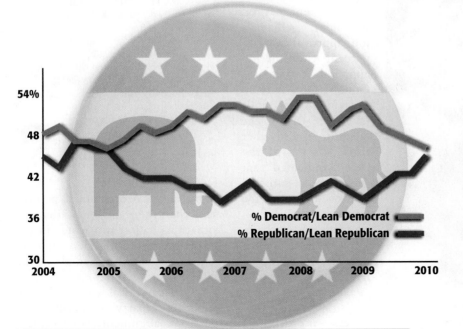

Party Identification, 2004–2010

% Democrat/Lean Democrat
% Republican/Lean Republican

54%
48
42
36
30

2004 2005 2006 2007 2008 2009 2010

Since the 2008 election, the party identification margin between the two parties has narrowed.
Source: Gallup.

governing party the political party or party coalition holding the reins of government in a democracy.

opposition party the political party out of power in a democracy.

The success of the Democratic Party in the 2006 and 2008 elections, for example, reflected popular displeasure with the performance of the Republican Congress (before the 2006 election) and the George W. Bush administration. In early 2008, fewer than one in three Americans approved of President Bush's performance as president, seriously damaging the prospects of Republican Party candidates in that year's election.[28] After the 2008 election, the Democratic Party controlled the White House and expanded its majorities in both houses of Congress. Democrats also saw significant gains at the state level. The 2010 midterm election is another example of voters holding the governing party accountable except this time it was the Democrats who were in charge and who suffered big losses. The Republican Party won control of the U.S. House, added seats in the Senate, and made substantial gains at the state level.

Political scientists Samuel Merrill, III, Bernard Grofman, and Thomas L. Brunell offer a theory to explain partisan cycles in American politics. They note that the average American voter is moderate—less liberal on most policy issues than the Democratic Party and less conservative than the Republicans. When the Democrats are in power, the public mood grows more conservative because the Democrats adopt policies that are more liberal than the policy preferences of the average voter. Over a period of time, the public grows dissatisfied and votes for change, putting a Republican in the White House and electing a Republican majority in Congress. The opposite happens when the Republicans are in power.

Indeed, the outcome of the 2010 election reflected the dissatisfaction of the nation with the party in charge. Polls taken just before the election found that Americans believed that the country was on the wrong track by a 64 percent to 31 percent margin. President Obama's job approval was 45 percent while the job approval rating for Congress was only 20 percent.[29] Exit polls taken the day of the election found that three fourths of the voters indicated that they were dissatisfied or even angry with the way the federal government was working. Why were people unhappy? It was primarily the economy. According to exit polls, 89 percent of voters said that the nation's economy was

Republican Congressman John Boehner of Ohio replaced Democrat Nancy Pelosi as speaker of the House after Republicans won a big victory in the 2010 election.

OFFICE HOURS
with PROFESSOR TANNAHILL

QUESTION: Why can't the Democrats and Republicans in Congress work together to solve the nation's problems instead of trying to score political points? If you listen to the Republicans, the Democrats never have a good idea, and vice versa. Where is the common ground?

ANSWER: Democrats and Republicans in Congress don't always work together because the voters who elect them don't trust the other party. The voter bases of the two parties are polarized on a broad range of issues, including taxes and spending, regulation, abortion, gay and lesbian rights, climate change, and foreign policy.[25] According to a Harris Poll conducted in early 2010, two-thirds of Republicans think that President Obama is a socialist (67 percent) and more than 40 percent believe he is a racist.[26] If you were a Republican member of Congress and many of the people who elected you think Obama is a racist and a socialist, would you cooperate with him on policy issues? I haven't seen any polling on how hardcore Democrats feel about Sarah Palin and other Republican leaders, but I suspect their views are pretty negative as well.

in bad shape. More than 40 percent said that their personal financial situations had grown worse in the last two years and 87 percent were worried or very worried about the direction of the economy.[30]

Other political sciences use the concepts of party era and political party realignment to explain changes in the party balance. A

Divided Government

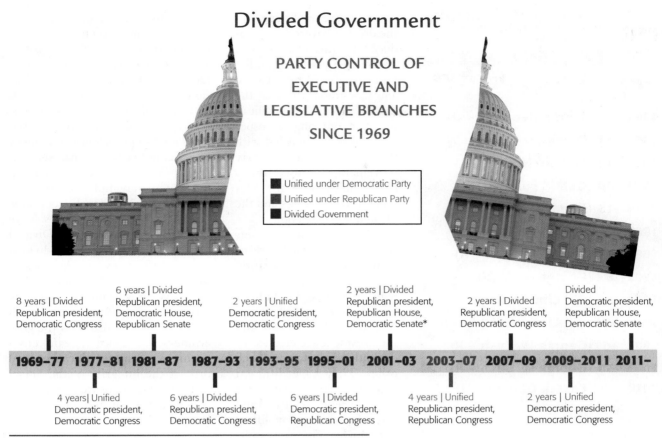

PARTY CONTROL OF EXECUTIVE AND LEGISLATIVE BRANCHES SINCE 1969

■ Unified under Democratic Party
■ Unified under Republican Party
■ Divided Government

8 years | Divided Republican president, Democratic Congress	6 years | Divided Republican president, Democratic House, Republican Senate		2 years | Unified Democratic president, Democratic Congress		2 years | Divided Republican president, Republican House, Democratic Senate*	2 years | Divided Republican president, Democratic Congress		Divided Democratic president, Republican House, Democratic Senate

1969–77 1977–81 1981–87 1987–93 1993–95 1995–01 2001–03 2003–07 2007–09 2009–2011 2011–

4 years| Unified Democratic president, Democratic Congress	6 years | Divided Republican president, Democratic Congress	6 years | Divided Democratic president, Republican Congress	4 years | Unified Republican president, Republican Congress	2 years | Unified Democratic president, Democratic Congress

Divided government is not unique to the current era but it has become more frequent.

*After the 2000 election, the Senate was evenly divided between the two parties, and the vote of Republican Vice President Richard Cheney enabled the GOP to claim majority status. In 2001, Republican Senator James Jeffords of Vermont switched his party allegiance from Republican to independent to allow the Democrats to claim the majority, which they held until 2003.

party era is a period of time characterized by a degree of uniformity in the nature of political party competition. A **party realignment** is a change in the underlying party loyalties of voters that ends one party era and begins another. The 1932 election in which the Democrat Franklin Roosevelt swept into office in the midst of the Great Depression is the classic example of a realigning election. The voters blamed the Republican Party for the Depression and turned control of government over to the Democrats, who held onto their majority status for nearly 50 years.

Divided Government

American elections sometimes result in **divided government**, which refers to the phenomenon of one political party controlling the legislative branch of government while the other holds the executive branch. Divided government can produce policy gridlock or cooperation. If party leaders in Congress and the president are unable to reach agreement on major policy issues, Congress may reject presidential initiatives while the president may veto measures passed by Congress, leaving the country in a policy gridlock. Alternatively, Congressional leaders and the White House may cooperate to adopt compromise policies.

Historical research shows that divided government is not unique to the current era, although it has become more frequent. The first instances of divided government occurred before the Civil War. In the nineteenth century, 16 of 50 elections produced divided government, with different parties controlling the White House and at least one chamber of Congress.[31] Between 1900 and 1952, 22 elections produced unified government; 4 resulted in divided government. Divided government has now become commonplace. Between 1952 and 2010, 11 elections resulted in unified government while 18 elections produced divided government.[32] (See figure above.) Divided government is common at the state level as well.

party era a period of time characterized by a degree of uniformity in the nature of political party competition

party realignment a change in the underlying party loyalties of voters that ends one party era and begins another.

divided government the phenomenon of one political party controlling the legislative branch of government while the other holds the executive branch.

MIDTERM GAINS AND LOSSES FOR THE PRESIDENT'S PARTY*

Year	Seats	President
1962	-4	(John F. Kennedy – D)
1966	-47	(Lyndon Johnson – D)
1970	-12	(Richard Nixon – R)
1974	-48	(Gerald Ford – R)
1978	-15	(Jimmy Carter – D)
1982	-26	(Ronald Reagan – R)
1986	-5	(Ronald Reagan – R)
1990	-8	(George H. W. Bush – R)
1994	-52	(Bill Clinton – D)
1998	+5	(Bill Clinton – D)
2002	+5	(George W. Bush – R)
2006	-30	(George W. Bush – R)
2010	-63	(Barack Obama – D)

Midterm elections are more likely to produce divided government than are presidential election years. With relatively few exceptions, the president's party loses seats in the House in a midterm election (see figure above). On ten occasions since 1894, midterm elections have produced divided government or added a second chamber to opposition control.[33] In 2006, for example, the Democratic Party won control of Congress, producing divided government after a period of unified Republican control. The 2008 election ended divided government because Democrats won control of both the White House and Congress. Divided government returned in 2011 after the Republican Party won a majority of seats in the U.S. House in the 2010 midterm election. Some observers are predicting that the divided government produced by this election will ensure two years of conflict between the White House and Congress. Many of the newly elected Republican members of Congress, especially members elected with the backing of the Tea Party movement, promised not to compromise with the Democrats in Congress and the Obama administration.

The Constitution sets the stage for divided government through its separation of powers among executive, legislative, and judicial branches of government. Members of Congress and the president are elected independently from each other. They have different constituencies, serve terms of different length, and stand for election at different times. Whereas candidates for president stress national issues involving foreign policy, defense, and the strength of the nation's economy, candidates for the House of Representatives focus on local issues, such as cleaning up an area waterway or the proposed closure of a regional military base. Local voters may choose the presidential candidate who they believe will work the hardest to cut taxes while voting for the candidate for Congress who promises to support increased federal spending in the region.[34]

think Do you prefer divided government, or would you rather have both the legislative and executive branches controlled by the same party?

At any given time, Party A may have an advantage on national issues while Party B is perceived by voters as being stronger on local issues. During the 1980s, presidential elections focused on defense, tax rates, and cultural values—issues that favored the Republicans. In contrast, races for Congress focused on more specific policy concerns, such as protecting Social Security, helping farmers or unemployed workers, and promoting local economic development. These issues gave Democrats the advantage.[35] Divided government reflected the divided issue preferences of Americans. Voters want low inflation, a less obtrusive government, and low taxes—positions associated with the GOP. Voters also want the government to ensure a safe environment, promote education, and protect the integrity of the Social Security and Medicare programs—issues that favor the Democratic Party.[36]

Divided government reflects the divided issue preferences of Americans

Political scientists disagree as to whether divided government is the result of conscious voter choice. Some research indicates that even though the proportion of voters who split their ticket in order to balance the House with a president of the other party is small, the number is large enough to affect election outcomes.[37] Other research, however, finds that voters who split their tickets in hopes of producing divided control of government are more than offset by people who cast straight tickets in order to minimize gridlock. In other words, strategic voting makes divided government less common, not more common.[38]

TAKING SIDES

Polarized Parties and American Government

Have political parties become too polarized?

Does party polarization in Congress reflect political polarization in the electorate?

OVERVIEW

The U.S. Congress is more politically polarized than any time in more than a century. The Democrats are coalescing around a liberal agenda and Republicans rallying around a conservative one. Within the parties, the high degree of ideological cohesion leads to partisan battles that often stall legislation. For example, while Democrats hold the presidency and a majority in Congress, they have difficulty passing legislation because they are unable to persuade any Republicans to support their initiatives. Both parties are pushing aside moderate candidates and centrist officials in favor of hardline conservatives for the GOP and committed liberals for the Democrats.

Is the electorate as polarized as the political parties have become? According to political scientist Morris Fiorina, the electorate is generally the same as it always has been: more moderate than the elected officials. Other political scientists argue that while the general population claims to be more moderate, people are actually voting more and more along ideological lines. The parties respond to this trend by choosing candidates who are more ideologically distinct and extreme.

 SUPPORTING building party consensus

 AGAINST building party consensus

Polarized parties pit two sides against each other. Americans have much more in common than the polarized system allows. Many Americans actually hold similar views, and when we look at election results we see many people winning in very close races. When elected officials who win in close elections claim mandates for their party, it leads to discord rather than deliberation.

Election results are not accepted. The more Americans are polarized, the less likely they are able to see that the other side has a legitimate claim to govern. Instead of accepting the 2008 election results, many Americans joined protest movements even before the new administration took office.

Party polarization impedes accountability. In a system where it is clear that one party is in control, any good or bad can be credited or blamed on that party in time for the next election. With party polarization in a separated system, there is no accountability. One party always blames the other party for all failures and credits its own membership for all successes, so the extent to which the government has failed or succeeded is unclear.

Competitive parties lead to more participation. One thing we know about politics is that if the parties are seen as distinct and are competitive with each other, then more people show up to vote and more people care about politics. Younger Americans have become more politically involved over the last decade, which may in large measure be due to the partisan polarization we see.

Representation means reflecting the ideological values of the people who elected you. The nation has conservative and liberal population bases. Members of each side have an expectation that when they elect someone, that official will represent their opinions, which is what representative democracy should be.

Party polarization slows down legislation inside Congress. The founders designed a separated system to prevent legislative tyranny, and partisan polarization helps to slow the legislative process. Divided government requires compromise, so party polarization gives us better government.

what we LEARNED

THE PARTY SYSTEM

10.1 *Why does the United States have a two-party system?*

The United States has a two-party system, which is the division of voter loyalties between two major political parties, resulting in the near exclusion of minor parties from seriously competing for a share of political power. Political scientists attribute America's two-party system to the nature of the country's election system, especially plurality elections and the Electoral College, as well as to the absence of fundamental social and political divisions.

PARTY ORGANIZATION

10.2 *What role do the national organizations play in promoting the success of their political parties?*

The national political party organizations recruit candidates, provide them with technical assistance and advice, and spend money on their behalf. Historically, the Republicans have enjoyed a fundraising advantage over the Democrats, but that advantage disappeared in 2008.

The national parties also produce platforms that demonstrate where the parties stand on issues. Since 1960, the parties have grown further apart philosophically, with the Democrats generally taking liberal positions and the Republicans expressing conservative views. Democrats believe that a strong government is needed to provide essential services and remedy social inequalities, while Republicans believe that a strong government interferes with business and threatens individual freedom.

VOTING PATTERNS

10.3 *What groups of people typically vote Democratic or Republican?*

Democrats do better among middle- and low-income people, minority voters, high-school dropouts, people with graduate degrees, women, younger people, single persons, gay/lesbian/bisexual individuals, people living in the Northeast and on the West Coast, liberals, Jews, people who seldom if ever attend religious services, and people living in urban areas. In contrast, Republicans are stronger with middle- and upper-income groups, white voters, people with bachelor's degrees, men, older people, married people, Southerners, conservatives, white evangelical Protestants, people who attend religious services regularly, and people living in rural areas.

PARTY STRENGTH AND THE PARTY BALANCE

10.4 *What factors affect the position of a political party in the American political system?*

The strength of a political party depends on its level of support among the electorate and the offices it holds. The two parties were at near parity in terms of party identification in 2010 and, after the 2010 midterm election, they shared power. Republicans controlled the U.S. House while Democrats enjoyed a majority of seats in the U.S. Senate and held the White House. Whereas the political party or party coalition holding the reins of government in a democracy is the governing party, the party out of power is the opposition party. Some political sciences use the concepts of party era and political party realignment to explain changes in the party balance. The phenomenon of one political party controlling the legislative branch of government while the other holds the executive branch is known as divided government.

From: Professor Tannahill
Add Cc | Add Bcc

Subject: Tips for Success

📎 Attach a file

BE A PROBLEM SOLVER:
Learn to be a problem solver, someone who finds solutions to problems and identifies new ways to get the job done, rather than someone who always turns to others to solve problems.

MySearchLab®

10.1 *Why does the United States have a two-party system?*

1 Which of the following is *not* a reason why the United States has a two-party system rather than a multiparty system?
  a. The plurality election system awards office to the candidate with the most votes, leaving candidates who finished a strong second or third with nothing.
  b. The Electoral College awards electoral votes only to candidates who win the most votes in each state.
  c. The United States is not deeply divided along social and political lines.
  d. Federal law limits the number of parties on the ballot to two.

2 An election system that awards office to the candidate with the most votes is known by which of the following terms?
  a. Proportional representation
  b. Party realignment
  c. Plurality election system
  d. Two-party system

3 Which of the following statements is true about Israel but is *not* true about the United States?
  a. If a political party gets 10 percent of the vote, it will get 10 percent of the seats in the national legislature.
  b. Candidates for the national legislature run from geographical areas called districts.
  c. Nearly all of the members of the national legislature are members of one of two major political parties.
  d. Voters may be reluctant to vote for a smaller party because they do not want to "throw their vote away" on a party that has no chance to gain representation.

10.2 *What role do the national organizations play in promoting the success of their political parties?*

4 Which of the following statements is true about party fundraising?
  a. The Democratic Party has historically raised more money than has the Republican Party.
  b. The Republican Party closed the fundraising gap with the Democrats in 2006 and especially 2008.
  c. The Republican Party has caught up with the Democrats because of Internet fundraising.
  d. None of the above

5 Which of the following candidates would be the most likely to benefit from financial support from the national party organization?
  a. A powerful committee chair facing only token opposition

  b. A candidate for an open seat locked in a close contest
  c. A challenger taking on an entrenched incumbent who will be very difficult to defeat
  d. A member of Congress running for re-election unopposed.

6 On which of the following issues do the Democratic Party and the Republican Party most closely agree?
  a. Immigration reform
  b. Energy Policy
  c. Support for Israel
  d. Affirmative Action

10.3 *What groups of people typically vote Democratic or Republican?*

7 Among which of the following income groups would you expect the Republican candidate for president to do best in the next presidential election?
  a. People making less than $30,000 a year
  b. People making between $30,000 and $60,000 a year
  c. People making between $100,000 and $150,000 a year
  d. People making more than $200,000 a year

8 Which of the following statements is true about the groups that support each of the two major political parties?
  a. Men are more likely than women to vote Democratic.
  b. The more education one has, the more likely that person is to vote Republican.
  c. White voters are more likely than are non-white voters to support Republican candidates.
  d. None of the above

9 Which of the following statements is true about voter preferences?
  a. Gay and lesbian voters tend to vote Republican.
  b. Married voters tend to vote Democratic.
  c. Women are more likely to vote Republican than are men.
  d. None of the above

10 Which of the following groups tends to vote Democratic?
  a. People who call themselves conservative
  b. Gays and lesbians
  c. People living in small towns and rural areas
  d. Men

11 Which of the following groups tend to vote Republican?
  a. People who attend religious services on a weekly basis
  b. Women
  c. People living in inner-city areas
  d. Jews

10.4 *What factors affect the position of a political party in the American political system?*

12 Which of the following is a period of time characterized by a degree of uniformity in the nature of political party competition?
  a. Plurality election system
  b. Party realignment
  c. Party era
  d. Proportional representation

13 Which of the following statements about party identification is accurate?
  a. Democrats outnumber Republicans by a ratio of two to one.
  b. Republicans outnumber Democrats by a ratio of two to one.
  c. Democrats slightly outnumber Republicans.
  d. Republicans slightly outnumber Democrats.

14 Which political party was the governing party of American national government after the 2008 election?
  a. The Republican Party, because the president was a Republican.
  b. The Democratic Party, because opinion polls showed a majority of Americans identified with the Democratic Party.
  c. The Democratic Party, because it held majorities in both houses of Congress and held the presidency.
  d. The Republican Party, because it held majorities in both houses of Congress and held the presidency.

15 Political Party A controls both houses of Congress, while Political Party B holds the presidency. This situation is an example of which of the following?
  a. Divided government
  b. Responsible parties
  c. Proportional representation
  d. Realignment

KNOW the score

14–15 correct:	Congratulations—you know your American government!
12–13 correct:	Your understanding of this chapter is weak—be sure to review the key terms and visit TheThinkSpot.
<12 correct:	Reread the chapter more thoroughly.

Answers: 1) d, 2) c, 3) a, 4) d, 5) b, 6) c, 7) d, 8) c, 9) d, 10) b, 11) a, 12) c, 13) c, 14) c, 15) a

11 CAMPAIGNS

ELECTIONS IN AMERICA

Learning Objective **11.1** How are elections conducted in the United States?

ELECTION CAMPAIGNS

Learning Objective **11.2** How are political campaigns organized?

CONGRESSIONAL ELECTIONS

Learning Objective **11.3** What are the similarities and differences between elections for the House and Senate?

PRESIDENTIAL ELECTIONS: THE NOMINATION

Learning Objective **11.4** What are the main steps in the contest for the presidential nomination of each party?

PRESIDENTIAL ELECTIONS: THE GENERAL ELECTION

Learning Objective **11.5** How does the Electoral College affect presidential elections?

HOW VOTERS DECIDE

Learning Objective **11.6** What factors affect voter choice?

Every 10 years, states with two or more U.S. House seats redraw congressional district boundaries to reflect population change. The process is both political and litigious (meaning it involves lawsuits). Texas was the big winner after the 2010 Census because it gained four seats to increase its representation in the House from 32 to 36 seats. With large majorities in both chambers of the Texas legislature and Republican Rick Perry in the governor's mansion, the Republican Party was in position to increase the ratio of Republicans to Democrats in the state's congressional delegation from 23 to 9

AND ELECTIONS

in 2011–2013 to a projected ratio of 26 to 10 after the 2012 election. Moreover, none of the districts appeared to be competitive between the two parties, ensuring that members of Congress would be chosen in primary elections, which are typically dominated by the most conservative voters (for Republicans) or the most liberal voters (for Democrats).[1]

Nonetheless, the Texas legislature might not have the last word on redistricting in the state. Minority rights groups filed suit, charging that the new districts illegally diminished minority voting rights. Even though 95 percent of the state's population growth between 2000 and 2010 was minority, mostly Hispanic, three of the four new congressional districts were expected to elect white members of Congress.[2]

The battle over redistricting introduces this chapter on elections in America. The chapter focuses on elections, considering types of elections, election districts and redistricting, political campaigns, congressional elections, presidential elections, the factors that influence voter choice, and the relationship between elections and public policy.

ELECTIONS IN AMERICA

11.1 *How are elections conducted in the United States?*

Americans have the opportunity to cast ballots in several types of elections.

Types of Elections

A **general election** is an election to fill state and national offices in November of even-numbered years. Voters choose among Democratic and Republican candidates, and sometimes third-party candidates and independent candidates not affiliated with any political party. Some states allow voters to cast a **straight-ticket ballot,** which refers to voters selecting the entire slate of candidates from one party only. In contrast, a **split-ticket ballot** involves voters casting their

ballots for candidates of two or more political parties.

Most general elections are plurality elections. In every state but Georgia, the candidate with the most votes wins the general election, regardless of whether the candidate has a majority of ballots cast. Georgia requires a **runoff,** which is a later election between the two candidates receiving the most votes when no candidate has won a majority in the initial election.

In most states, major parties choose their general election candi-

dates in primary elections scheduled a month or more before the November general election. A **primary election** is an election held to determine a party's nominees for the general election ballot. Democrats compete against other Democrats; Republicans compete against Republicans. In a number of states, a candidate must achieve a certain threshold level of support at a state party convention in order to qualify for the primary ballot. The candidate with the most votes wins the primary election in most states, regardless of whether the candidate has a majority. Some states, including most southern states, require a runoff between the top two candidates if no one receives a majority in the first vote.

general election an election to fill state and national offices held in November of even-numbered years.

straight ticket ballot voters selecting the entire slate of candidates of one party only.

split ticket ballot voters casting their ballots for the candidates of two or more political parties.

runoff an election between the two candidates receiving the most votes when no candidate got a majority in an initial election.

primary election an election held to determine a party's nominees for the general election ballot.

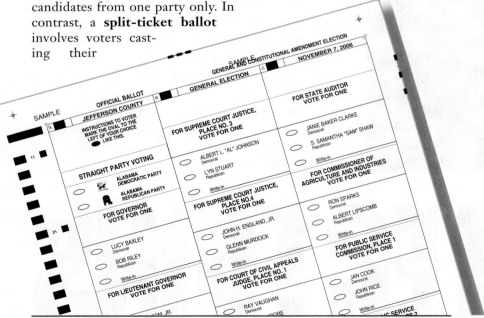

This sample ballot allows for a straight party vote. If a voter selects this option, she can fill in the party bubble to vote for all candidates of that party, rather than filling in her choices for each office on the ballot.

Some states conduct closed primaries; other states hold open primaries. A **closed primary** is an election system that limits primary election participation to registered party members. Only registered Republicans can vote in the Republican primary; participants in the Democratic primary must be registered Democrats. In contrast, an **open primary** is an election system that allows voters to pick the party primary of their choice without regard to their party affiliation. California has adopted a **jungle primary**, which is a primary election system in which all the candidates for an office run in the same primary regardless of political party affiliation (see *Breaking News*).

Election Districts

American voters select public officials in a combination of at-large and district elections. In an **at-large election,** citizens of an entire political subdivision, such as a state, vote to select officeholders. U.S. senators, state governors, and other state executive-branch officials are elected at-large in statewide elections. States that are so sparsely populated that they have only one representative in the U.S. House of Representatives, such as Alaska, Delaware, and Wyoming, choose their member of Congress in statewide at-large elections as well.

In a **district election,** a political subdivision, such as a state, is divided into geographic areas called districts, and each district elects one official. States with more than one U.S. representative choose their members of Congress from districts. Virginia for example, with 11 members of the U.S. House, has 11 U.S. congressional districts, each of which elects one representative. The members of state legislatures are also chosen in district elections.

Legislative district boundaries must be redrawn every ten years, after the national census is taken. Census data are used for apportioning the 435 seats of the U.S. House

The 2010 Reapportionment

Ten states lost one or more seats in the U.S. House of Representatives after the 2010 Census, while eight states gained one or more seats.

of Representatives among the states. **Apportionment** is the allocation of legislative seats among the states. States that grew rapidly since the last census gain seats in the House, whereas states that lost population or grew relatively slowly lose representation. After the 2010 Census, ten states lost one or more seats in the House, while eight states gained one or more seats. New York and other states that lost seats had to shuffle district boundaries to reduce their number of congressional districts. In contrast, Texas and other states that gained seats redrew district boundaries to increase the number of districts.

Legislative districts must also be redrawn if census data show population movement within a state. **Redistricting** is the process through which the boundaries of legislative districts are redrawn to reflect population movement. During the first half of the twentieth century, a number of states failed to redistrict despite dramatic population movement from rural to urban areas, because rural state legislators did not want to relinquish control. As a result, the population size of legislative districts

varied dramatically. In Illinois in the early 1960s, one U.S. congressional district in Chicago had a population of 914,053, while another district in rural southern Illinois contained

closed primary an election system that limits primary election participation to registered party members.

open primary an election system that allows voters to pick the party primary of their choice without regard to their party affiliation.

jungle primary a primary election system in which all the candidates for an office run in the same primary regardless of political party affiliation

at-large election a method for choosing public officials in which the citizens of an entire political subdivision, such as a state, vote to select officeholders.

district election a method for choosing public officials that divides a political subdivision, such as a state, into geographic areas called districts; each district elects one official.

apportionment the allocation of legislative seats among the states.

redistricting the process through which the boundaries of legislative districts are redrawn to reflect population movement.

California Voters Adopt Jungle Primary

California voters approved a state ballot proposition in 2010 creating a jungle primary, in which all the candidates for an office run in the same primary regardless of political party affiliation. The two candidates with the most votes then appear on the general election ballot. The proponents of the jungle primary, including California Governor Arnold Schwarzenegger, argued that it would help elect moderates as opposed to the liberal Democrats and conservative Republicans who emerge from the traditional primary system. In contrast, critics of the proposal, which included the leaders of all of the state's political parties, called it a gimmick that would confuse voters without improving the quality of elected officials.[3]

DISCUSSION

How does the jungle primary differ from a traditional primary? The traditional primary system is really two primary elections held simultaneously, a Republican primary and a Democratic primary, with the winners of each contest facing off in the general election. In a jungle primary, every candidate is on the same ballot without regard to party affiliation. The top two vote getters move on to the general election ballot.

Is it possible that the general election race could involve candidates from the same party? Yes. Two Democrats, two Republicans, or even two independents could emerge as the general election candidates.

Why does Governor Schwarzenegger believe that the new primary system will help elect moderates? The traditional primary system favors the election of very liberal Democrats and very conservative Republicans because primary election voters tend to be ideologically extreme. In a jungle primary, however, the primary electorate includes not just hard core party loyalists but independents as well. Candidates who take extreme positions on issues may lose out to more moderate candidates who can appeal to independent voters and even voters who identify with the other political party.[4]

Has this idea been tried before? Louisiana had a jungle primary for a number of years and the state of Washington adopted one in 2006, but those are relatively small states.

only 112,116 people.[5] Yet each district elected one representative to Congress.

The U.S. Supreme Court dealt with the issue of legislative reapportionment in a series of cases, the most important of which were *Baker v. Carr* (1962) and *Wesberry v. Sanders* (1964).[6] **Reapportionment** is the reallocation of legislative seats. In these and other cases, the Supreme Court established the doctrine of **one person, one vote**, which is the judicial ruling that the Equal Protection Clause of the Fourteenth Amendment to the U.S. Constitution requires that legislative districts be apportioned on the basis of population. The Supreme Court has also stipulated that legislative district boundaries be drawn to ensure nearly equal population size.

The Court's one-person, one-vote decisions have affected legislative representation and policy. When the rulings were first implemented in the 1960s, rural areas lost representation, whereas the nation's big cities gained seats. As a result, urban problems, such as housing, education, unemployment, transportation, and race relations gained priority on legislative agendas.[7] The distribution of public funds changed as well to conform closely to relative population size. Nationwide, the effect of redistricting was to shift $7 billion of public funds annually from rural to urban areas.[8]

Recent census figures have shown a shift of America's population away from inner cities to suburbs and surrounding metropolitan areas. The resulting redistricting changes have led to fewer representatives from constituencies demanding big government and more representatives from areas where people are wary of government. Congress and many state legislatures have grown more conservative.[9]

The 2010 midterm election, therefore, was particularly important because of the redistricting that will occur because of the 2010 Census. In 2011, states will use the data from the 2010 Census to redistrict both U.S. congressional seats and state legislative districts. Most states will redistrict through the legislative process; that is, the legislature will pass a redistricting bill and send it to the governor.[10] If one political party holds a majority of seats in the state legislature and controls the governor's office as well, it will be in good position to draw congressional districts designed to protect its incumbents from serious challenge from the other party while, perhaps, shifting some of the seats held by the other party into its column. When Democrats and Republicans share control—say, the Republicans control the legislature but the governor is a Democrat—they typically compromise on redistricting by agreeing to protect the incumbents of both parties.

Redistricting and the Voting Rights Act

Minority rights groups filed suit against the Texas redistricting plan under the **Voting Rights Act (VRA)** of 1965, a federal law designed to protect the voting rights of racial and ethnic minorities. The VRA makes it illegal to enact and enforce election rules and procedures that diminish the voting power of racial, ethnic, and language minority groups. Areas with a history of voting discrimination, including Texas, must submit redistricting plans to the U.S. Department of Justice for approval *before* they can go into effect.

In the late 1980s and early 1990s, the Department of Justice in the George H. W. Bush administration interpreted amendments to the VRA adopted in 1982 to require that state legislatures create legislative districts designed to maximize minority representation. In short,

Recent census figures have shown a shift of America's population away from inner cities.

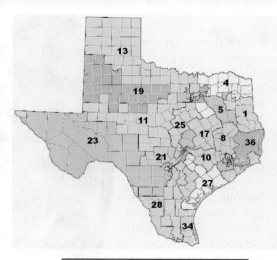

The Republican Party was positioned to control redistricting in a majority of states after the 2010 election because it held a majority of governorships and most state legislatures as well. For example, the Texas legislature, pictured above, firmly under Republican control, draws the boundaries for more than 36 U.S. Congressional districts.

the Justice Department declared that if a district *could* be drawn that would likely elect an African American or Latino candidate then it *must* be drawn. State legislatures would have to create the maximum possible number of **majority-minority districts**, which are legislative districts with populations that are more than 50 percent minority.[11]

Why would a Republican administration choose to implement the VRA to increase African American and Latino representation in Congress and state legislatures? After all, most minority lawmakers are Democrats. The reason was simple: The policy also helped the Republican Party to gain seats.[12] State legislatures

reapportionment the reallocation of legislative seats.

one person, one vote the judicial ruling that the Equal Protection Clause of the Fourteenth Amendment to the U.S. Constitution requires that legislative districts be apportioned on the basis of population.

Voting Rights Act (VRA) a federal law designed to protect the voting rights of racial and ethnic minorities.

majority-minority district legislative districts whose population is more than 50 percent African American and Latino.

redrew district lines to shift minority voters away from adjacent districts into new majority-minority districts. Because most African American and Latino voters are Democrats, the redistricting reduced Democratic voting strength in the surrounding districts, threatening the political survival of some white Democratic members of Congress. The Georgia congressional delegation, for example, went from one African American Democrat, eight white Democrats, and one white Republican before redistricting in 1991 to three African American Democrats and eight white Republicans after the 1994 election. Nationwide, the creation of majority-minority districts after the 1990 Census helped white Republicans pick up about nine seats in Congress, defeating white Democrats who were stripped of some of their minority voter support.[13]

think Is the Voting Rights Act still needed? Why or why not?

In the mid-1990s, the U.S. Supreme Court overruled the Justice Department's interpretation of the VRA. The Court responded to legal challenges filed against majority-minority districts created in Louisiana, Georgia, and other Southern states by ruling that state governments cannot use race as the predominant factor in drawing district lines without a compelling reason.[14] States are free to redistrict as long as the districts they draw do not diminish the political influence of minorities, but the VRA does not require states to create additional majority-minority districts in order to increase minority representation.[15] Furthermore, the Court ruled in 2003 that states have the

This political cartoon, drawn in 1812, depicts the electoral districts drawn to favor the candidates of Massachusetts Governor Elbridge Gerry.

leeway to create "coalitional districts" in which minority voters do not form a numerical majority, but are numerous enough so that coalitional voting will give a minority candidate a realistic opportunity to be elected.[16]

Gerrymandering

Redistricting can also be used to advance the interests of one political party or individual. In fact, the practice is so common that there is a word for it, **gerrymandering**, the drawing of legislative district lines for political advantage. The term dates from early nineteenth-century Massachusetts, when Governor Elbridge Gerry engineered the creation of a district so complicated that observers said it resembled a salamander: hence the term Gerry*mander*.

The courts have been **more** tolerant of **political** gerrymandering.

The federal courts have been more tolerant of political gerrymandering than they have been efforts to draw districts to increase minority representation in Congress. The U.S. Supreme Court has held that partisan gerrymandering is unconstitutional if it can be demonstrated that the "electoral system is arranged in such a manner that will consistently degrade a … group of voters' influence on the political process as a whole."[17] In practice, however, this standard is so high that it has never been satisfied. The U.S. Supreme Court has yet to find a political gerrymander unconstitutional.[18]

The latest redistricting controversy involves **midcycle redistricting**, which is the practice of redrawing legislative districts outside the regular redistricting cycle in order to gain political advantage. In 2003, Colorado and Texas adopted new redistricting schemes to replace legal redistricting plans already in place that had been used in the previous year's election. In Colorado, the Republican-controlled legisla-

gerrymandering the drawing of legislative district lines for political advantage.

midcycle redistricting redrawing legislative districts outside the regular redistricting cycle in order to gain political advantage.

ture and the Republican governor changed the boundaries of the state's Seventh Congressional District in order to help GOP Congressman Bob Beauprez win reelection. In 2002, Beauprez defeated his Democratic opponent by fewer than 300 votes. Meanwhile in Texas, the Republican legislature and the Republican governor redistricted in hopes of changing the ratio of the Texas Congressional delegation from a 17 to 15 Democratic advantage to a 22 to 10 Republican majority. Although the Colorado Supreme Court overturned the Colorado mid-cycle redistricting plan as a violation of the Colorado Constitution, the Texas plan survived, helping the Republicans to pick up five congressional seats in the 2004 election.

ELECTION CAMPAIGNS

11.2 *How are political campaigns organized?*

An election campaign is an attempt to get information to voters that will persuade them to elect a candidate or not to elect an opponent. Although many local election contests are modest affairs, presidential campaigns, statewide races, local elections in big cities, and many elections for Congress and state legislatures feature professional campaign consultants, sophisticated organizations, and big money.

The Role of Money

Money is the most controversial feature of American electoral politics.

The Cost of Campaigns.

Election campaigns cost money. In 2008, Obama and McCain together raised and spent more than $1 billion in their race for the White House, with Obama bringing in more than twice the money of his Republican opponent. Races for Congress are expensive as well. In 2010, the average House incumbent raised $1.5 million compared with less than $300,000 for the average challenger. The cost of Senate races varied, depending on the size of the state. Running for office is far more expensive in a large urban state with multiple media markets than it is in a small rural state without a major media market. In 2010, the average Senate incumbent raised $11.2 million compared with less than a million dollars for the average challenger.[19]

Money is a campaign necessity, but it does not guarantee success. In 2008, incumbent members of the House who won reelection outspent their opponent by an average $1.3 million to $300,000. Similarly, Senate incumbents who won reelection spent more than four times as much as their losing challengers, $8.4 million compared with $1.9 million. Nonetheless, money alone does not ensure victory. Republican Senator Norm Coleman of Minnesota raised and spent $21.8 million on his reelection campaign, more money than any candidate for the House or Senate on the ballot in 2008, but he lost an extremely close race to Democrat Al Franken.[20]

Critics charge that campaigns are too expensive. Many potential candidates for office choose not to run because they do not think they can raise the necessary funds. Incumbents, meanwhile, must devote an inordinate amount of time to fundraising. The critics of the current campaign funding system worry that public officials will make policy decisions with an eye to pleasing contributors rather than serving the policy interests of ordinary constituents.

In contrast, some policymakers believe that the problem with campaign spending is not the total amount of money spent but the disparity in resources among candidates. These policymakers favor reforming the campaign finance system to make it easier for candidates and parties to raise and spend money, which is used to spread their messages. Citizens need more information to make intelligent choices at the ballot box, they say, not less. An analysis of the campaigns for the U.S. House suggests that campaign spending enhances the quality of democracy. The study finds that campaign spending increases voter knowledge, improves the ability of the public to accurately identify the issue positions of the candidates, and increases voter interest in the campaign.[21]

> *Money is a campaign necessity, but it does not guarantee success.*

> think — **Are campaigns too expensive, or is spending the necessary means to increase voter knowledge?**

> The **largest** item in most campaign budgets is **advertising**.

The Campaign Budget.

The largest item in most campaign budgets is advertising, particularly on television. The cost of advertising time varies greatly, depending on the market and the medium. Television, especially network television

This still is from an Obama campaign advertisement broadcast in Iowa. The largest item in most campaign budgets is advertising, particularly on television.

supporters asking for the maximum contribution under federal law, which in 2008 was $2,300 per individual contributor.

George W. Bush developed a sophisticated system for raising money from individuals that netted millions of dollars for his two presidential campaigns. In 2000, more than 500 Bush supporters called Pioneers (mostly wealthy energy company officials, lobbyists, and corporate executives) raised $100,000 each in individual contributions up to $1,000, which was then the maximum amount an individual could give.[25] Each of the Pioneers tapped at least 100 people for contributions and earmarked their contribution checks with a special identification code in order to get credit. The Bush campaign rewarded Pioneers with

during primetime, is the most expensive. Cable television, radio, and newspapers are less costly. Advertising in larger markets, such as New York City or Los Angeles, is substantially more expensive than advertising in smaller markets, such as Baton Rouge, Louisiana, or Albuquerque, New Mexico. Running a serious political campaign in a populous state with several major media markets is many times more costly than running a campaign in a less populous state without a major media market.

Political campaigns have expenses other than advertising. Campaigns have offices with telephone banks, computers, fax machines, furniture, supplies, and utility costs. Campaigns hire consultants and employ professionals for fundraising, event coordination, media relations, Internet connection, and volunteer coordination. Candidates for president or statewide office also spend a good deal of money for travel. Fundraising itself is a campaign expense. In 2004, the Bush campaign spent $50 million on fundraising, $1 for every $4.87 raised.[22]

Sources of Campaign Money.
Wealthy individuals sometimes finance their own election campaigns. In 2010, Linda McMahon of

Connecticut ($50 million), Jeff Greene of Florida ($24 million), and Ron Johnson of Wisconsin ($9 million) headed a list of 14 candidates for the U.S. House or U.S. Senate that invested at least $2 million of their personal funds in an attempt to win elective office. Johnson and two of the other big-spending candidates won, but the other 11 all lost.[23] Self-financing is usually a sign of weakness because candidates with enough support to win office can raise money for their campaigns.

Candidates who are not wealthy enough to bankroll their own campaigns (or who choose to hold onto their money) must rely on others to finance their election efforts. Individual campaign contributors are the most important overall source of campaign cash, accounting for 60 percent of total receipts for U.S. House and Senate candidates, and more than 90 percent of the money raised by the two major-party presidential candidates in 2008, not counting federal funds.[24] Candidates raise money from individuals through direct solicitations, usually on the telephone or at fundraising dinners or receptions, by means of direct mail, and over the Internet. Candidates spend hours on the phone calling wealthy

Funding Sources for the 2008 Presidential Campaign

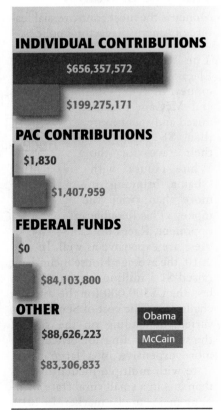

INDIVIDUAL CONTRIBUTIONS
$656,357,572
$199,275,171

PAC CONTRIBUTIONS
$1,830
$1,407,959

FEDERAL FUNDS
$0
$84,103,800

OTHER
$88,626,223
$83,306,833

Obama
McCain

*Neither candidate spent any of his own money.
Source: opensecrets.org.

special receptions and individual meetings with the candidate. Subsequently, President Bush appointed at least 19 of the Pioneers as ambassadors to other countries.[26] In 2004, with the contribution limit raised to $2,000 a person, the Bush campaign created a second category of fundraisers called Rangers, who agreed to raise at least $200,000 for the president's reelection.

Direct mail is another important fundraising tool. Typically, Candidate A sends a long, detailed letter to supporters warning of dire consequences if the other candidate wins the election. The only way to prevent the calamity and save the country, the letter declares, is to contribute money to Candidate A by writing a check today and inserting it in the return envelop included in the mailing. Direct mail is an expensive fundraising tool because it takes time and money to develop an address list of people who are likely to respond positively to appeals for campaign money. Mailing expenses are costly as well. Nonetheless, direct mail can be effective. For years, the Republican Party held a fundraising advantage over the Democrats because it had a more sophisticated direct mail operation.

The Internet is the latest innovation in campaign fundraising. Campaigns create a sharp-looking website designed to attract the attention of supporters who can donate online with a credit card and a few mouse clicks. The advantage of Internet fundraising is that it is relatively inexpensive, especially compared to direct mail. Campaigns can send e-mails again and again to supporters, giving them campaign updates and asking for funds at virtually no expense.[27] In 2008, Obama campaign raised millions of dollars in online contributions, mostly through small donations. Over half of the money the campaign raised came through donations of $200 or less.

As discussed in Chapter 9, interest groups give money directly to candidates through **political action committees (PACs)**, organizations created to raise and distribute

money in election campaigns. PACs are an important source of funds in races for the U.S. House, accounting for more than a third of the total money raised by House candidates. In contrast, PACs gave relatively little money directly to Senate or presidential candidates.[28] Federal law limits the amount of money that a PAC can give a candidate for federal office to $5,000 for each election.

The role of political parties in campaign fundraising has changed because of the adoption of the **Bipartisan Campaign Reform Act (BCRA)** of 2002, which is a campaign finance reform law designed to limit the political influence of big money campaign contributors. The BCRA, which is also known as "McCain-Feingold" after its two Senate sponsors, Senator John McCain and Senator Russ Feingold, prohibited political parties from raising **soft money**, funds raised by political parties that are not subject to federal campaign finance regulations. Before the adoption of the BCRA, parties raised hundreds of millions of dollars in unregulated, large contributions from individuals, corporations, and unions. The BCRA prohibited parties from raising soft money beginning with the 2004 election, forcing them to rely on **hard money**, funds raised subject to federal campaign contribution and expenditure limitations.[29]

Political parties primarily support their candidates with **independent expenditures**, which is money spent in support of a candidate but not coordinated with the candidate's campaign. Although parties can contribute a limited amount of money directly to candidates, they can make unlimited independent expenditures. Parties also back candidates by providing them with polling data and conducting get-out-the-vote efforts.

Much of the millions of dollars in soft money contributions that once went to political parties now goes to **527 committees**, which are organizations created by individuals

Former eBay CEO Meg Whitman spent more than $140 million of her own money in an unsuccessful bid to be elected governor of California. She lost to 72-year old former Governor Jerry Brown who became the oldest governor in California history.

and groups to influence the outcomes of elections by raising and spending money that candidates and political parties cannot legally raise. As long as 527 committees operate independently of political campaigns and stop short of explicitly calling for a candidate's election or defeat, they can raise and spend unlimited amounts of unregulated soft money. In the 2008 presidential campaign, 527 committees raised and spent millions of dollars to support one side or the other. America Votes, Fund for America, and Patriot

political action committee (PAC) organization created to raise and distribute money in election campaigns.

Bipartisan Campaign Reform Act (BCRA) a campaign finance reform law designed to limit the political influence of "big money" campaign contributors.

soft money the name given to funds that are raised by political parties that are not subject to federal campaign finance regulations.

hard money funds that are raised subject to federal campaign contribution and expenditure limitations.

independent expenditures money spent in support of a candidate but not coordinated with the candidate's campaign.

527 committee organization created to influence the outcomes of elections by raising and spending money that candidates and political parties cannot raise legally.

Majority were 527 committees that helped the Democrats by registering voters, organizing activists, and purchasing political advertisements. In the meantime, American Solutions for Winning the Future, Club for Growth, and RightChange.com were 527 committees that worked to support Republicans. In 2004, the 527 committee Swift Boat Veterans for Truth undermined Kerry's status as a decorated war hero and played a significant role in his eventual defeat. As long as 527 committees do not explicitly coordinate their work with either political party or presidential campaign, the BCRA does not apply to them.[30]

Finally, federal funds are an important source of campaign money for candidates for president. Although some reformers favor government funding for congressional elections, money is currently available only for presidential races. We discuss presidential campaign funding in more detail later in the chapter.

Campaign Organization and Strategy

Big-time campaigns are long, drawn-out affairs. Challengers begin planning and organizing their campaigns years before the election. Incumbents, meanwhile, never really stop campaigning. Many observers believe that American politics now features constant election campaigns because newly elected officeholders start work on their reelection the day they take the oath of office.

Campaigns start early because much has to be done. Candidates spend the early months of the race raising money, building an organization, seeking group endorsements, and planning strategy. Candidates often memorize a basic speech and rehearse answers to questions reporters might ask. One of the first tasks of a campaign is to prepare the candidate. This also often means outfitting the candidate with a new wardrobe, a new hairstyle, and a slimmer waistline. Some

Challengers begin planning their campaigns years before the election; incumbents never really stop campaigning.

critics of George W. Bush believe that he purchased his ranch in Crawford, Texas, in 1999 because it would provide an attractive backdrop for television reports on the candidate during the 2000 presidential election campaign. It would also help him project an image as a regular guy rather than the privileged son of a famous family and a graduate of Harvard and Yale.

An important goal for many campaigns is to improve the candidate's name recognition, especially if the candidate is not an incumbent. Citizens generally will not vote for someone with whom they are unfamiliar. Races for less visible offices may never move beyond the name-recognition stage. It helps if voters are already familiar with the candidate. Tom Osborne easily won a seat in Congress from Nebraska after retiring from a long and successful career as the head football coach at the University of Nebraska.

Besides building name recognition, campaigns attempt to create a favorable image of the candidate. Candidates air campaign advertisements that stress their qualifications

for the office and associate the candidate with popular themes and images. In 2008, for example, Senator McCain used his personal history as a prisoner of war in Vietnam as evidence that he was strong enough to be an effective commander in chief. Obama's image as an energetic, relatively young man helped reinforce his message of change and reform.

Campaigns try to create an unfavorable impression of the opponent. Negative campaigning is nothing new in American politics. Thomas Jefferson's enemies denounced him as the anti-Christ. Opponents accused President Grover Cleveland of beating his wife and fathering an illegitimate child. Critics attacked Theodore Roosevelt as a drunkard and a drug addict. In 1950, George Smathers defeated Senator Claude Pepper in Florida by calling Pepper "a shameless EXTROVERT" who has "a sister who was once a THESPIAN."[31] (If your dictionary is not handy, an extrovert is someone who is outgoing and a thespian is an actor.)

Research is mixed on the effectiveness of negative campaigning. Sometimes it works, but sometimes

One of the most controversial negative campaign advertisements was the "Daisy Girl" ad of 1964. Lyndon Johnson's campaign was criticized for trying to frighten voters by implying that candidate Barry Goldwater would start a nuclear war over Vietnam. You can view the clip at http://www.livingroomcandidate.org/.

it backfires. In general, negative campaigning is a more effective strategy for challengers than it is for incumbents, who are more successful with a positive campaign. Nonetheless, incumbents are often able to effectively counter a challenger's attacks. Political scientists find no evidence that personal attacks or attacks that distort the record are effective.[32]

Early in a campaign, candidates work to build name identification and establish their credibility by producing a message that is primarily positive. As the election approaches, candidates who trail in the polls often decide that positive advertising alone will not close the gap with their opponents, so they go on the attack in hopes of undermining their opponent's support.[33] Incumbents sometimes launch attack ad campaigns against their challengers early in the election season in hopes of creating a negative image for the challenger before the challenger has a chance to establish a positive identification. Candidates who suffer attack are likely to respond in kind because they know that voters presume that an unanswered attack is true.[34]

Campaign advertising increases citizen knowledge of issues and candidates, affects voter evaluations of candidates, and increases a candidate's share of the vote.[35] Campaign advertising broadcast close to the election has a greater impact than advertising early in the contest. Research shows that advertising has its greatest influence on people who are moderately aware of the campaign. The least politically alert do not get the message, whereas the best informed citizens have already made up their minds.[36]

Campaigns also try to focus voter attention to the issues on which their political party has an advantage.[37] **Issue ownership** is the concept that the public considers one political party more competent at addressing a particular issue than the other political party. The Democratic Party has an advantage on the environment, education, Social

Television is still the primary means for candidates to establish themselves and advertise their message, but the Internet is growing in importance. Mike Huckabee, a potential Republican presidential candidate in 2012 seen here addressing an MTV audience, maintains a big online presence, including a web site, blog, Facebook page, and Twitter feed.

Security, healthcare, and jobs; the Republicans are favored on taxes, law and order, and foreign policy.[38] During the 2008 presidential election, the Obama campaign stressed healthcare and the economy, especially unemployment and jobs, whereas the McCain campaign tried to shift the focus to taxes and foreign policy issues, particularly the war on terror.

Election campaigns for major offices are fought on the ground and in the air. Campaign professionals use the term **ground war** to refer to campaign activities featuring direct contact between campaign workers and citizens, such as door-to-door canvassing and personal telephone contacts. In 2008, the Obama and McCain campaigns deployed small armies of volunteers and paid campaign workers to register voters and get out the vote. Both parties concentrated their efforts on the **battleground states**, which are swing states in which the relative strength of the two major-party presidential candidates is close enough that either candidate could conceivably carry the state. The **air war** refers to campaign activities that involve the media, including television, radio, and the Internet. In 2008, campaign professionals focused their television

advertising on network shows and cable channels that data analyses showed were popular with people most likely to support the candidates of their party.

Social media have become the latest campaign battleground. Candidates create Facebook fan pages, open Twitter accounts, and upload campaign videos on YouTube. Social media enable candidates to communicate regularly and personally with supporters, increasing name identification and building enthusiasm. The social media are especially important for younger supporters, many of whom use social media as their main source of news.[39]

issue ownership the concept that the public considers one political party more competent at addressing a particular issue than the other political party.

ground war campaign activities featuring direct contact between campaign workers and citizens, such as door-to-door canvassing and personal telephone contacts.

battleground states swing states in which the relative strength of the two major-party presidential candidates is close enough so that either candidate could conceivably carry the state.

air war campaign activities that involve the media, including television, radio, and the Internet.

CONGRESSIONAL ELECTIONS

What are the similarities and differences between elections for the House and Senate?

In America's representative democracy, citizens elect the members of Congress. Whereas members of the House are elected to serve two-year terms, senators run for six-year terms. Because Senate terms are staggered, voters elect one-third of the Senate every two years.

House Elections

The most striking feature of elections for the U.S. House of Representatives is that most incumbents are reelected. Between 1954 and 2008, 93 percent of House incumbents seeking reelection won.[40] Even in 2010, a remarkably bad year for incumbents, 87 percent won reelection.[41]

Political scientists identify a number of factors that explain the success of incumbent House members seeking reelection:

- *Incumbency has built-in advantages.* Incumbents are almost always better known than challengers. They have the money to staff one or more district offices, allowances to pay for trips home during congressional sessions, and free postage to mail newsletters to constituents. They can also

Since 1986, more than **95 percent of incumbent** representatives seeking reelection **have won**.

build goodwill among constituents by bringing spending projects to the district, voicing the concerns of the district residents, and helping constituents navigate the bureaucracy.

- *Incumbents are almost always better funded.* To become known, challengers need to spend hundreds of thousands of dollars on their campaigns. Most serious candidates for Congress will not run unless they believe they have a realistic chance of winning, and that means raising more than $500,000.[42] Furthermore, incumbents try to scare off challengers by raising as much money as they can as early as they can.

- *Most incumbents are strong candidates.* They know how to run effective campaigns because they have run and won before. In contrast, many challengers are inexperienced campaigners.

- *Many congressional districts are safe for one party or the other.* In 2010, less than 20 percent of House

races were decided by 10 percentage points or less. Although some blame the prevalence of safe districts on the redistricting process, others attribute it to the phenomenon of communities growing more like-minded over time.[43]

Historically, the political party holding the White House loses seats in the House of Representatives in midterm elections. Between 1920 and 1980, the president's party lost ground in the House in 15 of 16 midterm elections, dropping an average of 35 seats. The phenomenon was so pronounced and appeared so regularly that political scientists developed theories to explain it. One set of theories focused on the withdrawal of coattails. The **coattail effect** is a political

franking privilege free postage provided members of Congress.

coattail effect a political phenomenon in which a strong candidate for one office gives a boost to fellow party members on the same ballot seeking other offices.

TAKE ✓ ACTION
Campaign Volunteers

Volunteers play an important role in election campaigns. They mail campaign literature to registered voters, telephone supporters to encourage them to vote, and drive citizens to the polls on Election Day. They are often the backbone of campaigns for local office.

Your assignment is to research campaign activity by volunteering for the candidate of your choice. Contact the local political party organizations to identify local campaigns that are seeking volunteers. To verify your volunteer work, bring your instructor a signed note from the campaign office manager indicating the time you spent on the campaign. Also, prepare a written report discussing your work and your impressions of the campaign, covering the following points:

- Identify the candidate and the office the candidate seeks, noting whether the candidate is the incumbent.
- Describe the campaign office, including the location, physical layout, and level of organization.
- Describe the other people working in the campaign as to age, gender, race, and ethnicity.
- List the tasks you completed for the campaign.
- Describe your impression of the experience, discussing whether you had a good time, whether you believe your work was important to the campaign's success, and if you ever plan to volunteer to work for a campaign again.

Brazil elects the members of its national legislature using a system in which each state is an at-large, multimember district. Citizens can cast their votes for either a party or a particular candidate. The number of seats a party wins is based on **proportional representation (PR)**, which is an election system that awards legislative seats to each party approximately equal to its popular voting strength. The candidates on the party slate with the most individual votes actually claim the seats. For example, if a party has enough combined party and candidate votes to win five seats, the five individual candidates on its party list who received the most votes are the individuals chosen to serve in the national legislature.[43]

The Brazilian electoral system provides for competition not just among political parties but also among candidates in the same party. In practice, legislative candidates focus on building their personal vote totals, often by campaigning in a geographical stronghold or targeting a particular group of voters, such as industrial workers or ethnic minorities. The electoral system affects policymaking because legislators worried about winning reelection focus their energy on **pork barrel spending**, which are expenditures to fund local projects that are not critically important from a national perspective. Political scientists also believe that the system increases the power of Brazil's president, who trades support on local projects for legislative votes on national issues.[44]

QUESTIONS

1 How does the Brazilian legislative electoral system differ from the American system?

2 Is the Brazilian system democratic? Why or why not?

3 Do you think Brazilian legislators focus more on pork barrel spending than do the members of the U. S. Congress? Why or why not?

---

phenomenon in which a strong candidate for one office gives a boost to fellow party members on the same ballot seeking other offices. Coattails are particularly important in election contests in which voters have relatively little information about either candidate, such as open-seat races for the U.S. House. In presidential election years, some of the people who turn out to cast their ballots for a popular presidential candidate either vote a straight ticket or support candidates from the same party as their presidential choice even though they have no real candidate preference. Two years later, without a presidential race on the ballot, many of the congressional candidates who benefited from the coattail effect lose without it. A second set of theories attempts to explain the tendency of the president's party to lose House seats in the midterm on the basis of ideological balancing. Moderate voters support the opposition party in order to restrain the president from pushing policies that they perceive to be ideologically extreme. Some voters may also use their vote at midterm to punish the president's party for poor performance, especially the performance of the economy.[45]

In 2010, the Democrats suffered the largest midterm loss for a president's party since 1938 when President Franklin D. Roosevelt watched his Democratic Party lose 72 House seats. The Democrats lost big in 2010 not just because a Democrat sat in the White House, but because many voters were worried about the economy. The incumbent party typically loses ground when the economy is weak. Furthermore, having gained House seats in the last two elections in 2006 and 2008, the Democrats found themselves defending most of the swing districts. At least President Obama could take solace in the knowledge that midterm elections are not predictive of the next president election. FDR easily won reelection in 1940 despite his party's thrashing at the polls in 1938.

Senate Elections

Senate races are more competitive than House elections. Incumbency is a factor in Senate contests, but it is not the overwhelming advantage that it is in House races. Furthermore, Senate races are typically closer than House contests, even when the incumbent wins. In 2008, 8 of 35 Senate races were decided by 10 percentage points or less.

Political scientists identify a number of differences between Senate and House races that account for the relatively greater vulnerability of Senate incumbents.

- *More diverse constituencies.* Senate constituencies are more diverse than most House constituencies and, hence, more competitive. U.S. House districts are often drawn to the clear electoral advantage of one party or the other. In contrast, senators must run at-large statewide, and both parties are capable of winning statewide races in any state.
- *Stronger challengers.* Incumbent senators generally face stronger challengers than House incumbents. A seat in the Senate is a prize that attracts the candidacies of governors, big-city mayors, members of the House, and well-known figures such as war heroes, sports stars, and show business

proportional representation (PR) an election system that awards legislative seats to each party approximately equal to its popular voting strength.

pork barrel spending expenditures to fund local projects that are not critically important from a national perspective.

celebrities. As a result, Senate challengers can usually attract enough media attention and raise sufficient money to run at least a minimal campaign.

- **Contests are national.** Finally, research has found that voters tend to perceive Senate races as national election contests. As a result, national issues often play a prominent role in Senate campaigns and national trends frequently affect Senate election outcomes.

In 2010, Republican political figures considering a possible race for the presidency in 2012 collected IOUs by campaigning on behalf of party candidates. Former Alaska Governor Sarah Palin endorsed more than a dozen Republican candidates for Congress or statewide office in 2010. Here, she is campaigning for Rick Perry, who was reelected as Governor of Texas.

PRESIDENTIAL ELECTIONS: THE NOMINATION

11.4 *What are the main steps in the contest for the presidential nomination of each party?*

The presidential election process consists of two distinct phases with different rules, requiring candidates to wage two separate campaigns. In the first phase of the presidential-election process, candidates compete for their political party's nomination, which is awarded at a national party convention by majority vote of the delegates in attendance. In the summer of a presidential election year, the party organizations in each state, the District of Columbia, and the various territories send delegates to select the party's nominee. The size of each state's convention delegation varies, depending on a formula set by the party that includes both the state's population and the success of the party in the state. The convention selects the presidential and vice-presidential nominees to run on the party's ticket in the November general election by majority vote of the delegates.

Until the conventions have done their work, the real contest is not between Democrats and Republicans, but among Democrats for the Democratic presidential nomination and among Republicans for their party's nomination. In 2008, New York Senator Hillary Rodham Clinton, Illinois Senator Barack Obama, and former North Carolina Senator John Edwards were the leading candidates for the Democratic nomination. Arizona Senator John McCain, former Massachusetts Governor Mitt Romney, former Arkansas Governor Mike Huckabee, and former New York City Mayor Rudy Giuliani contended for the GOP nomination. Because the convention delegates make the actual selection, candidates focus on the delegate-selection process in each state, hoping to get their supporters selected as delegates to the national convention.

The Delegate-Selection Process

The process of selecting delegates to the national party conventions varies from state to state. Most delegates are chosen in presidential preference primaries. A **presidential preference primary** is an election in which party voters cast ballots for the presidential candidate they favor and, in so doing, help determine the number of national convention delegates that candidate will receive. Democratic voters select among Democratic candidates; Republican voters choose among Republican presidential contenders.

Presidential primary elections typically attract fewer voters than does the general election. In 2008, 530,000 voters participated in the New Hampshire presidential preference primary, compared with 700,000 who turned out for the November general election in that state.[46] Primary election voters differ from general election voters in that primary voters identify strongly with the party in whose primary they vote. In contrast, the electorate for the general election includes a larger proportion of independents and people who identify weakly with a party.

The nature of the primary electorate affects the approaches candidates must take to winning

> Citizens who cast ballots in **primary elections** are not representative of **general election** voters.

presidential preference primary an election in which party voters cast ballots for the presidential candidate they favor and in so doing help determine the number of national convention delegates that candidate will receive.

A CLOSER LOOK
The Iowa Caucus

Caucus rules vary across states and between parties, but the Democratic caucus system in Iowa can serve as a useful example of how the system works. At the precinct location, supporters of each candidate gather in designated areas of the caucus room at the given time. Then there is a 30-minute period in which attendees try to convince others, particularly the undecided, to support the candidate of their choice. Debate is halted, and each candidate's supporters are counted. Candidates who fail to get a specified percentage of the vote are eliminated.

Then another 30-minute period is called so attendees can reorganize around the remaining candidates. In a caucus, a voter's second choice can be as important as his or her first choice. The voting closes after a head count of each group is made. The precinct allocates delegate seats in proportion to the number of voters, and each candidate's supporters choose their delegates for their allotted seats.

the nomination. People who identify strongly with the GOP are more conservative than voters as a group, whereas people who identify strongly with the Democratic Party are more liberal.[47] Consequently, Republican presidential contenders usually stress conservative themes during the nomination phase, whereas Democratic candidates emphasize liberal positions. Primary voters do not just consider policy preferences in choosing among candidates; they also evaluate each candidate's chances of winning the November general election.[48] The most liberal Democratic candidate and the most conservative Republican candidate may not win the nomination if large numbers of their party's primary voters believe they would not be strong candidates in the general election.

States that do not conduct presidential preference primaries use the caucus method to choose national convention delegates. The **caucus method of delegate selection** is a procedure for choosing national party convention delegates that involves party voters participating in a series of precinct and district or county political meetings. The process begins with party members attending local precinct meetings or caucuses that elect delegates to district or county meetings. The district/county meetings in turn select delegates for the state party convention. Finally, the state convention chooses national convention delegates.

Candidates use a different strategy for competing in caucus states than they employ in states with primary elections. Because caucus meetings require more time and effort than simply voting in a primary, the number of people who participate in them is generally fewer than primary participants and far fewer than the number of people who turn out for general elections. In 2008, for example, 350,000 people took part in the Iowa caucus compared with 1.5 million who voted in the general election.[49] Furthermore, most caucus participants are party activists who tend to be more liberal (in the Democratic Party) or more conservative (in the Republican Party) than party voters or the electorate as a whole. Consequently, in each party, ideologically extreme candidates (i.e., strong conservatives in the GOP, strong liberals in the Democratic Party) typically do better in caucus states.[50]

Candidates who do well in presidential preference primaries and caucuses win delegates pledged to support their nomination at the national convention. The Democratic Party awards delegates in rough proportion to a candidate's level of support as long as the candidate surpasses a 15 percent threshold. In contrast, Republican Party rules award delegates on a winner-take-all basis.

In addition to delegates selected through presidential preference primaries and caucuses, the national Democratic Party convention includes several hundred Democratic officeholders and party officials who are called **superdelegates**. The

caucus method of delegate selection a procedure for choosing national party convention delegates that involves party voters participating in a series of precinct and district or county political meetings.

superdelegates Democratic Party officials and officeholders selected to attend the national party convention on the basis of the offices they hold.

Allocation of Primary Delegates, by Party

Florida Republican Primary	Percentage of Votes	Percentage of Delegates Awarded
	McCain (36%)	100%
	Romney (31%)	0%
	Giuliani (15%)	0%
	Huckabee (13%)	0%
	Others (5%)	0%

Florida Republican Primary
The Republican Party awards convention delegates on a winner-take-all basis.

California Democratic Primary	Percentage of Votes	Percentage of Delegates Awarded
	Clinton (52%)	55%
	Obama (42%)	45%
	Others (6%)	0%

California Democratic Primary
The Democratic Party allocates state convention delegates proportionally.

2008 Democratic National Convention included 796 superdelegates, 19 percent of the total. Superdelegates are chosen on the basis of the offices they hold rather than their support for a particular candidate. In contrast to delegates selected through presidential preference primary elections and caucuses, superdelegates are officially uncommitted, or not pledged to support a specific candidate until the vote at the national convention. The superdelegate system ensures that Democratic officeholders and party leaders, who have a stake in what's best for the party, can attend the convention as delegates. The system bolsters the position of candidates who enjoy the support of party leaders. In 2008, superdelegates found themselves in a position to name a presidential nominee because the closeness of the Obama–Clinton race prevented either candidate from winning a majority of pledged delegates. Most superdelegates chose to go with Obama because he was the candidate who won the most pledged delegates.

think

Should superdelegates play a role in choosing a party's presidential nominee?

The Positioning Stage

The men and women who want to be president begin the process of seeking their party's nomination more than a year before any votes are cast. They assemble campaign teams, collect endorsements, establish campaign organizations in key primary and caucus states, build name recognition among party voters and activists, and raise money.

Raising money is particularly important for candidates during the primary positioning stage. Because the nomination process is front-loaded, candidates need to have millions of dollars on hand in order to conduct campaigns in dozens of states in the

space of just a couple of months. Furthermore, media attention mirrors fundraising success. Obama was able to compete against Clinton and eventually to win the nomination because of his remarkable fundraising operation. Although Obama trailed Clinton in the national polls at the end of 2007, he had raised nearly as much money as she and probably had the better organization in place.

Federal campaign finance laws allow for partial federal funding of presidential campaigns during the nomination stage. In order to qualify for federal matching funds, candidates must prove they are serious contenders by raising at least $5,000 in each of 20 states, in individual contributions of $250 or less. Once a candidate qualifies for federal funding, the government will match individual contributions dollar for dollar up to $250. Candidates who accept the money must agree to an overall pre-convention spending ceiling and state-by-state limits that vary, based on the population of a state. Candidates who reject federal funding are free to raise and spend as much money as they can.

Most serious presidential candidates no longer participate in the federal funding system because they are unwilling to accept the spending and fundraising limits. In 2008, candidates who took federal matching funds were limited to $50 million during the nomination period, including federal funds. In contrast, Obama and Clinton, both of whom

rejected federal funds, collected well over $250 million in campaign contributions for the nomination fight.[51]

The Invisible Primary

The **invisible primary** is the period between the time when candidates announce their intention to run for the presidency and the actual delegate-selection process begins. The men and women who want to be president begin the process of seeking their party's nomination more than a year before any votes are cast. They assemble campaign teams, collect endorsements, establish campaign organizations in key primary and caucus states, build name recognition among party voters and activists, and raise money. The latter is particularly important. Because the nomination process is front-loaded, candidates need to have millions of dollars on hand in order to conduct campaigns in dozens of states in the space of just a couple of months. Furthermore, media attention mirrors fundraising success. Obama was able to compete against Clinton and eventually to win the nomination because of his remarkable fundraising operation.

In 2008, Iowa and New Hampshire produced upset winners and upset losers. On the Republican side, Governor Romney spent heavily in Iowa and New Hampshire in

hopes of locking up the nomination early, but he was upset in both races, by Huckabee in Iowa and McCain in New Hampshire. Whereas Romney failed to meet expectations, both Huckabee and McCain exceeded them, and this success carried them further in the nomination process. Meanwhile, on the Democratic side, Iowa and New Hampshire narrowed the Democratic field to two main contestants—Clinton and Obama. The Obama campaign created an unprecedented grassroots campaign organization to build supporters and raise money. Obama won the Iowa caucus while Clinton finished third, behind John Edwards. Obama hoped to become the clear frontrunner for the nomination by winning the New Hampshire primary, held in early January, just a few days after the Iowa caucus. Riding a wave of favorable publicity generated by his Iowa caucus win, Obama moved up in the polls in New Hampshire and seemed poised to deliver another blow to the Clinton campaign.[52] Nonetheless, Clinton won a narrow victory in New Hampshire.

The contests in the weeks following Iowa and New Hampshire further help define the field. In 2008, the Nevada caucus and the South Carolina primary helped establish Clinton and Obama as the co-frontrunners for the Democrats, with Clinton winning Nevada and Obama taking South Carolina. As for the Republicans, Romney breathed life back into his candi-

think Do Iowa and New Hampshire play too great a role in the presidential nomination process?

dacy by winning in Nevada while McCain built on his victory in New Hampsure and established himself as the leading candidate by capturing the South Carolina primary.

Super Tuesday

Over the years, state legislatures around the country have moved their nomination contests to early in the year in hopes that their states will have more influence in the nomination process. In 2008, 24 states scheduled primaries or caucuses on Tuesday, February 5, including the big states of California, New York, Illinois, and New Jersey. Candidates with money, organization, and name recognition benefit from the frontloaded nomination process because they have the resources to compete in dozens of

states within a matter of a few days. Both Obama and Clinton were able to compete in 2008 because they had well-funded campaign organizations in place in all of the Super Tuesday states.

Super Tuesday often settles the nomination contest, at least for the Republicans, because of the party's winner-take-all delegate rule. With so many delegates at stake, one candidate usually wins enough delegates to claim the nomination or at least build an insurmountable delegate lead. Senator McCain became the inevitable Republican nominee because he won the most votes and, consequently, all of the delegates at stake in California, New York, New Jersey, and Illinois. The other major contenders soon dropped out of the race.

Barack Obama

John McCain

June

Hillary Clinton

Ron Paul

February

March

Mitt Romney

Mike Gravel

Mike Huckabee

The Democratic nomination can take longer to settle because the Democratic Party awards delegates on a proportional basis. In 2008, Clinton and Obama split the Super Tuesday contests. Even though Clinton won New York, California, and New Jersey, she earned only a few more delegates than did her opponent in each state because the vote was relatively close and the party's proportional rule ensured a near equal division of delegates between the two candidates. The two candidates emerged from the Super Tuesday voting nearly even in delegates won.

Some reformers propose to eliminate the advantage that front-loading gives to well-known or well-funded candidates by pacing primaries and caucuses throughout the winter and spring months of an election year. Spreading out the delegate selection process will increase the importance of voters in states holding primary elections later and reward candidates who can appeal to voters throughout the nation and not just in a few early contests.[53]

Post–Super Tuesday Contests

Obama emerged from Super Tuesday better positioned to win the nomination than did Clinton. The Clinton campaign assumed that she would effectively capture the nomination on Super Tuesday, whereas the Obama organization prepared for the nomination fight to continue well beyond the Super Tuesday voting. The Obama campaign created an organization in each of the states holding caucuses and primaries in the days and weeks immediately following Super Tuesday, but Clinton did not. Obama also took the fundraising lead. At the end of April 2008, more than halfway through the nomination process, Obama had raised $272 million compared with Clinton's $222 million.[54] Between February 5 and March 5, Obama won 11 consecutive contests, building a delegate lead of more than 150. Clinton

recovered to win primaries in Texas, Ohio, Pennsylvania, and other states, but Obama won contests as well, and she failed to close the gap. When the last primaries were held in early June, Obama had a clear delegate lead. Enough superdelegates announced their support to give him the nomination.

The Transition

The period from the end of the nomination contest until the national party conventions in midsummer is a time of transition. Once the frontrunner has enough delegates to ensure nomination, party leaders begin urging the remaining candidates still in the race to drop out in the name of party unity. In the meantime, the campaign of the eventual nominee begins to change focus. The candidate's speeches start to emphasize themes geared toward general election voters rather than the hardcore party voters who participate in primaries and caucuses. Campaign spokespersons redirect their attacks from their nomination opponents to the candidate of the other party. In 2008, the transition began for McCain shortly after Super Tuesday, whereas Obama had to wait until early June to being the transition phase.

The National Party Conventions

The national party conventions are the last step in the nomination process. The official role of a convention is to adopt a party platform and nominate a presidential and a vice-presidential candidate. Traditional wisdom holds that party platforms are meaningless documents, forgotten by Labor Day. To be sure, platforms often include general language because they represent compromise amont different factions within the party. Nonetheless, research shows that administrations fulfill about 70 percent of their platform promises.[55]

The most important business of a convention is the official selection

of the presidential nominee, ratifying the choice made during the primary season. Traditionally, the nomination takes place during primetime on the third evening of the convention. Festivities begin as speakers place the names of prospective nominees before the convention and their supporters respond with exuberant (and planned) demonstrations. Eventually, the time comes to call the roll of the states, and the delegates vote. A majority of the delegates must agree on a nominee. At every convention for more than 60 years, the delegates have selected a winner on the first ballot. Unless the nomination process changes dramatically, that pattern is likely to continue.

The final official business of the convention is to pick a vice-presidential candidate. Although the selection process is formally identical to the method for choosing a presidential nominee, the presidential candidate usually makes the choice weeks before the convention meets and the delegates ratify it. Above all else, presidential nominees look for running mates who will help them win in November. Historically, presidential candidates have tried to **balance the ticket**, which is an attempt to select a vice-presidential candidate who will appeal to different groups than the presidential nominee. Presidential candidates consider different types of balances in selecting a vice-presidential running mate, including racial, ethnic, religious, and gender diversity; regional balance; ideological balance; experience; factional balance (in hopes of healing divisions produced by a bruising primary battle); and personal characteristics, such as age, style, and personal appeal.[56] It is also helpful if the vice-presidential candidate comes from a populous state, such as California, Texas, New York, or Florida.

balance the ticket an attempt to select a vice-presidential candidate who will appeal to different groups of voters than the presidential nominee.

Both Obama and McCain used their vice-presidential selections to shore up perceived weaknesses. Obama chose Senator Joe Biden of Delaware, a 35-year veteran of the U.S. Senate and chair of the Senate Foreign Relations Committee. Obama wanted Biden to balance his own relative lack of experience, especially in foreign and defense policymaking. Obama may have also hoped that Biden, a Roman Catholic who was born in Pennsylvania, would attract white working-class voters in the Midwest and Catholic voters nationwide. McCain, meanwhile, surprised almost everyone by choosing Alaska's 44-year-old governor, Sarah Palin. McCain hoped to energize the conservative base of his party, because Palin is an outspoken opponent of abortion and gay marriage. He may have also hoped to attract the support of some women who were disappointed that Hillary Clinton did not win the Democratic nomination.

Biden probably did more to help Obama than did Palin to assist McCain. Except for occasional verbal missteps, Biden avoided controversy while campaigning vigorously for the ticket. Exit polls, surveys based on random samples of voters leaving the polling place, found that two-thirds of the electorate believed that Biden would be qualified to be president should it become necessary. Palin excited the conservative base of the Republican Party, attracting huge crowds at campaign events and mobilizing volunteers to work for the ticket, but her lack of experience and shaky interview performances left many observers questioning her fitness for the role of president. According to the exit polls, 60 percent of the electorate said she was not qualified to be president should it become necessary.[57]

The national party conventions are political rituals. The presidential candidates, vice-presidential choices, and platform positions are all known well in advance of the convention

Obama chose Delaware Senator Joe Biden, the chair of the Senate Foreign Relations Committee, as a running mate in hopes of balancing his own lack of foreign policy experience.

and approved without significant opposition. For roughly a week, each party presents itself and its candidates in the best possible light while criticizing the opposition. Nonetheless, conventions are important to the election process because many citizens decide how to vote in the general election at the time of the conventions.[58]

PRESIDENTIAL ELECTIONS: THE GENERAL ELECTION

11.5 *How does the Electoral College affect presidential elections?*

After the party conventions, the presidential election process enters its second and decisive phase. The field of presidential candidates has narrowed to one Democrat, one Republican, and several other candidates running on third-party tickets or as independents. The rules of the political game have changed as well, as each campaign considers what it must do to win an Electoral College majority.

The Electoral College

The **Electoral College** is the system established in the Constitution for the indirect election of the president and vice president. The framers of the Constitution disagreed on a procedure for selecting a president.

Some worried that congressional selection would make the chief executive subservient to Congress. Delegates at the constitutional convention from less populous states were afraid that popular election would afford their states little influence. Other delegates believed that voters scattered across the nation would vote for local favorites from their region of the country, overlooking better-qualified candidates from other states. The Electoral College was a compromise that reflected the division of power in a federal system, and ensured that presidents would respond to the interests of the states.[59]

*The Framers of the Constitution **disagreed** on a procedure for selecting a president.*

Under the Electoral College system, each state is entitled to as many electoral votes as the sum of its representatives in the U.S. House and Senate. Illinois, for example, with 18 representatives and 2 senators, has 20 electoral votes; Alabama, with 7 representatives and 2 senators, has 9. Altogether, the number of electoral votes is 538, based on 435 members of the House, 100

Electoral College the system established in the Constitution for indirect election of the president and vice president.

senators, and three electors for the District of Columbia. It takes a majority, 270 electoral votes, to elect a president.

Electors are individuals officially selected in each state to cast that state's electoral votes. Each state selects as many electors as it has electoral votes. The Framers of the Constitution anticipated that the members of the Electoral College would be experienced state leaders who would exercise good judgment in the selection of a president and vice president. In practice, however, the electors have been people chosen by party leaders to cast the state's electoral ballots for their party's nominees for president and vice president. Electors are usually long-time party activists selected as a reward for their service to the party. (The U.S. Constitution prohibits members of Congress from serving as electors.) Instead of exercising their own judgment to choose candidates for president and vice president, electors almost always cast their votes for their party's candidates.

The Constitution empowers the states to determine the manner of selecting their electors. Every state but Maine and Nebraska uses a winner-take-all election system. This means that the entire slate of electors backing the winning presidential candidate become the official set of electors for the state, regardless of the margin of victory. The states of Maine and Nebraska award electors based on the total statewide vote *and* the vote in each congressional district.

When voters choose among candidates in November, they are actually casting their ballots for electors pledged to support particular presidential and vice-presidential candidates. In 32 states, the names of the electors do not even appear on the ballot. A California voter casting a ballot for Obama in 2008 was really voting for a slate of 55 electors pledged to vote for the Obama–Biden ticket for president and vice president. A McCain voter in California cast a ballot for a different set of 55

electors, a slate pledged to back the McCain–Palin ticket.

The Electoral College meets to vote for presidential candidates more than a month after the popular vote. In December, the electors selected on Election Day in November gather in their state's capital city to officially mark their ballots for president and vice president. In January, Congress convenes in joint session (both chambers meeting together), opens the ballots, and announces the official outcome.

If no candidate receives a majority of electoral votes, Congress picks the president and vice president. The Constitution states that the House chooses the president from among the three presidential candidates with the most electoral votes. Each state delegation has one vote, and a majority (26 states) is needed for election. In the meantime, the Senate names the vice president from the top two vice-presidential candidates. Each senator has one vote and a majority is required for election.

The Fall Campaign

The goal of the general election campaign is to win 270 electoral votes. Each campaign targets states based on their electoral votes and the perception of the closeness of the race in the state, and allocates campaign resources accordingly.[60] Wyoming, Alaska, Montana, Delaware, and other states with few electoral votes receive little attention from the candidates, whereas California, Texas, New York, Florida, and other large states are preeminently important. If polls in a state show that one candidate leads the other by a substantial margin, then neither side is likely to devote many campaign resources to that state, focusing instead on places where the race is closer. In recent presidential elections, Texas, California, and New York have seen relatively little campaign activity because they have not been politically competitive. The Republicans have dominated presidential races in Texas, whereas the Democrats have had a

lock on California and New York. In contrast, Florida, Ohio, Pennsylvania, and Michigan have been battleground states.

The campaign funding rules are different for the general election period than they are during the primary season. Once the major party nominees are chosen, they are eligible for complete funding for the general-election campaign ($84.1 million in 2008). Candidates who accept the money may neither raise nor spend additional funds. In 2008, McCain accepted public financing. Obama refused it because he thought he would be able to raise and spend more money than federal funding would have provided. He was right. Obama raised several hundred million dollars for the general election campaign, giving him a substantial financial advantage over McCain.

The presidential and vice-presidential debates are often the most publicized events of the fall campaign. Debates affect people's views of the candidates, both because of the presentations made by the candidates themselves and because of media analyses.[61] Nonetheless, research shows that debates typically have little impact on election outcomes. The debate between John Kennedy and Richard Nixon is widely regarded as the turning point of the 1960 presidential race, but only because of the closeness of that contest. Most people who watched or heard the debate thought that the candidate they already favored had won. Most debates have little lasting effect on either voter preferences or knowledge about candidates and issues.

Most campaign events, not just debates, have relatively little impact on election outcomes because relatively few voters are open to persuasion. In both 2004 and 2008, more than 60 percent of the electorate decided how to vote before the

electors individuals selected in each state to officially cast that state's electoral votes.

Vice President Richard Nixon and Senator John Kennedy met in the first televised presidential debate in 1960.

The Results: Blue States and Red States

Some political observers believe that the United States is deeply and closely divided along regional lines into Republican **red states** and Democratic **blue states**, so named because of the colors used on the Electoral College map to show states that went Republican (red) or Democratic (blue). In this view, red states are pro-gun, pro-life, anti-gay Christian conservative strongholds opposed to government regulation and high taxes, whereas blue states are secular liberal bastions that favor gun control, abortion rights, gay rights, and well-funded government programs aimed at alleviating societal problems.

The Electoral College map graphically illustrates the blue state–red state divide. In 2004, President Bush won reelection by carrying every state in the South, every state in the Great Plains, and every state in the Rocky Mountains. Kerry won the Northeast and every state on the West Coast except Alaska. The two candidates split the Midwest. The 2004 electoral vote division closely resembled the 2000 election. The only states that flipped from one party to the other were New Mexico and Iowa, which went for Al Gore in 2000 but Bush in 2004, and New Hampshire, which switched from Bush in 2000 to Kerry in 2004.

In 2008, Obama broke out of the blue state–red state stalemate by winning a number of formerly red states. In addition to holding on to every state that Kerry took in 2004, Obama expanded his base in the Northeast by winning New Hampshire. He shored up his position in the Midwest, taking Ohio,

national party conventions.[62] Only 10 percent of the 2008 electorate made its voting choice within a week of election day.[63]

The electorate includes both base voters and swing voters. **Base voters** are rock-solid Republicans or hardcore Democrats, firmly committed to voting for their party's nominee. In contrast, **swing voters** are citizens who could vote either way. Base voters typically outnumber swing voters by a large margin. In 2004, polling indicated that 42 percent of voters were the Democratic base; 45 percent were the Republican base. Only 13 percent could be classified as swing voters.[64]

The base vote decides most elections. Bush won the 2004 election because his party had the larger base that year, and the Republicans did a better job than did the Democrats at turning out their base. Swing voters make a difference only when the base vote for each party is nearly equal in size and one candidate or the other attracts a substantial majority of

> In 2008, more than **60 percent** of the electorate decided how to vote *before* the national party conventions.

the swing vote. Political scientist William G. Mayer calculates that the swing vote was critical to the outcome of the close elections of 1976, 1980, 1992, and 2000, but other recent elections were decided by the base.[65] In 2008, voters identifying with the Democratic Party outnumbered Republican Party identifiers 39 percent to 32 percent, giving Obama a distinct advantage. Obama also capture 52 percent of independents, which represented 29 percent of the electorate.[66]

In the last few days of the campaign, the candidates frantically crisscross the country, making as many appearances as possible in large states that are expected to be close. Research shows that candidate appearances increase turnout, especially late in the campaign season, but have relatively little impact on voter choice.[67] Consequently, the candidates focus on party strongholds. Republicans hold rallies in the suburbs; Democrats campaign in inner-city neighborhoods.

base voters rock-solid Republicans or hardcore Democrats, firmly committed to voting for their party's nominee.

swing voters citizens who could vote for either party in an election.

red states Republican states

blue states Democratic states

Indiana, and Iowa. Obama made inroads in the South, the reddest region in the nation, winning Virginia, North Carolina, and Florida. Finally, he carved out a section of the Southwest, taking Colorado, New Mexico, and Nevada (see map below).

Political scientist Morris P. Fiorina believes that the red state–blue state division is overblown. He points out that most of the red states have major enclaves of blue voters, and vice versa. Even though Texas is a red state on the Electoral College map, many of its cities voted for Obama, as did the region along the border with Mexico. Meanwhile, many of the counties in California, a blue state, voted for McCain.

Electoral College Debate

The 2000 presidential election made the Electoral College the center of controversy, because the candidate with the most votes did not win the White House. Democratic presidential candidate Gore won the popular vote because he piled up huge margins of victory in the large states he won, such as California and New York, whereas George W. Bush won his biggest states, including Texas and Floria, by smaller margins. Bush also benefited from the federalism bonus that awards every state three electoral votes (because of its two senators and one representative) regardless of size. Because Bush carried 11 of 18 smaller states, he won more electoral votes than he would have received on the basis of population alone.[68] Bush took more electoral votes, and therefore the election.

Bush is not the only person to be elected president despite losing the national popular vote. In 1876, Samuel Tilden lost to Rutherford B. Hayes even though he received more popular votes than did his opponent. Similarly, Grover Cleveland won the popular vote in 1888 but lost the Electoral College—and the presidency—to Benjamin Harrison. The chances of a "wrong winner" electoral vote outcome are about one in three when the popular vote margin is 500,000 votes or fewer.[69] Nonetheless, election out-comes that close are rare. Only two presidential races in the twentieth century had popular vote margins of fewer than 500,000 votes—the Kennedy–Nixon election in 1960 and the Nixon–Humphrey contest in 1968.

Critics of the Electoral College warn that the electors may vote for persons other than their party's presidential and vice-presidential candidates. Fewer than half the states legally require the electors to cast their ballots for their party's nominees. The 2000 election was so close that two Bush electors could have changed the outcome had they switched their votes from Bush to Gore. Nonetheless, academic observers downplay the seriousness of this problem because most electoral vote margins are large enough that dozens of electors would have to change their votes to affect an election's outcome. Also, electors rarely prove unfaithful. Since 1789, only 10 out of nearly 22,000 electors have voted "against instructions."[70] None affected the outcome of an election.

Another criticism of the Electoral College is that Congress picks the president and vice president if no candidate receives a majority of the electoral vote. In 1824, the last time Congress named the president, the selection of John Quincy Adams over Andrew Jackson was marred by dark rumors of a backroom deal. It might also weaken the office of the presidency by making the incumbent dependent on congressional selection.[71] In recent years, the closest the nation has come to seeing an election go to Congress was in 1968, when independent candidate George Wallace won 46 electoral votes. In 1992, Ross Perot won 19 percent of the popular vote, but won no electoral votes because he failed to carry any states.

The strength of the Electoral College is that it conveys political legitimacy to the winner in closely fought presidential elections. Political legitimacy is the popular acceptance of a government and its

2008 Electoral College Results

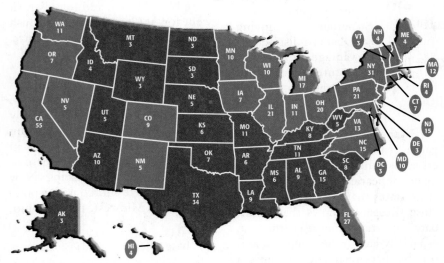

red states: states that voted for Republican John McCain for president in 2008

blue states: states that voted for Democrat Barack Obama in 2008

Obama won the election in 2008 by capturing a number of traditionally red states. The Electoral College vote was 365 for Obama, 173 for McCain.

*In Nebraska, Obama won a single electoral vote by carrying a congressional district in Omaha.

Vote Percentage for Winning Presidential Candidate

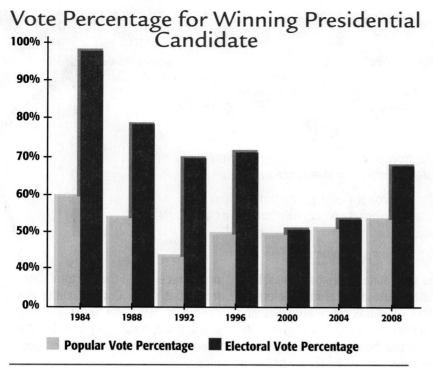

In every election, the winning candidate's electoral vote percentage was greater than his popular vote percentage, giving the candidate an appearance of greater majority support.

officials as rightful authorities in the exercise of power. If citizens and other public officials believe that a president lacks political legitimacy, the president will have difficulty exercising authority. The proponents of the Electoral College argue that it enhances the legitimacy of the president by ensuring that even close presidential elections produce a clear winner. For example, even though Bill Clinton took only 43 percent of the popular vote in 1992, he won 69 percent of the electoral vote. The Electoral College turned a badly divided popular vote, split 43 percent for Clinton to 38 percent for Bush to 19 percent for Perot, into a one-sided Electoral College victory. The morning after the election some newspapers even used the word *landslide* to describe Clinton's victory. The figure above compares the popular vote with the electoral vote percentage for the winning presidential candidate from 1984 through 2008. In every election, the winning candidate's electoral vote percentage was greater than the popular vote percentage. The defenders of the Electoral College believe that it is beneficial because it gives the winning presidential candidate the appearance of the majority support necessary to be an effective president.

Nonetheless, the 2000 election also showed that the Electoral College sometimes undermines the political legitimacy of a president. The outcome of the national Electoral College vote in 2000 depended on the result of the popular vote in Florida, which was too close to call. For more than a month, county canvassing boards, state officials, the Florida legislature, Florida judges, the Florida Supreme Court, and the U.S. Supreme Court struggled over ballot-counting issues. The outcome ultimately hinged on the decision whether and how to count more than 40,000 ballots that voting machines had failed to count. Many observers believed that a hand count of 40,000 additional ballots would give the election to Gore because most of the ballots were from counties that voted heavily for him. After a district court judge in Florida ruled against

a hand count, the Florida Supreme Court, all of whose members were Democrats, voted 4–3 to order a hand count. Within less than a day, the U.S. Supreme Court voted 5–4 to halt the count and disregard the ballots, giving the state of Florida, and the election, to Bush. The five justices in the majority were all appointees of President Reagan or President George H. W. Bush, the father of the presidential candidate who benefited from the decision.

Many observers believed that the involvement of the courts in the election outcome would undermine the legitimacy of the new president, regardless of the outcome of the dispute. Had Gore won because the Florida Supreme Court ordered a hand recount, Republicans would have charged that his victory was tainted by the intervention of a partisan court. As it were, many Democrats argued that Bush's election was illegitimate because of the intervention of a narrow partisan majority on the U.S. Supreme Court.

In the aftermath of the 2000 election, some members of Congress proposed constitutional amendments to abolish the Electoral College and replace it with direct popular election. The advocates of direct election point out that their system is simpler than the Electoral College and more democratic because it ensures that the candidate with the most votes nationwide wins. They also think direct election would increase turnout because every vote would count equally regardless of the state in which it was cast.[72]

Nonetheless, direct election of the president has its detractors. Some critics complain that candidates would make fewer public appearances, concentrating even more on television than they do now. Other opponents fear that a proliferation of independent and minor-party candidates would undermine the legitimacy of the eventual winner. Once again, consider the 1992 presidential election. Had Clinton won the

TAKING SIDES

Electoral College Reform

Should the selection of the president be in the hands of the people rather than the Electoral College?

Does the Electoral College system provide disproportionate influences to certain states or interests?

OVERVIEW

The founding fathers created the Electoral College because it was a way to ensure executive independence from Congress while balancing state interests. Unlike parliamentary models of government, in which the legislature chooses the executive leader from among its membership, a system of separated powers has to have an executive firmly independent from the legislature. The Electoral College also addressed the other main problem at the time of the founding by balancing the interests of the large states and small states. Each state is allocated as many electoral votes as it has representatives and senators in the U.S. Congress. Because the most populous states have the most seats in the House of Representatives, they also have the most electors, but every state, even the smallest states, receive at least three electoral votes.

All but two states employ a winner-take-all system for awarding their electoral votes. If a candidate wins by a slight margin in a state, he or she receives all the electoral votes from that state. Consequently, the candidate with the most popular votes nationwide may not be the candidate who wins the most electoral votes.

Proposals to reform the Electoral College often involve having states award their electors proportionally or by district, or giving bonus electors to the popular vote winner. A direct popular election plan would declare the person with the largest number of popular votes the winner.

SUPPORTING
reforming the Electoral College

The Electoral College fails to reflect the national popular will and goes against the concept of representation based on majority rule. If you are committed to the fundamental idea that the majority should prevail in a democracy, then the election of presidential candidates who lost the popular vote is a major problem. The candidate with the most votes should win the election.

The Electoral College limits voter choices. The winner-take-all mechanism of the Electoral College makes it extremely difficult for third-party or independent candidates ever to make much of a showing, reinforcing a two-party system and restricting choices available to the electorate.

The Electoral College is out of step with American politics. The president and vice president should be chosen in direct elections like all other elected officials in the country. The American people are capable of choosing their own leaders.

AGAINST
reforming the Electoral College

Contested elections would become impossible to overcome. The Electoral College protects us from endless recounts and challenges that would engage the more than 3,000 counties across the country. The recount in Florida alone in 2000 delayed the outcome of the election for months and was eventually halted by the Supreme Court.

The Electoral College protects national cohesiveness. The presidential candidates must appeal to coalitions of voters that are widely distributed in different states across the country. If candidates were elected by a national majority only, they could win by developing regions or groups of voters only, which would exacerbate regional differences and divisions.

A stable, two-party system exists because of the Electoral College. The design of the Electoral College, which forces parties to build broad coalitions to win, discourages the development of numerous, sometimes extremist smaller parties. A two-party system encourages parties and more divergent interests to coalesce around pragmatic views, and helps us keep stability in government and maintain our national identity.

amendment to abolish the Electoral College, despite the 2000 election. Constitutional amendments must be proposed by a two-thirds vote of the House and Senate and then ratified by three fourths of the states, margins not easily achieved. Will small states agree to an amendment that would reduce their influence in the presidential election process? Furthermore, interest groups that are disproportionately powerful in states with large numbers of electoral votes will oppose eliminating the Electoral College because it would reduce their influence. African Americans, Latinos, Jews, gay men and lesbians, and organized labor all enjoy considerable influence in large states rich in electoral votes. Because of the Electoral College, no candidate who hopes to win in California, for example, can afford to ignore the interests of Latino voters.

Florida voters protest the Court's decision to halt the count of disputed votes in the 2000 presidential election. Bush eventually received Florida's 25 electoral votes, and won the election 271–266 electoral votes.

presidency based on 43 percent of the popular vote instead of 69 percent of the electoral vote, would his administration have enjoyed the same level of political legitimacy as it did with his solid Electoral College victory?

Most political scientists think that it is unlikely that Congress and the states will adopt a constitutional

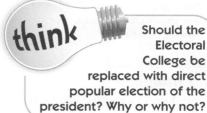

Should the Electoral College be replaced with direct popular election of the president? Why or why not?

HOW VOTERS DECIDE

 What factors affect voter choice?

Political scientists identify a number of factors influencing voter choice.

Party Identification

Voter choice is closely related to political party identification.[73] Democrats vote for Democratic candidates; Republicans back Republicans. In 2008, 89 percent of Republicans voted for McCain while 89 percent of Democrats backed Obama.[74] Keep in mind, however, that party identification is a complex phenomenon. People identify with one party or the other because they agree with its issue positions, have confidence in its leaders, or feel comfortable with groups associated with the party. When citizens decide to vote for Candidate A because Candidate A is a Democrat (or Republican), their choice is more than blind allegiance to a party label, it is also a response to the perceived issue positions and image of the party.

Issues

The role of issues varies, depending on the strength of a voter's party attachment and knowledge of the candidates' issue positions. Informed voters consider issues in selecting candidates, although they tend to be biased in favor in candidates who share their party identification. Well informed independents base their voting decisions strictly on how closely the candidates' issue positions match their own.[75] Less well-informed voters fall back on party identification. Poorly informed voters and people who are ambivalent on parties and issues base their voting decisions on other factors, such as their judgment about the state of

the economy.[76] At times, pressing national issues such as a war or economic crisis can become a priority in how citizens vote.

Personal Qualities and Image

Political science research shows that perceptions of a candidate's personal qualities influence voter choice. One study finds that voters evaluate presidential candidates on the basis on their mental image of what a president should be. According to the study, citizens want a president who is competent, honest, and reliable, and they pick the candidate they believe best matches those qualities.[77] Another study concludes that voters respond to candidates on the basis of their emotional evaluation of a candidate's moral leadership and competence.[78]

think What are the most important qualities a candidate for president should have in order to get your vote?

Many voters participating in the 2010 election wanted to send a message to President Obama and for most of them the message was negative. Only a fourth told polltakers that they were voting to support the president compared with 37 percent who said they were voting to oppose him.

Campaigns

Campaigns educate voters about candidates and issues.[79] Candidates who choose not to conduct a campaign or who lack the necessary funding to get their message across almost never win. Challengers for congressional seats who have less than a quarter million dollars to spend have less than a 1-percent chance of winning.[80]

Research shows that campaign tactics vary in effectiveness. Campaign advertising affects voters in concert with their party identification, making Democrats more likely to vote Democratic, and Republicans more likely to support GOP candidates. The issues that work best for the Democrats are education, childcare, and healthcare. In contrast, Republicans ben-

efit when they can shift the issue focus to taxes, morality, economic growth, and foreign policy.[81]

Political scientists believe that election campaigns affect election outcomes, but they are not as important as the state of the economy and the political context in which the race is run. The three most important underlying factors affecting the outcome of a presidential race are the following: 1) the incumbent president's approval rating in the months before the election; 2) the growth rate of the economy in the quarter prior to the election; and 3) the length of time the president's party has held the White House.[82] All three of these factors worked against McCain in the 2008 presidential campaign. He was a Republican trying to keep his party's hold on the White House for the third election in a row despite incumbent President Bush's low approval rating and a serious economic downturn. In 2008, 71 percent of the voters told pollsters that they disapproved of the way Bush was handling his job, and two-thirds of them cast

Important Issues in the 2010 Elections

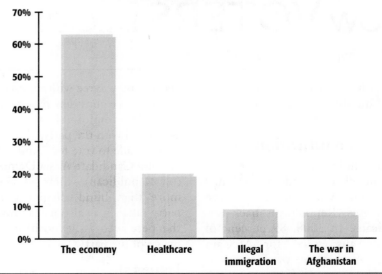

Voters leaving the polls were asked, "What was the most important issue to you this year?"

The overriding issue in the 2010 midterm election was the economy. When asked to identify their most important issue, more than 60 percent of voters said the economy.

Source: CNN exit polls

their ballots for Obama. Half the electorate described the economy as "poor" or "not so good"; 54 percent of them voted for Obama compared with 44 percent for McCain.[83]

Retrospective and Prospective Voting

Citizens make voting decisions based on their evaluations of the past and expectations for the future. **Retrospective voting** is the concept that voters choose candidates based on their perception of an incumbent candidate's past performance in office or the performance of the incumbent party. If voters perceive that things are going well, incum-bent officeholders and their party usually get the credit. They get the blame, though, if voters think the situation is poor. The economy is the most important factor affecting retrospective voter, but war and peace matter as well.[84] In 2008, 75 percent of the electorate told survey researches that the country was "seriously off on the wrong track"; 62 percent of them voted for Obama.[85]

Voter evaluations of candidates have a prospective component as well. **Prospective voting** is the concept that voters evaluate the incumbent officeholder and the incumbent's party based on their expectations of future developments.

One study finds that voter expectations of economic performance have a strong influence on voter choice.[86] Another study shows that voters reward or punish the pres-ident based on their view of the nation's economic prospects rather than the current standard of living.[87]

retrospective voting the concept that voters choose candidates based on their perception of an incumbent candidate's past performance in office or the performance of the incumbent party.

prospective voting the concept that voters evaluate the incumbent officeholder and the incumbent's party based on their expectations of future developments.

what we LEARNED

ELECTIONS IN AMERICA

11.1 *How are elections conducted in the United States?*

Americans have the opportunity to cast ballots in several types of elections. In most states, major parties choose their general election candidates in primary elections scheduled a month or more before the November general election. Some states have closed primaries; other states have open primaries.

American voters select public officials in a combination of at-large and district elections. Legislative district boundaries must be redrawn every ten years after the national census is taken. Legislative districts must also be redrawn because of population movement within a state. According to the one person, one vote rulings of the U.S. Supreme Court, legislative districts must be nearly equal in population. The Voting Rights Act (VRA) makes it illegal for state and local governments to enact and enforce election rules and procedures that diminish the voting power of racial, ethnic, and language minority groups.

Nonetheless, redistricting is highly political and can be used to advance the interests of a political party or a particular individual, a process known as gerrymandering.

ELECTION CAMPAIGNS

11.2 *How are political campaigns organized?*

An election campaign is an attempt to get information to voters that will persuade them to elect a candidate. Money is a campaign necessity, but it does not guarantee success. Wealthy candidates can fund their own campaigns, but most raise money from individual contributors and PACs. Political parties and 527 committees may also spend money to support or defeat candidates. Candidates spend the early months of the race raising money, building an organization, seeking group endorsements, planning strategy, and improving the candidate's name recognition, especially if the candidate is not an incumbent. Campaign advertising increases citizen knowledge of issues and candidates, affects voter evaluations of candidates, and increases a candidate's share of the vote.

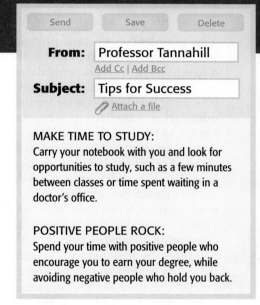

Send   Save   Delete

From: Professor Tannahill
Add Cc | Add Bcc

Subject: Tips for Success
📎 Attach a file

MAKE TIME TO STUDY:
Carry your notebook with you and look for opportunities to study, such as a few minutes between classes or time spent waiting in a doctor's office.

POSITIVE PEOPLE ROCK:
Spend your time with positive people who encourage you to earn your degree, while avoiding negative people who hold you back.

CONGRESSIONAL ELECTIONS

11.3 *What are the similarities and differences in elections for the House and Senate?*

The most striking feature of elections for the U.S. House of Representatives is that most incumbents are reelected. Incumbents are usually better known and better funded than their opponents. Voters typically like their representative even if they disapprove of the performance of Congress as a whole. Many House districts are safe for one or the other political party. Historically, the political party holding the White House loses seats in the House of Representatives in midterm elections. Senate races are more competitive than House elections, and incumbency is not as important. Senate constituencies are usually more diverse, and voters tend to perceive Senate races as national rather than local election contests.

PRESIDENTIAL ELECTIONS: THE NOMINATION

11.4 *What are the main steps in the contest for the presidential nomination of each party?*

The presidential election process consists of two distinct phases with different rules, requiring candidates to wage two separate campaigns. The first phase is the contest for the nomination. Republicans compete against other Republicans, Democrats against other Democrats in a series of primaries and caucuses designed to select delegates to each party's national nominating convention. Each candidate's goal is for his or her supporters to be chosen as convention delegates because the delegates, by majority vote, select the party's presidential nominee. In 2008, the presidential nomination process had six stages: 1) pre-primary positioning; 2) the early contests; 3) Super Tuesday; 4) post–Super Tuesday contests; 5) transition; and 6) the national party conventions.

MySearchLab®

PRESIDENTIAL ELECTIONS: THE GENERAL ELECTION

11.5 *How does the Electoral College affect presidential elections?*

After the party conventions, the presidential election process enters its second and decisive phase—the general election phase, which is a contest between the two major party tickets and, perhaps, a serious independent or third party candidate. Because the Electoral College determines the winner of the general election, the general election phase is actually 51 elections, a contest in every state and the District of Columbia. The winner is the candidate who can win a set of states whose combined electoral votes total at least 270, the majority of electoral votes at stake. With the exception of Maine and Nebraska, the candidate with the most votes in each state receives all of the state's electoral votes. In the general election phase, each campaign targets battleground states with large numbers of electoral votes at stake. Most elections are decided by the relative size of each party's base vote and how effective the party is at turning out its base.

The 2000 presidential election made the Electoral College the center of controversy because the winner of the popular vote, Al Gore, lost the election. George W. Bush captured a majority of Electoral College votes because he won a number of states by relatively small margins and because he carried more small states, each of which has three electoral votes regardless of its population. Critics of the Electoral College also worry about electors casting their ballots contrary to the will of the voters in their states and the prospect that Congress will pick a president and vice president if no candidate receives a majority of electoral votes. Reformers offer a number of alternatives to the Electoral College, including direct popular election, but no proposal has come close to winning the level of support needed to propose and ratify a constitutional amendment.

HOW VOTERS DECIDE

11.6 *What factors affect voter choice?*

Voter choice is closely related to political party identification. Informed voters base their voting decisions on ideology and the issue positions of the candidates; uninformed voters base their decisions on other factors, such as their judgment about the state of the economy. Perceptions of a candidate's personal qualities and image influence voter choice. Campaigns educate voters about candidates and issues. The three most important underlying factors affecting the outcome of a presidential race are: a) the incumbent president's approval rating in the months before the election; b) the growth rate of the economy in the quarter prior to the election; and c) the length of time the president's party has held the White House. Finally, citizens make voting decisions based on their evaluations of the past (retrospective voting) and expectations for the future (prospective voting).

11.1 *How are elections conducted in the United States?*

1 Luisa Cangelosi voted for the Republican candidate for president, the Democratic candidate for the U.S. Senate, and the Democratic candidate for the U.S. House. Ms. Cangelosi did which of the following?
   a. Violated the Voting Rights Act
   b. Voted in a presidential preference primary
   c. Voted a split-ticket ballot
   d. Voted in a primary election

11.2 *How are political campaigns organized?*

2 How often does reapportionment take place?
   a. Every 10 years, after the U.S. Census is taken
   b. Every four years, to coincide with the presidential election
   c. Whenever the population changes by more than 10 percent
   d. None of the above

3 Which of the following statements about the Voting Rights Act (VRA) is true?
   a. The VRA prohibits gerrymandering.
   b. The VRA does not apply to the entire country.
   c. The VRA only applies to the Northeast.
   d. None of the above

11.3 *What are the similarities and differences in elections for the House and Senate?*

4 Which of the following statements is true about the role of money in political campaigns?
   a. The candidate who spends the most money always wins.
   b. Advertising, especially television advertising, is the single largest expenditure in most campaign budgets.
   c. Candidates who provide most of their own campaign money usually win because they do not have to spend time fundraising.
   d. All of the above

5 Which of the following statements about negative campaigning is true?
   a. Negative campaigning is relatively new in American politics.
   b. Political scientists agree that negative campaigning decreases voter turnout.
   c. Political scientists agree that negative campaigning almost never works.
   d. None of the above

11.4 *What are the main steps in the contest for the presidential nomination of each party?*

6 Which of the following reasons helps explain why most incumbent members of the U.S. House are reelected?
   a. They usually have more money than their challenges.
   b. They are usually better known than their challengers.
   c. Many congressional districts are safe for one party or the other.
   d. All of the above

7 In 2008, a voter who was drawn to the polls out of excitement about the candidacy of Barack Obama decided to vote for the other Democratic candidates as well. This action illustrates which of the following concepts?
   a. Coattail effect
   b. Retrospective voting
   c. Rose garden strategy
   d. Split-ticket ballot

11.5 *How does the Electoral College affect presidential elections?*

8 How were the delegates to the 2008 Republican National Convention chosen?
   a. They were chosen by the Congress.
   b. They were chosen by the Electoral College.
   c. They were chosen by each state party, either through a presidential preference primary or a party caucus.
   d. They were chosen in a national primary election.

9 Which of the following plays the most important role in selecting the presidential nominees of the Democratic and Republican parties?
   a. Party activists and party voters
   b. Party bosses
   c. Each party's congressional delegation
   d. Independent voters

10 Why is doing well in the Iowa caucus and the New Hampshire primary important for candidates seeking their party's nomination for president?
   a. Candidates who do well in both states benefit from large numbers of convention delegates.
   b. Candidates who do well in both states benefit from a large amount of favorable publicity.
   c. Candidates who do well in both states benefit from a large number of electoral votes.
   d. All of the above

11 Alabama elects seven members of the House. How many electoral votes does Alabama have?

   a. Seven   b. Eight
   c. Nine   d. Eleven

12 Assume for the purpose of this question that a Democrat, a Republican, and a major independent candidate are running for president. In California, the Democrat gets 45 percent of the vote, the Republican gets 40 percent, and the independent receives the rest. How many of California's electoral votes will the Democratic candidate receive?
   a. All of them
   b. 45 percent of them
   c. None of them
   d. It depends on the outcome of the runoff between the Democrat and the Republican, the two top finishers

13 Under which of the following circumstances would Candidate A win the 2012 presidential election?
   a. Candidate A wins a majority of the popular vote nationwide.
   b. Candidate A carries more states than does any other candidate.
   c. Candidate A wins a plurality of the popular vote nationwide.
   d. Candidate A wins a majority of the electoral vote.

14 Person A tells survey researchers that she is a committed Democrat who decided to vote for the Democratic nominee for president well before the party's national convention. Person A is an example of which of the following?
   a. Base voter
   b. Swing voter
   c. Retrospective voter
   d. Independent voter

11.6 *What factors affect voter choice?*

15 Which of the following statements is an expression of retrospective voting?
   a. I voted for Candidate A because I like her promises and think she will do a good job in office.
   b. I voted for Candidate B because I like the way things are going and he is the incumbent.
   c. I voted for Candidate B because he is a Republican and I am a Republican.
   d. I voted for Candidate A because I agree with her on the issues.

KNOW the score

14–15 correct:	Congratulations—you know your American government!
12–13 correct:	Your understanding of this chapter is weak—be sure to review the key terms and visit TheThinkSpot.
<12 correct:	Reread the chapter more thoroughly.

Answers: 1) c, 2) a, 3) d, 4) b, 5) d, 6) d, 7) a, 8) c, 9) a, 10) b, 11) c, 12) a, 13) d, 14) a, 15) b

12 CONGRESS

BICAMERALISM

Learning Objective **12.1** How have structural differences affected the development of the House and Senate?

MEMBERSHIP

Learning Objective **12.2** What are the qualifications for and characteristics of members of Congress?

ORGANIZATION

Learning Objective **12.3** How is Congress organized in terms of leadership and committee structure?

THE LEGISLATIVE PROCESS

Learning Objective **12.4** What are the steps in the legislative process for a bill to become a law?

In early 2010, President Barack Obama and the Democratic Party leadership in Congress made history with the enactment of comprehensive healthcare reform. The legislation had two primary goals: first, to provide insurance coverage to most of the 32 million Americans without health insurance; and second, to slow the rapidly increasing cost of healthcare. The measure included a number of important provisions:

- Insurance companies will no longer be able to refuse coverage based on pre-existing conditions or to drop coverage of people who become ill.
- Businesses with 50 or more workers must provide health insurance coverage for their employees or pay a fine to the government.
- People who are not already covered must purchase a health insurance policy or pay an annual fine of $695. Families earning less than four times the federal poverty level—$88,200 a year in 2010—qualify for federal financial assistance to help them cover the cost.
- State governments will set up health insurance exchanges, which are marketplaces where businesses and individuals will be able to shop for insurance policies.

- Funding for the program comes from increasing tax rates on families making $250,000 a year ($200,000 for individuals) as well as a 10 percent tax on indoor tanning services.[1]

Healthcare reform was quite controversial. Whereas President Obama and most Democrats in Congress declared that the new law was a balanced solution to the nation's most pressing domestic policy priority, Republicans in Congress unanimously opposed the bill's passage, calling it an expensive government takeover of the healthcare industry. Republican leaders made healthcare reform an election issue, promising to repeal and replace the program if voters put them in power.

The enactment of healthcare reform provides a backdrop for studying the processes and politics of the U.S. Congress. This chapter highlights the differences in the two chambers of Congress. It profiles the membership of Congress and explains how Congress is organized. Finally, the chapter traces the steps of the legislative process, using the adoption of healthcare reform to illustrate the dynamics of the process.

BICAMERALISM

 How have structural differences affected the development of the House and Senate?

Article I of the U.S. Constitution declares that the legislative power of the United States is vested in a **bicameral** (two-house) legislature, consisting of the Senate and the House of Representatives. States enjoy equal representation in the U.S. Senate. California and Wyoming each have two senators, even though the population of California exceeds 36 million people and Wyoming has a population of just over half a million. The original Constitution originally stipulated that each state be represented by two senators chosen by its state legislature. The Seventeenth Amendment, ratified in 1913, provided for the direct popular election of senators. Today, the 50 states elect 100 senators, running statewide to serve six-year staggered terms, with one-third of the Senate standing for reelection each election year. Because senators run for election statewide, they have more diverse constituencies than do members of the House, most of whom run from relatively small districts.

The size of a state's delegation in the U.S. House depends on the state's population, but every state, no matter how small its population, must have at least one representative. California has more than 50 representatives in the House; Wyoming has one. In 1911, Congress capped the size of the House at 435 representatives. Today, the

House membership also includes non-voting delegates from the District of Columbia, American Samoa, the Virgin Islands, and Guam, as well as a resident commissioner from Puerto Rico. Representatives run from districts for two-year terms, with the entire House standing for reelection every other year.

The Constitution assigns certain responsibilities exclusively to the Senate. The Senate ratifies treaties by a two-thirds vote. It confirms presidential appointments of federal judges, ambassadors, and executive branch officials, all by majority vote. The only major appointment also requiring House approval is for the office of vice president. The Twenty-fifth Amendment provides that both the House and Senate confirm the president's nominee for vice president if the office becomes vacant.

The Senate and House share other duties. Both chambers must vote by a two-thirds margin to propose constitutional amendments, and both houses must agree by majority vote to declare war. The government can neither raise nor spend money without majority approval of both chambers, although bills that raise revenue must originate in the House. The Constitution specifies that the House of Representatives can **impeach** (formally accuse) an executive or judicial branch officeholder by majority vote. The accused official can be removed from office by a

two-thirds vote of the Senate. Legislation does not pass Congress unless it passes both the House and the Senate in identical form.

Because of their different constitutional structures and responsibilities, the House and Senate have developed into distinct legislative bodies. The Senate is often likened to a great debating society, where senators discuss the grand design of national policy. It is individualistic and dependent on informally devised decision-making practices. Many of the decisions made in the Senate require the approval of a **super-majority**, a voting majority that is greater than a simple majority. Because the Senate conducts much of its business under agreements requiring the unanimous consent of its members, individual senators enjoy considerable power over the legislative process.[2] Furthermore, the rules of debate in the Senate allow a minority of 41 senators to extend debate endlessly, preventing a measure from ever coming to a vote.

Members of the House have a reputation for devotion to technical expertise, personalized constituency

bicameral a two-house legislature.

impeach the act of formally accusing an official of the executive or judicial branches of an impeachable offense.

supermajority a voting margin that is greater than a simple majority.

House and Senate Comparisons

HOUSE

Members: 435

Apportioned among the states by population

Term length: Two years

Members must be:
- 25 years old
- U.S. citizen for at least seven years
- Legal resident of their state

Responsibilities:
- Initiates revenue-raising bills
- Impeaches federal officials by majority vote

Characteristics of Chamber:
- Members are constituency specialists who are typically more partisan than are members of the Senate
- House is majoritarian in that it decides most issues by simple majority vote

SENATE

Members: 100

Two senators per state

Term length: Six years

Members must be:
- 30 years old
- U.S. citizen for at least nine years
- Legal resident of their state

Responsibilities:
- Ratifies treaties
- Confirms many presidential appointments
- Tries impeachment cases and can remove officials by a two-thirds vote

Characteristics of Chamber:
- Members are constituency generalists who are typically less partisan than are members of the House
- Senate frequently requires a super majority to conduct business

---

service, and responsiveness to local political interests. Because of its size, the House is a relatively impersonal institution that depends on formal rules to structure the decision-making process. In contrast to the Senate, the House makes decisions by majority vote. As long as a measure enjoys the support of a bare majority of the members of the House, its opponents are powerless to stop it. The House is also considered a less prestigious body than the Senate. Members of the House frequently give up their seats to run for the Senate, but senators never leave their positions to run for the House.

MEMBERSHIP

 What are the qualifications for and characteristics of members of Congress?

The U.S. Constitution requires that members of the House be at least 25 years of age, American citizens for at least seven years, and residents of the state in which their district is located. Senators must be at least 30 years old, citizens for nine years, and residents of the state they represent. If disputes arise about qualifications or election results, each chamber of Congress determines the eligibility of its own members. The House and Senate can also expel a member for misconduct.

Profile of the Membership

Because of the impact of the Voting Rights Act (VRA) and changing social and cultural values, Congress is more diverse than at any time in its history.[3] As recently as 1965, the year the VRA became law, only six African Americans and four Latinos served in Congress. In contrast, the 112th Congress, which took office in 2011, was relatively diverse. Seventeen women, two Asian Americans, and two Latinos served in the Senate. The House of Representatives included 72 women, 42 African Americans, 24 Latinos, 9 Asian Americans, 1 Native American, 3 openly gay men, and 1 lesbian. Despite the influx of women and minority members over the last few decades, more than three-fourths of the members of the 112th Congress were white males of European ancestry.

Most members of Congress are older, affluent, established members of society. Almost every member of Congress is a college graduate and nearly two-thirds of the members hold advanced college degrees. Law and public service are the most popular professions, followed by business and education. Many members of the House and Senate are personally wealthy. The most commonly cited religious affiliations are Roman Catholic, Episcopalian, Methodist, Baptist, and Presbyterian. Most members of Congress

membership 223

Diversity in Congress

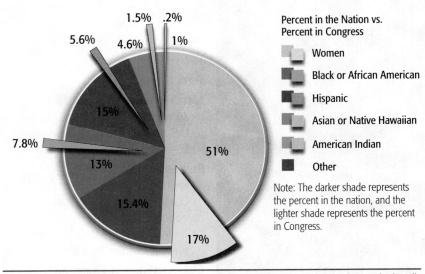

Percent in the Nation vs. Percent in Congress

- Women
- Black or African American
- Hispanic
- Asian or Native Hawaiian
- American Indian
- Other

5.6% 4.6% 1.5% .2%
1%
15%
7.8%
13%
15.4%
51%
17%

Note: The darker shade represents the percent in the nation, and the lighter shade represents the percent in Congress.

Although the membership of Congress is more diverse than ever, white males continue to be heavily over-represented.

have held elective office before coming to Congress. In the 112th Congress, the average age in the House was 57; it was 63 in the Senate.[4]

Compensation

Congress determines the compensation of its members. In 2011, rank and file members of the House and Senate received $174,000 a year, with members of the leadership earning higher salaries. Under a federal law enacted in 1989, lawmakers get an annual cost of living raise unless both the House and Senate vote to block it.

Congressional compensation is controversial. Many observers (including most members of Congress) believe that high pay is needed to attract good people. Although congressional salaries are more than adequate by most standards, senators and representatives earn less money than corporate executives and probably less than they could make working in private business, practicing law, or lobbying. Also, most members of Congress must maintain two residences—one in Washington, D.C., and another residence in their district or state. In contrast, the opponents of increasing congressional pay argue that high salaries are elitist. How can Congress be a representative institution, they ask, if its members earn several times more money than the average American makes? Furthermore, many critics believe that high salaries are unjustified considering the inability of Congress to solve some of the nation's most pressing problems.

In addition to their salaries, members of Congress have an allowance sufficient to cover regular trips home. They can also travel abroad for free on official business. Members enjoy free parking on Capitol Hill, free long-distance telephone use, and free postage for official correspondence—a perk known as the **franking privilege**. Members of Congress also benefit from a generous pension system.

think

Are members of Congress compensated too much, too little, or about the right amount?

Personal Styles

Traditionally, members of Congress got things done and advanced their careers by building relationships with colleagues, deferring to senior members, and bargaining. New members of Congress, especially in the House, were expected to learn the ropes from more experienced members before speaking out on policy matters. They earned respect from their colleagues by specializing in a particular policy area rather than trying to have an impact on a broad range of issues. Members of Congress were expected to cooperate with one another, exchanging favors and engaging in **logrolling**, an arrangement in which

franking privilege free postage provided to members of Congress.

Senators Richard Durbin (D, IL) and Charles Schumer (D, NY) share this rowhouse with two other congressmen to minimize expenses while they are in Washington, D.C.

Congressman Anthony Weiner, D., NY, resigned after accidently texting a lewd photo of himself to his public Twitter account. It was subsequently revealed that Weiner had sent sexually explicit photos of himself to several women.

two or more members of Congress agree in advance to support each other's favored legislation. The ideal lawmaker was someone who regarded the House or Senate as a career rather than a stepping-stone to higher office.[5]

In today's Congress, individual members have greater latitude than did their predecessors. Some members are skilled media entrepreneurs, using policy issues to gain media coverage so they can establish themselves as national political figures. They are less interested in passing legislation than in advancing their own political careers. Other members use the media to promote their legislative agendas. Through news conferences, press releases, televised speeches on C-Span, and other staged media events, they influence the legislative agenda, define policy alternatives, and shape public opinion about proposed legislation.[6]

Consider the careers of Minnesota Republican Congresswoman Michele Bachmann and Florida Democratic Congressman Alan Grayson. Bachmann is an outspoken social conservative who has become the darling of her party's activist base. In a speech that was seen by two million YouTube viewers, she wondered if healthcare reform would allow a 13-year-old girl to use a school sex clinic to get an abortion and "go home on the school bus that night." She

speculated in another speech that the reforms would deny healthcare to the ill: "So watch out if you are disabled." Grayson, meanwhile, is a combative liberal who has become a favorite of the base of the Democratic Party. He summarized the Republican healthcare plan in a YouTube video in three words: "Don't get sick." And if people do become ill, he said, the Republican plan was just as simple: "Die quickly."[7] Both Bachmann and Grayson have made themselves into political celebrities, able to raise substantially more money in campaign contributions than the average member of Congress can. In 2010, Bachmann raised more than $4.5 million while Grayson brought in $3.7 million.[8] Bachmann and Grayson have also become political lightening rods, attracting well-funded opponents. In 2010, Bachmann won reelection with 53 percent of the vote, but Grayson lost badly.

Home Styles

Most members of Congress believe that they have a responsibility to "vote their district," that is, take policy positions in accordance with the views of the majority of their constituents. Senators and representatives from agricultural states, for example, back farm support legislation whereas members of Congress from oil producing states support measures favored by the oil industry. Senators and representatives know that if they stray too far and too frequently from the policy preferences of the majority of their constituents, they may pay the price at the ballot box. Future election opponents will accuse them of "losing touch" with the folks back home and charge

them with voting against the interests of the state or district.[9] Consequently, members of Congress go home often, stress their local ties, and spend considerable time in their districts.[10]

Political scientist Richard F. Fenno points out that members of Congress perceive more than one constituency whose support they cultivate. The geographic constituency includes everyone who lives within the boundaries of a state (for a senator) or congressional district (for a representative). In sheer numbers, the geographic constituency is the largest—but the least important—constituency to the member of Congress because it includes many people who do not vote or who consistently support candidates of the other party.

The reelection constituency is those voters who support the senator or representative at the polls in general elections. It consists of loyal party voters and swing voters, including independents and people who identify with the other party but are willing to vote for candidates of the opposing party under certain circumstances. Incumbent members of Congress focus on this constituency, especially in districts that are competitive between the two major political parties. Representatives and senators who potentially face strong general election opposition often take moderate policy positions to win the support of swing voters, who are usually less conservative/less liberal than core party voters. Most of the Democrats in Congress who voted against healthcare reform represented competitive districts and they worried that a vote for healthcare reform would be used against them in the upcoming general election.

> Constituency pressure was a key factor in the battle over healthcare reform.

logrolling an arrangement in which two or more members of Congress agree in advance to support each other's favored legislation.

The primary constituency includes the people who would back the incumbent against a serious challenger in a party primary. Although any senator or member of Congress could face a primary election challenge, members of Congress who represent districts that are solidly Democratic or Republican are unlikely to have serious opposition in any election other than the primary. Consequently, GOP members of Congress from safe districts often take more conservative policy positions than do Republicans from competitive districts because they want to cultivate the support of Republican primary voters, who tend to be more conservative than the electorate as a whole. For similar reasons, Democrats from safe districts are frequently more liberal than are Democrats representing swing districts.[11] Congressional partisanship is more intense today than it was 20 or 30 years ago because most members of Congress win election from districts that are safe for candidates from their political party.[12]

Constituency pressure was a key factor in the battle over healthcare reform. Although polls showed that most Democratic voters favored healthcare reform, the measure was highly unpopular with Republicans, especially party activists who were stirred up by conservative talk show hosts and cable TV commentators.[13] Members of Congress are quite reluctant

Safe Districts and Congressional Partisanship

ELECTION YEAR	NO. CLOSE HOUSE RACES (decided by a margin of 10 percentage points or less)	AVERAGE WINNING PERCENTAGE
1992	111	64
1994	87	67
1996	80	64
1998	43	71
2000	42	69
2002	34	70
2004	31	69
2006	58	66
2008	46	67

Congressional partisanship is more intense today than it was 20 or 30 years ago, at least in part because most members of Congress win election from districts that are safe for candidates from their political party.

Source: Center for Responsive Politics, www.opensecrets.org.

to vote against the strong preferences of party activists on a high-profile issue such as healthcare reform because they worry about giving potential primary election opponents an issue that can be used against them. Moreover, interest groups are willing to recruit and fund primary challengers to incumbent members of Congress who do not support the party line on key issues.[14] Ultimately, on final passage, not a single Republican member of either the House or the Senate voted in favor of healthcare reform.

Members of Congress work to shore up constituent support through **constituency service**, actions taken by members of Congress and their staffs to attend to the individual, particular needs of constituents. Citizens sometimes ask

TAKE ✓ ACTION
Contacting Your Representative

Members of the U.S. House recognize that if they fail to represent the wishes of their constitutents satisfactorily, then they may risk reelection defeat. Your assignment is to participate in America's representative democracy by sending an e-mail message about a current policy issue to your representative in the U.S. House. You can find the name and e-mail address of your U.S. representative online at www.house.gov. The following guidelines will help you write an effective letter:

- Know what you are writing about. If you do not understand an issue, your message will have little impact.

Choose an issue discussed in the textbook or in the news, and research it sufficiently to speak about it intelligently.
- Use correct grammar. E-mail messages filled with grammatical errors and misspelled words will not have a positive impact.
- Make your point clearly and succinctly. Present your opinion and give the reasons behind your position in no more than a few paragraphs. Long, rambling messages are ineffective.

Submit a copy of your letter or e-mail message to your instructor. He or she will not grade you on your point of view, but will evaluate your work on the criteria stated above.

senators or representatives to resolve problems with federal agencies, such as the Social Security Administration (SSA) or the U.S. Citizenship and Immigration Services (USCIS). Constituents may ask members and their staffs to supply information about federal laws or regulations. Also, local civic clubs and other organizations frequently invite members of Congress to make public appearances at functions in their districts or states and meet with various groups of constituents about problems of local concern.

Membership Turnover

Members of Congress seeking reelection are usually successful, especially members of the House. Over the last 25 years, the reelection rate is 95 percent for House members and 80 percent for senators.[15] Members of Congress win reelection despite the general unpopularity of Congress because the voters make a distinction between the performance of their representative and the performance of Congress as an institution. Polls consistently show that the voters like their own member of Congress even when they disapprove of the actions of Congress as a whole.[16]

Despite relatively high reelection rates, Congress experiences significant turnover. In the 111th Congress, the average tenure for members of the House was 11 years; it was 13 years for members of the Senate.[17] Turnover is greater than statistics on incumbent reelection success rates suggest because many members decide not to seek reelection. Some members retire, some quit to run for higher office, and some leave Congress to pursue other opportunities, including work as lobbyists.

Many critics of Congress favor **term limitation**, which is the movement to restrict the number of terms public officials may serve. Term limitation advocates believe that career politicians grow cautious in office, constantly worrying about reelection. In contrast, officials who are prevented from holding office for more than a few years are free to adopt creative new ideas that may entail some political risk. The proponents of term limitation think that term limits will weaken the influence of special interest groups because officeholders will have less need to solicit money from interest groups to fund expensive reelection campaigns.

The opponents of term limitation argue that it is a gimmick that will cause harm rather than good. Term limits are undemocratic, they say, because they deny voters the chance to elect the candidates of their choice. If a majority of voters want to reelect an officeholder for a third, fourth, or even fifth term, they ask, should that not be their

The longest serving member of Congress is Representative John D. Dingell of Michigan. Dingell, who was born in 1924, first took office in 1955.

right? Furthermore, the opponents of term limitation worry that inexperienced officeholders will lack the knowledge and expertise to formulate effective public policy, and may have to rely on the advice of lobbyists and bureaucrats. Finally, the critics of term limitation warn that short-term officeholders may focus on securing future employment, and some future employers may be interest groups seeking special favors from government.[18]

constituency service the action of members of Congress attending to the individual, particular needs of constituents.

term limitation the movement to restrict the number of terms public officials may serve.

Approval Rating of Congress

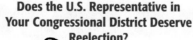

Do Most Members of Congress Deserve Reelection?

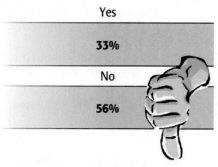

Yes

33%

No

56%

Does the U.S. Representative in Your Congressional District Deserve Reelection?

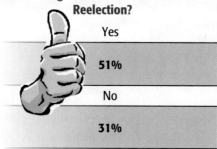

Yes

51%

No

31%

Source: USA Today/Gallup poll, October 2010.

ORGANIZATION

 12.3 *How is Congress organized in terms of leadership and committee structure?*

The organization of the House and Senate is based on political party.

Organization of the Floor

The "floor of the House" and "floor of the Senate" are the large rooms in which the members of each chamber assemble to do business. As a practical matter, the **floor** refers to the full House or full Senate taking official action. The organization of the floor refers to the structures that organize the flow of business conducted by the House or Senate as a whole.

The organization of the floor is based on party strength in each chamber. In the 111th Congress, which served from January 2009 through December 2010, the Democratic Party controlled both the House and the Senate. Democrats outnumbered Republicans in the House, 257 to 178. The party balance in the Senate was 57 Democrats, 41 Republicans, and two independents, both of whom voted with the Democrats to organize the chamber, effectively giving the Democrats a 59–41 advantage. After Republican Senator Arlen Specter of Pennsylvania switched parties in early 2009, the party balance in the Senate became 60 Democrats and 40 Republicans.

The sizable Democratic Party majorities in both the House and Senate during the 111th Congress were indispensable to the passage of healthcare reform because they allowed the Democrats to organize the floor of the House and Senate and dominate every congressional committee. Considering the determined opposition of almost every Republican to healthcare reform, the measure would almost certainly have failed had the Republican Party controlled either chamber of Congress or even if the margin between the two parties were closer, especially in the Senate.

The 2010 election changed the party balance in Congress. The Republican Party became the majority party in the House by adding more than 60 seats formerly held by Democrats. Although the Democrats continued to hold a majority of seats in the Senate, their margin fell to 53–47. House Republicans promised to do their best to repeal healthcare reform, but without control of either the Senate or the presidency, they are unlikely to achieve their goal.

Although the Constitution designates the vice president as the Senate's presiding officer, the legislative role of the vice president is relatively unimportant. The vice president may not address the Senate without permission of the chamber and votes only in case of a tie, which is rare. During eight years as vice president, Dick Cheney cast only eight tie-breaking votes in the Senate. More often than not, the vice president attends to other tasks, leaving the chore of presiding over the Senate to others.

The Constitution designates the **Senate president** *pro tempore* as the presiding officer of the Senate in the vice president's absence.

Congressional Leadership

SENATE	HOUSE
Vice President: *Joe Biden* **President Pro Tempore:** *Daniel Inouye (D, HI)*	**Speaker:** *John Boehner (R, OH)*
The vice president and Senate president pro tempore are constitutionally the presiding officers of the Senate, but, in practice, their role is more ceremonial than substantive.	The Speaker of the House is the presiding officer. The entire House membership selects the Speaker, but because almost all members vote for their party's candidate, the Speaker is invariably the leader of the majority party.
Majority Leader: *Harry Reid (D, NV)* **Majority Whip:** *Dick Durbin (D, IL)*	**Majority Leader:** *Eric Cantor (R, VA)* **Majority Whip:** *Kevin McCarthy (R, CA)*
The majority leader controls the business of the Senate. The whip is an assistant floor leader.	The majority party also has a majority leader and a majority whip to direct the agenda and votes on the floor.
Minority Leader: *Mitch McConnell (R, KY)* **Minority Whip:** *Jon Kyl (R, AZ)*	**Minority Leader:** *Nancy Pelosi (D, CA)* **Minority Whip:** *Steny Hoyer (D, MD)*
The minority leadership works to define a party program in its chamber, plan strategy, and, frequently, oppose the initiatives of the majority party leadership. The minority party in the Senate often has policy influence because of the filibuster, especially if it is united or the majority party is divided.	The minority party in the House seldom has policymaking influence, at least not if the majority party is united or nearly united, because the House works on a strictly majority basis. The minority party leadership speaks out on policy issues and plans strategy in hopes of eventually winning majority control of the chamber.

While the vice president and president *pro tempore* have largely ceremonial powers, the other congressional leaders have real power to direct how and when legislation reaches the floor.

floor the full House or full Senate taking official action.

Senate president *pro tempore* the presiding officer of the Senate in the vice president's absence.

Speaker Nancy Pelosi, D., California, presided over the passage of healthcare reform legislation in the House. Ironically, Republicans used the issue to help win control of the House in the 2010 election and that cost Pelosi her position as Speaker.

The Senate as a whole selects the president *pro tempore*, customarily electing the senator from the majority party with the greatest length of service, or **seniority**, in the chamber. In practice, the post of Senate president *pro tempore* is more honorary than substantive, and the rather tedious chore of presiding in the Senate is usually left to junior members of the majority party.

Real power on the floor of the Senate (and the House) is in the hands of the political party organizations. At the beginning of each session of Congress, the Republican and Democratic members of each chamber elect party leaders. In the Senate, the head of the majority party is called the **Senate majority leader**, and in the House of Representatives, the **Speaker of the House** is the presiding officer and the leader of the majority party. In the House, the second ranking figure in the majority party becomes the **House majority leader**. The minority party elects **minority leaders** in each house, and all leaders are assisted by **whips**, or assistant floor leaders.

The Senate majority leader and the Speaker of the House are the most important legislators in their respective chambers. Speaker Nancy Pelosi and Senate Majority Leader Harry Reid played a critical role in the adoption of healthcare refrom by managing the measure through the legislative procees to its eventual passage. The Senate majority leader and the Speaker appoint members to special committees and influence assignments to standing committees. They refer legislation to committee and control the flow of business to the floor. These latter two powers are especially important for the Speaker, who can use them to control the timing of legislation and determine the policy options available to House members voting on the floor. Although the Speaker cannot force passage of unpopular legislation, he or she can usually prevent consideration of a measure that he or she opposes, even when the measure enjoys enough support to pass the full House if it were to come to a vote.

The Senate majority leader and the Speaker hold positions of high visibility and great prestige, both in Congress and the nation. As party leaders, they work with fellow party members in Congress to set policy goals and to assemble winning coalitions. They consult widely with various party factions, working to compromise differences among party members and to maintain party unity. As national political leaders, the Senate majority leader and Speaker publicize the achievements of Congress, promote their party's positions in the media, and react to presidential initiatives.

Because party leadership posts are elective, the Senate majority leader and Speaker maintain their power by helping members achieve their goals: reelection, influence in national politics, policy enactment, and election to higher office. Party leaders create political action committees (PACs) to raise and distribute campaign money to fellow party members running for reelection. By playing the campaign money game, party leaders can support their parties in Congress while building personal loyalty among party members.[19] In the 2010 election, Speaker Pelosi's PAC to the Future contributed nearly $700,000 to Democratic congressional candidates. Meanwhile, Republican Leader John Boehner's PAC, Freedom Project, gave nearly $900,000 to Republican candidates.[20]

Leadership in Congress is both collegial and collective. It is collegial in the sense that the Senate majority leader and the Speaker of the House base their power on tact and persuasion rather than threats or criticism of other members. Leadership is collective in that top party leaders consult regularly with a broad range of party members, attempting to involve every party faction in setting party policy in the chamber.

Senate Majority Leader Harry Reid presided over the passage of healthcare reform legisaltion in the Senate. In 2010, Reid survived a tough reelection challenge from Sharron Angle, a Republican candidate backed by the Tea Party.

seniority length of service.

Senate majority leader the head of the majority party in the Senate.

Speaker of the House the presiding officer in the House of Representatives and the leader of the majority party in that chamber.

House majority leader the second-ranking figure in the majority party in the House.

minority leaders the heads of the minority party in the House or Senate.

whips assistant floor leaders in Congress.

The Speaker and majority leader are political party leaders as well, working to advance their parties' policy interests and to maintain their majority. When the Democratic Party controls Congress, the leadership promotes liberal policy alternatives while preventing the consideration of conservative bills (and vice versa when Republicans control). Although a Democratic majority in Congress cannot ensure the enactment of liberal legislation, it can usually prevent the passage of conservative measures.[21]

Members of Congress have a strong incentive to cooperate with their party leadership because the success of the members is tied to the success of their political party, especially in the House. Members of the majority party chair all committees and subcommittees, and have a greater opportunity for input on the details of legislation, at least in the House where the majority party tightly controls deliberations in committee and on the floor. Furthermore, the election prospects of senators and

Members of Congress have a strong incentive to cooperate with their party leadership because the success of the members is tied to the success of their political party.

members of the House from competitive districts depend at least in part on the standing of their political party in the eyes of the voters.[22] Democratic members of the House and Senate voted overwhelmingly in favor of healthcare reform not just because they favored the measure personally, but also because its defeat would be perceived as a defeat for their party and their party's president, weakening the position of the party in the 2010 midterm election.

The role of the minority party leadership in the House and Senate is similar to that of the majority party leadership. The minority leaders work to define a party program in their chamber, plan strategy, and unite party members behind party positions. They spend a good deal of time working to help their party become the majority party by recruiting candidates, raising money, planning strategy, and acting as the media spokespersons.[23] House Minority Leader John Boehner and Senate Minority Leader Mitch McConnell led the opposition to healthcare reform, uniting their party in Congress against the bill. After the measure passed, the Republican leaders called on the voters to elect a Republican majority in the House and Senate so the bill could be repealed.

The leadership of the minority party lacks the influence that their majority party counterparts enjoy, because the authority to control the flow of business to the floor lies with the majority party leadership. The influence of the minority leadership

Senate Minority Leader Mitch McConnell, R., Kentucky, and House Minority Leader John Boehner, R., Ohio led the Republican opposition to the adoption of healthcare reform. Boehner became speaker of the House in 2011 after the GOP won a majority of seats in the chamber in the 2010 election.

is especially limited in the House, where the rules enable a simple majority to conduct business. As long as the majority party in the House is united or nearly united, depending on the size of its majority, it can pass legislation without having to compromise with the minority party. Because the rules of the Senate allow a minority of senators, or sometimes even a single senator, to delay or defeat legislation, the minority party leadership plays a more substantive legislative role in the Senate than in the House.

The style of party leadership in Congress depends to a large degree on the occupant of the White House. When the opposition party controls the White House, congressional leaders act independently from, and frequently in opposition to, the White House. They scrutinize presidential appointments, aggressively investigate policy missteps, and critically evaluate presidential initiatives. In contrast, congressional leaders usually have a positive relationship when the same party controls both the legislative and executive branches of government. Congressional leaders worked closely with President George W. Bush to enact his policy proposals during his first six years in office when the Republican Party controlled the House and, with the exception of a short period of time, the Senate as well. In contrast, President Bush's relationship with Congress grew contentious after the 2006 election when Democrats won control of the House and Senate.

Committee and Subcommittee Organization

The detailed work of Congress takes place in committees. The advantage of the committee system is that it allows Congress to divide legislative work among a number of subgroups while giving individual members the opportunity to specialize, developing expertise in particular policy areas. The disadvantage of the committee system is that the division of broad issues into smaller subissues may impede the development of comprehensive and coordinated national policy. Because Congress deals with policy problems on a piecemeal basis, it tends to offer piecemeal solutions.

A **standing committee** is a permanent legislative committee with authority to draft legislation in a particular policy area or areas. The House Agriculture Committee, for example, deals with subjects related to agriculture, including rural economic conditions, crop insurance, agricultural trade, commodity futures trading, agricultural research and promotion, conservation, farm credit, welfare and food nutrition programs, and food safety inspection. The jurisdiction of the Senate Foreign Relations Committee includes matters relating to American national security policy, foreign policy, and international economic policy.

In addition to standing committees, Congress has special or select committees and joint committees. A **special or select committee** is a committee established for a limited time only. A **joint committee** is a committee that includes members from both houses of Congress. In contrast to standing committees, joint committees and special or select committees do not usually have the legislative authority to draft legislation. They can only study, investigate, and make recommendations.

Committees are divided into subcommittees. Not all committees have subcommittees, and not all bills are referred to subcommittee, but in the House in particular, subcommittees have become the center of legislative work. For example, the House Ways and Means Commit-

tee, which deals with tax issues, trade, and Social Security, has six subcommittees, each of which addresses a different aspect of the committee's responsibilities.

Senators typically have more committee assignments than do members of the House because the Senate has fewer members. Because senators are stretched thin, they pick and choose when to get involved in committee processes. Consequently, committee decisions in the Senate usually reflect the work of less than half the committee membership except on especially high-profile matters such as immigration reform or a major tax bill.[24] Because members of the House have fewer committee assignments than do their Senate counterparts, they are more likely to develop policy expertise in the issues dealt with by the committees on which they serve. As a result, committees play a more important role in the legislative process in the House than they do in the Senate.

When senators and representatives are first elected, they request assignment to standing committees that they believe will help them 1) win reelection, 2) gain influence in national politics, and 3) affect policy. Committees dealing with money qualify on all three counts and are in great demand. The money committees in the Senate are Appropriations, Budget, and Finance. In the House, the committees dealing with money are Appropriations, Budget, and Ways and Means. The other Senate committees that are considered prestigious assignments are Foreign Relations, Armed Services, and Judiciary.[25] In the House, members want to serve on the Energy and Commerce Committee because it deals with a broad range of important legislation. The Transportation and Infrastructure Committee is popular as well, because members see it as a way to

procure projects for their districts. Senators and representatives frequently request assignments on committees that deal with policy issues particularly relevant to their states and districts. Members of Congress from urban and financial centers are attracted to the banking committees; members from agricultural states favor membership on the agricultural committees. Finally, some members of Congress request particular committee assignments for personal reasons. For example, members of the House with prior military service may seek membership on the Armed Services Committee.[26]

Party committees in each chamber make committee assignments for members of their party. If members are unhappy with a

Senator Dianne Feinstein of California serves on four standing committees, one select committee, and a number of subcommittees. Here she speaks with Senator Byron Dorgan, D-ND., also a member of the Committee on Appropriations, on their way to a Democratic Caucus meeting.

standing committee a permanent legislative committee with authority to draft legislation in a particular policy area or areas.

special or select committee a committee established for a limited time only.

joint committee a committee that includes members from both houses of Congress.

The detailed work of Congress takes place in committees.

committee assignment, they may request a transfer when openings occur on committees they prefer. Committee switching is not especially common, particularly among senior members, because members who change committees must start over on the seniority ladder of the new committee. When committee members change committees, die, retire, or suffer defeat at the polls, other committee members volunteer for their subcommittee assignments in order of seniority. The most senior members get their choice; the least senior members get the leftovers.

The majority party controls each committee and subcommittee, which means they can hold a majority of the membership and the chairs of each committee and subcommittee. Before the 2010 election, the Democratic Party was the majority party in the House and Senate, and so Democrats chaired and accounted for a majority of the membership of each committee and subcommittee in both chambers. In 2010 the Republicans won a majority in the House, so beginning in 2011, Republicans chaired and were a majority in every House committee and subcommittee.

Each party has its own procedures for selecting committee chairs (for the majority party) and ranking members (for the minority party). Republican Party rules stipulate that the party committee that makes initial committee assignments nominates chairs or ranking members with confirmation by the **party caucus**, which is all of the party members of a chamber meeting as a group. The Republicans select chairs or ranking members based on party loyalty and ability to raise campaign money for party candidates, rather than using seniority as the sole basis for selection.[27] Republican party members who fail to meet their financial obligations to the party's campaign fund will be passed over for leadership positions.[28] Democrats, meanwhile, provide for the selection of committee chairs and ranking members by a secret-ballot vote of the party caucus. The Democrat with the most seniority on a particular committee usually wins the vote, except on those rare occasions when a senior member has alienated his or her colleagues. Both parties limit chairs and subcommittee chairs to six-year terms.

party caucus all of the party members of the House or Senate meeting as a group.

AROUND THE WORLD
Healthcare in Canada

Canada provides its citizens with universal healthcare, administered through the nation's provinces and territories. The provinces have some leeway to design their own plans; some assess their citizens a monthly premium or charge a fee for each visit to a physician, whereas others fund the program entirely from tax money. Coverage also varies somewhat from province to province and waits for services are longer in some areas than others.[29]

Although Canadian healthcare is publicly funded, it is privately provided. Citizens seeking medical services go to private physicians or visit hospitals and clinics that are either for-profit business or non-profits governed by boards of trustees. Many Canadians also have supplemental insurance coverage, often provided through their employers, to pay for services not covered or only partially covered by the national health system, including dental, optical, and prescription drug service.

Proponents of the Canadian system note that life expectancy is longer in Canada than it is in the United States and that infant mortality rates are lower. Furthermore, Canada devotes a smaller share of its GDP to healthcare than does the United States. In contrast, critics of the Canadian healthcare system complain that wait times for non-emergency services are sometimes long. Canadian medicine may also be relatively slow to adopt new treatments and technologies.[30]

QUESTIONS

1 Would you prefer the Canadian healthcare system to that in the United States?

2 What individuals and groups in the United States would support moving to a system similar to the Canadian system? Which would oppose?

3 Does the healthcare reform plan adopted by Congress and signed into law by President Obama move the United States closer to the Canadian system? Why or why not?

Filmmaker Michael Moore criticized the American healthcare system in his film *SICKO*.

THE LEGISLATIVE PROCESS

12.4 *What are the steps in the legislative process for a bill to become a law?*

The traditional image of the legislative process is that a member introduces a bill, it is referred to committee, it goes from committee to the floor, from the floor to a conference committee, and, if it passes every step, to the president. In today's Congress, the legislative process no longer conforms to the traditional "bill-becomes-a-law" formula, especially for major pieces of legislation, because Congress has modified the traditional process in order to increase the likelihood of passing major legislation. The key differences between the traditional model and the new model of legislative policy-making are the following:

- Major legislation is often written in the form of **omnibus bills**, which are complex, highly detailed legislative proposals covering one or more subjects or programs. The healthcare reform measure, for example, included provisions dealing with Medicaid, insurance regulation, healthcare delivery, and a set of tax increases to pay for the package. Congressional leaders assemble omnibus bills to attract as much support as possible.
- Pieces of major legislation are frequently referred to more than one standing committee. Involving several committees in the legislative process provides a measure's supporters with an opportunity to draft legislation that enjoys a broader base of support. Furthermore, the strategy avoids the danger of a hostile committee chair bottling up the bill in committee, which sometimes happens to measures referred to only one committee.
- The legislative leadership, especially in the House, coordinates the work of the standing committees and sets timetables to move legislation through the committee stage. They fashion the details of the legislation and develop a strategy for winning passage on the floor. Even after a bill clears committee, the leadership may change its provisions to broaden its base of support.
- A conference committee of dozens, maybe even hundreds, of members works out the final compromise language of the bill. Once again, the goal is to build a broad-enough coalition of support for the measure to ensure its passage.[31]

Origin and Introduction

In the 111th Congress, members introduced 13,675 bills and resolutions—8,789 in the House and 4,886 in the Senate.[32] A **bill** is a proposed law. Except for revenue raising bills, which must begin in the House, any bill may be introduced in either chamber. A **resolution** is a legislative statement of opinion on a certain matter. Resolutions may be introduced in either chamber. A member who introduces a measure is known as its **sponsor**. Bills and resolutions may have multiple sponsors, known as cosponsors. Rep. John Dingel of Michigan sponsored healthcare reform in the House. The measure had six co-sponsors. Over the years, legislative measures have grown longer and more complex. Since the 1940s, the length of the average bill has increased from 2.5 pages to more than 19 pages.[33] Omnibus bills are far longer. The healthcare reform act was 906 pages long.[34]

Although the formal introduction of legislation is a privilege limited to actual members of Congress, other political actors, including interest groups, the president, executive branch agencies, journalists, or

omnibus bills complex, highly detailed legislative proposals covering one or more subjects or programs.

bill a proposed law.

resolution a legislative statement of opinion on a certain matter.

sponsor a member who introduces a measure.

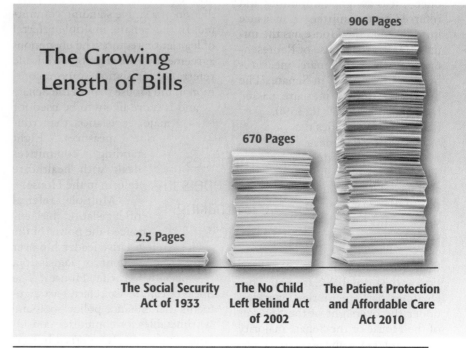

The Growing Length of Bills

906 Pages

670 Pages

2.5 Pages

The Social Security Act of 1933 | The No Child Left Behind Act of 2002 | The Patient Protection and Affordable Care Act 2010

Congressional leaders assemble lengthy omnibus bills, which are complex, highly detailed legislative proposals covering one or more subjects or programs, in order to attract as much support as possible.

constituents, may advance policy proposals or even draft the text of a bill. Many of the ideas contained in the healthcare reform bill had been discussed for years and some key aspects of the plan, including the individual mandate, were modeled on the Massachusetts healthcare reform plan.

Legislative activity is less today than it was 30 years ago. In the 1960s, senators and representatives introduced on average more than 50 bills and resolutions apiece during a two-year session of Congress. In contrast, the average member of Congress introduced only 26 measures in the 111th Congress.[35] The decline in legislative activity reflects a political climate that has grown skeptical of government solutions to the nation's problems. Many members of Congress, especially Republicans, won office by campaigning against government programs. Their goal is to reduce the scope of government activity rather than passing legislation to create new programs.

Committee and Subcommittee Action

Once a bill or resolution is introduced, it is assigned a number and referred to committee. A measure introduced in the House has the initials "H. R." for House of Representatives, whereas Senate measures begin with the "S." in Senate. The healthcare reform measure passed by Congress was H. R. 3590. (The number signifies the order in which a measure was introduced.) The sponsors of a bill also give it a popular title designed to put the measure in a favorable light. Democrats in Congress called their bill the Patient Protection and Affordable Care Act. The chamber parliamentarian, working under the oversight of the Speaker of the House or the Senate majority leader, refers the measure to a committee based on the subject covered by the bill or resolution.

Citizens and activists hoped to influence congressional deliberations on healthcare reform. Here, healthcare reform opponents and supporters argue their respective points of view.

Complex issues such as healthcare, immigration reform, international trade, and homeland security often cut across committee jurisdictions. Sometimes committees develop arrangements to cooperate or defer to one another.[36] At other times, the leadership employs **multiple-referral of legislation**, which is the practice of assigning legislation to more than one committee. The Speaker makes multiple-referral decisions in the House, and may also appoint an ad hoc (special) committee, or a taskforce, to consider a measure whose subject matter does not fit neatly within the jurisdiction of a single standing committee. In the Senate, multiple referral of legislation requires the unanimous agreement of the chamber. Multiple referral of legislation is more common in the House than in the Senate and is more likely to be used for major legislation than routine measures. Eight standing committees dealt with healthcare reform in the House.

Multiple referral of legislation has enhanced the power of the legislative leadership over the content of legislation, especially in the House. The Speaker can devise referral arrangements that enhance policy goals and set timetables for committee consideration of multiple referred bills. A multiple referred measure cannot continue in the legislative process until each committee dealing with it has finished its work. Furthermore, the Speaker can negotiate policy compromises among the various committees considering a multiple referred measure. In practice, multiple referral of legislation is also a means for moving legislation through the process because it enables the Speaker to intervene to prevent one committee from stalling a measure.[37]

Committees are gatekeepers in the lawmaking process, killing most of the bills and resolutions referred to them. In the 111th Congress, committees reported 1,249 measures to the floor of 13,675 bills and resolutions introduced, for a report rate of 9 percent.[38] Measures are more likely to receive detailed committee and subcommittee consideration if they are supported by committee chairs or legislative leadership, Congress as a whole, important interest groups, the general public, or the president. In contrast, measures that lack support or are opposed by the committee or party leadership seldom emerge from committee.

Committees and subcommittees do the detailed work of Congress. Once a measure is sent to committee or subcommittee, the chair and the ranking minority member ask their staffs to prepare separate reports on its merits. For major legislation, the committee or subcommittee chair

> Committees are gatekeepers in the lawmaking process.

multiple referral of legislation the practice of allowing more than one committee to consider legislation.

schedules hearings to allow the measure's supporters and opponents a chance to make their case. Full committees generally conduct Senate hearings; subcommittees hold most hearings in the House.

The next step is **legislative markup**. This is the process in which legislators go over a measure line-by-line, revising, amending, or rewriting it. In the House, markup usually takes place in subcommittee. Markup in the Senate generally occurs in full committee.

Once markup is complete, the subcommittee, and then the full committee, vote on whether to recommend passage. If the measure is voted down at either stage or members vote to **table** it (that is, postpone consideration), it is probably dead, at least for the session. If the measure is approved in subcommittee and committee, the next step is the floor of the full House or Senate.

The rules of the House provide a mechanism for members to bring to the floor a bill that has been tabled or defeated in committee. However, the procedure is seldom used and almost never successful. A bill's supporters can compel a committee to report a measure to the floor by means of a **discharge petition**, in which a majority of the members of the House of Representatives force a committee to report a bill to the floor of the House. Since 1910, only three measures forced from committee through the use of a discharge petition eventually became law.[39] Most members of Congress are reluctant to sign a discharge petition because they do not want to undermine committee authority. Furthermore, the threat of a discharge petition is sometimes enough to stimulate a committee to act on stalled legislation.

Floor Action

In the House, the process for moving measures from committee to the floor varies, depending on the type of measure involved. The House considers noncontroversial measures of relatively minor importance through a shortcut procedure on designated special days set aside for that purpose. Budget resolutions and **appropriation bills** may go directly from committee to the House floor. (An appropriation bill is a legislative authorization to spend money for particular purposes.)

The leadership brings some major pieces of legislation to the floor without committee consideration or with only cursory committee examination. If a measure was carefully studied in committee in the last session of Congress, the leadership may determine that no additional committee consideration is necessary. Sometimes, the leadership wants to move quickly for political reasons. In 2005, the House leadership put legislation on a fast track to provide aid for people affected by Hurricane Katrina, moving it directly to the floor without committee consideration.[40]

Most measures that clear standing committee must go to the Rules Committee before going to the floor. The **House Rules Committee** is a standing committee that

legislative markup the process in which legislators go over a measure line-by-line, revising, amending, or rewriting it.

table to postpone consideration of a measure during the legislative process.

discharge petition a procedure whereby a majority of the members of the House of Representatives can force a committee to report a bill to the floor of the House.

appropriation bill a legislative authorization to spend money for particular purposes.

House Rules Committee a standing committee that determines the rules under which a specific bill can be debated, amended, and considered on the House floor.

Committees do the detailed work of Congress. The House Rules Committee, seen here meeting on Capitol Hill, is one of the most powerful committees because it determines the rules under which bills come to the House floor.

determines the rules under which a specific bill can be debated, amended, and considered on the House floor. Because more measures clear committee than the full House has time to consider, the Rules Committee determines which measures go forward. Measures that are not assigned rules are not considered on the House floor and therefore have no chance of passage unless supporters can succeed in forcing the legislation out of the Rules Committee by means of a discharge petition.

When the Rules Committee refers a bill to the floor, it sets a time limit for debate and determines the ground rules for amendments. A rule that opens a measure to amendment on the House floor without restriction is an *open rule*. In contrast, a *closed rule* is a rule that prohibits floor consideration of amendments on the House floor. The measure must be voted up or down without amendment. In practice, most rules, especially rules for major pieces of legislation, are **structured rules**, which are rules that specify which amendments are allowed and under what conditions, the time available for debate, and/or the method of voting on amendments.[41] The Rules Committee limited debate on the healthcare reform bill to four hours, divided equally between proponents and opponents, and allowed consideration of two amendments—a Republican alternative bill, which failed, and an amendment to prohibit the expenditure of federal funds for healthcare coverage that included abortion services, which passed. The anti-abortion amendment was added to win the votes on final passage of a number of anti-abortion Democrats.[42]

Rules are a means for structuring debate on the House floor. Rules that force members to choose between comprehensive alternative pieces of legislation focus debate on big choices rather than the details of legislation. Rules can also prevent a measure's opponents from forcing

votes on the most unpopular provisions of a bill or offering amendments that the leadership opposes.[43] The Rules Committee is an important element of the Speaker's power. In contrast to other House committees, the Speaker personally appoints the majority party members of the Rules Committee, subject to approval by the party caucus, thereby ensuring control.

The role of the House Rules Committee in the legislative process is controversial. Its defenders contend that it enables the House to conduct business efficiently, especially in comparison with the plodding Senate, by allowing the chamber's majority to work its will. In contrast, critics charge that the majority party in the House uses the rules process to shut the minority party out of the legislative process entirely, bypassing intra-party discussion, debate, negotiation, and compromise necessary for the formulation of good legislation.[44]

Majority rules on the floor of the **House**.

Majority rules on the floor of the House. If all 435 members are present and voting, 218 votes are necessary for final passage of legislation, a simple majority. Healthcare reform passed the House 220–215. Democrats favored the measure 219–39. Every Republican except for Congressman Joseph Cao of New Orleans, Louisiana voted against the bill.

In the Senate, a measure typically reaches the floor through the mechanism of a **unanimous consent agreement (UCA)**, which is a formal understanding on procedures for conducting Senate business that requires acceptance by every member of the chamber. UCAs, like rules from the Rules Committee in the House, limit debate and determine the amendments that can be offered. Because a single senator can prevent the adoption of an agreement, UCAs reflect negotiation between the Senate leadership and the membership to consider the needs of every member. A member who objects to a UCA is said to have placed a hold. Members can work through the

majority leader's secretary to place holds anonymously, but that approach is rare. Often the purpose of a hold is to force some sort of concession, sometimes on an unrelated piece of legislation. The majority leader may choose to bring the measure to the floor despite the hold, but the motion to proceed may face a **filibuster,** an attempt to defeat a measure through prolonged debate. If that is overcome, then the bill itself may be filibustered. Nonetheless, senators usually get their legislation to the floor by accepting policy compromises or by threatening to place holds on legislation favored by the measure's opponents.

A senator can also bring a measure to the floor by offering it as an amendment to another bill. Senate rules allow consideration of **non-germane amendments**, unrelated to the subject matter of the original measure. (Non-germane amendments are not allowed in the House.) Senators sometimes propose these unrelated amendments in order to promote their particular policy preferences or embarrass their political opponents. A **killer amendment** is an amendment designed to make a measure so unattractive that it will lack enough support to pass. Opponents of term limitation, which Congress considered in 1995, offered an amendment that would count time already served in the calculation. Were it adopted, many members of Congress would effectively have voted themselves out office.[45] Killer amendments that succeed are rare.[46]

structured rules rules that specify the conditions for debate and amendments.

unanimous consent agreement (UCA) a formal understanding on procedures for conducting Senate business that requires acceptance by every member of the chamber.

filibuster an attempt to defeat a measure through prolonged debate.

non-germane amendments amendments which are unrelated to the subject matter of the original measure.

killer amendment an amendment designed to make a measure so unattractive that it will lack enough support to pass.

The rules of the **Senate** are designed to **maximize** the rights of **individual senators.**

Congress has a reputation as one of the great debating bodies of the world, but it is unusual for debates to sway many votes. The real work of Congress does not take place on the floor, but in committee and subcommittee, congressional offices, and elsewhere around the capital. Debates allow members to read into the record the case for and against a measure and to justify their own position to their constituents.

Floor proceedings are relatively less structured in the Senate than in the House. Although disgruntled House members can sometimes delay action through parliamentary maneuvers, the Rules Committee system generally ensures that House proceedings move forward in a predictable fashion. In contrast, the rules of the Senate are designed to maximize the rights of individual senators. One senator or a group of senators may use these rules to produce chaos on the Senate floor.

Indeed, senators sometimes take advantage of the rules to defeat legislation they oppose. Because Senate rules do not limit the amount of time a senator, or the chamber as a whole, can discuss a measure, a bill's opponents may filibuster. Under Senate rules, each senator who wishes to speak must be recognized and cannot be interrupted without consent. The Senate cannot vote on a piece of legislation until every senator has finished speaking.[47]

The procedure for ending a filibuster is known as **cloture**. A vote on cloture requires a three-fifths vote of the Senate membership (60 votes) to succeed. Although Senate rules limit post-cloture debate to 30 hours, a measure's opponents often delay action even longer through parliamentary maneuvering.

Filibusters have grown more common. From 1955 to 1960, the Senate experienced only two filibusters.[48] In contrast, recent sessions of Congress have averaged 28 filibusters each, with half of all major pieces of legislation facing a filibuster or a serious threat of a filibuster.[49] In the 111th Congress, the Republican Party in the Senate used the filibuster as a partisan weapon, and not just against healthcare reform. In 2009, Republicans filibustered 80 percent of major legislation.[50] Healthcare reform legislation was able to move forward to a final vote only after the chambers 60 Democratic senators voted to invoke colture, overcoming the unanimous opposition of the Senate's Republican members.

think Is the use of the filibuster a positive exercise of the minority voice, or does it undermine Congress's ability to produce legislation by majority?

The nature of the filibuster has changed. In the 1950s and 1960s, Senators conducting a filibuster engaged in long-winded debate, and Senate leaders kept the chamber in overnight marathon session in order to break the filibuster and move on with a vote. Today, Senators simply announce their intention to filibuster, and the Senate goes on with other business while the leadership works to gather sufficient support to invoke cloture. Sometimes, Senate leaders file a cloture petition to end debate even before a filibuster materializes. The increased use of the filibuster, particularly as a partisan weapon, has provoked controversy and debate about its proper role (see Taking Sides).

The Senate, similar to the House, decides the fate of legislation on final passage by majority vote. Although the proponents of a measure may need the support of 60 senators to bring a measure to a

Prominent Southern senators discuss strategy for their filibuster of the 1964 Civil Rights Act. The filibuster failed, and the Civil Rights Act was signed into law by President Lyndon Johnson.

cloture the procedure for ending a filibuster.

House Passes Medicare Reform Plan

The U.S. House has passed legislation to dramatically change the Medicare program. The reform plan passed largely along party lines in early 2011, with almost every Republican supporting it and almost every Democrat opposing it. Under the current Medicare program, the government picks up the cost of medical services for beneficiaries after they satisfy a deductible and cover the co-pay. Medical providers bill the government directly. Under the reform plan, seniors, beginning in 2022, would select from a set of approved private insurance plans. The government would pay a fixed amount to the insurance company for each recipient enrolled in its plans. Seniors who want health plans that cost more than the amount of money paid by the government would have to make up the difference themselves.

DISCUSSION

Republicans opposed healthcare reform when the Democrats pushed it, so why are they offering a healthcare reform plan of their own? Republicans want to reduce the size of government and cut spending. Medicare is too big and growing too rapidly for them to ignore it and still accomplish their budgetary goal.

Why do Democrats oppose the Republican reform? The Republican plan would decrease the cost of Medicare for the government by passing those costs along to recipients. Under the Republican plan, seniors would pay an ever-increasing share of their healthcare costs because the government payment to the insurance companies, which the Democrats call a voucher, would increase at the overall rate of inflation rather than the health industry rate of inflation, which is substantially greater.

Why do the Republicans support their plan? They take credit for having the courage to take on a difficult problem, and they believe that their plan will make seniors better off because it will save Medicare from possible bankruptcy. Republicans also believe that their plan will empower seniors to choose the most cost-efficient healthcare providers, driving down the cost of healthcare.[51]

Is the Republican plan popular? No. A Pew Research Center poll finds that people who know the most about the plan oppose it, 56 percent to 33 percent. People over 65 are against it as well, 51 percent to 25 percent, even though Congressman Ryan promises to allow anyone currently 55 years of age and over to stick with traditional Medicare.[52]

Will the Republican Medicare reform plan become law? Not anytime soon because Republicans don't currently control the Senate and don't hold the presidency.

vote because of the filibuster, once a final vote is taken, only a simple majority is necessary for final passage. Healthcare reform passed the Senate by a vote of 60–39, with every Democrat voting yes and every Republican voting no. (One Republican senator was absent when the vote was taken.)

Conference Committee Action

A measure does not pass Congress until it clears both the House and Senate in identical form. If the House and Senate pass similar, but not identical bills, the chamber that initially passed the measure can agree to the changes made by the other chamber, or the two houses can resolve their differences by adopting a series of reconciling amendments. When the differences between the two measures are too great for easy resolution, the two chambers appoint a **conference committee**, which is a special congressional committee created to negotiate differences on similar pieces of legislation passed by the House and Senate. Although Congress resorts to the conference committee process for only about 10 percent of the measures that ultimately become law, conference committees are typical for major legislation.[53]

The Speaker and the Senate majority leader appoint the members of a conference committee (called **conferees**) from lists given to them by committee leaders. The Speaker and majority leader typically appoint members of the standing committees that considered the bill, as well as Congress members who are sympathetic to the party's position.[54] Because of the increased use of mulitple referrals and the increasing tendency of Congress to write omnibus bills, the size of conference committees has grown, sometimes including dozens or even hundreds of members.

Republican Scott Brown won a special election to fill Ted Kennedy's vacant Senate seat in Massachusetts, promising to support a Republican filibuster to defeat healthcare reform. The election of Brown was full of ironies. Not only was Kennedy a lifelong proponent of healthcare reform, but the bill that Brown promised to derail was remarkably similar to the Massachusetts healthcare program, which Brown had supported when he served in the state legislature.

> A measure does not pass Congress until it clears both the House and Senate in identical form.

A conference committee is sometimes called the third house of Congress because it writes the final version of legislation. The conferees are not bound to stick with the version of the measures passed by either the House or the Senate. In practice, the final version of major legislation produced by a conference committee reflects not just a compromise between the House and Senate, but a compromise among the party leadership in each chamber, the president, and key interest groups with a stake in the legislation.

Once a majority of each chambers' conferees, voting separately, agree on a compromise, the revised measure, called the **conference report**, goes back to the floor of the House and Senate. The first chamber to vote on the conference report has three options: to accept, reject, or return to conference for more negotiations. If the first chamber accepts the measure, the second chamber has two options, to adopt or reject. If both chambers accept the conference report, the measure goes to the president.

The healthcare reform bills passed by the House and Senate were similar but not identical. Democratic leaders planned to create a conference committee where party leaders would negotiate a compromise final bill with significant input from the White House. Their plan was undone, however, by the results of a special election in Massachusetts to fill the seat that became vacant when Democratic Senator Ted Kennedy died. Much to the dismay of President Obama and Democrats in Congress, Scott Brown, a Republican, won the special election in early 2010. Brown promised to vote against cloture, preventing Senate Democrats from having the 60 votes necessary to end a Republican filibuster of the conference report.

conference committee a special congressional committee created to negotiate differences on similar pieces of legislation passed by the House and Senate.

conferees members of a conference committee.

conference report a revised bill produced by a conference committee.

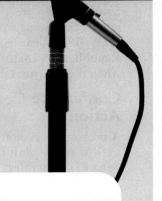

TAKING SIDES

Are Filibusters Good for Democracy?

Is the filibuster an unconstitutional rule of the U.S. Senate?

Given that the filibuster forces the Senate to operate with a supermajority, rather than a simple majority, is it undemocratic?

OVERVIEW

The founding fathers wrote the U.S. Constitution with the intent that some political decisions would be more difficult to make than others. Under the Constitution, some decisions require a plurality vote, some require a simple majority, and some require a supermajority. For Congress to override a president's veto, for example, both chambers need a two-thirds vote, a supermajority. The founders wanted to make it difficult to override a veto, so they required more agreement among members of Congress than just a simple majority. Congress passes legislation and the Senate confirms presidential appointments by simple majority because the framers wanted those decisions to be made more easily than overriding a veto.

Because of the filibuster, passing legislation now frequently requires a supermajority. A filibuster is an attempt to block or delay Senate action on a bill or another matter by debating it at length. The filibuster is a natural result of a strong respect for the right of every member of the Senate to speak his or her mind. The Senate created the cloture rule in 1917, which allows for a vote to end a filibuster. The number of Senators necessary to invoke cloture is three-fifths (60 votes), which is a supermajority.

Congress has recently become much more partisan in its behavior. Typically, the vast majority of one party votes against the overwhelming majority of the other party. In the Senate, the minority party, knowing the majority party can pass legislation without its vote, has increasingly threatened to filibuster legislation. As a result, majority leadership has had to find 60 votes in order to pass legislation or to confirm nominees, rather than the traditional 51 votes, because it needs to be able to invoke cloture.

SUPPORTING
filibusters as good for democracy

The Constitution says that each House may determine the rules of its proceedings. Each chamber has the ability to decide how to decide, so filibusters are not unconstitutional.

The U.S. Senate has always supported individuals and protected minority ideas. Because of the filibuster, members of both political parties must cooperate to get things done.

The filibuster encourages deliberation and strengthens legislation. Legislatures can move quickly in times of heightened crisis or when one party has control. Filibusters slow down any calamitous moves and force people to move deliberately and slowly, producing better legislation.

AGAINST
filibusters as good for democracy

Filibusters can be used to block legislation that the majority of Americans desire. Sometimes the people are progressing faster than the legislative institution, and out of touch senior members can block legislation that is good and necessary. For years, filibusters were used to block civil rights legislation.

Filibusters cause legislative gridlock. In December 2009, Senator Sheldon Whitehouse of Rhode Island noted that there had been more than 100 filibusters in one year.[55] This is an unhealthy situation for legislation, because it leads to the majority capitulating to the minority much more often than should be necessary and that frustrates the desire of voters.

Any change to the rules of governing needs to be constitutionally approved. The filibuster exists under the rules developed by the Senate on how the chamber should operate. Because the filibuster actually changing the way legislating is enacted, the practice is no longer simply an operating rule of the Senate, and requires a constitutional amendment.

Democratic congressional leaders and the president developed an alternative strategy for passing healthcare reform. First, the House voted to accept the version of healthcare reform passed by the Senate. The vote was 220–215, with every Republican voting no, and all but 39 Democrats voting yes. With this action, healthcare reform passed Congress because the measure had already passed the Senate. The bill went to the White House for President Obama's signature. Second, the House passed a budget reconciliation measure dealing with funding matters in the bill. The rules of Congress prohibit filibustering budget reconciliation bills. Although the budget reconciliation process was created to keep spending in line with overall budget goals, Republicans and Democrats in Congress have often used the process to enact policy measures (including the tax cut and Medicare reform legislation adopted during the George W. Bush administration). The Democrats used the reconciliation process to change some of the provisions in the Senate bill that House Democrats opposed. Without having to overcome a filibuster, Senate Democrats had more than enough votes to pass the reconciliation bill, and it too went to the president for signature. Finally, President Obama signed an executive order making it clear that tax money could not be used to purchase insurance policies as part of healthcare reform that covered abortion services. Obama took the action to win over the support of a number of anti-abortion Democrats in the House that threatened to vote against the Senate version of healthcare reform because they did not believe that its anti-abortion language was strong enough.

Presidential Action

The Constitution gives the president several options for dealing with legislation passed by Congress. If the president signs a measure, it becomes law. If the president does not sign the measure, it becomes law

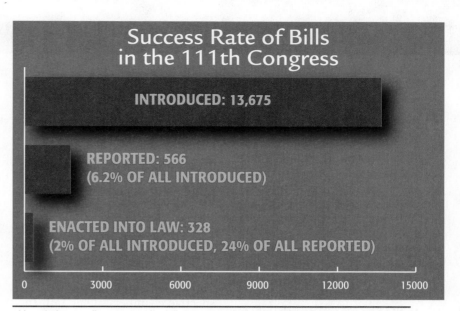

Although the overall success rate for bills is poor, most major pieces of legislation considered by Congress become law.

anyway after ten days unless Congress is adjourned, in which case it dies. When a president allows a measure to die without signature after Congress has adjourned, it is known as a **pocket veto**. If the president opposes a measure passed by Congress, the president can issue a **veto**, a refusal to approve a measure passed by the legislature. A president vetoes a bill by returning it to Congress with a statement of objections. If Congress overrides the veto by a two-thirds vote of each house, the measure becomes law anyway. Should either house fall short of two-thirds, the veto is sustained, and the measure has failed. Since the administration of Franklin Roosevelt, presidents have vetoed 1,349 measures, with Congress overriding 60 vetoes for an overirde rate of 4.4 percent.[56] Presidents are more likely to veto measures, and to have their vetoes overridden, when the opposition party controls Congress.[57]

The president must accept or reject a measure in its entirety. Congress takes advantage of this situation by passing omnibus bills combining provisions the president wants with measures the president would veto were they standing alone. A **rider** is a provision, unlikely to become law on its own merits, which is attached to an important measure so that it will ride through the legislative process. Appropriation bills are favorite vehicles for riders because they are must-pass legislation. For example, Congress enacted a smoking prohibition on commercial airline flights as a rider attached to an appropriation measure.[58]

The modifications in the legislative process adopted to increase the likelihood that major legislation will become law have been effective. Although the overall success rate for bills is poor, a majority of the major pieces of legislation considered by Congress become law. In the 111th Congress, only 328 bills of 13,675 measures introduced in the House and Senate became law, for a success rate of 2 percent.[59] However, over the last decade, 59 percent of *major* bills have become law.[60]

pocket veto the action of a president allowing a measure to die without signature after Congress has adjourned.

veto an action by the chief executive refusing to approve a measure passed by the legislature.

rider a provision, unlikely to become law on its own merits, that is attached to an important measure so that it will ride through the legislative process.

what we LEARNED

BICAMERALISM

12.1 *How have structural differences affected the development of the House and Senate?*

The U.S. has a bicameral legislature with a House and a Senate. Whereas states are equally represented in the Senate, representation in the House depends on a state's population. Senators run for election statewide to serve six-year terms; House members run from districts to serve two-year terms. Although the Constitution assigns certain responsibilities to the Senate, the two chambers share other tasks, including enacting legislation. The Senate is individualistic, with many important decisions requiring supermajority approval. Members of the House have a reputation for devotion to technical expertise, personalized constituency service, and responsiveness to local political interests.

MEMBERSHIP

12.2 *What are the qualifications for and characteristics of members of Congress?*

The U.S. Constitution requires that members of the House be no less than 25 years of age, American citizens for at least seven years, and residents of the state in which their district is located. Senators must be at least 30 years old, citizens for at least nine years, and residents of the state they represent. Although Congress is more diverse than at any time in its history, white males of European ancestry are still overrepresented. Traditionally, members of Congress got things done and advanced their careers by building relationships with colleagues, deferring to senior members, and bargaining. In today's Congress, some members have become skilled media entrepreneurs, using media coverage to establish themselves as national political figures. Members of Congress perform constituency service and cultivate ties with their districts,

which are important for their reelection. Despite the absence of term limits, congressional turnover is substantial because members often choose not to seek reelection.

ORGANIZATION

12.3 *How is Congress organized in terms of leadership and committee structure?*

The organization of the House and Senate is based on political party. The Senate majority leader and the Speaker of the House are the most important legislators in their respective chambers. They influence the membership of committees, refer legislation to committee, and control the flow of business to the floor, which is especially important in the House. The Speaker and majority leader are political party leaders, working to advance their party's policy interests and maintain their majority. Members of Congress have a strong incentive to cooperate with their party leadership because their success is tied to the success of their political party.

The detailed work of Congress takes place in committee and subcommittee. House members, with fewer committee assignments, are better able to specialize than are senators. Members of Congress request committee assignments from party committees responsible for assignment decisions, and committees dealing with money are in great demand. The majority party enjoys a majority on and chairs every committee and subcommittee. Each party has its own procedures for selecting committee chairs (for the majority party) and ranking members (for the minority party).

THE LEGISLATIVE PROCESS

12.4 *What are the steps in the legislative process for a bill to become a law?*

Today's Congress has adopted modifications in the traditional legislative process to increase the likelihood that it can pass major legislation.

Once a bill or resolution is introduced, it is assigned a number and referred to committee, where the detailed work of Congress takes place. Major legislation is often referred to more than one committee, especially in the House. Committees and subcommittees hold hearings, debate the details of legislation, and revise, amend, and rewrite a measure in a process known as legislative markup. In the House, most measures that clear standing committee go to the Rules Committee, which sets a time limit for debate and the ground rules for amendments. In the Senate, a measure typically reaches the floor through the mechanism of a unanimous consent agreement (UCA). A senator who opposes a measure may filibuster to delay and attempt to kill a bill. Cloture, the procedure for shutting off a filibuster, requires 60 votes.

A measure must pass the House and Senate in identical form before it has passed Congress. If the two chambers pass similar but not identical bills, one chamber can accept the version of the legislation passed by the other chamber, the two chambers can pass a series of reconciling amendments, or they can create a conference committee to negotiate a single measure, which must then be voted on again and passed by the House and Senate. After a bill passes Congress, it goes to the president who can sign, veto, or permit it to become law without signature.

TEST yourself

12.1 *How have structural differences affected the development of the House and Senate?*

1 Which of the following statements better describes the House than it does the Senate?
a. It makes most decisions strictly by majority vote.
b. It has a tradition as a great debating society where members enjoy broad freedom to voice their points of view.
c. It is an individualistic body where one member has considerable influence on the legislative process.
d. All of the above

2 Which of the following statements better describes the Senate than the House?
a. Every member stands for reelection every two years.
b. It is known as a great debating society.
c. Members of this chamber sometimes run for seats in the other chamber.
d. None of the above

12.2 *What are the qualifications for and characteristics of members of Congress?*

3 How did constituency pressure affect the vote on healthcare reform?
a. Many Republican members of Congress voted in favor of healthcare reform because polls showed strong support for the bill among independents.
b. Every Republican member of Congress voted against healthcare reform because polls showed strong opposition to the bill among Republicans, especially party activists.
c. Every Democratic member of Congress voted in favor of healthcare reform because polls showed strong opposition to the bill among Republicans, and Democrats enjoy making Republican voters angry.
d. Constituency attitudes about healthcare reform had no effect on congressional votes on the measure.

4 Which of the following statements about congressional turnover is *not* true?
a. Most members of Congress are reelected.
b. The reelection rate for House members is higher than it is for senators.
c. Congress experiences significant turnover because term limits restrict members to no more than 12 consecutive years in office.
d. Voters typically express a higher level of approval for their representative in Congress than they do for the institution as a whole.

12.3 *How is Congress organized in terms of leadership and committee structure?*

5 In practice, who is the most important leader in the U.S. Senate?
a. Speaker of the House
b. Senate president *pro tempore*
c. Senate majority leader
d. Vice president

6 Which of the following officials is the most important leader in the U.S. House?
a. Speaker of the House
b. Senate president *pro tempore*
c. Senate majority leader
d. Vice president

7 In which chamber of Congress does the minority leadership have the most influence and why?
a. In the House, because the rules the House require a two-thirds vote to approve most measures and that ensures that the two parties must work together
b. In the Senate, because the rules of the Senate give the minority substantial power to delay or defeat legislation, forcing the majority to work with the minority
c. In the House, because the Speaker of the House is independent of the two political parties
d. In the Senate, because the detailed work of the chamber takes place in committee

8 In 2010, the Democratic Party was the majority party in the House and Senate and a Democrat, Barack Obama, occupied the White House. Was the chair of the House Ways and Means Committee a Democrat or Republican? How do you know?
a. The chair could have been a Democrat or Republican depending on which member of the committee had the most seniority.
b. The chair was a Democrat because the president was Democrat.
c. The chair was a Democrat because Democrats were the majority party in the House.
d. The chair could have been a Democrat or a Republican depending on which member of the committee won a vote of the committee membership.

12.4 *What are the steps in the legislative process for a bill to become a law?*

9 Why do major legislative measures often take the form of omnibus bills?
a. Complex problems require complex solutions.

b. Government is so big that legislation must deal with a broad range of policy areas.
c. Congress is in session only part of the year and omnibus bills enable it to get more done in a short period of time.
d. Congressional leaders assemble omnibus bills in order to attract as much support as possible.

10 Legislative markup occurs at which stage of the legislative process?
a. On the floor
b. In committee
c. In conference committee
d. In the Rules Committee

11 What is the purpose of a discharge petition?
a. To end a filibuster.
b. To demand that a member of Congress be expelled for misconduct.
c. To force a committee to report a bill to the floor of the House.
d. To begin the impeachment process.

12 The opponents of a bill in the Senate have resorted to a filibuster to block it. How many votes will the measure's supporters need to invoke cloture and end the filibuster?
a. 51
b. 67
c. 60
d. 40

13 A conference committee agrees on a conference report. It passes the House, but it fails to pass the Senate. What is the status of the bill?
a. The measure goes to the president.
b. The measure is dead unless the Senate reconsiders it and passes it.
c. The House votes again on the measure and if it passes again, it goes to the president.
d. The president convenes a reconciliation committee involving the leadership of both the House and Senate.

14 Congress passes a bill that the president generally favors with the exception of one provision. What are the president's options?
a. The president can sign or veto the bill in its entirety.
b. The president can ask a conference committee to rewrite the bill.
c. The president can ask the Supreme Court to revise the bill.
d. The president can veto the offensive provision while signing the rest into law.

Answers: 1) a, 2) b, 3) b, 4) c, 5) c, 6) a, 7) b, 8) c, 9) d, 10) b, 11) c, 12) c, 13) b, 14) a

13 THE

THE **CONSTITUTIONAL** PRESIDENCY

Learning Objective **13.1** How does the Constitution define the office of the presidency?

PRESIDENTIAL **POWERS**

Learning Objective **13.2** What are the powers of the presidency?

THE **DEVELOPMENT** OF THE **MODERN PRESIDENCY**

Learning Objective **13.3** How did the modern presidency develop?

THE **ORGANIZATION** OF THE **PRESIDENCY**

Learning Objective **13.4** How does the presidential bureaucracy assist the chief executive in carrying out the duties of the office?

THEORIES OF **PRESIDENTIAL LEADERSHIP**

Learning Objective **13.5** What approaches do political scientists use to understand the concept of presidential power?

PRESIDENTIAL **POPULARITY**

Learning Objective **13.6** What factors affect presidential popularity?

Does President Barack Obama have the authority to commit U.S. armed forces to action in Libya without congressional authorization? In March 2011, President Obama joined an international effort to protect civilians and avert a humanitarian disaster in Libya after Muammar Qaddafi, the nation's ruler, declared his intent to go house-to-house to root out rebels trying to overthrow his government. The U.S. effort only involved air power, not ground forces. Moreover, in April, the United States turned over leadership of

PRESIDENCY

the operation to the **North Atlantic Treaty Organization (NATO)**, a military alliance consisting of the United States, Canada, and most European democracies.

The Constitution divides military power between the president and Congress. It names the president as commander in chief, but gives Congress sole authority to declare war. The last declared war, however, was World War II. All subsequent U.S. military operations, including that in Libya, have been initiated by the president. During the Vietnam War, Congress responded to what it considered to be an infringement of its constitutional power to declare war by enacting the **War Powers Act**, a law

limiting the president's ability to commit U.S. armed forces to combat abroad without consultation with Congress and congressional approval. Although Obama followed the provisions of the War Powers Act by informing Congress of the scope and expected duration of the Libyan operation, he failed to request authorization within 60 days as required by the law. The president asserted that the War Powers Act did not apply because the Libyan mission had become a NATO operation rather than an American military action. Did Obama overstep his authority?

The controversy over U.S. military action in Libya introduces this chapter on the presidency. The chapter begins with

the constitutional profile of the office. It examines its powers and responsibilities, traces the development of the modern presidency, and describes the organization of the executive branch. The chapter continues by exploring various theories of presidential leadership. It discusses presidential popularity and concludes by examining the presidency in the context of American politics.

North Atlantic Treaty Organization (NATO) a regional military alliance consisting of the United States, Canada, and most of the European democracies.

War Powers Act a law limiting the president's ability to commit American armed forces to combat abroad without consultation with Congress and congressional approval.

THE CONSTITUTIONAL PRESIDENCY

13.1 *How does the Constitution define the office of the presidency?*

The Constitution describes the office of the presidency in Article II.

Qualifications and Background

The Constitution declares that the president must be at least 35 years of age, a natural-born American citizen (as opposed to a naturalized citizen), and a resident of the United States for at least 14 years. Before the 2008 election, all the nation's presidents

had been white males of Western European ancestry. Two sets of presidents were father and son (John and John Quincy Adams and George and George W. Bush); two were grandfather and grandson (William Henry and Benjamin Harrison); and two were cousins (Theodore and Franklin D. Roosevelt). All but one, Roman Catholic John Kennedy, have been Protestant Christians. Most presidents have been fairly wealthy; the majority of them have

think — Should the United States consider amending the Constitution to allow naturalized (foreign-born) American citizens to become president?

been experienced politicians. Most presidents have come from states outside the South. In recent years,

Members of the "Birther Movement" are conspiracy theorists who charge that Barack Obama is not eligible to be president because he is not a natural born citizen. They believe he was born in Kenya or Indonesia and that his Hawaii birth certificate, pictured here, is a forgery.

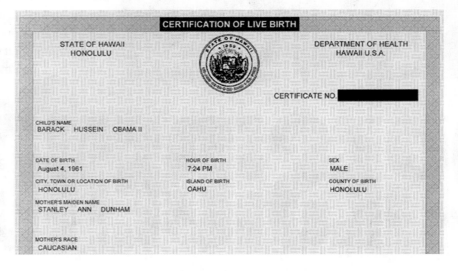

CERTIFICATION OF LIVE BIRTH

STATE OF HAWAII
HONOLULU

DEPARTMENT OF HEALTH
HAWAII U.S.A.

CERTIFICATE NO.

CHILD'S NAME
BARACK HUSSEIN OBAMA II

DATE OF BIRTH
August 4, 1961

HOUR OF BIRTH
7:24 PM

SEX
MALE

CITY, TOWN OR LOCATION OF BIRTH
HONOLULU

ISLAND OF BIRTH
OAHU

COUNTY OF BIRTH
HONOLULU

MOTHER'S MAIDEN NAME
STANLEY ANN DUNHAM

MOTHER'S RACE
CAUCASIAN

however, social barriers have begun to fall as the nation has elected a Roman Catholic (Kennedy), three Southerners (Jimmy Carter, Bill Clinton, and George W. Bush), and a divorced person (Ronald Reagan) to the White House. The election of Barack Obama, the son of a white woman from Kansas and a black immigrant from Kenya, shattered the barriers of race and ethnicity. Furthermore, Hillary Clinton's strong showing in the race for the Democratic presidential nomination suggests that gender is no longer a major barrier to the White House. The myth that anyone born in the United States can grow up to become president has come closer to reality than ever before in the nation's history.

Term of Office

The president's constitutional term of office is four years. The framers of the Constitution placed no limit on the number of terms that presidents could serve, believing that the desire to remain in office would compel them to do their best. George Washington, the nation's first chief executive, established a custom of seeking no more than two terms, which every president honored until Franklin D. Roosevelt broke tradition in the early 1940s. After Roosevelt, a Democrat, won election to a third and then a fourth term, unhappy Republicans launched a drive to amend the Constitution to limit the president to two terms. They succeeded with the ratification of the Twenty-second Amendment in 1951.

The proponents of the two-term limit argued that it prevented a president from becoming too powerful. In contrast, critics believed that the two-term limit unnecessarily weakened the office of the presidency by making a second-term president a **lame duck**, which is an official whose influence is diminished because the official either cannot or will not seek reelection. The opponents of the Twenty-second Amendment also complained that it

In 1998, the U.S. House made Bill Clinton the second president in the nation's history to be impeached. Like Andrew Johnson, the first president to be impeached, the Senate failed to remove him from office.

was undemocratic because it denied voters the right to reelect a president they admired.

think Do you think presidents should be permitted to run for more than two terms?

Impeachment and Removal

Impeachment is a process in which an executive or judicial official is formally accused of an offense that could warrant removal from office. The Constitution states that the president may be impeached for "treason, bribery, or other high crimes and misdemeanors." The founders foresaw two broad, general grounds on which a president could be impeached and removed from office. First, impeachment could be used against a president who abused the powers of office, thereby threatening to become a tyrant. Second, it could be employed against a president who failed to carry out the duties of the office.[1]

The actual process of impeachment and removal involves both houses of Congress. The House drafts articles of impeachment, a document listing the impeachable offenses that the House believes the president committed. Technically, *impeach* means to accuse; so when the House impeaches the president by majority vote, it is accusing the president of committing offenses that may warrant removal from office. The Senate then tries the president, with the chief justice of the Supreme Court presiding. The Senate must vote by a two-thirds majority to remove the president from office.

In 1868, Andrew Johnson became the first president to be impeached. When Johnson became president after Abraham Lincoln's assassination, he quarreled with the Republican Congress over which branch of government would control Reconstruction. Congress limited the president's power by passing the Tenure of Office Act,

lame duck an official whose influence is diminished because the official either cannot or will not seek reelection.

impeachment a process in which an executive or judicial official is formally accused of an offense that could warrant removal from office.

which stipulated that any official appointed by the president and confirmed by the Senate could not be removed from office until the Senate had confirmed a replacement. Johnson challenged the law by removing Secretary of War Edwin M. Stanton and appointing General Ulysses S. Grant as his interim successor. The House of Representatives responded by voting to impeach him, 126 to 47. The Senate voted 35 to 19 for conviction, just one vote short of the two-thirds vote necessary to remove President Johnson from office.

More than a century after Johnson survived impeachment, President Nixon faced possible impeachment because of the Watergate scandal. The affair began in June 1972 when five men were arrested breaking into the Democratic National Committee headquarters. The burglars were part of a conspiracy formed by Nixon aides to manipulate the Democratic Party's presidential nomination process. The cover-up eventually unraveled and the House Judiciary Committee recommended impeachment, but Nixon resigned before the full House could act.

In 1998, President Clinton became the second president to be impeached. Congress appointed Kenneth Starr as a special prosecutor to look into allegations of the president's involvement in a failed Arkansas land development called Whitewater when Clinton was governor of Arkansas. The investigation subsequently expanded to include allegations that Clinton had lied under oath about an alleged sexual liaison with White House intern Monica Lewinsky and that Clinton encouraged Lewinsky to lie as well. Starr charged that Clinton committed perjury by lying under oath. And he accused the president of obstructing justice by helping Lewinsky find a job after she left the White House. The House of Representatives impeached Clinton, but the Senate failed to convict and remove the president from office.

Presidential Succession and Disability

The vice president succeeds a president who is removed, resigns, or dies in office. After the vice president, the line of succession passes to the Speaker of the House, president *pro tempore* of the Senate, secretary of state, and then through the cabinet. In American history, nine vice presidents have succeeded to the presidency, but no Speakers or Senate presidents *pro tempore*. Furthermore, because of the Twenty-fifth Amendment, the order of succession probably will never

President Kennedy's assassination **focused attention** on the issue of presidential succession.

extend beyond the office of vice president.

The Twenty-fifth Amendment was ratified in 1967, after President Dwight Eisenhower's heart attack and President Kennedy's assassination focused attention on the issue of presidential succession and disability. The amendment authorizes the president to fill a vacancy in the office of vice president, subject to majority confirmation by both houses of Congress. This procedure was first used in 1973, when President Nixon nominated Gerald Ford to replace Vice President Spiro Agnew, who resigned under accusation of criminal wrongdoing. When Nixon himself resigned in 1974, Ford moved up to the presidency and appointed former governor of New York Nelson Rockefeller to be the new vice president.

Other provisions of the Twenty-fifth Amendment establish procedures for the vice president to become

The modern vice president is an important adviser to the president. Dick Cheney, left, vice president in the George W. Bush administration, is regarded the most powerful vice president in history. Joe Biden, pictured above, is vice president in the Obama administration.

acting president should the president become disabled and incapable of performing the duties of office. The president may declare disability by written notice to the Senate president *pro tempore* and the Speaker of the House. The vice president then becomes acting president until the president declares in writing the ability to resume the responsibilities of office. If the president is unable or unwilling to declare disability, the vice president can declare the president disabled in conjunction with a majority of the cabinet. Should the vice president/cabinet and president disagree on the question of the president's disability, Congress may declare the president disabled by two-thirds vote of each house.

The Vice Presidency

The Constitution gives the vice president two duties. The vice president is president of the Senate and votes in case of a tie. The vice president also becomes president of the United States if the office becomes vacant. For most of American history, however, the vice president was the forgotten person of Washington. In 1848, Daniel Webster, a prominent political figure of the time, rejected the vice presidential nomination of his party, by saying "I do not propose to be buried until I am dead."[2] Before the last half of the twentieth century, the

vice president had no staff and few responsibilities. The vice president represented the nation at selected ceremonial occasions, such as the funeral of a foreign leader, but had no policy responsibilities.

Today, the vice presidency has become a more visible and important office. The death in office of President Franklin Roosevelt, Eisenhower's heart attack, Kennedy's assassination, Nixon's resignation, and the assassination attempt against Reagan all called attention to the possibility that the vice president could become president at any time. A contemporary president who kept the vice president uninformed and uninvolved in policy issues would be generally regarded as an irresponsible chief executive. Furthermore, the vice presidency has become the most common path to the office of the presidency, either through succession or election. Since 1950, five presidents (Harry Truman, Lyndon Johnson, Nixon, Ford, and the elder Bush) held office as vice president prior to becoming president. Men and women of stature are now willing to serve as vice president.

Walter Mondale, who served under President Carter, is regarded as the first modern vice president. Carter used Vice President Mondale as an adviser, troubleshooter, and emissary to interest groups and

Congress. Since Mondale, every vice president has had an office in the White House, a sizable staff, and an open invitation to attend any meeting on the president's schedule. Presidents have used their vice presidents to chair commissions, debate political opponents, serve as emissaries to Congress, and give advice on policy matters. Vice President Dick Cheney was such a powerful figure in the George W. Bush administration that some critics accused him of being co-president.[3] Bush saw himself as chairman of the board with Cheney as a chief operating officer. Cheney developed great influence because he was detail-oriented and willing to assert himself. Many observers believe that Cheney was the architect of every significant policy initiative in the Bush administration, including the response to 9/11, energy policy, the war in Iraq, judicial nominations, the budget, and tax policy.[4] Vice President Joe Biden has become an important adviser for President Obama, especially on foreign and defense policy issues, such as the war in Afghanistan.

think Is it possible for the vice president to have too much influence?

PRESIDENTIAL POWERS

 13.2 *What are the powers of the presidency?*

The powers of the presidency have developed through the give-and-take of the political process. Although the Constitution outlines the powers of the office in Article II, many of its provisions are not clearly defined.[5] This ambiguity has enabled presidents to expand the limits of presidential power beyond the initial understanding of the authority granted the office.[6]

Diplomatic Powers

The Constitution gives the president, as **chief of state** (the official head of government), broad diplomatic authority to conduct foreign relations. The president has the power officially to recognize the governments of other nations and to receive and appoint ambassadors. For example, the United States broke off

diplomatic relations with China after the communist takeover in 1940. President Nixon stunned the world by flying to Beijing to begin the process of normalizing relations with the People's Republic of China as the legitimate government of mainland China. President Carter completed

chief of state the official head of government.

President Nixon's visit to China in 1972 startled the world, and was a coup for the president as the chief of state. Nixon was a strong anti-communist, and the communist government of China was considered a determined enemy of the United States.

Military Powers

The Constitution names the president commander in chief of the armed forces. As commander in chief, the president makes military policy, including decisions involving the use of force, operational strategy, and personnel. President Franklin Roosevelt, for example, chose the time and place of the Normandy invasion during World War II. Truman decided to drop the atomic bomb on Japan during World War II and fired General Douglas McArthur for publicly disagreeing with the administration's war policy during the Korean conflict. The first President Bush sent American forces to the Persian Gulf to roll back the Iraqi invasion of Kuwait. President George W. Bush ordered American forces to take military action against the Taliban government in Afghanistan and the al-Qaeda terrorists that it sheltered. He also ordered the American military to overthrow the government of Saddam Hussein in Iraq. President Obama demanded the resignation of General Stanley McChystal, the commander of U.S. forces in Afghanistan, after his remarks critical of Vice President Biden and other administration officials were quoted in *Rolling Stone* magazine.

The president's role as commander in chief embodies the doctrine of **civilian supremacy of the armed forces**, which is the concept that the armed forces should be under the direct control of civilian authorities. The doctrine of civilian supremacy is based on the belief that military decisions should be weighed in light of political considerations. The

the process and the two nations exchanged ambassadors. The only constitutional limitation on the president's power of diplomatic recognition is that ambassadorial appointments must be approved by majority vote of the Senate.

The Constitution empowers the president to negotiate treaties with other nations, subject to a two-thirds vote of ratification by the Senate. Since 1789, the Senate has rejected only 21 of more than 1,500 treaties submitted to it, but that figure underestimates the role of the Senate in the ratification process. Most treaties that lack sufficient support to pass the Senate are either withdrawn from consideration by the president or bottled up in committee. The Senate may make its approval of a treaty conditional, depending on the acceptance of amendments, interpretations, understandings, or other reservations. The president and the other countries involved must then decide whether to accept the conditions, renegotiate the provisions, or abandon the treaty altogether.[7]

Presidents use executive agreements to expand their diplomatic authority beyond the treaty power. An **executive agreement** is an international understanding between the president and foreign nations that does not require Senate ratification. Although the Constitution says nothing about executive agreements, the Supreme Court has upheld their use based on the president's diplomatic and military powers. Executive agreements are more numerous than treaties. The United States is currently a party to nearly 900 treaties and more than 5,000 executive agreements.[8] Many executive agreements involve relatively routine matters, such as the exchange of postal service between nations. Congress has passed legislation authorizing the executive branch to make executive agreements with other countries in certain fields, such as agriculture, trade, and foreign aid. Some executive agreements also require congressional participation because they involve changes in American law. Congress had to pass legislation authorizing the North American Free Trade Agreement (NAFTA), even though it was an executive agreement, because it required changes in American trade laws.

> The Constitution names the president **commander in chief** of the armed forces.

executive agreement an international understanding between the president and foreign nations that does not require Senate ratification.

civilian supremacy of the armed forces the concept that the armed forces should be under the direct control of civilian authorities.

concept of civilian supremacy also reflects the view that the preservation of representative democracy depends on keeping the military out of politics. In many nations, the armed forces are a powerful political force, and military men sometimes seize the reins of government from civilian authorities. The government of Burma (also known as Myanmar), for example, is a military government, headed by generals whose power depends on the support of the armed forces rather than the votes of the nation's people. In the United States, the president, a civilian, stands at the apex of the command structure of the armed forces. The government controls the military rather than the military controlling the government.

Presidents sometimes use their power as commanders in chief as the basis for exercising authority beyond the scope of direct military action. After Japan bombed Pearl Harbor in 1941 and the United States entered World War II, President Franklin Roosevelt issued an executive order authorizing the military to relocate all persons of Japanese ancestry from the West Coast to inland war relocation centers. More than 120,000 persons were interned, including 70,000 native-born American citizens. The Supreme Court upheld the constitutionality of the action, ruling that the government's need to prevent espionage outweighed the individual rights of the Japanese Americans.[9]

The controversy over U.S. military involvement in Libya is only the most recent quarrel between Congress and the president over military policy. In 1973, Congress, concerned over the Vietnam War, attempted to reassert its military authority with the War Powers Act.[10] The measure includes a number of important provisions:

- The president should consult with Congress "in every possible instance" before introducing U.S. forces into situations where hostilities would be likely.
- The president must make detailed, periodic reports on the necessity and scope of the operation.
- U.S. forces must be withdrawn after 60 days of the first reports of fighting (with a 30-day grace period to ensure safe withdrawal) unless Congress declares war or votes to authorize the presence of the U.S. forces.
- Congress can order the withdrawal of U.S. forces by majority vote of both houses at any time, even before the 60-day period has expired. This last provision was apparently invalidated by a 1983 Supreme Court decision that found similar measures unconstitutional.[11]

Since it's passage, the War Powers Act has been a source of conflict between the president and Congress. Whereas some members of Congress believe that the law requires that the president discuss the use of force with Congress and seek advice, presidents have generally only informed congressional leaders in advance of pending military actions. Chief executives have also tried to avoid the application of the War Powers Act by denying that the military actions they ordered fell under the scope of the law. Although President Obama complied with the law by notifying Congress of his plan to commit U.S. armed forces in Libya, he chose not to ask for authorization at the 60-day point because, he said, the action was no longer an American operation. The U.S. House responded by voting overwhelmingly to deny Obama authority to wage war in Libya, but it failed to pass a measure to cut off funding for the operation. Moreover, the Senate did not act on either measure, giving the president a free hand to carry on the Libya operation as he saw fit. Some observers pronounced the death of the War Powers Act.[12]

Professor Robert Kennedy believes that Congress has failed to provide a check and balance on the military power of the modern presidency. Even though the Constitution gives Congress broad authority, including the power to declare war, raise forces, and provide the funds for military operations, the legislative branch of government has largely abdicated its responsibility to check the war-making power of the chief executive. When presidents have chosen to act militarily, Congress has

think Should there be stricter limits on the president's authority as commander in chief, or does the president need the freedom to respond to security threats without having to take the time to go to Congress?

During World War II, President Roosevelt issued an executive order to authorize the relocation of Americans of Japanese descent to relocation camps.

either endorsed the endeavor or acquiesced in the president's action.[13] Even though many members of Congress, both Democrats and Republicans, believe that President Obama broke the law by failing to ask for authorization to remain in Libya, Congress failed to take meaningful action to force the president to retreat.

Inherent Powers

Inherent powers are those powers vested in the national government, particularly in the area of foreign and defense policy, which do not depend on any specific grant of authority by the Constitution, but rather, exist because the United States is a sovereign nation. Consider the Louisiana Purchase, which was the acquisition from France of a vast expanse of land stretching from New Orleans north to the Dakotas. President Thomas Jefferson justified his decision to acquire the territory on the basis of inherent powers because the Constitution says nothing about purchasing land from another country. Similarly, Lincoln claimed extraordinary powers to defend the Union during the Civil War on the basis of inherent powers. President George W. Bush used the doctrine of inherent powers to justify the use

of military tribunals to try enemy combatants captured in the war on terror, to designate U.S. citizens as enemy combatants and use aggressive interrogation techniques on them, to send terror suspects to countries that practice torture, and to authorize eavesdropping on American citizens by the National Security Agency (NSA).[14]

Presidential assertions of inherent powers are almost invariably controversial because they involve an expansion of government authority and presidential power not authorized by the Constitution. Critics of the Louisiana Purchase, for example, called Jefferson a hypocrite because he had long argued that the authority of the national government was limited to powers clearly delegated by the Constitution. Critics accused President Bush of exceeding his power and challenged his actions in the courts. As discussed in Chapter Four, the U.S. Supreme Court ruled that the president could not deprive detainees of their right to due process,[15] or put detainees on trial before military tribunals that had not authorized the action.[16] The Supreme Court also declared that terror suspects held at Guantánamo had a constitutional right to seek their release in federal court.[17]

Judicial Powers

The president plays a role in judicial policymaking. The president nominates all federal judges pending majority-vote confirmation by the Senate. The Senate usually approves nominees, but not without scrutiny, especially for Supreme Court selections. The Senate rejected two consecutive Supreme Court appointments by President Nixon before confirming his third choice. Similarly, the Senate rejected President Reagan's nomination of Robert Bork to the Supreme Court.

The power of appointment gives a president the opportunity to shape the policy direction of the judicial branch of American government, especially if a president serves two terms. During his eight years in office, President Clinton appointed 374 federal judges. George W. Bush named more than 300 judges during his presidency. Clinton and Bush each appointed two Supreme Court justices.[18] During his first two years in office, President Obama made two Supreme Court appointments, Sonia Sotomayor and Elena Kagan.

The Constitution empowers the president to grant pardons and reprieves. A **pardon** is an executive action that frees an accused or convicted person from all penalties for an offense. A **reprieve** is an executive action that delays punishment for a crime. With some exceptions, such as President Ford's pardon of former President Nixon, most presidential pardons and reprieves have not been controversial.

The Supreme Court challenged President George W. Bush's assertion of inherent power by ruling that terror suspects held at Guantánamo had a constitutional right to seek their release in federal court.

inherent powers powers vested in the national government, particularly in the area of foreign and defense policy, which do not depend on any specific grant of authority by the Constitution, but rather exist because the United States is a sovereign nation.

pardon an executive action that frees an accused or convicted person from all penalties for an offense.

reprieve an executive action that delays punishment for a crime.

Executive Powers

The president is the nation's **chief executive**, that is, the head of the executive branch of government. The Constitution grants the president authority to require written reports from department heads and enjoins the president to "take care that laws be faithfully executed." As head of the executive branch of government, presidents can issue executive orders to manage the federal bureaucracy. An **executive order** is a directive issued by the president to an administrative agency or executive department. Although the Constitution says nothing about executive orders, the courts have upheld their use based on law, custom, and the president's authority as head of the executive branch.

Presidents have used executive orders to enact important (and sometimes controversial) policies. President Lincoln, for example, used an executive order to issue the Emancipation Proclamation. President Eisenhower issued an executive order to send federal troops into Little Rock, Arkansas, in 1957 to protect African American youngsters attempting to attend a whites-only public high school. The first President Bush issued executive orders to prohibit abortion counseling at federally funded family planning centers. President Clinton, in turn, used an executive order to reverse the Bush order. President Obama issued executive orders to prohibit the use of torture in the interrogation of prisoners held in the war on terror and order the eventual closure of the detention camp at Guantánamo Bay, Cuba.

The president's power to issue executive orders is not unlimited. Presidents may issue executive orders only when they fall within the scope of the president's constitutional powers and legal authority. In 1952, for example, during the Korean War, the U.S. Supreme Court overturned an executive order by President Truman seizing the nation's steel mills to head off a strike that would have disrupted steel production and hurt the war effort. The Court declared that the president lacked the legal authority

After Arkansas Governor Orval Faubus defied an order of the U.S. Supreme Court to desegregate Little Rock Central High School, President Eisenhower issued an executive order to send federal troops to protect the African American students attempting to attend the school, and ensure that the Supreme Court ruling was honored.

to seize private property and that the president's power as commander in chief did not extend to labor disputes.[19] Congress can also overturn an executive order legislatively. Because the president would likely veto a measure reversing an executive order, Congress would need to vote to repeal the order and then to vote again by a two-thirds margin to override the veto.

Legislative Powers

Finally, the Constitution grants the president certain tools for shaping the legislative agenda. From time to time, it says, the president shall "give to Congress information of the state of the Union, and recommend to their consideration such measures as he shall judge necessary and expedient." Traditionally, the president makes a State of the Union address each January before a joint session of Congress and a national television audience. The speech gives the president the opportunity to raise issues and frame the terms of their discussion. Although the State of the Union address allows the president the opportunity to present himself or herself as the nation's chief legislator, it may also create unrealistic public expectations. In practice,

Congress approves only 43 percent of the policy initiatives included in the average State of the Union speech, either in whole or in part.[20]

The president can use the veto power to shape the content of legislation. The Constitution empowers the president to return measures to Congress along with objections. A vetoed measure can become law only if both the House and Senate vote to override by a two-thirds margin. The veto is a powerful weapon. Since 1789, Congress has overridden only 7 percent of presidential vetoes.[21] Nonetheless, political scientists consider the actual use of the veto a sign of weakness rather than strength because influential presidents can usually prevent passage of measures they oppose by threatening a veto.[22]

A **presidential signing statement** is a pronouncement issued

chief executive the head of the executive branch of government.

executive order a directive issued by the president to an administrative agency or executive department.

presidential signing statement a pronouncement issued by the president at the time a bill passed by Congress is signed into law.

by the president at the time a bill passed by Congress is signed into law. Presidents historically have used signing statements to comment on the bill they are signing, score political points, identify areas of disagreement with the measure, and discuss its implementation. President George W. Bush went further than any of his predecessors in using signing statements to expand the powers of his office. Bush signing statements identified more than 800 provisions in 500 measures that he signed into law but considered unconstitutional limitations on his authority as president and asserted his intention to ignore these provisions or treat them as advisory. Bush declared, for example,

*The Constitution requires that the president **sign** legislation or **veto** it in **its entirety**.*

that legislative provisions that establish qualifications for executive branch officials were advisory rather than mandatory because he believed that they unconstitutionally restricted the presidential power of appointment. He asserted his intention to withhold information from Congress and rejected legislative provisions that he believed would limit his power as commander in chief. Much to the unhappiness of congressional leaders, especially Democrats, President Obama has continued the use of signing statements to challenge the constitutionality of certain legislative provisions and to declare his intention not to enforce them.[23]

Presidential signing statements are controversial. Political scientist Phillip J. Cooper believes that signing statements are a vehicle for revising legislation without issuing a veto, which is subject to congressional override, and that violates the letter and spirit of the Constitution.[24] The American Bar Association (ABA) declared that Bush's use of signing statements was "contrary to the rule of law and our constitutional system of separation of powers" because the Constitution requires that the president sign legislation or veto it in its entirety.[25] In contrast, law professors Curtis A. Bradley and Eric A. Posner argue that signing statements are legal and useful because they provide a way for the president to disclose his or her views about the meaning and constitutionality of legislation.[26]

THE DEVELOPMENT OF THE MODERN PRESIDENCY

13.3 *How did the modern presidency develop?*

In the nineteenth century, the presidency was an institution on the periphery of national politics. Early presidents generally confined their initiatives to foreign affairs, leaving domestic policymaking to Congress. The nation's first chief executives did not negotiate with Congress over policy and rarely used the veto.[27] Three of the first six presidents vetoed no legislation at all.[28]

Andrew Jackson and Abraham Lincoln expanded the powers of the presidency. Jackson, who served as president from 1829 to 1837, vetoed legislation on policy grounds, issuing more vetoes than the first six presidents combined. He asserted his legislative leadership by asking the voters to elect different people to Congress who would be more supportive of his policy priorities.

President Lincoln, who held office during the Civil War from 1861 to 1865, used his authority as commander in chief to justify taking actions without congressional authorization. He declared martial law, ordered the blockade of southern ports, freed slaves in the rebelling territories, stationed troops in the South, and spent money not appropriated by Congress.

In the twentieth century, the role of the president grew as the role of the national government grew. Early twentieth-century presidents were more active than their nineteenth-century counterparts, especially Theodore Roosevelt and Woodrow Wilson. In foreign affairs, Roosevelt, who held office from 1901 to 1909, sent the navy halfway around the globe and schemed to acquire the Panama

Canal. Domestically, Roosevelt attacked monopolies, crusaded for conservation, and lobbied legislation through Congress. Wilson, who served from 1913 through 1921, was the first president to recommend a comprehensive legislative program to Congress. He was the first president to conduct face-to-face diplomacy with foreign leaders, negotiating the League of Nations Treaty. He also made direct policy appeals to the public, campaigning across the nation in support of the ratification of the League of Nations Treaty.[29]

*The **Great Depression** and **WWII** increased the scope of federal government activities.*

Franklin D. Roosevelt is regarded as the first modern president.

Franklin D. Roosevelt, who served from 1933 to 1945, is widely regarded as the first modern president. FDR, as President Franklin Roosevelt was known, was first elected during the Great Depression and held office through most of World War II. Both of these events served to increase the scope of federal government activities and centralize policymaking in the executive branch. The Depression generated public pressure for the national government to act to revive the nation's economy, help those Americans hardest hit by the collapse, and regulate business and industry in an effort to prevent recurrence of the disaster. FDR responded with the New Deal, a legislative package of reform measures that involved the federal government more deeply in the nation's economy. World War II also increased presidential power. The general public and Congress tend to defer to presidential leadership in the face of international threats, and Congress ceded many powers to the presidency during the war years.

The modern president is a chief executive who is active and visible. The modern president takes the lead in legislative policymaking, uses executive orders to act without congressional approval, has the support of an expanded presidential bureaucracy, and because of the increased role of the media, is the central figure of American government.

Political scientists Matthew Crenson and Benjamin Ginsberg identify a number of factors

AROUND THE WORLD

The Russian Presidency

Russia elects a president to a four-year term by popular vote. Russia has no vice president. The Russian Constitution makes the president the most powerful office in the government. The president appoints the prime minister to head the cabinet and to administer the government. The Duma, the lower chamber of the Russian parliament, must approve the president's choice for prime minister.

The Russian president plays a role in the legislative process somewhat similar to the role played by the American president in the legislative process. Measures passed by the parliament go to the president, who may sign or reject them. If the president rejects a bill, the parliament may vote to override the rejection by a two-thirds vote of both chambers. The president also has the power to make laws by decree. Presidential decrees may not contradict existing laws, and the parliament can rescind a presidential decree by majority vote.

The presidency was the dominant institution of Russian politics during the administration of Vladimir Putin, who served from 2000 through 2008. Putin consolidated power by crushing opposition and disqualifying his opponents on technicalities. The government also took control of the news media to ensure that Putin received flattering coverage while political opponents were either ignored or attacked.[30]

The importance of the presidency in Russian government is now in decline, ironically, because of Putin. The Russian Constitution limits the president to two four-year terms. So Putin promoted the candidacy of a handpicked successor, Dmitry Medvedev, a relatively unknown bureaucrat, and then Putin became prime minister. Because of the power Putin wields, some observers believe that the Russian system will evolve to resemble most parliamentary systems in which the real power is in the hands of the prime minister, with the president as the ceremonial head of state without significant decision-making influence.[31]

QUESTIONS

1 Is there a difference between the Russian president ruling by decree and the American president issuing executive orders?

2 Could a future American political leader execute a maneuver similar to that accomplished by Putin to stay in power despite the end of a second term in the White House?

3 What keeps the American president from taking actions similar to those taken by Putin?

Prime Minister Vladimir Putin and President Dmitry Medveidev. When Putin talks, Medvedev listens.

contributing to the emergence of the president as the chief actor in the political system. First, the United States has become a world power, thrusting foreign policy and national security issues to the top of the policy agenda. These are areas where the president's constitutional powers are stronger than they are in domestic policy. Second, the modern presidential selection process favors the election of assertive individuals with big ideas rather than individuals chosen primarily for their loyalty to their political parties. Finally, the executive branch of the national government has grown,

giving the president the means to expand influence.[32]

Political scientist Richard M. Skinner uses the term "partisan presidency" to describe the administrations of recent presidents, especially Reagan and George W. Bush. Skinner says that partisan presidents use the White House to further the interests of their political party. Rather than trying to build bipartisan coalitions, they work exclusively with the members of their own party in Congress to adopt their party's legislative agenda. President Bush, for example, worked with Republican congressional leaders

during his first term to pass Republican policy proposals without Democratic input or support.[33] After Democrats won control of Congress in the 2006 election, Bush and the Republican minority in Congress found themselves on the defensive. They could prevent the enactment of Democratic Party priorities, either by use of the filibuster in the Senate or a presidential veto, but they could no longer advance Republican initiatives. Those measures that did become law reflected compromise between the White House and the Democratic leadership in Congress.

THE ORGANIZATION
OF THE PRESIDENCY

13.4 *How does the presidential bureaucracy assist the chief executive in carrying out the duties of the office?*

he development of the modern presidency has been accompanied by a significant growth in the size and power of the presidential bureaucracy, that is, the White House staff and the Executive Office of the President. Early chief executives wrote their own speeches and even answered their own mail. They had only a few aides, whom they paid from their own funds. Thomas Jefferson, for example, had one messenger and one secretary. Eventually, Congress appropriated money for the president to hire aides and advisors, and the presidential bureaucracy grew. In the 1920s, the president had a staff of 30. By the 1950s, the number of presidential aides and advisors had grown to 250. Today, the combined staffs of the Executive Office and the White House number more than 2,000, and the president has grown to rely on them more and more.[34] The modern

president spends time bargaining with Congress while dealing with the media and the public. Reelection campaigns begin almost from the first day in office. Presidents have responded to the demands of the office by hiring aides with specialized expertise.[35]

White House Staff

The White House staff consists of personal aides, assistants, and advisors to the president, including a chief of staff, press secretary, speechwriter, appointments secretary, national security advisor, legislative liaison, counselor to the president, and various special assistants. They give the president advice on policy issues and politics, screen key appointments, manage press relations, organize the president's workday, and ensure that the president's wishes are carried out. The president selects the White House staff without Senate confirmation.

As with most presidential appointees (the exceptions are federal judges and regulatory commissioners), White House staff members serve at the president's pleasure, which means that the president can remove them at will.

Political and personal loyalty is usually the foremost criterion the president uses in selecting a staff. When George W. Bush became president, he recruited his staff primarily from his father's administration, his own administration as governor of Texas, and his presidential campaign. Andrew H. Card, Jr., the White House chief of staff during Bush's first term, was secretary of transportation in the first Bush administration. Similarly, President Obama selected Rahm Emanuel, a member of Congress from Chicago, Illinois, Obama's political home base, to serve as his chief of staff.

The White House staff focuses on politics as if the last presidential

Rahm Emanuel, a Democratic congressman from Chicago, was President Obama's first chief of staff. Emanuel left the administration in 2010 to run for mayor of Chicago.

campaign had never ended or the next one had already begun. Bush appointed Karl Rove, his campaign manager in the 2000 presidential election, to coordinate policy development in the White House in order to integrate policy with political strategy.[36] Similarly, Obama named David Axelrod, the chief political strategist of his 2008 election campaign, as a senior advisor in the White House. When healthcare reform appeared stalled in Congress, Obama turned to David Plouffe, his former campaign manager, to work as a political adviser to the White House.

Executive Office of the President

The **Executive Office of the President** is the group of White House offices and agencies that develop and implement the policies and programs of the president. Congress established the Executive Office in 1939 after a special investigative commission concluded that the responsibilities of the presidency were too great for any one individual. "The president needs help," the commission said. The legislation creating the Executive Office allowed the president to create and disband components without further congressional authorization. Consequently, the size and composition of the Executive Office changes somewhat from administration to administration. During the most recent Bush administration, the Executive Office had 14 units. President Obama's Executive Office has 11 units (see figure on the following page).[37]

The major agencies of the Executive Office are the National Security Council (NSC), Office of Management and Budget (OMB), Council of Economic Advisers (CEA), Council on Environmental Quality, Office of Science and Technology Policy, Office of the United States Trade Representative, and Office of Administration. The first two are the most prominent. The **National Security Council (NSC)** advises the chief executive on matters involving national security. It includes the president, vice president, secretaries of state and defense, and other officials whom the president may choose to include, such as the national security advisor, the head of the Joint Chiefs of Staff, and the director of the Central Intelligence Agency (CIA). Although the NSC was created primarily as an advisory body, in some administrations it has participated in policy formulation and implementation.

The **Office of Management and Budget (OMB)** is an agency that assists the president in preparing the budget. The OMB is an important instrument of presidential control of the executive branch. It assists the president in preparing the annual budget to be submitted to Congress, screens bills drawn up by executive branch departments and agencies to ensure that they do not conflict with the president's policy goals, monitors expenditures by executive branch departments, and evaluates regulations proposed by executive agencies. As with other federal agencies, most OMB personnel below the level of executive management are career employees chosen through a merit hiring system. The president appoints the director of the OMB and other top-level agency officials pending Senate confirmation.

Presidential Bureaucracy and Presidential Influence

The presidential bureaucracy is essential to the effective operation of the modern presidency. An efficient, knowledgeable White House staff is an important element of presidential power. Members of the staff not only advise the president on policy issues and political strategy, but they often act on behalf of the president in dealing with Congress, members of the executive branch bureaucracy, and the media. An efficient, professional staff can further the president's policy goals and create an image of presidential competence. A White House staff that is accessible to members of Congress and maintains open lines of communication will help promote the president's policies while keeping the president well-informed enough to prevent surprises.[38] In contrast, an

Executive Office of the President the group of White House offices and agencies that develop and implement the policies and programs of the president.

National Security Council (NSC) an agency in the Executive Office of the President that advises the chief executive on matters involving national security.

Office of Management and Budget (OMB) an agency that assists the president in preparing the budget.

How the White House Runs: The Executive Office of the President

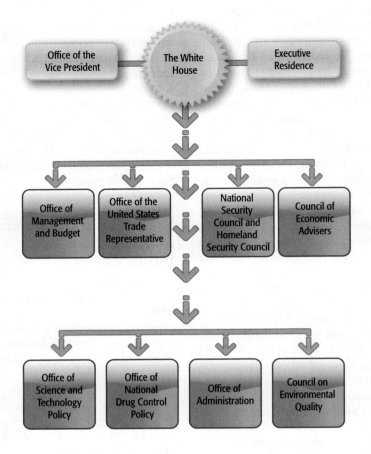

To be **effective**, a president must know which tasks **can be delegated** and which cannot.

delegates neither too little nor too much. Because a president's time, energy, and abilities are limited, the president must delegate some tasks. To be effective, a president must know which tasks can be delegated and which cannot. The president must also have a strong enough grasp of policy issues to recognize when the proposals of subordinates make sense and when they do not.[40]

President George W. Bush's decision to go to war against Iraq was based on a flawed decision-making process within the administration. Bush ordered the overthrow of Saddam Hussein because he believed that Iraq possessed weapons of mass destruction (WMD), which are nuclear, chemical, and biological weapons designed to inflict widespread military and civilian casualties. The United States had to act, the president declared, before Iraq gave WMD to terrorist groups that could then use them against the United States or its allies. The conclusion that Iraq possessed WMD, however, was wrong. The administration not only misinterpreted some of the intelligence it received, but also attempted to influence the nature of that intelligence to support its position. It sought evidence to prove that Iraq possessed WMD while ignoring information to the contrary. Furthermore, Bush decided to go to war without deliberating with his advisors as to whether war was necessary. The White House shut out Secretary of State Colin Powell from the decision-making process and ignored warnings from the military.[41]

inefficient staff makes the president appear incompetent. During the first two years of the Clinton administration, a disorganized White House staff contributed to the president's penchant for putting off decisions and failing to stick to decisions once they were made. As a result, Clinton developed a reputation for indecision and inconsistency, a reputation that contributed to substantial Democratic losses in the 1994 congressional elections. Leon Panetta, whom Clinton named chief of staff in 1994, brought discipline to the White House, enabling the president to rehabilitate his image and win re-election in 1996.[39]

The tendency of newly elected presidents to select old friends and campaign aides who are unfamiliar with Washington politics to serve in the White House often undermines the president's effectiveness. The problem is made worse if the president is also inexperienced in national politics. Healthcare reform was the foremost goal of Clinton's first term in office. The president appointed a task force chaired by Hillary Clinton to hold hearings and develop a plan to be presented to Congress. Because the task force lacked broad-based representation and conducted much of its work in secret, it failed to develop a plan with enough support to pass Congress, and the effort became an embarrassing failure.

The challenge for a president is to develop a leadership style that

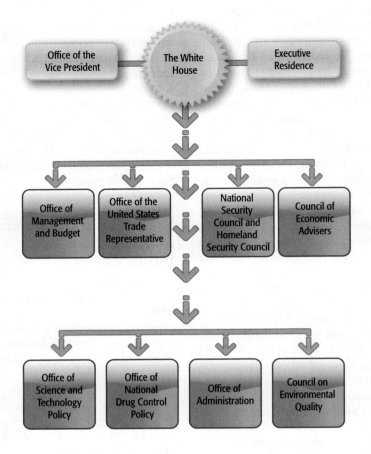

President Obama consults closely with his National Security Council and foreign policy advisors before making substantial foreign policy decisions. Here he speaks to reporters alongside General David Petraeus, then commander of U.S. forces in Afghanistan, and Robert Gates, who served as defense secretary.

THEORIES OF PRESIDENTIAL LEADERSHIP

 What approaches do political scientists use to understand the concept of presidential power?

Political scientists take different approaches to describing and explaining presidential leadership.

Presidential Character

Political scientist James David Barber believes that a president's performance in office depends on personality traits formed primarily during childhood, adolescence, and early adulthood. Barber classifies personality along two dimensions. The first dimension involves the amount of energy an individual brings to the office. Active presidents throw themselves into their work, immersing themselves in the details of the office, whereas passive presidents devote relatively little energy and effort to the job. The second dimension to Barber's personality classification scheme involves the president's attitude toward the job. Positive presidents enjoy their work. They have an optimistic, positive attitude. Negative presidents feel burdened by the weight of the office. They tend to be pessimists.

Barber uses these two dimensions to create four general types of presidential personalities: active–positive, active–negative, passive–positive, and passive–negative. According to Barber, the best type of personality for a president is active-positive. This president is self-confident, optimistic, flexible, and enjoys the job. Barber classifies FDR, Truman, Kennedy, Ford, Carter, George H. W. Bush, and Clinton as active-positive presidents.

Barber believes that the most dangerous chief executive is the active-negative president. This type of president puts great energy into work, but derives little pleasure from it. Barber says that active-negative presidents suffer from low self-esteem and tend to view political disputes in terms of personal success or failure. They are pessimistic, driven, and compulsive. Active-negative presidents tend to overreact to crises and continue failed policies long after it is clear they do not work because to admit error would be to lose control. Barber classifies Nixon, Hoover, and Johnson as active-negative presidents.

Barber lists two other categories of presidential personalities, passive-positive and passive-negative. Barber identifies Eisenhower as a passive-negative president, that is, one who is involved in politics out of a sense of duty. The passive-negative president avoids conflict and uncertainty and just plain dislikes politics. Finally, the passive-positive president is indecisive and superficially optimistic. This president tends to react rather than initiate. Barber classifies Reagan as passive-positive.[42]

Scholars identify a number of weaknesses with Barber's classification scheme. It is not always clear in which category a president should be placed. President Reagan can be labeled *passive* because of his inattentiveness and willingness to allow aides to carry a good deal of his workload. Nonetheless, the Reagan administration had a substantial impact on public policy, taking important initiatives in a wide range of policy areas. Is that the record of a passive president? Some critics complain that Barber's categories are so broad as to be little help in differentiating among presidents. Barber puts Presidents Franklin Roosevelt, Carter, and the first President Bush in the same category—active-positive. How helpful is Barber's classification scheme if

such different presidents fit in the same category? Historians typically rank Franklin Roosevelt among the best of the nation's presidents, whereas Carter and George H. W. Bush are considered only average. Finally, Barber's scheme ignores the political climate in which a president serves. The success or failure of a chief executive depends on a number of factors in addition to the president's personality traits.[43]

Leadership Style

Some scholars believe that the ability of a president to effectively use the powers of the office depends on leadership style. Political scientist Fred I. Greenstein takes this approach by identifying six qualities associated with effective presidential leadership:

- **Communication skills**. Greenstein identifies Franklin Roosevelt, Kennedy, Reagan, Clinton, and Obama as effective public communicators. In contrast, he says that both George H.W. Bush and George W. Bush were relatively ineffective communicators because they were prone to misstatements.

- **Organizational capacity**. According to Greenstein, Truman, Eisenhower, Kennedy, Ford, and the elder Bush had strong organizational skills, but Lyndon Johnson, Carter, and Clinton did not. Greenstein says that George W. Bush failed to create an organizational structure that would facilitate an effective decision-making process.

- **Political skill**. Greenstein says that Johnson was a skilled, determined political operator; in contrast, Carter had a poor reputation among fellow policymakers. Greenstein gives both George W. Bush and Obama high marks for being politically skilled.

- **Vision**. Eisenhower, Kennedy, Nixon, Reagan, and George W. Bush all had a capacity to inspire support for achieving a set of overarching goals. In the meantime, Greenstein believes that George H. W. Bush was weak in this area. Obama thus far has pursued policies that are influenced less by "abstract doctrine" than by "pragmatic efforts."

- **Cognitive skill**. Both Carter and Nixon were skilled at understanding complex issues by reducing them to their component parts. Truman and Reagan were less skilled. Greenstein faults George W. Bush for a management style that relied too heavily on his staff to provide the backup for his policy actions and that approach may have led him to error on the question of WMD in Iraq. Obama's cognitive style is marked by "intelligence, analytic detachment, and a capacity for complex thinking."[44]

- **Emotional intelligence**. Greenstein says that Eisenhower, Ford, and both Bushes were emotionally mature individuals able to focus on their responsibilities without distraction. In contrast, he labels Johnson, Nixon, Carter, and Clinton as "emotionally handicapped." Greenstien says that Obama is cool under pressure, but has difficulty conveying sympathy or compassion.[45]

Barber's Classification of Presidential Character

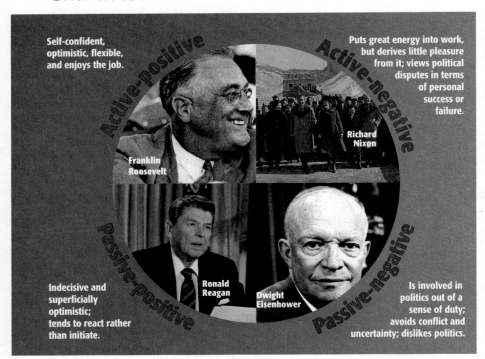

Self-confident, optimistic, flexible, and enjoys the job.

Active-positive

Active-negative

Puts great energy into work, but derives little pleasure from it; views political disputes in terms of personal success or failure.

Richard Nixon

Franklin Roosevelt

Passive-positive

Passive-negative

Indecisive and superficially optimistic; tends to react rather than initiate.

Ronald Reagan

Dwight Eisenhower

Is involved in politics out of a sense of duty; avoids conflict and uncertainty; dislikes politics.

The Power to Persuade

Political scientist Richard Neustadt believes that presidents succeed or fail based on their skills as political bargainers and coalition builders. Although the presidency is regarded as a powerful office, Neustadt points out that presidents lack authority to command public officials other than the members of the White House staff, some executive branch appointees, and the members of the armed forces. Under America's constitutional system, the members of Congress, federal judges, and state officials do not take orders from the president. Because presidents cannot command, they must convince other political actors to cooperate with them voluntarily. The power of the president, Neustadt says, is the power to persuade.

Presidents must bargain with other political actors and groups to try to win their cooperation. Presidents are brokers, consensus builders. In this task, presidents have several assets: they have a number of appointments to make; they prepare the budget; they can help supporters raise money for reelec-

> Because presidents cannot command, they must **convince other political actors to cooperate** with them voluntarily.

tion; and they can appeal to others on the basis of the national interest or party loyalty. To use these assets to their fullest, presidents must understand the dynamics of political power.[46]

Neustadt's approach can be used to explain the presidencies of Lyndon Johnson and Jimmy Carter. President Johnson learned as majority leader in the Senate how to build a political coalition to get legislation passed. In the White House, he put those skills to work and won passage for his legislative program, which was known as the Great Society. In contrast, President Carter never

mastered the mechanics of political power. He ran for president as an outsider, someone who was not tainted by Washington politics. Once in office, Carter appeared standoffish, and thought he could govern without bargaining. He was wrong. Politics involves negotiation, give-and-take, and compromise. Carter never understood that and consequently failed to accomplish many of his goals.

Going Public

Political scientist Samuel Kernell has updated the Neustadt approach. Kernell believes that contemporary presidents often must adopt a media-oriented strategy, which he calls "going public," if they are to achieve their goals in today's political environment. In 1981, for example, President Reagan went on television to ask citizens to contact their representatives in Congress to support his economic program. The public responded and Congress approved the president's budget proposals.

Media-oriented approaches are not new—Franklin Roosevelt was famous for his fireside chats on the radio—but the strategy has become more common. Modern communications and transportation technologies make going public relatively easy. Furthermore, today's presidential selection process tends to favor people who are better at public appeals than political bargaining. Perhaps most important, going public has become an easier and more efficient method for achieving political goals than bargaining. In the 1950s, a president pushing a policy agenda had to bargain with a handful of party leaders and committee chairs in Congress. Today, power in Congress

President John F. Kennedy was a skilled communicator. Here, in a speech at Rice University in 1962, Kennedy committed the nation to land an astronaut on the moon within the decade.

is more fragmented and the number of interest groups active in Washington politics has increased. As a result, it has become easier for presidents to go public than to engage in political bargaining.[47] Contemporary presidents advance their policy agendas through speeches, public appearances, political travel, and targeted outreach aimed at particular groups of voters.[48]

The George W. Bush administration illustrates both the strengths and limitations of the going public strategy. Bush effectively used the going public strategy to bring the threat of Iraq to the top of the public agenda and put pressure on Congress to approve his war policy. Intense public concern over Iraq made Democrats in Congress wary about opposing the president on Iraq because it could open them to the charge that they were soft on national defense. Nearly 40 percent of House Democrats and 57 percent of Senate Democrats joined nearly every Republican member of Congress in voting in favor of the resolution to authorize the use of military force in Iraq.[49] In contrast, President Bush's effort to reform Social Security failed because he was unable to convince a majority of the public that private retirement accounts were a good idea. As a result, it was easy for Democrats in Congress to oppose the president on the issue and difficult for

Republicans to support him. Going public is an ineffective strategy if the president's proposed initiative lacks public support.[50]

Unilateral Tools of Presidential Power

Professor Christopher S. Kelley says that presidents have certain "power tools" that allow the president to take unilateral action without direct congressional authorization or approval.[51] These tools include the following:

- **Executive orders**. They enable the president to adopt a number

of important policies without legislative approval.

- **Executive agreements**. They give the president an important tool for conducting foreign relations that does not require Senate.[52]
- **Presidential signing statements**. They enable the president to define the scope and limitations of legislation passed by Congress.
- **Recess appointments**. By filling vacancies during a period of time when Congress is in recess, the president can temporarily make appointments without the advice and consent of the Senate.[53]

TAKE ✔ ACTION
Why Do They Run?

Have you ever wondered why people seek political office? Do they want personal power? Do they hope to accomplish policy objectives? Are they motivated by a desire to serve the community?

Investigate the answers to these questions by interviewing an elected official in your area. Keep in mind that most public officials are busy, so local judges, school board members, community college trustees, and city council members may prove more accessible. Call or e-mail the official's office to introduce yourself and request 15 minutes or so for an interview, either on the phone or in person. Before you conduct the interview, learn as much as you can about the office and the official so you can make the most of the opportunity. Study the questions you want to ask so you will be able to speak in a conversational tone of voice.

Begin the interview by thanking the official for his or her time. Explain that you will report to your class on what you learn.

The following questions can serve as a guideline for your interview.

- Is this the first elected office you have held? (If not, ask what other posts the official has held.)
- Why did you decide to seek this office?
- About how many hours a week do you spend on the job?
- What do you like most about your position in local government?
- What do you like least about your position?
- Are you glad you sought this office and won? Why or why not?

Once you have completed the interview, thank the official again for his or her time. You will also want to write the official a thank-you letter for taking time to chat with you. Prepare a short oral report for your class on the interview, including your impressions of the official, and whether you are interested in running for office yourself.

PRESIDENTIAL POPULARITY

13.6 *What factors affect presidential popularity?*

Presidential popularity influences presidential power. A president's personal popularity affects the position of the president as a political broker and the ability of the president to appeal to the public for policy support. A president who is politically popular can offer more benefits and induce-

ments to other political actors for their cooperation than can an unpopular chief executive. Campaign help from a popular president is more valuable, and support for legislative proposals is more effective. Similarly, a popular president can claim to speak for the national interest with greater credibility.

A popular president enjoys more success with Congress than an unpopular chief executive. After September 11, 2001, President Bush's approval rating soared. Republican members of Congress eagerly associated themselves with the president, and Democrats were reluctant to oppose him. Congress passed legislation embodying the president's policy proposals dealing with taxes, the budget, government reorganization, Iraq, and the war on terror. By 2006, however, Bush's approval rating had fallen below 40 percent and members of Congress from both parties found it easy to oppose the president's legislative agenda. Democrats attacked Bush at every opportunity while Republican members of Congress boasted of their independence from the White House.

Presidential **popularity** influences presidential **power**.

New presidents are popular, at least for a few months. The tendency of a president to enjoy a high level of public support during the early months of an administration is known as the **honeymoon effect**. In the first few months of an administration, opposition political leaders and the press usually reserve judgment, waiting for the president to act before offering comment. Most voters, regardless of party affiliation, tell poll-takers that they approve of the president's performance in office because they have heard few complaints on which to base disapproval. President Obama enjoyed an initial approval rating of 68 percent; he averaged 63 percent during his first three months in office. Those figures were about average for recent presidents—higher than comparable numbers for Clinton, Reagan, and both Bushes, but lower than the ratings for Kennedy, Nixon, and Carter.

Once an administration begins making controversial policy decisions, however, opposition leaders and the media begin to criticize the president's performance. As the criticism mounts, the president's popularity invariably falls, especially among people who identify with the opposition political party.[54] Obama's honeymoon lasted about seven months, which is average for recent presidents. After beginning his presidency with approval ratings in the 60 percent range, Obama's popularity fell below 55 percent by late summer, 2009. Obama's honeymoon was

longer than that enjoyed by George W. Bush and Clinton, but shorter than the honeymoons of Richard Nixon and George H. W. Bush.[55]

Presidential approval responds to events. In domestic policy matters, presidential popularity rises with good news and falls with bad news, especially news concerning the economy. Although President Reagan was called the "Teflon President"—regardless of what went wrong, no blame stuck to him—he was an unpopular president during the recession of 1982. Only when the economy began to recover did Reagan's popular standing again exceed the 50 percent approval mark. President Clinton got off to such a slow start that the Democratic Party lost control of both houses of Congress in the 1994 midterm elections. Subsequently, a strong economy helped the president recover in the polls and win reelection in 1996 by a comfortable margin.

Presidential popularity rises dramatically during times of international crisis because of the **rally effect**, which is the tendency of the general public to express support for the incumbent president during a time of international threat. Political scientist John Mueller defines the rally effect as "being associated with an event which 1) is international and 2) involves the United States and particularly the president directly." Mueller says that the event must be "specific, dramatic, and sharply focused."[56] Mueller found that the "public seems to react to both 'good' and 'bad' international events in about the same way"—with a burst of heightened presidential approval.[57] For example, President George W. Bush's standing in the polls soared after September 11, 2001. The percentage of Americans who told survey researchers that they approved of Bush's performance in office leaped from 51 percent in early September to 90 percent later in the month.[58] Bush's popularity level also jumped when the United States invaded Iraq and then again when Saddam Hussein was captured.

The appearance and size of a rally effect depends on how the crisis

is presented to the public in terms of media coverage, comments from opposition political leaders, and statements from the White House.[59] When the nation appears threatened from abroad, the political criticism that generally accompanies presidential action is muted. The White House is able to get its interpretation of events before the public because opposition political leaders do not want to be accused of undermining the president during an international crisis. The public tends to support the president because the only messages it hears about the president's handling of the crisis are positive messages, usually conveyed by the White House itself or the president's allies in Congress.[60] Even though 9/11 was a national disaster, President Bush's approval rating soared because no one, at least initially, publicly raised

honeymoon effect the tendency of a president to enjoy a high level of public support during the early months of an administration.

rally effect the tendency of the general public to express support for the incumbent president during a time of international threat.

Presidential Approval Ratings

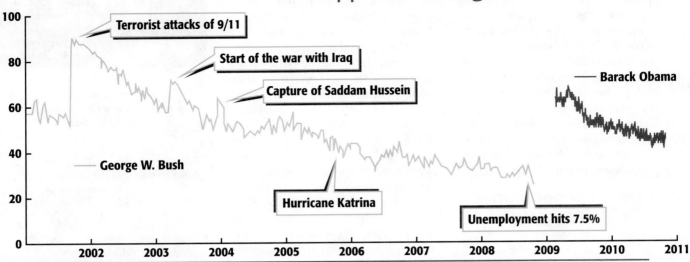

The approval rating for President George W. Bush rose dramatically after 9/11, a classic example of a rally effect. Bush saw his popularity sink to near record lows during the latter years of his administration. The opinion rating for President Obama showed a honeymoon followed by a slow but steady decline in popularity through 2009 and most of 2010.

Source: Gallup Poll and USA Today/Gallup Poll, available at http://www.pollingreport.com/BushJob1.htm and www.gallup.com.

questions about the administration's failure to foresee or prevent the terrorist attacks. Instead, the media were filled with images of the president comforting the families of the victims and declaring that the United States would bring to justice the people responsible for the attacks.[61]

The public responds differently to a domestic crisis than it does to an international crisis. Whereas opposition political leaders and the press typically withhold judgment in an international crisis, they are quick to criticize if something goes wrong domestically. Consider the reaction to Hurricane Katrina in August 2005 and its impact on President Bush's standing in the polls. Within days of the hurricane's coming ashore, opposition political leaders and the news media were blasting the Bush administration for inadequately responding to the disaster. Between late August and October 2005, the president's popularity rating fell by five percentage points.[62]

A rally effect has only a short-term impact on presidential popularity. According to a study conducted by the Gallup organization, a president's approval rating reverts to previous levels within seven months of

an international crisis unless other factors intervene, such as changing economic conditions.[63] At the beginning of an international crisis, the president enjoys near-unanimous support from members of the president's political party and strong support from independents and members of the other party. As the political climate returns to normal, the press and opposition party lead-

ers begin voicing criticism, initially about domestic policy matters and eventually about foreign affairs, as well. Although members of the president's party usually continue to support the incumbent, members of the other party and independents began to register their displeasure with the president's performance and the president's overall standing in the polls falls.[64]

President George W. Bush's popularity soared after 9/11. No one initially questioned the failure of the administration to prevent the attack. Instead, the media were filled with images of the president standing arm in arm with the first responders at Ground Zero.

TAKING SIDES

Signing Statements and Executive-Legislative Relations

Does presidential use of signing statements subvert the separation of powers?

Are signing statements unconstitutional?

OVERVIEW

Signing statements have been used by every president since James Monroe, so they are not a recent phenomenon. Signing statements are written pronouncements issued by the president when signing a bill into law and are printed in the U.S. Code along with the legislation. Essentially, they indicate the direction the president intends to take regarding the particular legislation. What has made them particularly controversial of late is the extent to which President George W. Bush used them to declare

certain provisions of a law unconstitutional; 87 percent of his 147 signing statements declared that some aspects of the law were unconstitutional and therefore would not be implemented by the executive branch.[65]

In 2006, for example, Congress passed a bill that would restrain the military's use of torture. In order to avoid having to veto the law, with the threat of his veto being overridden, President Bush signed the measure into law but issued a signing statement indicating that the executive

branch was in control of the military and thus Congress had no constitutional right to set rules about interrogating prisoners.

The American Bar Association released a report arguing that signing statements are akin to the line item veto, which the Supreme Court declared unconstitutional in 1998 in *Clinton v. New York City*. The ABA believes that if the president wants a line item veto, or if Congress wants to give him one, then a constitutional amendment is necessary.

 SUPPORTING
the use of signing statements

 AGAINST
the use of signing statements

Signing statements guide executive branch officials on how to interpret or administer a statute. The legislation that Congress passes is hardly comprehensive, and particular provisions are open to interpretation. An essential part of the president "executing" the laws is providing guidelines on how he thinks the law should be administered.

Executive review is important to the separated power system. Congress has the power and authority to make law, with some constitutional checks by both the judiciary and the president. If a president believes that parts of a law are unconstitutional, he can declare that he will selectively administer the law. Legal decision-making is a part of executive power.

Signing statements are public statements of policy intent. These statements allow the public to see the president's views on the effects of the law, and his plans for implementing it. They can be examined by both Congress and the people, and add to the conversation about legislation.

The Constitution requires that the president "shall take care that the laws be faithfully executed." Therefore, once a bill is passed in Congress and the president chooses to sign rather than veto it, the president is obligated to implement all its provisions and not just the ones he likes.

Allowing signing statements puts too much power in a unitary executive. This presidential power grab is an unconstitutional tipping of the balance of power away from the legislature, which the founders intended to be the locus of power in the federal government.

Legislative bargaining happens when all sides come to the table as equal parties. The president uses signing statements after all the negotiating has happened, which is a violation of bargaining. Congress conceded points to the president, but when his signing statement negates all of his own concessions, Congress will have no incentive to come to the table to bargain in the future.

what we LEARNED

THE CONSTITUTIONAL PRESIDENCY

13.1 *How does the Constitution define the office of the presidency?*

The Constitution declares that the president must be at least 35 years of age, a natural-born American citizen, and a resident of the U.S. for at least 14 years. The Twenty-Second Amendment declares that no president can be elected to more than two four-year terms. The House has the authority to impeach a president by majority vote, with the Senate deciding by a two-thirds vote whether to remove the president from office. The vice president succeeds a president who is removed, resigns, or dies in office.

PRESIDENTIAL POWERS

13.2 *What are the powers of the presidency?*

As chief of state, the president has broad diplomatic authority to conduct foreign relations. The president is commander in chief of the armed forces, and can take actions in the area of foreign and defense policy because of inherent powers vested in the national government. The president nominates all federal judges pending confirmation by the Senate and has the authority to grant pardons and reprieves. As chief executive, the president is empowered to issue executive orders, which presidents have used to enact important policies. The Constitution gives the president some tools for influencing the legislative process, including the veto.

THE DEVELOPMENT OF THE MODERN PRESIDENCY

13.3 *How did the modern presidency develop?*

Since the nineteenth century, the presidency has moved from the periphery of national politics to its center. Presidential power grows during time of crises, such as wars and economic depressions, because they increase public pressure for the government to act. Political scientists identify three factors responsible for the modern presidency: 1) the U.S. has emerged as a world power, 2) the presidential selection process favors individuals with big ideas rather than party loyalists, and 3) the executive branch of government has grown.

THE ORGANIZATION OF THE PRESIDENCY

13.4 *How does the presidential bureaucracy assist the chief executive in carrying out the duties of the office?*

The development of the modern presidency has been accompanied by a significant growth in the size and power of the presidential bureaucracy. The White House staff, which is chosen without need of Senate confirmation, gives the president advice on policy issues, screens key appointments, manages press relations, and organizes the president's workday. The Executive Office of the President is the group of White House offices and agencies that develop and implement the policies and programs of the president.

THEORIES OF PRESIDENTIAL LEADERSHIP

13.5 *What different approaches do political scientists use to understand the concept of presidential power?*

Political scientists take different approaches to describing and explaining presidential leadership. Barber believes that a president's performance in office depends on personality traits, classified along two dimensions—energy and attitude. Greenstein identifies six qualities associated with effective presidential leadership: communication skills, organizational skills, political skills, vision, cognitive skill, and emotional intelligence. Neustadt believes that presidents succeed or fail based on their skills as political bargainers and coalition builders. Kernell contends that contemporary presidents often must adopt a media-oriented strategy, which he calls "going public," if they are to achieve their goals in today's political environment. A number of political scientists point out that presidents have unilateral tools of power, such as executive orders or recess appointments.

PRESIDENTIAL POPULARITY

13.6 *What factors affect presidential popularity?*

Popular presidents are more influential than unpopular presidents. The tendency of a president to enjoy a high level of public support during the early stages of an administration is known as the honeymoon effect. Once a new president begins making policy decisions, opposition leaders and the media begin to criticize the performance and the president's popularity falls. In domestic policy matters, presidential popularity rises with good news and falls with bad news, especially news concerning the economy. Presidential popularity rises dramatically during times of international crisis because of the rally effect.

TEST yourself

13.1 *How does the Constitution define the office of the presidency?*

1   After winning reelection in 2004, President George W. Bush was a lame duck. What does that phrase mean?
   a.   President Bush was unpopular.
   b.   President Bush was ineligible to run for reelection.
   c.   President Bush had to deal with a Congress controlled by the opposition party.
   d.   President Bush faced impeachment charges.

2   Which of the following presidents was impeached and removed from office?
   a.   Andrew Johnson
   b.   Richard Nixon
   c.   Bill Clinton
   d.   None of the above

3   Which of the following statements about the vice presidency is true?
   a.   The vice president votes in the Senate only to break a tie.
   b.   The policymaking influence of the vice president today is significantly greater than it was 50 years ago.
   c.   In case of presidential disability, the vice president can become acting president.
   d.   All of the above

13.2 *What are the powers of the presidency?*

4   What is the difference between an executive agreement and a treaty?
   a.   Executive agreements do not require Senate ratification.
   b.   Treaties are more numerous than executive agreements.
   c.   The president negotiates treaties but members of Congress negotiate executive agreements.
   d.   None of the above

5   Which of the following statements about the War Powers Act is true?
   a.   It only applies to officially declared wars.
   b.   It requires the president to consult with Congress whenever possible before committing American forces to combat.
   c.   It has proved an effective check on the president's authority as commander in chief.
   d.   None of the above

6   What constitutional authority does the president have over the Supreme Court?
   a.   The president can fill vacancies by appointment subject to Senate confirmation.
   b.   The president can veto Supreme Court rulings subject to possible override by the Court.
   c.   The president can initiate removal proceedings against justices.
   d.   None of the above

7   A pronouncement issued by the president at the time a bill passed by Congress is signed into law is known as which of the following?
   a.   A veto statement
   b.   The state of the union address
   c.   A presidential signing statement
   d.   An executive order

13.3 *How did the modern presidency develop?*

8   Many political scientists believe that the era of the modern presidency began with the administration of which of the following presidents?
   a.   Franklin Roosevelt
   b.   Theodore Roosevelt
   c.   Abraham Lincoln
   d.   Woodrow Wilson

9   Which of the following statements best embodies the concept of the partisan presidency?
   a.   The president is stronger in foreign and defense policymaking than in domestic policymaking.
   b.   The president uses the White House to further the interests of his or her political party.
   c.   The presidency uses political bargaining to achieve policy goals.
   d.   The president works closely with congressional leaders of both political parties.

13.4 *How does the presidential bureaucracy assist the chief executive in carrying out the duties of the office?*

10   Which of the following presidential appointments does *not* require Senate confirmation?
   a.   A cabinet secretary
   b.   A federal judge
   c.   An ambassador
   d.   A member of the White House staff

11   Which of the following agencies is part of the Executive Office of the President?
   a.   Department of Justice
   b.   Federal Communication Commission (FCC)
   c.   Office of Management and Budget (OMB)
   d.   All of the above

13.5 *What approaches do political scientists use to understand the concept of presidential power?*

12   Which of the following political scientists analyzes presidential performance based on the personality traits of the president?
   a.   Samuel Kernell
   b.   Richard Neustadt
   c.   Fred I. Greenstein
   d.   James David Barber

13   Which of the following political scientists analyzes presidential performance based on the chief executive's skill as a political bargainer and coalition builder?
   a.   Samuel Kernell
   b.   Richard Neustadt
   c.   Fred I. Greenstein
   d.   James David Barber

13.6 *What factors affect presidential popularity?*

14   When a president first takes office, public opinion polls typically indicate that the president enjoys a high approval rating. Which of the following terms describes this phenomenon?
   a.   Honeymoon effect
   b.   Two-presidencies thesis
   c.   Coattail effect
   d.   Rally effect

15   President George W. Bush's approval rating soared after September 11, 2001. Which of the following terms would political scientists use to describe that phenomenon?
   a.   Two-presidencies thesis
   b.   Coattail effect
   c.   Honeymoon effect
   d.   Rally effect

KNOW the score

14–15 correct: Congratulations—you know your American government!

12–13 correct: Your understanding of this chapter is weak—be sure to review the key terms and visit TheThinkSpot.

<12 correct: Reread the chapter more thoroughly.

Answers: 1) b, 2) d, 3) d, 4) a, 5) b, 6) a, 7) c, 8) a, 9) b, 10) d, 11) c, 12) d, 13) b, 14) a, 15) d

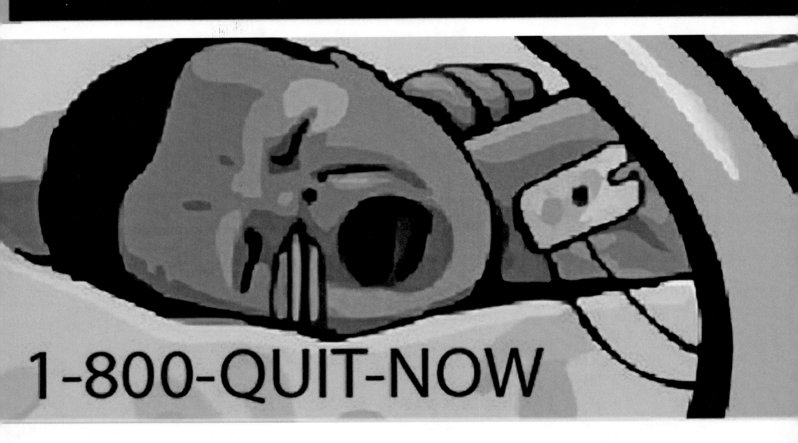

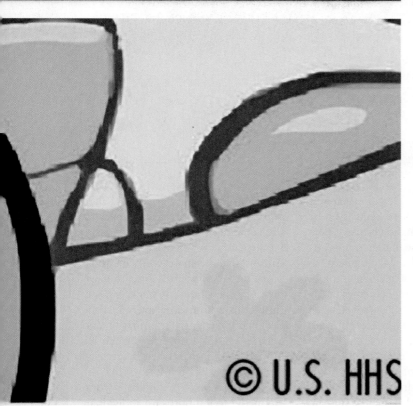

© U.S. HHS

The Food and Drug Administration (FDA) has adopted a regulation requiring tobacco companies to display larger, more prominent health warnings on all cigarette packaging and advertising in the United States. Beginning no later than September 2012, each cigarette package and advertisement must display one of nine different text warnings with accompanying color graphics. The warning labels must cover the top half of the front and back of a cigarette package and occupy at least 20 percent of advertising space. The FDA's goals in requiring the new warning labels are as follows:

* Increase awareness of the health risks associated with smoking, such as death, addiction, lung disease, cancer, stroke, and heart disease;
* Encourage smokers to quit; and
* Empower young people to say no to tobacco.[1]

The FDA hoped that the new warning labels with the graphic images would enable antismoking forces to regain momentum in the war against smoking. The old warnings had been unchanged

BUREAUCRACY

for 25 years. The adult smoking rate of 21 percent has not significantly improved since 2004, and one-fifth of high-school students smoke.

The FDA gets its authority to regulate tobacco packaging and advertising from Congress. In 2009, Congress passed and President Barack Obama signed the Family Smoking and Control Act to give the FDA authority to regulate the manufacture, distribution, and sale of tobacco products. The FDA adopted the new set of warning labels and accompanying graphics through the rulemaking process.

Reynolds American Inc., Lorillard, and other tobacco companies have responded to the new warning labels by filing suit, arguing that the FDA is violating their freedom of speech rights under the First Amendment. The companies contend that the dangers of smoking are well known and that the sole purpose of the new labels is to stigmatize smokers. A federal judge has ruled against the companies, but the case is on appeal and may eventually be decided by the U.S. Supreme Court.[2]

The controversy over the FDA's tobacco regulation introduces this chapter on the federal bureaucracy. The chapter begins by describing the major administrative units that make up the executive branch of American national government. It then examines federal personnel policies. The chapter explains the rulemaking process and discusses the politics of administrative policymaking from the perspectives of various important political actors, including the president, Congress, interest groups, and federal bureaucrats. Finally, the chapter compares and contrasts the concepts of subgovernments and issue networks.

ORGANIZATION
OF THE BUREAUCRACY

14.1 *What is the structure of the executive branch?*

The organization of the executive branch of American national government seems a bit haphazard. The Constitution is silent about the organization of the executive branch other than discussing the selection, powers, and responsibilities of the president and vice president. The agencies and departments that make up the rest of the executive branch have been created by Congress and the president through the legislative process over the last 220 years.

Cabinet Departments

The **cabinet departments** are major administrative units of the federal government that have responsibility for the conduct of a wide range of government operations. The 15 cabinet departments (in the order of their creation) are as follows: State, Defense, Treasury, Justice, Interior, Agriculture, Commerce, Labor, Housing and Urban Development (HUD), Transportation, Energy, Health and Human Services, Education, Veterans Affairs, and Homeland Security. The largest departments in terms of personnel are Defense and Veterans Affairs. In 2008, the Department of Defense had 682,000 civilian employees; the Department of Veterans Affairs employed 265,000 workers. In contrast, fewer than 4,210 employees worked for the Department of Education, the smallest department.[3] Each cabinet department includes a number of smaller administrative units with a variety of titles, such as bureau, agency, commission, administration, center, service, and institute. For example, the Department of Homeland Security includes Customs and Border Protection, Transportation Security Administration, Immigration and Customs Enforcement, U.S. Coast Guard, U.S. Secret Service, and Citizenship and Immigration Service.

With the exception of the head of the Justice Department, who is the attorney general, the people who lead the cabinet departments are called secretaries. The president appoints the secretaries and their chief assistants pending Senate confirmation. Although the Senate confirms most presidential appointments, the approval process has grown increasingly time-consuming. The average time between presidential nomination and Senate confirmation for executive branch appointees has increased steadily from 2.35 months for the nominees of President John Kennedy[4] to 9 months for individuals nominated by President George W. Bush.[5] Dozens of nominees remained unconfirmed more than a year after President Obama took office.

Confirmation delays have steadily increased, regardless of

cabinet departments major administrative units of the federal government that have responsibility for the conduct of a wide range of government operations.

Departments in the Presidential Cabinet

STATE Conducts foreign policy, including negotiating treaties and executive agreements

TREASURY Manages government finance

DEFENSE Provides for national defense

JUSTICE Enforces the law

INTERIOR Manages the nation's natural resources, including wildlife and public lands

AGRICULTURE Promotes agriculture, implements food and nutrition programs

COMMERCE Assists businesses and conducts the U.S. Census

LABOR Administers labor laws

HEALTH & HUMAN SERVICES Implements health, welfare, and old-age security programs

HOUSING AND URBAN DEVELOPMENT Manages urban and housing programs

TRANSPORTATION Oversees national transportation system, including highway and mass transit programs

ENERGY Manages energy policy and research

EDUCATION Administers federal education policy, including the No Child Left Behind Act

VETERANS AFFAIRS Administers programs aiding veterans

HOMELAND SECURITY Protects against terrorism and responds to natural disasters

party control of Congress and the White House, because of bureaucratic red tape and because individual senators have increased the use of a parliamentary procedure called a hold that allows an individual senator to privately delay a vote on a nomination. Holds are used as bargaining chips to extract concessions from the administration on unrelated matters or to retaliate over other issues.[6] In early 2010, for example, Republican Senator Richard Shelby of Alabama placed a blanket hold on more than 70 administration nominees because he was concerned about a pair of government spending projects in his home state. The holds had nothing to do with the qualifications of the nominees.[7] If a senator puts a hold on a nominee and refuses to remove it, the Senate can vote on confirmation only if the Senate as a whole invokes cloture and that is a time-consuming procedure that requires 60 votes.

Presidents can sometimes avoid the confirmation process by making appointments when the Senate is in recess. According to the Constitution, recess appointees serve until the end of the next session of the Senate. Senator Shelby dropped most of his holds after Obama made it known that he intended to use the 2010 Presidents' Day holiday to fill vacant positions with recess appointments.[8]

> Holds are used as **bargaining chips** to extract **concessions** from the Administration.

Presidents employ a number of criteria in selecting department heads. They look for knowledge, administrative ability, experience, loyalty, and congeniality. Some cabinet posts may be given to reward campaign assistance. Modern presidents want a cabinet that includes both men and women, and that reflects the ethnic and racial diversity of the United States. Presidents also seek individuals who fit the style and image of the department and who will be acceptable to the interest groups with which the department works most closely. The secretary of the treasury, for example, is typically someone with a background in banking or finance. The secretary of agriculture is a farmer, usually from the Midwest.

Finding qualified men and women who are willing to lead cabinet departments is often a challenge. Some potential cabinet officials will not accept an appointment because the position does not pay as well as executive positions in private industry and it lacks job security. Also, some potential cabinet secretaries turn down appointments because they and their families do not want to go through a long and often intrusive confirmation process.

The heads of the cabinet departments are part of the

President Obama meeting with his entire cabinet, including the vice president and the heads of the 15 cabinet departments.

president's cabinet, a body that includes the executive department heads and other senior officials chosen by the president, such as the U.S. ambassador to the United Nations. The policymaking role of the cabinet varies from president to president. President Dwight Eisenhower delegated considerable responsibilities to cabinet members. He met with his cabinet two or three times a month. In contrast, contemporary presidents seldom convene their cabinets, relying instead on the White House staff, the Executive Office of the President, and individual department heads. When President Obama considered his options for managing the war in Afghanistan, he assembled a diverse group of policy advisers, including political adviser David Axelrod, Secretary of State Hillary Clinton, Secretary of Defense Robert Gates, National Security Adviser General James Jones, White House Chief of Staff Rahm Emanuel, Central Intelligence Agency (CIA) Director Leon Panetta, and Vice President Joe Biden.[9]

Four cabinet officials—the secretary of state, secretary of defense, secretary of the treasury, and the attorney general—are known as the **inner cabinet** because of the importance of the policy issues their departments address.[10] Full cabinet meetings tend to become forums for presidential pep talks or show-and-tell sessions for cabinet members to discuss the latest developments in their departments. As for leading their departments, many secretaries soon learn that their departments are not easily led. Also, most department heads do not have the time to concentrate on the details of administration. They are too busy dealing with Congress, doing public relations work with their department's constituents, selling the president's program, and campaigning for the president's reelection.

Independent Executive Agencies

Congress and the president have created a number of **independent executive agencies**, executive branch

A Peace Corps volunteer spreads awareness about HIV/AIDS with a group of school children in Africa.

agencies that are not part of any of the 15 cabinet-level departments. The Environmental Protection Agency (EPA) is the federal agency responsible for enforcing the nation's environmental laws. The EPA is headed by an individual administrator, as are the Peace Corps, National Aeronautics and Space Administration (NASA), Central Intelligence Agency (CIA), Social Security Administration (SSA), and the Small Business Administration (SBA). The Federal Election Commission (FEC) is an independent executive agency headed by a multimember commission. The president appoints both individual agency heads and board members, pending confirmation by the Senate. The heads of independent executive agencies report directly to the president and serve at the president's pleasure.

Independent executive agencies perform a range of administrative and regulatory activities. The Peace Corps, for example, is an agency that administers an American foreign aid program under which volunteers travel to developing nations to teach skills and help improve living standards. The National Aeronautics and Space Administration (NASA) is the federal agency in charge of the space program. The Central Intelligence Agency (CIA) is the federal agency that gathers and evaluates foreign intelligence information in the interest of national security. The Environmental Protection Agency (EPA) is

the federal agency responsible for enforcing the nation's environmental laws. The Social Security Administration (SSA) is a federal agency that operates the Social Security system. The Small Business Administration (SBA) is a federal agency established to make loans to small businesses and assist them in obtaining government contracts. The Federal Election Commission (FEC) is the agency that enforces federal campaign finance laws.

Government Corporations

Government corporations are organizationally similar to private corporations except that the government rather than stockholders owns them. Their organizational rationale is that an agency that

president's cabinet an advisory group created by the president that includes the department heads and other officials chosen by the president.

inner cabinet the secretary of state, secretary of defense, secretary of the treasury, and the attorney general.

independent executive agencies executive branch agencies that are not part of any of the 15 cabinet-level departments.

government corporations corporations organizationally similar to private corporations, except that the government rather than stockholders owns them.

makes a product or provides a service should be run by methods similar to those used in the private sector. For example, the Postal Service is a government corporation responsible for mail service. An 11-member board of governors appointed by the president to serve nine-year, overlapping terms leads the agency. The board names a postmaster general to manage the day-to-day operation of the service. In addition to the Postal Service, the list of government corporations includes the National Railroad Passenger Corporation (Amtrak), a federal agency that operates intercity passenger railway traffic. The Federal Deposit Insurance Corporation (FDIC) is a federal agency established to insure depositors' accounts in banks and thrift institutions. The Tennessee Valley Authority (TVA) is a federal agency established to promote the development of the Tennessee River and its tributaries.

An important principle behind government corporations is that they should be self-financing, at least to a significant degree. In the case of the Postal Service, users pay most of the cost of operation by purchasing stamps and paying service charges. Not all government corporations,

however, are financially self-sufficient. Amtrak requires a subsidy from Congress to keep its trains rolling. Amtrak's critics argue that the agency should be forced to pay its own way or go out of business. If the demand for passenger rail is not sufficient to support Amtrak's operation, then the service should end. In contrast, the defenders of Amtrak believe that the agency provides an important service that should be continued. Furthermore, they point out that the government subsidizes automobile transportation by building highways and air transportation by constructing airports.

Foundations and Institutes

Foundations and institutes administer grant programs to local governments, universities, non-profit institutions, and individuals for research in the natural and social sciences or to promote the arts. The National Science Foundation (NSF) is a federal agency established to encourage scientific advances and improvements in science education. The National Endowment for the Arts (NEA) is a federal agency created to nurture cultural expression and promote appreciation of the arts. Foundations and institutes are

governed by multimember boards appointed by the president with Senate concurrence from lists of nominees submitted by various scientific and educational institutions.

Independent Regulatory Commissions

An **independent regulatory commission** is an agency outside the major executive departments that is charged with the regulation of important aspects of the economy. The Federal Trade Commission (FTC), for example, is an agency that regulates business competition, including enforcement of laws against monopolies and the protection of consumers from deceptive trade practices. The Federal Communications Commission (FCC) is an agency that regulates interstate and international radio, television, telephone, telegraph, and satellite communications, as well as licensing radio and television stations. The Securities and Exchange Commission (SEC) is an agency that regulates the sale of stocks and bonds as well as investment and holding

independent regulatory commission
an agency outside the major executive departments that is charged with the regulation of important aspects of the economy.

Where Do Federal Employees Work?

Largest Executive Departments	Number of employees
Defense	682,142
Veterans Affairs	265,390
Homeland Security	165,839
Treasury	111,335
Justice	107,970

Largest Independent Agencies	Number of employees
U.S. Postal Service	744,405
Social Security Administration	62,337
National Aeronautics and Space Administration	18,531
Environmental Protection Agency	18,127

Over 2.7 million people are employed by the federal government. The U.S. Postal Service and the Department of Defense are the largest federal employers.

Source: U.S. Office of Personnel Management, Federal Civilian Workforce Statistics—Employment and Trends, bimonthly.

Lloyd Blankfein, CEO of Goldman Sachs, testifies before a congressional committee after his company is charged with fraud by the Securities and Exchange Commission (SEC) in the wake of the financial crisis on Wall Street.

companies. The Equal Employment Opportunity Commission (EEOC) is an agency that investigates and rules on charges of employment discrimination.

> Congress has attempted to **insulate** independent regulatory commissions from **direct political pressure**.

Congress has attempted to insulate independent regulatory commissions from direct political pressure, especially from the White House. These agencies are headed by boards of three to seven members who are appointed by the president with Senate approval. In contrast to cabinet members and the heads of other executive departments, the president cannot remove regulatory commissioners. Instead, they serve fixed, staggered terms ranging from 3 to 14 years. As a result, a new president must usually wait several years before having much impact on the composition of the boards. Furthermore, the law generally requires that no more than a bare majority of board members be from the same political party.

Congress has designed independent regulatory commissions to provide closer, more flexible regulation than Congress itself can offer through specific language written into legislation. Congress has delegated authority to these agencies to control various business practices using broad, general language. Congress has authorized the FTC, for example, to regulate advertising in the "public

convenience, interest, or necessity." It has empowered the EEOC "to prevent any person from engaging in any unlawful employment practice."

Quasi-Governmental Companies

A **quasi-governmental company** is a private, profit-seeking corporation created by Congress to serve a public purpose. For example, Congress created the Federal National Mortgage Association (Fannie Mae) and Federal Home Loan Mortgage Corporation (Freddie Mac) to increase the availability of credit to home buyers. Fannie Mae and Freddie Mac are profit-making corporations run by 18-member boards of governors appointed by the president with Senate confirmation. They are exempt from state and federal taxation and enjoy a line of credit at the U.S. Treasury. Because of the perception that Congress would bail

them out if they got in financial trouble, Fannie Mae and Freddie Mac pay lower interest rates than they would if they were strictly private enterprises. Lower rates benefit home buyers, some of whom would not be able to qualify to purchase a home at all without the lower interest rate. The Export-Import Bank and the Government National Mortgage Association (Ginnie Mae) are other examples of quasi-governmental companies. The Export-Import Bank provides loan guarantees to foreign purchasers to enable them to acquire American goods. Ginnie Mae, meanwhile, purchases mortgages, pools them, and then issues mortgage-backed securities to investors.[11]

In 2008, Congress passed, and President George W. Bush signed, legislation to commit federal funds to Fannie Mae and Freddie Mac to ensure that they would not collapse under the weight of losses incurred in the housing foreclosure crisis. The federal government eventually took over the operation of Fannie Mae and Freddie Mac, at least temporarily, to prevent their financial collapse, which would have been catastrophic for the home mortgage industry. The action kept Fannie and Freddie in business, but potentially put taxpayers on the hook for billions of dollars in bad loans.

quasi-governmental company a private, profit-seeking corporation created by Congress to serve a public purpose.

The federal government was forced to provide financial support to Fannie Mae and Freddie Mac to keep them from going bankrupt under the weight of the home foreclosure crisis.

PERSONNEL

The size of the federal civilian bureaucracy has grown dramatically since the early days of the nation. In 1800, only about 3,000 persons worked for the U.S. government. That figure grew to 95,000 by 1881 and half a million in 1925. Today, the federal bureaucracy is the largest civilian workforce in the Western world, with 2.7 million civilian employees stationed in every state and city in the country and in almost every nation in the world.[12]

Since the early 1990s, the number of federal civilian employees has generally fallen. Between 1991 and 2001, the federal payroll decreased from 3.1 million to 2.7 million, a decline of nearly 13 percent. After September 11, 2001, the number of federal employees inched up. Congress passed, and the president signed, legislation to make airport baggage screeners federal employees, adding thousands of people to the federal payroll. Employment in other federal agencies that deal with security issues, including the Border Patrol, increased as well. The post-9/11 surge in federal employment peaked in 2003. The size of the federal workforce declined thereafter, before increasing slightly in 2008.

Although the official size of the federal workforce has generally declined since the early 1990s, the actual number of people employed directly and indirectly by the federal government has risen sharply over the same period of time. Political scientist Paul C. Light estimates that the true size of the federal civilian workforce is 14.6 million employees, not the 2.7 million on the official payroll.[13] In addition to civilian employees working directly for the federal government, Light's figure includes millions of contract workers, state and local government employees working on federally funded programs, and federal grant beneficiaries at colleges and universities. The federal government pays their salaries, but their names do not appear on federal personnel rosters. Contract workers collect taxes, prepare budget documents, take notes at meetings, and perform hundreds of other governmental functions. The Department of Defense even hires private security guards to protect military bases in the United States.[14] Furthermore, Congress and the president rely on millions of state and local bureaucrats to administer federal programs such as Medicaid and the Supplemental Nutrition Assistance Program.

Employment Practices

Employment practices in the early days of the nation emphasized character, professional qualifications, and political compatibility with the administration in office. Under President Andrew Jackson (1829–1837), political considerations became paramount. A new president would fire many of the employees of the previous administration and replace them with friends and supporters. To the victor belonged the spoils, they said, and federal jobs were the spoils. The method of hiring government employees from among the friends, relatives, and supporters of elected officeholders was known as the **spoils system**.

spoils system the method of hiring government employees from among the friends, relatives, and supporters of elected officeholders.

TAKE ✓ ACTION

Working for Uncle Sam

More than 2.7 million people work for the federal government in every state and city in the country and in almost every nation in the world. Even small towns are home to federal employees working for the U.S. Postal Service and other agencies. Find a friend, relative, or neighbor who works for the federal government. Chat with him or her about federal employment, and take notes so you can discuss the conversation in class. Use the following questions to guide your discussion:

• For which department or agency do you work, and how long have you been a federal employee?

• What are the advantages and disadvantages of working for the federal government as opposed to a private employer?

• Have you enjoyed your job with the government? Why or why not?

• Do you believe that federal employee compensation should be based on job performance?

• Would you recommend a career in the federal workforce to a college student?

When a disgruntled office seeker assassinated President James Garfield in 1881, Congress passed, and the new president signed, legislation to reform the federal hiring process. The legislation created a Civil Service Commission to establish a hiring system based on competitive examinations and to protect federal workers from dismissal for political reasons. Initially, the civil service system covered only about 10 percent of federal jobs, but Congress gradually expanded coverage to include more than 90 percent of federal workers.[15] In 1939, Congress enacted another reform, the **Hatch Act** (named after its author, Senator Carl Hatch of New Mexico), which was a measure designed to restrict the political activities of federal employees to voting and the private expression of views. The rationale behind the law was to protect government workers from being forced by their superiors to work for particular candidates.

Although civil service ended the spoils system, it, too, became the target of criticism. Many observers charged that the **civil service system** was too inflexible to reward merit, punish poor performance, or transfer civil servants from one agency to another without having to scale a mountain of red tape. In 1978, Congress and the president responded to complaints against the civil service system by enacting a package of reforms. The legislation established a Senior Executive Service (SES) composed of approximately 8,000 top civil servants who would be eligible for substantial merit bonuses but who could be transferred, demoted, or fired more easily than other federal employees. The reform measure replaced the old Civil Service Commission with two new agencies: an Office of Personnel Management to manage the federal workforce and a Merit Systems Protection Board to hear employee grievances.[16] The reforms also provided greater protection for whistleblowers—that is, workers who report wrongdoing or mismanagement—and streamlined procedures for dismissing incompetent employees.[17]

Congress and the president have given federal employees limited rights to organize. Federal workers won the right to form unions in 1912. Fifty years later, President John Kennedy signed an executive order giving federal workers the right to bargain collectively over a limited set of issues but not

Hatch Act a measure designed to restrict the political activities of federal employees to voting and the private expression of views.

civil service system a hiring system based on merit rather than political connections.

Evolution of the FEDERAL BUREAUCRACY

1789 | Congress authorizes the creation of the first federal agency, which it later renamed the Department of State.

1881 | A disgruntled federal office seeker assassinates President James Garfield.

1883 | Congress passes the Civil Service Reform Act (the Pendleton Act), to reform the federal hiring process on the basis of merit rather than patronage.

| 1780 | 1800 | 1820 | 1840 | 1860 | 1880 | 1900 | 1920 |

1829 | President Andrew Jackson ushers in the spoils system, in which political considerations became paramount in hiring government employees.

1933 | The size of the federal bureaucracy balloons during the New Deal era as President Franklin Delano Roosevelt and Congress create a series of federal agencies to regulate industry and put Americans back to work.

about pay or benefits. **Collective bargaining** is a negotiation between an employer and a union representing employees over the terms and conditions of employment. The civil service reform legislation adopted in 1978 guaranteed federal employees the right to bargain collectively over issues other than pay and benefits, but it prohibited federal workers from striking. In 1981, President Ronald Reagan fired more than 11,000 air traffic controllers for participating in a strike organized by the Professional Air Traffic Controllers Association (PATCO).

Democratic presidents typically have a more positive relationship with federal employee organizations than do Republican presidents. Labor unions in general are allied with the Democratic Party, whereas the GOP has stronger ties to management. Democratic President Bill Clinton, for example, issued an executive

think Does the regulation that federal employees cannot strike unfairly limit their bargaining power, or is it necessary to ensure government efficiency and public safety?

order directing federal agencies to develop partnerships with the employee unions. Clinton justified the approach as a means to reform government by making it more efficient. In contrast, President George W. Bush took an adversarial approach toward employee unions. He dissolved the partnership councils created during the Clinton administration and asked Congress to change personnel policies in light of the war on terror.[18]

When Congress created the Department of Homeland Security

(DHS) in 2002, it gave President Bush authority to relax civil service rules to make it easier for the administration to hire, transfer, promote, cross-train, discipline, and fire employees in the new department without having to worry about union rules and civil service procedures. The president argued that the administration needed more flexibility over personnel than the old civil service system provided in order to create a modern workforce capable of responding to the threat of international terrorism. In particular, the administration wanted to base annual salary increases on performance tied to job evaluations, rather than giving every employee an annual raise based on longevity. The Bush administration set out to create a pay-for-performance system not just for DHS but for the whole federal government that would replace the old general schedule system with its 15 GS levels and 10 steps within each level.[19] The new system would make it easier for managers to reward good work and punish poor performance while making it more difficult for unions to intervene on behalf of their members.[20] Soon after taking office, however, President Obama signed an executive order ending the performance-based pay system in DHS, and Congress, now under Democratic control, passed legislation to return DHS employees to the previous longevity based pay system.[21]

1939 | Congress authorizes the establishment of the Executive Office of the President (EOP) to assist in managing the bureaucracy, and passes the Hatch Act, which restricts the political activities of federal employees.

2002 | George W. Bush issues an executive order creating an Office of Homeland Security within the EOP, which is later elevated to a full cabinet department.

1940   1960   1980   2000

1965 | President Lyndon Johnson's Great Society programs result in the largest expansion of the federal bureaucracy since FDR's New Deal.

1978 | Congress enacts a package of reforms, including the creation of an Office of Personnel Management to manage the federal workforce and a Merit Systems Protection Board to hear Systems Protection Board to hear employee grievances.

think Does a performance-based pay system improve employee performance or is it just a way for managers to reward their friends?

collective bargaining a negotiation between an employer and a union representing employees over the terms and conditions of employment.

RULEMAKING

Independent regulatory commissions and regulatory agencies in the executive branch do much of their work through the rulemaking process. When Congress passes regulatory legislation, it frequently delegates authority to make rules for implementing the legislation to the bureaucracy. A **rule** is a legally binding regulation. **Rulemaking** is the regulatory process used by government agencies to enact legally binding regulations. For example, the Clean Air Act requires that the EPA adopt rules to protect the public from exposure to contaminants that are known to be hazardous to human health. On average, federal agencies produce between four and five thousand rules a year.[22]

The rulemaking process begins with an agency giving advance notice that it is considering issuing a rule in a particular policy area. The agency publishes the text of the proposed rule in the *Federal Register* and allows at least 30 days for the public to comment on the proposed rule. Concerned parties, usually interest groups affected by the proposed rule, submit written comments or offer testimony at public hearings. When an agency officially adopts a rule, it is published in the *Code of Federal Regulations*.

> When congress passes regulatory legislation, it **delegates authority** to make rules for implementing the legislation **to the bureaucracy**.

Rules are sometimes the product of formal negotiations among government agencies and affected interest groups. **Regulatory negotiation** is a structured process by which representatives of the interests that would be substantially impacted by a rule work with government officials to negotiate agreement on the terms of the rule. The goal of a regulatory negotiation is to produce an agreement to which all parties will sign.

The signed agreement stipulates that the parties participating in the negotiation will neither attempt to prevent the rule's adoption or challenge the rule in court once it is adopted.[23]

The Office of Management and Budget (OMB) is a regular participant in the rulemaking process. In 1981, President Ronald Reagan issued an executive order requiring that any executive branch agency issuing a new rule with an economic impact of $100 million or more must prepare a cost–benefit analysis and submit it to the OMB for approval. A **cost–benefit analysis** is an evaluation of a proposed policy or regulation based on a comparison of its expected benefits and anticipated costs. Reagan's order applied to executive branch agencies such as the EPA, but not to independent regulatory commissions such as the FCC. Although subsequent presidents have kept Reagan's requirement for a cost–benefit analysis of regulations, they have approached the issue from different perspectives. In Republican administrations, the OMB functions as an appeals court for business and trade groups worried about the impact of regulation on their activities. In contrast, environmentalists, consumer groups, and organized labor have more influence in the OMB review process during Democratic administrations.[24]

Congress exercises oversight of agency rules. Agencies must submit any proposed new rule to Congress, which has 60 days to overturn it through the legislative process subject to a presidential veto and a possible override attempt. If Congress does not act within 60 days, the rule goes into effect.

Federal courts also play a role in the rulemaking process. Individuals and groups unhappy with agency decisions sometimes turn to the federal courts for relief. Courts hear challenges not just from business groups who believe that federal regulations have gone too far, but also from consumer and environmental groups who argue that regulations are not strict enough. In general, the courts have ruled that agency decisions must be supported by evidence and reasoned explanations, and that the agencies must follow statutory requirements to give notice, hold hearings, and consult with parties outside the affected industries.[25]

rule a legally binding regulation.

rulemaking the regulatory process used by government agencies to enact legally binding regulations.

regulatory negotiation a process by which representatives of the interests that would be impacted by a rule work with government officials to negotiate the terms of the rule.

cost–benefit analysis an evaluation of a proposed policy or regulation based on a comparison of its expected benefits and anticipated costs.

The Office of Management and Budget (OMB) assists the president in the preparation of a budget proposal, which is presented to Congress in late January or early February.

INFLUENCES ON BUREAUCRATIC POLICYMAKING

14.4 *Who are the main political actors in bureaucratic policymaking, and how can they influence the process?*

Bureaucratic policymaking is a complex process involving the president, Congress, interest groups, and career bureaucrats. Each of the participants has a perspective and a set of political resources for achieving its goals. Political scientists explain the relationship among these groups using different concepts of administrative policymaking.

The President

Presidents have an important stake in the faithful and efficient implementation of federal programs, but they must work to influence the administrative process—and their success is not assured. Being chief executive does not entitle a president to command the federal bureaucracy so much as it offers the opportunity to influence policy implementation. President Jimmy Carter once ordered relevant federal agencies to develop guidelines to implement the administration's policy of discouraging industrial and commercial development in areas subject to repeated flooding. More than two years later, only 15 of 37 agencies most directly involved had written guidelines. Thirteen agencies were still working on the assignment, and 12 agencies had done nothing at all![26]

Presidents face a continuous struggle to have a major impact on bureaucratic policymaking. The federal bureaucracy is too large and spread out for easy oversight from the White House, and many federal programs are administered by state and local officials or by private contractors over whom the president has little direct authority. Presidents often lack the time to manage the bureaucracy and may not be interested in trying. It is more glamorous and politically rewarding, at least in the short run, to propose new policy initiatives than to supervise the implementation of programs already in place.

Presidents have several tools for influencing the bureaucracy. The president has the authority to name most of the top administrators in the bureaucracy, including department secretaries and undersecretaries, agency heads, and regulatory commissioners. President George W. Bush ordered each executive branch agency to create a regulatory policy office run by a presidential appointee to ensure that rules and other actions taken by the agency conformed to the president's policy priorities.[27] Except for members of the independent regulatory commissions, presidents also have the power to dismiss their appointees. The president can use the OMB to evaluate agency performance and screen rules proposed by executive branch agencies. The president proposes agency budgets and can ask Congress to reorganize the bureaucracy and propose agency budgets to Congress.

Consider the Reagan administration's efforts to reduce the regulatory activities of such agencies as the EPA, which President Reagan believed were excessive. The Reagan White House carefully screened the presidential appointees to head these agencies to ensure that they were business-oriented conservatives who would be loyal to the president. For example, Reagan selected an outspoken critic of the EPA to run the agency.[28] Reagan also attempted to limit regulatory activities by cutting agency budgets and reducing their personnel. At the president's urging, Congress reduced

> The federal bureaucracy is too large and spread out for easy oversight from the White House.

total EPA funding by 24 percent in 1982 alone, and the number of personnel authorized for clean air activities declined by 31 percent between 1980 and 1983.[29] Finally, the Reagan administration used the OMB to prevent the adoption of rules by executive-branch agencies that the White House considered burdensome to industry, such as pollution regulations for diesel vehicles.[30] Between 1981 and 1985, the OMB forced agencies to modify or withdraw 19 percent of proposed rules.[31]

Reagan's efforts to reduce regulatory activities enjoyed mixed success. In the short run, regulatory enforcement levels in the agencies Reagan targeted declined.[32] However, several Reagan appointees heading the agencies were eventually forced to resign amid allegations of improper or even illegal conduct, and Congress responded to the public controversy by conducting investigations and restoring budget cuts.[33] The experience of the Reagan administration demonstrates that a determined president can impact bureaucratic policymaking, but the president's success at influencing the bureaucracy depends on the role of other political actors, including Congress, interest groups, and agency administrators.

Congress

Congress has strong legal authority to oversee the actions of the federal bureaucracy. Congress can abolish an agency, reorganize its structure, change its jurisdiction, cut its budget, audit its expenditures, investigate its performance, and overrule its decisions. In short, Congress has

Angry public workers crowd into the Wisconsin state capitol to protest a plan to require state employees to pay more for their health insurance and pensions.

effective means for getting an agency's attention. The Smithsonian Institution is a national museum and educational institution chartered by Congress. When the Smithsonian's governing board failed to provide Congress with a satisfactory justification for an exclusive deal with Showtime Network to use materials in the Smithsonian collection to make films, the House Appropriations Committee cut $15 million from the agency's budget and sought a cap on salaries for agency administrators.[34]

Some political scientists believe that congressional oversight is generally ineffective. Congress is unable to provide clear, consistent policy oversight for the bureaucracy, they say, because Congress itself lacks consensus on administrative policy goals. Whereas some members of Congress will think an agency has gone too far, others will believe that it has not gone far enough. Furthermore, many political scientists believe that the increased attention of members of Congress to constituency service (the actions of members of Congress and their staffs attending to the individual, particular needs of constituents) has made senators and representatives more dependent on executive branch agencies for help in providing services to constituents. Members of Congress who have built mutually beneficial relationships with the bureaucracy are not going to undermine those relationships through aggressive oversight.[35]

In contrast, other political scientists believe that Congress has developed an effective method of oversight through a process that some observers call **fire-alarm oversight**. It is an indirect system of congressional surveillance of bureaucratic administration, characterized by rules, procedures, and informal practices that enable individual citizens and organized interest groups to examine administrative decisions, charge agencies with violating legislative goals, and seek remedies from agencies, courts, and Congress itself. In other words, Congress exercises oversight when the media, interest groups, or citizens call attention to a problem.

> Congress exercises oversight when the media, interest groups, or citizens call attention to a problem.

Interest Groups

Every agency has several, or perhaps dozens, of interest groups vitally concerned with the programs it administers. Broadcasters are concerned with the FCC. The airline industry, aircraft manufacturers, airline employee associations, and consumer groups have an interest in the Federal Aviation Administration (FAA). Western land interests and environmentalists monitor the activities of the Interior Department. Postal workers' unions, direct-mail advertisers, publishers, and consumer groups focus on the work of the Postal Service.

Interest groups have a number of tools for influencing the bureaucracy. Groups lobby bureaucratic agencies. They also lobby Congress

to pressure the bureaucracy on their behalf. Sometimes groups file lawsuits to block or reverse an agency's decisions.

Critics charge that federal agencies often become **captured agencies**, that is, agencies that work to benefit the economic interests they regulate rather than to serve the public interest. The Federal Maritime Commission, for example, historically has worked closely with shippers. The Federal Power Commission has been accused of acting on behalf of the electric-utility industry. Proponents of the captured-agencies thesis point to what they describe as a revolving door between industry and the bureaucracy as evidence of the comfortable relationship between the regulatory commissions and industry. Presidents appoint corporate lawyers and industry executives to serve as commissioners. When the commissioners eventually leave government, they often take jobs in the industries they once regulated.

Many political scientists believe that the captured-agencies thesis is too simplistic. Studies have found that capture is not the norm, and when it does occur, it does not always last.[36] Instead, a range of factors, including presidential appointments, congressional committees and subcommittees, judicial actions, economic conditions, and agency staffs affect agency decisions.[37] Professor Steven P. Croley notes that government agencies do not always take the side of special interests against the public interest. The FTC, for example, adopted the National Do Not Call Registry despite the opposition of the telemarketing

fire-alarm oversight an indirect system of congressional surveillance of bureaucratic administration that enables individual citizens and organized interest groups to examine administrative decisions, charge agencies with violating legislative goals, and seek remedies from agencies, courts, and Congress itself.

captured agencies agencies that work to benefit the economic interests they regulate rather than serving the public interest.

States Struggle with Underfunded Public Employee Pensions

State governments around the nation are trying to deal with underfunded public employee pension plans. Most or all of the public employees in California, Illinois, Texas, Ohio, Massachusetts, and several other states do not participate in the Social Security system. Public employees in those states rely on state pension plans for their retirement. Most states that do enroll their employees in the Social Security system supplement their retirement incomes with state pension plans. Nationwide, state pension systems are underfunded by an amount ranging from $700 billion to as much as $3 trillion.[38] The states with the greatest problems are West Virginia, Oklahoma, Illinois, New Hampshire, and Louisiana. States are responding to the problem by requiring workers to increase contributions, cutting retiree benefits, raising the retirement age, and reducing cost-of-living benefits for current retirees. If the pension gap is not closed, states will be forced to make up the difference with higher taxes or spending cuts in other budget areas.

DISCUSSION

How do state pension systems work? Public employees contribute money from their paychecks into a state pension fund and the state contributes to the fund as well. The money is then invested, and earnings are paid out to retirees. The principal is never spent.

Why are some pensions underfunded? The biggest single reason is the Great Recession. State employee pension funds are typically invested in diversified portfolios of stocks, bonds, real estate, and the like. During the 1990s and most of the early twenty-first century, the stock market did well and pensions grew. During the good times, some state legislatures reduced pension contributions and increased benefits. In 2008–2009, however, the stock market literally lost half its value. Real estate property values tumbled as well. Pension funds that were in good shape were suddenly underfunded.

Are public employee unions to blame for the problem? Employee unions are politically influential. Republicans argue that legislators, eager to win the political backing of employee unions, have promised pension benefits that are too generous. They believe that not only do pensions need to be cut but that the power of public employee unions needs to be curtailed. In Wisconsin, for example, the Republican governor and Republican-controlled legislature not only increased employee contributions while reducing pension benefits, but they also stripped public employee unions of the right to bargain over benefits. The move had the added benefit of weakening a group that supports the Democratic Party.

Why is the range of the projected future pension shortfall so broad? There is a big difference between $700 billion and $3 trillion. States will be paying pension benefits for decades to come. Whether there is a shortfall between benefits promised and the money available to cover them depends on the rate of return on investment for the pension funds. Strong future investment growth minimizes the problem; weak growth makes it worse. The different shortfall figures reflect differences in the level of optimism about future investment returns.

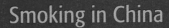
Health forces are losing the war against smoking in China. More than a million Chinese die every year from smoking-related causes; four of the five leading causes of death are smoking related. More than half of Chinese men smoke. (The smoking rate among women is much lower.)[39]

Smoking rates are high in China because the population is uninformed about the dangers of tobacco. Surveys show that less than one-fourth of Chinese believe that smoking causes cancer and other health problems. China has yet to conduct a nationwide antismoking campaign. It only recently adopted a ban on smoking in restaurants, bars, and other public places, but it is generally not enforced.[40] Warning labels on cigarette packages are in tiny type and written mostly in English, a language not understood by most Chinese consumers.

The Chinese government has a close financial relationship with the tobacco industry. The National Tobacco Corp., the company that produces Chinese cigarettes, is a government monopoly. It generates $93 billion in annual revenue and contributes more than 7 percent of Chinese government revenue from profits and taxes. The Chinese government limits competition from foreign imports and undermines efforts to discourage smoking. For example, the agency created to reduce smoking nationwide doesn't report to the ministry of health, but to the agency that runs the tobacco industry.[41] Health forces hope that the government will eventually get serious about reducing smoking because of the cost of smoking-related illnesses, but progress has been slow.[42]

QUESTIONS

1 Is it any business of the government if people smoke?

2 In the United States, the smoking rate for men once far exceeded the rate for women, but women have narrowed the gap. Why do you think that has happened?

3 Is it wrong for the U.S. government to promote the foreign export of American tobacco products?

More than half of Chinese men smoke.

industry.[43] The captured agencies thesis assumes that the political environment for each government agency consists of a single set of interest groups with a similar perspective, but that is not usually the case. The debate over the adoption of the National Do Not Call Registry involved not just an industry group, but also consumer organizations and the AARP.

Career Bureaucrats

Each agency has two sets of administrators—a small group of presidential appointees, typically called political appointees, and a larger group of career civil servants. Nineteen presidential appointees and 284 SES managers lead the Department of Health and Human Services. Five presidential appointees and 20 SES managers head the EEOC.[44] In contrast to presidential employees who serve no more than four or eight years, depending on the number of terms of the president who appoints them, SES managers are career bureaucrats who stay with a single agency for most of their careers. SES managers have interests of their own that may differ from those of the president and political administrators appointed to run their agencies. Career SES managers typically want to preserve and enhance their positions, their programs, and their budgets. Furthermore, agencies often attract employees who are personally committed to the mission of their department. Environmentalists work for the EPA, whereas people with agricultural backgrounds seek employment with the Department of Agriculture.

Career bureaucrats have resources for defending their turf. Sometimes career employees resort to subtle, behind-the-scenes resistance to policy changes they oppose, a sort of bureaucratic guerrilla warfare. In an organization as large as the federal bureaucracy, presidential initiatives can be opposed in a number of quiet ways. Changes may be delayed. Bureaucrats may follow the letter but not the spirit of directives. Officials may "forget" to pass along orders to subordinates. News of mistakes or internal bickering may be leaked to the press.[45]

Bureaucracy finds power in alliances with important members of Congress and interest groups. Executive branch agencies are some of the most vigorous and effective lobbyists. By assisting key members of Congress with problems involving constituent complaints, agencies build friendships. Furthermore, most agencies have interest group constituencies that are willing to use their political resources on behalf of the agency. Teacher groups lobby for the Department of Education, defense contractors fight for the defense budget, and medical professionals support the Public Health Service.

Executive branch officials know that they are more likely to achieve their goals if they can find a way to connect their policy preferences with the self-interest of members of Congress. Consider NASA's successful strategy for winning congressional support for continued funding of the International Space Station (ISS). NASA distributed work on the ISS to 68 prime contractors and 35 major subcontractors in 22 states, including California, Texas, Florida, New York, Illinois, Ohio, and Pennsylvania—all states with large, politically influential congressional delegations.[46]

Subgovernments and Issue Networks

Political scientists use different concepts to explain administrative policymaking. One approach to understanding the administrative process is the concept of subgovernment, or iron triangles. A **subgovernment**, or **iron triangle**, is a cozy, three-sided relationship among government agencies, interest groups, and key members of

Congress in which all parties benefit.

- On one point of the subgovernment triangle, the bureaucracy and interest groups benefit from a special relationship. Agencies enhance the economic status of the interest group through favorable regulation or the awarding of government contracts. Interest groups return the favor by lobbying Congress on behalf of the agency.
- On the second point of the triangle, interest groups and members of Congress enjoy a mutually beneficial relationship. Interest groups assist senators and members of the House by contributing to their reelection campaigns. In return, members of Congress vote to appropriate money for programs the interest groups support.
- The third point of the triangle focuses on the interaction between agencies and members of Congress. Politically wise bureaucrats know that it is important to keep key members of Congress happy by providing all the information they request, by

solving problems members of Congress bring to their attention, and by paying special notice to the needs of the home states and districts of key senators and representatives.

Consider the highway subgovernment. On one point of the highway triangle are interest groups that benefit from highway construction: auto manufacturers, the United Auto Workers Union (UAW), tire companies, asphalt and cement dealers, road contractors, long-haul trucking firms, the Teamsters Union, and oil companies. The second point is the Federal Highway Administration, which, of course, is interested in the preservation of the programs it administers. On the third point of the triangle are the congressional committees that consider highway-construction bills—the Environment and Public Works Committee in the Senate and the Committee on Transportation and Infrastructure in the House. Senators and representatives from states with extensive interstate highway systems, such as Texas, California, and Oklahoma, are also involved.

Each part of the subgovernment serves and is served by the other two. The members of Congress involved work to maintain federal support for highway construction and

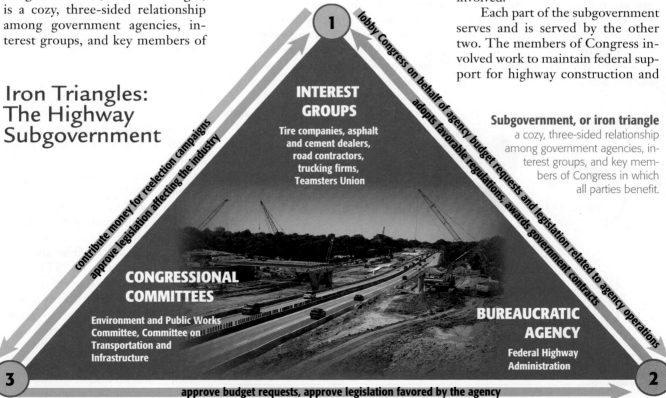

Iron Triangles: The Highway Subgovernment

1

lobby Congress on behalf of agency budget requests and legislation related to agency operations

adopts favorable regulations, awards government contracts

contribute money for reelection campaigns

approve legislation affecting the industry

INTEREST GROUPS

Tire companies, asphalt and cement dealers, road contractors, trucking firms, Teamsters Union

CONGRESSIONAL COMMITTEES

Environment and Public Works Committee, Committee on Transportation and Infrastructure

BUREAUCRATIC AGENCY

Federal Highway Administration

3

2

approve budget requests, approve legislation favored by the agency

helps committee members with constituency service

Subgovernment, or iron triangle
a cozy, three-sided relationship among government agencies, interest groups, and key members of Congress in which all parties benefit.

maintenance. The interest groups lobby Congress on behalf of highway programs, and their political action committees (PACs) contribute campaign money to members of Congress on key committees. The agency, meanwhile, makes sure that the districts and states of the members of Congress involved get their share of new highways and bridges. Also, if some town in the district wants a special favor, local officials call their representative or senator, who passes the request along to the agency. The agency is eager to please and happy to give the member of Congress the credit.

The political scientists who study subgovernments believe that a great deal of public policy is made through behind-the-scenes understandings among interest groups, key members of Congress, and the federal bureaucracy. When issues arise, the participants in the subgovernment settle the matter, with little input from political actors outside the triangle, including the president. The result is that public policy is tailored to the wishes of those groups most closely associated with the policy itself. Energy policy, they say, reflects the interests of the oil and gas industry. Highway programs are geared to match the concerns of the highway lobby.

In recent years, however, many political scientists have concluded

Issue Networks

think Do you think the influence of interest groups on government is good or bad? Explain your opinion.

that although subgovernments exist in American politics, their influence is less than it was during the 1940s and 1950s. Subgovernments prospered in a time when public policy was the work of a relatively small number of fairly autonomous participants: a handful of powerful committee chairs, a small number of interest groups, and a few agency administrators. Furthermore, most policy decisions were made outside public view.

Today's policy environment has changed. Power in Congress is centralized in the party leadership. Committee chairs are less influential. Interest groups are more numerous. Furthermore, new issues have arisen for which it is all but impossible to identify clearly the dominant actors, including energy, consumer protection, illegal immigration, and the environment.[47]

Political scientist Hugh Heclo believes that the concept of issue networks more accurately describes administrative policymaking today than the concept of subgovernments. An **issue network** is a group of political actors concerned with some aspect of public policy. Issue networks are fluid, with participants moving in and

out. They can include technical specialists, members of Congress, journalists, the president, interest groups, bureaucrats, academic experts, and individual political activists. Powerful interest groups may be involved, but they do not control the process. Instead, policy in a particular area results from conflict among a broad range of political actors both in and out of government.[48]

Consider the fate of the Highway Trust Fund. A subgovernment once dominated federal highway policy, but that is no longer the case. During the 1970s, the number of interest groups concerned with highway construction grew. Environmentalists worried about the effect of highway construction on the environment. Minority rights groups became alarmed about the impact of freeway construction on minority neighborhoods. Groups advocating energy conservation argued that government should divert money from highways to mass transit. In the meantime, congressional committees and subcommittees with jurisdiction over highway programs began to include members of Congress allied to groups opposed to highway spending. As a result, federal highway policy is now made in a more contentious, uncertain environment than before.[49] In 1991, Congress passed and the president signed the Intermodal Surface Transportation Efficiency Act (IS-TEA), granting states considerable leeway in deciding whether to spend federal transportation money for highways or mass transit. The legislation also required that states use a certain amount of money to fund "enhancement programs," which were local transportation-related projects designed to aid a community's quality of life, such as hike-and-bike trails. The passage of ISTEA reflected the participation of a broad range of interests concerned with transportation policy, not just the traditional set of interest groups involved with highway funding.[50]

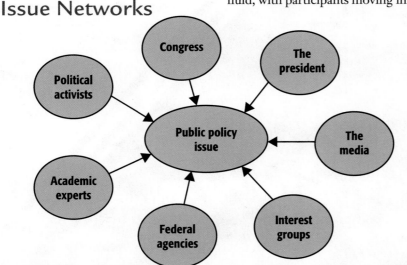

The concept of issue networks explains a more complicated relationship among a large number of political actors all actively involved in policymaking.

issue network a group of political actors that is actively involved with policymaking in a particular issue area.

TAKING SIDES

Regulating Executive Compensation

Should the government be allowed to limit compensations of chief executives of corporations?

Given the connections between the national economy and the success of private corporations, should business be regulated?

OVERVIEW

Executive pay began to skyrocket during the 1990s while the economy was doing well. In 2008–2009, as the economy collapsed, in some measure because of the behavior of by executives in major corporations, the public began to grow very angry with the amount of compensation that executives were receiving. This anger was particularly acute when it applied to those corporations that received billions of dollars in taxpayer funds in the 2008 Troubled Asset Relief Program (TARP) bailout. In the year following the bailout, employees at Wall Street firms earned more than $20 billion in bonus pay, which was 17 percent higher than in the previous year, according to New York State Comptroller Thomas DiNapoli. Furthermore, the 116 banks that received federal bailout funds paid their executives $1.6 billion, including benefits such as company jets and golf club memberships.[51]

President Obama has said that most of the $700 billion in TARP money has been repaid by businesses and that some businesses, like General Motors, were paying it back ahead of schedule. However, Obama has also called for a $500,000 salary cap for CEOs while their businesses are using taxpayer money, as well as legislation to allow shareholders input into executive compensation.

SUPPORTING government regulation of executive pay

Public corporations are responsible to the shareholders of the company. Once a company took federal money to stabilize its financial situation, the federal government became a major shareholder to whom the company must be responsible. Therefore, the federal government has the right and obligation to check what is happening in the company.

The economy is a public good. These large corporations are the underpinning of a national economy that belongs to everyone. Therefore, the federal government has the authority to use compensation to ensure that business executives are behaving properly, and to reward or punish behavior.

In a time of economic crisis, executives perceived as reaping more than they are worth create an unstable political environment. Executives should not receive bonuses when their companies are losing so much money that the government needs to bail them out.

AGAINST government regulation of executive pay

Executive compensation is part of a contractual obligation between the company and its employees. The federal government should not violate private business contracts based on its own assessment of individual performance. Bailout funds were used to rescue the businesses, which included their executives.

Government should not intervene in private business. The economy in America depends on the risk-taking behavior at major companies. The principles of market economy should be adhered to in both times of surplus and in times of crisis.

The American people can express their disapproval without government intervention. If there is public backlash against what CEOs are making, then the American people can vote with their dollars and not use those businesses. Information on the packages is available and people can choose to use a different business for the services provided.

ORGANIZATION OF THE BUREAUCRACY

14.1 *What is the structure of the executive branch?*

Congress and the president have created the agencies and departments that make up the executive branch over the last 220 years. The cabinet departments, including the Department of State and the Department of Defense, are the major administrative units of the federal government that have responsibility for the conduct of a wide range of government operations. Congress and the president have created a number of independent executive agencies that are not part of any of the 15 cabinet-level departments, such as the Environmental Protection Agency (EPA). Government corporations, such as the U.S. Postal Service, are organizationally similar to private corporations except that the government owns them rather than stockholders. Foundations and institutes administer grant programs to local governments, universities, non-profit institutions, and individuals for research in the natural and social sciences or to promote the arts. Independent regulatory commissions, such as the SEC, are agencies outside the major executive departments that are charged with the regulation of important aspects of the economy. Quasi-governmental companies, such as Fannie Mae and Freddie Mac, are private, profit-seeking corporations created by Congress to serve a public purpose, such as increasing the availability of credit to home buyers.

PERSONNEL

14.2 *How have federal employee personnel policies evolve?*

The size of the federal civilian bureaucracy has grown dramatically since the early days of the nation. Today, 2.7 million people work for the federal government, with mil-lions more working indirectly as private contractors, or as employees paid by federal grant money. When Andrew Jackson was president, federal employees were hired primarily on the basis of their political connections. After Garfield's assassination by a disappointed office seeker, Congress reformed the hiring process to emphasize merit. Congress subsequently established a Senior Executive Service (SES) of upper-level civil servants who would be eligible for big bonuses but could be more easily transferred, reassigned, etc.

RULEMAKING

14.3 *What are the steps in the rulemaking process?*

When Congress passes regulatory legislation, it frequently delegates authority to the bureaucracy to make legally binding rules to implement the legislation. Rules are sometimes the product of formal negotiations among government agencies and affected interest groups called regulatory negotiation. The OMB reviews rules before they go into effect. Congress can overturn rules before they go into effect through the legislative process subject to presidential veto and possible override.

INFLUENCES ON BUREAUCRATIC POLICYMAKING

14.4 *Who are the main political actors in bureaucratic policymaking, and how can they influence the process?*

Bureaucratic policymaking is a complex process involving the president, Congress, interest groups, and the bureaucracy itself. A president can have an impact on bureaucratic policymaking through appointive powers, the OMB, and his authority to propose budgets to Congress. Congress can abolish an agency, reorganize its structure, change its jurisdiction, cut its budget, audit its expenditures, investigate its performance, and overrule its decisions. Interest groups lobby agencies, lobby Congress, and sometimes file suits to influence administrative actions. Career bureaucrats have resources to defend their own interests, and find power in alliances with interest groups and key members of Congress.

Some political scientists believe that administrative policymaking reflects the activity of subgovernments or iron triangles, which are cozy, three-sided relationships among government agencies, interest groups, and key members of Congress in which all parties benefit. In recent years, however, many political scientists have concluded that the concept that best describes administrative policymaking is issue networks, which are groups of political actors that are concerned with some aspect of public policy.

| Send | Save | Delete |

From: Professor Tannahill
Add Cc | Add Bcc

Subject: Tips for Success
Attach a file

MUCH OF LIFE IS JUST SHOWING UP:
Go to class every day, arrive on time, pay attention, and don't leave early.

ENJOY:
Find a way to enjoy every class you take because students do better in subjects they like.

MySearchLab®

TEST yourself

14.1 *What is the structure of the executive branch?*

1 How did the Department of Defense, Federal Communication Commission, Postal Service, and other federal agencies come into existence?
   a. The president created them by executive order.
   b. The Constitution established them.
   c. They were established by court order.
   d. Congress and the president created them through the legislative process.

2 Which of the following is *not* a cabinet department?
   a. Environmental Protection Agency (EPA)
   b. Department of Homeland Security
   c. Department of Defense
   d. Department of Justice

3 Which of the following is *not* part of the inner cabinet?
   a. Secretary of state
   b. Secretary of Homeland Security
   c. Secretary of defense
   d. Attorney general

4 Which of the following is *not* an example of an independent executive agency?
   a. Peace Corps
   b. CIA
   c. FCC
   d. NASA

5 Which of the following is *not* an example of a government corporation?
   a. AMTRAK
   b. CIA
   c. Postal Service
   d. FDIC

6 The president has the authority to remove all but which one of the following government officials?
   a. Attorney general
   b. EPA administrator
   c. SEC commissioner
   d. Secretary of Transportation

7 Which of the following agencies is an example of a quasi-governmental company?
   a. Postal Service
   b. SEC
   c. AMTRAK
   d. Fannie Mae

14.2 *How have federal employee personnel policies evolved?*

8 The spoils system involved which of the following?
   a. Hiring friends, relatives, and political supporters to work for the government
   b. Giving government contracts to companies owned by friends, relatives, and political supporters
   c. Contracting out with private companies to implement government programs
   d. Forbidding government employees from engaging in political activities

9 Which of the following rights do federal employees enjoy?
   a. The right to form unions
   b. The right to vote for candidates of their choice
   c. The right to bargain collectively over issues other than pay and benefits
   d. All of the above

14.3 *What are the steps in the rulemaking process?*

10 Are private companies legally obligated to follow rules adopted by regulatory agencies?
   a. No. Only Congress has the authority to enact legally binding regulations.
   b. Yes, but only if the rules are ratified by Congress.
   c. Yes. Rules are legally binding.
   d. No, although many business follow them voluntarily.

11 Suppose the Department of Labor adopts a rule that a majority of the members of Congress oppose. What steps if any can Congress take to reverse the rule?
   a. Congress lacks the authority to overturn the rule.
   b. Congress can pass legislation to reverse the rule, but it would either require presidential approval or a vote by Congress to override a veto.
   c. Congress can ask the Supreme Court to overturn the rule.
   d. Congress can do nothing, but the president can veto the rule.

14.4 *Who are the main political actors in bureaucratic policymaking, and how can they influence the process?*

12 Suppose the president disagrees with the policy initiatives of a federal agency. What can the president do to exert control?
   a. The president can ask Congress to cut the agency's budget.
   b. The president can appoint administrators to head the agency who agree with the president's policy position.
   c. The president can ask Congress to reorganize the agency.
   d. All of the above

13 An agency that is accused of working too closely with the interest groups it is supposed to be regulating is known as which of the following?
   a. Issue network
   b. Captured agency
   c. Independent regulatory commission
   d. Iron triangle

14 Which of the following political actors is *not* part of a subgovernment or iron triangle?
   a. President
   b. Congress
   c. Interest group
   d. Government agency

15 Which of the following factors has contributed to an increase in the importance of issue networks and a decline in the significance of subgovernments?
   a. Committee chairs in Congress are less influential now than in the past.
   b. Interest groups are more numerous now than in the past.
   c. New issues have arisen that are not dominated by a single interest group.
   d. All of the above

KNOW the score

14–15 correct:	Congratulations—you know your American government!
12–13 correct:	Your understanding of this chapter is weak—be sure to review the key terms and visit TheThinkSpot.
<12 correct:	Reread the chapter more thoroughly.

Answers: 1) d, 2) a, 3) b, 4) c, 5) b, 6) c, 7) d, 8) a, 9) d, 10) c, 11) b, 12) d, 13) b, 14) a, 15) d

15 THE FEDERAL

JUDICIAL POLICYMAKING

Learning Objective 15.1 What role do courts and judges play in the policymaking process?

THE LOWER FEDERAL COURTS

Learning Objective 15.2 How is the federal court system organized?

THE U.S. SUPREME COURT

Learning Objective 15.3 How does the Supreme Court function?

POWER, POLITICS, AND THE COURTS

Learning Objective 15.4 What factors affect the policymaking power of the courts?

Betty Dukes was hoping to turn her life around when she took a part-time job as a greeter at Walmart. Through hard work, she thought she could win a promotion into management, but after years of little progress, she filed a gender discrimination lawsuit.[1] A federal judge ruled that the case could go forward as a class action lawsuit on behalf of 1.5 million current or former women Walmart employees.

A **class action lawsuit** is brought by one or more people on behalf of themselves and others who are in a similar situation. It enables a large number of individuals with relatively small claims to proceed because their pooled damages make the case worthwhile to attorneys, who earn fees based on a percentage of damages awarded. Dukes and the other women alleged that Walmart had created a male-dominated culture that led to discrimination against women. Even though 72 percent of Walmart employees were women, they made up only a third of management.[2] If Walmart lost, it could be ordered to pay billions of dollars in damages.[3] *Walmart v. Dukes*, however, was a big win for Walmart. The U.S. Supreme Court held that it could not proceed as a class action lawsuit because Walmart did not have a company policy regarding discrimination.[4] Betty Dukes and the other

class action lawsuit a lawsuit brought by one or more people on behalf of themselves and others who are in a similar situation.

COURTS

women could still sue, but they would have to prove that they were personally victims of discrimination as opposed to part of a large group of victimized women.[5]

This chapter considers the place of the courts in American government. It begins by examining the role of judges and courts in the policy process. The chapter traces the political history of the U.S. Supreme Court. It describes the federal court system, distinguishing between trial courts and appellate courts. The chapter examines district courts and then appellate courts, considering judicial selection and court jurisdiction. The chapter then turns to the U.S. Supreme Court, discussing judicial selection, judicial processes, and the impact of Court decisions. Finally, the chapter discusses the role of courts in the political system.

JUDICIAL POLICYMAKING

15.1 *What role do courts and judges play in the policymaking process?*

Courts make policy by interpreting the law and the Constitution.[6] When courts interpret the law, they modify policies adopted by the executive and legislative branches by aggressively expanding or narrowly restricting the provisions of a law. When courts interpret the Constitution, they exercise **judicial review**, which is the power of courts to declare unconstitutional the actions of the other branches and units of government. Altogether, the Supreme Court has overturned at least one provision in nearly 160 federal laws and 1,300 state laws and local ordinances.[7]

The Role of Courts and Judges

Controversy rages over the leeway courts should exercise in interpreting the Constitution. **Strict construction** is a doctrine of constitutional interpretation holding that the document should be interpreted narrowly. Advocates of strict construction believe that judges should stick closely to the literal meaning of the words in the Constitution and place themselves in harmony with the purpose of the framers. In contrast, **loose construction** is a doctrine of constitutional interpretation holding that the document should be interpreted broadly. Loose constructionists argue that strict construction is neither possible nor desirable. They point out that it is often difficult to ascertain original intent because no complete and accurate records exist to indicate what the authors of the Constitution had in mind. Furthermore, those records that are available show that the nation's founders often disagreed with each other about the Constitution's basic meaning.

A similar and related debate involves the role of judges. Conservative opponents of the Supreme Court sometimes accuse it of **judicial activism**, which is the charge that judges are going beyond their authority by making the law and not just interpreting it. For example, critics of *Roe v. Wade*, the Supreme Court's landmark abortion decision, call it an activist ruling because the U.S. Constitution does not specifically address the issue of abortion. Republican presidential candidates typically promise to nominate men and women to the Supreme Court who will practice **judicial restraint**, which is the concept that judges should defer to the policymaking judgment of the legislative and executive branches of government unless their actions clearly violate the law or the Constitution.

> The real controversy is that conservative and liberal judges disagree as to what the constitutional principles are.

Many political scientists believe that the debate between judicial activism and judicial restraint is more about politics than judicial behavior. Professors Kermit Roosevelt III and Thomas M. Keck contend that the accusation of judicial activism is a convenient line of attack for people who disagree with a court ruling for whatever reason.[8] The real dispute is not between the advocates of judicial activism and judicial restraint, but between liberal and conservative activism. All judges regard the Constitution as a charter of fundamental principles that courts are pledged to uphold. The real controversy is that conservative and liberal judges disagree as to what those principles are.[9]

judicial review the power of courts to declare unconstitutional the actions of the other branches and units of government.

strict construction a doctrine of constitutional interpretation holding that the document should be interpreted narrowly.

loose construction a doctrine of constitutional interpretation holding that the document should be interpreted broadly.

judicial activism the charge that judges are going beyond their authority by making the law and not just interpreting it.

judicial restraint the concept that judges should defer to the policymaking judgment of the legislative and executive branches of government unless their actions clearly violate the law or the Constitution.

Do you think the framers intended for a strict or loose interpretation of the Constitution? If you were a member of the Supreme Court, how would you approach the issue?

Political History of the Supreme Court

Throughout most of its history, the U.S. Supreme Court has been an active participant in some of the nation's most significant public policy debates. In its first decade, however, the Court was relatively unimportant. It decided only 50 cases from 1789 to 1800. Some of its members even resigned to take other, more prestigious jobs.[10]

After John Marshall was named chief justice, however, the Supreme Court's role in the policy process began to take shape. Under his leadership from 1801 to 1835, the Court claimed the power of judicial review in *Marbury v. Madison* (1803).[11] The Marshall Court ruled in favor of a strong national government in controversies concerning the relative power of the national government and the states. In *McCulloch v. Maryland* (1819), the Court struck down a Maryland tax on the national bank and gave broad scope to federal authority under the Constitution.[12]

Under Chief Justice Roger Taney (1836–1864), Marshall's successor, the Supreme Court's involvement in the slavery controversy led the Court away from support for a strong national government toward a states' rights position. In the infamous *Dred Scott* decision (1857), the Supreme Court held that the federal government had no power to prohibit slavery in the territories.[13]

After the Civil War, the Supreme Court protected the property rights of large corporations while ignoring the civil rights of African Americans. It scrutinized state and federal taxation and regulatory policies and found many of them unconstitutional. When southern states adopted policies designed to deny African Americans the right to vote, the Court was silent. When states adopted Jim Crow laws, legal provisions requiring the social segregation of African Americans in separate and generally unequal facilities, the Court legitimized their action in the famous segregation case of *Plessy v. Ferguson* (1896).[14]

In 1937, the Supreme Court changed course. In a remarkable turn of events, the Court began to uphold the constitutionality of New Deal legislation, broadly and consistently endorsing the right of government to regulate business and the nation's economy. After 1937, the agenda of the U.S. Supreme Court focused primarily on civil liberties and civil rights.

Under the leadership of Chief Justice Earl Warren (1953–1969), the Supreme Court adopted liberal policy positions on a number of civil liberties and civil rights issues. The Court strengthened the First Amendment guarantees of freedom of expression and religion, broadened the procedural rights of persons accused of crimes, and ruled decisively in favor of civil rights for African Americans and other minorities. In *Brown v. Board of Education of Topeka* (1954), the Court struck down laws requiring school segregation, overturning the *Plessy* decision.[15]

During Warren Burger's tenure as Chief Justice (1969–1986), the Supreme Court continued to focus primarily on civil liberties and civil rights. In some issue areas, such as abortion rights, capital punishment, education for the children of illegal aliens, affirmative action, school busing, and gender discrimination, the Burger Court broke new ground. In *Roe v. Wade*, the Court held that states could not prohibit abortion in the first two trimesters of pregnancy.[16] In other policy areas, however, particularly on issues involving the rights of persons charged with crimes, the Burger Court limited or qualified Warren Court positions.

The Supreme Court continued to defy labels during the tenure of Chief Justice Rehnquist (1986–2005). On some policy issue, the Rehnquist Court adopted conservative positions. The Court declared that government programs designed to remedy the effects of discrimination in government

The Supreme Court of the United States is the highest court in the land.

The Supreme Court in 2011. Top row (left to right): Justices Sonia Sotomayor, Stephen Breyer, Samuel Alito, Elena Kagan. Bottom row (left to right): Justices Clarence Thomas, Antonin Scalia, Chief Justice John Roberts, Justices Anthony Kennedy, Ruth Bader Ginsberg.

body as long as they did not grant minority applicants a set number of points.[22] The Rehnquist Court may be best remembered for *Bush v. Gore*, in which the Court decided by a 5–4 vote to halt the recount of Florida's vote, ending the 2000 presidential election and ensuring that George W. Bush would be the next president.

> The Supreme Court under Chief Justice Roberts is **closely divided** philosophically.

contracting were unconstitutional unless the government could demonstrate a compelling interest to justify their creation.[17] On other issues, however, the Rehnquist Court adopted liberal positions. The Court consistently blocked government efforts to include spoken prayer in school activities, ruling against clergy-led invocations and benedictions at graduation[18] as well as student-led prayers before high school football games.[19] The Rehnquist Court broke new ground on the issue of gay and lesbian rights by overturning the Texas

sodomy law that prohibited sexual relations between adults of the same gender even in the privacy of the home.[20]

The Rehnquist Court addressed a number of policy controversies by taking moderate, compromise positions. The Court allowed state governments to restrict abortion rights without overturning *Roe*. It struck down college admissions procedures that gave a numerical advantage to minority applicants,[21] but allowed college officials to consider race and ethnicity in order to achieve a diverse student

The Supreme Court under Chief Justice John Roberts is more conservative than its predecessor even though it remains closely divided philosophically.[23] On one hand, the Court pleased conservatives by upholding a federal ban on partial birth abortion, which is a procedure used in some late-term abortion.[24] On the other hand, the Court has satisfied liberals by holding unconstitutional a Louisiana law that provided for the death penalty for a defendant convicted of sexually assaulting a child who survived the assault.[25] Both both cases were decided 5-4 with Justice Anthony Kennedy providing the deciding vote.

THE LOWER FEDERAL COURTS

15.2 *How is the federal court system organized?*

The Constitution says relatively little about the organization of the federal court system. "The judicial Power of the United States," it declares, "shall be vested in one supreme Court, and in such inferior Courts as the Congress may from time to time ordain and establish." Over the years, Congress and the president have created the federal court system through the legislative process.

The figure on the following page diagrams the federal court system. Trial courts make up the lowest tier of federal courts. A **trial** is the

formal examination of a judicial dispute in accordance with law before a single judge. Trials involve attorneys, witnesses, testimony, evidence, judges, and, occasionally, juries. The U.S. district courts are the most important federal trial courts, hearing nearly all federal cases. The U.S. Court of Federal Claims and the U.S. Court of International Trade are specialized trial courts, created to deal with some of the more complex areas of federal law. The U.S. Court of Federal Claims hears disputes over federal contracts and cases involving claims for monetary damages against

the U.S. government; the U.S. Court of International Trade hears cases involving international trade and customs issues.

An **appeal** is the taking of a case to a higher court by the losing party in a lower-court decision. The procedures of appeals courts differ notably from those of trial courts. In

trial the formal examination of a judicial dispute in accordance with law before a single judge.

appeal the taking of a case from a lower court to a higher court by the losing party in a lower-court decision.

The U.S. Federal Courts

```
U.S. Supreme
Court
        │
U.S. Courts
of Appeals
  │     │     │
U.S. Court of    U.S. District    U.S. Court of
International Trade    Courts    Federal Claims
```

general, trial courts are concerned with questions of fact and the law as it applies to those facts. In contrast, appeals are based on issues of law and procedure. Appellate courts do not retry cases appealed to them. Instead, appellate court justices (juries do not participate in appellate proceedings) make decisions based on the law and the Constitution, the written and oral arguments presented by attorneys for the litigants in the lawsuit, and the written record of the lower-court proceedings. Also, appellate court justices usually make decisions collectively in panels of three or more judges rather than singly, as do trial court judges.

The U.S. courts of appeals and the U.S. Supreme Court are primarily appellate courts. The courts of appeals hear appeals from the federal trial courts and administrative agencies. The U.S. Supreme Court stands at the apex of the American court system. Although it has authority to try a limited range of cases, it is in practice an appellate court, hearing appeals from both the federal and state court systems.

District Courts

Congress has created 94 district courts, with at least 1 court in every state and 1 each in the District of Columbia, Guam, Northern Mariana Islands, Puerto Rico, and the Virgin Islands. Although only one judge presides in each courtroom, most of the districts have enough business to warrant more than one courtroom, each with its own judge.

The number of judges per district ranges from 1 to 28. Congress has authorized the appointment of 678 district court judges who, along with more than a hundred semi-retired senior judges, staff the district courts. In addition, each district court has a clerk, a U.S. marshal, and one or more bankruptcy judges, probation officers, court reporters, and magistrates attached to it.[26]

Selection of Judges. The president appoints federal judges subject to Senate confirmation by majority vote. **Senatorial courtesy**, the custom that senators have a veto on the nomination of judges to staff district courts located in their states, determines the selection of most district judges. When district court vacancies occur, senators from the states where the vacancies have occurred submit names to the president, who makes the formal nomination. The president can reject a senator's recommendation, but rarely does, especially when the senator belongs to the president's political party.

The Senate Judiciary Committee evaluates district court nominees. After the committee staff conducts a background check, the committee chair schedules a hearing to allow the nominee and interested parties an opportunity to be heard. The confirmation of district court judges is usually a quiet affair, with few nominees rejected. Confirmation is not neces-

sarily speedy, however, especially when the Senate and White House are in the hands of different political parties. Toward the end of a presidential term, the chair of the Senate Judiciary Committee and the Senate majority leader will sometimes delay the confirmation process in hopes that the White House changes parties and the new president can then fill pending vacancies. Even early in a term, the confirmation process takes anywhere from four months to two years, or even longer.[27]

Presidents typically nominate judges whose party affiliation and political philosophy are compatible with their own. Democratic presidents appoint Democratic judges; Republican presidents select Republicans. Some presidents also seek judges with particular political philosophies. In general, Republican presidents choose judges with conservative political philosophies, whereas Democratic presidents select liberal judges. Conservative judges tend to favor government interests over criminal defendants, interpret narrowly the constitutional guarantees of equal rights for women and minorities, support corporate interests against the claims of individual workers or consumers, and rule against federal government involvement in local policy issues. In contrast, liberal judges are more inclined to favor judicial underdogs, such as consumers, workers, criminal defendants, and members of minority groups. They tend to support the federal government in federalism disputes over the relative power of the states and the national government.[28]

Federal judges hold lifetime appointments, with "good behavior," as the Constitution puts it. They may not be retired involuntarily or removed for political reasons, but they are subject to impeachment by the

Federal judges hold **lifetime appointments,** with "good behavior."

senatorial courtesy the custom that senators from the president's party have a veto on judicial appointments from their states.

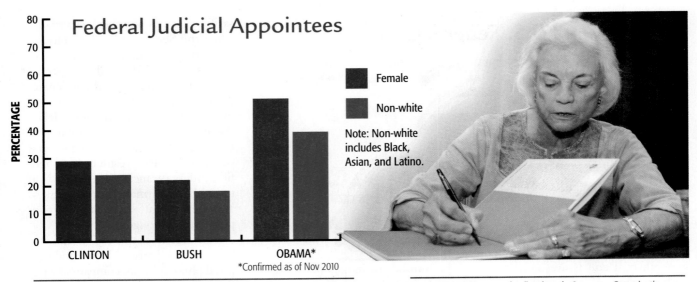

Federal Judicial Appointees

Legend:
- Female
- Non-white

Note: Non-white includes Black, Asian, and Latino.

CLINTON   BUSH   OBAMA*

*Confirmed as of Nov 2010

President Obama has appointed a higher percentage of women and minority judges than any president in history.

Source: Federal Judicial Center, www.fjc.gov

Sandra Day O'Connor, the first female Supreme Court justice, was nominated by President Reagan.

House and removal by the Senate. Although members of Congress occasionally threaten to impeach judges with whom they have policy disagreements, impeachment is rare and always directed against judges who are accused of misconduct. In American history, only seven federal judges have been impeached and removed from office. Most judges who get in trouble resign rather than face the humiliation of impeachment.[29]

Jurisdiction. The term **jurisdiction** refers to the authority of a court to hear and decide a case. The jurisdiction of district courts includes both civil and criminal matters. A **civil case** is a legal dispute concerning a private conflict between two parties—individuals, corporations, or government agencies. A **criminal case** is a legal dispute dealing with an alleged violation of a penal, or criminal, law. More than 80 percent of district court cases are civil disputes.[30] In sheer volume, the main chores of

the district courts are naturalizing new citizens and granting passport applications. District courts also have jurisdiction over bankruptcy cases filed under federal law, civil cases involving more than $75,000

jurisdiction the authority of a court to hear a case.

civil case a legal dispute concerning a private conflict between two parties—individuals, corporations, or government agencies.

criminal case a legal dispute dealing with an alleged violation of a penal law.

TAKE ✓ ACTION

A Day in Court

Learn about the judicial branch of government by visiting a courtroom in your community. Large cities will be home to federal courts and state courts, whereas small towns may have only municipal courts or justice of the peace courts. Go online to locate a court in your area and find out when it is in session. Visit the court for at least an hour. Then, write an essay in which you address the following questions:

- Which court did you visit (give its official title) and when did you go?
- Who was the presiding judge, by name and title?
- How many cases did you witness? Were the cases civil or criminal? How do you know? What issue(s) did the case(s) address?
- How many people were in the courtroom and who were they (defendants, lawyers, jurors, law officers, etc.)?

- Did the court run smoothly? Do you think the court ran fairly? Why do you say so?
- If you could make one change in the manner in which the court was run, what would it be?
- Did you have a good time? Discuss.

in which the U.S. government is a party, and—if either litigant requests it—lawsuits in which the parties live in different states and in which more than $75,000 is at stake. In these latter cases, federal judges apply the laws of the applicable state rather than federal law.

As for criminal matters, district courts try all cases involving violations of federal law as well as criminal offenses occurring on federal territory, federal reservations, or the high seas. District judges must also rule on *habeas corpus* petitions filed by inmates in both state and federal prisons. A **writ of *habeas corpus*** is a court order requiring government authorities either to release a person held in custody or demonstrate that the person is detained in accordance with law. *Habeas corpus* petitions allege that a prisoner is held contrary to law and ask a court to inquire into the matter. An inmate's attorney may charge, for example, that a state trial court erred in admitting certain evidence, thereby violating the Fourth and Fourteenth Amendments to the U.S. Constitution. If the judge sees merit in the petitioner's complaint, the judge can direct the jailer to reply, and a suit will be joined. Death row inmates often use *habeas corpus* petitions to avoid, or at least to delay, their execution. Litigants who lose their district court cases may appeal to a U.S. court of appeals. In practice, less than 20 percent of district court decisions are appealed.[31]

Courts of Appeals

The 13 U.S. courts of appeals (also known as circuit courts of appeals) are the primary intermediate appellate courts in the federal system, hearing appeals from the federal trial courts. A court of appeals serves each of 12 regions, which are called judicial circuits. A thirteenth circuit called the U.S. Court of Appeals for the Federal Circuit hears appeals in specialized cases, such as patent law, and cases appealed from the Court of International Trade and the Court of Federal Claims. The number of justices for each of the circuits ranges from three to twenty four. Altogether, 179 justices staff the courts of appeals along with another 40 senior justices.

Selection of Justices. The White House generally takes more care with nominations to the courts of appeals than it does with district court selections. Because the judicial circuits usually include several states, senatorial courtesy does not dictate the selection of justices on the courts of appeals.[32] Consequently, presidents are able to seek out men and women who not only share their political party affiliation but also their policy preferences.[33] When a vacancy occurs, a deputy attorney general gathers names of potential nominees, asking party leaders, senators, and members of the House for suggestions. Eventually, the deputy attorney general suggests a short list of names for the president's consideration, and the president makes a choice. The Senate examines appellate court nominees more closely than it considers district court selections, especially when the opposition party controls the Senate. Furthermore, as with district court nominees, delays are not unusual. The length of confirmation delays depends on the size of the president's opposition in the Senate, the proximity of the next presidential election, and whether the nominee is a woman or minority. Appellate court nominees who are women or minorities take twice as long to confirm as do white males.[34] The Senate is more likely to reject nominees when the opposition party controls the Senate, and in the last year of a president's term. Since 1950, the Senate has confirmed 94 percent of district and appellate court appointees when the president's party controls the Senate but only 80 percent of nominees when the opposition controls the Senate. The odds of confirmation in any event decline by 25 percent in a presidential election year.[35]

The confirmation process for courts of appeals judges has become an arena for conflict between the two political parties because of the importance and finality of the decisions of the appeals courts. Appellate courts decide thousands of cases per year, compared with fewer than a hundred decided by the U.S.

think

Do you think that federal judges should be periodically subject to reappointment or serve limited terms? Why or why not?

OFFICE HOURS
with PROFESSOR TANNAHILL

QUESTION: Why do court cases take so long to make it through the appeals process and reach the Supreme Court?

ANSWER: Although the court system sometimes moves quickly, most court cases spend years in the appeals process before the U.S. Supreme Court finally rules. *Brown v. Board of Education*, the landmark school desegregation case, was filed in Topeka, Kansas in February 1951, but wasn't decided by the Supreme Court until May 1954. The federal court system has three basic layers, and cases appealed from the state court systems typically pass through a multilayered system within the state, with numerous steps in the process at each stage. A cynic might also suggest that federal judges have no incentive to rush because they have lifetime appointments (with good behavior) and no federal judge has ever been impeached for working slowly.

Supreme Court, which agrees to hear relatively few appeals.[36] In addition, political parties in Congress are more ideologically polarized now than they were in the past. Republican members of Congress are almost all conservative, whereas their Democratic counterparts are almost all liberal. Most important votes in Congress break down along party lines, so it should be no surprise for judicial confirmation votes to become a partisan battleground as well. Finally, the stakes are high because of the close partisan balance on the courts, in which individual judges can tip the balance in a case.

Jurisdiction. The courts of appeals are exclusively appellate courts, usually hearing cases in panels of three justices each. They hear appeals from the U.S. district courts, the Court of International Trade, and the Court of Federal Claims. The courts of appeals also hear appeals on the decisions of the regulatory commissions, with the rulings of the National Labor Relations Board (NLRB) producing the most appeals. The courts of appeals are generally not required to hold hearings in every case. After reading the legal briefs in a case (a **legal brief** is a written legal argument) and reviewing the trial-court record, the appeals court may uphold the lower-court decision without hearing formal arguments.

> The courts of appeals have the final word on more than **95 percent** of the cases they hear.

When an appeals court decides to accept an appeal, the court usually schedules a hearing at which the attorneys for the two sides in the dispute present oral arguments and answer any questions posed by the justices. Appeals courts do not retry cases. Instead, they review the trial-court record and consider legal arguments. After hearing oral arguments and studying legal briefs, appeals court justices discuss the case and eventually vote on a decision, with a majority vote of the justices required to decide a case. The court may **affirm** (uphold) the lower court decision, reverse it, modify it, or affirm part of the lower court ruling while reversing or modifying the rest. Frequently, an appeals court may **remand** (return) a case to the trial court for reconsideration in light of the appeals court decision. The courts of appeals have the final word on more than 95 percent of the cases they hear because the Supreme Court rarely intervenes on appeal.[37]

legal brief a written legal argument.

affirm the action of an appeals court to uphold the decision of a lower court.

remand the decision of an appeals court to return a case to a lower court for reconsideration in light of an appeals court decision.

THE U.S. SUPREME COURT

15.3 *How does the Supreme Court function?*

The Supreme Court of the United States is the highest court in the land. Its rulings take precedence over the decisions of other federal courts. On matters involving federal law and the U.S. Constitution, the decisions of the U.S. Supreme Court take precedence over state court rulings as well.

The Constitution says nothing about the size of the Supreme Court, letting Congress and the president set its size legislatively. Through the years, the size of the Court has varied from five to ten justices. The present membership of nine justices has been in effect for more than a century. In the 1930s, President Franklin Roosevelt attempted to enlarge the Court in order to appoint new justices friendly to the New Deal, but his effort was popularly attacked as a court-packing plan and defeated by Congress. Since then, no serious efforts have been made to change the Court's size.

Today's Court includes a chief justice and eight associate justices. The justices are equal and independent, similar to nine separate law firms, but the chief justice is first among them. The chief presides over the Court's public sessions and private conferences. The chief justice can call special sessions of the Court and helps administer the federal court system. The chief justice also assigns justices the responsibility of writing the Court's majority opinion in cases when the chief votes with the majority.

The chief justice is a political leader who, to be successful, must deal effectively with political pressures both inside and outside the Court. Internally, the chief attempts to influence the other members of the Court. Externally, the chief justice lobbies Congress, responding and/or reacting to attacks against the Court. Regular sessions of the Supreme Court run from the first Monday in October until the end of June or early July. The summer months are a time for vacation and individual study by the Court's members, although the chief justice can call a special session to consider particularly pressing matters.

Jurisdiction

Technically, the Supreme Court can be both a trial court and an appellate court. The Constitution gives the Court a limited **original jurisdiction**, which is the set of cases a court

original jurisdiction the set of cases a court may hear as a trial court.

The Supreme Court in 2011

Justice	Year Born	Appoint-ment Year	Political Party	Law School	Appointing President	Religion	Senate Confirmation Vote
Antonin Scalia	1936	1985	R	Harvard	Reagan	Roman Catholic	98–0
Anthony Kennedy	1936	1988	R	Harvard	Reagan	Roman Catholic	97–0
Clarence Thomas	1948	1991	R	Yale	G. Bush	Roman Catholic	52–48
Ruth Bader Ginsburg	1933	1993	D	Columbia	Clinton	Jewish	96–3
Stephen Breyer	1938	1994	D	Harvard	Clinton	Jewish	87–9
John G. Roberts, Jr.	1955	2005	R	Harvard	G.W. Bush	Roman Catholic	78–22
Samuel A. Alito, Jr.	1950	2006	R	Yale	G.W. Bush	Roman Catholic	58–42
Sonia Sotomayor	1954	2009	I	Yale	Obama	Roman Catholic	68–31
Elena Kagan	1960	2010	D	Harvard	Obama	Jewish	63–37

may hear as a trial court. The Supreme Court may try "cases affecting ambassadors, other public ministers and consuls, and those in which a state shall be a party," except for cases initiated against a state by the citizens of another state or nation. In practice, however, the Court does not conduct trials. The Court shares jurisdiction with the U.S. district courts on the matters included in its original jurisdiction and leaves most of those cases for the district courts to decide.

The Court's appellate jurisdiction is set by law and, through the years, Congress has made the Supreme Court of the United States the nation's highest appellate court for both the federal and the state judicial systems. In the federal system, the courts of appeals generate the largest number of appeals by far. Cases may arise from the court of military appeals and special three-judge courts, which Congress has authorized to hear redistricting cases and some civil rights cases. Cases can also be appealed to the Supreme Court from the highest court in each state, usually the state supreme court.

Congress can reduce the jurisdiction of the Supreme Court if it chooses. After the Civil War, Congress removed the authority of the Court to review the constitutionality of Reconstruction legislation. Since then, Congress has been reluctant to tamper with the jurisdiction of the federal courts on grounds that it would interfere with the independence of the judicial branch. In recent years, most attempts to limit the jurisdiction of federal courts in cases involving such controversial issues as abortion, school prayer, busing, and the rights of criminal defendants have all failed.[38]

Selection of Justices

Nominating individuals to the Supreme Court is one of the president's most important responsibilities. Each appointment has the potential to affect public policy for years to come, particularly if the Court is closely divided or the president has the chance to name a new chief justice. Furthermore, it is an opportunity that may not come often. President Richard Nixon was able to appoint four justices in less than six years in office, but President Carter was unable to make any appointments during his four-year term.

The formal procedures for appointment and confirmation of Supreme Court justices are similar to those for appellate court justices except that they are generally performed more carefully and receive considerably more publicity.

The attorney general begins the task by compiling a list of possible nominees. The president narrows the list to a few names and the FBI conducts background checks on each.

In selecting individuals to serve on the Supreme Court, presidents look for nominees who share their political philosophy. When President Franklin Roosevelt finally had the chance to make appointments to the Supreme Court, he was careful to select nominees sympathetic to the

Supreme Court appointments have the potential to affect public policy for **years to come**.

Sonia Sotomayor, sworn in before the Senate Judiciary Committee in 2009, is the third female and first Latina justice.

New Deal. In contrast, President Reagan screened nominees to ensure their political conservatism.

The Senate scrutinizes Supreme Court nominations more closely than lower-court appointments. The Judiciary Committee staff and the staffs of individual senators carefully examine the nominee's background and past statements on policy issues. The committee conducts hearings at which the nominee, interest group spokespersons, and other concerned parties testify. The Senate as a whole then debates the nomination on the floor before voting to confirm or reject.

The confirmation process is highly political, with the White House and interest groups conducting public relations campaigns in hopes of putting pressure on wavering senators to confirm or reject the president's choice.[39] For example, the nomination of Clarence Thomas by President George H. W. Bush became a political tug-of-war between women's groups and the White House over Thomas's fitness to serve after Anita Hill, a former employee of Thomas at the Equal Employment Opportunity Commission (EEOC), accused him of sexual harassment.

Thomas eventually won confirmation by a narrow margin.

The Senate confirms most Supreme Court nominees. Since 1789, the Senate has approved 124 of 152 nominations. In the twentieth century alone, the rate was 52 of 62.[40] Senators routinely vote to confirm nominees who are perceived as well-qualified and whose political views are close to those of their constituents. When nominees are less qualified or hold controversial views, the outcome of the confirmation vote depends to a large degree on the political environment. Opponents of a nomination attempt to identify negative information about a nominee to justify rejection. They hope to expand the conflict over the nomination to the general public through committee hearings and the media. Consider the fate of Harriet Miers, President George W. Bush's first choice to replace the re-

tiring Sandra Day O'Connor on the Supreme Court. She asked the president to withdraw her nomination even before the Senate Judiciary Committee held hearings in the face of withering criticism from conservative commentators that she was both poorly qualified and insufficiently conservative for the job.

As with other judicial nominees, the Senate is most likely to reject Supreme Court nominees when the opposition party controls the Senate and/or when a nomination is made in the last year of a president's term.[41] When both these conditions apply, the failure rate for Supreme Court nominees is 71 percent.[42] The confirmation process has become so contentious that presidents have begun to seek out nominees who have written little so an to minimize the opportunity for opponents to build a case for rejection.

The backgrounds of individuals selected to serve on the Supreme Court are less diverse now than they once were. Historically, members of

Supreme Court Justice John Paul Stevens retired in 2010 after 35 years on the bench.

the Supreme Court came to the bench from a variety of backgrounds. Chief Justice Warren was governor of California. Justice Marshall was chief counsel for the National Association for the Advancement of Colored People (NAACP). In contrast, most justices chosen in the last 40 years have been federal judges, serving on the courts of appeal. Justice Kagan, a former solicitor general (the lawyer who represents the federal government before the Supreme Court) and Harvard Law School dean, is the only current member of the Court without prior judicial experience.

Life tenure means more today than it did **when the Constitution was written**.

Similar to other federal judges, members of the Supreme Court enjoy the ultimate in job security. With "good behavior," they can serve for life, and many have continued on the bench well past traditional retirement age. Associate Justice Hugo Black, for example, served until age 85; William O. Douglas stayed on the Court until he was 77, despite suffering a debilitating stroke; Justice Stevens retired from the Court in 2010 at the age of 90. Justices can be impeached and removed from office, but Congress is unlikely to act without clear evidence of misconduct. Politics or old age and ill health are probably not reason enough for Congress to initiate impeachment proceedings. Furthermore, because of advances in medicine, life tenure means more today than it did when the Constitution was written. Between 1789 and 1970, the average justice served fewer than 15 years, with vacancies occurring on average every 2 years. Since 1970, the average justice serves more than 26 years and a vacancy occurs every 3 years.[43] Because modern justices are serving longer, some Court observers advocate the adoption of term limits for Supreme Court jus-

tices in hopes of reducing the partisan intensity of the confirmation process and ensuring that each president has the opportunity to make one or two appointments.[44]

Deciding to Decide

Supreme Court justices set their own agenda. Each year, litigants appeal 7,000 to 10,000 cases to the Supreme Court, far more cases than the Court can reasonably handle. As a result, the justices screen the cases brought to them to decide which ones merit their attention.

Cases are the raw material from which the Supreme Court makes policy. An important judicial ground rule is that the Supreme Court must wait for a case to be appealed to it before it can rule. The Supreme Court does not issue advisory opinions. Although the members of the Court decide themselves what cases they will hear, their choices are limited to those cases that come to them on appeal. During the Civil War, for example, Chief Justice Taney, and perhaps a majority of the members of the Supreme Court, believed that the draft law was unconstitutional. They never had the opportunity to rule on the issue, however, because no case challenging the law ever reached the Court. Today, questions have been raised about the constitutionality of the limitations of the War Powers Act on the president's prerogatives as commander in chief, but the issue remains undecided because a case has yet to arise under the law.

The legal requirement that the Supreme Court can rule only when presented a case gives interest groups an incentive to promote and finance **test cases**, lawsuits initiated

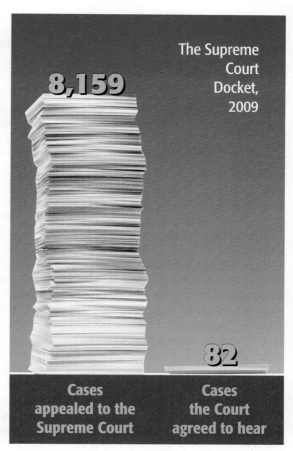

The Supreme Court Docket, 2009

8,159

82

Cases appealed to the Supreme Court

Cases the Court agreed to hear

to challenge the constitutionality of a legislative or executive act. *Brown v. Board of Education of Topeka*, for example, was a test case initiated by the NAACP. Linda Brown was a public school student who denied admission to a whites-only school near her home because of her race. The NAACP recruited the Brown family to file suit and provided the legal and financial resources necessary for carrying the case through the long and expensive process of trial and appeals.

Lawyers for losing parties in lower-court proceedings begin the process of appeal to the Supreme Court by filing petitions and submitting briefs explaining why their clients' cases merit review. Appellants must pay a filing fee and submit multiple copies of the paperwork, but the Court will waive these requirements when a litigant is too poor to hire an attorney or to cover the expenses of an appeal. The

test cases lawsuits initiated to assess the constitutionality of a legislative or executive act.

Court allows indigent appellants to file *in forma pauperis*, which is the process whereby an indigent litigant can file an appeal of a case to the Supreme Court without paying the usual fees. Frequently, pauper petitions come from prison inmates who study law books and prepare their own appeals. In 2008, 79 percent of the cases appealed to the Supreme Court were *in forma pauperis*.[45] The Court rejects most of these petitions, but a few make the Court's docket for full examination. When the Court decides to accept a case from the *in forma pauperis* docket, it appoints an attorney to prepare and argue the case for the indigent petitioner.

The actual selection process takes place in **conference**, a closed meeting attended by only the members of the Supreme Court. The justices decide which cases to hear based on the **Rule of Four**, a decision process used by the Supreme Court to determine which cases to consider on appeal, holding that the Court will hear a case if four of the nine justices agree to the review. In practice, the Supreme Court grants *certiorari*, or cert for short, which is the technical term for the Supreme Court's decision to hear arguments and make a ruling in a case, to only about 1 percent of all the cases appealed to it. In its 2009 term, the Court heard arguments on only 82 of the 8,159 cases appealed to it.[46]

What kinds of cases does the Supreme Court accept? The justices choose cases with legal issues of national significance that the Court has not already decided, cases involving conflicts among courts of appeals or between a lower court and the Supreme Court, and cases in which the constitutionality of a state or federal law is under attack. The Court rejects cases it considers trivial or local in scope, and cases that raise issues already decided by earlier rulings. The Court will not accept appeals from state courts unless the appellant can demonstrate that a substantial national constitutional question is involved.

In practice, the justices of the Supreme Court set their own rules for deciding which cases to accept, and then follow or interpret the rules as they see fit. For years, the Court refused to consider whether legislative districts that varied considerably in population size violated the Constitution. It was a political question, the justices said, declaring that the legislative and executive branches of government should address the issue rather than the judicial branch. In 1962, however, in *Baker v. Carr*, the Court chose to overlook its political-questions doctrine and rule on the dispute.[47]

In general, studies have found that the justices are more likely to accept a case when the U.S. government is the appellant, civil liberties or race related issues are involved, several interest groups file supporting briefs in a case, and lower courts disagree with one another. The members of the Supreme Court also choose cases that enable them to express their policy preferences with maximum impact. During the 1950s and 1960s, the Warren Court accepted cases to extend the guarantees of the Bill of Rights to the poor and other underdog litigants in both federal and state courts. In contrast, the more conservative Roberts Court often selects cases in order to adopt conservative policy positions. "Upperdogs," such as the government and business corporations, have been more successful in having their appeals heard.

Deciding the Case

The Supreme Court usually deals with the cases it chooses to hear in one of two ways. It decides some cases without oral arguments, issuing a ruling accompanied by an unsigned written opinion called a *per curiam opinion* that briefly explains the Court's decision. The justices may use this approach, for example, to reverse a lower-court ruling that is contrary to an earlier decision of the Court.

How a Case Gets to the Supreme Court

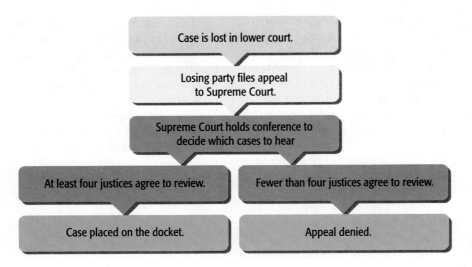

Case is lost in lower court.

Losing party files appeal to Supreme Court.

Supreme Court holds conference to decide which cases to hear

At least four justices agree to review. | Fewer than four justices agree to review.

Case placed on the docket. | Appeal denied.

in forma pauperis the process whereby an indigent litigant can file an appeal of a case to the Supreme Court without paying the usual fees.

conference a closed meeting attended only by the members of the Court.

Rule of Four a decision process used by the Supreme Court to determine which cases to consider on appeal, holding that the Court will hear a case if four of the nine justices agree to the review.

certiorari (cert) the technical term for the Supreme Court's decision to hear arguments and make a ruling in a case.

per curiam opinion an unsigned written opinion of a court.

How the Supreme Court Decides

Attorneys for the litigants submit briefs.

Other parties submit *amicus curiae* briefs.

Attorneys for the litigants present oral arguments.

Justices meet In closed conference to discuss and vote.

Designated justice drafts majority opinion.

Other justices in the majority may draft concurring opinions.

Justices in the minority may draft dissenting opinions.

Decision announced in open court.

The Court more extensively reviews the remainder of the cases it accepts. The attorneys for the litigants submit briefs arguing the merits of the case, and the Court schedules oral arguments. The Court may also receive *amicus curiae* (friend of the court) briefs, which are written legal arguments presented by parties not directly involved in the case, including interest groups and units of government. *Amicus* briefs offer the justices more input than they would otherwise receive and provide interest groups and other units of government an opportunity to lobby the Court. The justices sometimes use information contained in *amicus* briefs to justify their rulings.[48]

Attorneys for the litigants present oral arguments publicly to the nine justices in the courtroom of the Supreme Court building. The Court usually allows each side half an hour to make its case and to answer any questions the justices may ask. The members of the Court use the oral arguments to gather information about the case and to identify their policy options.[49] A few days after oral arguments, the justices meet in closed conference to discuss the case and to take a tentative vote. If the chief justice sides with the Court's majority on the initial vote, the chief either writes the majority opinion or assigns another justice the task. If the chief justice does not vote with the majority, the most senior justice in the majority is responsible for opinion assigning. The **majority opinion** is the official written statement of the Supreme Court, which explains and justifies its ruling and serves as a guideline for lower courts when similar legal issues arise in the future. The majority opinion is more important than the actual decision of the Court because the majority opinion establishes policy.

The majority opinion is a negotiated document among the justices who make up the majority on the deicion. While it is being written, other justices may be preparing and circulating concurring or dissenting opinions. A **concurring opinion** is a judicial statement that agrees with the Court's ruling but disagrees with the reasoning of the majority opinion. A justice may write a concurring opinion to point out what the Court did not do in the majority opinion and identify the issues that remain open for further litigation. A **dissenting opinion** is a judicial statement that disagrees with the decision of the court's majority. Justices write dissenting opinions in order to note disagreement with the Court's ruling, to emphasize the limits of the majority opinion, and to express the conscience of the individual justice. Only the majority opinion of the Court has legal force.

The Decision

Eventually, the positions of the justices harden or coalesce, and the Supreme Court announces its decision. The announcement takes place in open court, and the final versions of the majority, concurring, and dissenting opinions are published in the *United States Reports*. The Court decides cases by majority vote—9–0, 5–4, or anything in between.

Many observers believe that the strength of a Supreme Court decision depends on the level of agreement among the justices. *Brown v. Board of Education* was decided unanimously; the death or resignation of one or two justices was not going to reverse the majority on the issue should a similar case come before the Court in the near future. Furthermore, the Court issued only one opinion, the majority opinion written by Chief Justice Warren. The decision offered no comfort to anyone looking for a weakness of will on the Court. In contrast, the Court's decision in *Furman v. Georgia* (1972) was muddled. In *Furman*, the Court ruled that the death penalty, as then practiced, was discriminatory and hence unconstitutional. The Court did not say, however, that the death penalty, as such, was unconstitutional. The ruling's weakness, perhaps fragility, came from the closeness of the vote, five to four, and the number

> The majority opinion is more important than is the outcome of the case because the **majority opinion establishes policy**.

***amicus curiae* (friend of the court) brief** written legal argument presented by parties not directly involved in the case, including interest groups and units of government.

majority opinion the official written statement of the Supreme Court that explains and justifies its ruling and serves as a guideline for lower courts when similar legal issues arise in the future.

concurring opinion a judicial statement that agrees with the Court's ruling but disagrees with the reasoning of the majority opinion.

dissenting opinion a judicial statement that disagrees with the decision of the Court's majority.

Nigeria is an ethnically and religiously diverse country. The most important religions there are Islam, Christianity, Orisha, and Animism. After military rule ended in Nigeria in 1999 and the country established a federal system, 12 of the northern states adopted Sharia, Islamic law based on the Koran. Punishments under Sharia can be harsh. Adulterers may be stoned to death or flogged. Thieves may suffer the amputation of a hand. Public intoxication is punishable by flogging.

The adoption of Sharia in the northern states of Nigeria has been controversial. Even though Sharia applies only to Muslims, some aspects of it, including banning alcohol and prostitution, apply generally. Critics declare that the use of Sharia violates the principle of separation of state and religion. Furthermore, they charge that the status of women under Sharia and its imposition of harsh punishments cast the nation in an unfavorable light. They point to the 2002 case that provoked international outrage in which a divorced Muslim woman was sentenced to death after having a child out of wedlock. Islamic courts eventually overturned the sentence on the basis of a technicality. Sharia courts have subsequently avoided high-profile controversial cases.[50]

Amina Lawal and her lawyer appealed Lawal's Sharia sentence of death by stoning for adultery. The court overturned the verdict and Lawal was freed.

QUESTIONS

1 In a country as diverse as Nigeria, is it better for different regions to follow their own legal traditions or would it be preferable for the entire nation to have a uniform system?

2 Should a nation's laws be based on its religious traditions?

3 In what ways, if any, is American law grounded in Judeo-Christian legal traditions?

---

of opinions—four concurring and four dissenting opinions, besides the majority opinion. The justices could not agree on which facts were important in the case or what goals the Court should pursue.[51]

Implementation and Impact

Political scientists Charles Johnson and Bradley Canon divide the judicial policymaking process into three stages. First, higher courts, especially the U.S. Supreme Court, develop policies. Although major policy cases make headlines, the Supreme Court frequently clarifies and elaborates on an initial decision with subsequent rulings on related issues. Second, lower courts interpret the higher court rulings. In theory, lower federal courts apply

policies formulated by the U.S. Supreme Court without modification. In practice, however, Supreme Court rulings are often general, leaving room for lower courts to adapt them to the circumstances of specific cases. The third stage of Johnson and Canon's model of judicial policymaking is the implementation by relevant government agencies and private parties.[52] State legislatures had to rewrite death penalty statutes to comply with the *Furman* ruling, for example. Local school boards had the task of developing integration plans to comply with the *Brown* decision.

> **Unpopular**
> Supreme Court decisions are often met with **delay and subtle evasion**.

Although the implementation of Supreme Court rulings is not automatic, direct disobedience is rare because Court actions enjoy considerable symbolic legitimacy. When the Supreme Court ordered President Nixon to turn over key Watergate tapes to the special prosecutor, for example, Nixon complied. Had the president made a bonfire of them, as some observers suggested, he probably would have been impeached. Instead of defiance, unpopular Supreme Court decisions are often met with delay and subtle evasion.

Supreme Court decisions have their greatest impact when the Court issues a clear decision in a well-publicized case and its position enjoys strong support from other branches and units of government, interest groups, and public opinion.[53]

POWER, POLITICS, AND THE COURTS

What factors affect the policymaking power of the courts?

How much influence do federal courts have in the policymaking process? How responsive are they to public concerns? On different occasions in American history, various groups and individuals have attacked the federal courts as both too powerful and undemocratic. In the early 1930s, liberals said that the members of the Supreme Court were "nine unelected old men" who abused their power and tried to unravel the New Deal, despite strong popular support for President Roosevelt's program. In the 1960s and 1970s, conservatives complained about court rulings that gave rights to accused criminals, atheists, and political protesters, while preventing state and local governments from outlawing abortion or controlling the racial balance of local schools.

Both the Constitution and the law **check judicial authority**.

Political scientists who study the judicial branch identify a number of restrictions on the power of the federal courts. Both the Constitution and the law check judicial authority. The president appoints federal judges, and the Senate confirms their appointments. In the long run, Franklin Roosevelt won his battle with the Supreme Court by waiting for justices to die or retire and then replacing them with individuals friendly to New Deal policies. Voters who believe that the Supreme Court is too liberal or too conservative can eventually reverse the Court by electing conservative/liberal presidents and senators.

If Congress and the president believe that judicial rulings are wrong, they can undo the Court's work by changing the law or the Constitution. If Congress and the president disagree with the Court's interpretation of federal law, they can rewrite the law. In 1978, for example, the Supreme Court ruled that the completion of a dam on the Little Tennessee River would violate the Endangered Species Act because it threatened a tiny fish called the snail darter.[54] The following year, Congress legislated to reverse the Court.

Congress and the president cannot overrule Supreme Court decisions based on interpretations of the Constitution by simply passing legislation. **Statutory law**, which is law written by the legislature, does not supersede **constitutional law**, which is law that involves the interpretation and application of the Constitution. Amending the Constitution to overturn court rulings is a more difficult procedure than changing statutory law, of course, but it has been done. The Twenty-sixth Amendment, giving 18-year-olds the right to vote, was passed and ratified after the Supreme Court held that Congress could not legislatively lower the voting age because of constitutional restrictions.[55] Congress and the states have overturned four Supreme Court decisions by enacting constitutional amendments.[56]

The power of the federal courts is also limited by the practical nature of the judicial process. Courts are reactive institutions. They respond to policies adopted in other branches and at other levels of government, and then only when presented with a case to decide. The

Supreme Court cannot rule on the constitutionality of the War Powers Act, for example, until it has been given a case dealing with the issue.

Because the courts cannot enforce their own rulings, they must depend on the cooperation and compliance of other units of government and private parties to implement their decisions. Consider, for example, the difficulty in enforcing the Supreme Court's school prayer rulings. Despite the Supreme Court's longstanding decision against government-prescribed official prayers in public school classrooms, they continue to take place in a substantial number of schools, especially in the South, in rural and less educated communities, and in areas with relatively high concentrations of conservative Christians.[57]

Political scientist Robert Dahl believes that the courts are not out of step with Congress and the executive branch for long. Dahl conducted a study in which he traced the fate of 23 "important" laws that had been struck down by the Supreme Court. Three-fourths of the time, Dahl found that the original policy position adopted by Congress and the president ultimately prevailed. In most instances, Congress simply passed legislation similar to the measure that had been initially invalidated. And the second time around, the Court ruled the tweaked legislation constitutional. The role of the

statutory law law that is written by the legislature.

constitutional law law that involves the interpretation and application of the Constitution.

courts, Dahl said, is to legitimize the policy decisions made by the elected branches of government rather than to make policy on their own.[58]

In contrast, other political scientists believe that Dahl underestimated the policy influence of the courts. They note that whereas Dahl examined issues that he considered important, many so-called unimportant decisions are not unimportant at all, particularly to the groups most directly affected. Even on important matters, Dahl admits that court rulings affect the timing, effectiveness, and details of policy.[59]

think To what degree should Supreme Court justices consider public opinion in making their decisions?

The federal courts are important participants in America's policy process, but their influence depends on the political environment, the issue, and the political skills and values of the judges. One study concludes that the power of the federal courts, particularly the Supreme Court, hinges on their capacity to forge alliances with other political forces, including interest groups and the executive branch. In the 1960s, for example, the Supreme Court joined forces with civil rights groups and the White House under Presidents Kennedy and Johnson to promote the cause of African American civil rights.[60] Another study finds that federal judges are more likely to rule against presidential policy when the chief executive has lost popularity than when the president enjoys strong public support.[61]

The role of the courts varies from issue to issue. In today's policy process, the courts are most likely to defer to the other branches of government on issues involving foreign and defense policy, and economic policy. The courts are least likely to follow the lead of other branches and units of government on matters dealing with civil rights and civil liberties.

Legal scholar Jeffrey Rosen believes that the courts reflect the views of a majority of Americans on most issues. Judges can nudge the country in one policy direction or another, but they are sensitive to public opinion through pressure by Congress and the president. They recognize that their policy decisions will not be accepted by the country unless those decisions are perceived as being rooted in constitutional principles rather than the personal preferences of judges. On those occasions when courts stray too far away from mainstream public opinion, they get slapped down.[62]

High school football players in Odessa, Texas kneel in prayer after a game. Although it is unconstitutional for school authorities to organize prayers, students have a constitutional right to pray on their own initiative.

TAKING SIDES

Supreme Court Justices: Too Long on the Bench?

Is the lifetime term for Supreme Court justices too long?

Should a Constitutional amendment be added to give Supreme Court justices a single, fixed term?

OVERVIEW

Supreme Court justices are nominated by the president and confirmed by the U.S. Senate. Over the last couple of decades, the confirmation process has become much more rancorous and political than it had been in the past. Senate hearings for nominations are very public, with politicians, pundits, and interest groups weighing in on both sides. President Obama's first two Supreme Court nominee—Sonia Sotomayor and Elena Kagan—were confirmed largely along party lines, 68–31 for Sotomayor and 63–37 for Kagan.

Supreme Court justices also serve for life, because the founders wanted them to be removed from politics and able to make independent decisions. From 1789 to 1970, the average justice served for 16 years, but since 1970 the average justice has served 25.5 years.

In 2005, two law professors proposed the Supreme Court Renewal Act, which would require justices to rotate off the Supreme Court after 18 years—to either retire or serve on an appeals court. In 2009, the American Bar Association lent its support to the proposal.

 SUPPORTING a fixed term   AGAINST a fixed term

SUPPORTING a fixed term

The founders could not have foreseen the effect of the lifetime appointment clause. With dramatically increased life expectancy, people who make it to the bench stay there for a much longer time than the writers of the Constitution could have expected. Modern justices thus have a much greater effect on judicial interpretation than was originally intended.

The Supreme Court is not accountable to the American people. If the justices fall out of step with the views of the people, Americans have no way of reining them in. Term limits would allow change in a branch that needs it more often.

Partisan fights have led to more ideological appointees. Because the political system is so ideologically polarized, presidents nominate and Senators confirm—mostly along party line votess— ideologically committed justices. Unlike elected officials serving fixed term, the ideological justices stay for much longer than their ideological position is popular in the country at large.

AGAINST a fixed term

The Supreme Court is removed from the political process for a reason. The founders separated the function of interpreting law from the political process. Justices are generally selected and confirmed for their merit, that is, their ability to understand and interpret the law. Having justices step down to suit the changing winds of public opinion would add politics to the institution.

Longer terms create stability and continuity in important judicial rulings. Since more than 95 percent of cases are decided in state courts, Supreme Court justices are not responsible for the bulk of the judicial interpretation in this country. Therefore, it is important that these justices do serve a long time so that we have stability for those most crucial cases that do eventually reach the Court.

The longer justices serve together the better they get at making decisions. The justices indicate that they spend quite a bit of time talking to each other while making decisions. The more they can learn from, trust, and respect each other the better they will be at making the best decisions.

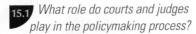

JUDICIAL POLICYMAKING

15.1 *What role do courts and judges play in the policymaking process?*

Courts make policy by interpreting the law and the Constitution. Courts interpret the Constitution by exercising judicial review. Some justices believe in strict construction, a narrow interpretation of the Constitution, while others favor loose construction, a broader interpretation. Justices also disagree about their role. Judicial activism is the charge that judges are going beyond their authority by making the law and not just interpreting it. Judicial restraint is the concept that judges should defer to the policymaking judgment of the legislative and executive branches of government unless their actions clearly violate the law or the Constitution. Many political scientists believe that all judges consider that the Constitution is a charter of fundamental principles that must be upheld but that liberal and conservative judges disagree as to what those principles are.

Over time, the Supreme Court shifts between periods of strict and loose construction, greater or less activity, decisions supporting a strong national government or states' rights, and rulings of a liberal or conservative nature. In recent years, the Court has had a close partisan balance, issuing some liberal and some conservative rulings.

THE LOWER FEDERAL COURTS

15.2 *How is the federal court system organized?*

The federal court system has three layers. The U.S. District Courts are trial courts, conducting all federal criminal and civil trials except those heard by the U.S. Court of Federal Claims and the U.S. Court of International Trade, which are specialized trial courts. The U.S. Courts of Appeals hear appeals from the federal trial courts and administrative agencies. These courts may affirm, reverse, or modify a lower court ruling. The U.S. Supreme Court, the highest court in the land, has the authority to try a limited range of cases but in practice is almost exclusively an appellate court.

The president appoints federal judges with senate confirmation, following the custom of senatorial courtesy. The overwhelming majority of district court nominees are approved, although the confirmation process is sometimes lengthy. All federal judges serve for life, "with good behavior."

THE U.S. SUPREME COURT

15.3 *How does the Supreme Court function?*

The Supreme Court is the highest court in the land. Congress has set the size of the court at nine—a presiding chief justice and eight associate justices. In practice, the Supreme Court is exclusively an appeals court, hearing cases brought to it from the courts of appeals and the highest court in each state, usually a state supreme court. The president fills vacancies on the Supreme Court by appointment, pending Senate confirmation. The confirmation process is often highly political. Similar to other federal judges, Supreme Court justices serve for life, "with good behavior."

The justices select which cases to hear among the thousands that are appealed. While the Court settles some cases quickly with *per curiam* opinions, most cases involve the justices reading briefs and hearing oral arguments. After an initial vote, the chief or the most senior justice in the majority writes or assigns the majority opinion. Justices may also write concurring and dissenting opinions. Although the Supreme Court decides cases by majority vote, many observers believe that the strength of a ruling depends on the level of agreement among the justices. After the Supreme Court sets policy, lower courts adapt the policies to particular circumstances. Government agencies and private parties implement the policies. Supreme Court decisions have their greatest impact when the position enjoys strong support from other branches and units of government, interest groups, and public opinion.

POWER, POLITICS, AND THE COURTS

15.4 *What factors affect the policymaking power of the courts?*

Political scientists who study the judicial branch identify a number of restraints on the power of the federal courts. Courts will eventually reflect the will of the voters because judges are appointed and confirmed by elected officials. Judicial decisions can be reversed by changing the law or the Constitution. Furthermore, courts are reactive institutions in that they must wait for a case before they can rule and they cannot enforce their own decisions.

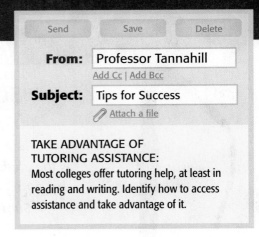

Send Save Delete

From: Professor Tannahill
Add Cc | Add Bcc
Subject: Tips for Success
Attach a file

TAKE ADVANTAGE OF TUTORING ASSISTANCE: Most colleges offer tutoring help, at least in reading and writing. Identify how to access assistance and take advantage of it.

15.1 *What role do courts and judges play in the policymaking process?*

1 The power of the courts to declare unconstitutional the actions of the other branches and units of government is known as which of the following?
  a. Loose construction
  b. Judicial review
  c. Strict construction
  d. Civil liberties

2 Which of the following statements most closely reflects the philosophy of loose construction of the Constitution?
  a. Judges should interpret the Constitution broadly to allow it to change with the times.
  b. Judges should recognize that their role is to interpret the law rather than make the law.
  c. Judges should stick to the literal meaning of the Constitution.
  d. Judges should closely follow the intent of the framers of the Constitution.

3 A liberal judge is more likely than a conservative judge to take which of the following policy actions?
  a. To rule in favor of the government and against criminal defendants
  b. To rule in favor of workers and against corporate interests
  c. To rule in favor of state governments in federalism disputes with the federal government
  d. All of the above

4 The Supreme Court claimed the power of judicial review in which of the following cases?
  a. *Marbury v. Madison*
  b. *McCulloch v. Maryland*
  c. *Brown v. Board of Education*
  d. *Plessy v. Ferguson*

15.2 *How is the federal court system organized?*

5 Which of the following federal courts is exclusively a trial court?
  a. District court
  b. Courts of appeal
  c. Supreme Court
  d. None of the above

6 The taking of a case from a lower court to a higher court by the losing party in a lower court decision is known as which of the following?
  a. Test case
  b. Judicial review
  c. Trial
  d. Appeal

7 How are U.S. district judges selected?
  a. They are career civil servants, chosen through a merit hiring process.
  b. They are appointed by the president subject to confirmation by the Senate.
  c. They are elected by the voters in the states where they serve.
  d. They are appointed by the president subject to confirmation by the House and Senate.

8 What is the term of office of a federal district judge?
  a. Two years
  b. Four years
  c. Six years
  d. Life, with "good behavior"

15.3 *How does the Supreme Court function?*

9 Suppose that Congress passes controversial legislation that some people believe is unconstitutional. When, if ever, will the Supreme Court address the issue?
  a. The Supreme Court will decide the issue when and if it accepts a case that involves a challenge to the constitutionality of the legislation.
  b. The Supreme Court reviews legislation passed by Congress before it takes effect.
  c. The Supreme Court will only review the legislation if Congress requests a review.
  d. Never.

10 Why was *Brown v. Board of Education* an example of a test case?
  a. The Supreme Court reversed an earlier decision (the *Plessy* case) when it decided *Brown*.
  b. The case was prepared, presented, and financed by an interest group.
  c. An interest group submitted a legal brief that discussed issues raised by the case.
  d. *Brown* is considered a landmark decision in constitutional law.

11 A Supreme Court justice agrees with the outcome of a case but disagrees with the legal reasoning presented in the majority opinion. Which of the following actions would the justice take?
  a. File a friend of the court brief
  b. Write a concurring opinion
  c. Write a majority opinion
  d. Write a dissenting opinion

12 Assuming that the Supreme Court is fully staffed and that every justice participates in a decision, how many justices must agree to decide the outcome of a case?
  a. Four
  b. Five
  c. Six
  d. Nine

15.4 *What factors affect the policymaking power of the courts?*

13 Suppose that a majority of the members of the Supreme Court believe that a recent action by the president violates the Constitution. What can they do?
  a. They can do nothing until a case arises that involves the issue and the case is appealed to the Supreme Court.
  b. Nothing. The Supreme Court can review the acts of Congress but not the actions of the president.
  c. The Supreme Court can issue an opinion declaring the president's action unconstitutional.
  d. The Supreme Court can invite parties to file a challenge against the president's action.

14 What power does the Supreme Court have to enforce its rulings?
  a. The Court can order law enforcement personnel to enforce its rulings.
  b. The Court must rely on the other branches and units of government to enforce its rulings.
  c. Court rulings do not need to be enforced because compliance is voluntary.
  d. None. Court rulings are regularly ignored.

15 Which of the following is a check on the power of the Supreme Court?
  a. The president can appoint and the Senate can confirm new justices to fill vacancies on the Court.
  b. The House and Senate can propose an amendment to the Constitution to overturn a judicial interpretation of the Constitution.
  c. Congress and the president can rewrite a law to reverse a judicial interpretation of an act of Congress.
  d. All of the above

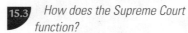

KNOW the score

14–15 correct:	Congratulations—you know your American government!
12–13 correct:	Your understanding of this chapter is weak—be sure to review the key terms and visit TheThinkSpot.
< 12 correct:	Reread the chapter more thoroughly.

Answers: 1) b, 2) a, 3) b, 4) a, 5) a, 6) d, 7) b, 8) d, 9) a, 10) b, 11) b, 12) b, 13) a, 14) b 15) d

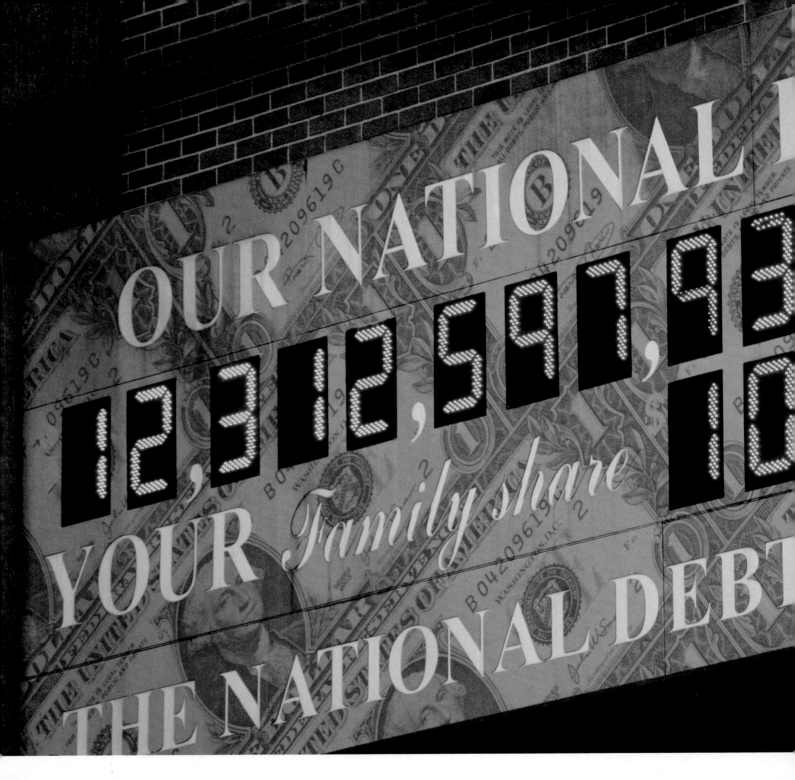

16 ECONOMIC

The federal government is spending more money than it collects in taxes, much more. In 2010, federal expenditures exceeded revenues by $1.3 trillion. It was the largest federal **budget deficit**, which is the amount by which expenditures exceed revenues, since the end of World War II, when the government borrowed huge sums of money to

POLICYMAKING

fund the war effort.[1] Furthermore, the Congressional Budget Office (CBO) projects that the cumulative deficit between 2010 and 2020 will be nearly $10 trillion.[2] Although most economists agree that running a budget deficit is sometimes an appropriate economic policy, they warn that large annual deficits incurred over a long period of time threaten the nation's economic health.

Policymakers disagree about economic policy. President Barack Obama and his Democratic allies in Congress believe that the country needs to adopt a long-term plan for reducing the deficit, including both tax increases and spending reductions. In the short run, however,

they contend that the government should increase spending in order to stimulate the economy and reduce the unemployment rate, which exceeded 9 percent in 2010. In contrast, Republicans counter that government spending and the deficit are the real threat to the economy. They say that the best way to attack the deficit and help the economy is by cutting government spending.

The debate over government spending and the budget deficit introduces this chapter on economic policymaking. The chapter begins by discussing the goals of economic policy. It identifies the most significant revenue sources of the federal government. The

chapter examines some of the key issues facing the nation's tax system and the reforms that have been proposed for addressing those issues. It discusses budget deficits and the national debt, and their potential effect on the health of the economy. The chapter then examines the major spending priorities of the federal government. It discusses how the government makes fiscal policy, as well as the policymaking role of the Federal Reserve System. Finally, the chapter details the economic policymaking process.

budget deficit the amount by which annual budget expenditures exceed annual budget receipts.

THE GOALS OF ECONOMIC POLICY

16.1 *What are the primary goals of American economic policy?*

Policymakers adopt economic policies in order to achieve the goals of funding government services, encouraging/discouraging private sector activity, redistributing income, and promoting economic growth with stable prices.

Fund Government Services

Americans disagree over spending priorities and the appropriate level of funding for federal activity. In fiscal year 2010, which ran from October 1, 2009 through September 30, 2010, the federal government spent $3.5 trillion funding government programs, including healthcare, Social Security, and national defense.[3] In general, liberals believe that government can play a positive role in addressing the needs of society. They favor programs to improve the nation's health, education, and welfare. In contrast, conservatives believe that the role of government should be limited to the provision of basic services. They support spending for

national defense and to promote economic development, but they are wary about spending for social programs, especially by the federal government, because they think that high taxes and big government suppress economic growth.

Consider the controversy over the National Endowment for the Arts (NEA), which is a government agency created to nurture cultural expression and promote appreciation of the arts. The NEA helps fund art exhibitions, drama productions, and musical performances all over the United States. Many conservative members of Congress want to end funding for the NEA. Why should taxpayers support art, they ask, especially art that may offend them? In contrast, liberal members of Congress defend the NEA. Government should support the arts, they declare, because it enriches the cultural life of the nation and enhances local economic development. Sometimes art will be controversial, but the government should not dictate to artists what their art should embody.

think

Do you think that tax money should support the National Endowment for the Arts (NEA)? Why or why not?

Encourage/Discourage Private Sector Activity

Congress and the president use economic policy to encourage some private sector activities while discouraging others. By making home mortgage interest and real estate taxes deductible, the federal government promotes housing construction and home ownership. Similarly, the government uses tax breaks to encourage people to give money to charity, save for retirement, and invest in state and local government bonds. Congress and the president also use tax policy to discourage certain activities. Increasing cigarette taxes, for example, reduces the smoking rate for teenagers.

Raising gasoline taxes saves energy and decreases pollution by discouraging driving.

A **subsidy** is a financial incentive given by government to an individual or a business interest to accomplish a public objective. The federal government encourages people to go to college by providing students with low-interest loans. It keeps the U.S. merchant marine in business by requiring that goods shipped between American ports travel on American-flag vessels with American crews rather than less expensive foreign-registered ships. Government subsidizes farm production, cattle grazing on western lands, offshore oil production, and marketing American products and goods overseas.

The government operates a number of agricultural subsidy programs. It gives some farmers price-support loans. Farmers borrow money from the government, using their crops as collateral. The value of the crops and hence the amount of money the farmer can borrow is determined by a target commodity price set by the U.S. Department of Agriculture (USDA). If the market price rises above the target price, the farmer sells the crop, repays the loan, and makes a profit. If the market price falls below the target price, the government pays farmers the difference between the two prices,

either in cash or in certificates for government stored commodities. The government also subsidizes farmers by intervening to limit commodity production, thus dri-

think If you were in Congress, would you favor tax subsidies for home ownership? Attending college? Offshore drilling? Producing renewable energy? Growing sugarcane?

ving up market prices. No one can grow peanuts, for example, without a federal license.

Tax incentives and subsidies are controversial. Their defenders argue that tax incentives and subsidies enable the government to accomplish worthwhile goals, such as promoting home ownership and the export of American-made goods. In contrast, the critics of tax incentives and subsidies charge that they are based more on politics than the desire to achieve worthwhile policy goals. Tax breaks and subsidies drive up taxes and product costs for ordinary Americans and consumers. Congress and the president persist in reauthorizing and funding farm programs because of the political power of agricultural interest groups.[4]

American agricultural producers benefit from billions of dollars in subsidies.

Redistribute Income

Income redistribution involves government taking items of value, especially money, from some groups of people and then giving items of value, either in cash or services, to other groups of people. Those people who favor income redistribution believe that government has an obligation to reduce the income gap between the poorest and wealthiest income groups in the nation. They advocate the adoption of programs that provide benefits based on need and a tax structure whose burden falls most heavily on business and the wealthy. Furthermore, many scholars believe that extreme levels of income inequality are incompatible with democracy. They note that the world's democracies tend to be countries with a large middle class, whereas countries that are divided between a small group of very rich families and a huge group of the very poor typically do not have democratic governments. In contrast, the opponents of income redistribution believe that government should adopt tax systems and spending programs designed to foster economic development because, in the long run, economic development will benefit all segments of society, including low-income groups, more than programs designed to redistribute wealth. In practice, they warn, programs designed to redistribute wealth hinder economic development, hurting everyone. They believe that government has a role to ensure a level playing field in which everyone can compete fairly to get ahead, but that government should not intervene to dictate economic winners and losers.

subsidy a financial incentive given by government to an individual or a business interest to accomplish a public objective.

income redistribution government taking items of value, especially money, from some groups of people and then giving items of value, either in cash or services, to other groups of people.

> Extreme levels of income inequality seem **incompatible with democracy**.

Many government programs redistribute income. Healthcare reform transfers wealth from upper-income earners to low- and middle-income people.[5] Social Security, a federal pension and disability insurance program, transfers money from current wage earners and their employers to retirees and people with disabilities.

Promote Economic Growth with Stable Prices

A final goal of economic policy is to promote economic growth by avoiding depression, minimizing the severity of recession, and controlling inflation.[6] A **depression** is a severe and prolonged economic slump characterized by decreased business activity and high unemployment. It is more severe than a **recession**, which is an economic slowdown characterized by declining economic output and rising unemployment. **Inflation** is a decline in the purchasing power of the currency. Consider the response of the government to the severe recession of 2008–2009. Early in 2008, Congress passed and President George W. Bush signed legislation to give most taxpayers a $600 tax rebate in hopes that they would spend the money and thus boost the economy. Later in the year, with economic conditions worsening, the Bush administration loaned billions of dollars to companies to keep them from failing, including GM and Chrysler. Meanwhile, Congress authorized the U.S. Department of the Treasury to spend $700 billion to bail out the financial industry in hopes that banks and mortgage companies would begin making

loans again, freeing the credit market. The Federal Reserve reduced **interest** rates to near zero and loaned money to financial institutions as well. In early 2009, Congress passed and President Barack Obama signed a $787 billion stimulus package of tax cuts and spending programs designed to get the economy moving again. Finally, Congress passed and the president signed a measure in 2010 to give $26 billion to states to minimize the number of teachers who lose their jobs and to help states cover the cost of providing healthcare to low-income people.

Government efforts to manage the economy are controversial. Liberal economists believe that the government can play a positive role in promoting economic growth with stable prices. They credit the actions of the Bush and Obama administrations with saving the nation from

another Great Depression. Although the recession was severe, so severe that it is often called the Great Recession, it could have been much worse.[7] In contrast, conservatives argue that government interventions in the economy are counterproductive. Government bailouts and stimulus spending drive up the deficit, they say, without making the economy more efficient. In their view, the best government policies for promoting economic growth are low taxes, low spending, and minimal regulation.

depression a severe and prolonged economic slump characterized by decreased business activity and high unemployment.

recession an economic slowdown characterized by declining economic output and rising unemployment.

inflation a decline in the purchasing power of the currency.

interest money paid for the use of money.

The Obama administration created a web site to track stimulus spending so the public could see that the money was being used to create jobs and was not being wasted. You can look up projects in your area at www.recovery.gov.

REVENUES:
HOW GOVERNMENT RAISES MONEY

16.2 *What are the most important sources of revenue for the federal government?*

In 2010, the U.S. government raised $2.2 trillion in revenue. As the figure on the right shows, the individual income tax and payroll taxes together generated nearly 85 percent of federal government revenue. The corporate income tax along with a variety of other sources accounted for the remainder.

Individual Income Tax

The individual income tax is the largest single source of revenue for the national government, producing 43.2 percent of the nation's total tax revenue in fiscal year (budget year) 2010. The income tax system divides taxable income into brackets and applies a different tax rate to the portion of income falling into each bracket, with higher incomes taxed at higher rates than lower incomes.

Income tax rates are a source of political controversy. When President Bill Clinton left office in 2001, the tax tables included five brackets with tax rates of 15, 28, 31, 36, and 39.6 percent. Shortly after taking office, President George W. Bush proposed and Congress passed a major income tax cut that increased the number of brackets to six and reduced the rates to 10, 15, 25, 28, 33, and 35 percent. They also agreed to repeal the **estate tax**, which is a tax levied on the value of an inheritance. Congress and the president subsequently reduced taxes on dividend income, and exempted or deferred taxes on interest income from savings. In order to avoid a Senate filibuster, Republican leaders phased the tax cuts in over the following decade and then allowed them all to expire in 2011. President Obama has proposed making the Bush tax cuts permanently for everyone but families earning more than $250,000 a year and individuals making more than $200,000 annually. He would

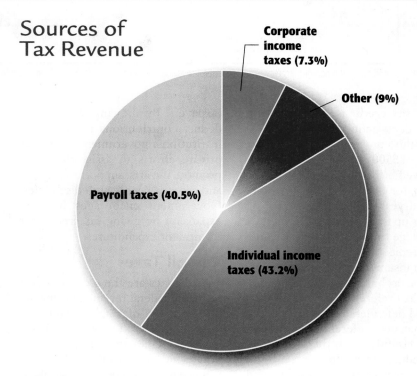

Sources of Tax Revenue

- Corporate income taxes (7.3%)
- Other (9%)
- Payroll taxes (40.5%)
- Individual income taxes (43.2%)

Source: Office of Management and Budget

use the extra revenue to reduce the deficit. Republicans, meanwhile, want to make all the Bush tax cuts permanent, arguing that increasing taxes would hurt the economy.

Because of tax preferences, not all income is taxable. A **tax preference** is a tax deduction or exclusion that allows individuals to pay less tax than they would otherwise. Tax preferences include tax exemptions, deductions, and credits. A **tax exemption** is the exclusion of some types of income from taxation. For example, veterans' benefits, pension contributions and earnings, and interest earned on state and local government bonds are exempt from the income tax. Taxpayers are also allowed to claim personal exemptions for themselves and their dependents. In 2010, the personal exemption was $3,650 for every taxpayer and each dependent.

A **tax deduction** is an expenditure that can be subtracted from a taxpayer's gross income before figuring the tax owed. Taxpayers can itemize deductions for such expenditures as home mortgage interest payments, charitable contributions, and state and local real estate taxes. For example, a family that contributes $5,000 to charity reduces its taxable income by $5,000.

estate tax tax levied on the value of an inheritance.

tax preference a tax deduction or exclusion that allows individuals to pay less tax than they would otherwise.

tax exemption the exclusion of some types of income from taxation.

tax deduction an expenditure that can be subtracted from a taxpayer's gross income before figuring the tax owed.

Payroll taxes, the second-largest source of federal revenue, support the Social Security and Medicare programs.

A **tax credit** is an expenditure that reduces an individual's tax liability by the amount of the credit. A tax credit of $500 reduces the amount of tax owed by $500. The Hope Scholarship, for example, grants first- and second-year college students tax credits up to $1,500 to cover the cost of college tuition and fees. A family tax credit of $5,000 to purchase health insurance reduces the family's income tax burden by $5,000.

Tax preferences have both critics and defenders. Their opponents say that tax preferences erode taxpayer confidence in the income tax and reduce tax receipts. In 2010, tax preferences reduced individual and corporate income tax collections by nearly $1 trillion.[8] Defenders of tax preferences point out that they are a mechanism that government can use to promote certain activities or assist particular groups of taxpayers. By allowing taxpayers to deduct contributions to charitable institutions, government promotes private efforts to assist the poor, promote the arts, support education, and care for people with disabilities. Government encourages business expansion by giving tax credits for investment expenditures.

Payroll Taxes

Payroll taxes are the second-largest source of federal revenue, producing 40.5 percent of total revenues in 2010. The payroll tax rate, which is levied on wages and salaries but not other sources of income, is 15.3 percent, with 7.65 percent withheld from the employee's paycheck and an equivalent 7.65 percent paid by the employer. Most workers pay more in payroll taxes than they pay in personal income taxes. A single worker earning $30,000 a year in wages, for example, paid $4,590 in payroll taxes in 2010 compared with less than $3,000 in income taxes. The payroll tax supports both the Social Security and Medicare programs, with 12.4 percent going to finance Social Security and 2.9 percent set aside for Medicare. Wage earners and their employers paid Social Security payroll taxes on the first $106,800 of an employee's annual salary in 2010. They paid the Medicare payroll tax on all wage income. In 2010, Congress expanded the payroll tax to cover income other than wages and salaries to help fund healthcare reform. Beginning in 2012, families earning $250,000 or more a year ($200,000 for individuals) will pay a 3.8 percent Medicare payroll tax on investment income.

tax credit an expenditure that reduces an individual's tax liability by the amount of the credit.

TAKE ✓ ACTION

Tax Breaks for College Students

The Hope Credit and Lifetime Learning Credit are tax breaks for college students. Your assignment is to research the tax rules to determine whether you or your parents can benefit from these credits. You can find information about these credits online at the IRS website, www.irs.gov. Research these tax breaks for college students, review your family's tax situation, and answer the following questions:

• How do the Hope Credit and Lifetime Learning Credit programs differ?

• Who qualifies? Do you have to be a full-time student? Are the credits available for both public and private school students?

• If parents have two children in college at the same time, can they claim a tax credit for each of them?

• Can you claim the cost of this textbook as an educational expense? Why or why not?

• Do you or your parents qualify for either the Hope Credit or the Lifetime Learning Credit? Why or why not?

• If you qualify for either, how will the credit affect your tax liability?

• Did you or your parents claim a credit last year? Will you claim it next year?

Corporate Income Taxes and Other Revenue Sources

In 2010, the national government derived 16.3 percent of its tax revenue from corporate income taxes, excise taxes, and miscellaneous revenue sources. The corporate income tax, which generated 7.3 percent of federal tax revenues in 2010, has four brackets—15 percent on the first $50,000 of taxable earnings, 25 percent on income between $50,000 and $75,000, 34 percent on earnings between $75,000 and $10 million, and 35 percent on income greater than $10 million. Because the 15 percent and 25 percent rates apply only to income below $75,000, most corporate profits are taxed at the higher rates. **Excise taxes** are taxes levied on the manufacture, transportation, sale, or consumption of a particular item or

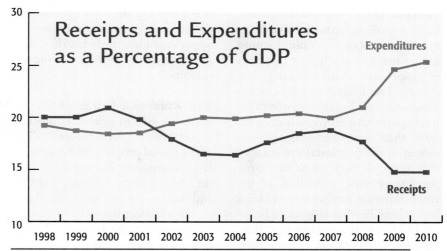

Receipts and Expenditures as a Percentage of GDP

In 2010, government expenditures exceeded 25 percent of GDP while government receipts were only 15 percent of GDP.

Source: Office of Management and Budget.

What We Pay for in a Gallon of Gasoline

14% — Taxes (federal and state)

13% — Distribution and marketing costs and profits

9% — Refining costs and profits

64% — Crude oil

Excise taxes on gasoline are used for road maintenance and transportation projects. Federal and state governments collect on average $0.40 for each gallon of gasoline sold.

Source: U.S. Department of Energy.

set of related items. The government assesses excise taxes on gasoline, alcohol, tobacco, tires, airplane tickets, and a number of other items. The government also raises revenue through customs duties, fines, penalties, and inheritance taxes.

Tax Issues and Proposed Reforms

Policymakers face a number of issues in government finance.

Tax Burden. Are taxes too high? Economists believe that the best way to evaluate the size of the nation's tax burden is to consider it in proportion to the nation's **gross domestic product (GDP),** which is the total value of goods and services produced by a nation's economy in a year. The figure above graphs both government receipts and government expenditures relative to GDP from 1998 through 2010. Receipts rose during the 1990s, peaking at 20.9 percent in 2000. Tax receipts fell during the early years of the twenty-first century both because of a recession in 2002 and because of tax cuts passed by Congress and signed by President George W. Bush. In 2010, the federal tax burden stood at 14.8 percent of the nation's GDP. National, state, and local taxes combined represented 24.8 percent of GDP.[9]

Observers disagree about the weight of the nation's tax burden. Scholars who believe that the taxes are either too low or about right note that the tax burden in the United States is relatively light compared to the tax burden in many other industrialized nations. France (49.6 percent), Germany (43.4 percent), Italy (45.9 percent), Japan (35 percent), and the United Kingdom (41.9 percent) all allocate more of their national income to government than does the United States.[10] In contrast, other scholars contend that Americans are overtaxed and they warn that high tax rates depress economic growth. In general, Republicans believe that high taxes undermine economic prosperity, whereas Democrats resist tax cuts because they want to ensure that the government has sufficient revenue to fund government services.

> The tax burden in the U.S. is **relatively light** compared to many other industrialized nations.

Tax Fairness. Social scientists classify taxes as progressive, proportional, or regressive based on

excise taxes taxes levied on the manufacture, transportation, sale, or consumption of a particular item or set of related items.

gross domestic product (GDP) the total value of goods and services produced by a nation's economy in a year, excluding transactions with foreign countries.

how a particular tax affects different income groups. A **progressive tax** is a levy that taxes people earning higher incomes at a higher rate than it does individuals making less money. The federal income tax is a progressive tax because people earning higher incomes pay a higher tax rate than persons making less money. A **proportional tax** is a levy that taxes all persons at the same percentage rate, regardless of income, whereas a **regressive tax** is a levy whose burden falls more heavily on lower-income groups than on wealthy taxpayers. Economists generally classify sales and excise taxes as regressive taxes because lower-income persons spend a greater proportion of their earnings on items subject to taxation than do upper-income persons.

Observers disagree about the fairest tax system. The advocates of progressive taxation often defend the concept on the basis of the **ability-to-pay theory of taxation**, which is the approach to government finance that holds that taxes should be based on an individual's ability to pay. Well-to-do persons can better afford taxes than lower-income individuals, so they should pay more.[11] Furthermore, the advocates of income redistribution point out that a progressive tax helps to narrow the income differential between the poor and the affluent.

Other experts on public finance believe that the best tax system is one that encourages economic growth. They favor sales and excise taxes because those levies discourage people from spending their money on consumer goods. They want people to save and invest their incomes. They also believe that progressive taxes such as the income tax are harmful to the economy because they reduce the amount of money middle- and upper-income individuals have available to invest in economic development.

Tax Reform. Critics of the nation's tax system offer a number of prescriptions for reform. The advocates of progressive tax systems favor increasing income tax rates on corporations and upper-income taxpayers while cutting taxes for people at the lower end of the income ladder. They also support reducing or eliminating deductions that allow upper-income persons and corporations to avoid paying taxes. In contrast, the opponents of progressive income tax systems charge that raising taxes on upper-income families and corporations would hurt the economy by discouraging savings and investment.

Instead of making the income tax more progressive, some reformers favor making it proportional. They want the United States to replace the current income tax system with a **flat tax**, which is an income tax that assesses the same percentage tax rate on all income levels above a personal exemption while allowing few if any deductions. The advocates of the flat tax prefer it to the current income tax system because it is simpler and because it would close loopholes that allow wealthy individuals to escape taxation.

Not everyone thinks the flat tax is a good idea. Critics charge that it would increase the tax bite on middle-income Americans while cutting taxes for the wealthy. The current income tax system is graduated in that it assesses a higher tax rate on higher incomes than on lower incomes. A flat tax that was designed to generate the same amount of revenue as the current income tax system would lower taxes on wealthy families while increasing taxes for lower- and middle-income families. Another criticism of the flat tax is that it would eliminate popular tax deductions. If homeowners cannot deduct mortgage interest and real estate taxes, the cost of owning a home would rise significantly. Charities, religious organizations, colleges, and universities would suffer because gifts to them would no longer be tax deductible. Businesses that lose tax breaks would probably pass along their additional costs to consumers.

Some reformers want to replace the income tax with a national **sales tax**, which is a levy assessed on the retail sale of taxable items. Because the national sales tax could be collected through the systems that the states now use to collect state and local sales taxes, the IRS could be eliminated and taxpayers would no longer have to spend time and money keeping tax records. Furthermore, a national sales tax would provide a powerful incentive for savings and investment because investment income would not be taxed. Nonetheless, the proposal for a national sales tax has its share of critics. Opponents point out that a national sales tax rate would have to be set at 18 to 20 percent on top of existing state and local sales taxes in order to raise as much money as the current personal income tax. Also, the burden of the sales tax would fall most heavily on low- and

> The burden of a **sales tax** would fall most heavily on **low- and middle-income** wage earners.

think Do you think people who make more money should pay a greater proportion of their earnings in taxes than people with lower incomes?

progressive tax a levy that taxes people earning higher incomes at a higher rate than it does individuals making less money.

proportional tax a levy that taxes all persons at the same percentage rate, regardless of income.

regressive tax a levy whose burden falls more heavily on lower-income groups than on wealthy taxpayers.

ability-to-pay theory of taxation the approach to government finance that holds that taxes should be based on an individual's ability to pay.

flat tax an income tax that assesses the same percentage tax rate on all income levels.

sales tax a levy assessed on the retail sale of taxable items.

middle-income wage earners because they spend a greater proportion of their earnings on retail purchases, which are taxed. In contrast, upper-income families who devote a greater share of their earnings to real estate purchases and investments in stocks and bonds, transactions that are not typically subject to sales taxes, would pay less than they do now.

Some members of Congress have begun discussing the possible adoption of a **value added tax (VAT),** which is a tax on the estimated market value added to a product or material at each stage of its manufacture or distribution, ultimately passed on to the consumer. Assume that a manufacturer buys raw material for $1,000 and uses it to create a consumer product worth $1,500. The value added is $500 and that amount is subject to the tax. The VAT is similar to a sales tax, but more difficult to evade because manufacturers pay the tax rather than consumers. The VAT, which is used extensively around the world, can raise a great deal of money. It is also relatively invisible to consumers (and voters) because it is included in the final cost of an item rather than added on at the point of purchase similar to a sales tax. Critics charge that the VAT is regressive for the same reason that sales taxes are regressive—low-income people spend more of their incomes on items subject to the tax than do upper-income people.[12]

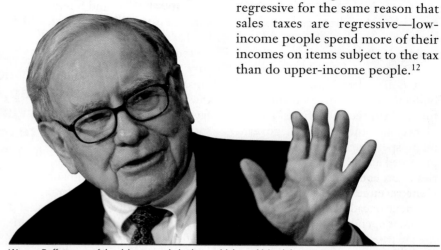

Warren Buffett, one of the richest people in the world, has criticized the U.S. tax system. He noted that his $46 million income was taxed at a rate of 17.7 percent, while his secretary's $60,000 was taxed at 25 percent, because of the different ways in which the tax code treats investment gains versus ordinary income.

DEFICITS AND THE DEBT

16.3 *What is the relationship of federal deficit and the national debt to the nation's economy and economic growth?*

The terms *budget deficit, budget surplus,* and *balanced budget* all refer to the relationship between annual budget revenues and budget expenditures. In contrast to a budget deficit, which is the amount of money by which annual budget *expenditures* exceed annual budget *receipts,* a **budget surplus** is the sum by which annual budget *receipts* exceed annual budget *expenditures.* If budget receipts equal budget expenditures, the government has a **balanced budget.** Finally, the **national debt** is the accumulated indebtedness of the federal government. An annual budget deficit increases the debt by the amount of the deficit, whereas a surplus decreases the debt. In 2010, for example, federal budget receipts were $2.2 trillion compared with outlays of $3.5 trillion, for a budget deficit of $1.3 trillion.[13] As a result, the national debt grew by $1.3 trillion during 2010.

By graphing both budget receipts and budget outlays as a percentage of GDP, the figure on p. 315 also graphs the relative size of budget deficits and surpluses between 1998 and 2010. The government began the period with a surplus and some economists actually predicted that it was on course to pay off the national debt. The surplus turned into deficit in 2002 and the deficit grew wider until 2006 when rising tax revenues began to close the gap. In 2008, 2009, and 2010, the deficit gap expanded dramatically as expenditures rose while revenues fell.

> Budget **deficits and surpluses** reflect both the health of the nation's economy and policy decisions.

Changes in budget deficits and surpluses reflect fluctuations in the health of the nation's economy and the policy decisions of Congress and the president. The widening budget gap of the late 2000s and 2010 is a direct result of the Great Recession. During a recession, tax revenues fall because personal income and corporate profits are down. In the meantime, expendi-

value added tax (VAT) a tax on the estimated market value added to a product or material at each stage of its manufacture or distribution.

budget surplus the sum by which annual budget receipts exceed annual budget expenditures.

balanced budget budget receipts equal budget expenditures.

national debt the accumulated indebtedness of the federal government.

tures increase as welfare payments and unemployment compensation claims rise. For opposite reasons, economic booms increase government revenues while decreasing expenditures. The mounting surpluses of the late 1990s and 2000 were largely the result of an economic boom that produced rapidly growing tax collections.

Deficits and surpluses also reflect policy decisions. The record budget surpluses of 2000 and 2001 turned into record deficits because of tax cuts and increased government spending. George W. Bush proposed and Congress passed a series of tax cuts that reduced government revenues by $5 trillion over the next decade. Meanwhile, government spending soared. Some of the increased expenditures were earmarked to conduct the war on terror, fight wars in Afghanistan and Iraq, and provide for homeland security. The president and Congress added hundreds of billions of dollars more to the budget imbalance by increasing spending for education, transportation, healthcare, and farm subsidies.[14]

When the federal budget is in deficit, the Department of the Treasury borrows money to close the gap between revenues and expenditures. Much of the money needed to cover the deficit is borrowed from surplus funds in other federal accounts, such as the Social Security Old Age and Survivors Insurance (OASI) Trust Fund, which by law must be invested in U.S. Treasury securities. The government borrows the rest of the money from public sources, such as savings and loan institutions, corporations, insurance companies, commercial banks, state and local governments, foreign investors, foreign governments, and individual Americans.[15] In mid-2010, the national debt stood at $13 trillion, including $8.5 trillion publicly held and $4.5 trillion held in U.S. government accounts.[16]

The national government pays interest on debt that is owed to the public. In 2010, the government paid $188 billion in interest on the debt, 5 percent of expenditures. As the size of the debt grows and as the record low interest rates of 2009–2010 inevitably increase,

*Economists generally agree that deficit spending is an **appropriate government response** to a recession.*

interest payments will go up. The Office of Management and Budget (OMB) estimates that interest on the debt will be $571 billion in 2015, a figure representing 13 percent of government expenditures.[17] Even if the federal budget is balanced in 2015, a development no one currently predicts, American taxpayers will be paying billions not for current government services but to finance earlier spending.

The relationship of the deficit and the national debt to economic growth is complex. Economists generally agree that deficit spending is an appropriate government response to a recession. People thrown out of work during a recession reduce their spending and that causes others to lose their jobs as the economy spirals downward. Business reduces its spending as well because of the slowing economy. The government can help reverse the cycle by running a deficit.[18] Congress and the president followed this strategy in 2008-2010 when they adopted economic stimulus packages designed to pump money into the economy with spending programs and tax cuts. Many economists also believe that deficits can be justified if the money is spent on projects that enhance long-term economic growth, such as improving transportation and education. In theory, at least, these sorts of programs pay for themselves by generating future tax revenues.

The deficit becomes an economic crisis if and when investors decide that the U.S. government is no longer a safe place to invest their money. U.S. government securities have long been considered the safest investment in the world. Nonetheless, many economists worry that investors will not always be so optimistic about the ability of the U.S. government to repay its debts, especially as the government borrows trillions of additional dollars in the years ahead. At some

Many economists justify deficit spending if it creates new jobs and generates future revenue. A portion of the federal stimulus package was earmarked for renewable energy research, and the federal government subsidizes the installation of solar panels with a tax credit.

Governments borrow money by selling various types of securities to investors. These securities are essentially promissory notes that the government will repay the debt with interest on a certain date. In 2010, the Greek government faced a debt crisis when it found itself unable to pay or refinance its debt. Investors were wary of loaning more money to Greece because the Greek national debt was larger than its GDP and growing rapidly.[19] The Greek debt crisis threatened not just Greece but the world economy. If Greece defaulted on its debt, the investors, which included banks in Europe and the U.S., would lose their money. In addition, future investors would be wary about loaning money to governments in general, driving up interest rates worldwide.[20]

Other members of the European Union (EU) and the International Monetary Fund (IMF) eventually agreed to help Greece finance its debt. They put together a financial plan of more than $100 billion to guarantee loans to Greece. Investors would now be willing to lend to Greece because their investments were guaranteed by the IMF and EU countries with better credit. In exchange for the guarantee, the Greek government agreed to raise taxes, crack down on tax evasion, and cut spending.

The Greek bailout was widely unpopular. Greece was rocked by violent protests against pay cuts and layoffs of government workers, an increase in the retirement age, and a series of tax increases.[21] Meanwhile, people in other EU countries, especially

Germany, resented having their tax dollars put at risk to support what they regarded as irresponsible budget policies in Greece.[22]

QUESTIONS

1 How closely does the debt situation in the United States resemble that of Greece?

2 Would you be willing to pay higher taxes and receive fewer services in order to reduce the federal budget deficit?

3 Do you think candidates in the United States (or anywhere, for that matter) would be successful if they ran for office promising to cut spending and increase taxes? Why or why not?

Greek police battle demonstrators opposed to the layoff of government workers and an increase in the retirement age.

point, investors may demand substantially higher interest rates before they loan the U.S. government their money, dramatically increasing the cost of the debt to U.S. taxpayers. In the worst possible scenario, Chinese, Japanese, and other foreign investors will tell U.S. officials that they will no longer loan the U.S. government money unless it dramatically increases taxes and cuts spending in order to reduce its deficit. Those steps would likely harm the U.S. economy.[23]

Congress and the president can act to close the budget gap before the nation faces a debt crisis, but the policy options—increased taxes and/or reduced spending—are politically unpopular. Most Republican members of Congress are adamantly opposed to increasing taxes. In fact, many Republican leaders favor additional tax cuts. Although Republicans support reducing government spending to cut the deficit, most Republican members of Congress are reluctant

to specify which programs should be cut and by how much. Moreover, they generally oppose reductions in defense expenditures. Democrats, meanwhile, stand firmly opposed to any cuts in Social Security, Medicare, or other major programs. Although most Democrats voted in favor of increasing taxes on upper-income families and individuals in 2010, they used the money to fund healthcare reform rather than reduce the deficit.

EXPENDITURES: HOW

GOVERNMENT SPENDS MONEY

As the pie chart on the right shows, federal government expenditures in 2010 were closely divided among five budget categories—healthcare (22.3 percent), Social Security (19.4 percent), national defense (19.3 percent), income security (18.4 percent), and everything else (20.1 percent). The "everything else" category included transportation, agriculture, energy, housing, education, and interest on the debt.

Healthcare

Although health expenditures include money for medical research and disease control, by far the largest federal health programs are Medicare and Medicaid. More than 45 million people participate in the Medicare program at an annual cost of $457 billion, including premiums and deductibles paid by program participants, and general revenue expenditures.[24] Medicare benefits can include compulsory hospitalization insurance, medical insurance, and prescription drug coverage, funded through a combination of premiums deducted from Social Security checks, payroll tax, and other deductables and co-pays.[25]

The aging of the baby-boom generation, which is an exceptionally large number of Americans born after the end of World War II, is a demographic time bomb for the Medicare program. Between 2010 and 2030, the Medicare rolls will more than double, adding huge costs to the system.[26] Furthermore, inflation in the healthcare industry is driving up the cost of medical care faster than wages are rising to provide tax revenues to cover the cost. The addition of the prescription drug benefit to Medicare makes the program's financial crisis more severe because the cost of prescription

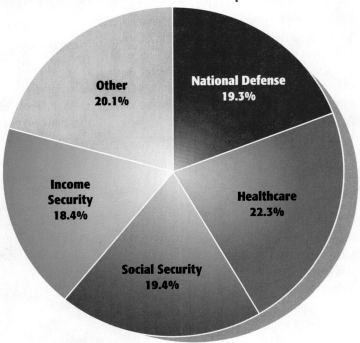

Federal Government Expenditures

Source: Office of Management and Budget.

drugs is rising more rapidly than healthcare costs in general. The Medicare Board of Trustees estimates that program expenditures will exceed assets by 2012.[27]

In order to preserve the financial integrity of the Medicare system, Congress and the president will have to adopt reforms involving benefit reductions, tax increases, and greater charges to recipients. The most commonly offered reform proposals include reducing government payments to hospitals and doctors, increasing the 2.9 percent payroll tax, pushing back the age at which beneficiaries can qualify for benefits from 65 to 67, and increasing premiums for retirees who are better off financially.

Preserving the Medicare program is a political necessity, but none of the alternatives will be politically easy to adopt. Medicare

enjoys strong public and interest group support. The Medicare Board of Trustees estimates it would take a reduction of program expenditures of 53 percent, an in-

With the aging of the baby-boom generation and rising healthcare costs, ensuring the solvency of Medicare is an important issue Congress and the president will need to tackle.

crease in program revenues of 134 percent, or some combination of tax increases and benefit cuts to ensure the program's long-term solvency.[28] If Congress and the president do nothing, the Medicare shortfall will add to the budget deficit.

Medicaid is another large and rapidly growing federal healthcare program. In 2010, Medicaid served 58 million people at a cost to the federal government of $277 billion. The poor—particularly pregnant women, mothers, and their young children—are the largest group of recipients, accounting for three-fourths of Medicaid beneficiaries. Nearly two-thirds of Medicaid spending, however, goes to the other 25 percent of recipients—the blind, disabled, and impoverished elderly—because their medical needs are greater, and therefore more expensive to meet. All told, Medicaid covers the cost of healthcare for one in every three children. It pays for 40 percent of births and funds two-thirds of the nursing home care in the country.[29]

The CBO estimates that Medicaid costs will double over the next decade. It projects that Medicaid enrollment of elderly persons will increase by an average of 2.5 percent a year over the next ten years because of the aging of the baby-boom generation. Rising Medicaid costs also reflect inflation in the healthcare industry, which has been greater than in the economy as a whole, particularly with the introduction of expensive new technologies and prescription drugs.[30]

Finally, the healthcare reform legislation passed by Congress and signed into law by President Obama in 2010 will significantly affect almost all elements of American healthcare. The most important features of the new legislation are in the below table.

Social Security

Are you counting on Social Security for your retirement? Six in ten of all Americans who are not now retired and three fourths of adults below the age of 35 believe that Social Se-

curity will be unable to pay them a benefit when they retire.[31] Congress created the program in 1935 to provide limited coverage to workers in industry and commerce upon their retirement at age 65. Through the years, Congress has extended the program's scope and increased its benefits. Even before the first benefit checks were mailed, Congress expanded coverage to include the aged spouse and children of a retired worker, as well as the young children and spouse of a covered worker upon the worker's death. Congress subsequently added disability insurance to the package and provided for early retirement.

Congress and the president have also increased Social Security benefits, especially over the last 35 years. They raised benefits 15 percent in 1970, 10 percent in 1971, and 20 percent in 1972. Beginning in 1975, Congress and the president indexed benefits to the consumer price index (CPI), a measure of inflation that is based on the changing cost of goods

Patient Protection and Affordable Care Act

Insurance reform	Insurance companies will no longer be able to refuse coverage based on pre-existing conditions or drop coverage of people who become ill. Young people will be able to remain on their parents' insurance plans until they reach 26.
Employer mandate	Businesses with 50 or more workers must provide health insurance coverage for their employees or pay a fine to the government. Small businesses can receive tax credits to help cover the cost of insuring their employees.
Medicaid expansion	The measure expands Medicaid to cover childless adults earning at least 133 percent of the federal poverty level ($29,327 for a family of four in 2010), adding 10 million to 14 million people to Medicaid rolls.[32]
Individual mandate	Most people who are not already covered will be required to purchase a health insurance policy or pay an additional tax of $695. Families earning less than four times the federal poverty level, which was $88,200 a year in 2010, qualify for federal financial assistance to help them cover the cost.
Insurance exchanges	State governments will set up health insurance exchanges, which are marketplaces where businesses and individuals will be able to shop for insurance policies. Insurance companies will compete for customers by providing quality products at affordable prices.
Medicare reform	Eliminates the "donut hole" in prescription drug benefits, providing more complete coverage.
Cost control mechanisms	Insurance companies will pay a 40 percent tax on expensive plans known as "Cadillac plans." These plans require little or no out-of-pocket expense, so beneficiaries have no incentive to control costs.
Funding	The estimated cost of healthcare reform is $940 billion over the next decade, which will be covered by increasing tax rates on families making $250,000 a year ($200,000 for individuals). The measure raises additional revenue by taxing the so-called Cadillac insurance plans and from a 10 percent tax on indoor tanning services.[33]

When Congress created Social Security in 1935, the tax rate was 2 percent (1 percent for the employer and 1 percent for the employee) with a wage threshold (ceiling on which the tax is assessed) of $3,000.

and services. In 2009, for example, Social Security recipients enjoyed a 6.2 percent cost-of-living adjustment in their benefit checks because the CPI rose 6.2 percent in 2008. A **cost-of-living adjustment (COLA)** is a mechanism designed to regularly increase the size of a payment to compensate for the effects of inflation. In 2008, the average retired worker received a monthly Social Security check of $1,079.[34]

The Social Security program can most accurately be described as a tax on workers to provide benefits to elderly retirees and disabled persons. Contrary to popular belief, Congress did not create Social Security as a pension/savings plan in which the government would simply refund the money that retirees contributed over the years along with interest. Instead, current payroll taxes pay the benefits for current recipients. Because the initial tax rate was relatively low, current retirees draw substantially more money in Social Security benefits than they paid in payroll taxes. The average retired person today gets back all the money he or she paid into Social Security, with interest, in

about seven years. Because tax rates are higher today, workers who are now in their thirties will likely pay more money in taxes during their lifetimes than they will collect in benefits after they retire.

Even though payroll taxes were initially low, the Social Security trust funds maintained healthy surpluses into the early 1970s. With the baby-boom generation coming of age and more women entering the workforce than ever before, the pool of workers paying taxes into the system grew more rapidly than did the number of retirees collecting benefits. Furthermore, the system benefited from a healthy economy and rising wages.

Eventually, demographic and economic changes combined with political decisions to drive the Social Security system into near bankruptcy. Early retirement, increased longevity, and falling birthrates served to swell the ranks of Social Security beneficiaries while slowing the increase in the number of employees paying taxes. When Social Security was created, the average worker retired at age 69 and lived another eight years. Today, the average worker retires at 64 and draws retirement benefits for 19 years.[35] In the meantime, Congress and the president increased benefits and pegged future increases in Social Security payments to the inflation rate. When the economy slumped and inflation soared in the late 1970s, the Social Security system faced a financial crisis.

In 1983, Congress and President Reagan responded to the situation by adopting a Social Security bailout plan that increased payroll taxes significantly while somewhat

limiting future benefit payments. The plan provided for an increase in the retirement age by small annual increments after the year 2000 until the retirement age reaches 67. Also, the bailout legislation provided that half the benefits of upper-income recipients would be counted as taxable income for income tax purposes. In 1993, Congress increased the share of taxable Social Security for middle- and upper-income recipients from 50 to 85 percent.

> In 1950, 16 workers paid taxes for every person drawing benefits. By 2030, the ratio will be only 2 to 1.

The goal of the Social Security bailout plan was not only to keep the program solvent for the short term, but also to ensure its long-range stability despite unfavorable demographic trends. In 1950, 16 workers paid taxes for every person drawing benefits. In 2000, the ratio was down to 3 to 1. By the year 2030, when the baby boom generation will have retired, the ratio of workers to retirees will be only 2 to 1.[36] The architects of the bailout plan hoped that the payroll tax increases would be sufficient to allow the Social Security trust funds to build up sizable surpluses that could be used to pay benefits well into the twenty-first century. At the end of 2009, the Social Security trust funds held assets worth $2.5 trillion.[37]

Although the bailout plan has put Social Security in the black for now, the retirement of the baby boom generation threatens the system's long-term financial viability. Benefit payments regularly begin to exceed payroll tax revenue in 2016, and the trust funds will be exhausted by 2037. At that point, payroll taxes will generate only 78 percent of the cost of the program.[38] Because trust fund assets are held in treasury notes,

cost-of-living adjustment (COLA) a mechanism designed to regularly increase the size of a payment to compensate for the effects of inflation.

Congress Raises the Debt Limit

In early August 2011, Congress barely averted a possible economic catastrophe by passing legislation at the last possible moment to raise the debt limit. The measure authorized the U.S. Department of the Treasury to borrow additional money to pay the nation's bills while cutting government spending by $917 billion over the next 10 years. Moreover, Congress created a 12-member commission of House and Senate members, evenly divided between the two parties, to identify $1.2 trillion to $1.4 trillion in additional deficit reduction, potentially including both spending cuts and revenue increases. If the commission fails to agree or if Congress refuses to adopt its recommendations, automatic spending cuts kick in affecting domestic spending, national security expenditures, and to a limited degree, Medicare. Both Social Security and Medicaid were spared from automatic cuts.[39]

DISCUSSION

What is the debt ceiling? The debt ceiling is an authorization to borrow money to close the gap between government revenues and expenditures. Raising the debt ceiling does not increase the deficit. Congress and the president created the deficit earlier when they chose to spend more money than they were willing to generate in taxes. Raising the debt ceiling simply authorizes the government to borrow to make up the difference between revenues and approved expenditures.

Why is voting to raise the debt ceiling controversial? Congress has raised the debt ceiling many times before without great controversy. It became controversial in 2011 when Republicans in Congress declared that they would not agree to raise the ceiling unless President Obama and Democrats in Congress agreed to cut the budget deficit by at least an equivalent amount.

Why was reducing the deficit so difficult? It was difficult because the president and the two parties in Congress have radically different perspectives. Republicans in Congress wanted big cuts in domestic spending, including Social Security and Medicare, but few if any cuts in defense expenditures. Most importantly, they adamantly refused to consider revenue increases of any kind. Democrats in Congress were willing to accept cuts in domestic expenditures as long as they were part of a balanced package that included both defense cuts and additional revenues generated by closing tax loopholes and increasing taxes on the wealthy. They were dead set against cuts in Medicare, Social Security, and Medicaid. President Obama, meanwhile, pushed for a grand compromise including spending cuts in domestic and defense budgets, reforms in Social Security and Medicare, and more revenues.

Did the compromise solve the debt problem? Most economists believe that long-term deficit reduction will involve both increased revenues and cuts in spending, including the big entitlement programs of Medicare, Medicaid, and Social Security. The 2011 compromise was just a first step toward deficit reduction because it only shaved $3 trillion out of a projected $10 trillion in additional debt over the next 10 years. Many economists complain that the debt deal failed to do anything in the short run to promote economic growth.[40]

the key date for policymakers is 2016 rather than 2037.[41] Once the annual cost of Social Security benefits exceeds payroll tax revenues, benefits will have to be reduced unless Congress and the president make up the shortfall from general revenues.

think If you were a member of Congress, what actions would you favor to ensure the long-term solvency of the Social Security program?

A number of reformers want to go beyond tinkering with benefits and funding mechanisms to change the basic structure of Social Security. Some reformers want to make Social Security a **means-tested program**, which is a government program that provides benefits to recipients based on their financial need. Under the current system, recipients qualify for benefits based on their age and contributions, regardless of personal wealth or other income. If Social Security were a means-test program, benefit levels would be based on the financial need of the recipients. The advantage of this approach is that it would reduce benefits without hurting low-income retirees. The disadvantage is that middle- and upper-income taxpayers might be unwilling to continue supporting the program if their benefits were decreased.

Many conservatives favor reforming Social Security through **privatization**, which is a process that involves the government contracting with private business to implement government programs. President George W. Bush proposed supplementing Social Security with a pension plan system in which workers would invest some of the money they would have contributed to Social Security in private savings accounts. Bush and other proponents of privatization believe that employees would have a better return on an investment in stocks and bonds than

they could count on from the Social Security system. The returns on the private accounts would cushion the impact of future reductions in Social Security benefits. In contrast, the critics of privatization warn that private investments carry risk. Falling stock prices could endanger retirement income. Furthermore, even if privatization succeeds in the long run, the government would have to put additional funds into the Social Security system to make up for the money diverted into private accounts.

National Defense

National defense is the third-largest category of federal government expenditures. This budget category includes funding for the Department of Defense as well as nuclear weapons-related activities of the Department of Energy and defense-related expenditures by several other agencies, such as the Coast Guard and the Federal Bureau of Investigation (FBI). Chapter 17 examines defense spending in detail.

Income Security

The income security category of federal government spending encompasses a variety of domestic spending programs, including unemployment insurance, federal retirement, and, with the major exception of Medicaid, most welfare programs. Federal civilian retirement and federal military retirement collectively represent almost half the expenditures in the category. **Welfare programs**, which are government programs that provide benefits to individuals based on their economic status, account for most of the rest. Welfare programs are means-tested programs.

The most important welfare programs are the Earned Income Tax Credit (EITC), Food Stamps, Supplemental Security Income (SSI), and Temporary Assistance to Needy Families (TANF). The Earned Income Tax Credit (EITC) is designed to give cash assistance to low-income working families by refunding some or all of the taxes they pay and, if their wages are low, giv-

ing them a payment rather than assessing a tax. The Supplemental Nutrition Assistance Program (SNAP) is a federal program (once called the Food Stamp program) that provides vouchers to low-income families and individuals that can be used to purchase food from grocery stores. Supplemental Security Income (SSI) provides money to low-income people who are elderly, blind, or disabled, and who do not qualify for Social Security benefits. Temporary Assistance to Needy Families (TANF) provides temporary financial assistance and work opportunities to needy families.

> The goal of **welfare reform** was to move recipients from the welfare rolls to the workforce.

Federal welfare policy changed in the mid-1990s with the adoption of welfare reform. Before 1996, the unofficial goal of the nation's welfare system was to provide welfare recipients with a minimum standard of living.[42] In 1996, Congress passed and President Bill Clinton signed sweeping welfare reform legislation that explicitly changed the underlying philosophy of American welfare policy. Instead of attempting to supply low-income individuals and families with cash and benefits sufficient to meet basic human needs, the goal of welfare reform was to move recipients from the welfare rolls to the workforce. The legislation limited the amount of time able-bodied adult recipients could draw benefits by placing a lifetime limit of five years on welfare assistance. Childless adults between the ages of 18 and

means-tested program a government program that provides benefits to recipients based on their financial need.

privatization a process that involves the government contracting with private business to implement government programs.

welfare programs government programs that provide benefits to individuals based on their economic status.

The Food Stamp program, now called the Supplemental Nutrition Assistance Program (SNAP), delivers benefits through debit cards which can be used for food purchases. In 2010, the food stamp program fed one in four children in America.

Welfare reform has helped reduce the welfare rolls, but it has not eliminated poverty. Most of the people who have made their way off welfare lack the skills necessary to get jobs that pay much more than $7 or $8 an hour. As a result, they remain dependent on government assistance, especially EITC.[44] The number of TANF recipients fell dramatically from 14.2 million in 1994 to 3.8 million in 2008, before increasing to 4.4 million in 2009 in the midst of the Great Recession. Critics of welfare reform are alarmed by the slow rise in the number of TANF recipients in 2009–2010, despite rising unemployment rates. They worry that states are making it difficult for people to enroll in TANF because the amount of federal money provided to the states does not increase as the number of recipients increases.[45]

50 could receive SNAP (Food Stamp) benefits for no more than three months in any three-year period. The heads of families on welfare would have to find work within two years, or the family would lose benefits. Unmarried teenage mothers would have to live at home and stay in school in order to collect benefits. States were given the option to deny assistance to children born to welfare recipients in order to discourage welfare mothers from having additional children.

Welfare reform has shifted the focus of government assistance to the poor from cash benefits to services designed to help poor people get and keep jobs. Cash assistance now counts for less than half of all spending under TANF. Instead, states are using their welfare dollars to help meet the transportation needs of welfare recipients to get to work, to address drug abuse and mental health problems, and to provide childcare for single parents.[43]

think

Should states cut off welfare benefits to women who have children while on welfare?

FISCAL POLICYMAKING

16.5 *How do Congress and the president make fiscal policy?*

Fiscal policy is the use of government spending and taxation for the purpose of achieving economic goals. Congress and the president make fiscal policy when they adopt the annual budget and enact tax laws.

Ground Rules for Budgeting

Congress and the president must operate under certain ground rules as they formulate and adopt an annual budget. Budget expenditures are classified as mandatory or discretionary. **Mandatory spending** refers to budgetary expenditures that are mandated by law, including entitlements, contractual commitments made in previous years, and interest on the debt. **Entitlements**

are programs such as Social Security in which anyone who qualifies is entitled to collect benefits, so that money will be spent and must be budgeted. **Discretionary spending** includes budgetary expenditures that are not mandated by law or contract, including annual funding for education, the Coast Guard, space exploration, highway construction, defense, foreign aid, and the Federal Bureau of Investigation (FBI). More than 60 percent of total government expenditures are mandatory.

More than **60 percent** of total government expenditures are **mandatory**.

Between 1990 and 2002, Congress and the president, first President George H. W. Bush and then President Clinton, prepared the

fiscal policy the use of government spending and taxation for the purpose of achieving economic goals.

mandatory spending budgetary expenditures that are mandated by law, including entitlements and contractual commitments made in previous years.

entitlement program a government program providing benefits to all persons qualified to receive them under law.

discretionary spending budgetary expenditures that are not mandated by law or contract, such as annual funding for education, highway construction, or national defense.

annual budget on the basis of negotiated budget agreements that established spending limits for the discretionary part of the budget. The negotiated budget agreement set strict spending caps for three spending areas—domestic, defense, and international expenditures—and prohibited shifting money among the categories.[46] As a result, the annual budget debate revolved around the distribution of a predetermined amount of money among items within the three categories. Instead of debating spending priorities between domestic and defense spending, for example, Congress and the president considered how to allocate budget resources among budget items within each category.

The budget agreements also included a **PAYGO** provision, which is a pay-as-you-go budget rule that requires that any tax cut or spending increase be offset by tax increases or spending cuts elsewhere in the budget. In 2002, however, Congress and the president allowed the budget agreement to expire so they could enact tax cuts and increase spending without adopting corresponding tax increases and budget reductions. Without the discipline of a budget agreement, federal spending increased dramatically, from 18.5 per-cent of GDP in 2001 to 25.4 percent in 2010.[47] Spending associated with homeland security, the war on terror, and wars in Iraq and Afghanistan drove up the cost of government, of course, but the absence of a budget agreement made it easier for Congress and the president to increase spending for education, agriculture, transportation, healthcare, and other programs. Although Congress reinstated PAYGO rules in 2010, it provided for several large exceptions to the rule, including any expenditure that Congress decided to declare an emergency.

think Should the federal government be required to create a balanced budget, in which expenditures are no greater than receipts on an annual basis?

The Budget Process

The White House begins the process of formulating a budget in March, a year and a half before the start of the fiscal year, when the president sets economic goals and establishes over-all revenue and expenditure levels. The president may map plans for spending initiatives in some areas, retrenchments in others.

Once the president has set administration priorities, the OMB sends spending guidelines to the various departments of the executive branch and directs them to prepare detailed budgets. Several months later, the agencies send the OMB their budget proposals, which often exceed the original ceiling. The OMB questions the size of some of the spending requests, and the agencies respond by justifying their proposals. The head of the agency, the director of the OMB, and a member of the White House staff (and perhaps even the president) negotiate a final budget request for inclusion in a detailed budget proposal, which the president submits to Congress in January or February. The budget document, which is the size of a telephone book for a large city, includes specific spending recommendations to fund every agency of the federal government and for all federal activities.

Discretionary expenditures must be approved through the **appropriations process**, which is the procedure through which Congress legislatively provides money for a particular purpose. Appropriation bills begin in the appropriations committees in each house although, by tradition, the House Appropriations Committee takes the lead in the process. Congress appropriates money annually. The House Appropriations Committee divides the discretionary part of the budget into 13 separate categories for assignment to its 13 subcommittees, and passes 13 separate appropriation bills. Spending for entitlement programs is included in the budget but does not go through the appropriations process.

PAYGO a pay-as-you-go budget rule that requires that any tax cut or spending increase be offset by tax increases or spending cuts elsewhere in the budget.

appropriations process the procedure through which Congress legislatively allocates money for a particular purpose.

MUSEUM HOURS
9:45 a.m. - 5:30 p.m.

Due to the Federal Government shutdown, the Smithsonian Institution must be closed.

We regret the inconvenience.

Non-essential parts of the federal government shut down in 1995 because of a budget standoff between the Republican Congress and Democratic President Bill Clinton.

Spending programs must be authorized, regardless of whether they are entitlements or programs funded by discretionary spending. The **authorization process** is the procedure through which Congress legislatively establishes a program, defines its general purpose, devises procedures for its operation, specifies an agency to implement the program, and indicates an approximate level of funding for the program (but does *not* actually provide money). The standing legislative committees in each chamber, such as Agriculture or Armed Services, consider authorization bills. Congress may authorize a program for one year only or for several years. The budget timetable calls for Congress and the president to complete work on the budget by October 1, the beginning of the fiscal year.

Congress and the president adopt tax measures through the legislative process with the constitutional stipulation that revenue-raising bills must originate in the House. Consequently, tax legislation must pass the House before it passes the Senate. The Ways and Means Committee has jurisdiction over tax measures in the House. In the Senate, the Finance Committee considers tax bills.

MONETARY POLICYMAKING AND THE ROLE OF THE FED

16.6 *What is the policymaking role of the Federal Reserve System?*

Most Americans are concerned about interest rates. Consumers pay interest on credit card debt and when they borrow money to purchase vehicles or homes. Investors earn interest on the money they save. Interest rates also affect the economy. Low interest rates encourage companies to borrow money to expand their operations. Low interest rates for automobile loans and home mortgage interest promote consumer automobile and home purchases. In contrast, high interest rates promote savings and discourage borrowing by business and consumers alike.

Many economists believe that the government can influence the performance of the nation's economy by adjusting interest rates. Increasing interest rates can cool inflation by slowing down economic activity, whereas cutting interest rates can stimulate economic growth. The government affects interest rates through its control of the money supply. **Monetary policy** is the control of the money supply for the purpose of achieving economic goals.

The **Federal Reserve System (the Fed)** is is the central banking system of the United States with authority to establish banking poli-

cies and influence the amount of credit available in the economy. It consists of 12 Federal Reserve banks, each located in one of the nation's 12 Federal Reserve districts. A seven-member board of governors is appointed by the president with Senate confirmation to serve fixed, overlapping terms of 14 years. The president designates one member of the board as the chair to serve a four-year term, pending Senate confirmation. President George W. Bush appointed economist Ben Bernanke to chair the Fed in 2006. Obama named Bernanke to serve a second term as chair in 2009.

Congress has ordered the Fed to make policy with two goals: full employment and price stability. The Federal Open Market Committee (FOMC) is a committee of the Federal Reserve that meets eight times a year to review the economy and to adjust monetary policy to achieve the goals. The FOMC is a 12-member group that includes the seven members of the Federal Reserve board, the president of the Federal Reserve Bank of New York, and four of the eleven other Federal Reserve Bank presidents who serve on a rotating basis. If the FOMC determines that the demand for goods and services is growing faster than businesses can

authorization process the procedure through which Congress legislatively establishes and defines a program, but does not actually provide funding for it.

monetary policy the control of the money supply for the purpose of achieving economic goals.

Federal Reserve System (Fed) the central banking system of the United States with authority to establish banking policies and influence the amount of credit available in the economy.

supply them, it tightens monetary supply to fight inflation. It does this by reducing the funds available to banks for loans and by raising interest rates to make businesses and individuals less willing to borrow money. In contrast, if the FOMC believes that businesses are not selling as many goods and services as they can produce and fewer people have jobs than want them, it eases monetary policy to prevent recession. It lowers interest rates by increasing the funds that banks can lend, hoping to encourage businesses and consumers to borrow to make purchases.

The Fed moved aggressively in 2008–2009 to shore up the economy and stave off financial crisis. As economic activity slowed throughout 2008, the Fed lowered interest rates. By late 2008, the federal funds rate,

In 2008–2009, the Fed moved aggressively under the direction of Fed Chairman Ben Bernanke, pictured above, to shore up the banking system in hopes of keeping the Great Recession from becoming the next Great Depression.

functioning smoothly. The Fed financed the private acquisition of Bear Stearns, a global investment bank. It assisted with the government takeover of Fannie Mae and Freddie Mac, the giant mortgage lenders. It brokered the sale of investment firm Merrill Lynch to Bank of America and bailed out American International Group (AIG), a giant insurance and financial services corporation. Altogether, the Fed loaned $1.6 trillion.[48]

The Fed's actions were controversial. Bernanke and many economists believe that the Fed helped save the nation from another Great Depression. The Great Recession with nearly 10 percent unemployment was painful but nothing in comparison with the 25 percent unemployment of the Great Depression of the 1930s. Moreover, most of the money the Fed loaned to banks and other financial institutions was paid back with interest.[49] In contrast, critics blame the Fed for failing to anticipate the nature and severity of the financial crisis. They also complain that the Fed put taxpayer dollars at risk bailing out the institutions whose risky lending practices were responsible for the financial crisis.[50]

which is the rate at which banks charge each other for loans, was effectively zero percent. Nonetheless, the economy continued to falter in the face of a serious financial crisis. According to Fed Chair Bernanke, virtually every large financial institution in the world was in danger of going bankrupt and that likely would have led to another Great Depression. The Fed acted to prop up U.S. banks and other financial institutions by loaning them money with the goal of keeping the financial markets

MAKING ECONOMIC POLICY

16.7 *How is American economic policy made?*

The most important elements of the environment for economic policymaking are public opinion, the strength of the economy, and party control of the executive and legislative branches of government. Americans "vote their pocketbooks." That is, they reelect incumbent officeholders if the economy is strong, but turn them out of office if the economy is weak.[51]

Conventional wisdom holds that Americans **"vote their pocketbooks."**

The strength of the economy expands or limits the policy options available to economic policymakers. A growing economy generates revenue that can be used to fund new spending programs or provide tax cuts. Strong economic growth in the mid- and late-1990s did at least as much to eliminate the budget deficit as the policy choices of elected officials. In contrast, a weak economy reduces the options available to policymakers. Although the president and Congress may want to respond to a recession by cutting taxes or increasing government programs to help the unemployed,

they will not have the money to fund tax cuts or new programs unless they borrow it.

It matters which party controls Congress. Democrats generally back policies designed to assist their traditional support groups: organized labor, inner-city voters, and lower- and middle-income families. Republicans, meanwhile, steer economic policy to benefit their support groups: business people and professionals, suburban voters, and middle- and upper-income families. When Congress and the presidency are in the hands of different parties, economic policy typically reflects compromise between the parties.

Agenda Setting

A number of political actors participate in elevating economic issues to the official policy agenda. Candidates often highlight economic issues during election campaigns. Interest groups such as AARP stress the need to preserve Social Security and Medicare. Business groups are concerned about tax issues and government regulation. The media emphasize economic developments, such as the unemployment rate or the size of the deficit. Finally, economic developments set the agenda as well. High unemployment rates focus the attention of policymakers on creating jobs. Policymakers discuss energy when the price of a gallon of gasoline goes up.

Policy Formulation, Adoption, and Legitimation

Economic policy formulation takes place in congressional committees, executive branch agencies, and the White House. It involves officials from all levels of government as well as a wide range of interest group participants. The president and the president's staff, department heads, and the OMB prepare detailed budget proposals for submission to Congress. The appropriations committees in each house draft budget legislation; standing committees work on authorization measures. The Ways and Means Committee in the House and the Finance Committee in the Senate deal with tax measures. Conference committees iron out the final details for most appropriation bills, tax measures, and authorization bills. The Fed formulates monetary policy.

Individual members of Congress focus on issues important to their states and districts. Farmbelt senators and representatives pay special attention to legislation affecting agriculture. Members with defense bases or defense industries in their districts are concerned with the defense appropriation. The congressional leadership uses **earmarks**, provisions that direct funds be spent for particular purposes, to win support for appropriation bills that might not otherwise pass.[52]

Interest groups also take part in policy formulation. Corporations lobby Congress to affect the impact of tax policies on their firms. Weapons manufacturers attempt to influence decisions on defense spending. AARP participates in negotiations over reform of the Medicare program and changes in Social Security.

The executive and legislative branches of American national government are primarily responsible for the adoption of fiscal policy. The judiciary plays a relatively small role. Congress and the president create government programs and appropriate money to fund them. They raise funds through taxation and borrowing. The Fed adopts monetary policies.

Political battles over economic policymaking do not always end with policy adoption but continue into the policy legitimation stage of the policy process. Consider the fight over healthcare reform. No sooner had President Obama signed the bill into law than he began a speaking tour designed to explain the measure and sell it to the nation. Democratic members of Congress who supported the bill held events in their districts as well, discussing the benefits of healthcare reform to their communities. In contrast, Republican leaders in Congress reiterated their opposition and called for the bill's repeal. Meanwhile, a number of state officials opposed to healthcare reform filled lawsuits that challenged the measure's constitutionality.

Policy Implementation, Evaluation, and Change

The implementation of economic policy involves nearly the whole of government in America. The Treasury Department, especially the IRS, is responsible for tax collection and borrowing. The Federal Reserve and

earmarks provisions that direct that funds be spent for particular purposes.

Evaluation of economic policy is an important job of Congress, and Elizabeth Warren has been tapped as a "Sheriff of Wall Street." Warren headed the Congressional Oversight Panel, created to investigate the U.S. banking bailout, and is helping develop a new Consumer Financial Protection Bureau.

TAKING SIDES:

Balancing the Budget

Should Congress be required to balance the budget every year, thus eliminating deficits?

Would a constitutional amendment be the best way to solve the debt problem?

OVERVIEW

As of May 20, 2010, the outstanding public debt of the United States was $13 trillion, which was about $40,000 per citizen.[53] In general, the debt has accumulated because American citizens prefer having services without paying for them. A number of factors in recent years have caused the deficit to balloon and the debt to grow, including the cost of fighting two wars, the rising cost of providing public services, and the tax cuts enacted during the Bush Administration.

Some members of Congress have proposed a constitutional amendment to balance the budget which would prohibit the federal government from spending more money than it brings in on an annual basis. Similar amendments were proposed in 1936, 1995, and 2004, but none passed Congress.

 SUPPORTING requiring a balanced budget

Thirteen trillion dollars in debt is bad for the economy. The more debt a nation has, the less money it has to save and reinvest in the nation's economy, which affects its ability to pay for federal programs. The debt is so large that a constitutional amendment is needed to rein in a Congress that cannot control itself.

Politics is a battle over scarce resources. Resources are supposed to be scarce, not infinite. When the legislature is allowed to use infinite future resources, it is not required to legislate well. A constitutional amendment to balance the budget would force Congress to make real choices about policies rather than simply funding everything

Large debts cause foreign policy problems for the United States. Our national debt is owned by Japan, China, the UK, and oil-exporting countries.[54] When we then try to encourage other nations to behave in accordance with the interests of the United States, the fact that we have no economic power to leverage means we have less influence.

 AGAINST requiring a balanced budget

A balanced budget amendments prevents Congress and the president from responding to an economic crisis. Recessions, such as the recent Great Recession, increase spending while decreasing revenue. If Congress were operating under a balanced budget amendment in 2008–2009, it would have had to raise taxes and cut spending instead of taking action to stimulate the economy. The result would likely have been another Great Depression.

Congress needs to have flexibility to legislate. Congressional spending provides services for American citizens, and Congress needs to have access to the funds necessary to do its job. A balanced budget amendment would impair the legislative branch's ability to make decisions about policy.

A constitutional amendment to balance the budget can freeze government operations. In 1995, the government was shut down over a budget battle, putting important services on hold. These types of crises would become more common and more problematic as Congress would be constitutionally required to fix a budget at a certain point.

its member banks implement monetary policy. Money is spent by the agencies of the executive branch and, through federal programs, by an array of state and local governments. State governments, for example, are responsible for implementing federal transportation policies, Medicaid, and most welfare programs.

Congress and the president often leave considerable discretion to officials who implement economic policies. Welfare reform initially allowed states considerable flexibility to design their welfare programs. For example, states could grant hardship exemptions to individual recipients who had exhausted their benefits or were unable to find work. In general, the legislation set goals and allowed state governments to develop their own strategies for achieving the goals. States

which met the goals would receive financial rewards; states falling short of goals would suffer penalties. States have considerable leeway to implement healthcare reform as well.

Both the executive and legislative branches of American government have mechanisms for evaluating economic policy. The OMB assesses the operation of programs within the executive branch for the president, whereas the Government Accountability Office (GAO) performs a similar role for Congress, investigating agency activities and auditing expenditures. Outside of the GAO, however, efforts at oversight are haphazard and unsystematic. Furthermore, when they do occur, they tend to focus on nickel-and-dime matters, such as expense accounts and limousine use,

or on well-publicized abuses, such as cost overruns on weapons systems purchased by the Pentagon.

Economic policies change because of changes in party control of Congress and the presidency, and because of changes in the state of the economy. Healthcare reform legislation would not have passed in 2010 without a Democratic president and sizable Democratic majorities in both the House and Senate. Certainly, the measure would not have been funded by increasing taxes on upper-income individuals and families had Democrats not been in charge. Economic policies change with variations in the state of the economy. When the economy slowed in 2008, Congress and the president adopted a stimulus plan and the Fed cut interest rates.

what we LEARNED

THE GOALS OF ECONOMIC POLICY

16.1 *What are the primary goals of American economic policy?*

The first goal of economic policy is to fund government services. A second goal is to encourage/discourage private sector activity. The government taxes behavior it wishes to discourage, such as smoking, and subsidizes activities it wants to promote, such as homeownership. A third goal of economic policy is to redistribute income, and a final goal is to promote economic growth by avoiding depression, minimizing the severity of recession, and controlling inflation.

REVENUES: HOW GOVERNMENT RAISES MONEY

16.2 *What are the most important sources of revenue for the federal government?*

The individual income tax is the largest source of revenue for the national government. Other sources of federal revenue include the corporate income tax and excise taxes levied on such items as gasoline, tobacco, and airplane tickets. In general, Republicans believe that high taxes undermine economic prosperity, whereas Democrats resist tax cuts because they want to ensure that the government has sufficient revenue to fund essential government services.

Social scientists identify three general types of taxes: progressive, proportional, and regressive. The federal income tax is progressive; sales and excise taxes are considered regressive. Critics of the nation's tax system offer a number of prescriptions for reform, including progressive tax systems, a flat tax, a national sales tax, or a value added tax (VAT). Critics of the flat tax, a national sales tax, and the VAT contend that they would shift the tax

Send   Save   Delete

From: Professor Tannahill
Add Cc | Add Bcc

Subject: Tips for Success
Attach a file

HAVE GOALS:
Declare a major if you don't have one already because students without goals seldom succeed. You can switch majors later if you change your mind.

burden from middle- and upper-income earners to lower- and middle-income families.

DEFICITS AND THE DEBT

16.3 *What is the relationship of federal deficit and the national debt to the nation's economy and economic growth?*

Changes in budget deficits and surpluses reflect fluctuations in the health of the nation's economy and the policy decisions of Congress and the president. The government must pay interest on publicly held debt, which in 2010 amounted to 5 percent of expenditures. Economists generally agree that deficit spending is an appropriate government response to a recession and deficit spending that finances economic growth may be acceptable as well. A debt crisis would take place if and when investors decide that the U.S. government is no longer a safe place to invest their money. Congress and the president could take steps now to head off a possible debt crisis, but they are reluctant to act because the options, increased taxes and/or spending cuts, are politically unpopular and may also slow economic growth.

EXPENDITURES: HOW GOVERNMENT SPENDS MONEY

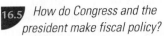 **What are the most important spending priorities of the federal government?**

The most important spending priorities in 2010 were healthcare, Social Security, national defense, and income security. Medicare and Medicaid are by far the largest federal healthcare programs. The retirement of the baby-boom generation threatens the long-term solvency of Medicare, Medicaid, and Social Security. National defense includes funding for the Department of Defense as well as nuclear-weapons related activities of the Department of Energy. The income security category of federal government spending encompasses a variety of domestic spending programs, including unemployment insurance, federal retirement, and most welfare programs. Since the adoption

of welfare reform in the late 1990s, the goal of welfare has changed from ensuring that poor people have basic necessities to moving the poor from welfare to work.

FISCAL POLICYMAKING

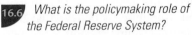 **How do Congress and the president make fiscal policy?**

Fiscal policy is the use of government spending and taxation for the purpose of achieving economic goals. The ground rules that Congress and the president must follow in formulating fiscal policy are that mandatory expenditures such as entitlement programs must be budgeted for, and budget agreements such as PAYGO must be followed. The OMB assists the president in preparing a budget, which is submitted to Congress at the beginning of the year. Only discretionary expenditures must be approved through the appropriations process. Spending programs must be authorized, regardless of whether they are entitlements or programs funded by discretionary spending. Congress and the president adopt tax bills through the legislative process.

MONETARY POLICYMAKING AND THE ROLE OF THE FED

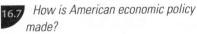 **What is the policymaking role of the Federal Reserve System?**

The Federal Reserve System (the Fed) is the central banking system of the United States with authority to establish banking policies and influence the amount of credit available in the economy. Congress has ordered the Fed to make monetary policy with the aim of achieving two

goals: full employment and price stability. The Fed moved aggressively in 2008–2009 to shore up the economy and stave off a financial crisis by lowering interest rates and by loaning money to banks and other financial institutions.

MAKING ECONOMIC POLICY

How is American economic policy made?

The most important elements of the environment for economic policymaking are public opinion, the strength of the economy, and party control of the executive and legislative branches of government. A number of political actors participate in setting the agenda for economic policymaking, including candidates for office, interest groups, and the media. Events, such as recessions and bouts with inflation, set the agenda as well. Economic policy formulation takes place in congressional committees, executive branch agencies, and the White House.

Whereas the executive and legislative branches of American national government are primarily responsible for the adoption of fiscal policy, the Fed adopts monetary policy. Political battles over economic policymaking do not always end with policy adoption but continue into the policy legitimation stage of the policy process. The implementation of economic policy involves nearly the whole of government in America, including the Federal Reserve System, executive branch agencies, and state and local governments. Both the executive and legislative branches of American government have mechanisms for evaluating economic policy.

MySearchLab®

TEST yourself

16.1 What are the primary goals of American economic policy?

1 A financial incentive given by government to an individual or a business interest to accomplish a public objective is known by which of the following terms?
   a. Entitlement
   b. Welfare program
   c. Subsidy
   d. Progressive taxation

2 "The nation is suffering a severe economic slump. Many companies have gone out of business and unemployment is at a record high." That statement describes which of the following?
   a. Inflation
   b. Recession
   c. Depression
   d. Supply-side economics

16.2 What are the most important sources of revenue for the federal government?

3 Which of the following is the most important tax source of revenue for the U.S. government?
   a. Sales taxes
   b. Payroll taxes
   c. Corporate income taxes
   d. Individual income taxes

4 Federal taxes on gasoline, tires, and airplane tickets are examples of which of the following?
   a. Progressive taxes
   b. Excise taxes
   c. Payroll taxes
   d. Tax preferences

5 The federal income tax is an example of which of the following?
   a. Progressive tax
   b. Regressive tax
   c. Proportional tax
   d. Excise tax

6 An income tax that assesses the same percentage tax rate on all income levels above a personal exemption while allowing few if any deductions is a definition of which of the following?
   a. Progressive tax
   b. Value added tax (VAT)
   c. Excise tax
   d. Flat tax

16.3 What is the relationship of federal deficit and the national debt to the nation's economy and economic growth?

7 Assume that federal government revenues are $2.5 trillion and expenditures are $3 trillion. Which of the following statements is accurate?
   a. The budget is balanced.
   b. The government ran a surplus of $0.5 trillion.
   c. The government ran a deficit of $0.5 trillion.
   d. The national debt is $0.5 trillion.

8 Why does a recession increase the size of a budget deficit?
   a. Individual income tax collections fall because people who have lost their jobs make less money on which to pay taxes.
   b. Corporate income tax collections fall because corporations make smaller profits or even lose money.
   c. Spending increases because more people qualify for welfare benefits.
   d. All of the above

16.4 What are the most important spending priorities of the federal government?

9 Which of the following is *not* one of the top five major expenditure categories in the federal budget?
   a. Foreign aid
   b. Social Security
   c. National defense
   d. Healthcare

10 Is Social Security a means-tested program?
   a. No, because eligibility does not depend on income.
   b. No, because it is funded by a special tax rather than general revenues.
   c. Yes, because everyone who meets certain criteria is eligible.
   d. Yes, because the program is jointly administered by the national government and the states.

16.5 How do Congress and the president make fiscal policy?

11 Which of the following terms is best described in the following sentence: "Congress can only spend a dollar if it saves a dollar elsewhere"?
   a. Privatization
   b. Discretionary spending
   c. Pork barrel spending
   d. PAYGO

12 "Budgetary expenditures that are not mandated by law or contract" is the definition for which of the following terms?
   a. Privatization
   b. Discretionary spending
   c. Pork barrel spending
   d. PAYGO

16.6 What is the policymaking role of the Federal Reserve System?

13 Which of the following is primarily responsible for setting monetary policy?
   a. The Fed
   b. Office of Management and Budget
   c. Department of the Treasury
   d. Congress

14 The Fed took which of the following actions in response to the deepening recession in late 2008?
   a. Loaned banks money
   b. Increased interest rates
   c. Raised taxes
   d. All of the above

16.7 How is American economic policy made?

15 Which of the following units of government is *least* involved in the adoption of economic policies?
   a. Congress
   b. Supreme Court
   c. President
   d. Fed

KNOW the score

14–15 correct:	Congratulations! You know your American government!
12–13 correct:	Your understanding of the chapter is weak—be sure to review the key terms and visit TheThinkSpot.
<12 correct:	Reread the chapter more thoroughly.

Answers: 1) c, 2) c, 3) d, 4) b, 5) a, 6) d, 7) c, 8) d, 9) a, 10) a, 11) d, 12) b, 13) a, 14) a, 15) b

17 FOREIGN

CONTEXT OF AMERICAN FOREIGN AND DEFENSE POLICY

Learning Objective **17.1** Who are the political actors that make up the international community, and how does the United States pursue its foreign policy goals within that community?

THE HISTORY OF AMERICAN FOREIGN AND DEFENSE POLICY

Learning Objective **17.2** What is the history of American foreign and defense policy?

AMERICAN FOREIGN AND DEFENSE POLICY STRATEGIES

Learning Objective **17.3** What are the two main ways in which America engages in world affairs, and what strategies does it utilize for national defense?

MAKING FOREIGN AND DEFENSE POLICY

Learning Objective **17.4** How is American foreign and defense policy made?

The United States and its allies believe that Iran is trying to build a nuclear weapon, and that a nuclear Iran would threaten world peace. The United States considers Iran to be a **rogue state**, which is a nation that threatens world peace by sponsoring international terrorism and promoting the spread of weapons of mass destruction (WMD), including chemical, biological, and nuclear weapons. American policymakers worry that an Iran armed with nuclear weapons would bully its neighbors, perhaps setting off regional arms races, and might even use a nuclear weapon against the United States or its allies.

rogue state a nation that threatens world peace by sponsoring international terrorism and promoting the spread of weapons of mass destruction.

AND DEFENSE POLICYMAKING

The United States and its allies have several options for dealing with the Iranian nuclear threat, but none appear likely to be effective. They could impose economic sanctions against Iran by limiting trade with the country, but not all of the world's major trading nations are willing to participate.[1] They could seek to engage the government of Iran diplomatically with the goal of convincing the nation's leaders that Iran would be better off politically, economically, and militarily if it were perceived as a member in good standing of the international community. In 2009, the Obama administration attempted to open a dialogue with the Iranian government, but the talks went nowhere.[2] Finally, the United States or Israel (be-cause it feels directly threatened by the prospect of an Iranian nuclear weapon) could launch missile strikes against Iran aimed at destroying its nuclear capacity before it is able to construct a weapon. The strikes might prove ineffective, however, and Iran could retaliate by disrupting oil shipments through the Persian Gulf, seriously damaging the economies of Western Europe and the United States.

The threat of nuclear weapons development in Iran is a major foreign and defense policy challenge for the United States, and introduces Chapter 17 on the foreign and defense policies of the United States. **Foreign policy** is public policy that concerns the relationship of the United States to the international political environment. **Defense policy** is public policy that concerns the armed forces of the United States. The chapter begins with a description of the international environment, and lists the goals and tools of American foreign policy. The chapter traces the history of American foreign and defense policy. It then examines the current strategies for the foreign policy and defense policy of the United States, and identifies the important players and elements in American foreign policymaking.

foreign policy public policy that concerns the relationship of the United States to the international political environment.

defense policy public policy that concerns the armed forces of the United States.

CONTEXT OF AMERICAN FOREIGN AND DEFENSE POLICY

17.1 *Who are the political actors that make up the international community, and how does the United States pursue its foreign policy goals within that community?*

The important players on the international scene include not only the world's nations, but also a number of influential multinational organizations and nongovernmental organizations. It is within this community that the United States pursues its foreign and defense policy goals, using a variety of tools.

The International Community

Since the seventeenth century, the nation-state has been the basic unit of the international community. A **nation-state** is a political community, occupying a definite territory, and having an organized government. Other nations recognize its independence and respect the right of its government to exercise authority within its boundaries, free from external interference. Today, more than 190 countries comprise the world community of nations.[3]

Political scientists divide the world's nations into three groups based on their level of economic development. The United States, Canada, Japan, and the countries of Western Europe are **postindustrial societies**, nations whose economies are increasingly based on services, research, and information rather than on heavy industry. India, China, South Korea, Brazil, and a number of other countries are modernizing industrial states that are emerging as important economic powers. Finally, many of the countries of Asia, Africa, and Latin America are preindustrial states with an average standard of living well below that in postindustrial societies.[4]

The United States has diplomatic relations with almost all of the world's nations. The term **diplomatic relations** refers to a system of official contacts between two nations in which the countries exchange ambassadors and other diplomatic personnel and operate embassies in each other's country. Iran, Cuba, and North Korea are among the few nations with which the United States does not have formal diplomatic relations.

In addition to the governments of the world, more than a hundred transnational (or multinational) organizations are active on the international scene. The best

nation-state a political community occupying a definite territory and having an organized government.

postindustrial societies nations whose economies are increasingly based on services, research, and information rather than heavy industry.

diplomatic relations a system of official contacts between two nations in which the countries exchange ambassadors and other diplomatic personnel and operate embassies in each other's country.

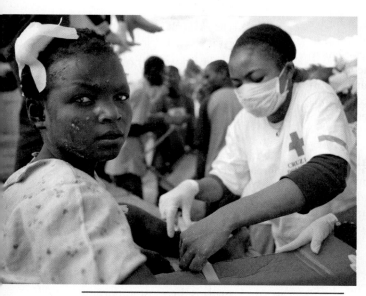

An aid worker from the American Red Cross, an NGO, provides medical assistance to earthquake survivors in Haiti.

known of these is the **United Nations (UN)**, an international organization founded in 1945 as a diplomatic forum to resolve conflicts among the world's nations. In practice, the UN has not always been effective at maintaining the peace. The UN Security Council, the organization charged with maintaining peace and security among nations, has frequently been unable to act because each of its five permanent members (Russia, China, Britain, France, and the United States) has a veto on its actions. The Security Council has been unable to persuade Iran to give up its nuclear weapons program, at least in part, because the permanent members disagree on how best to approach the problem.

Some of the UN's most important accomplishments have come in the areas of disaster relief, refugee relocation, agricultural development, loans for developing nations, and health programs. The UN has several agencies that carry out these and other tasks, including the World Health Organization (WHO), an international organization created to control disease worldwide worldwide. The WHO is a world clearinghouse for medical and scientific information. It sets international standards for drugs and vaccines and, at government request, helps fight disease in any country. The WHO is in the forefront of the battle against the spread of AIDS in the developing world.

The UN and its affiliated agencies are funded through dues and assessments charged to member nations. The amount of each nation's contribution depends, in general, on the strength of the nation's economy. The United States has the largest assessment because the American economy is the world's largest. As a result, the United States is also the UN's most influential member.[5]

A number of other international organizations are important to American foreign and defense policies. The **North Atlantic Treaty Organization (NATO)** is a military alliance consisting of the United States, Canada, and most of the European democracies. The United States and its allies formed NATO after World War II to defend against the threat of a Soviet attack on Western Europe. With the collapse of the Soviet Union, NATO has expanded to include many of the nations that were once part of the Soviet bloc. The United States, Canada, and the established democracies of Western Europe hope that the inclusion of these nations in the NATO alliance will strengthen their commitment to democratic institutions and capitalist economic structures. The United States wants NATO to become a global security organization that is capable either of taking military action or of providing humanitarian relief anywhere in the world.

The World Trade Organization (WTO) is an international organization that administers trade laws, and provides a forum for settling trade disputes among nations. It promotes international trade by sponsoring negotiations to reduce tariffs and other barriers to trade. (A tariff is a tax on imported goods.) The WTO also arbitrates disputes over trade among its 145 member nations. For example, the WTO has sponsored negotiations to allow modernizing countries to make generic versions of lifesaving drugs for their own use and for export to countries too poor either to make the drugs themselves or to purchase them from pharmaceutical companies. Wealthy nations, led by the United States, want to sharply limit the number of diseases covered by the drugs in order to protect the intellectual property rights of pharmaceutical companies. In contrast, developing nations, such as Brazil, China, and India, argue that governments should have the right to determine which diseases constitute public health crises in their countries.[6]

think Should pharmaceutical companies be required to provide low-cost drugs to treat HIV and other life-threatening illnesses in poor countries where people cannot afford to pay the price that people in wealthier countries pay?

The International Monetary Fund (IMF) is an international organization created to promote economic stability worldwide. It provides loans to nations facing economic crises, usually on the condition that they adopt and implement reforms designed to bring long-term economic stability. In 2008, for example, the IMF loaned Iceland more than $2 billion to stabilize that country's banking system hard hit by the world financial crisis.

United Nations (UN) an international organization founded in 1945 as a diplomatic forum to resolve conflicts among the world's nations.

North Atlantic Treaty Organization (NATO) a regional military alliance consisting of the United States, Canada, and most of the European democracies.

Nongovernmental organizations (NGOs) are international organizations committed to the promotion of a particular set of issues. Greenpeace, Friends of the Earth, World Wide Fund for Nature, and the Nature Conservancy are NGOs that address environmental issues. Save the Children is an NGO concerned with the welfare of children. NGOs vary in their relationship to the international community. NGOs such as the International Red Cross and Doctors Without Borders work in partnership with national governments to assist the victims of natural disasters or political turmoil. Other NGOs lobby national governments over policy issues such as the effort to ban the importation of genetically modified foods. Some NGOs encourage consumers to boycott retailers who sell goods produced under exploitative working conditions in developing countries. They organize protests at international meetings of the WTO to push for the incorporation of health and safety conditions in international trade agreements.[7]

Foreign Policy Goals

The United States has consistently pursued three foreign and defense policy goals throughout its history: national security, economic prosperity, and the projection of American values abroad.[8]

National Security. The foremost goal of American foreign and defense policies is national security. A basic aim of the foreign policy of any nation is to preserve its sovereignty and to protect its territorial integrity. No nation wants to be overrun by a foreign power or dominated by another nation. Although the United States is today the world's foremost military power, it still has national security concerns. The terrorist attacks of September 11, 2001, demonstrated the vulnerability of the United States. Although Iran is not capable of mounting a direct attack on the United States, it could threaten American interests in the Middle East. It could also give or sell nuclear weapons to terrorist groups.

Economic Prosperity. National prosperity is another goal of American foreign and defense policy. This goal includes encouraging free markets, promoting international trade, and protecting American economic interests and investments abroad. Because the American economy is closely entwined with the global economy, it is essential to the nation's economic health that the United States has access both to foreign suppliers of goods and services, and to foreign markets for American products. The nation's military involvement in the Persian Gulf, for example, has been motivated at least in part by a desire by the United States to protect access to the region's oil fields.

International trade has grown increasingly important to the economy of the United States. Trade now accounts for 25 percent of the nation's output of goods and services, compared to only 11 percent in 1970. The United States exported $1.6 trillion worth of goods and services in 2009 while importing $1.9 trillion worth. Canada is the most important trading partner of the United States, followed by China, Mexico, Japan, and Germany.[9]

Trade is controversial in the United States because it produces winners and losers. Consumers benefit from trade because they have the opportunity to purchase a broad range of goods at competitive prices. American manufacturers of medical instruments, farm equipment, pharmaceuticals, oil drilling equipment, and electronics benefit because they sell their products abroad. In contrast, inefficient small farmers, old steel mills, and the nation's clothing and textile manufacturers suffer because they do not compete effectively against international competition. Furthermore, some liberal groups in the United States oppose trade because they believe it rewards international corporations that exploit low-wage workers in developing countries and that it leads to environmental degradation around the globe.

Both political parties have favored the growth of trade because they believe that the economic gains from trade outweigh the costs. President Bill Clinton, despite the opposition of a majority of the members of his own political party, won congressional support

U.S. Navy SEALS shot and killed Osama bin Laden in 2011 and gathered intelligence that they hope to use to disrupt the al-Qaeda terror network.

> The **American economy** is closely entwined with the **global economy**.

nongovernmental organizations (NGOs) international organizations committed to the promotion of a particular set of issues.

for the **North American Free Trade Agreement (NAFTA)**, an international accord among the United States, Mexico, and Canada to lower trade barriers among the three nations. The George W. Bush administration negotiated the Central America Free Trade Agreement (CAFTA) with Nicaragua, Honduras, Costa Rica, El Salvador, and Guatemala to phase out tariffs among participating nations on manufactured goods, agricultural commodities, chemicals, an construction equipment.

Promoting American Ideals Abroad. A final general goal of American foreign and defense policy is the promotion of American ideas and ideals abroad. Historically, American policymakers have justified military interventions as efforts to protect freedom and promote democracy. Many of the nation's foreign policies today are designed to further the causes of democracy, free-market capitalism, and human rights. For years, the United States has attempted to isolate Cuba economically and diplomatically in hopes of either driving the Castro regime out of power or of forcing Castro to bring democracy and free-market capitalism to the island.

Spreading democracy was at the center of the foreign policy of the George W. B ush administration. When American forces failed to uncover WMD in Iraq, President Bush offered the promotion of democracy as the new justification for the invasion. Democracies are stronger economically and more stable politically than undemocratic governments, he declared. Consequently, their residents have few incentives to join terrorist organizations. Bush also endorsed the theory of the democratic peace, which is the concept that democracies

International Trade

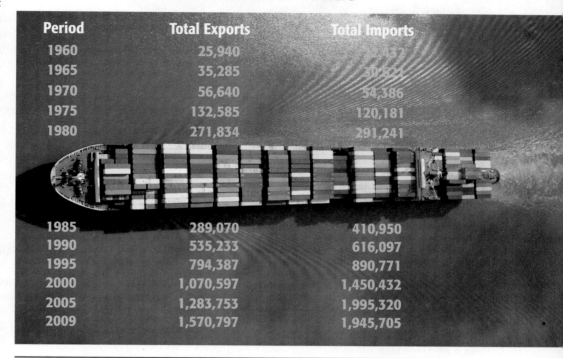

Period	Total Exports	Total Imports
1960	25,940	
1965	35,285	
1970	56,640	54,386
1975	132,585	120,181
1980	271,834	291,241
1985	289,070	410,950
1990	535,233	616,097
1995	794,387	890,771
2000	1,070,597	1,450,432
2005	1,283,753	1,995,320
2009	1,570,797	1,945,705

The table above shows the monetary value of American imports and exports, in millions of dollars. You can see that the value of goods and services traded between the United States and other countries has risen dramatically, especially in the last decade. Because imports have risen more rapidly than exports, the United States has a sizable trade deficit.

Source: U.S. Census Bureau, Foreign Trade Division.

do not wage war against other democracies.[10]

Critics of the Bush administration warned that an emphasis on democratization is unrealistic, naïve, and counterproductive. Implanting democracy in countries without a democratic tradition may be impossible because people may be unwilling to make the compromises necessary for democracy to work. The various tribal and religious factions in Iraq fought with each other despite the introduction of democracy after the fall of Saddam. Furthermore, democracy may result in the election of regimes hostile to American interests. In much of the Arab world, including Egypt and Saudi Arabia, free elections would likely produce the selection of distinctly anti-American Islamic governments. Finally, American pressure to democratize may alienate allies in the war on terror. The United States depends on the cooperation of undemocratic regimes in

Egypt and Saudi Arabia to combat terrorism.

Foreign Policy Tools

The United States pursues its foreign and defense policy goals through military, economic, cultural, and diplomatic means. Since the end of World War II, the Armed Forces of the United States have intervened militarily in various countries around the world. The United States has also given military assistance in the form of arms and advisors to friendly governments fighting against forces hostile to the interests of the United States. For example, the United States has provided military aid to the government of Colombia in its war against guerrilla forces supported by international narcotics

North American Free Trade Agreement (NAFTA) an international accord among the United States, Mexico, and Canada to lower trade barriers among the three nations.

Fidel Castro, left, and his brother Raul have ruled Cuba since 1959 despite American political and economic efforts to force them from power. An embargo limiting trade and business with Cuba has been in effect since 1960.

The U.S. pursues its foreign policy goals through military, economic, cultural, and diplomatic means.

traffickers. After September 11, 2001, the United States supplied military aid, including American advisors, to the government of the Philippines in its war against insurgent forces, which may have ties to al-Qaeda.

Besides the actual use of military force, the United States has pursued its policy goals by forming defense alliances and transferring military hardware to other nations. Since the end of World War II, the United States has participated in a number of defense alliances, including NATO and SEATO (the Southeast Asia Treaty Organization). America is also the world's major distributor of weapons, accounting for more than 68 percent of weapon sales worldwide in 2008. The Unites Arab Emirates, Morocco, Taiwan, India, Iraq, Saudia Arabia, Egypt, South Korea, and Brazil are among the major

purchasers of American arms.[11] Some international arms sales are private transactions between American firms and foreign governments. Most sales, however, are government-to-government transactions in which the U.S. Department of Defense acts as a purchasing agent for a foreign government wanting to buy American-made weapons.

The United States also attempts to achieve foreign policy

goals through economic means, such as trade and foreign aid. Trade can be used to improve international relations. One method the United States employed to improve relations with China was to encourage a trade relationship. In contrast, America has erected trade barriers against foreign governments it wishes to pressure or punish. The United States attempts to isolate Cuba and North Korea economically. Trade sanctions could also be employed against Iran.

The United States also uses foreign aid to achieve foreign policy goals. Although the United States is the world's largest donor, its level of giving as a share of national income is among the lowest of the developed nations, less than half that of European countries.[12] The size of the foreign aid budget is also relatively small, less than one percent of the federal budget—and most of this money goes to further the nation's foreign policy aims. In 2008, the primary recipients of U.S. foreign aid were, in order of importance, Iraq, Afghanistan, Israel, Egypt, and Colombia.[13] Each nation is important to American foreign policy. The United States is trying to build effective governments in Iraq and Afghanistan while American forces fight wars in those

The United States uses foreign aid to further its image abroad. Here, an Afghani family benefits from American food aid.

countries. Israel and Egypt are countries critical to Middle Eastern peace. Meanwhile, the United States assists Colombia in its war against drug traffickers and terrorists.

Foreign policy goals can sometimes be realized through cultural means, including the promotion of tourism and student exchanges, goodwill tours, and international athletic events. For example, the process of improving relations between the United States and China in the 1970s was facilitated by cultural exchanges. In fact, one of the first contacts between the two nations was the visit of an American table tennis team to China—"ping-pong diplomacy," the pundits called it. The Olympic Games, meanwhile, are not just a sporting event but also a forum for nations to make political statements. The United States boycotted the 1980 Moscow Olympics to protest the Soviet invasion of Afghanistan. The Soviet Union returned the favor in 1984 by staying home when the games were held in Los Angeles.

Finally, foreign policy goals can also be achieved through diplomacy, which is the process by which nations carry on political relations with each other. Ambassadors and other embassy officials stationed abroad provide an ongoing link between governments. The UN, which is headquartered in New York City, offers a forum in which the world's nations can make diplomatic contacts, including countries that may not have diplomatic relations with one another. Diplomacy can also be pursued through special negotiations or summit meetings among national leaders.

THE HISTORY OF AMERICAN FOREIGN AND DEFENSE POLICY

 17.2 *What is the history of American foreign and defense policy?*

American foreign policy is best understood within the context of its historical development.

From Isolationism to Internationalism

For almost a century, the principle theme of American foreign policy toward Europe was **isolationism**, which is the view that the United States should minimize its interactions with other nations. In his farewell address in 1796, retiring President George Washington warned the nation to avoid "entangling alliances" with other countries. President James Monroe articulated the policy in his **Monroe Doctrine** of 1823, which was a declaration of American foreign policy opposing any European intervention in the Western Hemisphere and affirming the American intention to refrain from interfering in European affairs. The United States was far from a world power in the early nineteenth century. Americans devoted their energies to subduing and developing North America and did not welcome European interference. However, isolationism contained an element of hypocrisy because it did not apply to American actions in the Western Hemisphere. The United States reserved for itself the right to interfere in the affairs of the nations of the Americas.

President George Washington warned the nation to avoid **"entangling alliances"** with other countries.

And interfere it did. America fought a war with Mexico in order to annex the area that is now California, Arizona, and New Mexico. President Theodore Roosevelt intervened in Colombia to create the nation of Panama so the United States could build a canal. In the twentieth century, America intervened militarily in several Latin American nations, including Cuba, El Salvador, Nicaragua, the Dominican Republic, Grenada, and Panama.

The United States began to break out of its isolationism toward nations outside the Western Hemisphere in the 1890s. America had developed trading interests around the world that it wanted to protect. Eventually, World War I and World War II thrust the United States to the forefront of international affairs. Because of improved technology, isolationism was more difficult, if not impossible, to achieve. Modern communications and transportation had shrunk the world. More important, the United States emerged from World War II as a great power, militarily and economically. It was the only nation with nuclear weapons and the only major industrial country whose economic foundations had not been battered by war. With important military, political, and economic interests around the globe, the United States could no longer afford isolationism.

isolationism the view that the United States should minimize its interactions with other nations.

Monroe Doctrine a declaration of American foreign policy opposing any European intervention in the Western Hemisphere and affirming the American intention to refrain from interfering in European affairs.

The Cold War

The relationship between the United States and the Soviet Union was the dominant element of American foreign policy after World War II. The **Cold War**, which was the period of international tension between the United States and the Soviet Union lasting from the late 1940s through the late 1980s, was both an ideological and political struggle. It pitted communism against capitalism, and dictatorship against democracy. The leaders of both the United States and the Soviet Union pictured the international competition as a contest between different ways of life, one representing good and the other representing evil. The Cold War was also a bipolar (two-sided) struggle between the world's two remaining military superpowers. The other great powers of the prewar era—Germany, France, the United Kingdom, and Japan—had either been destroyed or weakened by the war. That left a political vacuum into which the war's

> The **Cold War** was a bipolar struggle between the world's two remaining military **superpowers**.

survivors, the United States and the Soviet Union, sought to enter.

America pursued a strategy of **containment**, which sought to keep the Soviet Union from expanding its sphere of control and preserve the balance of power in Europe and Asia. The United States offered military and economic assistance to nations threatened by communist subversion. Not only did the U.S. send weapons and financial aid to foreign countries such as Greece and Turkey, but also committed American fighting forces abroad in countries such as Korea and Vietnam. Both wars were costly, lengthy, and unpopular. Neither war was a success. The Korean War ended in stalemate with the Korean peninsula divided between North and South. The Vietnam War ended with the victory of communist forces after the withdrawal of American military units.

The Cuban missile crisis of 1962 was the climactic event of the Cold War. The Soviet Union remained inferior to the United States in nuclear weaponry, so Soviet leader Nikita Khrushchev installed missiles in Cuba, just 90 miles from American soil. When the United States discovered the Soviet move, President John Kennedy responded with a naval blockade. The stage was set for a nuclear confrontation, but the Soviets backed down, withdrawing their missiles. The two nations were eyeball-to-eyeball on the brink of nuclear war, said Secretary of State Dean Rusk, and the Soviets blinked.

In the late 1960s and early 1970s, the United States and Soviet Union entered an era of improved relations known as **détente**.

The two superpowers increased trade and cultural relations, and exchanged scientific information in such fields as cancer research, weather forecasting, and space exploration.[14] Perhaps the most important aspect of détente was arms control. Both the United States and the Soviet Union found advantage in slowing the arms race. Arms control saved money and, perhaps, reduced the probability of nuclear war.

In 1968, the United States and the Soviet Union signed the **Nuclear Non-Proliferation Treaty**, which is an international agreement designed to prevent the spread of nuclear weapons. Under terms of the treaty, the five nations that then possessed nuclear weapons (the United States, Soviet Union, China, France, and Great Britain) agreed not to deliver nuclear weapons or weapons technology to other nations; non-nuclear countries agreed not to seek or develop nuclear weapons. All of the world's nations are parties to the Nuclear Non-Proliferation Treaty except for Cuba, Israel, India, and Pakistan.[15] Iran stands accused of violating the treaty.

During the 1970s, the administrations of Presidents Richard Nixon, Gerald Ford, and Jimmy Carter attempted to adapt American foreign policy to adjust to what they saw as the long-term decline of American economic and military power. The cornerstone of this policy was the Nixon Doctrine. Although the United States would help small nations threatened by communist aggression with economic and military

Cold War the period of international tension between the United States and the Soviet Union lasting from the late 1940s through the late 1980s.

containment U.S. policy which sought to keep the Soviet Union from expanding its sphere of control and preserve the balance of power in Europe and Asia.

détente an era of improved relations between the Soviet Union and the United States.

Nuclear Non-Proliferation Treaty an international agreement designed to prevent the spread of nuclear weapons.

Customers gather in a store's electronics department to watch President John F. Kennedy deliver a televised address to the nation on the status of the Cuban Missile Crisis in 1962.

aid, those countries must play a major role in their own defense. The Carter administration stressed the importance of human rights. Carter declared that American trade, aid, and alliances would be based at least in part on the way in which other governments treated their own citizens. In the aftermath of the Vietnam War, Carter wanted to return an air of morality to American foreign policy. From a practical standpoint, the president hoped to pressure repressive noncommunist governments to reform their policies.

When Ronald Reagan became president, he promised an end to the self-doubt and decline that had infected United States foreign policy in the 1970s. He regarded world politics as a bipolar rivalry between the United States and the Soviet Union, and called for a resolute national will and a military buildup. The Reagan Doctrine called for the United States to offer military aid to groups attempting to overthrow communist governments anywhere in the world. Reagan hoped that the Soviets would eventually have to choose between reducing their commitments abroad and economic collapse at home. Rejecting the Carter emphasis on human rights, Reagan offered practically unconditional support to anti-communist governments, even those that were undemocratic. He ordered an invasion of the Caribbean country of Grenada to overthrow a government friendly to Cuba, and directed air strikes against the North African nation of Libya in retaliation for that country's alleged support of terrorism.

During Reagan's second term, the key feature of American foreign policy was once again caution. Congress was no longer willing to fund the military buildup, public opinion cooled on some aspects of the president's foreign policy, and firsthand experience in dealing with the realities of international affairs forced Reagan to modify his foreign policy focus.

In the late 1980s, a new Soviet leader, Mikhail Gorbachev, recog-

President Reagan, speaking in West Berlin near the Berlin Wall in 1987, called on the Soviet Union and its leader, Mikhail Gorbachev, to free Eastern Europe from Soviet control. "Mr. Gorbachev," Reagan said, "tear down this wall."

nized that while the Soviet Union was a military superpower, its economy was a shambles. Gorbachev reasoned that economic reforms would not succeed unless some of the enormous human and material resources devoted to the Soviet military could be diverted to the domestic economy. Gorbachev declared that the Soviet Union would not intervene militarily in the internal affairs of other nations, and ordered the withdrawal of Soviet military units from Afghanistan and Eastern Europe.

Although the fall of the Berlin Wall in 1989 may have been the single most dramatic development, nearly every nation in the region underwent major political and economic change. Without the backing of the Soviet military, communist regimes in one country after another collapsed under popular pressure to be replaced by reform governments promising democratic elections, individual freedom, and fewer economic controls.[16] When given the opportunity for political change, a number of Soviet republics, including Lithuania, Estonia, Belarus, Georgia, and the Ukraine, declared their independence from Russian control. In late 1991, Russia and some of the other republics dissolved the Soviet Union, ending the Cold War.

The collapse of the Soviet Union left the United States as the world's only superpower. Developing nations in Latin American, Africa, Asia, and Eastern Europe turned to the American model of political and economic development. Meanwhile, Russia, China, and other countries that had once been part of the communist bloc opened their economies to international trade and investment, creating a global economy, which is the integration of national economies into a world economic system in which companies compete worldwide for suppliers and markets.

9/11 and the War on Terror

The war on terror began on September 11, 2001, when terrorists took over four American passenger airplanes. They flew two of them into the World Trade Towers in New York City and a third into the Pentagon in Washington, D.C. A fourth plane crashed in Pennsylvania after passengers fought back against the hijackers. The events of 9/11 changed the

The events of 9/11 changed the environment for American foreign and defense policy by demonstrating that the United States is vulnerable to attack despite its status as the world's sole superpower.

environment for American foreign and defense policy by demonstrating that the United States is vulnerable to attack despite its status as the world's sole superpower. No nation could match American military might, but international terror organizations such as al-Qaeda could inflict significant casualties and seriously disrupt the world economy.

The war on terror raises a number of important issues for American policymakers to address:

• **Fighting international terrorism.** Terror organizations do not have home countries. The challenge for the U.S. armed forces is to find and root out terrorist organizations before they can strike against Western interests. After 9/11, the United States and its allies invaded Afghanistan to overthrow the Taliban government because it was either unwilling or unable to expel the al Qaeda terrorist forces operating from Afghan soil. Allied forces easily forced the Taliban from power, but most Taliban and al Qaeda fighters escaped in rugged, lawless territory along the Afghan-Pakistan border. The Taliban soon regrouped and launched an insurgency against the new Afghan government and allied forces. In 2010, the American military commander in the region warned that the war was in danger of being lost, and President Obama ordered an additional 30,000 troops to the region, bringing the total American force commitment to nearly 100,000.

• **Controlling the spread of WMD.** In 2003, President George W. Bush ordered U.S. forces to invade Iraq and overthrow the government of Saddam Hussein even though Iraq had had nothing to do with 9/11. Bush believed that Iraq had WMD and worried that Saddam would share them with enemies of the United States. Al-Qaeda with a nuclear weapon would be a potential catastrophe. As it turned out, Iraq did not have WMD. The United States did overthrow Saddam Hussein, but troops soon became embroiled in a protracted war against insurgents.

• **Preventing the development of failed states. A failed state** is a country where the government no longer effectively functions. Failed states can become havens for terrorist groups, may threaten regional security, and may disrupt regional economies. Somalia, Chad, and Sudan are generally considered failed states. [17] American policymakers worry that Iraq and Afghanistan may become failed states as well if American forces leave before their governments are ready to govern effectively.

• **Limiting regional conflicts.** The United States has an interest in resolving regional conflicts in the Middle East, Southeast Asia, Africa, and elsewhere because they may disrupt regional economies and provide opportunities for terror groups to establish footholds.

• **Dealing with rogue states.** Rogue states, such as Iran and North Korea, are a threat to world peace because they sponsor international terrorism and threaten to spread WMD.

failed states nation-states in which the government no longer effectively functions, threatening regional security and economies.

Did Obama Show Weakness by Bowing to the Japanese Emperor?

When President Obama visited Japan in late 2009, he greeted Japanese Emperor Akihito with a low bow. Conservative commentators in the United States attacked the president for showing deference to the emperor. Karl Rove, an adviser to former President George W. Bush, said that the bow displayed weakness.[18] Another conservative critic declared that the "United States now willingly prostrates itself before the rest of the world."[19] In contrast, the Obama administration defended the bow as a symbol of a foreign policy based on "mutual interest and mutual respect" rather than confrontation.[20]

DISCUSSION

Japan still has an emperor? Japan is a constitutional monarchy similar to the United Kingdom. The emperor is the symbolic head of state and has no real power. The prime minister is the head of the government.

Why would Obama bow to Akihito? Bowing is a traditional form of greeting in Japan. Obama's bow was a sign of respect.

Why did Obama's bow upset conservatives? Karl Rove and other conservatives believe that the United States should follow a unilateralist approach to achieving its foreign policy goals. The United States should act only in its own interests without asking permission of anyone. Conservatives attacked Obama for bowing before the emperor because, in their view, it undermined America's status as the world's foremost political, economic, and military power.

What is Obama's approach to foreign policymaking? Obama is an internationalist. He believes that the United States can best achieve its foreign policy goals through cooperation and coordination with other countries. In his view, showing respect for other nations, including bowing to Emperor Akihito, is a sign of strength rather than weakness.

AMERICAN FOREIGN AND
DEFENSE POLICY STRATEGIES

17.3 *What are the two main ways in which America engages in world affairs, and what strategies does it utilize for national defense?*

The terrorist attacks of September 11, 2001, provide the backdrop for American foreign policy in the post–Cold War world. American policymakers generally agree that the United States must be closely engaged in world affairs not only to protect its economic interests abroad but also to guard the American homeland against assault by terrorist organizations or rogue states. Policymakers also concur that the United States should exert leadership in international affairs because it is the world's foremost military and economic power. As former Secretary of State Madeleine Albright phrased it, the United States is the world's "indispensable nation" in that its participation is essential to solving the world's military, economic, and humanitarian problems.[21] Policymakers disagree, however, on how closely the United States should work with its allies and the other nations of the world.

Approaches to Foreign Policy

Some policymakers believe that the United States should follow a **unilateralist** approach to achieving its foreign policy goals, by acting alone if necessary. The advocates of a unilateralist approach argue that because the United States has the world's most powerful military and largest economy, it can assert itself internationally. Other nations will have no choice but to accept the leadership of the United States and adapt to American preferences.[22]

❝When it comes to our security, we really don't need anybody's permission.❞
—George W. Bush

President George W. Bush pursued a unilateralist foreign policy, at least during his first term. Bush justified attacking Iraq without UN support because the United States believed that Saddam Hussein had WMD that he could give to terrorists who could then use them to kill tens of thousands of Americans. "When it comes to our security," said Bush, "we really don't need anybody's permission."[23] Similarly, the Bush administration rejected a series of global agreements that enjoyed overwhelming international support, including the Global Warming Treaty, the Biological Diversity Treaty, the Mine Ban Treaty, and the International Criminal Court. The United States refused to ratify the Global Warming Treaty because it believed that it put too much of the burden for reducing emissions of carbon dioxide and other greenhouse gases on the United States. It rejected the Biological Diversity Treaty because it argued that the agreement did not go far enough to protect the patent rights of bioengineering companies. The United States opposed the Mine Ban Treaty because it claimed that it needed landmines to protect American troops in South Korea. The United States rejected the International Criminal Court Treaty because it did not want Americans subject to international criminal court prosecution.

Other policymakers, however, believe that the United States should take an **internationalist** approach to achieving its foreign policy goals by working in close concert with the global community. After World War II, the United States and its allies established the UN, NATO, the IMF, and other international institutions to keep the peace, deter aggression, and promote economic develop-

ment. The advocates of an internationalist approach to American foreign policy believe that the United States should work with these institutions and with its allies to address the problems of international terrorism, nuclear proliferation, and rogue states.

President Obama favors an internationalist foreign policy, reversing many of the policies of the Bush administration. The themes of the Obama administration are partnership, engagement, and common interests with other nations. President Obama has made it clear that the United States will approach international issues from a perspective of cooperation with other countries and not just with America's traditional allies in Western Europe and Japan, but also with emerging global powers, such as China, India, Russia, Brazil, Turkey, Indonesia, and South Africa. The Obama administration has also been trying to engage countries with whom the United States has had poor relations, especially in the Muslim world, including Syria and even Iran. President Obama delivered

unilateralist an approach to foreign policy that advocates acting in one's own best interests, alone if necessary.

internationalist an approach to foreign policy that supports working in close concert with the global community.

An Egyptian man applauds as he listens to President Obama speak at Cairo University in 2009. In his speech, Obama discussed the various issues of contention between the United States and the Muslim world and spoke of the need for dialogue and understanding.

an address in Cairo, Egypt, during his first year in office in which he discussed the various issues of contention between the United States and the Muslim world and spoke of the need for dialogue and understanding.[24]

Defense Spending

Foreign policy goals determine defense strategies. Military capabili-ties, meanwhile, influence a nation's foreign policy by expanding or limiting the options available to policy-makers. The figure below depicts United States defense spending from 1960 through 2010 as a percentage of the gross domestic product (GDP), the total value of goods and services produced by a nation's economy in a year, excluding transactions with foreign countries. In general, defense spending rises during wartime and falls during peacetime. Defense expenditures peaked relative to the size of the economy during the Korean War in the early 1950s and the Vietnam War in the late 1960s. After the end of both the Korean and Vietnam conflicts, defense spending fell. The only exception to the pattern of rising defense spending during wartime and falling defense expenditures during peacetime occurred during the early 1980s when President Reagan proposed and Congress passed the largest peacetime increase in military spending in the nation's history. Defense spending fell again in the 1990s after the collapse of the Soviet Union and the end of the Cold War. Since September 11, 2001, defense expenditures have increased as Congress and the president fund the war on terror as well as military operations in Afghanistan and Iraq. In 2010, the Obama administration proposed reducing defense spending in the years ahead as American forces leave Iraq and, eventually, Afghanistan as well.

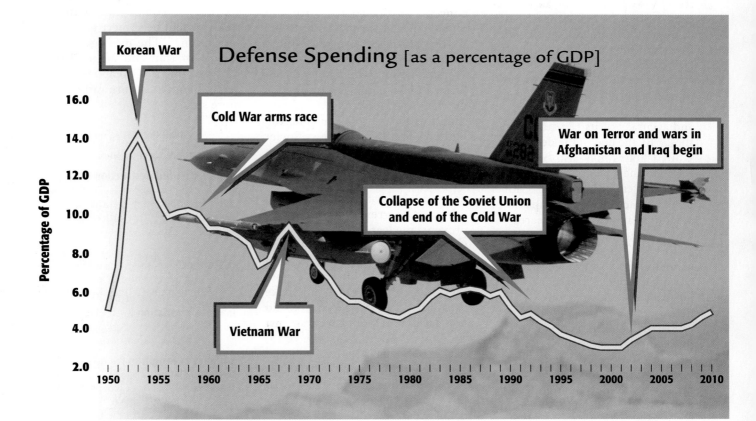

Defense Spending [as a percentage of GDP]

Korean War

Cold War arms race

War on Terror and wars in Afghanistan and Iraq begin

Collapse of the Soviet Union and end of the Cold War

Vietnam War

Percentage of GDP

16.0 14.0 12.0 10.0 8.0 6.0 4.0 2.0

1950 1955 1960 1965 1970 1975 1980 1985 1990 1995 2000 2005 2010

Defense Forces

America's defense strategy is based on **strategic** (nuclear) and **conventional** (non-nuclear) **forces**.

Strategic Forces. The United States has 5,200 nuclear weapons.[25] More than half are currently active and deployed, ready to be carried to their targets through a variety of delivery systems. The U.S. Air Force can deliver at least 320 nuclear missiles by plane—B-52s or B-2s. The U.S. Navy has more than 2,000 nuclear missiles on submarines, with at least a third of the subs on patrol at any one time. The U.S. Army has 1,450 nuclear weapons configured for cruise missile delivery. Other missiles sit in silos located in 12 states and six European countries, ready for launch.[26]

In 2010, President Obama and Russian President Dmitra A. Medvedev signed an arms control treaty. If ratified, each nation within seven years will be allowed to deploy no more than 1,550 strategic warheads and 700 launchers. The treaty also provides for an inspection system to allow each side to monitor the other's compliance.[27] President Obama believes that the United States can maintain its security despite the reductions by relying more heavily on missile defense and by improving the reliability and accuracy of its remaining missiles.[28] By the end of the decade, the United States may also be able to rely on a new class of non-nuclear weapons called Prompt Global Strike, which would be capable of reaching anywhere on earth in under an hour with great accuracy and force. The weapon, which will generate the localized destructive power of a nuclear warhead, could be used to destroy an Iranian nuclear site.[29]

Many defense theorists believe that nuclear weapons promoted world peace during the Cold War because no national leader acting rationally would risk initiating a nuclear holocaust. This concept was formalized in the doctrine of **mutual assured destruction (MAD)**, which was the belief that the United States and the Soviet Union would be deterred from launching a nuclear assault against each other for fear of being destroyed in a general nuclear war.

> American leaders explain the concept of deterrence as **"peace through strength."**

Even if one country were able to destroy the other country without suffering a single retaliatory strike, the environmental damage from the nuclear attack would be catastrophic to the entire planet.

Deterrence was the organizing principle of American defense policy during the Cold War. It was the ability of a nation to prevent an attack against itself or its allies by threat of **massive retaliation**, the concept that the United States will strike back against an aggressor with overwhelming force. American leaders often explained the concept of deterrence with the phrase "peace through strength." By preparing for war, the United States would ensure the peace. Weaker nations would be deterred from attacking the United States because America enjoyed military superiority. In the meantime, the United States and the Soviet Union would be deterred from attacking each other because both countries possessed nuclear arsenals capable of destroying the other. Deterrence worked to prevent nuclear war during the Cold War because both the United States and the Soviet Union believed that the other side possessed an effective second-strike capability. The Soviet Union did not dare launch an attack against the United States (and vice versa) because Soviet leaders believed that enough American nuclear forces would survive the initial Soviet strike to destroy their country.

Deterrence is an imperfect defense strategy in the post–Cold War world because of rogue states and, especially, terrorist organizations. Although deterrence continues to be an effective defense strategy against the threat of nuclear attack by Russia or China, some defense analysts believe that it may be ineffective against rogue states whose leaders are sometimes prone to engage in high-risk behavior. Terrorist organizations, meanwhile, are unlikely to be deterred by the threat of massive retaliation because they lack a home base that the United States could attack.[30]

In 2010, the Obama administration announced a new nuclear strategy aimed at enhancing deterrence against Iran and North Korea. The United States declared that it would not use nuclear weapons against nonnuclear countries that are in compliance with the Nuclear Nonproliferation Treaty even if they attack the United States. Instead, the United States would respond with conventional weapons. In contrast, Iran and North Korea, countries that are out of compliance with the treaty, would be subject to nuclear retaliation.[31] The message for the leaders of Iran and North Korea was that nuclear weapons would make them less secure rather than more secure.

strategic forces nuclear forces.

conventional forces non-nuclear forces.

mutual assured destruction (MAD) the belief that the United States and the Soviet Union would be deterred from launching a nuclear assault against each other for fear of being destroyed in a general nuclear war.

deterrence the ability of a nation to prevent an attack against itself or its allies by threat of massive retaliation.

massive retaliation the concept that the United States will strike back against an aggressor with overwhelming force.

military preemption the defense policy that declares that the United States will attack hostile nations or groups that represent a potential threat to the security of the United States.

AROUND THE WORLD

Nuclear Weapons in Pakistan

Pakistan became a nuclear power in 1998 when it successfully tested several nuclear weapons. International observers believe that it has now produced enough fissile material to make as many as 50 nuclear devices.[32] Pakistan has also purchased or developed medium-range ballistic missiles that are capable of striking cities in neighboring India. Pakistan and India are longstanding enemies, having fought three wars since 1948. The two nations remain locked in a bitter dispute over control of the border region of Kashmir. By developing nuclear weapons, Pakistan hopes to establish itself as a regional power and to claim leadership of the Muslim world as the first Muslim nation to have the bomb.

The United States opposes Pakistan's nuclear weapons program because of the danger that the next war between Pakistan and India will be a nuclear war and because of the fear that Pakistani nuclear weapons may fall into the hands of terrorists. The government of Pakistan is unstable, and senior officials in the Pakistani military are known for being sympathetic with the former Taliban government of Afghanistan and with Osama bin Laden.[33] The U.S. had imposed economic sanctions on Pakistan after the nuclear tests, but lifted the sanctions after 9/11 in exchange for Pakistani cooperation in the war against the Taliban.

QUESTIONS

1 Does Pakistan's having nuclear weapons make a war between Pakistan and India more or less likely? Why?

2 Is the United States hypocritical to oppose nuclear weapons in Pakistan, considering that the United States is the world's foremost nuclear power?

3 Is a nuclear Pakistan a threat to world peace? Why or why not?

Protesters in Karachi, Pakistan, burn an Indian flag.

President George W. Bush responded to the terrorist attacks of September 11, 2001, by announcing that the United States had adopted the policy of **military preemption**, which is the defense policy that declares that the United States will attack nations or groups that represent a potential threat to the security of the United States. Under certain circumstances, military preemption could even involve the United States using nuclear weapons against a potential enemy threat. President Bush justified the policy of preemption as follows:

Given the goals of rogue states and terrorists, the United States can no longer solely rely on a reactive posture as we have

in the past. The inability to deter a potential attacker, the immediacy of today's threats, and the magnitude of potential harm that could be caused by our adversaries' choice of weapons do not permit that option. We cannot let our enemies strike first.[34]

The American attack against Iraq to overthrow the regime of Saddam Hussein was the first application of the doctrine of military preemption. The United States went to war not because Iraq posed an immediate threat to national security, but because of the possibility that Iraq could give weapons of mass destruction to terrorists. "The people of the United States will not live at the mercy of an outlaw regime that

threatens the peace with weapons of mass murder," said President Bush.

The policy of military preemption is controversial, especially against rogue states. Critics question the assertion that deterrence is ineffective against rogue states. The leaders of Iran and other enemies of the United States are not suicidal. Overwhelming military force deters rogue states as effectively as it does other nations. Just because American policymakers may not always understand Iranian politics does not mean that that nation or its leaders behave irrationally.[35] Saddam Hussein was an evil dictator, but was he really an immediate threat to the United States? Critics also warn that the

Preemption in Iran

It is more important to . . .

	Total %	Rep %	Dem %	Ind %
Prevent Iran from developing nuclear weapons, even if means taking military action	61	71	51	66
Avoid military conflict, even if Iran may develop nuclear weapons	24	16	31	32

Location of Installed Test Centrifuges

Control Room

Main Location of Rails for Production of Enriched Uranium

Administration building and staff sleeping quarters

Public opinion polls show that Americans are open to using preemptive force to stop Iran from developing nuclear weapons. These satellite photos show suspected nuclear development sites in Iran.

Source: Pew Research Center for the People & the Press, October 2009.

consistent application of the doctrine of preemption would involve the United States in perpetual war. Iran has greater weapons capability than Iraq had. Does the United States plan to go to war against Iran as it did Iraq? Finally, the critics of preemption worry that other nations will use the doctrine of preemption to justify attacking their neighbors.[36]

Conventional Forces. For decades, the United States maintained a large standing army in order to defend against a possible conventional arms attack by the Soviet Union in Western Europe. More than two million men and women served in the U.S. Armed Forces through the 1980s. After the end of the Cold War, the United States scaled back its conventional forces, cutting the size of its Armed Forces sharply in the early 1990s. With the dissolution of the Soviet Union, the chances of great armies clashing on the scale of World War II were remote. The United States instead was more likely to be embroiled in asymmetrical warfare, which is a conflict in which the military capabilities of the two belligerents differ significantly, such as the current conditions in Iraq and Afghanistan. Nonetheless, the United States kept the basic structure of a large military intact, with 1.4 million troops in uniform. Pentagon planners believed that substantial military forces were still needed to fulfill the mission of fighting regional wars, promoting regional stability, keeping the peace, and participating in humanitarian relief efforts.

Donald Rumsfeld, the secretary of defense in the George W. Bush administration from 2001 through the end of 2006, advocated restructuring the U.S. military. He believed that the U.S. Armed Forces could rely on speed, mobility, and firepower rather than the giant armies characteristic of twentieth-century warfare.[37] Rumsfeld put his theory into action in Afghanistan, where American airpower, including an unmanned aircraft called the Predator, defeated Taliban and al-Qaeda forces by using precision weapons operating at extremely long range, with targeting information gathered on the ground, in the air, and from space. American troops on the ground initially served as spotters for airpower and acted as liaisons to local Afghan militia. The United States employed the same strategy in Iraq, using highly mobile ground forces to slice through Iraqi defenses by use of overwhelming firepower, much of it delivered by air.

Rumsfeld's critics believe that the United States still needs substantial conventional forces and that, in fact, the U.S. military is too small. Although firepower and mobility enabled the United States to defeat the Taliban and the Iraqi Army in short order, American forces were insufficient to stabilize either nation. As a result, the United States and its allies remained embroiled in protracted warfare against insurgent forces in both Afghanistan and Iraq years after the initial invasion.

In 2009, the U.S. Navy rescued an American sea captain from a group of Somali pirates who were holding him hostage aboard a vessel in the Persian Gulf. These events demonstrated the continued need for conventional forces, despite the greater threat of WMDs.

International events are the most important environmental factors affecting foreign and defense policymaking. Today, the most important event shaping American foreign and defense policy are the terrorist attacks of September 11, 2001. Survey research shows that although most Americans support an active role for the United States in world affairs, the general public is more cautious about American involvement abroad than are foreign policy leaders in government, the media, business, and academia.[38]

Agenda Setting

Events, public opinion, the media, interest groups, Congress, and the president all play a role in setting the agenda for foreign and defense policymaking. Events affect the agenda for foreign and defense policymaking because of their impact on public opinion. Some issues, such as the bombing of Pearl Harbor or 9/11, become important because of media coverage. Many interest groups participate in foreign and defense policymaking. Corporate and trade groups focus on trade policy, seeking protection from foreign competition or working against restrictive trade policies that threaten their businesses. Environmental groups emphasize international environmental issues.

Historically, the president has taken the lead in foreign and defense policy matters.[39] During the 1960s and 1970s, a series of presidents worked to persuade Congress and the nation of the importance of American intervention in Vietnam. After September 11, 2001, President George W. Bush announced a new American policy of preemption and focused on disarming Iraq. Bush used his second inaugural address to identify democratization as a principal goal of American foreign policy.

During the Cold War presidents could generally count on bipartisan support for foreign policy issues, but congressional consensus has become much less frequent since the war in Vietnam.[40] Since 9/11, there has been consensus on the importance of eliminating al-Qaeda, but disagreement over how best to deal with rogue states.[41] Consider the controversy over the war in Iraq. When the president ordered the U.S. military to invade Iraq to overthrow Saddam Hussein, Congress offered support and voted to provide additional money to fund the war and help rebuild Iraq. As the situation in Iraq worsened and public opinion began to turn against the war, individual members of Congress spoke out against administration policies and Congressional committees initiated investigations of the Iraqi prisoner abuse scandal at Abu Ghraib Prison, and over allegations that Halliburton and other private contractors had overcharged the U.S. government for work performed in Iraq.

Policy Formulation, Adoption, and Legitimation

The president and Congress share constitutional authority to formulate and adopt foreign and defense policy. The president negotiates treaties, but the Senate must ratify them. The president can request money for foreign aid and defense, but Congress must appropriate the funds. The president is commander in chief of the U.S. Armed Forces, but Congress declares war.

The president often initiates foreign and defense policies, with Congress acting to modify or, occasionally, reject policies formulated in the executive branch. Presidents take the lead in foreign and defense policy legitimation, frequently with an address directly to the American people. For example, when President George W. Bush decided to order the invasion of Iraq, he explained and justified his action in a televised address from the White House. Presidents are usually successful in building initial support for a policy because they frame the issue in terms of national defense and support for the troops.[42] Congress is more likely to support presidential initiatives in foreign and defense policy when the president's party controls Congress, when the president enjoys a relatively high approval rating, and during times of international crisis. After September

Congressional committees investigated allegations of Iraqi prisoner abuse at Abu Ghraib Prison in Iraq.

11, 2001, President George W. Bush benefited from an atmosphere of international crisis, strong public support, and Republican majorities in the House and the Senate after the 2002 election. However, after Democrats won a majority in Congress in the 2006 election, Bush faced a Congress, and general public, hostile to his administration's foreign and defense policies.

Policy Implementation, Evaluation, and Change

The executive branch is primarily responsible for the implementation of foreign policy. The Department of State, Department of Defense, the CIA, and the National Security Council are prominently involved. The State Department is chiefly responsible for the diplomatic realm of foreign policy, which includes representing the United States' interests abroad, running the embassies, and negotiating agreements and treaties. The Department of Defense coordinates and runs the military services. The heads of each branch of the military are part of the Joint Chiefs of Staff, an important advisory group to the president. The CIA is the primary intelligence gathering agency, and the National Security Council (NSC) is a group of senior advisors and cabinet offi-

cials that helps coordinate policy among the agencies.

The government has no systematic, ongoing mechanism for evaluating foreign and defense policies. Congress monitors expenditures, but often limits its policy oversight to high-profile issues, such as the war in Iraq, or issues that impact the home districts of members, such as the decision to close a local military base. Scandals also receive considerable attention. Other efforts at evaluation take place in the executive branch, in academia, and by the news media.

In general, foreign and defense policies are probably more difficult to evaluate than policies in other areas. It is not always possible to determine whether policy goals have been met. In the absence of war, for example, any evaluation of the effectiveness of particular defense strategies has to be somewhat speculative. Another problem is that many of the details of policy implementation are secret. Only now, years after the events took place, is information available so that historians can begin to evaluate American foreign policy in the years immediately following World War II.

Secretary of State Hillary Rodham Clinton, left, shakes hands with Indonesian Foreign Minister Hassan Wirajuda after a press conference following their meeting in Jakarta, Indonesia.

Foreign and defense policies change because of changes in the policymaking environment and because of policy evaluation. After the collapse of the Soviet Union, the United States policy of containment was no longer necessary. American policymakers also change course because of the perception that previous policy approaches have failed. After the failure to find WMD in Iraq, for example, the United States will be reluctant to act preemptively against another country unless proof of threat is overwhelming.

TAKE ✓ ACTION

America In the Eyes of the World

What do people in other countries think about the United States? This class project is to interview international students and other foreign nationals about the perceptions of people in their home countries about the United States. International students who are part of the class can take the lead, interviewing their friends and helping American students understand the information they receive. The interviews should focus on the following subject areas:

- Culture. How influential is American culture (television, films, music, etc.) in your country? Do people admire American culture, or does it offend them? Do they worry that American culture will overwhelm their own culture?

- Economics. Do people in your country believe that they benefit from the economic power of the United States, or do they think that they are hurt economically by the United States?
- Foreign policy. What do people in your country think about American foreign policy? Do they consider the United States to be a force for good, or do they believe the United States acts unfairly in its own interest?

After the interviews are complete, your instructor will ask students to discuss what they learned from the activity. In which of the three areas were attitudes about the United States the most and least positive? How did points of view vary from region to region? Why might people from other nations think as they do about the United States?

TAKING SIDES

The Arab Spring

*Do the recent uprisings in the Middle East constitute
a pro-democracy movement?
Should the United States embrace these movements?*

OVERVIEW

In December 2010, a young Tunisian man set fire to himself to protest government corruption after police seized his vegetable cart. The act sparked a revolution that overthrew the president of Tunisia within less than a month. Protests spread throughout the Arab world, where unemployment rates soared and stable dictatorships and monarchies had tightly controlled political activities for decades. Even countries that had established nominal democracies, such as Egypt, censored the press and repressed opposition. Yet, due in part to access to the Internet and mobile devices, groups were able not only to organize widespread demonstrations, but also to get images and information out of the country so that international pressure could be brought to bear. In mid-February 2011, demonstrators in Tahrir Square in Cairo and across the country forced Egyptian President Hosni Mubarak to step down and hand over control of the government to the military. Not long after that, a civil war erupted in Libya and major uprisings broke out in Syria, Yemen, and Bahrain. Other regimes weathered less significant but unprecedented expressions of civil unrest. President Obama praised demonstrators in Tunisia, but initially hesitated when it came to Egypt. He was torn between an idealist embrace of a potentially democratic movement and a realist skepticism regarding the final outcome of the protests and the long-term impact on the stability of the region.

 SUPPORTING
the Arab Spring

 AGAINST the Arab
Spring

Americans should support the spread of democratic freedoms. The demonstrators in Tahrir Square and elsewhere throughout the Middle East are not only protesting against their economic situation, but also against corrupt and repressive regimes.

New governments in the region may improve human rights. In Middle Eastern countries, women face significant gender-based violence and legalized discrimination, with laws that give husbands control over a woman's right to work or travel independently. Egyptian women's rights activists participated in the Tahrir Square protests and hope to bring about change.

The spread of democratic regimes may bring peace to the region. As a general rule, democratic countries do not go to war with other democratic countries. Democratic revolutions in the Middle East could help avert future wars.

Many protesters do not espouse democratic values. The Muslim Brotherhood, a group that advocates for the creation of an Islamic state, participated in the Tahrir Square protests. They are Egypt's largest organized opposition group.

The Arab Spring has not yet given rise to democratic regimes. In Egypt, President Hosni Mubarak's resignation left power in the hands of the Supreme Council for the Armed Forces, military rulers who have stated that they are preparing the country for democratic elections. Protests, however, have continued in Tahrir Square against military rule. The new prime minister in Tunisia, meanwhile, resigned and has left a power vacuum.

The Arab Spring may weaken U.S. interests and allies in the area and strengthen Iran. Egyptian President Hosni Mubarak was an ally of the United States, playing a leading role in a pro-Western alliance and facilitating Israeli–Palestinian negotiations. Saudi Arabia, a long-time U.S. ally, intervened on behalf of the Bahrain government against the protesters in order to contain political unrest.

CONTEXT OF AMERICAN FOREIGN AND DEFENSE POLICY

17.1 *Who are the political actors that make up the international community, and how does the United States pursue its foreign policy goals within that community?*

The nation-state is the basic unit of the international community. In addition to the governments of the world, more than a hundred transnational (or multinational) organizations are active on the international stage, including the United Nations (UN) and its various components, such as the WHO. Nongovernmental organization, including Greenpeace, International Red Cross, and even terror organizations, are important international political actors as well.

The United States has consistently pursued three foreign and defense policy goals throughout its history: national security, economic prosperity, and the projection of American values abroad. The United States pursues these goals through military, economic, cultural, and diplomatic means. In addition to the actual use of force, the United States forms defense alliances, promotes trade with other nations, uses foreign aid to win international backing, and engages in diplomacy.

THE HISTORY OF AMERICAN FOREIGN AND DEFENSE POLICY

17.2 *What is the history of American foreign and defense policy?*

For almost a century, the principle theme of American foreign policy was isolationism. After WWII, the relationship between the United States and the Soviet Union was the dominant element of American foreign policy, as the two nations were locked in the Cold War from the late 1940s until the collapse of the Soviet Union in 1991. The collapse of the Soviet Union ended the Cold War and left the United States as the world's only superpower. The events of 9/11 changed the environment for American foreign and defense policy by demonstrating that the United States is vulnerable to attack despite its status as the world's sole superpower. The war on terror raises a number of important issues for American policymakers, including controlling the spread of WMD, preventing failed states, limiting regional conflicts, dealing with rogue states, and fighting international terrorism.

AMERICAN FOREIGN AND DEFENSE POLICY STRATEGIES

17.3 *What are the two main ways in which America engages in world affairs, and what strategies does it utilize for national defense?*

American policymakers generally agree that the United States must be fully engaged in world affairs, but they disagree on how closely the United States should work with its allies and the other nations of the world. The George W. Bush administration followed a unilateralist approach to achieving its foreign policy goals, while the Obama administration has taken an internationalist approach.

America's defense strategy is based on strategic (nuclear) and conventional (non-nuclear) forces. In general, defense spending increases during wartime and falls during peacetime. Since 9/11, defense expenditures have increased as Congress and the president fund the war on terror as well as military operations in Afghanistan and Iraq. Deterrence was the organizing principle of American defense policy during the Cold War, but it is an imperfect strategy today because of rogue states and, especially, terrorist organizations. Terrorists have no home country to be attacked in retaliation and may be willing to die for their cause.

MAKING FOREIGN AND DEFENSE POLICY

17.4 *How is American foreign and defense policy made?*

International events are the most important environmental factors affecting foreign and defense policymaking. Events, public opinion, the media, interest groups, Congress, and the president all play a role in setting the agenda for foreign and defense policymaking. The president and Congress share constitutional authority to formulate and adopt foreign and defense policy. Presidents take the lead in foreign and defense policy legitimation. The executive branch is primarily responsible for the implementation of foreign policy. The government has no systematic, ongoing mechanism for evaluating foreign and defense policies. Finally, foreign and defense policies change because of changes in the policymaking environment and because of policy evaluation.

MySearchLab®

TEST yourself

17.1 *Who are the political actors that make up the international community, and how does the United States pursue its foreign policy goals within that community?*

1 Which of the following is an international organization created to promote economic stability worldwide?
   a. NATO
   b. United Nations
   c. WHO
   d. IMF

2 Greenpeace, Friends of the Earth, World Wide Fund for Nature, and the Nature Conservancy are all examples of which of the following?
   a. Nation-states
   b. Rogue states
   c. Nongovernmental organizations
   d. All of the above

3 Which of the following is the most important trading partner of the United States?
   a. China
   b. Germany
   c. Mexico
   d. Canada

4 Which of the following nations is *not* a major recipient of U.S. foreign aid?
   a. Iraq
   b. Afghanistan
   c. Iran
   d. Israel

17.2 *What is the history of American foreign and defense policy?*

5 The American policy of keeping the Soviet Union from expanding its sphere of control was known as which of the following?
   a. Balance of power
   b. Containment
   c. Deterrence
   d. Military preemption

6 Which of the following presidents asked Congress for a substantial increase in defense spending during peacetime in order to force the Soviet Union to choose between economic collapse and the end of the Cold War?
   a. Richard Nixon
   b. Ronald Reagan
   c. George H. W. Bush
   d. Bill Clinton

7 Which of the following nations is currently considered a superpower?
   a. Russia
   b. China
   c. United States
   d. All of the above

8 The government of Country X has lost popular support. It controls the capital city, but not the rest of the country, where regional warlords are in charge. Armed gangs threaten the peace in parts of the country. Country X is an example of which of the following?
   a. Failed state
   b. Rogue state
   c. Post-industrial society
   d. Non-governmental organization

17.3 *What are the two main ways in which America engages in world affairs, and what strategies does it utilize for national defense?*

9 "Because the United States is the world's only superpower, it can assert itself internationally and other nations will have no choice but to go along." The above statement most closely reflects which of the following approaches to foreign policy?
   a. Isolationist approach
   b. Internationalist approach
   c. Multinational approach
   d. Unilateralist approach

10 Which of the following is an argument offered by those people who believe that the United States should take an internationalist approach to foreign policy?
   a. The United States should act in its own best interests rather than compromising with other nations.
   b. As the world's most powerful nation, the United States does not have to accommodate the interests of other countries.
   c. The United States needs the support of other nations if it hopes to accomplish its foreign policy goals.
   d. All of the above

11 Which of the following statements is true about American defense spending?
   a. In general, defense spending rises during wartime and falls during peacetime.
   b. As a percentage of GDP, defense spending is greater today than at any time since World War II.

   c. Defense spending has been falling in recent years despite the war on terror and wars in Afghanistan and Iraq.
   d. All of the above

12 "The Soviet leaders did not dare launch a nuclear attack against the United States because the American counterattack would have destroyed the Soviet Union and vice versa." The above statement is an expression of which of the following?
   a. Military preemption
   b. Isolationism
   c. Mutual assured destruction (MAD)
   d. Nuclear winter

13 Which president is most closely associated with the concept of military preemption?
   a. Richard Nixon
   b. George W. Bush
   c. Bill Clinton
   d. Ronald Reagan

17.4 *How is American foreign and defense policy made?*

14 Which of the following officials has historically taken the lead in American foreign and defense policymaking?
   a. President
   b. Speaker of the House
   c. Chief Justice of the United States
   d. Secretary of Defense

15 Which of the following statements best describes bipartisanship?
   a. Congress and the president work closely together.
   b. The House and Senate work closely together.
   c. Republicans and Democrats work closely together.
   d. The United States and Russia work closely together.

KNOW the score

14–15 correct:	Congratulations! You know your American government!
12–13 correct:	Your understanding of the chapter is weak—be sure to review the key terms and visit TheThinkSpot.
<12 correct:	Reread the chapter more thoroughly.

Answers: 1) d, 2) c, 3) d, 4) c, 5) b, 6) b, 7) c, 8) a, 9) d, 10) c, 11) a, 12) c, 13) b, 14) a, 15) c

THE DECLARATION
OF INDEPENDENCE

In Congress, July 4, 1776

The unanimous Declaration of the thirteen united States of America.

When in the Course of human events, it becomes necessary for one people to dissolve the political bands which have connected them with another, and to assume among the Powers of the earth, the separate and equal station to which the Laws of Nature and of Nature's God entitle them, a decent respect to the opinions of mankind requires that they should declare the causes which impel them to the separation.

We hold these truths to be self-evident, that all men are created equal, that they are endowed by their Creator with certain unalienable Rights, that among these are Life, Liberty and the pursuit of Happiness. That to secure these rights, Governments are instituted among Men, deriving their just powers from the consent of the governed. That whenever any Form of Government becomes destructive of these ends, it is the Right of the People to alter or to abolish it, and to institute new Government, laying its foundation on such principles and organizing its powers in such form, as to them shall seem most likely to effect their Safety and Happiness. Prudence, indeed, will dictate that Governments long established should not be changed for light and transient causes; and accordingly all experience hath shown, that mankind are more disposed to suffer, while evils are sufferable, than to right themselves by abolishing the forms to which they are accustomed. But when a long train of abuses and usurpations, pursuing invariably the same Object evinces a design to reduce them under absolute Despotism, it is their right, it is their duty, to throw off such Government, and to provide new Guards for their future security. Such has been the patient sufferance of these Colonies; and such is now the necessity which constrains them to alter their former Systems of Government. The history of the present King of Great Britain is a history of repeated injuries and usurpations, all having in direct object the establishment of an absolute Tyranny over these States. To prove this, let Facts be submitted to a candid world.

He has refused his Assent to Laws, the most wholesome and necessary for the public good.

He has forbidden his Governors to pass Laws of immediate and pressing importance, unless suspended in their operation till his Assent should be obtained; and when so suspended, he has utterly neglected to attend to them.

He has refused to pass other Laws for the accommodation of large districts of people, unless those people would relinquish the right of Representation in the Legislature, a right inestimable to them and formidable to tyrants only.

He has called together legislative bodies at places unusual, uncomfortable, and distant from the depository of their Public Records, for the sole purpose of fatiguing them into compliance with his measures.

He has dissolved Representative Houses repeatedly, for opposing with manly firmness his invasions on the rights of the people.

He has refused for a long time, after such dissolutions, to cause others to be elected; whereby the Legislative Powers, incapable of Annihilation, have returned to the People at large for their exercise; the State remaining in the mean time exposed to all the dangers of invasion from without, and convulsions within.

He has endeavoured to prevent the population of these States; for that purpose obstructing the Laws for Naturalization of Foreigners; refusing to pass others to encourage their migrations hither, and raising the conditions of new Appropriations of Lands.

He has obstructed the Administration of Justice, by refusing his Assent to Laws for establishing Judiciary Powers.

He has made Judges dependent on his Will alone, for the tenure of their offices, and the amount and payment of their salaries.

He has erected a multitude of New Offices, and sent hither swarms of Officers to harass our people, and eat out their substance.

He has kept among us, in times of peace, Standing Armies without the Consent of our legislatures.

He has affected to render the Military independent of and superior to the Civil Power.

He has combined with others to subject us to a jurisdiction foreign to our constitution, and unacknowledged by our laws; giving his Assent to their acts of pretended Legislation:

For quartering large bodies of armed troops among us:

For protecting them, by a mock Trial, from Punishment for any Murders which they should commit on the inhabitants of these States:

For cutting off our Trade with all parts of the world:

For imposing taxes on us without our Consent:

For depriving us in many cases, of the benefits of Trial by Jury:

For transporting us beyond Seas to be tried for pretended offences:

For abolishing the free System of English Laws in a neighbouring Province, establishing therein an Arbitrary government, and enlarging its Boundaries so as to render it at once an example and fit instrument for introducing the same absolute rule into these Colonies:

For taking away our Charters, abolishing our most valuable Laws, and altering fundamentally the Forms of our Governments:

For suspending our own Legislature, and declaring themselves invested with Power to legislate for us in all cases whatsoever.

He has abdicated Government here, by declaring us out of his Protection and waging War against us.

He has plundered our seas, ravaged our Coasts, burnt our towns, and destroyed the lives of our people.

He is at this time transporting large armies of foreign mercenaries to compleat the works of death, desolation and tyranny, already begun with circumstances of Cruelty and perfidy scarcely paralleled in the most barbarous ages, and totally unworthy the Head of a civilized nation.

He has constrained our fellow Citizens taken Captive on the high Seas to bear Arms against their Country, to become the executioners of their friends and Brethren, or to fall themselves by their Hands.

He has excited domestic insurrections amongst us, and has endeavoured to bring on the inhabitants of our frontiers, the merciless Indian Savages, whose known rule of warfare, is an undistinguished destruction of all ages, sexes and conditions.

In every stage of these Oppressions We have Petitioned for Redress in the most humble terms: Our repeated Petitions have been answered only by repeated injury. A Prince, whose character is thus marked by every act which may define a Tyrant, is unfit to be the ruler of a free people.

Nor have we been wanting in attentions to our British brethren. We have warned them from time to time of attempts by their legislature to extend an unwarrantable jurisdiction over us. We have reminded them of the circumstances of our emigration and settlement here. We have appealed to their native justice and magnanimity, and we have conjured them by the ties of our common kindred to disavow these usurpations which, would inevitably interrupt our connections and correspondence. They too have been deaf to the voice of justice and of consanguinity. We must, therefore, acquiesce in the necessity, which denounces our Separation, and hold them, as we hold the rest of mankind, Enemies in War, in Peace Friends.

We, therefore, the Representatives of the United States of America, in General Congress, Assembled, appealing to the Supreme Judge of the world for the rectitude of our intentions, do, in the Name, and by authority of the good People of these Colonies, solemnly publish and declare, That these United Colonies are, and of Right ought to be Free and Independent States; that they are Absolved from all Allegiance to the British Crown, and that all political connection between them and the State of Great Britain, is and ought to be totally dissolved; and that as Free and Independent States, they have full Power to levy War, conclude Peace, contract Alliances, establish Commerce, and to do all other Acts and Things which Independent States may of right do. And for the support of this Declaration, with a firm reliance of the Protection of Divine Providence, we mutually pledge to each other our Lives, our Fortunes and our sacred Honor.

THE CONSTITUTION
OF THE UNITED STATES OF AMERICA

We the people of the United States, in Order to form a more perfect Union, establish justice, insure domestic Tranquility, provide for the common defence, promote the general Welfare, and secure the Blessings of Liberty to ourselves and our Posterity, do ordain and establish this Constitution for the United States of America.

Article I

Section 1

All legislative Powers herein granted shall be vested in a Congress of the United States, which shall consist of a Senate and House of Representatives.

Section 2

The House of Representatives shall be composed of Members chosen every second Year by the People of the several States, and the Electors in each State shall have the Qualifications requisite for Electors of the most numerous Branch of the State Legislature.

No person shall be a Representative who shall not have attained to the Age of twenty five Years, and been seven Years a Citizen of the United States, and who shall not, when elected, be an Inhabitant of that State in which he shall be chosen.

Representatives and direct Taxes shall be apportioned among the several States which may be included within this Union, according to their respective Numbers, which shall be determined by adding to the whole Number of free Persons, including those bound to Service for a Term of Years, and excluding Indians not taxed, three fifths of all other Persons.* The actual Enumeration shall be made within three years after the first Meeting of the Congress of the United States, and within every subsequent Term of ten Years, in such Manner as they shall by Law direct. The Number of Representatives shall not exceed one for every thirty Thousand, but each State shall have at Least one Representative; and until such enumeration shall be made, the State of New Hampshire shall be entitled to chuse three, Massachusetts eight, Rhode-Island and Providence Plantations one, Connecticut five, New-York six, New Jersey four, Pennsylvania eight, Delaware one, Maryland six, Virginia ten, North Carolina five, South Carolina five, and Georgia three.

When vacancies happen in the Representation from any State, the Executive Authority thereof shall issue Writs of Election to fill such Vacancies.

The House of Representatives shall chuse their Speaker and other Officers; and shall have the sole Power of Impeachment.

Section 3

The Senate of the United States shall be composed of two Senators from each State, chosen by the Legislature thereof, for six Years; and each Senator shall have one Vote.

Immediately after they shall be assembled in Consequence of the first Election, they shall be divided as equally as may be into three Classes. The Seats of the Senators of the first Class shall be vacated at the Expiration of the second Year, of the second Class at the Expiration of the fourth Year, and of the third Class at the Expiration of the sixth Year, so that one third may be chosen every second Year; and if Vacancies happen by Resignation, or otherwise, during the Recess of the Legislature of any State, the Executive thereof may make temporary Appointments until the next Meeting of the Legislature, which shall then fill such Vacancies.†

No Person shall be a Senator who shall not have attained to the Age of thirty Years, and been nine Years a Citizen of the United States, and who shall not, when elected, be an Inhabitant of that State in which he shall be chosen.

The Vice President of the United States shall be President of the Senate, but shall have no Vote, unless they be equally divided.

The Senate shall chuse their other Officers, and also a President pro tempore, in the Absence of the Vice President, or when he shall exercise the Office of the President of the United States.

The Senate shall have the sole Power to try all impeachments. When sitting for that Purpose, they shall be on Oath or Affirmation. When the President of the United States is tried, the Chief Justice shall preside: And no person shall be convicted without the Concurrence of two thirds of the Members present.

Judgment in Cases of Impeachment shall not extend further than to removal from Office, and disqualification to hold and enjoy any Office of honor, Trust or Profit under the United States; but the Party convicted shall nevertheless be liable and subject to Indictment, Trial, Judgment and Punishment, according to Law.

---

*Other persons being black slaves. Modified by Amendment XIV, Section 2.

†Provisions changed by Amendment XVII.

Section 4

The Times, Places and Manner of holding Elections for Senators and Representatives, shall be prescribed in each State by the Legislature thereof; but the Congress may at any time by Law make or alter such Regulations, except as to the Places of chusing Senators.

The Congress shall assemble at least once in every Year, and such Meeting shall be on the first Monday in December, unless they shall by Law appoint a different Day.*

Section 5

Each House shall be the Judge of the Elections, Returns and Qualifications of its own Members, and a Majority of each shall constitute a Quorum to do Business; but a smaller number may adjourn from day to day, and may be authorized to compel the Attendance of absent Members, in such Manner, and under such Penalties as each House may provide.

Each House may determine the Rules of its Proceedings, punish its Members for disorderly Behaviour, and, with the Concurrence of two thirds, expel a Member.

Each House shall keep a Journal of its Proceedings, and from time to time publish the same, excepting such Parts as may in their Judgment require Secrecy; and the Yeas and Nays of the Members of either House on any question shall, at the Desire of one fifth of those Present, be entered on the Journal.

Neither House, during the Session of Congress, shall, without the Consent of the other, adjourn for more than three days, nor to any other Place than that in which the two Houses shall be sitting.

Section 6

The Senators and Representatives shall receive a Compensation for their Services, to be ascertained by Law, and paid out of the Treasury of the United States. They shall in all Cases, except Treason, Felony and Breach of the Peace, be privileged from arrest during their Attendance at the Session of their respective Houses, and in going to and returning from the same; and for any Speech or Debate in either House, they shall not be questioned in any other Place.

No Senator or Representative shall, during the Time for which he was elected, be appointed to any civil Office under the Authority of the United States, which shall have been created, or the Emoluments whereof shall have been encreased, during such time; and no Person holding any Office under the United States shall be a Member of either House during his Continuance in Office.

Section 7

All Bills for raising Revenue shall originate in the House of Representatives; but the Senate may propose or concur with Amendments as on other Bills.

Every Bill which shall have passed the House of Representatives and the Senate, shall, before it become a Law, be presented to the President of the United States;

*Provisions changed by Amendment XX, Section 2.

If he approves he shall sign it, but if not he shall return it, with his Objections, to that House in which it shall have originated, who shall enter the Objections at large on their Journal, and proceed to reconsider it. If after such Reconsideration two thirds of that House shall agree to pass the Bill, it shall be sent, together with the Objections, to the other House, by which it shall likewise be reconsidered, and if approved by two thirds of that House, it shall become a Law. But in all such Cases the Votes of both Houses shall be determined by Yeas and Nays, and the Names of the Persons voting for and against the Bill shall be entered on the Journal of each House respectively. If any Bill shall not be returned by the President within ten Days (Sundays excepted) after it shall have been presented to him, the Same shall be a Law, in like Manner as if he had signed it, unless the Congress by their Adjournment prevent its Return, in which Case it shall not be a Law.

Every Order, Resolution, or Vote to which the Concurrence of the Senate and House of Representatives may be necessary (except on a question of Adjournment) shall be presented to the President of the United States; and before the Same shall take Effect, shall be approved by him, or being disapproved by him, shall be repassed by two thirds of the Senate and House of Representatives, according to the Rules and Limitations prescribed in the Case of a Bill.

Section 8

The Congress shall have Power To lay and collect Taxes, Duties, Imposts and Excises, to pay the Debts and provide for the common Defence and general Welfare of the United States; but all Duties, Imposts and Excises shall be uniform throughout the United States;

To borrow Money on the credit of the United States;

To regulate Commerce with foreign Nations, and among the several States, and with the Indian Tribes;

To establish a uniform Rule of Naturalization, and uniform Laws on the subject of Bankruptcies throughout the United States;

To coin Money, regulate the Value thereof, and of foreign Coin, and fix the Standard of Weights and Measures;

To provide for the Punishment of counterfeiting the Securities and current Coin of the United States;

To establish Post offices and post Roads;

To promote the Progress of Science and useful Arts, by securing for limited Times to Authors and Inventors the exclusive Right to their respective Writings and Discoveries;

To constitute Tribunals inferior to the supreme Court;

To define and punish Piracies and Felonies committed on the high Seas, and Offences against the Law of Nations;

To declare War, grant Letters of Marque and Reprisal, and make Rules concerning Captures on Land and Water;

To raise and support Armies, but no Appropriation of Money to that Use shall be for a longer Term than two Years;

To provide and maintain a Navy;

To make Rules for the Government and Regulation of the land and naval Forces;

To provide for calling forth the Militia to execute the Laws of the Union, suppress Insurrections and repel Invasions;

To provide for organizing, arming, and disciplining, the Militia, and for governing such Part of them as may be employed in the Service of the United States, reserving to the States respectively, the Appointment of the Officers, and the Authority of training the Militia according to the discipline prescribed by Congress;

To exercise exclusive Legislation in all Cases whatsoever, over such District (not exceeding ten Miles square) as may, by Cession of particular States, and the Acceptance of Congress, become the Seat of Government of the United States, and to exercise like Authority over all Places purchased by the Consent of the Legislature of the State in which the Same shall be, for the Erection of Forts, Magazines, Arsenals, dock-Yards, and other needful Buildings;—And

To make all Laws which shall be necessary and proper for carrying into Execution the foregoing Powers, and all other Powers vested by this Constitution in the Government of the United States, or in any Department or Officer thereof.

Section 9

The Migration or Importation of such Persons as any of the States now existing shall think proper to admit, shall not be prohibited by the Congress prior to the Year one thousand eight hundred and eight, but a Tax, or duty may be imposed on such Importation, not exceeding ten dollars for each Person.

The privilege of the Writ of Habeas Corpus shall not be suspended, unless when in Cases of Rebellion or Invasion the public Safety may require it.

No Bill of Attainder or ex post facto Law shall be passed.

No Capitation, or other direct, Tax shall be laid, unless in Proportion to the Census or Enumeration herein before directed to be taken.

No Tax or Duty shall be laid on Articles exported from any State.

No Preference shall be given by any Regulation of Commerce or Revenue to the Ports of one State over those of another; nor shall Vessels bound to, or from, one State, be obliged to enter, clear, or pay Duties in another.

No Money shall be drawn from the Treasury, but in Consequence of Appropriations made by Law; and a regular Statement and Account of the Receipts and Expenditures of all public Money shall be published from time to time.

No Title of Nobility shall be granted by the United States: And no Person holding any Office of Profit or Trust under them, shall, without the Consent of the Congress, accept of any present, Emolument, Office, or Title, of any kind whatever, from any King, Prince, or foreign State.

Section 10

No State shall enter into any Treaty, Alliance, or Confederation; grant Letters of Marque and Reprisal; coin Money; emit Bills of Credit; make any Thing but gold and silver Coin a Tender in Payment of Debts; pass any Bill of Attainder, ex post facto Law, or Law impairing the Obligation of Contracts, or grant any Title of Nobility.

No State shall, without the Consent of the Congress, lay any Imposts or Duties on Imports or Exports, except what may be absolutely necessary for executing its inspection Laws: and the net Produce of all Duties and Imposts, laid by any State on Imports or Exports, shall be for the Use of the Treasury of the United States; and all such Laws shall be subject to the Revision and Control of the Congress.

No State shall, without the Consent of Congress, lay any Duty of Tonnage, keep Troops, or Ships of War in time of Peace, enter into any Agreement or Compact with another State, or with a foreign Power, or engage in War, unless actually invaded, or in such imminent Danger as will not admit of delay.

Article II

Section 1

The executive Power shall be vested in a President of the United States of America. He shall hold his Office during the Term of four Years, and, together with the Vice President, chosen for the same Term, be elected, as follows:

Each State shall appoint, in such Manner as the Legislature thereof may direct, a Number of Electors, equal to the whole Number of Senators and Representatives to which the State may be entitled in the Congress; but no Senator or Representative, or Person holding an Office of Trust or Profit under the United States, shall be appointed an Elector.

The Electors shall meet in their respective States, and vote by Ballot for two Persons, of whom one at least shall not be an Inhabitant of the same State with themselves. And they shall make a List of all the Persons voted for, and of the Number of Votes for each; which List they shall sign and certify, and transmit sealed to the Seat of the Government of the United States, directed to the President of the Senate. The President of the Senate shall, in the Presence of the Senate and House of Representatives, open all the Certificates, and the Votes shall then be counted. The Person having the greatest Number of Votes shall be the President, if such Number be a Majority of the whole Number of Electors appointed; and if there be more than one who have such Majority, and have an equal Number of Votes, then the House of Representatives shall immediately chuse by Ballot one of them for President; and if no Person have a Majority, then from the five highest on the List the said House shall in like Manner chuse the President. But in chusing the President, the Votes shall be taken by States, the Representation from each State having one Vote; a quorum for this Purpose shall consist of a Member or Members from two thirds of the States, and a Majority of all the States shall be necessary to a Choice. In every Case, after the Choice of the President, the Person having the greatest Number of Votes of the Electors shall be the Vice President. But if there should remain two or more who have equal Votes, the Senate shall chuse from them by Ballot the Vice President.*

The Congress may determine the Time of chusing the Electors, and the Day on which they shall give their Votes; which Day shall be the same throughout the United States.

No Person except a natural born Citizen, or a Citizen of the United States, at the time of the Adoption of this Constitution, shall be eligible to the Office of President; neither shall any Person be eligible to that Office who shall not have attained to the Age of thirty five Years, and been fourteen Years a Resident within the United States.

In Case of the Removal of the President from Office, or of his Death, Resignation, or Inability to discharge the Powers and Duties of the said Office, the Same shall devolve on the Vice President, and the Congress may by Law provide for the Case of Removal, Death, Resignation or Inability, both of the President and Vice President, declaring what Officer shall then act as President, and such Officer shall act accordingly, until the Disability be removed, or a President shall be elected.

The President shall, at stated Times, receive for his Services, a Compensation, which shall neither be encreased nor diminished during the Period for which he shall have been elected, and he shall not receive within that Period any other Emolument from the United States, or any of them.

Before he enter on the Execution of his Office, he shall take the following Oath or Affirmation:—"I do solemnly swear (or affirm) that I will faithfully execute the Office of President of the United States, and will to the best of my Ability, preserve, protect and defend the Constitution of the United States."

Section 2
The President shall be Commander in Chief of the Army and Navy of the United States, and of the Militia of the several States, when called into the actual Service of the United States; he may require the Opinion, in writing, of the principal Officer in each of the executive Departments, upon any Subject relating to the Duties of their respective Offices, and he shall have Power to grant Reprieves and Pardons for Offences against the United States, except in Cases of Impeachment.

He shall have Power, by and with the Advice and Consent of the Senate, to make Treaties, provided two thirds of the Senators present concur; and he shall nominate, and by and with the Advice and Consent of the Senate, shall appoint Ambassadors, other public Ministers and Consuls, Judges of the supreme Court, and all other Officers of the United States, whose Appointments are not herein otherwise provided for, and which shall be established by Law: but the Congress may by Law vest the Appointment of such inferior Officers, as they think proper in the President alone, in the Courts of Law, or in the Heads of Departments.

The President shall have Power to fill up all Vacancies that may happen during the Recess of the Senate, by granting Commissions which shall expire at the end of their next Session.

Section 3
He shall from time to time give to the Congress Information of the State of the Union, and recommend to their Consideration such Measures as he shall judge necessary and expedient; he may, on extraordinary occasions, convene both Houses, or either of them, and in Case of Disagreement between them, with Respect to the Time of Adjournment, he may adjourn them to such Time as he shall think proper; he shall receive Ambassadors and other public Ministers; he shall take Care that the Laws be faithfully executed, and shall Commission all the Officers of the United States.

Section 4
The President, Vice President and all civil Officers of the United States, shall be removed from Office on Impeachment for, and Conviction of, Treason, Bribery, or other high Crimes and Misdemeanors.

Article III
Section 1
The judicial Power of the United States, shall be vested in one supreme Court, and in such inferior Courts as the Congress may from time to time ordain and establish. The Judges, both of the supreme and inferior Courts, shall hold their Offices during good Behaviour, and shall, at stated Times, receive for their Services, a Compensation, which shall not be diminished during their Continuance in Office.

Section 2
The judicial Power shall extend to all Cases in Law and Equity, arising under this Constitution, the Laws of the United States, and Treaties made, or which shall be made, under their Authority;—to all Cases affecting

*Provisions superseded by Amendment XII.

Ambassadors, other public Ministers and Consuls;—to all cases of admiralty and maritime Jurisdiction;—to Controversies to which the United States shall be a Party;—to Controversies between two or more States;—between a State and Citizens of another State;—between Citizens of different States;—between Citizens of the same State claiming Lands under Grants of different States, and between a State, or the Citizens thereof, and foreign States, Citizens or Subjects.*

In all Cases affecting Ambassadors, other public Ministers and Consuls, and those in which a State shall be Party, the supreme Court shall have original Jurisdiction. In all the other Cases before mentioned, the supreme Court shall have appellate Jurisdiction, both as to Law and Fact, with such Exceptions, and under such Regulations as the Congress shall make.

The Trial of all Crimes, except in Cases of Impeachment, shall be by Jury; and such Trial shall be held in the State where the said Crimes shall have been committed, but when not committed within any State, the Trial shall be at such Place or Places as the Congress may by law have directed.

Section 3
Treason against the United States, shall consist only in levying War against them, or in adhering to their Enemies, giving them Aid and Comfort. No person shall be convicted of Treason unless on the Testimony of two Witnesses to the same overt Act, or on Confession in open Court.

The Congress shall have Power to declare the Punishment of Treason, but no Attainder of Treason shall work Corruption of Blood, or Forfeiture except during the Life of the Person attained.

Article IV
Section 1
Full Faith and Credit shall be given in each State to the public Acts, Records, and judicial Proceedings of every other State. And the Congress may by general Laws prescribe the Manner in which such Acts, Records and Proceedings shall be proved, and the Effect thereof.

Section 2
The Citizens of each State shall be entitled to all Privileges and Immunities of Citizens in the several States.

A Person charged in any State with Treason, Felony, or other Crime, who shall flee from Justice, and be found in another State, shall on Demand of the executive Authority of the State from which he fled, be delivered up, to be removed to the State having Jurisdiction of the Crime.

No Person held to Service or Labour in one State, under the Laws thereof, escaping into another, shall, in Consequence of any Law or Regulation therein, be discharged from such Service or Labour, but shall be delivered up on Claim of the Party to whom such Service or Labour may be due.

*Clause changed by Amendment XI.

Section 3
New States may be admitted by the Congress into this Union; but no new State shall be formed or erected within the Jurisdiction of any other State; nor any State be formed by the Junction of two or more States, or Parts of States, without the Consent of the Legislatures of the States concerned as well as of the Congress.

The Congress shall have Power to dispose of and make all needful Rules and Regulations respecting the Territory or other Property belonging to the United States; and nothing in this Constitution shall be so construed as to Prejudice any Claims of the United States, or of any particular State.

Section 4
The United States shall guarantee to every State in this Union a Republican Form of Government, and shall protect each of them against Invasion; and on Application of the Legislature, or of the Executive (when the Legislature cannot be convened) against domestic Violence.

Article V
The Congress, whenever two thirds of both Houses shall deem it necessary, shall propose Amendments to this Constitution, or, on the Application of the Legislatures of two thirds of the several States, shall call a Convention for proposing Amendments, which, in either Case, shall be valid to all Intents and Purposes, as Part of this Constitution, when ratified by the Legislatures of three fourths of the several states, or by Conventions in three fourths thereof, as the one or the other Mode of Ratification may be proposed by the Congress; Provided that no Amendment which may be made prior to the Year One thousand eight hundred and eight shall in any Manner affect the first and fourth Clauses in the Ninth Section of the first Article; and that no State, without its Consent, shall be deprived of its equal Suffrage in the Senate.

Article VI
All Debts contracted and Engagements entered into, before the Adoption of this Constitution, shall be as valid against the United States under this Constitution, as under the Confederation.

This Constitution, and the Laws of the United States which shall be made in Pursuance thereof; and all Treaties made, or which shall be made, under the Authority of the United States, shall be the supreme Law of the Land; and the Judges in every State shall be bound thereby, any Thing in the Constitution or Laws of any State to the Contrary notwithstanding.

The Senators and Representatives before mentioned, and the Members of the several State Legislatures and all executive and judicial Officers, both of the United States and of the several States, shall be bound by Oath or Affirmation to support this Constitution; but no religious

Test shall ever be required as a Qualification to any Office or public Trust under the United States.

Article VII

The Ratification of the Conventions of nine States shall be sufficient for the Establishment of this Constitution between the States so ratifying the Same.

Done in Convention by the Unanimous Consent of the States present the Seventeenth Day of September in the Year of our Lord one thousand seven hundred and Eighty seven and of the Independence of the United States of America the Twelfth.* In Witness whereof We have hereunto subscribed our Names.

*The Constitution was submitted on September 17, 1787, by the Constitutional Convention, was ratified by the conventions of several states at various dates up to May 29, 1790, and became effective on March 4, 1789.

AMENDMENTS
TO THE CONSTITUTION
(The First Ten Amendments Form the Bill of Rights)

Amendment I [1791]

Congress shall make no law respecting an establishment of religion, or prohibiting the free exercise thereof; or abridging the freedom of speech, or of the press, or the right of the people peaceably to assemble, and to petition the Government for a redress of grievances.

Amendment II [1791]

A well regulated Militia being necessary to the security of a free State, the right of the people to keep and bear Arms, shall not be infringed.

Amendment III [1791]

No Soldier shall, in time of peace, be quartered in any house, without the consent of the Owner, nor in time of war, but in a manner to be prescribed by law.

Amendment IV [1791]

The right of the people to be secure in their persons, houses, papers, and effects, against unreasonable searches and seizures, shall not be violated, and no Warrants shall issue, but upon probable cause, supported by Oath or affirmation, and particularly describing the place to be searched, and the persons or things to be seized.

Amendment V [1791]

No person shall be held to answer for a capital or otherwise infamous crime, unless on a presentment or indictment of a Grand Jury, except in cases arising in the land or naval forces, or in the Militia, when in actual service in time of War or public danger; nor shall any person be subject for the same offence to be twice put in jeopardy of life or limb; nor shall be compelled in any criminal case to be a witness against himself, nor be deprived of life, liberty, or property, without due process of law; nor shall private property be taken for public use, without just compensation.

Amendment VI [1791]

In all criminal prosecutions, the accused shall enjoy the right to a speedy and public trial, by an impartial jury of the State and district wherein the crime shall have been committed, which district shall have been previously ascertained by law, and to be informed of the nature and cause of the accusation; to be confronted with the witnesses against him; to have compulsory process for obtaining witnesses in his favor, and to have the Assistance of Counsel for his defence.

Amendment VII [1791]

In Suits at common law, where the value in controversy shall exceed twenty dollars, the right of trial by jury shall be preserved, and no fact tried by a jury, shall be otherwise reexamined in any court of the United States, than according to the rules of the common law.

Amendment VIII [1791]

Excessive bail shall not be required, nor excessive fines imposed, nor cruel and unusual punishments inflicted.

Amendment IX [1791]

The enumeration in the Constitution, of certain rights, shall not be construed to deny or disparage others retained by the people.

Amendment X [1791]

The powers not delegated to the United States by the Constitution, nor prohibited by it to the States, are reserved to the States respectively, or to the people.

Amendment XI [1798]

The Judicial power of the United States shall not be construed to extend to any suit in law or equity, commenced or prosecuted against one of the United States by Citizens of another State, or by Citizens of Subjects of any Foreign State.

Amendment XII [1804]

The Electors shall meet in their respective states and vote by ballot for President and Vice-President, one of whom, at least, shall not be an inhabitant of the same state with themselves; they shall name in their ballots the person voted for as President, and in distinct ballots the person voted for as Vice-President, and they shall make distinct lists of all persons voted for as President, and of all persons voted for as Vice-President, and of the number of votes for each, which lists they shall sign and certify, and transmit sealed to the seat of the government of the United States, directed to the President of the Senate;—The President of the Senate shall, in the presence of the Senate and House of Representatives, open all the certificates and the votes shall then be counted;—The person having the greatest number of votes for President, shall be the President, if such number be a majority of the whole number of Electors appointed; and if no person have such majority, then from the persons having the highest numbers not exceeding three on the list of those voted for as President, the House of Representatives shall choose immediately, by ballot, the President. But in choosing the President, the votes shall be taken by states, the representation from each state having one vote; a quorum for this purpose shall consist of a member or members from two-thirds of the states, and a majority of all the states shall be necessary to a choice. And if the House of Representatives shall not choose a President whenever the right of choice shall devolve upon them, before the fourth day of March next following, then the Vice-President shall act as President, as in the case of the death or other constitutional disability of the President.—The person having the greatest number of votes as Vice-President, shall be the Vice-President, if such number be a majority of the whole number of Electors appointed, and if no person have a majority, then from the two highest numbers on the list, the Senate shall choose the Vice-President; a quorum for the purpose shall consist of two-thirds of the whole number of Senators, and a majority of the whole number shall be necessary to a choice. But no person constitutionally ineligible to the office of President shall be eligible to that of Vice-President of the United States.

Amendment XIII [1865]
Section 1

Neither slavery nor involuntary servitude, except as a punishment for crime whereof the party shall have been duly convicted, shall exist within the United States, or any place subject to their jurisdiction.

Section 2

Congress shall have power to enforce this article by appropriate legislation.

Amendment XIV [1868]
Section 1

All persons born or naturalized in the United States, and subject to the jurisdiction thereof, are citizens of the United States and the State wherein they reside. No State shall make or enforce any law which shall abridge the privileges or immunities of citizens of the United States; nor shall any State deprive any person of life, liberty, or property, without due process of law; nor deny to any person within its jurisdiction the equal protection of the laws.

Section 2

Representatives shall be apportioned among the several States according to their respective numbers, counting the whole number of persons in each State, excluding Indians not taxed. But when the right to vote at any election for the choice of electors for President and Vice President of the United States, Representatives in Congress, the Executive and Judicial officers of a State, or the members of the Legislature thereof, is denied to any of the male inhabitants of such State being twenty-one years of age, and citizens of the United States or in any way abridged, except for participation in rebellion or other crime, the basis of representation therein shall be reduced in the proportion which the number of such male citizens shall bear to the whole number of male citizens twenty-one years of age in such State.

Section 3

No person shall be a Senator or Representative in Congress, or elector of President and Vice President, or hold any office, civil or military, under the United States or under any State, who, having previously taken an oath, as a member of Congress, or as an officer of the United States, or as a member of any State legislature or as an executive or judicial officer of any State to support the Constitution of the United States, shall have engaged in insurrection or rebellion against the same, or given aid or comfort to the enemies thereof. But Congress may by a vote of two-thirds of each House, remove such disability.

Section 4

The validity of the public debt of the United States, authorized by law, including debts incurred for payment of pensions and bounties for services in suppressing insurrection or rebellion, shall not be questioned. But neither the United States nor any State shall assume or pay any debt or obligation incurred in aid of insurrection or rebellion against the United States, or any claim for the loss or emancipation of any slave; but all such debts, obligations and claims shall be held illegal and void.

Section 5

The Congress shall have the power to enforce, by appropriate legislation, the provisions of this article.

Amendment XV [1870]

Section 1

The right of citizens of the United States to vote shall not be denied or abridged by the United States or by any State on account of race, color, or previous condition of servitude.

Section 2

The Congress shall have power to enforce this article by appropriate legislation.

Amendment XVI [1913]

The Congress shall have power to lay and collect taxes on incomes, from whatever source derived, without apportionment among the several States, and without regard to any census or enumeration.

Amendment XVII [1913]

The Senate of the United States shall be composed of two Senators from each State, elected by the people thereof, for six years; and each Senator shall have one vote. The electors in each State shall have the qualifications requisite for electors of the most numerous branch of the State legislatures.

When vacancies happen in the representation of any State in the Senate, the executive authority of such State shall issue writs of election to fill such vacancies: *Provided*, That the legislature of any State may empower the executive thereof to make temporary appointments until the people fill the vacancies by election as the legislature may direct.

This amendment shall not be so construed as to affect the election or term of any Senator chosen before it becomes valid as part of the Constitution.

Amendment XVIII [1919]

Section 1

After one year from the ratification of this article the manufacture, sale, or transportation of intoxicating liquors within, the importation thereof into, or the exportation thereof from the United States and all territory subject to the jurisdiction thereof for beverage purposes is hereby prohibited.

Section 2

The Congress and the several States shall have concurrent power to enforce this article by appropriate legislation.

Section 3

This article shall be inoperative unless it shall have been ratified as an amendment to the Constitution by the legislatures of the several States, as provided in the Constitution, within seven years from the date of the submission hereof to the States by the Congress.

Amendment XIX [1920]

The right of citizens of the United States to vote shall not be denied or abridged by the United States or by any State on account of sex.

Congress shall have power to enforce this article by appropriate legislation.

Amendment XX [1933]

Section 1

The terms of the President and Vice President shall end at noon on the 20th day of January, and the terms of Senators and Representatives at noon on the 3rd day of January, of the years in which such terms would have ended if this article had not been ratified; and the terms of their successors shall then begin.

Section 2

The Congress shall assemble at least once in every year, and such meeting shall begin at noon on the 3rd day of January, unless they shall by law appoint a different day.

Section 3

If, at the time fixed for the beginning of the term of the President, the President elect shall have died, the Vice President elect shall become President. If a President shall not have been chosen before the time fixed for the beginning of his term, or if the President elect shall have failed to qualify, then the Vice President elect shall act as President until a President shall have qualified; and the Congress may by law provide for the case wherein neither a President elect nor a Vice President elect shall have qualified, declaring who shall then act as President, or the manner in which one who is to act shall be selected, and such person shall act accordingly until a President or Vice President shall have qualified.

Section 4

The Congress may by law provide for the case of the death of any of the persons from whom the House of Representatives may choose a President whenever the right of choice shall have devolved upon them, and for the case of the death of any of the persons from whom the Senate may choose a Vice-President whenever the right of choice shall have devolved upon them.

Section 5

Sections 1 and 2 shall take effect on the 15th day of October following the ratification of this article.

Section 6

This article shall be inoperative unless it shall have been ratified as an amendment to the Constitution by the legislatures of three-fourths of the several States within seven years from the date of its submission.

Amendment XXI [1933]

Section 1
The eighteenth article of amendment to the Constitution of the United States is hereby repealed.

Section 2
The transportation or importation into any State, Territory, or possession of the United States for delivery or use therein of intoxicating liquors, in violation of the laws thereof, is hereby prohibited.

Section 3
This article shall be inoperative unless it shall have been ratified as an amendment to the Constitution by conventions in the several States, as provided in the Constitution, within seven years from the date of the submission hereof to the States by the Congress.

Amendment XXII [1951]

Section 1
No person shall be elected to the office of the President more than twice, and no person who has held the office of President, or acted as President, for more than two years of a term to which some other person was elected President shall be elected to the office of the President more than once. But this Article shall not apply to any person holding the office of President when this Article was proposed by the Congress, and shall not prevent any person who may be holding the office of President or acting as President, during the term within which this Article becomes operative from holding the office of President or acting as President during the remainder of such term.

Amendment XXIII [1961]

Section 1
The District constituting the seat of Government of the United States shall appoint in such manner as the Congress may direct:

A number of electors of President and Vice President equal to the whole number of Senators and Representatives in Congress to which the District would be entitled if it were a State, but in no event more than the least populous State; they shall be in addition to those appointed by the States, but they shall be considered, for the purposes of the election of President and Vice President, to be electors appointed by a State; and they shall meet in the District and perform such duties as provided by the twelfth article of Amendment.

Section 2
The Congress shall have power to enforce this article by appropriate legislation.

Amendment XXIV [1964]

Section 1
The right of citizens of the United States to vote in any primary or other election for President or Vice President, for electors for President or Vice President, or for Senator or Representative in Congress, shall not be denied or abridged by the United States or any State by reason of failure to pay any poll tax or other tax.

Section 2
The Congress shall have the power to enforce this article by appropriate legislation.

Amendment XXV [1967]

Section 1
In case of the removal of the President from office or his death or resignation, the Vice President shall become President.

Section 2
Whenever there is a vacancy in the office of the Vice President, the President shall nominate a Vice President who shall take the office upon confirmation by a majority vote of both houses of Congress.

Section 3
Whenever the President transmits to the President pro tempore of the Senate and the Speaker of the House of Representatives his written declaration that he is unable to discharge the powers and duties of his office, and until he transmits to them a written declaration to the contrary, such powers and duties shall be discharged by the Vice President as Acting President.

Section 4
Whenever the Vice President and a majority of either the principal officers of the executive departments or of such other body as Congress may by law provide, transmit to the President pro tempore of the Senate and the Speaker of the House of Representatives their written declaration that the President is unable to discharge the powers and duties of his office, the Vice President shall immediately assume the powers and duties of the office as Acting President.

Thereafter, when the President transmits to the President pro tempore of the Senate and the Speaker of the House of Representatives his written declaration that no inability exists, he shall resume the powers and duties of his office unless the Vice President and a majority of either the principal officers of the executive department or of such other body as Congress may by law provide, transmit within four days to the President pro tempore of the Senate and the Speaker of the House of Representatives their written declaration that the President is unable to discharge the powers and duties of his office. Thereupon Congress shall decide the issue, assembling within 48 hours for that purpose if not in session. If the Congress, within 21 days after receipt of the latter written declaration, or, if Congress is not in session, within 21 days after Congress is required to assemble, determines by two-thirds vote of both houses that the President is unable to discharge the powers and duties of his office, the Vice President shall continue to discharge the same as Acting President; otherwise, the President shall resume the powers and duties of his office.

Amendment XXVI [1971]
Section 1
The right of citizens of the United States, who are 18 years of age or older, to vote shall not be denied or abridged by the United States or any state on account of age.

Section 2
The Congress shall have the power to enforce this article by appropriate legislation.

Amendment XXVII [1992]
No law varying the compensation for the service of Senators and Representatives shall take effect until an election of Representatives shall have intervened.

CHOOSING
THE PRESIDENT

Election Year	Elected to Office			
	President	**Party**	**Vice President**	**Party**
1789	George Washington		John Adams	Parties not yet established
1792	George Washington		John Adams	Federalist
1796	John Adams	Federalist	Thomas Jefferson	Democratic-Republican
1800	Thomas Jefferson	Democratic-Republican	Aaron Burr	Democratic-Republican
1804	Thomas Jefferson	Democratic-Republican	George Clinton	Democratic-Republican
1808	James Madison	Democratic-Republican	George Clinton	Democratic-Republican
1812	James Madison	Democratic-Republican	Elbridge Gerry	Democratic-Republican
1816	James Monroe	Democratic-Republican	Daniel D. Tompkins	Democratic-Republican
1820	James Monroe	Democratic-Republican	Daniel D. Tompkins	Democratic-Republican
1824	John Quincy Adams Elected by House of Representatives because no candidate received a majority of electoral votes.	National Republican	John C. Calhoun	Democratic
1828	Andrew Jackson	Democratic	John C. Calhoun	Democratic
1832	Andrew Jackson	Democratic	Martin Van Buren	Democratic
1836	Martin Van Buren	Democratic	Richard M. Johnson First and only vice president elected by Senate (1837), having failed to receive a majority of electoral votes.	Democratic

Major Opponents		Electoral Vote		Popular Vote
For President	**Party**			
		Washington	69	Electors selected by
		Adams	34	state legislatures
George Clinton	Democratic-Republican	Washington	132	Electors selected by
		Adams	77	state legislatures
		Clinton	50	
Thomas Pinckney	Federalist	Adams	71	Electors selected by
Aaron Burr	Democratic-Republican	Jefferson	68	state legislatures
		Pinckney	59	
John Adams	Federalist	Jefferson	73	Electors selected by
Charles Cotesworth Pinckney	Federalist	Adams	65	state legislatures
Charles Cotesworth Pinckney	Federalist	Jefferson	162	Electors selected by
		Pinckney	14	state legislatures
Charles Cotesworth Pinckney	Federalist	Madison	122	Electors selected by
George Clinton	Eastern Republican	Pinckney	47	state legislatures
De Witt Clinton	Democratic-Republican (antiwar faction) and Federalist	Madison	128	Electors selected by state legislatures
		Clinton	89	
Rufus King	Federalist	Monroe	183	Electors selected by
		King	34	state legislatures
		Monroe	231	Electors selected by
		John Quincy Adams	1	state legislatures
Andrew Jackson	Democratic	Adams	84	113,122
Henry Clay	Democratic-Republican	Jackson	99	151,271
		Clay	37	47,531
William H. Crawford	Democratic-Republican	Crawford	41	40,856
John Quincy Adams	National Republican	Jackson	178	642,553
		Adams	83	500,897
Henry Clay	National Republican	Jackson	219	701,780
William Wirt	Anti-Masonic	Clay	49	482,205
		Wirt	7	100,715
		Floyd	11	Delegates chosen by South Carolina legislature
Daniel Webster	Whig	Van Buren	170	764,176
Hugh L. White	Whig	Harrison	73	550,816
William Henry Harrison	Anti-Masonic	White	26	146,107
		Webster	14	41,201
		Mangum	11	Delegates chosen by South Carolina legislature

Election Year	Elected to Office			
	President	**Party**	**Vice President**	**Party**
1840	William Henry Harrison Died in 1841; succeeded by John Tyler.	Whig	John Tyler Assumed presidency in 1841; vice president's office was left vacant.	Whig
1844	James K. Polk	Democratic	George M. Dallas	Democratic
1848	Zachary Taylor Died in 1850; succeeded by Millard Fillmore.	Whig	Millard Fillmore Assumed presidency in 1850; vice president's office was left vacant.	Whig
1852	Franklin Pierce	Democratic	William R. King	Democratic
1856	James Buchanan	Democratic	John C. Breckenridge	Democratic
1860	Abraham Lincoln	Republican	Hannibal Hamlin	Republican
1864	Abraham Lincoln Died in 1865; succeeded by Andrew Johnson.	National Union/ Republican	Andrew Johnson Assumed presidency in 1865; vice president's office was left vacant.	National Union/ Republican
1868	Ulysses S. Grant	Republican	Schuyler Colfax	Republican
1872	Ulysses S. Grant	Republican	Henry Wilson	Republican
1876	Rutherford B. Hayes Contested result settled by special election commission in favor of Hayes.	Republican	William A. Wheeler	Republican
1880	James A. Garfield Died in 1881; succeeded by Chester A. Arthur.	Republican	Chester A. Arthur Assumed presidency in 1881; vice president's office was left vacant.	Republican
1884	Grover Cleveland	Democratic	Thomas A. Hendricks	Democratic
1888	Benjamin Harrison	Republican	Levi P. Morton	Republican
1892	Grover Cleveland	Democratic	Adlai Stevenson	Democratic

Major Opponents		Electoral Vote		Popular Vote
For President	**Party**			
Martin Van Buren	Democratic	Harrison	234	1,274,624
James G. Birney	Liberty	Van Buren	60	1,127,781
Henry Clay	Whig	Polk	170	1,338,464
James G. Birney	Liberty	Clay	105	1,300,097
		Birney	—	62,300
Lewis Cass	Democratic	Taylor	163	1,360,967
Martin Van Buren	Free-Soil	Cass	127	1,222,342
		Van Buren	—	291,263
Winfield Scott	Whig	Pierce	254	1,601,117
John P. Hale	Free-Soil	Scott	42	1,385,453
		Hale	—	155,825
John C. Fremont	Republican	Buchanan	174	1,832,955
Millard Fillmore	American (Know-Nothing)	Fremont	114	1,339,932
		Fillmore	8	871,731
John Bell	Constitutional Union	Lincoln	180	1,865,593
Stephen A. Douglas	Democratic	Breckinridge	72	848,356
John C. Breckinridge	Democratic	Douglas	12	1,382,713
		Bell	39	592,906
George B. McClennan	Democratic	Lincoln	212	2,218,388
		McClennan	21	1,812,807
		Eleven secessionist states did not participate.		
Horatio Seymour	Democratic	Grant	286	3,598,235
		Seymour	80	2,706,829
		Texas, Mississippi, and Virginia did not participate.		
Horace Greeley	Democratic and Liberal Republican	Grant	286	3,598,235
Charles O'Connor	Democratic	Greeley	80	2,834,761
James Black	Temperance	Greeley died before the Electoral College met. His electoral votes were divided among the four minor candidates.		
Samuel J. Tilden	Democratic	Hayes	185	4,034,311
Peter Cooper	Greenback	Tilden	184	4,288,546
Green Clay Smith	Prohibition	Cooper	—	75,973
Winfield S. Hancock	Democratic	Garfield	214	4,446,158
James B. Weaver	Greenback	Hancock	155	4,444,260
Neal Dow	Prohibition	Weaver	—	305,997
James G. Blaine	Republican	Cleveland	219	4,874,621
John P. St. John	Prohibition	Blaine	182	4,848,936
Benjamin F. Butler	Greenback	Butler	—	175,096
		St. John	—	147,482
Grover Cleveland	Democratic	Harrison	233	5,447,129
Clinton B. Fisk	Prohibition	Cleveland	168	5,537,857
Alson J. Streeter	Union Labor			
Benjamin Harrison	Republican	Cleveland	277	5,555,426
James B. Weaver	Populist	Harrison	145	5,182,600
John Bidwell	Prohibition	Weaver	22	1,029,846

	President	Party	Vice President	Party
1896	William McKinley	Republican	Garret A. Hobart	Republican
1900	William McKinley Died in 1901; succeeded by Theodore Roosevelt.	Republican	Theodore Roosevelt Assumed presidency in 1901; vice president's office was left vacant.	Republican
1904	Theodore Roosevelt	Republican	Charles W. Fairbanks	Republican
1908	William Howard Taft	Republican	James S. Sherman	Republican
1912	Woodrow Wilson	Democratic	Thomas R. Marshall	Democratic
1916	Woodrow Wilson	Democratic	Thomas R. Marshall	Democratic
1920	Warren G. Harding Died in 1923; succeeded by Calvin Coolidge.	Republican	Calvin Coolidge Assumed presidency in 1923; vice president's office was left vacant.	Republican
1924	Calvin Coolidge	Republican	Charles G. Dawes	Republican
1928	Herbert C. Hoover	Republican	Charles Curtis	Republican
1932	Franklin D. Roosevelt	Democratic	John N. Garner	Democratic
1936	Franklin D. Roosevelt	Democratic	John N. Garner	Democratic
1940	Franklin D. Roosevelt	Democratic	Henry A. Wallace	Democratic
1944	Franklin D. Roosevelt Died in 1945; succeeded by Harry S. Truman.	Democratic	Harry S. Truman Assumed presidency in 1945; vice president's office was left vacant.	Democratic
1948	Harry S. Truman	Democratic	Alben W. Barkley	Democratic
1952	Dwight D. Eisenhower	Republican	Richard M. Nixon	Republican
1956	Dwight D. Eisenhower	Republican	Richard M. Nixon	Republican

For President	Party			
William Jennings Bryan	Democratic, Populist, and National Silver Republican	McKinley	271	7,102,246
		Bryan	176	6,492,559
Joshua Levering	Prohibition			
John M. Palmer	National Democratic			
William Jennings Bryan	Democratic and Fusion Populist	McKinley	292	7,218,039
		Bryan	155	6,358,345
Wharton Barker	Anti-Fusion Populist	Woolley	—	209,004
Eugene V. Debs	Social Democratic	Debs	—	86,935
John G. Woolley	Prohibition			
Alton B. Parker	Democratic	Roosevelt	336	7,626,593
Eugene V. Debs	Socialist	Parker	140	5,082,898
Silas C. Swallow	Prohibition	Debs	—	402,489
		Swallow	—	258,596
William Jennings Bryan	Democratic	Taft	321	7,676,258
Eugene V. Debs	Socialist	Bryan	162	6,406,801
Eugene W. Chafin	Prohibition	Debs	—	420,380
		Chafin	—	252,821
William Howard Taft	Republican	Wilson	435	6,296,547
Theodore Roosevelt	Progressive (Bull Moose)	Roosevelt	88	4,118,571
Eugene V. Debs	Socialist	Taft	8	3,486,720
Eugene W. Chafin	Prohibition			
Charles E. Hughes	Republican	Wilson	277	9,127,695
Allen L. Benson	Socialist	Hughes	254	8,533,507
J. Frank Hanly	Prohibition			
Charles W. Fairbanks	Republican			
James M. Cox	Democratic	Harding	404	16,133,314
Eugene V. Debs	Socialist	Cox	127	9,140,884
		Debs	—	913,664
John W. Davis	Democratic	Coolidge	382	15,717,553
Robert M. LaFollette	Progressive	Davis	136	8,386,169
		LaFollette	13	4,184,050
Alfred E. Smith	Democratic	Hoover	444	21,391,993
Norman Thomas	Socialist	Smith	87	15,016,169
Herbert C. Hoover	Republican	Roosevelt	472	22,809,638
Norman Thomas	Socialist	Hoover	59	15,758,901
Alfred M. Landon	Republican	Roosevelt	523	27,752,869
William Lemke	Union	Landon	8	16,674,665
Wendell L. Wilkie	Republican	Roosevelt	449	27,263,448
		Wilkie	82	22,336,260
Thomas E. Dewey	Republican	Roosevelt	432	25,611,936
		Dewey	99	22,013,372
Thomas E. Dewey	Republican	Truman	303	24,105,182
J. Strom Thurmond	States' Rights Democratic	Dewey	189	21,970,065
		Thurmond	39	1,169,063
Henry A. Wallace	Progressive	Wallace	—	1,157,326
Adlai E. Stevenson	Democratic	Eisenhower	442	33,936,137
		Stevenson	89	27,314,649
Adlai E. Stevenson	Democratic	Eisenhower	457	35,585,245
		Stevenson	73	26,030,172

	President	Party	Vice President	Party
1960	John F. Kennedy Died in 1963; succeeded by Lyndon B. Johnson	Democratic	Lyndon B. Johnson Assumed presidency in 1963; vice president's office was left vacant.	Democratic
1964	Lyndon B. Johnson	Democratic	Hubert H. Humphrey	Democratic
1968	Richard M. Nixon	Republican	Spiro T. Agnew	Republican
1972	Richard M. Nixon Resigned in 1974; succeeded by Gerald R. Ford.	Republican	Spiro T. Agnew Resigned in 1974; replaced by Gerald R. Ford, who was in turn replaced by Nelson Rockefeller.	Republican
1976	James E. Carter	Democratic	Walter Mondale	Democratic
1980	Ronald Reagan	Republican	George Bush	Republican
1984	Ronald Reagan	Republican	George Bush	Republican
1988	George H. Bush	Republican	J. Danforth Quayle	Republican
1992	William J. Clinton	Democratic	Albert Gore, Jr.	Democratic
1996	William J. Clinton	Democratic	Albert Gore, Jr.	Democratic
2000	George W. Bush	Republican	Richard Cheney	Republican
2004	George W. Bush	Republican	Richard Cheney	Republican
2008	Barack Obama	Democratic	Joseph Biden	Democratic

Major Opponents		Electoral Vote		Popular Vote
For President	**Party**			
Richard M. Nixon	Republican	Kennedy	303	34,227,096
		Nixon	219	34,108,546
		Byrd (Ind. Dem.)*	15	—
Barry M. Goldwater	Republican	Johnson	486	43,126,584
		Goldwater	52	27,177,838
Hubert H. Humphrey	Democratic	Nixon	301	31,770,237
George C. Wallace	American	Humphrey	191	31,270,533
	Independent	Wallace	46	9,906,141
George S. McGovern	Democratic	Nixon	520	46,740,323
		McGovern	17	28,901,598
		Hospers (Va.)	1	—
Gerald R. Ford	Republican	Carter	297	40,830,763
Eugene McCarthy	Independent	Ford	240	39,147,793
		McCarthy	—	756,631
James E. Carter	Democratic	Reagan	489	43,899,248
John B. Anderson	Independent	Carter	49	35,481,435
Ed Clark	Libertarian	Anderson	—	5,719,437
Walter Mondale	Democratic	Reagan	525	54,451,521
David Bergland	Libertarian	Mondale	13	37,565,334
Michael Dukakis	Democratic	Bush	426	47,946,422
		Dukakis	112	41,016,429
George H.W. Bush	Republican	Clinton	370	44,908,233
H. Ross Perot	Independent	Bush	168	39,102,282
		Perot	—	19,217,213
Robert Dole	Republican	Clinton	379	45,590,703
H. Ross Perot	Independent	Dole	159	37,816,307
		Perot	—	7,866,284
Albert Gore, Jr.	Democratic	Bush	271	50,456,141
Ralph Nader	Green	Gore	266	50,996,039
Patrick Buchanan	Reform	Nader	—	2,882,807
		Buchanan	—	448,868
John Kerry	Democratic	Bush	286	62,028,194
Ralph Nader	Green	Kerry	252	59,027,612
Michael Badnarik	Libertarian	Nader	—	460,650
		Badnarik	—	396,888
John McCain	Republican	Obama	365	69,456,897
Ralph Nader	Green	McCain	173	59,934,814
		Nader		

*Byrd received 15 electoral votes although he was not a candidate for the presidency.

GLOSSARY

527 committees organizations created by individuals and groups to influence the outcomes of elections by raising and spending money that candidates and political parties cannot legally raise.

Ability-to-pay theory of taxation the approach to government finance that holds that taxes should be based on an individual's ability to pay.

Access the opportunity to communicate directly with legislators and other government officials in hopes of influencing the details of policy.

Advocacy groups organizations created to seek benefits on behalf of groups of persons who are in some way incapacitated or otherwise unable to represent their own interests.

Affirm the action of an appeals court to uphold the decision of a lower court.

Affirmative action steps taken by colleges, universities, and private employers to remedy the effects of past discrimination.

Agents of socialization those factors that contribute to political socialization by shaping formal and informal learning.

Air war campaign activities that involve the media, including television, radio, and the Internet.

Amicus curiae (friend of the court) briefs written legal arguments presented by parties not directly involved in the case, including interest groups and units of government.

Anti-clericalism a movement that opposes the institutional power of religion, and the involvement of the church in all aspects of public and political life.

Antifederalists Americans opposed to the ratification of the new Constitution because they thought it gave too much power to the national government.

Appeal the taking of a case from a lower court to a higher court by the losing party in a lower-court decision.

Apportionment the allocation of legislative seats among the states.

Appropriation bill a legislative authorization to spend money for particular purposes.

Appropriations process the procedure through which Congress legislatively allocates money for a particular purpose.

At-large election a method for choosing public officials in which the citizens of an entire political subdivision, such as a state, vote to select officeholders.

Attack journalism an approach to news reporting in which journalists take an adversarial attitude toward candidates and elected officials.

Authorization process the procedure through which Congress legislatively establishes and defines a program, but does not actually provide funding for it.

Baby-boom generation the exceptionally large number of Americans born during the late 1940s, 1950s, and early 1960s.

Balance the ticket an attempt to select a vice-presidential candidate who will appeal to different groups of voters than the presidential nominee.

Balanced budget budget receipts equal budget expenditures.

Base voters rock-solid Republicans or hardcore Democrats, firmly committed to voting for their party's nominee.

Battleground states swing states in which the relative strength of the two major-party presidential candidates is close enough so that either candidate could conceivably carry the state.

Biased sample a sample that tends to produce results that do not reflect the true characteristics of the universe because it is unrepresentative of the universe.

Bicameral legislature a two-house legislature.

Bill a proposed law.

Bill of attainder a law declaring a person or a group of persons guilty of a crime and providing for punishment without benefit of a judicial proceeding.

Bill of Rights the first ten amendments to the U.S. Constitution.

Bipartisan Campaign Reform Act (BCRA) a campaign finance reform law designed to limit the political influence of "big money" campaign contributors.

Block grant program a federal grant program that provides money for a program in a broad, general policy area.

Blue states Democratic states

Broadcast media television and radio.

Budget deficit the amount by which annual budget expenditures exceed annual budget receipts.

Budget surplus the sum by which annual budget receipts exceed annual budget expenditures.

Bundling a process in which an interest group gathers checks from individual supporters and sends them to candidates in a bundle, allowing an interest group to route more money than the group alone could contribute.

Cabinet departments major administrative units of the federal government that have responsibility for the conduct of a wide range of government operations.

Cap and trade an approach to pollution control in which the government sets a limit on the amount of emissions allowed (the cap) and then permits companies to buy and sell emissions allowances (the trade).

Capital punishment the death penalty.

Capitalism an economic system characterized by individual and corporate ownership of the means of production and a market economy based on the supply and demand of goods and services.

Captured agencies agencies that work to benefit the economic interests they regulate rather than serving the public interest.

Card check method of union authorization that allows union organizers to collect employee signatures on authorization forms instead of holding a secret ballot election.

Categorical grant program a federal grant program that provides funds to state and local governments for a fairly narrow, specific purpose.

Caucus method of delegate selection a procedure for choosing national party convention delegates that involves party voters participating in a series of precinct and district or county political meetings.

Cause groups organizations whose members care intensely about a single issue or small group of related issues.

Certiorari (cert) the technical term for the Supreme Court's decision to hear arguments and make a ruling in a case.

Checks and balances the overlapping of the powers of the branches of government designed to ensure that public officials limit the authority of each other.

Chief executive the head of the executive branch of government.

Chief of state the official head of government.

Citizen groups organizations created to support government policies that they believe will benefit the public at large.

Civil case a legal dispute concerning a private conflict between two parties—individuals, corporations, or government agencies.

Civil liberties the protection of the individual from the unrestricted power of government.

Civil rights the protection of the individual from arbitrary or discriminatory acts by government or by individuals based on that person's group status, such as race and gender.

Civil service system a hiring system based on merit rather than political connections.

Civil union a legal partnership between two men or two women that gives the couple all the benefits, protections, and responsibilities under law as are granted to spouses in a traditional marriage.

Civilian supremacy of the armed forces the concept that the armed forces should be under the direct control of civilian authorities.

Class action lawsuit a class action lawsuit is a lawsuit brought by one or more people on behalf of themselves and others who are in a similar situation.

Closed primary an election system that limits primary election participation to registered party members.

Cloture the procedure for ending a filibuster.

Coattail effect a political phenomenon in which a strong candidate for one office gives a boost to fellow party members on the same ballot seeking other offices.

Cold War the period of international tension between the United States and the Soviet Union lasting from the late 1940s through the late 1980s.

Collective bargaining a negotiation between an employer and a union representing employees over the terms and conditions of employment.

Commerce Clause the constitutional provision giving Congress authority to "regulate commerce . . . among the several states."

Compulsory voting the legal requirement that citizens participate in national elections.

Concurrent powers powers of government that are jointly exercised by the national government and state governments.

Concurring opinion a judicial statement that agrees with the Court's ruling but disagrees with the reasoning of the majority opinion.

Confederation a league of nearly independent states.

Conferees members of a conference committee.

Conference a closed meeting attended only by the members of the Court.

Conference committee a special congressional committee created to negotiate differences on similar pieces of legislation passed by the House and Senate.

Conservatism the political philosophy that government power undermines the development of the individual and diminishes society as a whole.

Constituency the district from which an officeholder is elected.

Constituency service the action of members of Congress attending to the individual, particular needs of constituents.

Constitution the fundamental law by which a state or nation is organized and governed, and to which ordinary legislation must conform.

Constitutional amendment a formal, written change or addition to the nation's governing document.

Constitutional law law that involves the interpretation and application of the Constitution.

Containment U.S. policy which sought to keep the Soviet Union from expanding its sphere of control and preserve the balance of power in Europe and Asia.

Conventional forces non-nuclear forces.

Cost–benefit analysis an evaluation of a proposed policy or regulation based on a comparison of its expected benefits and anticipated costs.

Cost-of-living adjustment (COLA) a mechanism designed to regularly increase the size of a payment to compensate for the effects of inflation.

Criminal case a legal dispute dealing with an alleged violation of a penal law.

De facto segregation racial separation resulting from factors other than law, such as housing patterns.

De jure segregation racial separation required by law.

Defense policy public policy that concerns the armed forces of the United States.

Delegated or enumerated powers the powers explicitly granted to the national government by the Constitution.

Democracy a system of government in which ultimate political authority is vested in the people.

Depression a severe and prolonged economic slump characterized by decreased business activity and high unemployment.

Détente an era of improved relations between the Soviet Union and the United States.

Deterrence the ability of a nation to prevent an attack against itself or its allies by threat of massive retaliation.

Developing countries nations with relatively low levels of per capita income.

Diplomatic relations a system of official contacts between two nations in which the countries exchange ambassadors and other diplomatic personnel and operate embassies in each other's country.

Direct democracy a political system in which the citizens vote directly on matters of public concern.

Discharge petition a procedure whereby a majority of the members of the House of Representatives can force a committee to report a bill to the floor of the House.

Discretionary spending budgetary expenditures that are not mandated by law or contract, including annual funding for education, the Coast Guard, space exploration, highway construction, defense, foreign aid, and the Federal Bureau of Investigation (FBI).

Disfranchisement the denial of voting rights.

Dissenting opinion a judicial statement that disagrees with the decision of the Court's majority.

District election a method for choosing public officials that divides a political subdivision, such as a state, into geographic areas called districts; each district elects one official.

Divided government the phenomenon of one political party controlling the legislative branch of government while the other holds the executive branch.

Double jeopardy the government trying a criminal defendant a second time for the same offense after an acquittal in an earlier prosecution.

Due process of law the constitutional principle holding that government must follow fair and regular procedures in actions that could lead to an individual's suffering loss of life, liberty, or property.

Earmarks provisions that direct that funds be spent for particular purposes.

Electioneering participating in the electoral process through endorsements or financial support of candidates.

Electoral College the system established in the Constitution for indirect election of the president and vice president.

Electors individuals selected in each state to officially cast that state's electoral votes.

Entitlement program a government program providing benefits to all persons qualified to receive them under law.

Environmental Protection Agency (EPA) the federal agency responsible for enforcing the nation's environmental laws.

Equal Protection Clause a provision of the Fourteenth Amendment of the U.S. Constitution that declares that "No State shall ... deny to any person within its jurisdiction the equal protection of the laws."

Estate tax tax levied on the value of an inheritance.

Ex post facto law a retroactive criminal statute that operates to the disadvantage of accused persons.

Excise taxes taxes levied on the manufacture, transportation, sale, or consumption of a particular item or set of related items.

Exclusionary rule the judicial doctrine stating that when the police violate an individual's constitutional rights, the evidence obtained as a result of police misconduct or error cannot be used against the defendant.

Executive agreement an international understanding between the president and foreign nations that does not require Senate ratification.

Executive Office of the President the group of White House offices and agencies that develop and implement the policies and programs of the president.

Executive order a directive issued by the president to an administrative agency or executive department.

Executive power the power to enforce laws.

Exit polls surveys based on random samples of voters leaving the polling place.

External political efficacy the assessment of an individual of the responsiveness of government to his or her concerns.

Extradition the return from one state to another of a person accused of a crime.

Factions special interests who seek their own good at the expense of the common good.

Failed states nation-states in which the government no longer effectively functions, threatening regional security and economies.

Fairness Doctrine an FCC regulation repealed in 1987 that required broadcasters to present controversial issues of public importance in "an honest, equal, and balanced manner."

Federal Communications Commission (FCC) government agency that regulates the broadcast media using the public airwaves.

Federal grant program a program through which the national government gives money to state and local governments to spend in accordance with set standards and conditions.

Federal mandate a legal requirement placed on a state or local government by the national government requiring certain policy actions.

Federal preemption of state authority an act of Congress adopting regulatory policies that overrule state policies in a particular regulatory area.

Federal Reserve System (the Fed) the central banking system of the United States with authority to establish banking policies and influence the amount of credit available in the economy.

Federal system a political system that divides power between a central government, with authority over the whole nation, and a series of state governments.

Federalist Papers a series of essays written by James Madison, Alexander Hamilton, and John Jay advocating the ratification of the Constitution.

Federalists Americans who supported the ratification of the Constitution.

Federation/federal system a political system that divides power between a central government, with authority over the whole nation, and a series of state governments.

Filibuster an attempt to defeat a measure through prolonged debate.

Fire-alarm oversight an indirect system of congressional surveillance of bureaucratic administration that enables individual citizens and organized interest groups to examine administrative decisions, charge agencies with violating legislative goals, and seek remedies from agencies, courts, and Congress itself.

Fiscal policy the use of government spending and taxation for the purpose of achieving economic goals.

Flat tax an income tax that assesses the same percentage tax rate on all income levels.

Floor the full House or full Senate taking official action.

Foreign policy public policy that concerns the relationship of the United States to the international political environment.

Formula grant program a grant program that awards funding on the basis of a formula established by Congress.

Framing the process by which a communication source, such as a news organization, defines and constructs a political issue or public controversy.

Franking privilege free postage provided members of Congress.

Free-rider barrier the concept that individuals will have little incentive to join and contribute to a group if benefits go to members and nonmembers alike.

Friendly Incumbent Rule a policy whereby an interest group will back any incumbent who is generally supportive of the group's policy preferences, without regard for the party or policy views of the challenger

Frostbelt the northeastern and midwestern regions of the United States.

Full Faith and Credit Clause the constitutional provision requiring that states recognize the official acts of other states, such as marriages, divorces, adoptions, court orders, and other legal decisions.

Fundamental right a constitutional right that is so important that government cannot restrict it unless it can demonstrate a compelling or overriding public interest for so doing.

Gender gap differences in party identification and political attitudes between men and women.

General election an election to fill state and national offices held in November of even-numbered years.

Gerrymandering the drawing of legislative district lines for political advantage.

Global economy the integration of national economies into a world economic system in which companies compete worldwide for suppliers and markets.

Global warming the gradual warming of the Earth's atmosphere, reportedly caused by the burning of fossil fuels and industrial pollutants.

Governing party the political party or party coalition holding the reins of government in a democracy.

Government corporations corporations organizationally similar to private corporations, except that the government rather than stockholders owns them.

Grandfather clause a provision that exempted those persons whose grandfathers had been eligible to vote at some earlier date from tests of understanding, literacy tests, and other difficult-to-achieve voter qualification requirements.

Gross domestic product (GDP) the total value of goods and services produced by a nation's economy in a year, excluding transactions with foreign countries.

Ground war campaign activities featuring direct contact between campaign workers and citizens, such as door-to-door canvassing and personal telephone contacts.

Hard money funds that are raised subject to federal campaign contribution and expenditure limitations.

Hatch Act a measure designed to restrict the political activities of federal employees to voting and the private expression of views.

Hate-crimes law a legislative measure that increases penalties for persons convicted of criminal offenses motivated by prejudice based on race, religion, national origin, gender, or sexual orientation.

Honeymoon effect the tendency of a president to enjoy a high level of public support during the early months of an administration.

House majority leader the second-ranking figure in the majority party in the House.

House Rules Committee a standing committee that determines the rules under which a specific bill can be debated, amended, and considered on the House floor.

Impeach the act of formally accusing an official of the executive or judicial branches of an impeachable offense.

Impeachment a process in which an executive or judicial official is formally accused of an offense that could warrant removal from office.

Implied powers those powers of Congress not explicitly mentioned in the Constitution, but derived by implication from the delegated powers.

In forma pauperis the process whereby an indigent litigant can file an appeal of a case to the Supreme Court without paying the usual fees.

Income redistribution government taking items of value, especially money, from some groups of people and then giving items of value, either in cash or services, to other groups of people.

Independent executive agencies executive branch agencies that are not part of any of the 15 cabinet-level departments.

Independent expenditures   money spent in support of a candidate but not coordinated with the candidate's campaign.

Independent regulatory commission   an agency outside the major executive departments that is charged with the regulation of important aspects of the economy.

Inflation   a decline in the purchasing power of the currency.

Inherent powers   powers vested in the national government, particularly in the area of foreign and defense policy, which do not depend on any specific grant of authority by the Constitution, but rather exist because the United States is a sovereign nation.

Inner cabinet   the secretary of state, secretary of defense, secretary of the treasury, and the attorney general.

Interest   money paid for the use of money.

Interest group   an organization of people who join together voluntarily on the basis of some interest they share for the purpose of influencing policy.

Internal political efficacy   the assessment by an individual of his or her personal ability to influence the policymaking process.

Internationalist   an approach to foreign policy that supports working in close concert with the global community.

Isolationism   the view that the United States should minimize its interactions with other nations.

Issue network   a group of political actors that is actively involved with policymaking in a particular issue area.

Issue ownership   the concept that the public considers one political party more competent at addressing a particular issue than the other political party.

Jim Crow laws   legal provisions requiring the social segregation of African Americans in separate and generally unequal facilities.

Joint committee   a committee that includes members from both houses of Congress.

Judicial activism   the charge that judges are going beyond their authority by making the law and not just interpreting it.

Judicial power   the power to interpret laws.

Judicial restraint   the concept that judges should defer to the policymaking judgment of the legislative and executive branches of government unless their actions clearly violate the law or the Constitution.

Judicial review   the power of courts to declare unconstitutional the actions of the other branches and units of government.

Jungle primary   a primary election system in which all the candidates for an office run in the same primary regardless of political party affiliation

Jurisdiction   the authority of a court to hear a case.

Killer amendment   an amendment designed to make a measure so unattractive that it will lack enough support to pass.

Lame duck   an official whose influence is diminished because the official either cannot or will not seek reelection.

Latent opinion   what public opinion would be at election time if a political opponent made a public official's position on the issue the target of a campaign attack.

Legal brief   a written legal argument.

Legislative markup   the process in which legislators go over a measure line-by-line, revising, amending, or rewriting it.

Legislative power   the power to make laws.

Libel   false written statements

Liberalism   the political philosophy that favors the use of government power to foster the development of the individual and promote the welfare of society.

Limited government   the constitutional principle that government does not have unrestricted authority over individuals.

Lobbying   the communication of information by a representative of an interest group to a government official for the purpose of influencing a policy decision.

Logrolling   an arrangement in which two or more members of Congress agree in advance to support each other's favored legislation.

Loose construction   a doctrine of constitutional interpretation holding that the document should be interpreted broadly.

Majority opinion   the official written statement of the Supreme Court that explains and justifies its ruling and serves as a guideline for lower courts when similar legal issues arise in the future.

Majority-minority district   legislative districts whose population is more than 50 percent African American and Latino.

Mandatory spending   budgetary expenditures that are mandated by law, including entitlements and contractual commitments made in previous years.

Margin of error (or sample error)   a statistical term that refers to the accuracy of a survey.

Massive retaliation   the concept that the United States will strike back against an aggressor with overwhelming force.

Matching funds requirement   the legislative provision that the national government will provide grant money for a particular activity only on the condition that the state or local government involved supplies a certain percentage of the total money required for the project or program.

Means-tested program   a government program that provides benefits to recipients based on their financial need.

Medicaid   a federal program designed to provide health insurance coverage to low-income persons, people with disabilities, and elderly people who are impoverished.

Medicare   a federally funded health insurance program for the elderly.

Midcycle redistricting   redrawing legislative districts outside the regular redistricting cycle in order to gain political advantage.

Military preemption   the defense policy that declares

that the United States will attack hostile nations or groups that represent a potential threat to the security of the United States.

Minimum wage   the lowest hourly wage that an employer can legally pay covered workers.

Minority business set-aside   a legal requirement that firms receiving government grants or contracts allocate a certain percentage of their purchases of supplies and services to businesses owned or controlled by members of minority groups.

Minority leaders   the heads of the minority party in the House or Senate.

Miranda warning   Before questioning, accused persons must be warned that 1) they have a right to remain silent; 2) that any statements they give may be used against them; and 3) that they are entitled to the presence of an attorney, either retained or appointed.

Mixed economy   an economic system that combines private ownership with extensive intervention.

Monetary policy   the control of the money supply for the purpose of achieving economic goals.

Monroe Doctrine   a declaration of American foreign policy opposing any European intervention in the Western Hemisphere and affirming the American intention to refrain from interfering in European affairs.

Multiparty system   the division of voter loyalties among three or more major political parties.

Multiple referral of legislation   the practice of allowing more than one committee to consider legislation.

Mutual assured destruction (MAD)   the belief that the United States and the Soviet Union would be deterred from launching a nuclear assault against each other for fear of being destroyed in a general nuclear war.

National debt   the accumulated indebtedness of the federal government.

National Security Council (NSC)   an agency in the Executive Office of the President that advises the chief executive on matters involving national security.

National Supremacy Clause   the constitutional provision that declares that the Constitution and laws of the United States take precedence over the constitutions and laws of the states.

National Voter Registration Act (NVRA)   a federal law designed to make it easier for citizens to register to vote; also known as the Motor Voter Act.

Nation-state   a political community occupying a definite territory and having an organized government.

Natural rights   the belief that individual rights transcend the power of government.

Necessary and Proper Clause/Elastic Clause   the Constitutional provision found in Article I, Section 8 that declares that "[Congress shall have the power] to make all laws which shall be necessary and proper for carrying into execution the foregoing powers, and all other powers vested by this Constitution in the government of the United States, or in any department or office thereof."

New Deal   a legislative package of reform measures proposed by President Franklin Roosevelt for dealing with the Great Depression.

New media   alternative media sources, such as the Internet, cable television, and satellite radio.

Nongovernmental organizations (NGOs)   international organizations committed to the promotion of a particular set of issues.

North American Free Trade Agreement (NAFTA)   an international accord among the United States, Mexico, and Canada to lower trade barriers among the three nations.

North Atlantic Treaty Organization (NATO)   a regional military alliance consisting of the United States, Canada, and most of the European democracies.

Nuclear Non-Proliferation Treaty   an international agreement designed to prevent the spread of nuclear weapons.

Objective journalism   a style of news reporting that focuses on facts rather than opinion, and presents all sides of controversial issues.

Office of Management and Budget (OMB)   an agency that assists the president in preparing the budget.

Omnibus bills   complex, highly detailed legislative proposals covering one or more subjects or programs.

One person, one vote   the judicial ruling that the Equal Protection Clause of the Fourteenth Amendment to the U.S. Constitution requires that legislative districts be apportioned on the basis of population.

Open primary   an election system that allows voters to pick the party primary of their choice without regard to their party affiliation.

Opposition party   the political party out of power in a democracy.

Original jurisdiction   the set of cases a court may hear as a trial court.

Pardon   an executive action that frees an accused or convicted person from all penalties for an offense.

Parental choice   an educational reform aimed at improving the quality of schools by allowing parents to select the school their children will attend.

Party caucus   all of the party members of the House or Senate meeting as a group.

Party era   a period of time characterized by a degree of uniformity in the nature of political party competition

Party platform   a statement of party principles and issue positions.

Party realignment   a change in the underlying party loyalties of voters that ends one party era and begins another.

PAYGO   a pay-as-you-go budget rule that requires that any tax cut or spending increase be offset by tax increases or spending cuts elsewhere in the budget.

Per capita   per person.

Per curiam opinion   an unsigned written opinion of a court.

Plurality election system   a method for choosing public officials that awards office to the candidate with the most votes; it favors a two-party system.

Pocket veto   the action of a president allowing a measure to die without signature after Congress has adjourned.

Political action committee (PAC)   an organization created to raise and distribute money in election campaigns.

Political culture   the widely held, deeply rooted political values of a society.

Political efficacy   the extent to which individuals believe that they can influence the policymaking process.

Political elites   the people who exercise a major influence on the policymaking process.

Political left or left wing   liberal.

Political legitimacy   the popular acceptance of a government and its officials as rightful authorities in the exercise of power.

Political movement   a group of people that wants to convince other citizens and/or government officials to take action on issues that are important to the group.

Political participation   an activity that has the intent or effect of influencing government action.

Political party   a group of individuals who join together to seek government office in order to make public policy.

Political right or right wing   conservative.

Political socialization   the process whereby individuals acquire political knowledge, attitudes, and beliefs.

Pork barrel spending   expenditures to fund local projects that are not critically important from a national perspective.

Postindustrial societies   nations whose economies are increasingly based on services, research, and information rather than heavy industry.

Poverty threshold   the amount of money an individual or family needs to purchase basic necessities, such as food, clothing, healthcare, shelter, and transportation.

Power of the purse   the authority to raise and spend money.

President's cabinet   an advisory group created by the president that includes the department heads and other officials chosen by the president.

Presidential preference primary   an election in which party voters cast ballots for the presidential candidate they favor and in so doing help determine the number of national convention delegates that candidate will receive.

Presidential signing statement   a pronouncement issued by the president at the time a bill passed by Congress is signed into law.

Primary election   an election held to determine a party's nominees for the general election ballot.

Print media   newspapers and magazines.

Prior restraint   government action to prevent the publication or broadcast of objectionable material

Private sector   the privately owned segment of the economy.

Privatization   a process that involves the government contracting with private business to implement government programs.

Privileges and Immunities Clause   the constitutional provision prohibiting state governments from discriminating against the citizens of other states.

Probable cause   the reasonable suspicion based on evidence that a particular search will uncover contraband.

Progressive tax   a levy that taxes people earning higher incomes at a higher rate than it does individuals making less money.

Project grant program   a grant program that requires state and local governments to compete for available federal money.

Proportional representation (PR)   an election system that awards legislative seats to each party approximately equal to its popular voting strength.

Proportional tax   a levy that taxes all persons at the same percentage rate, regardless of income.

Prospective voting   the concept that voters evaluate the incumbent officeholder and the incumbent's party based on their expectations of future developments.

Public opinion   combined personal opinions of adults toward issues of relevance to government.

Public sector   the government-owned segment of the economy.

Quasi-governmental company   a private, profit-seeking corporation created by Congress to serve a public purpose.

Racially restrictive covenants   private deed restrictions that prohibited property owners from selling or leasing property to African Americans or other minorities.

Rally effect   the tendency of the general public to express support for the incumbent president during a time of international threat.

Random sample   a sample in which each member of the universe has an equal likelihood of being included.

Reapportionment   the reallocation of legislative seats.

Recession   an economic slowdown characterized by declining economic output and rising unemployment.

Red states   Republican states

Redistricting   the process through which the boundaries of legislative districts are redrawn to reflect population movement.

Regressive tax   a levy whose burden falls more heavily on lower-income groups than on wealthy taxpayers.

Regulatory negotiation   a process by which representatives of the interests that would be impacted by a rule work with government officials to negotiate the terms of the rule.

Religious left   those who hold liberal views because of their religious beliefs.

Religious right   those who hold conservative views because of their religious beliefs.

Remand   the decision of an appeals court to return a case to a lower court for reconsideration in light of an appeals court decision.

Representative democracy/republic a political system in which citizens elect representatives to make policy decisions on their behalf.

Reprieve an executive action that delays punishment for a crime.

Republican in name only (RINO) an accusation that a Republican candidate or elected official is insufficiently conservative to merit the support of party activists

Reserved/residual powers the powers of government left to the states.

Resolution a legislative statement of opinion on a certain matter.

Retrospective voting the concept that voters choose candidates based on their perception of an incumbent candidate's past performance in office or the performance of the incumbent party.

Rider a provision, unlikely to become law on its own merits, that is attached to an important measure so that it will ride through the legislative process.

Right-to-work laws statutes that prohibit union membership as a condition of employment.

Rogue state a nation that threatens world peace by sponsoring international terrorism and promoting the spread of weapons of mass destruction.

Rule a legally binding regulation.

Rule of Four a decision process used by the Supreme Court to determine which cases to consider on appeal, holding that the Court will hear a case if four of the nine justices agree to the review.

Rule of law the constitutional principle that holds that the discretion of public officials in dealing with individuals is limited by the law.

Rulemaking the regulatory process used by government agencies to enact legally binding regulations.

Runoff an election between the two candidates receiving the most votes when no candidate got a majority in an initial election.

Sales tax a levy assessed on the retail sale of taxable items.

Sample a subset of a universe.

Selective incorporation the process through which the U.S. Supreme Court interpreted the Due Process Clause of the Fourteenth Amendment of the U.S. Constitution to apply most of the provisions of the national Bill of Rights to the states.

Senate majority leader the head of the majority party in the Senate.

Senatorial courtesy the custom that senators from the president's party have a veto on judicial appointments from their states.

Seniority length of service.

Separate but equal the judicial doctrine holding that separate facilities for whites and African Americans satisfy the equal protection requirement of the Fourteenth Amendment.

Separation of powers the division of political power among executive, legislative, and judicial branches.

Shield law a statute that protects journalists from being forced to disclose confidential information in a legal proceeding.

Signaling role a term that refers to the accepted responsibility of the media to alert the public to important developments as they happen.

Slander false spoken statements

Social Security a federal pension and disability insurance program funded through a payroll tax on workers and their employers.

Socialism an economic system characterized by governmental ownership of the means of production and control of the distribution of goods and services.

Soft money the name given to funds that are raised by political parties that are not subject to federal campaign finance regulations.

Sound bite a short phrase taken from a candidate's speech by the news media for use on newscasts.

Sovereignty the authority of a state to exercise its legitimate powers within its boundaries, free from external interference.

Speaker of the House the presiding officer in the House of Representatives and the leader of the majority party in that chamber.

Special or select committee a committee established for a limited time only.

Split ticket ballot voters casting their ballots for the candidates of two or more political parties.

Spoils system the method of hiring government employees from among the friends, relatives, and supporters of elected officeholders.

Sponsor a member who introduces a measure.

Standard of living the goods and services affordable to and available to the residents of a nation.

Standing committee a permanent legislative committee with authority to draft legislation in a particular policy area or areas.

States' rights an interpretation of the Constitution that favors limiting the authority of the federal government while expanding the powers of the states.

Statutory law law that is written by the legislature.

Straight ticket ballot voters selecting the entire slate of candidates of one party only.

Strategic forces nuclear forces.

Strict construction a doctrine of constitutional interpretation holding that the document should be interpreted narrowly.

Strict judicial scrutiny the judicial decision rule holding that the Supreme Court will find a government policy unconstitutional unless the government can demonstrate a compelling interest justifying the action.

Structured rules rules that specify the conditions for debate and amendments.

Subgovernment, or iron triangle a cozy, three-sided relationship among government agencies, interest groups, and key members of Congress in which all parties benefit.

Subsidy   a financial incentive given by government to an individual or a business interest to accomplish a public objective.

Suffrage   the right to vote.

Sunbelt   the southern and western regions of the United States.

Superdelegates   Democratic Party officials and officeholders selected to attend the national party convention on the basis of the offices they hold.

Supermajority   a voting margin that is greater than a simple majority.

Superpower   a country powerful enough to influence events throughout the world.

Survey research   the measurement of public opinion.

Suspect classifications   distinctions among persons that must be justified on the basis of a compelling government interest that cannot be achieved in a less restrictive fashion.

Swing voters   citizens who could vote for either party in an election.

Table   to postpone consideration of a measure during the legislative process.

Tax credit   an expenditure that reduces an individual's tax liability by the amount of the credit.

Tax deduction   an expenditure that can be subtracted from a taxpayer's gross income before figuring the tax owed.

Tax exemption   the exclusion of some types of income from taxation.

Tax preference   a tax deduction or exclusion that allows individuals to pay less tax than they would otherwise.

Tea Party movement   a loose network of conservative activists organized to protest high taxes, excessive government spending, and big government in general.

Term limitation   the movement to restrict the number of terms public officials may serve.

Test case   a lawsuit initiated to assess the constitutionality of a legislative or executive act.

Test of understanding   a legal requirement that citizens must accurately explain a passage in the U.S. Constitution or state constitution before they could register to vote.

Third party   a minor party in a two-party system.

Trade associations   organizations representing the interests of firms and professionals in the same general field.

Trial   the formal examination of a judicial dispute in accordance with law before a single judge.

Two-party system   the division of voter loyalties between two major political parties.

Tyranny of the majority   the abuse of the minority by the majority.

Unfunded mandate   requirement imposed by Congress on state or local governments without providing federal funding to cover its cost.

Unicameral legislature   a one-house legislature.

Unilateralist   an approach to foreign policy that advocates acting in one's own best interests, alone if necessary.

Unitary government   a governmental system in which political authority is concentrated in a single national government.

United Nations (UN)   an international organization founded in 1945 as a diplomatic forum to resolve conflicts among the world's nations.

Universe   the population survey researchers wish to study.

Value added tax (VAT)   a tax on the estimated market value added to a product or material at each stage of its manufacture or distribution.

Veto   an action by the chief executive refusing to approve a measure passed by the legislature.

Voter mobilization   the process of motivating citizens to vote.

Voting age population (VAP)   the number of U.S. residents who are 18 years of age or older.

Voting eligible population (VEP)   the number of U.S. residents who are legally qualified to vote.

Voting Rights Act (VRA)   a federal law designed to protect the voting rights of racial and ethnic minorities.

War Powers Act   a law limiting the president's ability to commit American armed forces to combat abroad without consultation with Congress and congressional approval.

Warrant   an official authorization issued by a judicial officer.

Welfare programs   government programs that provide benefits to individuals based on their economic status.

Whips   assistant floor leaders in Congress.

White primary   an electoral system used in the South to prevent the participation of African Americans in the Democratic primary.

Writ of habeas corpus   a court order requiring government authorities either to release a person held in custody or demonstrate that the person is detained in accordance with law.

Writ of mandamus   a court order directing a public official to perform a specific act or duty.

Zone of acquiescence   the range of policy options acceptable to the public on a particular issue.

NOTES

Chapter 1

[1]U.S. Census Bureau, "Center of Population, 1790–2010," available at http://2010.census.gov.

[2]U.S. Census Bureau, "Growth and Movement of United States Population," available at http://2010.census.gov.

[3]U.S. Census Bureau, "States Ranked by Population Size: 1900, 1950, and 2000," *Demographic Trends in the Twentieth Century*, p. 29, available at www.census.gov; U.S. Census Bureau, "Resident Population of the United States, the District of Columbia, and Puerto Rico: 2010 Census," available at www.census.gov.

[4]U.S. Census Bureau, "Resident Population Projection by Sex and Age: 2010–2050," *2008 Statistical Abstract*, available at www.census.gov.

[5]U.S. Census Bureau, *The Population Profile of the United States: 2010*, available at www.census.gov.

[6]U.S. Census Bureau, "Projected Population of the United States, by Race and Hispanic Origin: 2000 to 2050," available at www.census.gov.

[7]U.S. Census Bureau, "Census Bureau Data Show Key Population Changes Across Nation," available at www.census.gov.

[8]U.S. Citizenship and Immigration Services (USCIS), *Fiscal Year 2008 Yearbook of Immigration Statistics*, available at http://uscis.gov/graphics/.

[9]Jeffrey S. Passel and D'Vera Cohn, "U.S. Unauthorized Immigration Flows Are Down Sharply Since Mid-Decade," Pew Hispanic Center, September 1, 2010, available at http://pewhispanic.org.

[10]Ibid.

[11]Chistopher Rudolph, *National Security and Immigration: Policy Develops in the United States and Western Europe Since 1945* (Stanford, CA: Stanford University Press, 2006), pp. 126–142.

[12]Mari-Claude Blanc-Chaléard, "Old and New Migrants in France: Italians and Algerians," in Leo Lucassen, David Feldman, and Jochen Oltmer, eds., *Paths of Integration: Migrants in Western Europe (1880–2004)* (Amsterdam: Amsterdam University Press, 2006), p. 54.

[13]Alec G. Hargreaves, *Multi-Ethnic France: Immigration, Politics, Culture, and Society* (NY: Routledge, 2007), p. 201.

[14]Robert H. Frank, "Income Inequality and the Protestant Ethic," in Victor Nee and Richard Swedberg, eds., *Capitalism* (Stanford, CA: Stanford University Press, 2007), pp. 73–73.

[15]U.S. Census Bureau, *Income, Poverty, and Health Insurance Coverage in the United States: 2009*, available at www.census.gov.

[16]U.S. Department of Health and Human Services, "2008 Annual Update of the HHS Poverty Guidelines," available at www.hhs.gov.

[17]U.S. Census Bureau, *Income, Poverty, and Health Insurance Coverage in the United States: 2009*.

[18]Ibid.

[19]U.S. Census Bureau, "Population by Country or Area: 1990–2010," *The 2009 Statistical Abstract*, available at www.census.gov.

[20]Stockholm International Peace Research Institute, "Military Expenditure Data, 1999-2008," available at www.sipri.org.

[21]World Bank, "World GDP 2009," available at http://data.worldbank.org.

[22]David Barboza, "G.M,. Eclipsed at Home, Soars to the Top in China," *New York Times*, July 22, 2010, available at www.nytimes.com.

[23]Powell, "The Other GM," p. 2.

[24]Peter Whoriskey, "Revamped GM Loses $1.2 Billion," *Washington Post*, November 17, 2009, available at www.washingtonpost.com.

[25]David Finkel, "The American Dream, Revisited," *Washington Post National Weekly Edition*, December 22, 2003-January 4, 2004, p. 19.

[26]Scott Burns, "Jobs and Benefits Are a la Carte Now," *Dallas Morning News*, May 18, 2004, available at www.dallasnews.com.

[27]"Factbox: National Assembly Elections in Vietnam," May 17, 2007, available at www.reuters.com.

[28]Michael Slackman, "Testing Egypt, Mubarak Rival Is Sent to Jail," *New York Times*, December 25, 2005, available at www.nytimes.com.

[29]M. Steven Fish, *Democracy Derailed in Russia: The Failure of Open Politics* (New York, NY: Cambridge University Press, 2005), p. 71.

[30]Robert A. Dahl, *Polyarchy: Participation and Opposition* (New Haven, CT: Yale University Press, 1971), p. 3.

[31]Jeffrey Passel, "Trends in Unauthorized Immigration," Pew Hispanic Center, October 2, 2008, available at http://pewhispanic.org.

[32]Steven A. Camarota, "Immigration, Both Legal and Illegal, Puts Huge Strain on the Country," Center for Immigration Studies, available at www.cis.org.

Chapter 2

[1]Gordon S. Wood, *The Creation of the American Republic 1776–1787* (Chapel Hill, NC: University of North Carolina Press, 1969), pp. 131–148.

[2]Donald S. Lutz, "The Changing View of the Founding and a New Perspective on American Political Theory," *Social Science Quarterly* 68 (December 1987): 669–686.

[3]Wood, pp. 601–14.

[4]Lutz, p. 677.

[5]*The Federalist*, No. 51.

[6]Ibid.

[7]Richard Neustadt, *Presidential Power*, rev. ed. (New York, NY: Wiley, 1976), p. 33.

[8]Edward C. Carmines and Lawrence C. Dodd, "Bicameralism in Congress: The Changing Partnership," in Lawrence C. Dodd and Bruce I. Oppenheimer, eds., *Congress Reconsidered*, 3rd ed. (Washington, DC: Congressional Quarterly Press, 1985), pp. 414–436.

[9]Robert A. Dahl, *A Preface to Democratic Theory*, expanded edition (Chicago, IL: University of Chicago Press, 2006), p. 137.

[10]Paul Finkelman, "James Madison and the Bill of Rights: A Reluctant Paternity," in Gerhard Casper, Dennis J. Hutchison, and David Strauss, eds., *The Supreme Court Review* (Chicago, IL: University of Chicago Press, 1990), pp. 309–311.

[11]Richard Labunski, *James Madison and the Struggle for the Bill of Rights* (New York, NY: Oxford University Press, 2006), pp. 96–255.

[12]Leonard Levy, *Judgments: Essays on American Constitutional History* (Chicago, IL: Quadrangle Books, 1972), p. 17.

[13]*Marbury v. Madison*, 1 Cranch 137 (1803).

[14]Richard H. Fallon, Jr., *The Dynamic Constitution: An Introduction to American Constitutional Law* (New York, NY: Cambridge University Press, 2004), p. 193.

[15]*Plessy v. Ferguson*, 163 U.S. 537 (1896).

[16]*Brown v. Board of Education of Topeka*, 347 U.S. 483 (1954).

[17]Thomas A. Birkland, *An Introduction to the Policy Process: Theories, Concepts, and Models of Public Policy Making* (Armonk, NY: M.E. Sharpe, 2001), p. 39.

[18]Charles A. Beard, *An Economic Interpretation of the Constitution of the United States* (New York, NY: Macmillan, 1913).

[19]James L. Sundquist, *Constitutional Reform and Effective Government*, rev. ed. (Washington, DC: Brookings Institution, 1986), pp. 5–6.

[20]Peter F. Nardulli, "The Constitution and American Politics: A Developmental Perspective," in Peter F. Nardulli, ed., *The Constitution and American Political Development* (Chicago, IL: University of Chicago Press, 1992), p. 12.

[21]Jeffrey M. Jones, "Majority Continues to Consider Iraq War a Mistake," February 6, 2008, available at www.gallup.com.

Chapter 3

[1]Karen Adelberger, "Federalism and Its Discontents: Fiscal and Legislative Power-Sharing in Germany, 1948–1999," *Regional and Federal Studies* 11 (Summer 2000): 43–68.

[2]Jan Erk, *Explaining Federalism: State, Society and Congruence in Austria, Belgium, Canada, Germany, and Switzerland* (New York: Routledge, 2008), pp. 58–70.

[3]Joseph F. Zimmerman, "The Nature and Political Significance of Preemption," *PS: Political Science & Politics*, July 2005, p. 361.

[4]Josh Goodman, "The Costliest Ride," *Governing*, July 2009, pp. 50–52.

[5]Terence Chea, "Budget Cuts Devastate California Higher Education," KPBS, August 5, 2009, available at www.kpbs.org.

[6]Elliot Parker, "Going the Wrong Way," *Las Vegas Sun*, June 12, 2011, available at www.lasvegassun.com.

[7]*McCulloch v. Maryland*, 4 Wheaton 316 (1819).

[8]*Dred Scott v. Sandford*, 19 Howard 393 (1857).

[9]*United States v. Lopez*, 514 U.S. 549 (1995).

[10]*Printz v. United States*, 521 U.S. 98 (1997).

[11]*United States v. Morrison*, 529 U.S. 598 (2000).

[12]Office of Management and Budget, "Summary Comparison of Total Outlays for Grants to State and Local Governments, 1940 to 2014," *The Budget for Fiscal Year 2011, Historical Tables*, available at www.whitehouse.gov/omb/budget.

[13]Larry N. Gerston, *American Federalism: A Concise Introduction* (Armonk, NY: M.E. Sharpe, 2007), p. 69.

[14]Frances E. Lee, "Bicameralism and Geographic Politics: Allocating Funds in the House and Senate," *Legislative Studies Quarterly* 29 (May 2004): 185–214.

[15]National Association of State Budget Officers, "The Fiscal Survey of the States," June 2010, available at www.nasbo.org.

[16]Paul Posner, "The Politics of Coercive Federalism in the Bush Era," *Publius: The Journal of Federalism* 37 (Summer 2007): p. 399.

[17]Gerston, *American Federalism: A Concise Introduction*, p. 20.

[18]Molly Stauffer and Carl Tubbesing, "The Mandate Monster," *State Legislatures*, May 2004, pp. 22–23.

[19]http://medicalmarijuana.procon.org/view.resource.php?resourceID=000884.

Chapter 4

[1]Website of Westboro Baptist Church, available at www.godhatesfags.com.

[2]Adam Cohen, "Why Spewing Hate at Funerals Is Still Free Speech," *Time*, September 29, 2010, available at www.time.com.

[3]Walter M. Weber, "*Snyder v. Phelps*: Testing the Free Speech Clause in the Westboro Baptist Funeral Picketing Case," October 28, 2010, available at http://writ.news.findlaw.com.

[4]Ben Nuckols, "Albert Snyder, Marine Father, Wages Court Battle Against Funeral Protests," April 13, 2010, available at www.huffingtonpost.com.

[5]*Pruneyard Shopping Center v. Robins*, 447 U.S. 74 (1980).

[6]Richard H. Fallon, Jr., *The Dynamic Constitution: An Introduction to American Constitutional Law* (New York, NY: Cambridge University Press, 2004), pp. 60–61.

[7]Patrick M. Garry, *Wrestling with God: The Court's Tortuous Treatment of Religion* (Washington, DC: Catholic University of America Press, 2006), pp. 70–72.

[8]*Everson v. Board of Ewing Township*, 330 U.S. 1 (1947).

[9]*Zelman v. Simmons-Harris*, 536 U.S. 639 (2002).

[10]*Engel v. Vitale*, 370 U.S. 421 (1962).

[11]*Van Orden v. Perry*, 545 U.S. 667 (2005).

[12]*McCreary County v. American Civil Liberties Union*, 545 U.S. 844 (2005).

[13]*Santa Fe School District v. Doe*, 530 U.S. 290 (2000).

[14]*Cantwell v. Connecticut*, 310 U.S. 296 (1940) and *Martin v. Struthers*, 319 U.S. 141 (1943).

[15]*Cantwell v. Connecticut*, 310 U.S. 296 (1940) and *Martin v. Struthers*, 319 U.S. 141 (1943).

[16]*Employment Division, Oregon Department of Human Resources v. Smith*, 493 U.S. 378 (1990).

[17]Suzanna Sherry, "The First Amendment and the Right to Differ," in David J. Bodenhammer and James W. Ely, Jr., *The Bill of Rights in Modern America* (Bloomington, IN: Indiana University Press, 2008), pp. 49–66.

[18]*Snyder v. Phelps*, No. 9-751 (2011).

[19]*Brandenburg v. Ohio*, 395 U.S. 444 (1969).

[20]*Cohen v. California*, 403 U.S. 15 (1971).

[21]*Cohen v. California*, 403 U.S. 15 (1971).

[22]*Madsen v. Women's Health Center*, 512 U.S. 753 (1994).

[23]"Hate Is Not Speech: A Constitutional Defense of Penalty Enhancement for Hate Crimes," *Harvard Law Review* 106 (April 1993): 1314–31.

[24]*Wisconsin v. Mitchell*, 508 U.S. 47 (1993).

[25]*Texas v. Johnson*, 491 U.S. 397 (1989).

[26]*United States v. Eichman*, 396 U.S. 310 (1990).

[27]*Miller v. California*, 413 U.S. 15 (1973).

[28]*New York Times v. Sullivan*, 376 U.S. 254 (1964).

[29]*Near v. Minnesota*, 283 U.S. 697 (1931).

[30]*New York Times v. United States*, 403 U.S. 713 (1971).

[31]*McDonald v. Chicago*, 08-1521 (2010).

[32]*District of Columbia v. Heller*, 554 U.S. 290 (2008).

[33]*District of Columbia v. Heller*.

[34]*Griswold v. Connecticut*, 381 U.S. 479 (1965).

[35]*Roe v. Wade*, 410 U.S. 113 (1973).

[36]*Webster v. Reproductive Health Services*, 492 U.S. 490 (1989).

[37]Adam Liptak, "Hate Speech or Free Speech? What Much of West Bans is Protected in the U.S." *New York Times*, June 11, 2008, available at www.nytimes.com.

[38]*Planned Parenthood of Southeastern Pennsylvania v. Casey*, 505 U.S. 833 (1992).

[39]*Lawrence v. Texas*, 539 US 558 (2003).

[40]*Illinois v. Wardlow*, 528 U.S. 119 (2000).

[41]*United States v. Ross*, 456 U.S. 798 (1982).

[42]*United States v. Ross*, 456 U.S. 798 (1982).

[43]*Mapp v. Ohio*, 367 U.S. 643 (1961).

[44]Adam Liptak, "U.S. Alone in Rejecting All Evidence if Police Err," *New York Times*, July 19, 2008, available at www.nytimes.com.

[45]*Massachusetts v. Shepherd*, 468 U.S. 981 (1984) and *United States v. Leon*, 468 U.S. 897 (1984).

[46]*Arizona v. Fulminante*, 499 U.S. 270 (1991).

[47]*Herring v. United States*, 7-513 (2009).

[48]*Miranda v. Arizona*, 384 U.S. 436 (1966).

[49]Gary L. Stuart, *Miranda: The Story of America's Right to Remain Silent* (Tucson, AR: University of Arizona Press, 2004), p.100.

[50]*Harris v. New York*, 401 U.S. 222 (1971).

[51]*New York v. Quarles*, 467 U.S. 649 (1984).

[52]*Moran v. Burdine*, 475 U.S. 412 (1986).

[53]*Kansas v. Hendricks*, 521 U.S. 346 (1997).

[54]Quoted in *Time*, July 7, 1997, p. 29.

[55]*Berghuis v. Thompkins*, No. 08-1470 (2010).

[56]*Globe Newspaper Co. v. Superior Court*, 457 U.S. 596 (1982).

[57]*Chancler v. Florida*, 449 U.S. 560 (1981).

[58]*Williams v. Florida*, 399 U.S. 78 (1970).

[59]*Snyder v. Louisiana*, No. 06-10119 (2008).

[60]*Gideon v. Wainwright*, 372 U.S. 335 (1963).

[61]*Tollett v. Henderson*, 411 U.S. 258 (1973).

[62]*Solem v. Helm*, 463 U.S. 277 (1983).

[63]*Kennedy v. Louisiana*, 554 U.S. (2008).

[64]*Graham v. Florida*, No. 08-7412 (2010).

[65]*Furman v. Georgia*, 408 U.S. 238 (1972).

[66]*Gregg v. Georgia*, 428 U.S. 153 (1976).

[67]http://www.deathpenaltyinfo.org/.

[68]Frank Newport, "In U.S., Two-Thirds Continue to Support Death Penalty," Gallup Report, 2009, www.gallup.com.

[69]Bureau of Justice Statistics, "Capital Punishment Statistics," available at www.ojp.usdoj.gov.

[70]James S. Leibman, *A Broken System: Error Rates in Capital Cases, 1973–1995*, available at www.thejusticeproject.org.

[71]Ibid.

[72]Bureau of Justice Statistics, "Capital Punishment 2005," available at www.ojp.usdoj.gov.

[73]"Supreme Court Bars Executing Mentally Retarded," June 20, 2002, available at cnn.com.

[74]*Atkins v. Virginia*, 536 U.S. 304 (2002).

[75]Otis H. Stephens, Jr., "Presidential Power, Judicial Deference, and the Status of Detainees in an Age of Terrorism," in David B. Cohen and John W. Wells, eds., *American National Security and Civil Liberties in an Era of Terrorism* (New York, NY: Palgrave MacMillan, 2004), p. 82.

[76]*Korematsu v. United States*, 323 U.S. 214 (1944).

[77]Kal Raustiala, *Does the Constitution Follow the Flag?* (New York, NY: Oxford University Press, 2009), pp. 190–206.

[78]Death Penalty Information Center, available at www.deathpenaltyinfo.org.

[79]*Hamdan v. Rumsfeld*, 548 U.S. 557 (2006).

[80]*Boumediene v. Bush*, 553 U.S. (2008).

Chapter 5

[1]"Surveying the Land," *Advocate*, August 2009, p. 57.

[2]Mike O'Sullivan, "San Francisco Gay Marriage Court Case Could Have National Impact," Voice of America, January 13, 2010, available at www1.voanews.com.

[3]Elder Witt, *The Supreme Court and Individual Rights*, 2nd ed. (Washington, DC: Congressional Quarterly Press, 1988), pp. 223–226.

[4]*Plessy v. Ferguson*, 163 U.S. 537 (1896).

[5]*Cumming v. Richmond County Board of Education*, 175 U.S. 528 (1899).

[6]*Missouri ex rel Gaines v. Canada*, 305 U.S. 337 (1938).

[7]*Sweatt v. Painter*, 399 U.S. 629 (1950).

[8]*McLaurin v. Oklahoma State Regents*, 339 U.S. 637 (1950).

⁹*Brown v. Board of Education of Topeka*, 347 U.S. 483 (1954).

¹⁰*Brown v. Board of Education of Topeka*, 349 U.S. 294 (1955).

¹¹Gerald Rosenberg, "Substituting Symbol for Substance: What Did *Brown* Really Accomplish?" *P.S. Political Science & Politics* (April 2004): 205.

¹²Quoted in Harrell R. Rodgers, Jr., and Charles S. Bullock III, *Law and Social Change* (New York, NY: McGraw-Hill, 1972), p. 71.

¹³*Alexander v. Holmes County Board of Education*, 396 U.S. 19 (1969).

¹⁴Rosenberg, "Substituting Symbol for Substance," p. 206.

¹⁵National Center for Education Statistics, available at http://nces.ed.gov.

¹⁶*Public Agenda for Citizens*, available at www.publicagenda.org.

¹⁷"The Most Underreported Story of 2009," *Time*, December 28, 2009– January 4, 2010.

¹⁸"School Segregation on the Rise," *Harvard Gazette News*, July 19, 2001, available at www.new.harvard.edu/gazette.

¹⁹*Millikin v. Bradley*, 418 U.S. 717 (1974).

²⁰*Missouri v. Jenkins*, 515 U.S. 70 (1995).

²¹*Parents Involved in Community Schools v. Seattle School District No. 1*, 551 U.S. 701 (2007).

²²*In re Griffiths*, 413 U.S. 717 (1973); *Examining Board of Engineers, Architects and Surveyors v. de Otero*, 426 U.S. 572 (1976); *Bernal v. Fainter*, 467 U.S. 216 (1984).

²³Henry Weinstein, "Airport Screener Curb Is Rejected," *Los Angeles Times*, November 16, 2002, available at www.latimes.com.

²⁴*Bradwell v. Illinois*, 16 Wall 130 (1873).

²⁵Philippa Smith, "The Virginia Military Institute Case," in Sibyl A. Schwarzenbach and Patricia Smith, eds., *Women and the Constitution: History, Interpretation, and Practice* (New York, NY: Columbia University Press, 2003), p. 343.

²⁶*United States v. Virginia*, 518 U.S. 515 (1996).

²⁷*Rostker v. Goldberg*, 453 U.S. 57 (1981).

²⁸Stephen Schwartz, "Shari'a in Saudi Arabia, Today and Tomorrow," in Paul Marshall, ed., *Radical Islam's Rules: The Worldwide Spread of Extreme Shari'a Law* (Lanham, MD: Rowman & Littlefield, 2005), pp. 33–34.

²⁹Mai Yamani, "Muslim Women and Human Rights in Saudi Arabia," in Eugene Cotran and Mai Yamani, eds., *The Rule of Law in the Middle East and the Islamic World: Human Rights and the Judicial Process* (London, UK: I. B. Tauris, 2000), pp. 137-145.

³⁰Damien McElroy, "Saudi Arabia to Lift Ban on Women Drivers," *Daily Telegraph*, January 21, 2008, available at www.telegraph.co.uk.

³¹*Romer v. Evans*, 517 U.S. 620 (1996).

³²*Smith v. Allwright*, 321 U.S. 649 (1944).

³³*Guinn v. United States*, 238 U.S. 347 (1915).

³⁴*Louisiana v. United States*, 380 U.S. 145 (1965).

³⁵*Harper v. State Board of Elections*, 383 U.S. 663 (1966).

³⁶Quoted in Alfred H. Kelley and Winfred A. Harbison, *The American Constitution: Its Origins and Development* (New York, NY: Norton, 1970), p. 460.

³⁷Quoted in Witt, *The Supreme Court and Individual Rights*, p. 247.

³⁸*Civil Rights Cases*, 109 U.S. 3 (1883).

³⁹*Heart of Atlanta Motel v. United States*, 379 U.S. 241; and *Katzenbach v. McClung*, 379 U.S. 294 (1964).

⁴⁰*Buchanan v. Warley*, 245 U.S. 60 (1917).

⁴¹*Shelley v. Kraemer*, 334 U.S. 1 (1948).

⁴²Augustus B. Cochran III, *Sexual Harassment and the Law* (Lawrence, KS: University of Kansas Press, 2004), p. 114.

⁴³*Oncale v. Sundowner Offshore Services, Inc.*, 523 U.S. 75 (1998).

⁴⁴*Boy Scouts of America, et. al. v. Dale*, 530 U.S. 640 (2000).

⁴⁵Frank Newport, "For First Time, Majority of Americans Favor Legal Gay Marriage," May 20, 2011, available at www.gallup.org.

⁴⁶Sandhya Somashekhar and Peyton Craighill, "Slim Majority Back Gay Marriage, Post-ABC Poll Says," *Washington Post*, March 18, 2011, available at www.washingtonpost.com.

⁴⁷*City of Richmond v. J. A. Croson Co.*, 488 U.S. 469 (1989).

⁴⁸*Adarand Constructors v. Pena*, 515 U.S. 200 (1995).

⁴⁹*Regents of the University of California v. Bakke*, 438 U.S. 265 (1978).

⁵⁰*Gratz v. Bollinger*, 539 U.S. 244 (2003).

⁵¹*Grutter v. Bollinger*, 539 U.S. 306 (2003).

⁵²http://www.washingtontimes.com/news/2008/oct/09/minorities-in-college-leveling-despite-rise/.

⁵³National Center for Education Statistics, available at www.nces.edu.gov.

⁵⁴"Higher Education," Public Agenda for Citizens, available at www.publicagenda.org.

Chapter 6

¹Anthony Leiserowitz, "American Opinions on Global Warming: Summary," Yale School of Forestry and Environmental Studies, 2007, available at http://environment.yale.edu.

²"Beyond Red and Blue: The Political Typology," Pew Research Center for the People & the Press, May 4, 2011, available at http://people-press.org.

³Edward Greenberg, "Orientations of Black and White Children to Political Activity," *Social Science Quarterly* 5 (December 1970): 561–571.

⁴David O. Sears and Nicholas A. Valentino, "Politics Matters: Political Events as Catalysts for Pre-adult Socialization," *American Political Science Review* 91 (March 1997): 45-65.

⁵M. Kent Jennings, "Political Knowledge Over Time and Across Generations," *Public Opinion Quarterly* 60 (Summer 1996): 228-252.

⁶Eric Plutzer, "Becoming a Habitual Voter: Inertia, Resources, and Growth in Young Adulthood," *American Political Science Review* 96 (March 2002): 54.

⁷Richard G. Niemi and Jane Junn, *Civic Education: What Makes Students Learn* (New Haven, CT: Yale University Press, 1998), p. 148.

⁸Cynthia Gordon, "Al Gore's Our Guy: Linguistically Constructing a Family Political Identity," *Discourse and Society* 15 (2004): 607-631.

⁹M. Kent Jennings, Laura Stoker, and Jake Bowers, "Politics across Generations: Family Transmission Reexamined," *Journal of Politics* 71 (April 2009): 782-799.

[10]Paul Allen Beck and M. Kent Jennings, "Family Traditions, Political Periods, and the Development of Partisan Orientations," *Journal of Politics* 53 (August 1991): 742-763.

[11]Niemi and Junn, *Civic Education*, p. 148.

[12]Edward Metz and James Youniss, "A Demonstration that School-Based Required Service Does Not Deter—But Heightens—Volunteerism," PS: *Political Science & Politics* (April 2003): 281-286.

[13]Molly W. Andolina, Krista Jenkins, Cliff Zukin, and Scott Keeter, "Habits from Home, Lessons from School: Influences on Youth Civic Engagement," *Social Education* 67 (October 2003): 278-279.

[14]Edgar Lott, "Civic Education, Community Norms, and Political Indoctrination," *American Sociological Review* 28 (February 1963): 69-75.

[15]Steve Crabtree, "Religiosity Highest in World's Poorest Nations," August 31, 2010, available at www.gallup.com.

[16]Robert Wuthnow, "Mobilizing Civic Engagement: The Changing Impact of Religious Involvement," in Theda Skocpol and Morris P. Fiorina, eds., *Civic Engagement in American Democracy* (Washington, DC: Brookings Institution Press, 1999), p. 352.

[17]Frederick C. Harris, "Something Within: Religion as a Mobilizer of African-American Political Activism," *Journal of Politics* 56 (February 1994): 42-68.

[18]Kenneth D. Wald, Dennis E. Owen, and Samuel S. Hill, Jr., "Churches as Political Communities," *American Political Science Review* 82 (June 1988): 531-548.

[19]Kenneth D. Wald, Dennis E. Owen, and Samuel S. Hill, Jr., "Political Cohesion in Churches," *Journal of Politics* 52 (February 1990): 197-215.

[20]Katharine Q. Seelye and Janet Elder, "Strong Support Is Found for Ban on Gay Marriage," *New York Times*, December 21, 2003, available at www.nytimes.com.

[21]Paul Allen Beck, Russell J. Dalton, Steven Greene, and Robert Huckfeldt, "The Social Calculus of Voting: Interpersonal, Media, and Organizational Influences on Presidential Choices," *American Political Science Review* 96 (March 2002): 57-73.

[22]Herbert P. Hyman, *Political Socialization* (Glencoe, IL: Free Press, 1959), pp. 109-115.

[23]Clyde Wilcox, "Feminism and Anti-Feminism Among Evangelical Women," *Western Political Quarterly* 42 (March 1989): 147-160.

[24]Ibid., p. 185.

[25]Shanto Iyengar and Donald R. Kinder, *News That Matters: Television and American Opinion* (Chicago: University of Chicago Press, 1987), pp. 112-113.

[26]Jon A. Krosnick and Donald R. Kinder, "Altering the Foundations of Support for the President Through Priming," *American Political Science Review* 84 (June 1990): 497-512.

[27]John R. Alford, Carolyn L. Funk, and John R. Hibbing, "Are Political Orientations Genetically Transmitted?" *American Political Science Review* 99 (May 2005): 153-167.

[28]Jeffrey M. Stonecash, *Political Polling: Strategic Information in Campaigns* (Lanham, MD: Rowman & Littlefield, 2003), pp. 141-143.

[29]Richard Morin, "Look Who's Talking," *Washington Post National Weekly Edition*, July 19-25, 1993, p. 37.

[30]Richard Morin, "The Jokers Stacking the Deck," *Washington Post Nation Weekly Edition*, August 17, 1998, p. 42.

[31]Megan Thee, "Cellphones Challenge Poll Sampling," *New York Times*, December 7, 2007, available at www.nytimes.com.

[32]Herbert Asher, *Polling and the Public: What Every Citizen Should Know*, 6th ed. (Washington, DC: CQ Press, 2004), pp. 82-86.

[33]Larry M. Bartels, "Democracy with Attitudes," in Michael B. MacKuen and George Rabinowitz, eds., *Electoral Democracy* (Ann Arbor, MI: University of Michigan Press, 2003), pp. 56-57.

[34]Frank Newport, "Six out of 10 Americans Say Homosexual Relations Should Be Recognized as Legal," May 15, 2003, available at www.gallup.com.

[35]Asher, *Polling and the Public*, p. 61.

[36]Richard Morin, "What Informed Public Opinion?" *Washington Post National Weekly Edition*, April 10-16, 1995, p. 36.

[37]Howard Schuman and Jean Converse, "The Effects of Black and White Interviewers on Black Response in 1968," *Public Opinion Quarterly* 35 (Spring 1971): 44-68; and Shirley Hatchett and Howard Schuman, "White Respondents and Race of Interviewer Effects," *Public Opinion Quarterly* 39 (Winter 1975): 523-528.

[38]Asher, *Polling and the Public*, p. 96.

[39]*Gallup Poll Monthly*, July 1992, pp. 8-9.

[40]Matthew Warshaw, "Starting from Scratch: Making Research a Reality in Afghanistan," available at www.publicopinionpros.norc.org.

[41]Julie Ray and Rajesh Srinivasan, "Nearly Half of Afghans Think More U.S. Troops Will Help," Gallup, September 30, 2009, available at www.gallup.com.

[42]George H. Gallup, Jr., "How Many Americans Know U.S. History? Part I," October 21, 2003, available at www.gallup.com.

[43]Lydia Saad, "More Americans Plugged into Political News," September 28, 2009, available at www.gallup.com.

[44]Pew Research Center for the People & the Press.

[45]Saad, "More Americans Plugged into Political News;" Keeter and Suls, "Political Knowledge Update."

[46]Morin, "Tuned Out, Turned Off," p. 7.

[47]Samuel A. Stouffer, *Communism, Conformity, and Civil Liberties: A Cross Section of the Nation Speaks Its Mind* (Garden City, NY: Doubleday, 1955), pp. 28-42.

[48]James W. Prothro and C. W. Grigg, "Fundamental Principles of Democracy: Bases of Agreement and Disagreement," *Journal of Politics* 22 (Spring 1960): 276-294.

[49]Robert Chandler, *Public Opinion: Changing Attitudes on Contemporary Social and Political Issues*, A CBS News Reference Book (New York, NY. R. R. Bowker, 1972), pp. 6-13.

[50]Clyde Z. Nunn, Harry J. Crockett, Jr., and J. Allen Williams, Jr., *Tolerance for Nonconformity: A National Survey of Americans' Changing Commitment to Civil Liberties* (San Francisco, CA. Jossey-Bass, 1978); James A. Davis, "Communism, Conformity, Cohorts, and Categories: American Tolerance in 1954 and 1972-73," *American Journal of Sociology* 81 (November 1975): 491-513.

[51]Jeffrey J. Mondak and Mitchell S. Sanders, "Tolerance and Intolerance, 1976-1998," *American Journal of Political Science* 47 (July 2003): 492-502.

[52]John Mueller, "Trends in Political Tolerance," *Public Opinion Quarterly* 52 (Spring 1988): 19.

[53]Donald Philip Green and Lisa Michele Waxman, "Direct Threat and Political Tolerance," *Public Opinion Quarterly* 51 (Summer 1987): 149-165.

[54]James L. Gibson, "Enigmas of Intolerance: Fifty Years after Stouffer's *Communism, Conformity, and Civil Liberties,*" *Perspectives on Politics* 4 (March 2006): 21-34.

[55]David G. Barnum and John L. Sullivan, "The Elusive Foundations of Political Freedom in Britain and the United States," *Journal of Politics* 52 (August 1990): 719-739.

[56]Dennis Chong, "How People Think, Reason, and Feel about Rights and Liberties," *American Journal of Political Science* 37 (August 1993): 867-899.

[57]"The ANES Guide to Public Opinion and Electoral Behavior," available at www.electionstudies.org.

[58]Pew Research Center for the People & the Press, "Public Trust in Government: 1958-2010," available at http://people-press.org.

[59]Pew Research Center for the People & the Press, "Distrust, Discontent, Anger and Partisan Rancor," April 11, 2010, available at http://people-press.org.

[60]"The NES Guide to Public Opinion and Electoral Behavior," available at www.electionstudies.org

[61]Ibid.

[62]Ruy A. Teixeira, *Why Americans Don't Vote: Turnout Decline in the United States 1960-1984* (New York, NY. Greenwood Press, 1987), p. 78.

[63]Lydia Saad, "In 2010, Conservatives Still Outnumber Moderates, Liberals," June 25, 2010, available at www.gallup.com.

[64]"The NES Guide to Public Opinion and Electoral Behavior," available at www.electionstudies.org

[65]Lydia Saad, "Special Report: Ideologically, Where Is the U.S. Moving?," July 6, 2009, available at www.gallup.com.

[66]The Gallup Poll, available at www.gallup.com.

[67]Eugene R. Wittkopf and Michael R. Maggiotto, "Elites and Masses: A Comparative Analysis of Attitudes Toward America's World Role," *Journal of Politics* 45 (May 1983): 303-334.

[68]Scott B. Blinder, "Dissonance Persists: Reproduction of Racial Attitudes among Post-Civil Rights Cohorts of White Americans," *American Politics Research* 35 (May 2007): 299-335.

[69]Frank Newport, "Little 'Obama Effect' on Views About Race Relations," October 29, 2009, available at www.gallup.com.

[70]Frank Newport, "Blacks as Conservative as Republicans on Some Moral Issues," December 3, 2008, available at www.gallup.com.

[71]Caryle Murphy and Alan Cooperman, "Seeking to Reclaim the Moral High Ground," *Washington Post National Weekly Edition*, May 29-June 4, 2006, p. 12.

[72]James L. Guth, John C. Green, Corwin E. Smith, and Margaret M. Poloma, "Pulpits and Politics: The Protestant Clergy in the 1988 Presidential Election," in Guth and Green, eds., *The Bible and the Ballot Box* (Boulder, CO: Westview Press, 1991), pp. 73-93.

[73]Frank Newport and Lydia Saad, "Religion, Politics Inform Americans' Views on Abortion," April 3, 2006, available at www.gallup.com.

[74]Allen D. Hertzke and John David Rausch, Jr., "The Religious Vote in American Politics: Value Conflict, Continuity, and Change," in Craig, *Broken Contract?*, p. 191.

[75]Frank Newport, "Religious Intensity Remains Powerful Predictor of Politics," December 11, 2009, available at www.gallup.com.

[76]Saad, " 'Conservatives' Are Single-Largest Ideological Group."

[77]Amy Goldstein and Richard Morin, "The Squeaky Wheel Gets the Grease," *Washington Post National Weekly Edition*, October 28-November 3, 2002, p. 34.

[78]Thomas C. Wilson, "Trends in Tolerance Toward Rightist and Leftist Groups, 1976-1988," *Public Opinion Quarterly* 58 (Winter 1994): 539-556.

[79]Timur Kuran and Edward J. McCaffery, "Sex Differences in the Acceptability of Discrimination," *Political Research Quarterly* 61 (July 2008): 228-238.

[80]Laurel Elder and Steven Greene, "The Myth of 'Security Moms' and 'Nascar Dads,' Parenthood, Political Stereotypes, and the 2004 Election," *Social Science Quarterly* 88 (March 2007), p. 11.

[81]V. O. Key, Jr., *Public Opinion and American Democracy* (New York: Alfred Knopf, 1961), p. 499.

[82]James A. Stimson, *Public Opinion in America: Moods, Cycles, and Swings* (Boulder, CO: Westview Press, 1991), pp. 19-21.

[83]Kenneth D. Wald, James W. Button, and Barbara A. Rienzo, "The Politics of Gay Rights in American Communities: Explaining Antidiscrimination Ordinances and Policies," *American Journal of Political Science* 40 (November 1996): 1152-1178.

[84]Karlyn Bowman, "Public Opinion on the War with Iraq," American Enterprise Institute, March 19, 2009, available at www.aei.org.

[85]Program on International Policy Attitudes, available at www.pipa.org.

Chapter 7

[1]Sean M. Theriault, *Party Polarization in Congress* (New York, NY: Cambridge University Press, 2008), pp. 3–9.

[2]"The ANES Guide to Public Opinion and Electoral Behavior," available at www.electionstudies.org.

[3]Michael P. McDonald, United States Election Project, available at http:// elections.gmu.edu.

[4]Sidney Verba, Kay Lehman Schlozman, and Henry E. Brady, *Voice and Equality: Civic Volunteerism in American Politics* (Cambridge, MA: Harvard University Press, 1995), p. 51.

[5]André Blais, *To Vote or Not to Vote?* (Pittsburgh, PA: University of Pittsburg Press, 2000), pp. 12-13.

[6]Henry E. Brady, Sidney Verba, Kay Lehman Schlozman, "Beyond SES: A Resource Model of Political Participation," *American Political Science Review* 89 (June 1995): 3.

[7]Andrea Louise Campbell, "Self-Interest, Social Security, and the Distinctive Participation Patterns of Senior Citizens," *American Political Science Review* 96 (September 2002): 565–574.

[8]Ibid.

[9]Verba, Schlozman, and Brady, *Voice and Equality: Civic Volunteerism in American Politics*, p. 354.

[10]Ibid.

[11]Thomas M. Holbrook and Scott D. McClurg, "The Mobilization of Core Supporters: Campaigns, Turnout, and Electoral Composition in the United States Presidential Elections," *American Journal of Political Science* 49 (October 2005): 689–703.

[12]Melissa R. Michelson, Lisa García Bedolla, and Margaret A. McConnell, "Heeding the Call: The Effect of Targeted Two-Round Phone Banks on Voter Turnout," *Journal of Politics* 71 (October 2009): 1549-1563.

[13]Blais, *To Vote or Not to Vote?* p. 13.

[14]U.S. Census Bureau, "Voting and Registration in the Election of November 2008," available at www.census.gov.

[15]APSA Task Force Report, "American Democracy in an Age of Rising Inequality," p. 656.

[16]U.S. Census Bureau, "Voting and Registration in the Election of November 2008."

[17]Sam Roberts, "2008 Surge in Black Voters Nearly Erased Racial Gap," *New York Times*, July 21, 2009, available at www.nytimes.com.

[18]U.S. Census Bureau, "Voting and Registration in the Election of November 2008."

[19]Jeff Manza and Christopher Uggen, *Locked Out: Felon Disenfranchisement and American Democracy* (New York, NY: Oxford University Press, 2006), pp. 76–80.

[20]Matt A. Barreto, "¡Sí Se Puede! Latino Candidates and the Mobilization of Latino Voters," *American Political Science Review* 101 (August 2007): 425-441.

[21]U.S. Census Bureau, "Voting and Registration in the Election of November 2008."

[22]Verba, Schlozman, and Brady, *Voice and Equality: Civic Volunteerism in American Politics*, p. 255.

[23]Richard Morin, "Tuned Out, Turned Off," *Washington Post National Weekly Edition*, February 5–11, 1996, p. 6.

[24]Daniel Setiawan, "After Six-Year Fight, Perry Signs Voter ID into Law," *Texas Observer*, May 27, 2011, available at www.texasobserver.com.

[25]Tom Curry, "Voter ID Debate Could Change 2012 Landscape, May 25, 2011, available at www.msnbc.com.

[26]Crawford v. Marion County Election Board, 553 U.S. 181 (2008).

[27]Stephen Ansolabehere, "Effects of Identification Requirements on Voting: Evidence from the Experience of Voters on Election Day," PS: Political Science & Politics (January 2009): 127–130.

[28]James G. Gimpel, Karen M. Kaufmann, and Shanna Pearson-Markowitz, "Battleground States Versus Blackout States: The Behavioral Implications of Modern Presidential Campaigns," *Journal of Politics* 69 (August 2007): 786–797.

[29]Lydia Saad, "More Americans Plugged into Political News," September 28, 2009, available at www.gallup.com.

[30]International Institute for Democracy and Electoral Assistance, available at www.idea.int.

[31]Gary W. Cox, "Electoral Rules and the Calculus of Mobilization," *Legislative Studies Quarterly* 24 (August 1999): 387–419.

[32]G. Bingham Powell, Jr., "American Voter Turnout in Comparative Perspective," *American Political Science Review* 80 (March 1986): 17–43.

[33]Jan E. Leighley and Jonathan Nagler, "Unions, Voter Turnout, and Class Bias in the U.S. Electorate, 1964–2004," *Journal of Politics* 69 (May 2007): 430–441.

[34]Verba, Schlozman, and Brady, *Voice and Equality: Civic Volunteerism in American Politics*, p. 72.

[35]Ibid.

[36]Petrocek and Shaw, "Nonvoting in America: Attitudes in Context,"pp. 71–72.

[37]Mark N. Franklin, "Electoral Engineering and Cross-National Turnout Differences: What Role of Compulsory Voting?" *British Journal of Political Science* 29 (January 1999): 205.

[38]Australian Electoral Commission, "2007 Federal Election Voter Turnout by Division," available at www.aec.gov.au.

[39]M. Mackerras and I. McAllister,"Compulsory Voting, Party Stability, and Electoral Advantage in Australia," *Electoral Studies* 18 (June 1999): 217–233.

[40]Gary C. Jacobson, *A Divider, Not a Uniter: George W. Bush and the American People* (New York, NY. Pearson Longman, 2007).

[41]Jack H. Nagel and John E. McNulty, "Partisan Effects of Voter Turnout in Presidential Elections," *American Politics Quarterly* 28 (July 2000): 408–429.

[42]William Crotty, "Political Participation: Mapping the Terrain," in Crotty, ed., *Political Participation and American Democracy*, pp. 7–15.

[43]Michael M. Gant and William Lyons, "Democratic Theory, Nonvoting, and Public Policy," *American Politics Quarterly* 21 (April 1993): 185–204.

[44]Thomas E. Cavanagh, "When Turnout Matters: Mobilization and Conversion as Determinants of Election Outcomes," in Crotty, *Political Participation and American Democracy*, p. 106.

[45]Peter L. Francia, Rachel E. Goldberg, John C. Green, Paul S. Herrnson, and Clyde Wilcox, "Individual Donors in the 1996 Federal Elections," in John C. Green, ed., *Financing the 1996 Election* (Armonk, NY: M. E. Sharpe, 1999), p. 128.

[46]Verba, Schlozman, and Brady, *Voice and Equality: Civic Volunteerism in American Politics*, pp. 475–493.

[47]Theda Skocpol, *Diminished Democracy: From Membership to Management in American Civic Life* (Norman, OK: University of Oklahoma Press, 2003), pp. 6–13, 224–244.

[48]APSA Task Force Report, "American Democracy in an Age of Rising Inequality," p. 657.

[49]*Voting: Some Procedural Changes and Informational Activities Could Increase Turnout* (Washington, DC: General Accounting Office, 1990), p. 2.

[50]Sean Richey, "Voting by Mail: Turnout and Institutional Reform in Oregon," *Social Sciences Quarterly* 89 (December 2008): 902–915.

[51]Ronald D. Michaelson, Illinois State Board of Elections, quoted in Peter Baker, "An All-Time High for Ballot Box No-Shows," *Washington Post National Weekly Edition*, November 11–17, 1996, p. 11.

[52]Michael D. Martinez and David Hill, "Did Motor Voter Work?" *American Politics Quarterly* 27 (July 1999): 296–315.

[53]Cynthia Rugeley and Robert A. Jackson, "Getting on the Rolls: Analyzing the Effects of Lowered Barriers on Voter Registration," *State Politics and Policy Quarterly* 9 (Spring 2009): 56–78.

[54]International Institute for Democracy and Electoral Assistance, "Voter Turnout," www.idea.int/vt/.

[55]Ibid.

[56]U.S. Census Bureau, "Voting and Registration in the Election of November 2008."

[57]International Institute for Democracy and Electoral Assistance, "Voter Turnout."

Chapter 8

[1]"Partisanship and Cable News Audience," October 30, 2009, Pew Center for the People & the Press, available at http://peope-press.org.

[2]Jim Galloway, "Documenting the Media Migration to Separate Corners," *Atlanta Courier Journal*, April 27, 2008, available at www.acj.com.

[3]Quoted in Galloway, "Documenting the Media Migration to Separate Corners."

[4]Michael Smerconish, "Media Enabling Political Polarization," June 16, 2010, available at http://host.madison.com.

[5]Ted Koppel, "Olbermann, O'Reilly, and the Death of Real News," *Washington Post*, November 14, 2010, available at www.washingtonpost.com.

[6]Project for Excellence in Journalism, available at www.stateofthenewsmedia.org.

[7]"Annual Report," available at www.tribune.com.

[8]"Press Freedom Index 2009," available at www.rsf.org.

[9]Ibid.

[10]Erika Franklin Fowler and Kenneth M. Goldstein, eds., "Free Media in Campaigns," in Stephen C. Craig, ed., *The Electoral Challenge: Theory Meets Practice* (Washington, DC: CQ Press, 2006), pp. 112–115.

[11]Richard Perez-Pena, "U.S. Newspaper Circulation Falls 10%," *New York Times*, October 26, 2009, available at www.nytimes.com.

[12]"The State of the News Media 2009," available at www.stateofthenews media.org.

[13]Pew Center for the People & the Press, available at http://people-press.org.

[14]Jose Antonio Vargas, "Obama Raised Half a Billion Online," *Washington Post*, November 20, 2008, available at www.washingtonpost.com.

[15]Elizabeth Gorman, "Obama Cashes in Online Political Capital for Sotomayor," ABC News, May 29, 2009, available at www.abcnews.com.

[16]Quoted in *Texas Observer*, June 12, 2009, p. 15.

[17]*Red Lion Broadcasting v. FCC*, 395 U.S. 367 (1969).

[18]Broadcast Decency Enforcement Act of 2005, PL no. 109-235.

[19]Doris A. Graber, *Mass Media and American Politics*, 7th ed. (Washington, DC: CQ Press, 2006), p. 77.

[20]Bruce Miroff, "The Presidential Spectacle," in Michael Nelson, ed., *The Presidency and the Political System*, 8th ed. (Washington, DC: CQ Press, 2006), p. 277.

[21]Alessandra Stanley, "For President, Five Programs, One Message," *New York Times*, September 21, 2009, available at www.nytimes.com.

[22]White House Press Release, "President Arrives in Alabama, Briefed on Hurricane Katrina," September 2, 2005, available at www.whitehouse.gov.

[23]Pew Research Center.

[24]Farnsworth and Lichter, *The Nightly News Nightmare*, pp. 118–161.

[25]Pew Research Center's Project for Excellence in Journalism, "How the Press Reported the 2008 Presidential Election," October 22, 2008, available at www.journalism.org.

[26]Farnsworth and Lichter, *The Nightly News Nightmare*, pp. 118–161

[27]Pew Center for the People & the Press, "Partisanship and Cable News Audiences," October 30, 2009, available at http://people-press.org.

[28]Kim Fridkin Kahn and Patrick J. Kenney, "The Slant of the News: How Editorial Endorsements Influence Campaign Coverage and Citizens' Views of Candidates," *American Political Science Review* 96 (June 2002): 381–394.

[29]Tim Groeling and Samuel Kernell, "Is Network News Coverage of the President Biased?" *Journal of Politics* 60 (November 1998): 1063–1087; Larry Sabato, "Is There an Anti-Republican, Anti-Conservative Media Tilt?" *Campaigns and Elections*, September 1993, p. 16.

[30]Thomas E. Patterson, "Bad News, Period," *PS: Political Science and Politics*, March 1996, pp. 17–20.

[31]Elizabeth A. Skewes, *Message Control: How News Is Made on the Presidential Campaign Trail* (Lanham, MD: Rowman & Littlefield Publishers, 2007), p. 13.

[32]Pew Research Center for the People & the Press, "Internet Overtakes Newspapers as News Outlets," December 23, 2008, available at http://pewresearch.org.

[33]Pew Research Center for the People & the Press, "Key News Audiences Now Blend Online and Traditional News Sources," August 17, 2008, available at http://pewresearch.org.

[34]Paul Farhi, "Political Pundits, Overpopulating the News Networks, *Washington Post*, February 19, 2008, available at www.washingtonpost.com.

Chapter 9

[1]Lori Montgomery, "Among GOP, Anti-Tax Orthodoxy Runs Deep," Washington Post, June 5, 2011, available at www.washingtonpost.com.

[2]Mancur Olson, *The Logic of Collective Action* (Cambridge, MA: Harvard University Press, 1971).

[3]Kelly D. Patterson and Matthew M. Singer, "Targeting Success: The Enduring Power of the NRA," in Allan J. Ciglar and Burdett A. Loomis, eds., *Interest Group Politics* (Washington, DC: CQ Press, 2007), pp. 41-42.

[4]Anthony J. Nownes, *Total Lobbying: What Lobbyists Want (and How They Try to Get It)*, (New York, NY: Cambridge University Press, 2006), p. 13.

[5]U.S. Census Bureau, "Union Members by Selected Characteristics: 1985–2008," The *2010 Statistical Abstract*, available at www.census.gov.

[6]Peter L. Francia, "Protecting America's Workers in Hostile Territory: Unions and the Republican Congress," in Paul S. Herrnson, Ronald G. Shaiko, and Clyde Wilcox, eds., *The Interest Group Connection: Electioneering, Lobbying, and Policymaking in Washington*, 2nd ed. (Washington, DC: CQ Press, 2005), p. 214.

[7]*Dukes v. Wal-Mart, Inc.*, 04-16688 (9th Cir. Feb. 6, 2007).

[8]American Federation of Labor-Congress of Industrial Organizations, available at www.aflcio.org.

[9]Caryle Murphy and Alan Cooperman, "Seeking to Reclaim the Moral High Ground," *Washington Post National Weekly Edition*, May 29–June 4, 2006, p. 12.

[10]John C. Green and Nathan S. Bigelow, "The Christian Right Goes to Washington: Social Movement Resources and the Legislative Process," in Herrnson, Shaiko, and Wilcox, eds., *The Interest Group Connection*, pp. 191–206.

[11]Roderi Ai Camp, *Politics in Mexico: The Democratic Consolidation* (New York, NY: Oxford University Press, 2007), p. 89.

[12]Ibid., pp. 144–145.

[13]Daniel C. Levy and Kathleen Bruhn, *Mexico: The Struggle for Democratic Development*, 2nd ed. (Berkeley, CA: University of California Press, 2006), pp. 123–124.

[14]Federal Election Commission, "Summary of PAC Financial Activity, 2007–2008," available at www.fec.gov.

[15]Federal Election Commission, "Top 50 PAC Disbursements," available at www.fec.gov.

[16]Federal Election Commission, "PAC Financial Activity, 2007–2008," available at www.fec.gov.

[17]Ibid.

[18]Professor James A. Thurber, quoted in Jeffrey H. Birnbaum, "Mickey Goes to Washington," *Washington Post National Weekly Edition*, February 25–March 2, 2008, p. 6.

[19]Steve Hargreaves, "Exxon 2008 Profit: A Record $45 Billion," January 30, 2009, CNN Money, available at www.cnn.com.

[20]Ronald G. Shaiko, "Making the Connection: Organized Interests, Political Representation, and the Changing Rules of the Game in Washington Politics," in Herrnson, Shaiko, and Wilcox, eds., *The Interest Group Connection*, p. 32.

[21]Center for Responsive Politics, available at www.opensecrets.org.

[22]Rogan Kersh, "The Well-Informed Lobbyist: Information and Interest Group Lobbying," in Ciglar and Loomis, ed., *Interest Group Politics*, pp. 390–406.

[23]John R. Wright, "Contributions, Lobbying, and Committee Voting in the U.S. House of Representatives," *American Political Science Review* 84 (June 1990): 417–438.

[24]Thomas B. Edsall, "A Chill but Not the Cold Shoulder," *Washington Post National Weekly Edition*, January 16–22, 2006, p. 15.

[25]Dan Eggen and Philip Rucker, "Loose Network of Activists Drives Reform Opposition," *Washington Post*, August 16, 2009, available at www.washingtonpost.com.

[26]Ruth Markus and Charles R. Babcock, "Feeding the Election Machine," *Washington Post National Weekly Edition*, February 17, 1997, p. 7.

[27]Steven E. Schier, *By Invitation Only: The Rise of Exclusive Politics in the United States* (Pittsburgh, PA: University of Pittsburgh Press, 2000), p. 179–181.

[28]John M. Broder, "Court Rejects Moratorium on Drilling in the Gulf," *New York Times*, July 8, 2010, available at www.nytimes.com.

[29]John M. Broder, "U.S. Issues Revised Offshore Drilling Ban," *New York Times*, July 12, 2010, available at www.nytimes.com.

[30]Richard Monastersky, "Protesters Fail to Slow Animal Research," *Chronicle of Higher Education*, April 18, 2008, pp. A1, A26–A28.

[31]Tom Arrandale, "The Mid-Life Crisis of the Environmental Lobby," *Governing*, April 1992, pp. 32–36.

[32]Diana Evans, "Before the Roll Call: Interest Group Lobbying and Public Policy Outcomes in House Committees," *Political Research Quarterly* 49 (June 1996): 287–304.

[33]Pew Research Center for the People & the Press, "Public Support Falls for Religion's Role in Politics," August 21, 2008, available at http://pewresearch.org.

[34]Alan Wisdom, "Political Gaps Strain Churches," The Institute on Religion and Democracy, available at www.theird.org/Page.aspx?pid=1383.

Chapter 10

[1]Marc Caputo, "GOP Poll: Tea Party Movement Could Cost Republicans in 2012," *Miami Herald*, June 22, 2011, available at www.miamiherald.com.

[2]Octavio Amorim Neto and Gary W. Cox, "Electoral Institutions, Cleavage Structures, and the Number of Parties," *American Journal of Political Science* 41 (January 1997): 149–74.

[3]Maurice Duverger, *Political Parties* (New York, NY: Wiley, 1954), p. 217.

[4]A. James Reichley, "The Future of the American Two-Party System at the Beginning of a New Century," in John C. Green and Rick Farmer, eds., *The State of the Parties: The Changing Role of Contemporary American Parties*, 4th ed. (Lanham, MD: Rowman & Littlefield, 2003), pp. 20–21.

[5]Michael Toner, "The Impact of the New Campaign Finance Law on the 2004 Presidential Election," in Larry Sabato, ed., *Divided States of America: The Slash and Burn Politics of the 2004 Presidential Election* (New York, NY: Pearson Longman, 2006), p. 197.

[6]Center for Responsive Politics, available at www.opensecrets.org.

[7]Timothy P. Nokken, "Ideological Congruence versus Electoral Success: Distribution of Party Organization Contributions in Senate Elections, 1990–2000," *American Politics Research* 31 (January 2003): 3–26.

[8]Exit poll data, available at www.cnn.com.

[9]Ibid.

[10]Juan Castillo, "Latinos Deliver on Potential, Turn Out Big for Obama," *Austin American-Statesman*, November 6, 2008, available at www.statesman.com.

[11]David L. Leal, Stephan A. Nuño, Jongho Lee, and Rodolpho O. de la Garza, "Latinos, Immigration, and the 2006 Midterm Election," *PS: Political Science & Politics* (April 2008): 312.

[12]Exit poll data.

[13]Ibid.

[14]Ibid.

[15]Ibid.

[16]Jongho Lee and Harry P. Pachon, "Leading the Way: An Analysis of the Effect of Religion on the Latino Vote," *American Politics Research* 35 (March 2007): 252–272.

[17]John C. Green, Lyman A. Kellstedt, Corwin E. Smidt, and James L. Guth, "How the Faithful Voted: Religious Communities and the Presidential Vote," in David E. Campbell, ed., *A Matter of Faith: Religion in the 2004 Presidential Election* (Washington, DC: Brookings Institution Press, 2007), pp. 1–28.

[18]Exit poll data.

[19]Frank Newport, "Church Attendance and Party Identification," Gallup News Service, May 18, 2005, available at www.gallup.com.

[20]Exit poll data.

[21]Ibid.

[22]Ibid.

[23]Ibid.

[24]Morris P. Fiorina, *Culture War? The Myth of a Polarized America*, 2nd ed. (New York, NY: Pearson Education, 2006), pp. 61–70.

[25]Joseph Bafumi and Robert Y. Shapiro, "A New Partisan Voter," Journal of Politics 71 (January 2009): 1–24.

[26]No Surprise That Harris Poll Finds Republicans Believe GOP Smears of Obama," Media Matters forAmerica, March 25, 2010, available at www.mediamatters.com.

[27]Gallup, available at www.gallup.com.

[28]"Bush Approval Static, Congress' Sinks Further," March 14, 2008, available at www.gallup.com.

[29]"RCP Poll Averages," available at www.realclearpolitics.com.

[30]Gary Langer, "2010 Elections Exit Poll Analysis: The Political Price of Economic Pain," ABC News, November 3, 2010, available at www.abcnews.go.com.

[31]Joel H. Silbey, "Divided Government in Historical Perspective, 1789–1996," in Peter F. Golderisi, ed., *Divided Government: Change, Uncertainty, and the Constitutional Order* (Lanham, MD: Rowman & Littlefield, 1996), pp. 9–34.

[32]Morris Fiorina, *Divided Government*, 2nd ed. (Cambridge, MA: Harvard University Press, 1996), p. 7.

[33]Andrew E. Busch, *Horses in Midstream: U.S. Midterm Elections and Their Consequences, 1894–1998* (Pittsburgh, PA: University of Pittsburgh Press, 1999), pp. 15–22.

[34]John R. Petrocik and Joseph Doherty, "The Road to Divided Government: Paved Without Intention," in Golderisi, ed., *Divided Government: Change, Uncertainty, and the Constitutional Order*, p. 105.

[35]Gary C. Jacobson, "The Persistence of Democratic House Majorities," in Gary W. Cox and Samuel Kernell, eds., *The Politics of Divided Government* (Boulder, CO: Westview Press, 1991), pp. 57–84.

[36]Gary C. Jacobson, "Divided Government and the 1994 Elections," in Golderisi, ed., *Divided Government: Change, Uncertainty, and the Constitutional Order*, p. 62.

[37]Walter R. Mebane, Jr., "Combination, Moderation, and Institutional Balancing in American Presidential Elections," *American Political Science Review* 94 (March 2000): 37–57.

[38]Michael Peress, "Strategic Voting in Multi-Office Elections," *Legislative Studies Quarterly* 33 (November 2008): 619–640.

Chapter 11

[1]Stephen Ansolabehere and Maxwell Palmer, "Texas Redistricting—Evaluation of Plan C141," Harvard Election Data Archive, available at http://projects.iq.harvard.edu.

[2]Thanh Tan, "House Passes Congressional Redistricting Map," Texas Tribune, June 14, 2011, available at www.texastribune.org.

[3]Aaron Blake, "Assessing the Effects of California's Proposition 14," Washington Post, June 10, 2010, available at www.washingtonpost.com.

[4]E. J. Schultz, "Parties Weigh Impact of Open Primaries," Fresno Bee, June 14, 2010, available at www.fresnobee.com.

[5]Robert E. Cushman and Robert F. Cushman, *Cases in Constitutional Law*, 3rd ed. (New York: Appleton-Century-Crofts, 1968), p. 42.

[6]*Baker v. Carr*, 369 U.S. 186 (1962) and *Wesberry v. Sanders*, 376 U.S. 1 (1964).

[7]Thomas Brunell and Bernard Grofman, "The Partisan Consequences of *Baker v. Carr* and the One Person, One Vote Revolution," in Lisa Handley and Bernie Grofman, eds., *Redistricting in Comparative Perspective* (New York, NY: Oxford University Press, 2008), pp. 225–236.

[8]Stephen Ansolabehere, Alan Gerber, and James Snyder, "Equal Money: Court-Ordered Redistricting and Public Expenditures in the American States," *American Political Science Review* 96 (December 2002): 767–777.

[9]Harold Wolman and Lisa Marckini, "The Effect of Place on Legislative Roll-Call Voting: The Case of Central-City Representatives in the U.S. House," *Political Science Quarterly* 81 (September 2000): 763–781.

[10]Michael P. McDonald, "United States Redistricting: A Comparative Look at the 50 States," in Lisa Handley and Bernie Grofman, eds., *Redistricting in Comparative Perspective*, (New York, NY: Oxford University Press, 2008) p. 56.

[11]Mark Monmonier, *Bushmanders and Bullwinkles: How Politicians Manipulate Electronic Maps and Census Data to Win Elections* (Chicago, IL: University of Chicago Press, 2001), p. 62.

[12]David Lublin and D. Stephen Voss, "Racial Redistricting and Realignment in Southern State Legislatures," *American Journal of Political Science* 44 (October 2000): 792–810.

[13]David T. Canon, *Race, Redistricting, and Representation: The Unintended Consequences of Black Majority Districts* (Chicago, IL: University of Chicago Press, 1999), p. 257.

[14]*Shaw v. Reno*, 509 U.S. 630 (1993) and *Miller v. Johnson*, 515 U.S. 900 (1995).

[15]*Reno v. Bossier Parish School Board*, 528 U.S. 320 (2000).

[16]*Georgia v. Ashcroft*, 539 U.S. 461 (2003).

[17]*Davis v. Bandemer*, 478 U.S. 109 (1986).

[18]Richard L. Engstrom, "The Post-2000 Round of Redistricting: An Entangled Thicket within the Federal System," *Publius: The Journal of Federalism* 32 (Fall 2002): 60–64.

[19]Center for Responsive Politics, available at www.opensecrets.org.

[20]Ibid.

[21]John J. Coleman and Paul F. Manna, "Congressional Campaign Spending and the Quality of Democracy," *Journal of Politics* 62 (August 2000): 757–789.

[22]Ken Herman, "Campaigns Spend Millions to Seek Yet More Millions," *Austin American-Statesman*, August 22, 2004, available at www.statesman.com.

[23]Center for Responsive Politics, available at www.opensecrets.org.

[24]Federal Election Commission, available at www.fec.gov.

[25]Richard A. Oppel, Jr., "Campaign Documents Show Depth of Bush Fund-Raising," *New York Times*, May 5, 2003, available at www.nytimes.com.

[26]Wayne Slater, "Elite Donors Lifted Bush," *Dallas Morning News*, May 5, 2003, available at www.dallasnews.com.

[27]Kirsten A. Foot and Steven M. Schneider, *Web Campaigning* (Cambridge, MA: MIT Press, 2006), pp. 197–198.

[28]Center for Responsive Politics, available at www.opensecrets.org.

[29]Michael J. Malbin, *The Election After Reform: Money, Politics, and the Bipartisan Campaign Reform Act* (Lanham, MD: Rowman & Littlefield, 2006), pp. 3–4.

[30]Glen Justice and Jim Rutenberg, "Advocacy Groups Step Up Costly Battle of Political Ads," *New York Times*, September 25, 2004, available at www.nytimes.com.

[31]Kerwin C. Swint, *Mudslingers: The Top 25 Negative Political Campaigns of All Time* (Westport, CT: Praeger, 2006), p. 47.

[32]Richard R. Lau and Gerald M. Pomper, "Effectiveness of Negative Campaigning in U.S. Senate Elections," *American Journal of Political Science* 46 (January 2002): 47–66.

[33]David E. Damore, "Candidate Strategy and the Decision to Go Negative," *Political Research Quarterly*, 55 (September 2002): 669–685.

[34]Stephen Ansolabehere and Shanto Iyengar, "Winning Through Advertising: It's All in the Context," in James A.
Thurber and Candice J. Nelson, eds., *Campaigns and Elections American Style* (Boulder, CO: Westview, 1995), p. 109.

[35]Lynda Lee Kaid, "Political Advertising," in Stephen C. Craig, ed., *The Electoral Challenge: Theory Meets Practice* (Washington, DC: CQ Press, 2006), p. 82.

[36]Gregory A. Huber and Kevin Arceneaux, "Identifying the Persuasive Effects of Presidential Advertising," *American Journal of Political Science* 51 (October 2007): 957–977.

[37]John R. Petrocik, William L. Benoit, and Glenn J. Hansen, "Issue Ownership and Presidential Campaigning," *Political Science Quarterly* 118 (Winter 2004-2004): 599–626.

[38]Jeremy C. Pope and Jonathan Woon, "Measuring Changes in American Party Reputation, 1939–2004," *Political Research Quarterly* 62 (December 2009): 653–661.

[39]Doug Beizer, "Social Media Swings Tight Mass. Senate Race," *Federal Computer Week*, January 20, 2010, available at http://fcw.com.

[40]Paul R. Abramson, John H. Aldrich, and David W. Rohde, *Change and Continuity in the 2008 Election* (Washington, DC: CQ Press, 2010), p. 229.

[41]Alexander C. Hart, "Election by Numbers," Washington Post, November 5, 2010, available at www.washingtonpost.com.

[42]Michael E. Toner and Melissa L. Laurenza, "Emerging Campaign Finance Trends and Their Impact on the 2006 Midterm Election," in Larry J. Sabato, ed., The Sixth Year Itch: The Rise and Fall of the George W. Bush Presidency (New York: Pearson, 2008), p. 132.

[43]Bill Bishop and Robert Cushing, "The Big Sort: Migration, Community, and Politics in the United States of 'Those People,'" in Ruy Teixeira, ed., Red, Blue, and Purple America (Brookings Institution Press, 2008), p. 69.

[44]Barry Ames, "Electoral Rules, Constituency Pressures, and Pork Barrel: Bases of Voting in the Brazilian Congress," *Journal of Politics* 57 (May 1995): 324–343.

[45]Robert S. Erikson and Gerald C. Wright, "Voters, Candidates, and Issues in Congressional Elections," in Lawrence C. Dodd and Bruce I. Oppenheimer, eds., *Congress Reconsidered*, 7th ed. (Washington, DC: CQ Press, 2001), p. 72.

[46]Secretary of State of New Hampshire, available at www.sos.nh.gov.

[47]John S. Jackson, Nathan S. Bigelow, and John C. Green, "The State of Party Elites: National Convention Delegates, 1992–2000," in John C. Green and Rick Farmer, eds., *The State of the Parties: The Changing Role of Contemporary American Parties* (Lanham, MD: Rowman & Littlefield, 2003), pp. 54–78.

[48]Paul R. Abramson, John H. Aldrich, Phil Paolino, and David W. Rohde, "Sophisticated Voting in the 1988 Presidential Primaries," *American Political Science Review* 86 (March 1992): 55–69.

[49]"State-by-state Election Results," available at www.govote.com.

[50]Barbara Norrander, "Nomination Choices: Caucus and Primary Outcomes, 1976–88," *American Journal of Political Science* 37 (May 1993): 343–364.

[51]Federal Election Commission.

[52]Jackie Calmes, "Clinton Braces for Second Loss; Union, Senators May Back Obama," *Wall Street Journal*, January 8, 2008, available at www.wsj.com.

[53]Lonna Rae Atkeson and Cherie D. Maestas, "Meaningful Participation and the Evolution of the Reformed Presidential Nominating System," *PS: Political Science & Politics*, January 2009, pp. 59–64.

[54]Federal Election Commission.

[55]Gerald M. Pomper, "Parliamentary Government in the United States: A New Regime for a New Century?" in Green and Farmer, eds., *The State of the Parties*, p. 273.

[56]Jody C. Baumgartner, *The American Vice Presidency Reconsidered* (Westport, CT: Praeger, 2006), p. 78.

[57]Exit Poll Data, available at www.cnn.com.

[58]Gerald M. Pomper, "The New Role of the Conventions as Political Rituals," in Costas Panagopoulos, ed., *Rewiring Politics: Presidential Nominating Conventions in the Media Age* (Baton Rouge, LA: LSU Press, 2007), pp. 189–197.

[59]Randall E. Adkins and Kent A. Kirwan, "What Role Does the 'Federalism Bonus' Play in Presidential Selection?" *Publius: The Journal of Federalism* 32 (Fall 2002): 71–90.

[60]Daron R. Shaw, *The Race to 270: The Electoral College and the Campaign Strategies of 2000 and 2004* (Chicago, IL: University of Chicago Press, 2006), p. 143.

[61]Kim J. Fridkin, Patrick J. Kenney, Sarah Allen Gershon, Karen Shafer, and Gina Serignese Woodall, "Capturing the Power of a Campaign Event: The 2004 Presidential Debate in Tempe," *Journal of Politics* 69 (August 2007): 770–785.

[62]Michael Dimock, April Clark, and Juliana Menasce Horowitz, "Campaign Dynamics and the Swing Vote in the 2004 Election," in William G. Mayer, ed., *The Swing Voter in American Politics* (Washington, DC: Brookings Institution, 2008), p. 58.

[63]Exit Poll Data.

[64]Mayer, ed., *The Swing Voter in American Politics*, p. 19.

[65]Ibid.

[66]Exit Poll Data.

[67]Jeffrey M. Jones, "Does Bringing Out the Candidate Bring Out the Vote?" *American Politics Quarterly* 26 (October 1998): 395–419.

[68]Ibid.

[69]David W. Abbott and James P. Levine, *Wrong Winner: The Coming Debacle in the Electoral College* (New York, NY: Praeger, 1991), p. 32.

[70]Lawrence D. Longley and Neal R. Peirce, *The Electoral College Primer 2000* (New Haven, CT: Yale University Press, 1999), p. 24.

[71]George C. Edwards III, *Why the Electoral College is Bad for America* (New Haven, CT: Yale University Press, 2004), p. 150.

[72]Ann N. Crigler, Marion R. Just, and Edward J. McCaffery, *Rethinking the Vote: The Politics and Prospects of American Electoral Reform* (New York, NY: Oxford University Press, 2004).

[73]Warren E. Miller, "Party Identification, Realignment, and Party Voting: Back to the Basics," *American Political Science Review* 85 (June 1991): 557–68.

[74]John R. Petrocik, "Reporting Campaigns: Reforming the Press," in Thurber and Nelson, eds., *Campaigns and Elections American Style*, p. 128.

[75]Stephen A Jessee, "Partisan Bias, Political Information and Spatial Voting in the 2008 Presidential Election," *Journal of Politics* 72 (April 2010): 327–340.

[76]Scott J. Basinger and Howard Lavine, "Ambivalence, Information, and Electoral Choice," *American Political Science Review* 99 (May 2005): 169–184.

[77]Arthur H. Miller, Martin P. Wattenberg, and Oksana Malachuk, "Schematic Assessments of Presidential Candidates," *American Political Science Review* 80 (June 1986): 521–540.

[78]George E. Marcus, "The Structure of Emotional Response: 1984 Presidential Candidates," *American Political Science Review* 82 (September 1988): 737–761.

[79]Thomas M. Holbrook, "Do Campaigns Matter?" in Stephen C. Craig, ed., *The Electoral Challenge: Theory Meets Practice* (Washington, DC: CQ Press, 2006), pp. 12–13.

[80]Edward Roeder, "Not Only Does Money Talk, It Often Calls the Winners," *Washington Post National Weekly Edition*, September 26–October 2, 1994, p. 23.

[81]Brian F. Schaffner, "Priming Gender: Campaigning on Women's Issues in U.S. Senate Elections," *American Journal of Political Science* 49 (October 2005): 803–817.

[82]Alan I. Abramowitz, "Can McCain Overcome the Triple Whammy?" May 29, 2008, Larry J. Sabato's Crystal Ball 2008, available at www.centerforpolitics.org.

[83]Exit Poll Data.

[84]David Karol and Edward Miguel, "The Electoral Cost of War: Iraq Casualties and the 2004 U.S. Presidential Election," *Journal of Politics* 69 (August 2007): 633–648.

[85]Exit Poll Data.

[86]Brad Lockerbie, "Prospective Voting in Presidential Elections, 1956–1988," *American Politics Quarterly* 20 (July 1992): 308–325.

[87]Michael B. MacKuen, Robert S. Erikson, and James A. Stimson, "Peasants or Bankers? The American Electorate and the U.S. Economy," *American Political Science Review* 86 (September 1992): 597–611.

Chapter 12

[1]Karen Tumulty and Kate Pickert with Alice Park, "America, The Doctor Will See You Know," *Time*, April 5, 2010, pp. 24–32.

[2]Charles B. Cushman, Jr., *An Introduction to the U.S. Congress* (Armonk, NY: M.E. Sharpe, 2006), p. 5.

[3]Robert V. Remini, *The House: The History of the House of Representatives* (New York, NY: HarperCollins, 2006), p. 496.

[4]Mildred Amer and Jennifer E. Manning, "Membership in the 111th Congress: A Profile," Congressional Research Service, December 31, 2008, available at http://assets.opencrs.com.

[5]Donald R. Matthews, *U.S. Senators and Their World* (New York, NY: Vintage Books, 1960), pp. 116–117.

[6]Burdett Loomis, *The New American Politician: Ambition, Entrepreneurship, and the Changing Face of Political Life* (New York, NY: Basic Books, 1988), pp. 233–244.

[7]Quoted in Michael Scherer and Jay Newton-Small, "Welcome to the Fun House," *Time*, November 9, 2009, p. 41.

[8]Center for Responsive Politics, available at www.opensecrets.org.

[9]Brandice Canes-Wrone, David W. Brady, and John F. Cogan, "Out of Step, Out of Office: Electoral Accountability and House Members' Voting," *American Political Science Review* 96 (March 2002): 127–140.

[10]Sally Friedman, *Dilemmas of Representation: Local Politics, National Factors, and the Home Styles of Modern U.S. Congress Members* (Albany, NY: State University of New York Press, 2007), pp. 223–225.

[11]Richard F. Fenno, *Home Style* (Boston, MA: Little, Brown, 1978), p. 18.

[12]Richard G. Forgette, *Congress, Parties, and Puzzles: Politics as a Team Sport* (New York, NY: Peter Lang, 2004), p. 174.

[13]Lydia Saad, "By Slim Margin, Americans Support Healthcare Bill's Passage," Gallup, March 23, 2010, available at www.gallup.com.

[14]Michael H. Murekami, "Divisive Primaries: Party Organizations, Ideological Groups, and the Battle Over Party Unity," *PS: Political Science & Politics*, October 2008, pp. 918–923.

[15]Center for Responsive Politics, available at www.opensecrets.org.

[16]John R. Hibbing and Christopher W. Larimer, "What the American Public Wants Congress to Be," in Lawrence C. Dodd and Bruce I. Oppenheimer, eds., *Congress Reconsidered*, 8th ed. (Washington, DC: CQ Press, 2005), p. 63.

[17]"Membership of the 111th Congress: A Profile."

[18]Rebekah Herrick and Samuel H. Fisher III, *Representing America: The Citizen and the Professional Legislator in the House of Representatives* (Lanham, MD: Lexington Books, 2007), pp. 93–96.

[19]Kristin Kanthak, "Crystal Elephants and Committee Chairs: Campaign Contributions and Leadership Races in the U.S. House of Representatives," *American Politics Research* 35 (May 2007): 389–406.

[20]Center for Responsive Politics, available at www.opensecrets.org.

[21]Gary W. Cox and Mathew D. McCubbins, *Setting the Agenda: Responsible Party Government in the U.S. House of Representatives* (New York, NY: Cambridge University Press, 2005), pp. 1–9.

[22]Gary W. Cox and Mathew D. McCubbins, *Legislative Leviathan: Party Government in the House*, 2nd ed. (New York, NY: Cambridge University Press, 2007), pp. 256–257.

[23]Eric S. Heberlig and Bruce A. Larson, "Party Fundraising, Descriptive Representation, and the Battle for Majority Control: Shifting Leadership Appointment Strategies in the U.S. House of Representatives, 1990–2002," *Social Science Quarterly* 88 (June 2007): 404–421.

[24]Barbara Sinclair, "The New Role of U.S. Senators," in Dodd and Oppenheimer, eds., *Congress Reconsidered*, 8th ed., p. 5.

[25]Laura W. Arnold, "The Distribution of Senate Committee Positions: Change or More of the Same?" *Legislative Studies Quarterly* 26 (May 2001): 227–248.

[26]Scott A. Frisch and Sean Q. Kelly, *Committee Assignment Politics in the U.S. House of Representatives* (Norman, OK: University of Oklahoma Press, 2006), pp. 328–330.

[27]Paul R. Brewer and Christopher J. Deering, "Musical Chairs: Interest Groups, Campaign Fund-Raising, and Selection of House Committee Chairs," in Paul S. Herrnson, Ronald G. Shaiko, and Clyde Wilcox, eds., *The Interest Group Connection: Electioneering, Lobbying, and Policymaking in Washington*, 2nd ed. (Washington, DC: CQ Press, 2005), pp. 141–146.

[28]Jeff Zeleny, "Of Party Dues and Deadbeats on Capitol Hill," *New York Times*, October 1, 2006, available at www.nytimes.com.

[29]Health Canada, available at www.hc-sc.gc.ca.

[30]Gerard W. Boychuk, *National Health Insurance in the United States and Canada* (Washington, DC: Georgetown University Press, 2008), pp. 3–21.

[31]Barbara Sinclair, *Unorthodox Lawmaking: New Legislative Processes in the U.S. Congress*, 3rd ed. (Washington, DC: Congressional Quarterly Press, 2007), pp. 5–8.

[32]Congressional Record, Daily Digest, "Résumé of Congressional Activity, 110th Congress," available at www.senate.gov/reference/resources/pdf/110_1.pdf.

[33]Roger H. Davidson and Walter J. Oleszek, *Congress and Its Members*, 7th ed. (Washington, DC: CQ Press, 2000), p. 31.

[34]Steven Brill, "On Sale: Your Government. Why Lobbying Is Washington's Best Bargain," *Time*, July 12, 2010, p. 32.

[35]"Résumé of Congressional Activity, 110th Congress."

[36]John Baughman, *Common Ground: Committee Politics in the U.S. House of Representatives* (Stanford, CA: Stanford University Press, 2006), pp. 175–179.

[37]Sinclair, *Unorthodox Lawmaking*, p. 12.

[38]"Résumé of Congressional Activity, 110th Congress."

[39]Davidson and Oleszek, *Congress and Its Members*, 7th ed. p. 242.

[40]Sinclair, *Unorthodox Lawmaking*, p. 19.

[41]Matthew Green and Daniel Burns, "What Might Bring Regular Order Back to the House?" *PS: Political Science & Politics*, April 2010, pp. 223–226.

[42]Ibid., p. 22.

[43]Ibid., p. 32.

[44]Thomas E. Mann and Norman J. Ornstein, *The Broken Branch: How Congress Is Failing America and How to Get It Back on Tract* (New York, NY: Oxford University Press, 2006), p. 170.

[45]John D. Wilerson, "'Killer' Amendments in Congress," *American Political Science Review* 93 (September 1999): 535–552.

[46]Charles J. Finocchiaro and Jeffery A. Jenkins, "In Search of Killer Amendments in the Modern U.S. House," *Legislative Studies Quarterly* 33 (May 2008): 263–294.

[47]Gregory J. Wawro and Eric Schickler, *Filibuster: Obstruction and Lawmaking in the U.S. Senate* (Princeton, NJ: Princeton University Press, 2006), pp. 13–14.

[48]Christopher J. Deering, "Leadership in the Slow Lane," *PS: Policy and Politics* (Winter 1986): 37–42; Bruce I. Oppenheimer,

"Changing Time Constraints on Congress: Historical Perspectives on the Use of Cloture." in Lawrence C. Dodd and Bruce I. Oppenheimer, eds., *Congress Reconsidered*, 4th ed. (Washington, DC: Congressional Quarterly Press, 1989), pp. 393–413.

[49]Sinclair, *Unorthodox Lawmaking*, p. 69.

[50]Peter Beinart, "Why Washington's Tied Up in Knots," *Time*, March 1, 2010, p. 23.

[51]Carl Hulse, "Ryan Defends Medicare Proposal," New York Times, May 16, 2001, available at www.nytimes.com.

[52]"Opposition to Ryan Medicare Plan from Older, Attentive Americans," Pew Research Center for the People & the Press, June 6, 2011, available at http://pewresearch.org.

[53]Sinclair, *Unorthodox Lawmaking*, p. 76.

[54]Jeffrey Lazarus and Nathan W. Monroe, "The Speaker's Discretion: Conference Committee Appointments in the 97th through 106th Congresses," *Political Research Quarterly* 60 (December 2007): 593–606.

[55]Sheldon Whitehouse, "Whitehouse Decries GOP Tactics in Health Care Debate," December 20, 2009, available at www.whitehouse.senate.gov.

[56]Samuel B. Hoff, "Saying No: Presidential Support and Veto Use, 1889–1989," *American Politics Quarterly* 19 (July 1991): 317.

[57]Based on the data included in John Woolley and Gerhard Peters, "The American Presidency Project."

[58]Dan Morgan, "Along for the Rider," *Washington Post National Weekly Edition*, August 19–25, 2002, p. 15.

[59]"Résumé of Congressional Activity, 110th Congress."

[60]Sinclair, *Unorthodox Lawmaking*, p. 272.

Chapter 13

[1]Michael J. Gerhardt, *The Federal Impeachment Process: A Constitutional and Historical Analysis* (Princeton, NJ: Princeton University Press, 1995), p. 105.

[2]Quoted in Michael Nelson, "Choosing the Vice President," *PS: Political Science & Politics* (Fall 1988): 859.

[3]Jody C. Baumgartner, *The American Vice Presidency Reconsidered* (Westport, CT: Praeger, 2006), p. 133.

[4]Joel K. Goldstein, "The Rising Power of the Modern Vice Presidency," *Presidential Studies Quarterly* 38 (September 2008): 374–389.

[5]Harold J. Krent, *Presidential Powers* (New York, NY: New York University Press, 2005), pp. 215–216.

[6]Ryan J. Barilleaux, "Venture Constitutionalism and the Enlargement of the Presidency," in Christopher S. Kelley, *Executing the Constitution: Putting the President Back Into the Constitution* (Albany, NY: State University of New York, 2206), pp. 40–42.

[7]"Learning About the Senate: Treaties," available at www.senate.gov.

[8]Ibid.

[9]*Korematsu v. United States*, 323 U.S. 214 (1944).

[10]Public Law 93-148 (1973).

[11]*Immigration and Naturalization Service (INS) v. Chadha*, 462 U.S. 919 (1983).

[12]Bruce Ackerman and Oona Hathaway, "Death of the War Powers Act?" *Washington Post*, May 17, 2011, available at www.washingtonpost.com.

[13]Robert Kennedy, *The Road to War: Congress' Historic Abdication of Responsibility* (New York: Praeger, 2010), pp. 132–134.

[14]Louis Fisher, "The Scope of Inherent Powers," in Edwards and King, *The Polarized Presidency of George W. Bush*, p. 53.

[15]*Hamdi v. Rumsfeld*, 542 U.S. 507 (2004).

[16]*Hamdan v. Rumsfeld*, 548 U.S. 557 (2006).

[17]*Boumediene v. Bush*, 553 U.S. 723 (2008).

[18]Administrative Office of the U.S. Courts, "Federal Judicial Vacancies," available at www.uscourts.gov.

[19]*Youngstown Sheet and Tube Co. v. Sawyer*, 343 U.S. 579 (1952).

[20]Donna R. Hoffman and Alison D. Howard, *Addressing the State of the Union: The Evolution and Impact of the President's Big Speech* (Boulder, CO: Lynne Rienner, 2006), p. 194.

[21]Harold W. Stanley and Richard G. Niemi, *Vital Statistics on American Politics 2007–2008* (Washington, DC: CQ Press, 2008), p. 268.

[22]Rebecca A. Deen and Laura W. Arnold, "Veto Threats as a Policy Tool: When to Threaten?" *Presidential Studies Quarterly* 32 (March 2002): 30–45.

[23]Charlie Savage, "Obama's Embrace of a Bush Tactic Riles Congress," *New York Times*, August 8, 2009, available at www.nytimes.com.

[24]Phillip J. Cooper, "George W. Bush, Edgar Allan Poe, and the Use and Abuse of Presidential Signing Statements," *Presidential Studies Quarterly* 35 (September 2005): 515–532.

[25]Robert Pear, "Legal Group Faults Bush for Ignoring Parts of Bills," *New York Times*, July 24, 2006, available at www.nytimes.com.

[26]Curtis A. Bradley and Eric A. Posner, "Presidential Signing Statements and Executive Power," *Constitutional Commentary* 23 (Winter 2006): 307–364.

[27]Nolan McCarty, "Presidential Vetoes in the Early Republic: Changing Constituitonal Norms or Electoral Reform?" *Journal of Politics* 71 (April 2009): 369–384.

[28]Michael A. Sollenberger, *Presidential Vetoes, 1789–Present: A Summary Overview*, Congressional Research Service, available at www.house.gov.

[29]Kevan M. Yenerall, "Executing the Rhetorical Presidency: William Jefferson Clinton, George. W. Bush, and the Contemporary Face of Presidential Power," in Kelly, *Executing the Constitution*, pp. 132–133.

[30]M. Steven Fish, *Democracy Derailed in Russia: The Failure of Open Politics* (New York, NY: Cambridge University Press, 2005), pp. 30–80.

[31]Clifford J. Levy, "With Tight Grip on Ballot, Putin Is Forcing Foes Out," *New York Times*, October 14, 2007, available at www.nytimes.com.

[32]Matthew Crenson and Benjamin Ginsberg, *Presidential Power: Unchecked and Unbalanced* (New York, NY: W.W. Norton, 2007), pp. 11–13.

[33]Richard M. Skinner, "The Partisan Presidency," in John C. Green and Daniel J. Coffey, eds., *The State of the Parties*, 5th ed. (Lanham, MD: Rowman & Littlefield, 2007), pp. 331–341.

[34]John P. Burke, "The Institutional Presidency," in Michael Nelson, ed., *The Presidency and the Political System*, 8th ed. (Washington, DC: CQ Press, 2006), p. 386.

[35]Matthew J. Dickinson and Matthew J. Lebo, "Reexamining the Growth of the Institutional Presidency, 1940–2000," *Journal of Politics* 69 (February 2007): 206–219.

[36]Matthew J. Dickinson, "The Executive Office of the President: The Paradox of Politicization," in Aberbach and Peterson, eds., *The Executive Branch*, p. 154.

[37]The Executive Office of the President, available at www.whitehouse.gov/administration/eop.

[38]Dickinson and Lebo, "Reexamining the Growth of the Institutional Presidency, 1940–2000," pp. 206–219.

[39]Paul J. Quirk, "Presidential Competence," in Nelson, *The Presidency and the Political System*, 8th ed., pp. 156–158.

[40]Ibid., pp. 179–89.

[41]James. P. Pfiffner, "Intelligence and Decision Making Before the War with Iraq," in Edwards and King, *The Polarized Presidency of George W. Bush*, p. 235.

[42]James David Barber, *The Presidential Character*, 4th ed. (Englewood Cliffs, NJ: Prentice-Hall, 1992); "Carter and Reagan: Clues to Their Character," *U.S. News & World Report*, October 27, 1980, pp. 30–33.

[43]Michael Nelson, "The Psychological Presidency," in Nelson, ed., *The Presidency and the Political System*, 8th ed., pp. 170–194.

[44]Fred I. Greenstein (2009) "The Leadership Style of Barack Obama: An Early Assessment," *The Forum*: Vol. 7: Iss. 1, Article 6.

[45]Fred I. Greenstein, *The Presidential Difference: Leadership Style from FDR to Barack Obama*, 3rd ed. (Princeton, NJ: Princeton University Press, 2009).

[46]Richard E. Neustadt, *Presidential Power: The Politics of Leadership* (New York, NY: Wiley, 1980).

[47]Samuel Kernell, *Going Public: New Strategies of Presidential Leadership*, 3rd ed. (Washington, DC: Congressional Quarterly Press, 1997).

[48]Joseph A. Pike and John Anthony Maltese, *The Politics of the Presidency*, 6th ed. (Washington, DC: CQ Press, 2004), p. 118.

[49]Scott B. Blinder, "Going Public, Going to Baghdad: Presidential Agenda-Setting and the Electoral Connection in Congress," in Edwards and King, eds., *The Polarized Presidency of George W. Bush*, pp. 336–344.

[50]Brandice Canes-Wrone, *Who Leads Whom? Presidents, Policy, and the Public* (Chicago, IL: University of Chicago Pres, 2006), p. 185.

[51]Kelly, *Executing the Constitution*, pp. 4–5.

[52]Steven A. Shull, *Policy by Other Means: Alternative Adoption by Presidents* (College Station, TX: Texas A&M University Press, 2006), pp. 30–35.

[53]Ryan C. Black, Anthony J. Madonna, Ryan J. Owens, and Michael S. Lynch, "Adding Recess Appointments to the President's 'Tool Chest' of Unilateral Powers," *Political Research Quarterly* 60 (December 2007): 645–654.

[54]Raymond Tatalovich and Alan R. Gitelson, "Political Party Linkages to Presidential Popularity: Assessing the 'Coalition of Minorities' Thesis," *Journal of Politics* 52 (February 1990): 241.

[55]Jeffrey M. Jones, "Obama Honeymoon Continues; 7 Months is Recent Average," July 3, 2009, available at www.gallup.com.

[56]John E. Mueller, *War, Presidents, and Public Opinion* (New York, NY: Wiley, 1973), p. 208.

[57]Ibid., p. 212.

[58]Jeffrey M. Jones, "Bush's High Approval Ratings Among Most Sustained for Presidents," *Gallup Poll Monthly*, November 2001, p. 32.

[59]William D. Baker and John R. O'Neal, "Patriotism or Opinion Leadership? The Nature and Origins of the 'Rally 'round the Flag' Effect," *Journal of Conflict Resolution* 45 (October 2001): 661–687.

[60]Richard Brody, "International Crises: A Rallying Point for the President?" *Public Opinion*, December/January 1984, pp. 41–43, 60.

[61]Marc J. Hetherington and Michael Nelson, "Anatomy of a Rally Effect: George W. Bush and the War on Terrorism," *PS: Political Science & Politics* (January 2003): 37–42.

[62]Gallup Poll, "Presidential Job Approval in Depth," available at www.gallup.com.

[63]*Gallup Poll Monthly*, June 1991, p. 27.

[64]Frank Newport, "Bush Job Approval Update," Gallup News Service, July 29, 2002, available at www.gallup.com.

[65]Charlie Savage, "Bush Challenges Hundreds of Laws," *Boston Globe*, April 30, 2006, available at www.boston.com.

Chapter 14

[1]Food and Drug Administration, "Cigarette Health Warnings," available at www.fda.gov.

[2]Betsy McKay and David Kesmodel, "Labels Give Cigarette Packs a Ghoulish Makeover," Wall Street Journal, June 22, 2011, available at http://wsj.com.

[3]U.S. Census Bureau, "Federal Civilian Employment by Branch and Agency," *The 2009 Statistical Abstract*, available at www.census.gov.

[4]G. Calvin MacKenzie, "The Real Invisible Hand: Presidential Appointees in the Administration of George W. Bush," *PS: Political Science & Politics*, March 2002, p. 28.

[5]Paul C. Light, "Late for Their Appointments," *New York Times*, November 16, 2004, available at www.nytimes.com.

[6]Nolan McCarty and Rose Razaghian, "Advice and Consent: Senate Responses to Executive Branch Nominations, 1885–1996," *American Journal of Political Science* 43 (October 1999): 1122–1143.

[7]Scott Wilson and Ed O'Keefe, "Administration Faults GOP Tactic of Blocking Presidential Appointments," *Washington Post*, February 5, 2010, available at www.washingtonpost.com.

[8]Manu Raju, "Reid Ready to Play at Recess," February 7, 2010, available at www.politico.com.

[9]Peter Baker, "How Obama Came to Plan for 'Surge' in Afghanistan," *New York Times*, December 6, 2009, available at www.nytimes.com.

[10]Joseph A. Pika and John Anthony Maltese, *The Politics of the Presidency*, 6th ed. (Washington, DC: CQ Press, 2004), p. 230.

[11]Jonathan G. S. Koppel, *The Politics of Quasi-Government* (New York: NY: Cambridge University Press, 2003), pp. 187–195.

[12]"Federal Civilian Employment, by Branch and Agency: 1990 to 2006," *Statistical Abstract of the United States 2000.*

[13]Paul C. Light, "The New True Size of Government," Robert F. Wagner Graduate School, New York University, available at http://wagner.nyu.edu.

[14]Scott Shane and Ron Nixon, "In Washington, Contractors Take on Biggest Role Ever," *New York Times*, February 4, 2007, available at www.nytimes.com.

[15]O. Glenn Stahl, *Public Personnel Administration*, 8th ed. (New York, NY: Harper & Row, 1983), p. 42.

[16]Joel D. Aberbach and Bert A. Rockman, "Senior Executives in a Changing Political Environment," in James P. Pfiffner and Douglas A. Brook, eds., *The Future of Merit: Twenty Years After the Civil Service Reform Act* (Washington, DC: Woodrow Wilson Center Press, 2000), pp. 81–97.

[17]Joel D. Aberbach and Bert A. Rockman, "Senior Executives in a Changing Political Environment," in James P. Pfiffner and Douglas A. Brook, eds., *The Future of Merit: Twenty Years After the Civil Service Reform Act* (Washington, DC: Woodrow Wilson Center Press, 2000), pp. 81–97.

[18]James R. Thompson, "Federal Labor-Management Relations Under George W. Bush: Enlightened Management or Political Retribution?" in James S. Bowman and Jonathan P. West, eds., *American Public Service: Radical Reform and the Merit System* (Boca Raton, FL: RC Press, 2007), p. 240.

[19]Christopher Lee, "An Overhaul, Not a Tune-Up," *Washington Post National Weekly Edition*, June 16–22, 2003, p. 30.

[20]Ann Gerhart, "Homeland Insecurity," *Washington Post National Weekly Edition*, April 4–10, 2005, pp. 6–7.

[21]2010 Defense Authorization Act, Public Law 111-84.

[22]Cornelius M. Kerwin, *Rulemaking: How Government Agencies Write Law and Make Policy*, 3rd ed. (Washington, DC: CQ Press, 2003), p. 21.

[23]Alana S. Knaster and Philip J. Harter, "The Clean Fuels Regulatory Negotiation," *Intergovernmental Perspective* (Summer 1992): 20–22. *Intergovernmental Perspective* (Summer 1992): 20–22).]

[24]Terry M. Moe, "The Presidency and the Bureaucracy: The Presidential Advantage," in Michael Nelson, ed., *The Presidency and the Political System*, 6th ed. (Washington, DC: CQ Press, 2000), pp. 465–468.

[25]Alan B. Morrison, "Close Reins on the Bureaucracy: Overseeing the Administrative Agencies," in Herman Schwartz, ed., *The Burger Years* (New York, NY: Viking, 1987), pp. 191–205.

[26]Ron Duhl, "Carter Issues an Order, But Is Anybody Listening?" *National Journal*, June 14, 1979, pp. 1156–1158.

[27]Robert Pear, "Bush Directive Increases Sway on Regulation," *New York Times*, January 30, 2007, available at www.nytimes.com.

[28]Marissa Martino Golden, *What Motivates Bureaucrats? Politics and Administration during the Reagan Years* (New York, NY: Columbia University Press, 2000), pp. 152–159.

[29]B. Dan Wood, "Principals, Bureaucrats, and Responsiveness in Clean Air Enforcement," *American Political Science Review* 82 (March 1988): 218.

[30]Kay Lehrman Schlozman and John T. Tierney, *Organized Interests and American Democracy* (New York, NY: Harper & Row, 1986), p. 353.

[31]Joseph Cooper and William F. West, "Presidential Power and Republican Government: The Theory and Practice of OMB Review of Agency Rules," *Journal of Politics* 50 (November 1988): 864–895.

[32]Ibid., p. 811.

[33]Ibid., pp. 806–807, 818–821.

[34]Edward Wyatt, "House Panel Challenges Smithsonian," *New York Times*, May 11, 2006, available at www.nytimes.com.

[35]Michael D. Reagan and John G. Salzone, *The New Federalism*, 2nd ed. (New York: Oxford University Press, 1981), chap. 3.

[36]Schlozman and Tierney, *Organized Interests and American Democracy*, pp. 341–346.

[37]Terry M. Moe, "Control and Feedback in Economic Regulation: The Case of the NLRB," *American Political Science Review* 79 (December 1985): 1094–1116; Jeffrey E. Cohen, "The Dynamics of the 'Revolving Door' on the FCC," *American Journal of Political Science* 30 (November 1986): 689–708.

[38]Frank Keegan, "Public Pensions: $700 Billion 'Problem' or $3 Trillion 'Crisis?'" March 29, 2011, available at http://statehousenewsonline.com.

[39]BBC, "China to Ban Smoking in Public Places," March 24, 2011, available at http://news.bbc.co.uk.

[40] Benjamin Haas, "China Smoking Ban May Have Little Effect," Los Angeles Times, April 30, 2011, available at http://articles.latimes.com.

[41]William Wan, "In China, Battling State-Owned Big Tobacco," The Star, July 4, 2011, available at www.star.com.jo.

[42]William Wan, "China's Anti-Smoking Activists Try a New Argument: That It's Bad for the Economy," Washington Post, June 26, 2011, available at www.washingtonpost.com.

[43]Steven P. Croley, *Regulation and Public Interests: The Possibility of Good Regulatory Government* (Princeton, NJ: Princeton University Press, 2008), pp. 214–230.

[44]Colin Campbell, "The Complex Organization of the Executive Branch: The Legacies of Competing Approaches to Administration," in Joel D. Aberbach and Mark A. Peterson, eds., *The Executive Branch* (New York, NY: Oxford University Press, 2005), p. 254.

[45]Dennis D. Riley and Bryan E. Brophy-Baermann, *Bureaucracy and the Policy Process* (Lanham, MD: Rowman & Littlefield Publishers, 2006), p. 98.

[46]Jeffrey Kluger, "Space Pork," *Time*, July 24, 2000, pp. 24–26.

[47]Jeffrey M. Berry, "Subgovernments, Issue Networks, and Political Conflict," in Richard A. Harris and Sidney M. Milkis, *Remaking American Politics* (Boulder, CO: Westview Press, 1989), pp. 239–260.

[48]Hugh Heclo, "Issue Networks and the Executive Establishment," in Anthony King, ed., *The New American Political System*

(Washington, DC: American Enterprise Institute, 1978), pp. 87–124.

⁴⁹John R. Provan, "The Highway Trust Fund: Its Birth, Growth, and Survival," in Theodore W. Taylor, ed., *Federal Public Policy* (Mt. Airy, MD: Lomond Publications, 1984), pp. 221–258.

⁵⁰Jonathan Walters, "Revenge of the Highwaymen," *Governing*, September 1997, p. 13.

⁵¹"$1.6 Billion Went to Bailed Out Bank Execs," December 22, 2008, available at www.msnbc.msn.com.

Chapter 15

¹Paul Elias, "Betty Dukes, Wal-Mart Greeter, Leads Class Action Lawsuit," May 1, 2010, available at www.huffingtonpost.com.

²Jeffrey Toobin, "Betty Dukes v. Walmart," New Yorker, June 20, 2010, available at www.newyorker.com.

³Daniel Fisher, "Wal-Mart v. Dukes Asks Court to Fix the World," March 28, 2011, available at http://blogs.forbes.com.

⁴Walmart Stores v. Dukes, No. 10-277 (2011).

⁵Adam Serwer, "Walmart v. Dukes: The Difficulty of Proving the Old Boy Network Exists," American Prospect, June 20, 2011, available at http://prospect.org.

⁶Richard L. Pacelle, Jr., *The Role of the Supreme Court in American Politics: The Least Dangerous Branch* (Boulder, CO: Westview Press, 2002), p. 35.

⁷Harold W. Stanley and Richard G. Niemi, *Vital Statistics on American Politics 2007–2008* (Washington, DC: Congressional Quarterly Press, 2008), p. 301.

⁸Kermit Roosevelt III, *The Myth of Judicial Activism: Making Sense of Supreme Court Decisions* (New Haven, CT: Yale University Press, 2006), p. 3.

⁹Thomas M. Keck, *The Most Activist Supreme Court in History: The Road to Modern Judicial Conservatism* (Chicago, IL: University of Chicago Press, 2004), pp. 286–289.

¹⁰Robert A. Carp, Ronald Stidham, and Kenneth L. Manning, *Judicial Process in America*, 6th ed. (Washington, DC: Congressional Quarterly Press, 2004), p. 28.

¹¹*Marbury v. Madison*, 1 Cranch 137 (1803).

¹²*McCulloch v. Maryland*, 4 Wheaton 316 (1819).

¹³*Dred Scott v. Sandford*, 19 Howard 393 (1857).

¹⁴*Plessy v. Ferguson*, 163 U.S. 537 (1896).

¹⁵*Brown v. Board of Education of Topeka*, 347 U.S. 483 (1954).

¹⁶*Roe v. Wade*, 410 U.S. 113 (1973).

¹⁷*City of Richmond v. J. A. Croson Co.*, 488 U.S. 469 (1989).

¹⁸*Lee v. Weisman*, 505 U.S. 577 (1992).

¹⁹*Santa Fe School District v. Doe*, 530 U.S. 290 (2000).

²⁰*Lawrence v. Texas*, 539 U.S. 558 (2003).

²¹*Gratz v. Bollinger*, 539 U.S. 244 (2003).

²²*Grutter v. Bollinger*, 539 U.S. 306 (2003).

²³Adam Liptak, "Court Under Roberts Is Most Conservative in Decades," *New York Times*, July 24, 2010, available at www.nytimes.com.

²⁴*Gonzalez v. Carhart*, 550 U.S. 124 (2007).

²⁵*Kennedy v. Louisiana*, 554 U.S. ___(2008).

²⁶Carp, Stidham, and Manning, *Judicial Process in America*, pp. 43–44.

²⁷Karl Derouen, Jr., Jeffrey S. Peake, and Kenneth Ward, "Presidential Mandates and the Dynamics of Senate Advice and Consent, 1885–1996," *American Politics Research* 33 (January 2005): 106–131.

²⁸Cass R. Sunstein, David Schkade, Lisa M. Ellman, and Andres Sawicki, *Are Judges Political? An Empirical Analysis of the Federal Judiciary* (Washington, DC: Brookings Institution, 2006), pp. 147–149.

²⁹Ibid., p. 141.

³⁰Ibid., p. 52.

³¹Ibid., p. 53.

³²Ashlyn Kuersten and Donald Songer, "Presidential Success through Appointments to the United States Courts of Appeal," *American Politics Research* 31 (March 2003): 119.

³³Michael W. Giles, Virginia A. Hettinger, and Todd Peppers, "Picking Federal Judges: A Note on Policy and Partisan Selection Agendas," *Political Research Quarterly* 54 (September 2001): 623–641.

³⁴David C. Nixon and David L. Gross, "Confirmation Delay for Vacancies on the Circuit Courts of Appeal," *American Politics Research* 29 (May 2001): 246–274.

³⁵John N. Paden, Muslim Civic Cultures and Conflict Resolution: The Challenge of Democratic Federalism in Nigeria (Washington, DC: Brookings Institution Press, 2005), pp. 139–174.

³⁶R. Jeffrey Smith, "Back-Bench Politics," *Washington Post National Weekly Edition*, December 15–21, 2008, p. 7.

³⁷Joan Biskupic, "Barely a Dent on the Bench," *Washington Post National Weekly Edition*, October 24–30, 1994, p. 31.

³⁸Charles Gardner Geyh, *When Courts and Congress Collide: The Struggle for Control of America's Judicial System* (Ann Arbor, MI: University of Michigan Press, 2006), p. 19.

³⁹Quoted in Henry J. Abraham, *Justices and Presidents: A Political History of Appointments to the Supreme Court* (New York, NY: Oxford University Press, 1974), p. 246.

⁴⁰Timothy R. Johnson and Jason M. Roberts, "Presidential Capital and the Supreme Court Confirmation Process," *Journal of Politics* 66 (August 2004): 663–683.

⁴¹Keith E. Whittington, "Presidents, Senates, and Failed Supreme Court Nominations," *2006 The Supreme Court Review* (Chicago, IL: University of Chicago Press, 2006), pp. 412–422.

⁴²John Massaro, *Supremely Political: The Role of Ideology and Presidential Management in Unsuccessful Supreme Court Nominations* (Albany, NY: State University of New York Press, 1990), p. 136.

⁴³Mark Silverstein, "Bill Clinton's Excellent Adventure: Political Development and the Modern Confirmation Process," in Howard Gillman and Cornell Clayton, eds., *The Supreme Court in American Politics: New Institutional Interpretation* (Lawrence, KS: University of Kansas Press, 1999), p. 145.

⁴⁴Linda Myers, "Law Professors Propose Term Limits for Supreme Court Justices," January 27, 2005, available at www.cornell.edu.

⁴⁵U.S. Supreme Court, "2009 Year-End Report on the Federal Judiciary," available at www.supremecourtus.gov.

⁴⁶Ibid.

[47]*Baker v. Carr*, 369 U.S. 186 (1962).

[48]Lee Epstein and Jack Knight, "Mapping Out the Strategic Terrain: The Informational Role of *Amici Curiae*," in Cornell W. Clayton and Howard Gillman, *Supreme Court Decision-Making, New Institutional Approaches* (Chicago, IL: University of Chicago Press, 1999), p. 229.

[49]Timothy R. Johnson, "Information, Oral Arguments, and Supreme Court Decision Making," *American Politics Research* 29 (July 2001): 331–351.

[50]Sarah A. Binder and Forrest Maltzman, "Congress and the Politics of Judicial Appointments," in Lawrence C. Dodd and Bruce I. Oppenheimer, *Congress Reconsidered*, 8th ed. (Washington, DC: CQ Press, 2205), pp. 302–305.

[51]*Furman v. Georgia*, 408 U.S. 238 (1972).

[52]Charles A. Johnson and Bradley C. Canon, *Judicial Policies: Implementation and Impact* (Washington, DC: Congressional Quarterly Press, 1984), ch. 1.

[53]Gerald N. Rosenberg, *The Hollow Hope: Can Courts Bring About Social Change?* (Chicago, IL: University of Chicago Press, 1991), pp. 336–338.

[54]*Tennessee Valley Authority v. Hill*, 437 U.S. 153 (1978).

[55]*Oregon v. Mitchell*, 400 U.S. 112 (1970).

[56]Carp, Stidham, and Manning, *Judicial Process in America*, p. 371.

[57]Kevin T. McGuire, "Public Schools, Religious Establishments, and the U.S. Supreme Court: An Examination of Policy Compliance," *American Politics Research* 37 (January 2009): 50-74.

[58]Robert Dahl, "Decision-Making in a Democracy: The Supreme Court as a National Policy-Maker," *Journal of Public Law* 6 (Fall 1957): 279–295.

[59]Johnson and Canon, *Judicial Policies*, pp. 231–232.

[60]Mark Silverstein and Benjamin Ginsberg, "The Supreme Court and the New Politics of Judicial Power," *Political Science Quarterly* 102 (Fall 1987): 371–388.

[61]Craig R. Ducat and Robert L. Dudley, "Federal District Judges and Presidential Power During the Postwar Era," *Journal of Politics* 51 (February 1989): 98–118.

[62]Jeffrey Rosen, *The Most Democratic Branch: How the Courts Serve America* (New York, NY: Oxford University Press, 2006), pp. 7–8.

Chapter 16

[1]Congressional Budget Office, available at www.cbo.gov.

[2]Congressional Budget Office, "Budget Projections," March 24, 2010, available at www.cbo.gov.

[3]"A New Era of Responsibility: The President's Budget, FY2010," available at www.whitehouse.gov.

[4]Randal R. Rucker and E. C. Pasour, Jr., "The Growth of U.S. Farm Programs," in Price V. Fishback, et. al., *Government & the American Economy: A New History* (Chicago, IL: University of Chicago Press, 2007), p. 483.

[5]David Leonhardt, "In Health Care Bill, Obama Attacks Wealth Inequality," *New York Times*, March 23, 2010, available at www.nytimes.com.

[6]Chris J. Dolan, John Frendreis, and Raymond Tatalovich, *The Presidency and Economic Policy* (Lanham, MD: Rowman & Littlefield, 2008), p. 3.

[7]Paul Krugman, "Averting the Worst," *New York Times*, August 10, 2009, available at www.nytimes.com.

[8]Office of Management and Budget, *Budget of the United States Government, Analytical Perspectives, Fiscal Year, 2011*, available at www.omb.gov.

[9]"A New Era of Responsibility: The President's Budget, FY2010," available at www.whitehouse.gov.

[10]U.S. Census Bureau, "Gross Public Debt, Expenditures, and Receipts by Country: 1990–2006," *The 2008 Statistical Abstract*, available at www.census.gov.

[11]Anthony J. Cataldo II and Arline A. Savage, *U.S. Individual Federal Income Taxation: Historical, Contemporary, and Prospective Policy Issues* (Oxford, UK: Elsevier Science, 2001), pp. 39–40.

[12]Shawn Tully, "VAT Trap: The Inevitable Fix for the Deficit," *Fortune*, February 10, 2010, available at www.cnnmoney.com.

[13]Congressional Budget Office, available at www.cbo.gov.

[14]David Leonhardt, "For U.S., a Sea of Perilous Red Ink, Years in the Making," *New York Times*, June 10, 2009, available at www.nytimes.com.

[15]U.S. Department of the Treasury, "Major Foreign Holders of U.S. Securities," available at www.ustreas.gov.

[16]Bureau of the Public Debt, available at www.treasurydirect.gov.

[17]Office of Management and Budget, *President's Budget: Historical Tables*.

[18]Robert H. Frank, "When 'Deficit' Isn't a Dirty Word," *New York Times*, March 22, 2009, available at www.nytimes.com.

[19]"Greece's Financial Crisis Explained," CNN, March 26, 2010, available at www.cnn.com.

[20]David McHugh, "Q & A on the Greek Debt Crisis," Bloomberg Businessweek, March 4, 2010, available at www.businessweek.com.

[21]"Greece's Austerity Measures," BBC, May 5, 2010, available at www. bbc.co.uk.

[22]Kate Connolly, "Greek Debt Crisis: The View from Germany," Guardian, February 11, 2010, available at www.guardian.co.uk.

[23]Robert J. Samuelson, "With Health Bill, Obama Has Sown the Seeds of a Budget Crisis," *Washington Post*, March 29, 2010, available at www.washingtonpost.com.

[24]Congressional Budget Office, "CBO's March 2008 Baseline: Medicare," available at www.cbo.gov.

[25]Centers for Medicare and Medicaid Services, available at www.cms.hhs.gov.

[26]Congressional Budget Office, "Budget Options," available at www.cbo.gov.

[27]*Social Security and Medicare Boards of Trustees 2009 Annual Reports*, available at www.ssa.gov.

[28]Ibid.

[29]Congressional Budget Office, "Fact Sheet for CBO's March 2009 Baseline: Medicaid," available at www.cbo.gov.

[30]Donald B. Marron, "Medicaid Spending Growth and Options for Controlling Costs," Testimony before the Senate Select Committee on Again, available at www.cbo.gov.

[31]"Social Security," Gallup Poll, available at www.gallup.com.

[32]John Buntin, "Dueling Diagnosis," *Governing*, February 2010, p. 24.

[33]Karen Tumulty and Kate Pickert with Alice Park, "America, The Doctor Will See You Know," *Time*, April 5, 2010, pp. 24–32.

[34]Social Security Administration, available at www.ssa.gov.

[35]Jesse J. Holland, "Raise Retirement Age to Save Social Security?" *Business Week*, August 1, 2008, available at www.businessweek.com.

[36]*Social Security and Medicare Boards of Trustees 2008 Annual Reports*.

[37]Social Security Administration, Trust Fund Data, available at www.ssa.gov.

[38]*Social Security and Medicare Boards of Trustees 2008 Annual Reports*.

[39]Mary Williams Walsh, "Social Security to See Payout Exceed Pay-in This Year," New York Times, March 24, 2010, available at www.nytimes.com.

[40]"Social Security History," Social Security Administration, available at www.ssa.gov.

[41]June O'Neill, "The Trust Fund, the Surplus, and the Real Social Security Problem," in Michael D. Tanner, ed., *Social Security and its Discontents: Perspectives on Choice* (Washington, DC: CATO Institute, 2004), pp. 37–38.

[42]William A. Kelso, *Poverty and the Underclass: Challenging Perceptions of the Poor in America* (New York, NY: New York University Press, 1994), p. 4.

[43]Robert Pear, "Welfare Spending Shows Huge Shift from Checks to Services," *New York Times*, October 13, 2003, available at www.nytimes.com.

[44]Congressional Budget Office, "The Budget and Economic Outlook: An Update," available at www.cbo.gov.

[45]Jason Deparle, "Welfare Aid Not Growing as Economy Drops Off," *New York Times*, February 2, 2009, available at www.nytimes.com.

[46]Roger H. Davidson and Walter J. Oleszek, *Congress and Its Members*, 7th ed. (Washington, DC: CQ Press, 2000), p. 372.

[47]Office of Management and Budget, *Budget of the United States Government, Fiscal Year 2009*.

[48]Interview with Ben Bernanke, *Time*, December 28, 2009–January 4, 2010, pp. 76–78.

[49]Michael Grunwald, "Ben Bernanke," *Time*, December 28, 2009–January 4, 2010, pp. 47–62.

[50]Sewell Chan, "Is Ben Bernanke Having Fun Yet?" *New York Times*, May 14, 2010, available at www.nytimes.com.

[51]Alan I. Abramowitz, "Can McCain Overcome the Triple Whammy?" May 29, 2008, Larry J. Sabato's Crystal Ball 2008, available at www.centerforpolitics.org.

[52]Jonathan Weisman, "Bush Puts the Kibosh on Lawmakers' Pet Projects—Later," *Washington Post National Weekly Edition*, February 4–10, 2008, p. 7.

[53]"The Debt to the Penny and Who Holds It," available at www.treasurydirect.gov.

[54]Ibid.

Chapter 17

[1]Borzou Daragahi, "Clinton Offers New Tactic in Iran Sanctions," *San Francisco Chronicle*, February 10, 2010, available at www.sfgate.com.

[2]Peter Beinart, "Shrinking the War on Terrorism," *Time*, December 14, 2009, pp. 42–45.

[3]Marcus Franda, *The United Nations in the Twenty-First Century: Management and Reform Processes in a Troubled Organization* (Lanham, MD: Rowman & Littlefield, 2006), p. 1.

[4]Robert Cooper, *The Postmodern State and the World Order* (London: Demos, 2000), p. 22.

[5]Courtney B. Smith, *Politics and Process at the United Nations: The Global Dance* (Boulder, CO: Lynne Rienner, 2006), p. 28.

[6]Elizabeth Becker, "Trade Talks Fail to Agree on Drugs for Poor Nations," *New York Times*, December 21, 2002, available at www.nytimes.com.

[7]Jonathan P. Doh and Hildy Teegan, *Globalization and NGOs: Transforming Business, Government, and Society* (Westport, CT: Praeger, 2003), pp. 3–9, 206–219.

[8]Terry L. Deibel, *Foreign Affairs Strategy: Logic for American Statecraft* (New York, NY: Cambridge University Press, 2007), p. 271.

[9]"United States Foreign Trade Highlights," International Trade Administration, U.S. Department of Commerce, available at www.ita.doc.gov.

[10]Marvin Zonis, "The 'Democracy Doctrine' of President George W. Bush," in Stanley A. Renshon and Peter Suedfeld, eds., *Understanding the Bush Doctrine: Psychology and Strategy in an Age of Terrorism* (New York, NY: Routledge, 2007), p. 232.

[11]Congressional Research Service, *Conventional Arms Transfers to Developing Nations, 1996–2003*, August 26, 2004, available at www.fas.org/man/crs.

[12]Celia W. Dugger, "U.S. Challenged to Increase Aid to Africa," *New York Times*, June 5, 2005, available at www.nytimes.com.

[13]U.S. Census Bureau, "U.S. Government Foreign Grants and Credits by Country: 2000–2008," *2010 Statistical Abstract*, available at www.census.gov.

[14]Philip J. Allen, ed., *Pitirim A. Sorokin in Review* (Durham, NC: Duke University Press, 1963).

[15]"Treaty on the Non-proliferation of Nuclear Weapons," available at www.un.org.

[16]Coil D. Blacker, "The New United States-Soviet Detente," *Current History* 88 (October 1989): 321–325, 357–359.

[17]The Failed States Index 2010, Foreign Policy, August 4, 2010, available at www.foreignpolicy.com.

[18]"Karl Rove Says Obama's Bow to Japanese Emperor Akihito was Inappropriate," Daunting Ideas, November 16, 2009, available at http://dauntingideas.com.

[19]John Johnson, "Obama Bows to Emperor," November 14, 2009, available at www.newser.com.

[20]Michael Scherer, "The Deference Debate," *Time*, November 30, 2009, p. 18.

[21]Robert J. Lieber, *Eagle Rules? Foreign Policy and American Primacy in the Twenty-First Century* (Upper Saddle River, NJ: Pearson, 2002), pp. 5–6.

[22]Stanley A. Renshon, "The Bush Doctrine Reconsidered," in Renshon and Suedfeld, eds., *Understanding the Bush Doctrine*, p. 2.

[23]Quoted in G. John Ikenberry, "Is American Multilateralism in Decline?" *Perspectives on Politics* 1 (September 2003): 534.

[24]Peter Beinart, "Shrinking the War on Terrorism," *Time*, December 14, 2009, pp. 42–45.

[25]*Time*, July 13, 2009, p. 14.

[26]Isaiah Wilson III, "What Weapons Do They Have and What Can They Do?" *PS: Political Science & Politics* (July 2007): 473.

[27]Peter Baker and Dan Bilefsky, "Russia and U.S. Sign Nuclear Arms Reduction Pact," *New York Times*, April 8, 2010, available at www.nytimes.com.

[28]David E. Sanger and Thom Shanker, "White House Is Rethinking Nuclear Policy," *New York Times*, February 28, 2010, available at www.nytimes.com.

[29]David E. Sanger and Thom Shanker, "U.S. Faces Choice on New Weapons for Fast Strikes," *New York Times*, April 22, 2010, available at www.nytimes.com.

[30]Willie Curtis, "Illusionary Promises and Strategic Reality: Rethinking the Implications of Strategic Deterrence in a Post 9/11 World," in Renshon and Suedfeld, eds., *Understanding the Bush Doctrine*, pp. 133–143.

[31]David E. Sanger. "Obama's Nuclear Strategy Intended as a Message," *New York Times*, April 6, 2010, available at www.nytimes.com.

[32]David Albright, "Securing Pakistan's Nuclear Weapons Complex," Institute for Science and International Security, October 2001, available at www.isis-online.org/publications/terrorism/stanleypaper.html.

[33]Farzana Shaikh, "Pakistan's Nuclear Bomb: Beyond the Non-Proliferation Regime," *International Affairs* 78 (January 2002): 29-48.

[34]David E. Sanger. "Obama's Nuclear Strategy Intended as a Message," *New York Times*, April 6, 2010, available at www.nytimes.com.

[35]Steven Mufson, "Rogue States: A Real Threat?" *Washington Post National Weekly Edition*, June 12, 2000, p. 15.

[36]John Dumbrell, "The Bush Doctrine," in George C. Edwards III and Philip John Davies, *New Challenges for the American Presidency* (New York: Longman, 2004), pp. 232–234.

[37]ThomE. Ricks, "A New Way of War," *Washington Post National Weekly Edition*, December 10–16, 2001, p. 6.

[38]Richard Morin, "A Gap in Worldviews," *Washington Post National Weekly Edition*, April 19, 1999, p. 34.

[39]Cecil V. Crabb, Jr., Glenn J. Antizzo, and Leila E. Serieddine, *Congress and the Foreign Policy Process* (Baton Rouge, LA: Louisiana State University Press, 2000), p. 189.

[40]James Meernik, "Presidential Support in Congress: Conflict and Consensus on Foreign and Defense Policy," *Journal of Politics* 55 (August 1993): 569–87.

[41]Robert S. Litwak, *Regime Change: U.S. Strategy Through the Prism of 9/11* (Baltimore, MD: Johns Hopkins University Press, 2007), p. 48.

[42]"Service Members Legal Defense Network, "About Don't Ask Don't Tell,'"available at www.sldn.org.

PHOTO CREDITS

Table of Contents:
v: nico_blue /iStockphoto; vi: (tl) AP Photo/Gerald Herbert; (tc): Jim Goldstein/ Danita Delimont/Alamy; (tr) AP Photo/Paul Sakuma; vii: (tl) SAUL LOEB/ AFP/Getty Images; (tc) Donna Abu-Nasr/AP Photo; (tr) Jeff Greenberg/The Image Works; viii: (tl) Bill Clark/Roll Call/Getty Images; (tc) AP Photo/Cliff Owen; (tr) Dave Einsel/Getty Images; ix: (tl) YURI GRIPAS/Reuters/Landov; (tc) P-59 Photos/Alamy; (tr) Exactostock / SuperStock; x: (tl) Joe Raedle/News-makers/Getty Images; (tc) Getty Images; (tr) Getty Images.

Introduction
2–3 Jim West / Alamy; 4 Bill Fritsch/Brand X/Corbis; 7 AP Photo/Gerald Herbert.

Chapter 1
10–12 Jim Goldstein/Danita Delimont/Alamy; 12 Solus-Veer/Corbis; 14 Judy Ben Joud/Shutterstock; 15 Justin Sullivan/Getty Images; 16 Cedric Joubert/AP Photo; 17 Damian Dovarganes/AP Photo; 18 Rolf Haid/dpa/Landov; 19 Greg Baker/AP Photo; 20 (tl) Kevin Lee/Bloomberg/Getty Images; (br) Tim Boyle/Getty Images; 22 Bill Pugliano/Getty Images; 26–27 AP Photo/Alex Brandon.

Chapter 2
28 The Colonial Williamsburg Foundation; 29 (tr) Mike Bentley/iStockphoto; (b) AP Photo/Paul Sakuma; 30 Mario Perez / ABC / Everett Collection; 32 Stock Montage/Hulton Archive/Getty Images; 34 ANDY RAIN/EPA/Landov; 37 Craig Brewer/Photodisc/ Jupiter images; 38 (tl) Hulton Archive/Getty Images; (tr) AP Photo; 40 Afton Almaraz/AP Photo; 41 Public Domain.

Chapter 3
46–47 Jack Kurtz/ZUMA Press/Newscom; 49 Brooks Kraft/Corbis News/ Corbis; 50 Kuttig-People/Alamy; 54 (bl) Photos.com; (br) Yellowj/Shutterstock; 56 Justin Sullivan/Getty Images; 58 Pakhnyushcha/Shutterstock.

Chapter 4
62–63 Noah Addis/Corbis; 65 Nancy Kaszerman/ZUMA Press/Newscom; 66 (l) Bob Daemmrich/Corbis; 66 (r) Bob Daemmrich/Corbis; 67 UPI/Monika Graff/ Landov; 68 Christina Dicken/Chronicle-Tribune/AP Photo; 70 KARL-JOSEF HILDENBRAND/dpa/Landov; 71 Susan Steinkamp/CORBIS; 72 Stephane Cardinale/Sygma/Corbis; 73 AP Photo/Evan Vucci; 79 PAUL BUCK/AFP/ Getty Images; 80 (tl) Northwestern University Library [http://www.library.northwestern.edu/govpub/collections/wwii-posters/img/ww1646-72]; (br) SAUL LOEB/AFP/Getty Images; 81 AP Photo/Don Heupel.

Chapter 5
84–85 Blend Images/Hill Street Studios/Getty Images; 87 Time & Life Pictures/ Getty Images; 88 Bettmann/Corbis; 89 Andersen Ross/Blend Images/ PhotoLibrary; 90 Antonio Nava/Landov; 91 (t) AP Photo/Emilio Morenatti; (b) Donna Abu-Nasr/AP Photo; 92 Bettman/Corbis; 93 (bl) North Wind Picture Archives; (br) Hulton Archive/Getty Images; (t) Hulton Archive/Getty Images; 94 Bettman/Corbis; 96 Andy Mead/Icon SMI/Corbis; 99 Steph Goralnick/ Flickr/Getty Images; 100 AP Photo/Paul Sancya.

Chapter 6
104–105 ilker canikligil/Shutterstock; 107 Michael Newman/Photo Edit; 108 John Sundlof/Alamy; 108 John Sundlof/Alamy; 110 Jeff Siner/The Charlotte Observer/AP Photo; 111 (bl) Mitchell Gerber/CORBIS; (t) Stockbyte/Getty Images; 113 (t) Underwood Archives/Alamy; (b) SHAH MARAI/AFP/Getty Images; 116 w86/ZUMA Press/Newscom; 117 Izzy Schwartz/Photdisc/Getty Images; 118 Bettmann/CORBIS; 119 CORBIS; 121 Pete Stone/CORBIS; 122 Digital Vision/Getty Images; 124 SvenMartson / The Image Works.

Chapter 7
128–129 Frederic Larson/San Francisco Chronicle/Corbis; 130 Douglas McFadd/Stringer/Getty Images News/Getty Images; 131 Bill Clark/Roll Call/Getty Images; 132 (b) MR. MONOPOLY © 1935, 2011 Hasbro. All Rights Reserved; 132 (t) Paul Hawthorne/Getty Images; 133 Andresr/Shutterstock; 135 (l) Wally McNamee/CORBIS; 135 (c) Bettmann/CORBIS; 135 (r) Clinton Campaign/AP Photo; 136 suravid/Shutterstock; 137 UANG XIAOYONG/ Xinhua/Landov; 138 Jeff Greenberg/The Image Works.

Chapter 8
142–143 James Leynse/Corbis; 144 Ryan Noble/ZUMA Press/CORBIS; 145 AP Photo/Jose Goitia; 146 Pearson Education; 147 (tr) AP Photo/Charles Dharapak; (bl) Alex Wong/Getty Images; (c) Reuters/CORBIS; (bc) Matthew Cavanaugh/epa/Corbis; (br) Cafe Press/AP Photo; 148 Jeff Kravitz/FilmMagic/ Getty Images; 149 AP Photo/J. Scott Applewhite; 150 (t) x99/ZUMA Press/Newscom; (b) Comedy Central/Courtesy the Everett Collection; 151 Paramount Pictures/Photofest.

Chapter 9
156–157 Chris Fitzgerald / Candidate Photos/Newscom; 159 AP Photo/Paul Sakuma; 160 (t) Roger L. Wollenberg/UPI/Newscom; (b) QI HENG/Xinhua/ Landov; 161 (t) AP Photo/Rob Carr; (b) Carrie Devorah/WENN/Newscom; 162 (t) Alex Wong/Getty Images; (tr) AP Photo/Peter Cosgrove, File; (b) APPhoto/Gregory Bull; 163 (l) Chuck Savage/Corbis; (r) PeterHvizdak/The Image Works; 164 League of Conservation Voters; 167 (b) Scott Maxwell/ LuMaxArt/Shutterstock; (bl) AP Photo/Gerald Herbert; (tr) AP Photo/Craig Lassig; 168 Jennie Book/Shutterstock; 169 Jason Kempin/WireImage/ Gettyimages; 170 William B. Plowman/NBC NewsWire via AP Images.

Chapter 10
174–175 Peter Casolino/Alamy; 176 Jason Kirk/Getty Images; 177 Shai Ginott/CORBIS; 178 Chip Somodevilla/Getty Images; 179 Lynn Goldsmith/CORBIS; 180 WHITNEY CURTIS/EPA/Landov; 181 Jeff Haynes/Polaris/Newscom; 182 FRANK E. LOCKWOOD/MCT/Landov; 183 Shutterstock; 184 AP Photo/Cliff Owen; 185 David Coleman/Alamy.

Chapter 11
190–191 AP Photo/Reed Saxon; 192 Probate Court, Jefferson County, AL; 196 North Wind Picture Archives; 198 Clinton Campaign/AP Photo; 199 AP Photo/Lenny Ignelzi; 200 Lyndon Baines Johnson Library Collection; 201 Scott Gries/Getty Images; 204 Dave Einsel/Getty Images; 205 Dave Weaver/AP Photo; 206–207 (bkgd) Daniel Mandic/Shutterstock; 206 (bc) Ethan Miller/ Getty Images; (bc) Alex Wong/Getty Images; (br) Moose/AdMedia/Newscom; 207 (bl) Soren McCarty/WireImage/Getty Images; (bc) Chris Fitzgerald/ CandidatePhotos/Newscom; (bc) David McNew/Getty Images; (br) Alex Wong/Getty Images; (cr) Stefan Zaklin/epa/Corbis; (cr) Yoan Valat/epa/Corbis; (br) TOSHIFUMI KITAMURA/AFP/Getty Images; 209 AP Photo/Heather Ainsworth; 211 Bettmann/CORBIS; 215 AP Photo/Beth A.Keiser; 216 Mark Peterson/Redux.

Chapter 12
220–221 AP Photo/J. Scott Applewhite; 223 AP Photo/Susan Walsh; 224 Doug Mills/The New York Times/Redux Pictures; 225 Dennis Van Tine/Retna Ltd./ CORBIS; 227 (b) Pearson Education; (t) Chip Somodevilla/Getty Images; 229 (t) Brooks Kraft/Corbis News/Corbis; (b) Bill Clark/CQ-Roll Call Group/Getty Images; 230 Kevin Dietsch/Upi/Landov Media; 231 Newscom; 232 (c) Lions Gate/Courtesy Everett Collection; 233 Ian Tragen/Shutterstock; 234 Darren McCollester/Getty Images; 235 YURI GRIPAS/Reuters/Landov; 237 Bettmann/ CORBIS; 239 AP Photo/Steven Senne.

Chapter 13
244–245 P-59 Photos/Alamy; 246 Chicago Tribune/MCT/Newscom; 247 Martin H. Simon/Corbis; 248 (bl) AP Photo; 248 (br) Brooks Kraft/Corbis News/Corbis; 250 AP Photo; 251 Seattle Post-Intelligencer Collection; Museum of History and Industry/CORBIS; 252 AP Photo/Lynne Sladky; 253 Bettmann/ CORBIS; 255 (tl) Bettmann/CORBIS; (br) Alexander Natruskin/Pool/epa/ Corbis; 257 SAUL LOEB/AFP/Getty Images; 259 Doug Mills/The New York Times/Redux Pictures; 260 (bl) CORBIS; 260 (br) ASSOCIATED PRESS; (tl) Bettmann/CORBIS; (tr) AP Photo; 261 NASA Archive/Alamy; 264 Associated Press.

Chapter 14
268–269 EPA/FDA/LANDOV; 271 AP Photo/Gerald Herbert; 272 AP Photo/Gerald Herbert; 273 David R. Frazier/The Image Works; 274 (tl) Orjan F. Ellingvag/Dagens Naringsliv/Corbis News/Corbis; (br) Exactostock / SuperStock; 276 The Library of Congress; 277 Joe Marquette/AP Photo; 278 Joshua Roberts/Bloomberg via Getty Images; 280 DAVID BANKS/UPI/ Newscom; 282 Boaz Rottem/Alamy; 283 AP Photo/Eric Rowley.

Chapter 15

288–289 Jeff Greenberg / Alamy; **391** Jeff Greenberg / Alamy; **292** Steve Petteway, Collection of the Supreme Court of the United States; **294** (tr) Jack Kurtz/ZUMA/Corbis; (br) Comstock/Jupiter Images; **298** (tl) KEVIN DIETSCH/UPI/Landov; (br) AFP/Getty Images; **302** LUC GNAGO/ Reuters/ Landov; **304** Joe Raedle/Newsmakers/Getty Images.

Chapter 16

308–309 AP Photo/Mark Lennihan; **311** Rick Lew/Getty Images; **312** Public Domain; **314** Bonnie Kamin / PhotoEdit; **315** Picsfive/Shutterstock; **317** Matthew Cavanaugh/epa/Corbis; **318** Tudor Stanica/Shutterstock; **319** Uriel Sinai/Getty Images; **320** Yellow Dog Productions/Getty Images; **322** The

Library of Congress; **325** Getty Images; **326** AP Photo/Doug Mills; **328** Scott J. Ferrell/Congressional Quarterly/Alamy; **329** Chip Somodevilla/Getty Images.

Chapter 17

334–335 AFP/Getty Images; **337** Talia Frenkel/UPI/Newscom; **338** AP Photo; **339** Diego Lezama Orezzoli/Corbis; **340** (t) ALEJANDRO ERNESTO/ EPA/Newscom; (b) Paula Bronstein/Getty Images; **342** Ralph Crane/Time Life Pictures/Getty Images; **343** INTERFOTO / Alamy; **344** Sean Adair/ Reuters/Landov; **347** (t) KHALED DESOUKI/AFP/Getty Images; (b) Transtock/Corbis; **349** RIZWAN TABASSUM/AFP/Getty Images; **350** (t) MICHAEL CRABTREE/Reuters/ Landov; (b) Megan E. Sindelar/U.S. Navy/Getty Images; **351** AP Photo; **352** AP Photo/Dita Alangkara.

TEXT CREDITS

Chapter 11

195 "Texas District Viewer" Screenshot: "Texas District Viewer" from TEXAS DISTRICT VIEWER website. Copyright © 2011 by Texas Legislative Council. Reprinted with permission; **201** "MTV/MySpace's 'Closing Arguments' Presi-dential Forum" Screenshot: "MTV/MySpace's 'Closing Arguments' Presidential Forum" from LIFE MAGAZINE website. Copyright © 2011 by Life Magazine. Reprinted by permission.

INDEX

Note: Page numbers in italics followed by *f* and *t* indicate figure and table respectively.